Churchill

A PHOTOGRAPHIC PORTRAIT

Other books by Martin Gilbert

Churchill

A PHOTOGRAPHIC PORTRAIT

by Martin Gilbert

HOUGHTON MIFFLIN COMPANY BOSTON 1974

FIRST PRINTING   A

FIRST AMERICAN EDITION

Library of Congress Cataloging in Publication Data
Gilbert, Martin, 1936-   comp.
    Churchill; a photographic portrait.
    1. Churchill, Sir Winston Leonard Spencer, 1874-
1965—Portraits, caricatures, etc. I. Title.
DA566.9.C5G444   1974   942.082'092'4   74-4204
ISBN 0-395-19405-9

Printed in the United States of America

Preface

My aim in these pages has been to portray, in a single photographic volume, something of the variety and span of Churchill's life; to show him in many different moods, and on many divers occasions. Although not all the major incidents of Churchill's long career were recorded in photographs, or even drawn by cartoonists, it is still possible to present, in visual form, a surprisingly large number of specific events from all periods of his life.

Although Churchill was much photographed, many of the original negatives have been destroyed, and many of the prints lost, since 1900. The natural ravages of time, the man-made processes of clearing-up and 'weeding out', the accident of fire, and the fierce destruction of the Blitz, have combined to eliminate for all time many important Churchill photographs. This process of destruction continues. During the course of my researches, a senior assistant in a leading photographic agency remarked: 'Periodically we go through destroying things. We do it every week. We haven't the space for them. We destroy precious, irreplaceable things.' Such destruction is commonplace, and, in view of the fact that negatives can easily be stored in university archives, it is also unnecessary. Much of the material lost by the current, continuing destruction is lost forever. Nevertheless, the number of surviving photographs is substantial, providing adequate scope for any single-volume selection.

Nearly half of the photographs in this volume come from Churchill's personal photograph albums. I have supplemented this important source with photographs from the Churchill papers, from the albums of his contemporaries, from institutions, and from several news agency archives. In November 1968, when I began to assemble this material, I appealed for photographs in over forty national and local newspapers. As a result of the ready response, I obtained much extra material, and the final selection of 364 photographs and cartoons was made from a total collection of over 5,000—sufficient to make at least another twelve volumes.

Throughout his political life, and particularly before 1940, Churchill was a popular subject for cartoonists; it was often their portrayal of him that lodged in the public mind. I have taken most of the cartoons from his own voluminous press cutting albums, which also contain several original photographs. On most pages I have tried to provide a quotation relevant to the illustrations, or to their themes. Most of these quotations come from material in the Churchill papers; some from the archives of his contemporaries; some from his speeches, and some from his books. I have listed the sources, both for the photographs and for the quotations, at the end of the volume.

I am particularly grateful to Baroness Spencer-Churchill, who allowed me to borrow her own photograph album, and to talk to her about the photographs. I am also grateful to Winston S. Churchill MP, Sir Winston Churchill's grandson, for putting his grandfather's photograph albums and press cutting books at my disposal.

In the early stages of my research I was greatly helped and encouraged by the late Field Marshal Earl Alexander of Tunis, and by Field Marshal Viscount Montgomery of Alamein, both of whom let me use their extensive photograph collections, and answered my many questions about the events portrayed in them. I am also extremely grateful to those individuals who provided photographs which I have used in this volume, or who gave me information which enabled me to trace photographs. In particular I should like to thank J. R. A. Bailey; Therize Borry; A. Butterworth; Peregrine S. Churchill; John Davie; John Freeman; D. Freeman; Major-General Sir Edmund Hakewill Smith; Miss Grace Hamblin; James Harvey; Lady Patricia Kingsbury; Mrs Constance Mainprice; A. Massen; Paul Maze; J. J. Moss; Mr Rance; Sir Geoffrey Shakespeare; Harry Skinner; Mr and Mrs H. Sornsen; the 2nd Viscount Trenchard; Dr J. Van Roey; Ava, Viscountess Waverley; and Peter Woodard.

Nearly two-thirds of the photographs in this volume are from private sources. But the book could not have been completed without the help of those news agencies in whose care are many of the most important photographs, often in the form of glass plate negatives. The following news agencies, institutions, and archives provided material: Acme News Pictures; Associated Newspapers; Barratts Photo Press; Bassano & Vandyk; Camera Press; The Cardiff Naturalists Society; Central Press Photos; The Czechoslovak Army Film & Photo Service; The Daily Mirror Picture Service; European Picture Service; Fox Photos; Paris Match; The Press Association; The Radio Times Hulton Picture Library; The Imperial War Museum; The London News Agency; The Sport and General Press Agency; Syndication International; Thomson Newspapers; Time Incorporated; Topical Press Agency; and United Press International.

The selection of the photographs, the cartoons and the quotations is my own. But I am grateful to Miss Susie Sacher, who advised me on the selection, the layout and the cover; to Mrs Charmian Allam, who did all the typing; and to Miss Mary Tyerman, who provided detailed information about several of the incidents portrayed in the photographs. My particular thanks are due to Jerry Moeran, of Studio Edmark, Oxford, and to his assistant Miss Jean Hunt, who prepared many of the prints used for this volume from faded or damaged originals, and who copied all the cartoons from the original press cuttings.

It has not always been possible to give the precise date of a particular photograph, or to identify all the people in it. I would be extremely grateful to any reader who can provide more precise dating, or any further identification. I should also welcome new photographs for use in future editions, or in the remaining volumes of the official biography.

Merton College
Oxford
29 August 1973

MARTIN GILBERT

Churchill

A PHOTOGRAPHIC PORTRAIT

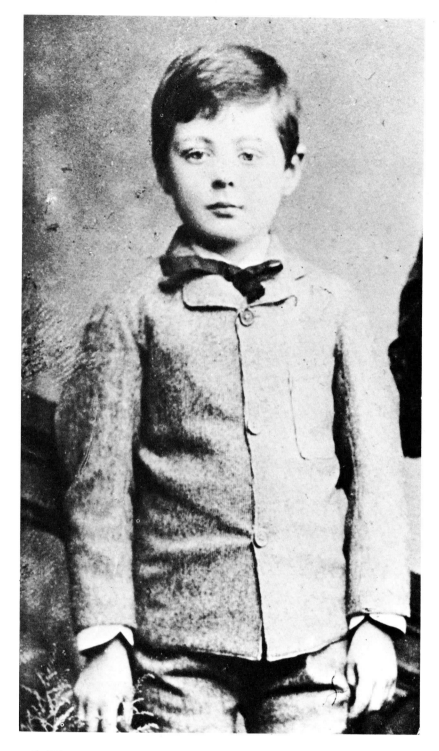

1 Winston Leonard Spencer Churchill was born on 30 November 1874, at Blenheim Palace. This photograph was taken in Dublin, when Churchill was five.

2 Churchill's mother, Lady Randolph Churchill, an American by birth. In 1874, when her son Winston was born, she was twenty years old. A central figure in fashionable society, she saw little of her son during his childhood. In his memoirs, published in 1930, Churchill wrote: '*She shone for me like the Evening Star. I loved her dearly – but at a distance.*'

3 Churchill in 1881, in his sailor suit. Throughout his childhood he was fascinated by armies and fleets. On 4 January 1882 he wrote to his mother from Blenheim Palace: '*I thank you very much for those beautiful presents those Soldiers and Flags and Castle they are so nice. . . .*' On 1 April 1882 he wrote again: '*I have been playing out of doors at making encampments which is great fun. I pretend to pitch a tent and make the umbrella do for it.*' On 6 February 1883 he wrote: '*I am longing for another feudal castle.*'

4 Churchill's father, Lord Randolph Churchill; a photograph taken in about 1884 when Lord Randolph was thirty-five. In 1885, while his father was in India, Churchill wrote to him: '*When are you coming home again. I hope it will not be long. I am at school now and am getting on pretty well. Will you write and tell me about India what it's like. It must be very nice and warm out there now, while we are so cold in England. Will you go out on a tiger Hunt while you are there? Are the Indians very funny? . . . Try and get me a few stamps for my stamp album, Papa. Are there many ants in India if so, you will have a nice time, what with ants mosquitos. Every body wants to get your signature will you send me a few to give away? I am longing to see you so much.*' In 1885 Lord Randolph had become Secretary of State for India; in the following year he was made Chancellor of the Exchequer and Leader of the House of Commons. Although young, he was one of the most popular and forceful speakers of his time, and seen by many as a future Conservative Prime Minister.

6 Lady Randolph Churchill with her two sons, Jack and Winston; a photograph taken in 1889, when Jack was nine and Winston fourteen. On 1 January 1891, Churchill wrote to his mother from Banstead Manor, near Newmarket, where he and his brother were on holiday together: '*We have slaughtered many rabbits – About 11 brace altogether. Tomorrow we slay the rats. The Pond is frozen 8 inches – The ground is covered with 4 inches of snow. Pipes are frozen – Oil freezes in the kitchen. No wind. V-happy. V. well. We are enjoying ourselves very much. We exist on onions and Rabbits & other good things.*' Jack, who became stockbroker, died in 1947.

5 Mrs Everest, Churchill's nurse from 1875. In his memoirs Churchill wrote: '*Mrs Everest it was who looked after me and tended all my wants. It was to her I poured out my many troubles . . .*' On 29 July 1888, when he was thirteen, Churchill wrote to his mother, from Harrow School: '*Could you let Everest come down, bring my clothes. . . . Do let Everest come, because my ideas of packing are very limited. . . . If you will let Everest come please telegraph by what train she will arrive or I shall not know what to do.*'

7 Churchill as a schoolboy; a photograph probably taken in 1889. His school reports caused his parents continual anxiety. On 12 June 1890 his mother wrote to him: '. . . *your work is an insult to your intelligence. If you would only trace out a plan of action for yourself & carry it out & be determined to do so – I am sure you could accomplish anything you wished. It is that thoughtlessness of yours which is your greatest enemy.*'

8

Lord Randolph Churchill in 1893, the year
before his death at the age of forty-five, and
the year in which his son succeeded in
entering Sandhurst. On hearing the news of
his son's success, Lord Randolph, who was
already very ill, wrote to him, on 9 August
1893: *'There are two ways of winning in an
examination, one creditable the other the
reverse. You have unfortunately chosen the
latter method, and appear to be much pleased
with your success. The first extremely dis-
creditable feature of your performance was
missing the infantry, for in that failure is
demonstrated beyond refutation your slovenly
happy-go-lucky harum scarum style of work
for which you have always been distinguished at
your different schools. . . . With all the advantages you had, with all the abilities which
you foolishly think yourself to possess & which
some of your relations claim for you, with all
the efforts that have been made to make your
life easy & agreeable & your work neither
oppressive or distasteful, this is the grand result
that you come up among the 2nd rate & 3rd
rate class who are only good for commissions
in a cavalry regiment. . . . I am certain that if
you cannot prevent yourself from leading the
idle useless unprofitable life you have had
during your schooldays & later months, you
will become a mere social wastrel one of the
hundreds of the public school failures, and you
will degenerate into a shabby unhappy &
futile existence. If that is so you will have to
bear all the blame for such misfortunes
yourself.'*

9 Churchill with two fellow officer-cadets at the Royal Military College, Sandhurst. On 3 September 1893, after three days as a cadet, he wrote to his father: '*The Discipline is extremely strict – Far stricter than Harrow. Hardly any law is given to juniors on joining. No excuse is ever taken – not even with a plea of "didn't know" after the first few hours: and of course no such thing as unpunctuality or untidiness is tolerated. Still there is something very exhilarating in the military manner in which everything works; and I think that I shall like my life here during the next 18 months very much.*' Later in his letter Churchill wrote: '*The dinner is very grand – and the names of the dishes are written in French on the menu. There is nothing else French about them.*'

10 Churchill in fancy dress at Sandhurst, 11 May 1894. Two days earlier he had written to his mother: '*Please try to get me a costume and send it by the guard of the train at 11.45. I will meet it. Try to get a gorrilla or something amusing.*'

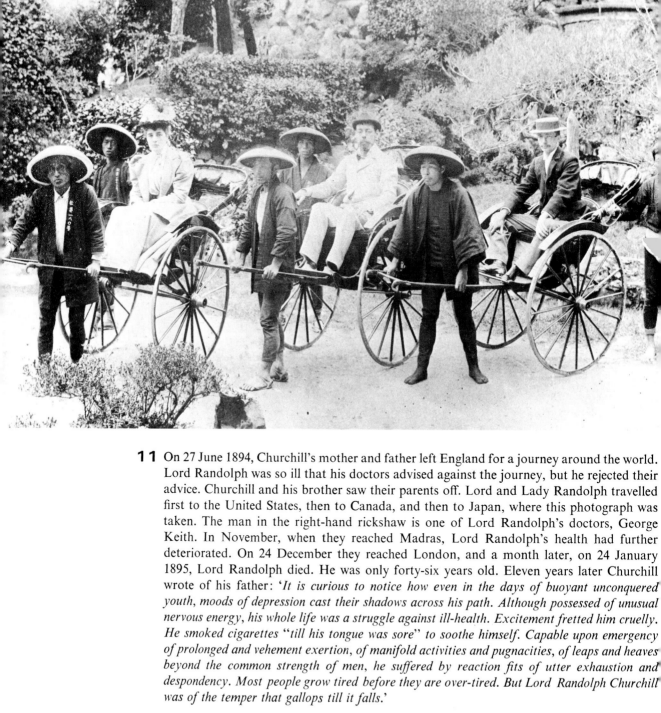

11 On 27 June 1894, Churchill's mother and father left England for a journey around the world. Lord Randolph was so ill that his doctors advised against the journey, but he rejected their advice. Churchill and his brother saw their parents off. Lord and Lady Randolph travelled first to the United States, then to Canada, and then to Japan, where this photograph was taken. The man in the right-hand rickshaw is one of Lord Randolph's doctors, George Keith. In November, when they reached Madras, Lord Randolph's health had further deteriorated. On 24 December they reached London, and a month later, on 24 January 1895, Lord Randolph died. He was only forty-six years old. Eleven years later Churchill wrote of his father: '*It is curious to notice how even in the days of buoyant unconquered youth, moods of depression cast their shadows across his path. Although possessed of unusual nervous energy, his whole life was a struggle against ill-health. Excitement fretted him cruelly. He smoked cigarettes "till his tongue was sore" to soothe himself. Capable upon emergency of prolonged and vehement exertion, of manifold activities and pugnacities, of leaps and heaves beyond the common strength of men, he suffered by reaction fits of utter exhaustion and despondency. Most people grow tired before they are over-tired. But Lord Randolph Churchill was of the temper that gallops till it falls.*'

12 Churchill and his mother; a photograph taken shortly after Lord Randolph's death, when Churchill himself was only twenty years old. Three years later in 1898, he wrote in his book 'The River War', of the Mahdi: '*Solitary trees, if they grow at all, grow strong; and a boy deprived of a father's care often develops, if he escapes the perils of youth, an independence and vigour of thought which may restore in after life the heavy loss of early days.*'

14 On 11 September 1896 Churchill sailed with the Fourth Hussars to India, reaching Bombay on 2 October. He remained in India for nearly two years, during which time he was in action on the North-West Frontier. On several occasions, in the midst of battle, he was nearly killed. On 19 September 1897 he wrote to his mother: '*I rode on my grey pony all along the skirmish line where everyone else was lying down in cover. Foolish perhaps but I play for high stakes and given an audience there is no act too daring or too noble. Without the gallery things are different. I will write again soon if all goes well, if not you know my life has been a pleasant one, quality not quantity is after all what we should strive for. Still I should like to come back and wear my medals at some big dinner or some other function.*'

13 A month before his father's death Churchill had taken the final Sandhurst examination. He passed it, coming 20th in the list of 130 candidates. His best marks were for Tactics, Fortifications and Riding. On 19 February 1895 he joined the Fourth Hussars at Aldershot, and on the following day was Gazetted a 2nd Lieutenant. His pay was £120 a year. Even during his first year as a soldier, his thoughts were on politics. On 16 August 1895 he wrote to his mother: '*It is a fine game to play – the game of politics – and it is well worth waiting for a good hand before really plunging. At any rate – four years of healthy and pleasant existence, combined with both responsibility & discipline can do no harm to me – but rather good. The more I see of soldiering the more I like it, but the more I feel convinced that it is not my métier. Well, we shall see – my dearest Mamma.*'

15

At the beginning of 1898 Churchill pleaded
with his mother to use her influence to help
him to join Lord Kitchener's expedition for
the reconquest of the Sudan. '*It is a pushing
age*', he wrote to his mother on 10 January,
'*and we must shove with the best*.' On 14
March, when he was twenty-five, he published
an account of the war on the Indian frontier,
entitled 'The Malakand Field Force'. In
July the War Office attached him as a
Lieutenant to the 21st Lancers. On 2 August
he was in Cairo, where this photograph was
taken. A month later, on 2 September, he
took part in the cavalry charge of the 21st
Lancers at the battle of Omdurman, writing
to his mother two days after the battle: '*I was
under fire all day and rode through the charge.
You know my luck in these things. I was about
the only officer whose clothes, saddlery, or
horse were uninjured. I fired 10 shots with my
pistol – all necessary – and just got to the end
of it as we cleared the crush. I never felt the
slightest nervousness and felt as cool as I do
now. I pulled up and reloaded within 30 yards
of their mass and then trotted after my troop
who were then about 100 yards away. I am
sorry to say I shot 5 men for certain and two
doubtful. . . . Nothing touched me. I destroyed
those who molested me and so passed out without any disturbance of body or mind.*'

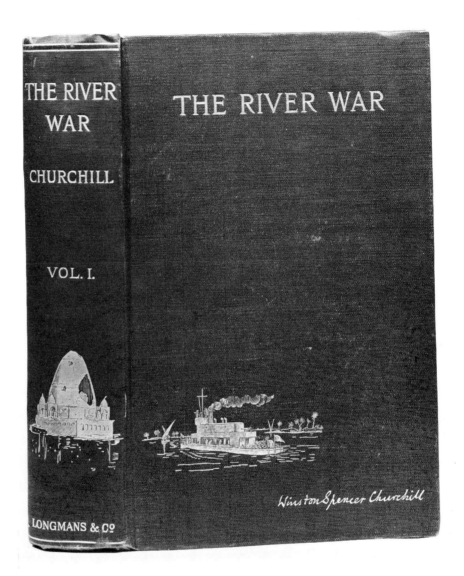

16 Immediately after the battle of Omdurman, Churchill began to write an account of the whole Sudan campaign. '*I work all day & every day at the book . . .*' he wrote to his mother on 21 December 1898. '*My hand gets so cramped. I am writing every word twice & some parts three times. It ought to be good since it is the best I can do.*' Entitled 'The River War', Churchill's book (his second) was published in England on 6 November 1899, and in the United States a month later.

18 Within four months of Churchill's defeat at Oldham, war broke out in South Africa between the British and the Boers. Churchill arranged to go to South Africa as war correspondent of the 'Morning Post'. He was paid £250 a month, a sum believed to be the highest ever paid up till then for a journalistic assignment. On 31 October 1899, he reached Cape Town. On 3 November he wrote to his mother: '*a fierce and bloody struggle is before us in which at least ten or twelve thousand lives will be sacrificed. . . .*' He himself was on his way to the scene of action, telling his mother: '*I shall believe I am to be preserved for future things.*'

17 Determined to enter politics, Churchill resigned his commission on 3 May 1899 after only four years in the Army. On 20 June he was adopted as Conservative candidate for Oldham. In his election address, dated 24 June, he declared: '*I regard the improvement of the condition of the British people as the main end of modern government.*' On 2 July he wrote to his friend Pamela Plowden about the election campaign: '*. . . it has been a strange experience and I shall never forget the succession of great halls packed with excited people until there was not room for a single person more – speech after speech, meeting after meeting – three even four in one night – intermittent flashes of Heat & Light & enthusiasm – with cold air and the rattle of a carriage in between: a great experience. And I improve every time – I have hardly repeated my-self at all. And at each meeting I am conscious of growing powers and facilities of speech. . . .*' The result was declared on 6 July; Churchill had been defeated, the Liberals victorious.

19 On 15 November 1899, at the invitation of Captain Aylmer Haldane, Churchill travelled by armoured-train on a reconnaissance through Boer-held territory. The train was derailed by the Boers, and Churchill, although only a war correspondent, at once offered Haldane his services. In his official report of the ambush Haldane wrote: '*For an hour efforts to clear the line were unsuccessful, as the trucks were heavy and jammed together, and the break-down gang could not be found, but Mr Churchill with indomitable perseverance continued his difficult task. . . . I would point out that while engaged on the work of saving the engine, for which he was mainly responsible, he was frequently exposed to the full fire of the enemy. I cannot speak too highly of his gallant conduct.*' The engine escaped; but Churchill, Haldane, and fifty others were captured. This photograph shows the derailed wagons on the day after the ambush.

20

Churchill's part in the armoured-train ambush was widely reported. This artist's drawing was published in the 'Saturday Herald' on 18 November 1899, only three days after the ambush. Its caption read: '*Young Churchill, a newspaper correspondent, at the battle of the armoured train, was obliged to seize a rifle and give the demoralised English soldiers a brave example. "Can't ye stand like men!" was his scornful cry.*'

"CAN'T YE STAND LIKE MEN!"

Arrivée à Pretoria des prisonniers du train blindé d'Estcourt (Lord Churchill à gauche en casquette).

La Guerre Anglo-Boer

Ed. Nels, Bruxelles. Serie Transvaal III

22 A Belgian postcard, showing the arrival of the armoured-train prisoners at Pretoria. Churchill is standing by the edge of the platform, wearing a flat cap. On 18 November 1899, three days after his capture, Churchill wrote to his mother from the State Model School, in which the prisoners were confined: '*Dearest Mamma, A line to explain that I was captured in the armoured train at Frere on the 15th, with some 50 officers and soldiers and some other non-combatants and platelayers and such like. As I was quite unarmed and in possession of my full credentials as a Press correspondent, I do not imagine they will keep me. . . . You need not be anxious in any way but I trust you will do all in your power to procure my release. After all this is a new experience – as was the heavy shell fire.*'

21 This artist's reconstruction of the armoured-train ambush was published in the 'Daily News Weekly' on 25 November 1899. The caption read: '*All the survivors praise Mr Winston Churchill's heroic conduct. He called for volunteers to help detach one of the wrecked trucks from the engine, and worked with them under the fire of three guns. When the wreckage was cleared the engine driver, who was wounded in the head, began to retire, but Mr Churchill called to him to come back, saying, "A man is never hit twice." The man brought back the engine, and Mr Churchill then helped to carry the wounded to the tender, and accompanied them back to Frere. There he jumped down with a rifle, and ran towards the enemy.*'

23 Churchill in captivity; Pretoria, 18 November 1899. He at once asked the Boers to release him, as he was a journalist and not a soldier, but the Boers refused. Of his time in prison he later wrote, in 'My Early Life': '*I certainly hated every minute of my captivity more than I have ever hated any other period in my whole life. . . . Looking back on those days, I have always felt the keenest pity for prisoners and captives.*' On 12 December 1899 Churchill, Haldane and Sergeant Major Brockie tried to escape over the wall of the prison; only Churchill succeeded in getting away. A Boer official in Pretoria offered a reward of £25 '*to anyone who brings the escaped prisoner of war Churchill dead or alive to this office*'. But Churchill managed to leave Boer territory, first on foot and then by train, undetected.

24

The news of Churchill's escape caused an even greater sensation than his capture had done. On 1 January 1900 an artist in the 'Illustrated Police News' gave his impression of the escape, and of Churchill's subsequent journey to the coast.

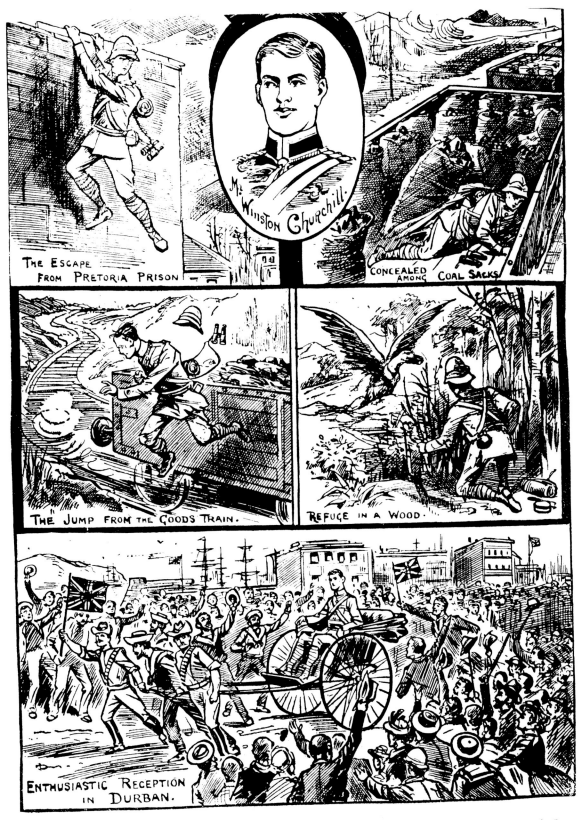

THE ESCAPE OF BRAVE WINSTON CHURCHILL
FROM PRETORIA.

SIXTY HOURS OF TERRIBLE ANXIETY AND DARING ADVENTURES

26 General Buller's headquarters were only a few miles from the scene of the armoured-train ambush. Having rejoined the army, as a Lieutenant in the South African Light Horse, Churchill revisited the scene of his capture, which had just come under British control. On 6 January 1900 he wrote to his mother: *'There is a great battle – the greatest yet fought – impending here. And of course, I cannot run the risk of missing it. . . . These are anxious days, but when one is quite sure that one is filling ones proper place in the scheme of the world affairs, we may await events with entire composure. I should never care to go home to England, unless we are victorious here.'*

25 Churchill reached Durban on 23 December 1899, where he described his escape to an enthusiastic crowd. On the following day he set out for General Buller's headquarters, having decided to rejoin the army once more. On 26 December, General Buller wrote to Lady Londonderry: *'Winston Churchill turned up here yesterday escaped from Pretoria. He really is a fine fellow and I must say I admire him greatly. I wish he was leading irregular troops instead of writing for a rotten paper. We are very short of good men, as he appears to be, out here. . . .'*

27 A photograph of Churchill while he was a Lieutenant in the South African Light Horse (during the brief period when he tried to grow a moustache). In January he took part in the battle of Spion Kop, writing to Pamela Plowden on 28 January: '*For good or ill I am com-mitted and I am content. I do not know whether I shall see the end or not, but I am quite certain that I will not leave Africa until the matter is settled. I should forfeit my self respect forever if I tried to shield myself like that behind an easily obtained reputation for courage. No possible advantage politically could compensate – besides believe me none would result. My place is here: here I stay – perhaps forever.*' And he added: '*The scenes on Spion Kop were among the strangest and most terrible I have ever witnessed.*'

28 In his letter to Pamela Plowden on 28 January Churchill wrote: '*I had five very dangerous days – continually under shell & rifle fire and once the feather in my hat was cut through by a bullet. But – in the end I came serenely through.*' And on 25 February he wrote to her: '*I was vy nearly killed two hours ago by a shrapnel. But though I was in the full burst of it God preserved me. Eight men were wounded by it. I wonder whether we shall get through and whether I shall live to see the end. There is a continual stream of wounded flowing by here to the hospitals – nearly a thousand in the last two days and five hundred before. The war is vy bitter but I trust we shall not show ourselves less determined than the enemy. My nerves were never better and I think I care less for bullets every day.*'

30 General Buller had allowed Churchill to remain a war correspondent as well as a soldier. Not only did he fight in the battles of 1900, but he also reported on them for the 'Morning Post'. This photograph shows sixteen of the war correspondents who covered the war. Immediately above Churchill is his friend J. B. Atkins, of the 'Manchester Guardian'; on Churchill's right, Basil Gotto of the 'Daily Express', on his left, F. W. Walker, also of the 'Daily Express'. In the front row are W. B. Wollin of the 'Sphere' (with pipe), J. O. Knight of the Chicago 'Times and Herald', and Ernest Prater of the 'Sphere'.

29 On 28 January 1900 Churchill's mother reached Durban on the hospital ship 'Maine', which had been purchased for £40,000 by a group of Anglo-Americans. Earlier, on 6 January, Churchill had written to her: '*I am so glad & proud to think of your enterprise & energy in coming out to manage the "Maine". Your name will long be remembered with affection by many poor broken creatures.*' One of Lady Randolph's first patients was her son Jack, for whom Churchill had secured a commission in the South African Light Horse, and who was wounded on 12 February 1900. '*He is unhappy at being taken off the board so early in the game*', Churchill wrote to his mother on 13 February. In this photograph, Jack poses with his mother on board the 'Maine'.

31 On 15 May 1900, while Churchill was still on active service in South Africa, a volume of his war despatches was published in London, entitled 'London to Ladysmith via Pretoria'. The book earned him more than £2,000. On the day of publication he wrote to his aunt Mrs Jack Leslie: '*I have had so many adventures that I shall be glad of a little peace and security. I have been under fire now in forty separate affairs, in this country alone and one cannnot help wondering how long good luck will hold. But I stand the wear and tear pretty well and indeed my health, nerve and spirits were never better than now at the end of seven months war.*'

32 Churchill sailed from Cape Town on 7 July 1900, reaching England on 20 July. His political ambitions were well understood by his contemporaries. This drawing by Spy was published in 'Vanity Fair' on 10 July, while he was still on his way home. The caption read: '*He is a clever fellow who has the courage of his opinions . . . He can write and he can fight, . . . he has hankered after Politics since he was a small boy, and it is probable that his every effort, military or literary, has been made with political bent . . . He is something of a sportsman; who prides himself on being practical rather than a dandy; he is ambitious; he means to get on, and he loves his country. But he can hardly be the slave of any Party.*'

PARK HALL, CARDIFF.

The Committee of the Cardiff Naturalists Society beg to announce that Mr.

Winston Churchill, M.P.

Will give his deeply interesting Lecture. entitled :

"THE WAR AS I SAW IT"

on

THURSDAY EVENING, NOVEMBER 29th, 1900, at 8.

The Lecture will be illustrated by Lantern Slides from Photos.

Mr. J. J. NEALE (*President of the Cardiff Naturalists Society*), will preside.

Doors open at 7.30.   Lecture at 8.   Carriages at 9.45.

RESERVED SEATS—Balcony, Front Row, 7 6; Other Seats in Balcony, 5/ ; Area, 3 6; UNRESERVED SEATS, 2 -.

Plan of the Hall may be seen and Tickets obtained at Mr. Wm. Lewis's, Duke Street.

34   As soon as he had become a Member of Parliament, Churchill began a series of lectures on the South African War, both in England, where he earned £3,782 in 35 days, and in the United States, where he earned an average of £50 a night for over 30 nights. During 1899 and 1900 he had earned a total of £10,000 by his books, his journalism and his lectures.

33   On 25 July 1900, five days after reaching England from South Africa, Churchill was again adopted as Conservative candidate for Oldham. On 31 July he wrote to his brother Jack: '*I went to the House of Commons yesterday where I was treated with great civility by many people. . . . I have greatly improved my position in England by the events of last year. . . . The newspapers all give me paragraphs wherever I make a speech and a great many of the country newspapers write leading articles upon it.*' Churchill was elected to Parliament on 1 October 1900, two months before his twenty-sixth birthday.

35 Churchill as Conservative MP for Oldham. His first Parliamentary speeches were an attack on his own Party's proposal to increase British military expenditure. On 13 May 1901 he told the House of Commons: '*I have frequently been astonished since I have been in this House to hear with what composure and how glibly Members and even Ministers, talk of a European war . . . a European war can only end in the ruin of the vanquished and the scarcely less fatal commercial dislocation and exhaustion of the conquerors.*'

36

A cartoon in 'Punch', by E. T. Reed, published on 10 September 1902. Throughout 1902 Churchill continued to be dissatisfied with Conservative policies. In January, after reading Seebohm Rowntree's book 'Poverty: A Study of Town Life', he noted privately that '*this festering life at home makes world-wide power a mockery*'. In Parliament he advocated a generous peace with the Boers. On 10 October 1902 he described to Lord Rosebery his ideal of a Middle Party '*free at once from the sordid selfishness & callousness of Toryism on the one hand & the blind appetites of the Radical masses on the other*'.

" Yes, men of Oldham."

" It never got over my escape."

" The duties of confidential adviser to Lord Roberts are not light."

" That's how I fetch Oldham."

38 Churchill with two friends, Henry Wilson (later Field Marshal Sir Henry Wilson) and, in the wheelchair, Auberon Herbert (later Lord Lucas). Herbert, who had lost a leg in the South African war, was killed in action while flying behind the German lines on 4 November 1916; Wilson was shot dead in London by two Sinn Fein assassins on 22 June 1922.

37 Churchill at Blenheim with the Duchess of Marlborough, formerly Consuelo Vanderbilt. During 1903 and 1904 he often stayed at Blenheim, writing a biography of his father. The book, entitled 'Lord Randolph Churchill', was published in two volumes on 2 January 1906. The publishers paid Churchill £8,000 for it. In it Churchill wrote of *'an England of wise men who gaze without self-deception at the failings and follies of both political parties, of brave and earnest men who find in neither faction fair scope for the effort that is in them'*.

39 A photograph of Churchill in 1904, taken after he had joined the Liberal Party. On 24 October 1903 he wrote to his friend Lord Hugh Cecil: '*I am an English Liberal. I hate the Tory party, their men, their words & their methods. I feel no sort of sympathy with them. . . .*' On 31 May 1904 he crossed the floor of the House of Commons to become a Liberal. During 1904 and 1905, he spoke throughout Britain, championing Free Trade, and denouncing the Conservatives. On 13 May 1905 he told a Manchester audience that the Conservative Party was '*a party of great vested interests, banded together in a formidable confederation, corruption at home, aggression abroad . . . dear food for the million, cheap labour for the millionaire*'.

HESITATING.

"Mr. Winston Churchill's inclusion in the Liberal party, though not formally concluded, is regarded as inevitable."—Daily Papers.

40   A cartoon in the 'Manchester Daily Despatch' of 19 March 1904, shortly before Churchill crossed to the Liberal benches. The chicken in the Liberal hen-coop is Sir Henry Campbell-Bannerman, then Leader of the Opposition.

THE NEW BOY.

OLIVER CHURCHILL BEGINS A NEW CAREER.

41   A cartoon in the 'Pall Mall Gazette' of 7 June 1904, after Churchill had joined the Liberals. Campbell-Bannerman is at the stove, with John Morley (standing) and H. H. Asquith (seated) on his left. Lloyd George is seated, far right.

43 On 10 December 1905 Churchill became Under-Secretary of State for the Colonies in Campbell-Bannerman's Liberal Government. On 13 January 1906 he was elected as Member of Parliament for Manchester North-West. During 1906 he played a leading part in the conciliation of South Africa. He is seen here at the meeting of Colonial Prime Ministers, held in London on 8 May 1907. Asquith is sitting below him, Lloyd George at the far right. On Churchill's left are the Permanent Under-Secretary of State at the Colonial Office, Sir Francis Hopwood, and the South African Prime Minister Louis Botha (to whose daughter, it was rumoured in the press – Churchill had become engaged). The Colonial Secretary, Lord Elgin, is seated at the centre of the group (with white beard).

42 Churchill entrusted his literary earnings to the banker, Sir Ernest Cassel, telling him: '*feed my sheep*'. Under Cassel's guidance, Churchill's investments prospered. This photograph shows Churchill and Cassel together in 1906. After his death in September 1921 Churchill wrote to Cassel's granddaughter Edwina (later Lady Mountbatten): '*He was a valued friend of my father's & I have taken up that friendship & have held it all my grown life. I had the knowledge that he was vy fond of me & believed in me at all times – especially in hard times. I had a real & deep affection for him. ...*'

44 to 50 Churchill with his constituents, at a garden party in Manchester, 23 August 1907.

51 As Under-Secretary of State for the Colonies, Churchill decided to visit East Africa. He travelled out in October 1907, through Malta and Cyprus, combining work, sightseeing and hunting. Here he is in Malta, in formal dress with his Private Secretary, Eddie Marsh, who served with him in every Government office that he held from 1905 to 1929. Marsh often advised Churchill not to send letters and telegrams which he believed were best unsent. On 4 January 1906 Churchill's aunt Leonie Leslie had written to him: '*I heard of you through Mr Marsh and I am so glad you make "si bon menage" together. He seems delighted to be with you – and already fond of you! Which is a good thing, as one can work so much better for anyone one cares for.*' Twenty years later, on 2 May 1928, T. E. Lawrence wrote to a friend about Marsh: '. . . *many people despise him; I've found him sincere always; and he serves Winston with all his might.*'

52 Churchill and Marsh on horseback in the Sudan. On 6 November 1907, Churchill wrote to his mother: '*What a difference to the fag of a London day. My heart bounds up with every day I spend in the open air.*'

53

On arrival at Mombasa station, Churchill was greeted by the Colony's officials, and watched by the settlers. In his letter to his mother of 6 November, he wrote: '*Everything moves on the smoothest of wheels for me. A special train with dining & sleeping cars was at my disposal all the way. Whenever I wished to stop, it stopped.*'

Churchill sailed o
the Nile at Kha
toum, and visite
the battlefield c
Omdurman, wher
he had fough
twelve years before
While at Khartour
his manservan
Scrivings, die
suddenly of foo
poisoning. After th
funeral, Churchil
wrote to his mother
'It was a melanchol
& startling event; e
to me who hav
become so deper
dent upon this poo
man for all the littl
intimate comforts o
my daily life, it ha
been a most keen &
palpable loss. . . . .
thought as I walke
after the coffin a
Khartoum – I alway.
follow funeral.
there – how easily i
might have been
might then still be
me.

54 At Khartoum, Churchill visited the buildings which had been shelled during the war of 1898, in which he had fought as a young officer. Here he poses in front of a shell-scarred wall. The city had been bombarded in 1898 by British gunboats which had sailed up the Nile. During his journey of 1907, Churchill sent several dozen long memoranda back to the Colonial Office. One senior civil servant there, Sir Francis Hopwood, wrote to the Colonial Secretary, Lord Elgin, about Churchill: '*He is most tiresome to deal with & will I fear give trouble – as his father did – in any position to which he may be called. The restless energy, uncontrollable desire for notoriety & the lack of moral perception make him an anxiety indeed!!*'

56 On 5 April 1908 H. H. Asquith became Prime Minister, and seven days later Churchill entered the Cabinet as President of the Board of Trade. Because of his appointment, he had to stand for re-election to Parliament. This photograph shows him campaigning in his constituency. Manchester North-West. But on 23 April he was defeated by his unsuccessful Conservative opponent of two years previously. To Miss Clementine Hozier, with whom he had fallen in love, he wrote on 27 April: *'I am glad to think you watched the battle from afar with eye sympathetic to my fortunes. Now I have to begin all over again. . . .'*

Daily Mirror

THE MORNING JOURNAL WITH THE SECOND LARGEST NET SALE.

No. 1,414. | Registered at the G.P.O. as a Newspaper. | MONDAY, MAY 11, 1908. | One Halfpenny.

ASK FOR the Special Extra
BEAUTY NUMBER
of the "DAILY MIRROR."
PRICE ONE PENNY.
NOW ON SALE.

MR. WINSTON CHURCHILL FINDS "A SAFE SEAT" AT LAST: REJECTED IN MANCHESTER, HE IS ELECTED M.P. FOR DUNDEE.

57   Churchill soon found a new constituency, Dundee, for which he was elected on 9 May 1908. The 'Daily Mirror' of 11 May recorded his success.

59 Churchill became a Privy Councillor on 1 May 1907; here he is seen with John Morley in Privy Council uniform, on their way to St James's Palace, 6 July 1908.

58 Churchill in 1908.

60

In 1908, on his return from East Africa, Churchill joined the Cabinet, as President of the Board of Trade. Aged thirty-three, he was one of the youngest Cabinet Ministers of his time. Four months after entering the Cabinet, he became engaged to Miss Clementine Hozier. In a letter to his bride-to-be, on 8 August 1908, he described himself as '*stupid and clumsy*' in his relations with women, and '*quite self-reliant and self-contained*'.

61 A photograph of Miss Clementine Hozier, taken during her engagement. On 12 August 1908 Churchill wrote to his future mother-in-law, Lady Blanche Hozier: '*I am not rich nor powerfully established, but your daughter loves me & with that love I feel strong enough to assume this great & sacred responsibility; & I think I can make her happy & give her a station & career worthy of her beauty & virtues.*'

Zur Vermählung des englischen Handelsministers.

Mrs. Winston Churchill, geb. Miß Clementine Hozier. Oben: Mr. Winston Churchill.

62 A German newspaper illustration, after Churchill's wedding on 12 September 1908. On the following day Churchill wrote to his mother *'What a relief to have got that ceremony over! & so happily.'*

63

Churchill on his wedding day: arriving at St Margaret's, Westminster, with his best man, Lord Hugh Cecil. Lloyd George was among those who signed the register. The Churchills spent their honeymoon first at Blenheim, then at Baveno on Lake Maggiore, and finally in Venice.

64

Churchill and his wife during their first year of marriage. On 6 September 1909 he wrote to her: '*I am so much centred in my politics, that I often feel I must be a dull companion, to anyone who is not in the trade too. It gives me so much joy to make you happy – & I often wish I were more various in my topics.*'

65 Churchill and Lloyd George (top left) watch a demonstration of the Brennan Monorail at the White City on 4 November 1910. Augustine Birrell is standing below Lloyd George. Asquith, his daughter Violet, Sir Ernest Cassel, and Clementine Churchill were also present. This is one of the only photographs showing Churchill and Lloyd George together before 1911. At the end of 1908 Churchill had joined Lloyd George in opposing the increased naval expenditure demanded by the First Lord of the Admiralty, Reginald McKenna, for they were both strongly opposed to the creation of an arms race with Germany, and wanted to concentrate Government spending on social reform. In 1886 Lord Randolph had resigned over the Government's military expenditure, and had never held public office again. On 21 December 1908 Lloyd George wrote to Churchill: '*I cannot go away without expressing to you my deep obligation for the assistance you rendered me in smashing McKenna's fatuous estimates & my warm admiration for the splendid way in which you tore them up. I am a Celt & you will forgive me for telling you that the whole time you were raking McK's squadron I had a vivid idea in my mind that your father looked on with pride at the skilful & plucky way in which his brilliant son was achieving victory in a cause for which he had sacrificed his career & his life.*'

66
Churchill and
McKenna on
their way to a
Cabinet meeting
at the end of
1909.

67 Churchill was a keen supporter of the Territorial Army. Here four members of the Churchill family pose for a photograph at a Territorial camp of the Queen's Own Oxfordshire Hussars: The 9th Duke of Marlborough, Viscount Churchill, Winston Churchill and Jack Churchill. Churchill went every year to camp and to manœuvres. On 15 September 1909, while a guest at manœuvres in Germany, he wrote to his wife: '*Much as war attracts & fascinates my mind with its tremendous situations – I feel more deeply every year – & can measure the feeling here in the midst of arms – what vile & wicked folly & barbarism it all is.*'

68 While at manœuvres in Germany, Churchill was the guest of the Kaiser, with whom he is here seen shaking hands.

A MINISTER "CAPTURED" BY A SUFFRAGETTE:
MR. WINSTON CHURCHILL AND MISS MAY DREW.

Miss Drew was one of the Suffragettes who visited the House of Commons
the other day, and was more fortunate than some of her sisters in the
cause, for she "captured" Mr. Winston Churchill as that Minister was
leaving the House, walked with him for a considerable distance, and
"lectured" him the while. Mr. Churchill "bore up" well under the strain,
and appeared interested.—[PHOTOGRAPH BY L.N.A.]

69 A page from the 'Illustrated London News', 10 April 1909.

70 On 14 November 1909 a militant suffragette, Miss Theresa Garnett, attacked Churchill with a dog whip at Bristol railway station. The blow caught him across the face, and also dented his hat. As detectives pulled her away, she called out: '*You brute, why don't you treat British women properly?*' Two days later the 'Manchester Evening News' published this drawing of the incident. On 12 July 1910 Churchill spoke, and voted, against the Bill to give women the vote. Suffragette threats continued. On 1 February 1913 Churchill wrote to his wife: '*Be vy careful not to open suspicious parcels arriving by post. . . . On the other hand do not leave them lying unopened in the house. They shd be dealt with carefully & promptly. These harpies are quite capable of trying to burn us out.*'

71 Throughout his two years at the Board of Trade, Churchill had been a strong advocate of State aid to the sick and the unemployed. Among his measures was the setting up of Labour Exchanges, to help the unemployed to find work. On 1 February 1910 he and his wife visited the first seventeen Labour Exchanges, all of which had been opened that day. This picture shows them at the Whitechapel Exchange. Nearly two years earlier, on 14 March 1908, he had written to Asquith: '*Dimly across gulfs of ignorance I see the outline of a policy wh I call the Minimum Standard. . . . Underneath, though not in substitution for, the immense disjoined fabric of social safeguards & insurances which has grown up by itself in England, there must be spread – at a lower level – a sort of Germanised network of State intervention & regulation.*'

72 Sir Edward Grey, Churchill and Lord Crewe coming away from a Cabinet meeting following the Liberal victory in the General Election of 14 February 1910. The election had been fought by the Liberals in order to challenge the House of Lords, which had been blocking much of the Liberals' social legislation. In the campaign, Churchill travelled throughout the country denouncing the powers of the Lords. On 1 February 1910, at the height of the campaign, Asquith had written to Churchill: '*Your speeches from first to last have reached a high-water mark, and will live in history.*' In one of these speeches, made at Leven on 9 January 1910, Churchill had declared, of Lord Lansdowne: '*His career represents privilege and favour from beginning to end; consistent and unbroken spoon-feeding from start to finish—that is the royal road to favour and employment. He is the representative of a played out, obsolete, anachronistic Assembly, a survival of a feudal arrangement utterly passed out of its original meaning – a force long since passed away, which only now requires a smashing blow from the electors to finish it for ever.*' On the day of the election victory, Churchill was appointed Home Secretary. He was thirty-five years old.

73 Mrs Lloyd George, Lloyd George, Churchill and William Clarke (Lloyd George's Secretary), on the way to the House of Commons for Lloyd George's Budget, 27 April 1910. Churchill wanted strong measures against the House of Lords if it rejected the Budget. *'The time has come for the total abolition of the House of Lords'*, he had written to Asquith on 14 February 1910. The Budget passed the House of Commons by 324 votes to 231; the House of Lords, accepting the verdict of the election, agreed to it without even a division. That night Churchill wrote to Edward VII: *'Everyone is tired out by the unceasing strain, and the holiday of a month is the dearest wish of most Members of the House of Commons.'*

74

A cartoon by Max Beerbohm, 1910. Churchill, standing in the grounds of Blenheim Palace, is saying to his cousin, the Duke of Marlborough: *'Come come! As I said in one of my speeches, "there is nothing in the Budget to make it harder for a poor hard-working man to keep a decent home in comfort".'*

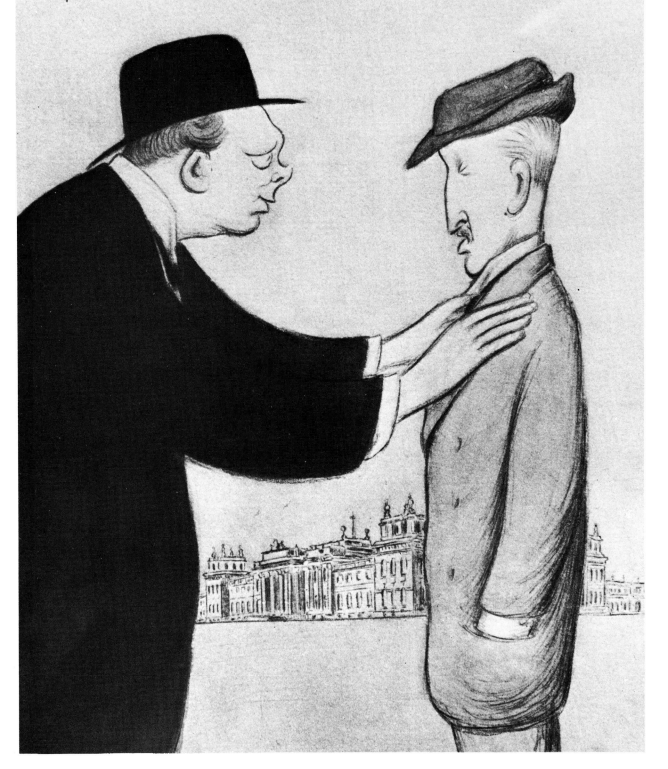

75 Churchill and his cousin the Duke of Marlborough go to Buckingham Palace on 6 May 1910, the day after the death of Edward VII, to attend the Privy Council meeting on the accession of the new King, George V. On 10 February 1911 Churchill wrote to George V advocating Labour Colonies for 'tramps and wastrels', and commenting: 'It must not however be forgotten that there are idlers and wastrels at both ends of the social scale.' The King intimated in reply that he regarded the proposal as 'socialistic' and the comment as 'superfluous'.

20 TURN 'EM OUT!

(Copyright.)

76 A playing card designed by E. T. Reed, the 'Punch' cartoonist, for the game of 'PANKO or VOTES FOR WOMEN'. The game took the form of 'Suffragists v. Anti-Suffragists'. Churchill is shown in his Privy Councillor's robes.

77 Churchill's first child, Diana, was born on 11 July 1909. On 12 September he wrote to his wife: '*I wonder what she will grow into, & whether she will be lucky or unlucky to have been dragged out of chaos. She ought to have some rare qualities both of mind & body. But these do not always mean happiness or peace.*' Four months later there was a brief moment of friction between husband and wife, and on 10 November he wrote to her: '*Dearest it worries me vy much that you should seem to nurse such absolutely wild suspicions wh are so dishonouring to all the love & loyalty I bear you & will please god bear you while I breathe. They are unworthy of you & me. And they fill my mind with feelings of embarrassment to wh I have been a stranger since I was a schoolboy. . . . You ought to trust me for I do not love & will never love any woman in the world but you and my chief desire is to link myself to you week by week by bonds which shall ever become more intimate & profound. Beloved I kiss your memory – your sweetness & beauty have cast a glory upon my life.*'

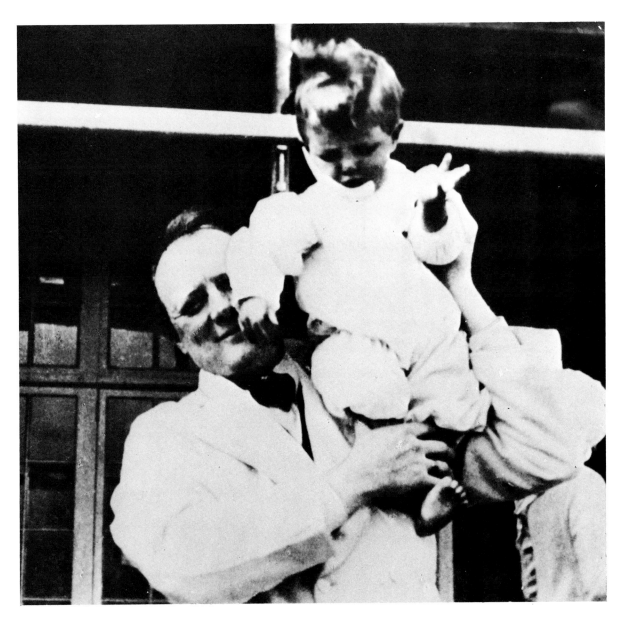

78 Churchill's second child, Randolph – his only son – was born on 28 May 1911. Five days later Churchill wrote, to his wife, from Blenheim Park where he was in camp with the Oxfordshire Hussars: '*Many congratulations are offered me upon the son. With that lack of jealousy wh ennobles my nature, I lay them all at your feet.*' And he added that he hoped that his son would not be backward in his feeding. '*At his age*', he explained, '*greediness & even swinishness at table are virtues.*' This photograph shows Churchill and his son together at the seaside in the summer of 1912.

81   Postcards of 'The Battle of Stepney' were sold in large numbers, and the incident was recorded in an early cinema newsreel. This photograph was circulated widely as a postcard. Eddie Marsh is standing next to Churchill (both in top hats). In the House of Commons the Conservative Leader, A. J. Balfour, criticized Churchill's action: *'He was, I understand in military phrase, in what is known as the zone of fire – he and a photographer were both risking valuable lives. I understand what the photographer was doing, but what was the right honourable gentleman doing?'*

79   Scots Guards covering 100 Sidney Street, a house in the East End of London where two armed burglars were trapped on 3 January 1911. The burglars had killed three of the policemen who tried to arrest them, and had begun to fire on the police from the house. Because the burglars had rifles and the police were only armed with revolvers, Churchill had – at the request of the War Office – given authority for a detachment of Scots Guards to go to the scene.

80   Churchill himself arrived in Sidney Street shortly after the soldiers. Later that day he wrote, to Asquith: *'It was a striking scene in a London street – firing from every window, bullets chipping the brickwork, police and Scots Guards armed with loaded weapons artillery brought up etc.'* In a note written seven days later he recalled: *'I made it my business, however, after seeing what was going on in front to go round the back of the premises and satisfy myself that there was no chance of the criminals effecting their escape through the intricate area of walls and small houses at the back of No 100 Sidney Street. This took some time, and when I returned to the corner of Sidney Street I was told that the house had caught on fire, and I could see smoke coming out from the top-floor window.'*

82 The fire at 100 Sidney Street. In his letter to Asquith, Churchill wrote: '*I thought it better to let the House burn down than spend good British lives in rescuing those ferocious rascals.*' After the fire had burnt itself out the police entered the building, and found two bodies. One had been shot, the other asphyxiated.

83

Churchill giving evidence at the Sidney Street inquest on 18 January 1911. He had been much criticized in the Press for having conducted the operation and given orders to the police and firemen. He told the Coroner: '*A junior officer of the Fire Brigade (Station Officer Edmonds) came up to me where I was standing and said that the Fire Brigade had arrived, and that he understood he was not to put out the fire at present. Was this right? or words to that effect. I said, "Quite right; I accept full responsibility." I wish to make it clear that these words refer to the specific question asked me, and that I confirmed and supported the police in their action. From what I saw, it would have meant loss of life and limb to any fire brigade officer who had gone within effective range of the building. . . . I did not in any way direct or over-ride the arrangements that the police authorities had made. I gave no directions to alter arrangements already made by them.*' Sydney Holland (later Viscount Knutsford), who was with Churchill throughout the siege, wrote to him six days before the Inquest: '*The only possible excuse for anyone saying that you gave orders is that you did once and very rightly go forward and wave back the crowd at the far end of the road. If those miscreants had come out there would have been lots of people shot by the soldiers. And you did also give orders that you and I were not to be shot in our hindquarters by a policeman who was standing with a 12 bore behind you!*'

84 Churchill talking to Lord Northcliffe at the Hendon Aviation Meeting, 12 May 1911. Clementine Churchill is on the left, shielding her eyes. Churchill was an early and eager advocate of flying. As early as 25 February 1909 he had told the Aerial Navigation sub-Committee of the Committee of Imperial Defence that the problem of the use of aeroplanes '*was a most important one*', and he had urged his colleagues to avail themselves of the Wright Brothers' expertise. At the Hendon Meeting Churchill watched the aviator Grahame-White drop a bomb on an area marked out to resemble the deck of a ship. The demonstration was organised by the Parliamentary Aerial Defence Committee.

85 Churchill and McKenna (in top hat) at the Hendon Aviation Meeting. The hatless man is the pilot and aeroplane instructor Grahame-White. On 24 October 1911 Churchill left the Home Office to become First Lord of the Admiralty. As First Lord he devoted much energy to building up the Royal Naval Air Service and was encouraged in his decision by Admiral of the Fleet Lord Fisher (then retired), who wrote to him on 10 November 1911: '*Aviation supersedes small cruisers & Intelligence vessels. You told me you would push aviation – you are right. . . .*' Churchill responded readily to Fisher's enthusiasm. Over two years earlier in a letter to his wife on 30 May 1909, he had described – after attending an Army Field Day in Berkshire – his attitude to military, naval and air matters: '*These military men vy often fail altogether to see the simple truths underlying the relationships of all armed forces, & how the levers of power can be used upon them. Do you know I would greatly like to have some practice in the handling of large forces. I have much confidence in my judgment on things, when I see clearly, but on nothing do I seem to feel the truth more than in tactical combinations. It is a vain and foolish thing to say – but you will not laugh at it. I am sure I have the root of the matter in me. . . .*'

87 Lord Fisher and Churchill on their way to the launching of HMS 'Centurion', 18 November 1911. This was the first King George V Class battleship to be launched after Churchill became First Lord. Six months later Churchill persuaded Fisher to become Chairman of the Royal Commission on Oil Supply, writing to him on 11 June 1912: '*This liquid fuel problem has got to be solved, and the natural inherent, unavoidable difficulties are such that they require the drive and enthusiasm of a big man. . . . You have got to find the oil: to show how it can be stored cheaply: how it can be purchased regularly and cheaply in peace; and with absolute certainty in war. . . . I recognize it is little enough I can offer you. But your gifts, your force, your hopes, belong to the Navy, with or without return; and as your most sincere admirer, and as the head of the Naval Service, I claim them now, knowing well you will not grudge them. You need a plough to draw. Your propellers are racing in air.*'

86 Churchill as First Lord of the Admiralty; a photograph taken at the time of his appointment on 24 October 1911, five weeks before his thirty-fifth birthday. Four days later the 'Observer' declared: '*We are afraid of Mr Churchill because he is weak and rhetorical . . . his moods are not to be depended upon. We cannot detect in his career any principles or even any consistent outlook upon public affairs. His ear is always to the ground; he is the true demagogue, sworn to give the people what they want, or rather, and that is infinitely worse, what he fancies they want. No doubt he will give the people an adequate Navy if they insist upon it.*' This was typical of Conservative comment at the time.

88 Churchill with Prince Louis of Battenberg (Second Sea Lord, 1911–12). This photograph shows them at Dover on 25 April 1912, when they inspected the harbour defences. On 29 October 1914, after Prince Louis had resigned as First Sea Lord, Churchill wrote to him: '*The Navy of today, and still more the Navy of tomorrow, bears the imprint of your work.*'

Churchill on board the Royal yacht 'Victoria and Albert', at Spithead, 9 July 1912, for the Naval Review. Asquith was also present, and that evening Churchill wrote to his wife: '*The PM is quite indefatigable & has been on his legs all day. He loves this sort of life & is well suited to it. He would have made a much better Admiral than most I have to get along with. Prince Louis looked vy imposing on his splendid Thunderer.*' Churchill spent several months at sea each year, in 1912, 1913 and 1914, mostly on board the Admiralty yacht 'Enchantress'. On 30 January 1913 he wrote to his wife from the Firth of Tay: '*I wish you were here. . . . Don't be disloyal to me in thought. I have no one but you to break the loneliness of a bustling and bustled existence.*' And on 2 November 1913 he wrote to her from Portland: '*We are an enormous crowd on board and every cabin chock full. . . . Wind & rain & sea = crowds of men talking shop = cold & sleet = more shop. But it amuses me – I am a fool who shd not have been born.*'

90

Lady Randolph Churchill, her son, and Eddie Marsh at Earls Court on Armada Day, 29 July 1912, on board a model of Sir Francis Drake's ship 'Revenge'.

91 Holiday time. Churchill at Cannes, setting off for golf with the American actress Maxine Elliot, February 1913.

92 Golfing at Cannes.

93 Clementine Churchill, her husband, and Millicent Duchess of Sutherland on the front at Monte Carlo, February 1913.

94 Churchill and his wife arriving at the Channel Islands, 1913, having just landed from the 'Enchantress'.

THE "OFFICIAL" TOUR ENDED

Mr. Asquith and Mr. Winston Churchill arriving at Victoria Station
last week on their return from the Mediterranean

95 During May 1913 Churchill steamed on the 'Enchantress' to the Eastern Mediterranean and
the Adriatic, visiting British naval squadrons and stations. Among those who went with him
was the Prime Minister, H. H. Asquith. This photograph was published in the 'Bystander',
on 4 June 1913.

UNDER HIS MASTER'S EYE.

SCENE—*Mediterranean, on board the Admiralty yacht " Enchantress."*

MR. WINSTON CHURCHILL. "ANY HOME NEWS?"

MR. ASQUITH. "HOW CAN THERE BE WITH YOU HERE?"

96 A cartoonist's view of the cruise of the 'Enchantress'. This cartoon appeared in 'Punch' on 21 May 1913. (In December 1908 Churchill had published an account of his African tour, entitled 'My African Journey'; in this cartoon the book at his side is called 'My journey in Africa'.)

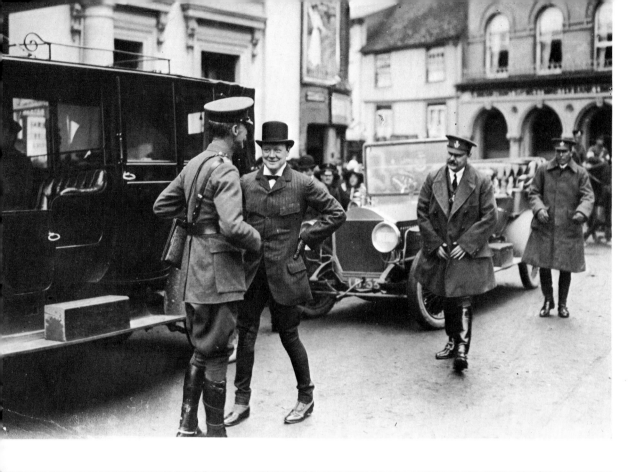

Churchill's two children, Randolph (in pram) and Diana, walking with their nannies out- **99**
side Admiralty House. In 1913 an unsuccessful attempt was made by suffragettes to kidnap
the young Randolph (then aged two) from his pram. Churchill was devoted to his two
children. On 23 July 1913 he wrote to his wife, from on board the 'Enchantress': '*Tender
love to you my sweet one & to both those little kittens & especially that radiant Randolph.
Diana is a darling too: & I repent to have expressed a preference. But somehow he seems a more
genial generous nature: while she is mysterious and self conscious. They are vy beautiful &
will win us honour some day when everyone is admiring her & grumbling about him.*'

97 General Sir Ian Hamilton, Churchill, his brother Jack, and his close friend, the Conservative MP F. E. Smith, at Buckingham in September 1913, during Army manœuvres.

98 Clementine Churchill, Admiral Hood (Churchill's Naval Secretary), Churchill and Eddie
Marsh at Lords. Admiral Hood was killed at the Battle of Jutland in 1916.

100

Churchill and Lord Fisher leaving a meeting of the Committee of Imperial Defence in 1913. Fisher encouraged Churchill to press his colleagues for substantial increases in British naval power. On 28 August 1913 Churchill drew up detailed plans to create a War Fleet of 79 battleships by 1920 (instead of the 59 which up till then had been planned for). He believed that if such a fleet were built, the Germans would be deterred from taking any aggressive action which might involve Britain. But at the same time Churchill offered to halt this programme if the Germans were willing, for their part, to accept a 'naval holiday'. The German Government refused his offer.

101

Churchill with his friend Jack Seely (then Secretary of State for War) watching the Review of the Brigade of Guards in Hyde Park, 28 April 1913.

102 A German view of Churchill's naval policy, published in the weekly magazine 'Ulk' on 28 November 1913. Churchill's veils are marked '*For an increase in the navy*' and '*Against an increase in the navy*', and the caption reads: '*What then will result from Churchill's dance of the veils? A naked egoist!*'

The problem of the hour. What shall we give? Christmas presents for notabilities. — No. 1.

103 A cartoonist's view of Churchill's flying activities. This cartoon was published in the 'Birmingham Evening Despatch' on 1 December 1913. Throughout 1913 and 1914 Churchill learned to fly, and at the same time worked to improve the performance of aeroplanes, and the power of the Royal Naval Air Service. In a letter to his wife on 23 October 1913, after a day of flying practice, he wrote: '*It is vy satisfactory to find such signs of progress in every branch of the Naval air service. In another year – if I am spared ministerially – there will be a gt development. When I have pumped in another million the whole thing will be alive & on the wing.*'

104
and
105
Two photographs of Churchill on 23 February 1914, after he had gone on a practice flight at Eastchurch. The weekends which he spent flying were a delight to him. After an earlier practice on 23 October 1913 he wrote to his wife: *'It has been as good as one of those old days in the S. African war, & I have lived entirely in the moment, with no care for all those tiresome party politics & searching newspapers, & awkward by-elections. . . . For good luck before I started I put your locket on.'*

106

Churchill on his way to the Cabinet, 22 January 1914. His proposals for increased Naval expenditure to meet the rapidly increased German naval construction, had provoked strong opposition from Lloyd George, and divided the Cabinet. The crisis continued for more than a month. On 26 January Churchill wrote to Lloyd George: '*While I am responsible, what is necessary will have to be provided. The estimate of 1914–15 have been prepared with the strictest economy. For all expenditure incurred or proposed there is full warrant & good reason. There is no act of Admiralty administration for which I am responsible wh cannot be vindicated to the House of Commons. I cannot buy a year of office by a bargain under duress about estimates of 1915–16. No forecasts beyond the year have ever been made by my predecessors; & I have no power – even if I were willing – to bind the Board of Admiralty of 1915 to any exact decision. I recognise your friendship, but I ask no favours & I shall enter into no irregular obligations.*'

107

A cartoon by E. T. Reed, published in the 'Bystander' on 28 January 1914, at the height of the naval estimates crisis. From left to right: Lloyd George, Haldane, Asquith, Grey and Churchill. Within two weeks the majority of Churchill's proposals for a larger Navy had been accepted by the Cabinet. On 2 February Churchill wrote to Asquith: '*I do not love this naval expenditure & am grieved to be found in the position of taskmaster. But I am myself the slave of facts & forces wh are uncontrollable unless naval efficiency is frankly abandoned. The result of all this pressure & controversy leaves me anxious chiefly lest the necessary services have been cut too low.*' On 10 February, when the crisis was over, Churchill wrote to his mother: '*. . . it has been a long and wearing business wh has caused me at times vy gt perplexity*'.

"We All Go the Same Way Home!"

THE ONLY QUESTION STANDING OVER FOR DECISION BEING——WHICH WAY IS IT?

108 Churchill on board ship at Dover, 8 April 1914, on his way to Spain, where he was to play Polo as the guest of King Alfonso.

109 Churchill on his polo pony during his visit to Spain. He also worked during his holiday, writing to Prince Louis of Battenberg from Madrid on 14 April 1914: '*Freedom from politics and pouches has enabled me to deal comprehensibly with the various Staff questions now pending & I have spent several days on the task. Will you kindly read my memo. . . .*'

110 Churchill crossing Horse Guards Parade.

111 In the summer of 1914 Churchill took Field-Marshal Sir John French (Commander-in-Chief designate of the British Expeditionary Force) to inspect naval installations in Scotland.

112 Churchill's support for expansion of the Royal Naval Air Service was vigorous and widely approved. This cartoon by Bernard Partridge, entitled 'Neptune's Ally', was published in 'Punch' on 25 May 1914, shortly after Churchill's return from Spain, when it was reported in the Press that he was continuing with his flying practice.

113 On 29 May 1914 Churchill wrote to his wife from Portsmouth: '*My darling one, I have been at the Central Flying School for a couple of days – flying a little in good & careful hands & under perfect conditions. So I did not write you from there as I know you wd be vexed.*' In her reply, Clementine Churchill begged him to stop flying altogether. He accepted her plea, writing from the 'Enchantress' on 6 June: '*I will not fly any more. . . .*' and adding: '*This is a wrench, because I was on the verge of taking my pilot's certificate. It only needed a couple of calm mornings; & I am confident of my ability to achieve it vy respectably. I shd greatly have liked to reach this point wh wd have made a suitable moment for breaking off. But I must admit that the numerous fatalities of this year wd justify you in complaining if I continued to share the risks – as I am proud to do – of these good fellows. So I give it up decidedly for many months & perhaps for ever. This is a gift – so stupidly am I made – wh costs me more than anything wh cd be bought with money. So I am vy glad to lay it at your feet, because I know it will rejoice & relieve your heart. Anyhow I can feel I know a good deal about this fascinating new art. I can manage a machine with ease in the air, even with high winds, & only a little more practice in landings wd have enabled me to go up with reasonable safety alone. I have been up nearly 140 times, with many pilots, & all kinds of machines, so I know the difficulties the dangers & the joys of the air – well enough to appreciate them, & to understand all the questions of policy wh will arise in the near future. . . . Though I had no need & perhaps no right to do it – it was an important part of my life during the last 7 months, & I am sure my nerve, my spirits & my virtue were all improved by it. But at your expense my poor pussy cat! I am so sorry.*'

114

Sir Edward Grey and Churchill walking across the Horse Guards Parade on the eve of war in 1914. Churchill insisted, against much Ministerial opposition, that it was in Britain's interest to support France to repel a German attack, and on 28 July he ordered the Fleet to take up its War Stations in the North Sea. That night he wrote to his wife: '*Everything tends towards catastrophe & collapse. I am interested, geared up & happy. Is it not horrible to be built like that? The preparations have a hideous fascination for me. I pray to God to forgive me for such fearful moods of levity.*'

115

'Full Steam Ahead'; a cartoon of Churchill by Poy, published on 4 August 1914. On 24 August, as the Germans swept through Belgium, Churchill telegraphed to Admiral Jellicoe: '*We have not entered this business without resolve to see it through. You may rest assured that our action will be proportionate to the gravity of the need. I have absolute confidence in the final result.*'

FULL STEAM AHEAD!

BRAVO WINSTON!

The Rapid Naval Mobilisation and Purchase of the Two Foreign Dreadnoughts Spoke Volumes for your Work and Wisdom.

MR. WINSTON CHURCHILL, FIRST LORD OF THE ADMIRALTY
AND (INSET) HIS CHARMING AND BEAUTIFUL WIFE

If you listen to the opinion of the navy in general upon Mr. Churchill you will be thankful that such a man has been in control of our navy in the immediate past. Mrs. Churchill must be a proud woman. Mr. Churchill has fought and overcome the Little Navyites in the past so that our fleet may fight and overcome our foes in the future

116 Churchill on the eve of war; a photograph published in the 'Tatler' on 12 August 1914, with an inset photograph of Clementine Churchill.

WINSTON CHURCHILL,
NATUS 1874.

For Character Sketch, see page 551.

117 A drawing of Churchill, published in 'Everyman' on 21 August 1914, at a time when his decision to send the Fleet to its War Stations before the outbreak of war was widely praised. In the 'Everyman' 'Character Sketch', an anonymous Member of Parliament wrote of Churchill: *'Those who have worked with him declare that there never was a Minister of the Crown so eager and swift in his work; and if they find a fault in him as a worker it is that he is apt to forget that all men are not endowed with his high talents and amazing energy. In times of relaxation he is never idle, and in times of great pressure he spares neither himself nor those around him, but he has the supreme gift of making his assistants in all ranks give the best of their labour freely to the task of the moment. Rumour tells us that he is heartless in his ambition and careless of every interest but his own. To that description his own closest associates, political, official, and personal, give the lie; and they will tell you that he is at once the most exacting and the most generous chief whom they have ever served.'*

WINSTON IN THE WAR
He is only Forty!

By T. P.

COLONEL SEELY AND MR. CHURCHILL DRIVING THROUGH THE STREETS OF BESIEGED ANTWERP.

118 On 3 October the Belgians planned to evacuate Antwerp. With the approval of Lord Kitchener and Sir Edward Grey, Churchill hurried to the city to rally its Belgian and British defenders. This photograph was published on 12 December 1914 in 'Great Deeds of the War'. The article was by T. P. O'Connor, the Irish Nationalist MP. With Churchill is his friend General Seely, a former Liberal Secretary of State for War.

119

Churchill at Antwerp. For three days he took virtual charge of the defence, helping to delay the German advance. Both while he was at Antwerp, and on his return, Churchill asked Asquith to be relieved of his Office and given a military command. Asquith refused, writing to a friend (Venetia Stanley) on 7 October: '*He is a wonderful creature, with a curious dash of schoolboy simplicity . . . and what someone said of genius – "a zigzag streak of lightning in the brain".*'

120 Churchill's third child, Sarah, was born on the day he returned from Antwerp. This family photograph, taken at Admiralty House towards the end of 1914, shows Churchill, his daughter Diana, his wife, his daughter Sarah (on her mother's lap), his son Randolph, his mother, his nephew Peregrine, his sister-in-law Lady Gwendeline, his nephew John-George, and his brother Jack, home briefly on leave. In October 1914 Jack had gone to the front with the Queen's Own Oxfordshire Hussars. On 9 November Churchill wrote to him from the Admiralty: '*I feel so acutely the ignoble position of one who merely cheers from the bank the gallant efforts of the rowers. But I cannot stir. The combinations at this moment are of the highest interest and importance. . . . Have no fear for the result. We have got the dirty dogs tight. The end is a long way off: but it is certain, tho' not in sight. . . . My dear I am always anxious about you. It wd take the edge off much if I cd be with you. I expect I shd be vy frightened but I wd dissemble.*'

121 Churchill, Kitchener and Lloyd George: a cartoon by Poy, published on Churchill's 40th birthday, 30 November 1914. That day, Margot Asquith wrote in her diary: '*Winston Churchill was 40 today. . . . He has done a good deal for a man of forty. . . . He never shirks, hedges, or protects himself – though he thinks of himself perpetually. He takes huge risks. He is at his very best just now; when others are shrivelled with grief – apprehensive, silent, irascible and self-conscious morally; Winston is intrepid, valourous, passionately keen and sympathetic, longing to be in the trenches – dreaming of war, big, buoyant, happy, even. It is very extraordinary, he is a born soldier.*' On 5 December 1914 Asquith wrote to Venetia Stanley about a new plan with which Churchill was involved: '*His volatile mind is at present set on Turkey & Bulgaria, & he wants to organize a heroic adventure against Gallipoli and the Dardanelles. . . .*' In May 1915 when Churchill had been forced to leave the Admiralty, Lord Kitchener told him: '*Well there is one thing at any rate they cannot take from you. The Fleet was ready.*'

123 On 19 February 1915 the War Cabinet agreed that troops should be sent to the Dardanelles (though not in the quantities which Churchill believed were essential if success were to be assured). On 25 February George V and Churchill went to Blandford, in Dorset, where the King inspected the Royal Naval Division before it sailed to the Dardanelles. This photograph was made into a postcard for the troops to send home with a farewell message. On the following day Churchill warned the War Council that if further troops were not sent, Britain would find herself '*face to face with a disaster*'.

22

urchill in February 1915, at the time when he and his naval advisers were preparing their bitious plan of attack at the Dardanelles, in the hope of capturing Constantinople, cing Turkey to surrender and persuading the neutral Balkan States (Bulgaria, Greece d Rumania) to attack Germany and Austria–Hungary. The War Cabinet had approved plan (to attack with ships alone) on 13 January 1915, despite Churchill's vehement tests that troops would be needed to follow up any naval success.

A VICTIM OF VAPOUR.

THE
COMPRESSION
VAPOUR BATH.
(Royal Navy Patent)

THE
BIG-POT
BOILER.

IRATE PATIENT: "This is ruining my system. Turn off the tap or I'll murder somebody."
SUAVE ATTENDANT: "Ah, he feels it! Now for a little more pressure."

124 While the final plans were being made for the Dardanelles operation, the public applauded the Navy's success in setting up a blockade of the German ports, and driving all German ships from the Atlantic, the Pacific and the Indian Ocean. This cartoon, showing the Kaiser's discomfiture, was published in the 'Manchester Dispatch' on 19 February 1915.

A PET AVERSION.

(*After the picture by Phiz, in "The Old Curiosity Shop," of Quilp and Kit's effigy.*)

125 A cartoon published in the 'Westminster Gazette' on 25 February 1915, showing the Kaiser in action against Churchill, with the Crown Prince watching. The caption read: '*Mr Winston Churchill has a prominent place in the hate of British Ministers expressed in Germany.*'

126 Churchill's brother Jack sailed for the Dardanelles on 13 March 1915, on the Staff of the military Commander-in-Chief, Sir Ian Hamilton. This photograph was taken some weeks after the troops had landed on the Gallipoli Peninsula on 25 April 1915.

127 At the Dardanelles, the naval attack of 18 March 1915 failed to break through the Turkish minefields, and the subsequent military landings of 25 April failed to gain more than a foothold on the rugged Gallipoli Peninsula. On 15 May Lord Fisher resigned and the Conservatives threatened to start the first controversial debate of the war. In the Cabinet crisis that followed, Asquith agreed to form a Coalition with the Conservatives, who, as a condition of their acceptance, demanded Churchill's removal from the Admiralty. Here he is seen, during the crisis, walking to 10 Downing Street. On the morning of 21 May Churchill wrote to Asquith: '*I did not believe it was possible to endure such anxiety. None of the ordinary strains of war – wh I have borne all these months – are comparable to this feeling. . . . I can only look to you. Let me stand or fall by the Dardanelles – but do not take it from my hands.*' Later than same day, Churchill accepted that his career as First Lord was over, writing to Asquith: '*I am grateful to you for yr kindness to me & belief in my vision of things.*'

128

Churchill walking across Horse Guards Parade with his successor as First Lord, the former Conservative Prime Minister, A. J. Balfour. On 26 May Churchill wrote to Balfour about the future of the Gallipoli campaign: '*The military operations shd proceed with all possible speed so that the period of danger may be shortened. Whatever force is necessary, can be spared, and can be used, shd be sent at once, & all at once. . . . Punishment must be doggedly borne.*'

"WHERE IS LANCASTER
AND WHAT IS A DUCHY?"

130 While at the Admiralty, Churchill had taken the initiative in pressing for an armoured, mechanical vehicle which could crush barbed wire and penetrate the German trench lines. On 28 June 1915 he and Lloyd George went to Wormwood Scrubs to watch the trial of the Killen–Strait barbed wire cutter, a forerunner of the tank. Churchill is half hidden behind the post; Lloyd George is in bowler hat. But Churchill felt acutely his lack of authority. On 20 September he wrote to his friend Jack Seely: '*It is odious to me to remain here watching sloth & folly, with full knowledge & no occupation.*'

129

On 27 May 1915 Churchill became Chancellor of the Duchy of Lancaster in Asquith's Coalition Government. It was a post without any real power. This photograph was printed in the 'Bystander' on 2 June. Clementine Churchill later recalled: '*When he left the Admiralty he thought he was finished. . . . I thought he would die of grief.*'

132 Churchill and his wife listen to Lord Kitchener at the Guildhall, 9 July 1915. Horatio Bottomley (hands clasped) is just behind Churchill. Kitchener appealed for further volunteers to serve on the western front. In Cabinet, Churchill argued – with Lloyd George's support – that it was essential to introduce conscription, but Kitchener insisted that the voluntary system was adequate. On 4 October 1915 Churchill threatened to resign from the Cabinet unless Kitchener were removed, writing to Asquith: '*The experiment of putting a great soldier at the head of the War Office in time of war has not been advantageous.*' Churchill argued that Lloyd George should be made Secretary of State for War, on account of his '*drive and penetrating insight*'. Asquith declined to make any such change.

131

Churchill with two of the Conservative Ministers who joined the Coalition in May 1915; Lord Lansdowne and Lord Curzon. He continued to advocate further military effort at the Dardanelles, writing to all his Cabinet colleagues on 18 June: '*There can be no doubt that we now possess the means and the power to take Constantinople before the end of the summer if we act with decision and with a due sense of proportion. The striking down of one of the three hostile Empires against which we are contending, and the fall to our arms of one of the most famous capitals in the world, with the results which must flow therefrom, will, conjoined with our other advantages, confer upon us a far-reaching influence among the Allies, and enable us to ensure their indispensable co-operation. Most of all, it will react on Russia. It will give the encouragement so sorely needed. It will give the reward so long desired. It will render a service to an Ally unparalleled in the history of nations. It will multiply the resources and open the channel for the re-equipment of the Russian armies. It will dominate the Balkan situation and cover Italy. It will resound through Asia. Here is the prize, and the only prize, which lies within reach this year. It can certainly be won without unreasonable expense, and within a comparatively short time. But we must act now, and on a scale which makes speedy success certain.*' But the renewed assault at Gallipoli, on 6 August, failed to drive the Turks from the Peninsula, and at the end of the year the British abandoned their attempts to break through to Constantinople.

133 to 136 Churchill and his wife at Enfield, 18 September 1915, when Churchill addressed munitions workers. During his speech he told them: '*We cannot understand the inscrutable purposes which have plunged these evils upon the world, and have involved all the nations of Europe in a catastrophe measureless in its horror. But we know that if in this time of crisis and strain we do our duty, we shall have done all that is in human power to do – and we shall so bear ourselves in this period – all us of, whatever part we play on the stage of the world's history – we shall bear ourselves so that those who come after us will find amid the signs and scars of this great struggle that the liberties of Europe and of Britain are still intact and inviolate; when those looking back upon our efforts such as they have been, will say of this unhappy but not inglorious generation, placed in a position of extraordinary trial, that it did not fail in the test, and that the torch which it preserved lights the world for us today.*'

137 Lloyd George and Churchill in Whitehall, October 1915. A month later Churchill was excluded from the newly formed inner War Cabinet, and resigned from the Government altogether, writing to Asquith on 11 November: '*I have a clear conscience which enables me to bear any responsibility for past events with composure. Time will vindicate my administration of the Admiralty, and assign me my due share in the vast series of preparations and operations which have secured us the command of the seas.*'

138 Having resigned from Asquith's Government, Churchill rejoined the Army and crossed to France, where he was attached for training to the Grenadier Guards. On 5 December 1915 he visited the French front line, together with his friend Captain Edward Louis Spears (third from left). On Churchill's left is General Fayolle (commanding the 33rd Corps), and behind the General is a German prisoner (in cap). That night Churchill wrote to his wife: '*I lunched with the HQ of the 33rd Corps and cheered them all up about the war & the future. The general insisted on our being photographed together – me in my French steel helmet – & to make a background German prisoners were lined up. . . .*' Churchill was full of admiration for Spears' bravery, writing to him a year later, in October 1916: '*I read your name this morning in the casualty list for the 4th time with keen emotion. . . . I cannot tell you how much I admire and reverence the brilliant & noble service you are doing & have done for the country. You are indeed a Paladin worthy to rank with the truest knights of the great days of romance. Thank God you are alive. Some good angel has guarded you amid such innumerable perils & brought you safely thus far along this terrible & never ending road.*'

139 On 4 January 1916 Churchill was appointed Lieutenant-Colonel, commanding the 6th Royal Scots Fusiliers. For six months he commanded them, first in training, then in the front line. This photograph, taken in Armentieres on 11 February, shows him with his 2nd in command, Sir Archibald Sinclair. Four days later Churchill wrote to his wife: '*Last night . . . after dinner, I had a splendid walk with Archie all over the top of the ground. We left the trenches altogether & made a thorough examination of all the fields, tracks, ruins etc immediately behind our line. You cannot show yourself here by day, but in the bright moonlight it is possible to move about without danger (except from random bullets) & to gain a vy clear impression. Archie was a vy good guide. We also went out in front of our own parapet into the No man's land & prowled about looking at our wire & visiting our listening posts. This is always exciting.*'

141

Humiliated by the hostile reaction to his speech, Churchill returned to the front. This photograph shows him in London on the eve of his return. Depressed at the turn of events, he wrote to his wife on 26 March 1916, from the trenches: '*So much effort, so many years of ceaseless fighting & worry, so much excitement & now this rough fierce life here under the hammer of Thor, makes my older mind turn for – the first time I think to other things than action. . . . Sometimes also I think I wd not mind stopping living vy much. I am so devoured by egoism that I wd like to have another soul in another world & meet you in another setting. . . . But I am not going to give in or tire at all. I am going on fighting to the vy end in any situation open to me from wh I can most effectively drive on this war to victory.*'

140

Churchill as Lieutenant-Colonel, 6th Royal Scots Fusiliers. On 6 March 1916, while he was in London on leave, he went to the House of Commons and denounced the Government's conduct of the naval war, warning MPs that: '*Blood and money, however lavishly poured out, would never repair the consequences of what might be even an unconscious relaxation of effort. . . . To lose momentum is not merely to stop but to fall.*' On 8 March Margot Asquith wrote to A. J. Balfour: '*I've never varied in my opinion of Winston I'm glad to say. He is a hound of the lowest sense of political honour, a fool of the lowest judgement & contemptible. He cured me of oratory in the House & bored me with oratory in the home.*'

The Right Hon. Winston S. Churchill, M.P.

143 Churchill speaking at Chelmsford, 9 September 1916. For six months he had argued in favour of a more vigorous conduct of the war, and had also sought to defend himself from the hostile cry: '*What about the Dardanelles?*', which was hurled at him on many public occasions. During his speech at Chelmsford he said: '. . . *in all classes of our countrymen there is no division of opinion as to what the ultimate outcome will be.* [Hear, hear.] *The great strength which our country has shown is a source of pride to everyone. The unanimity with which our Empire has rallied to the Mother Land in the great cause justifies and vindicates British institutions.* [Applause.] *It is over two years since the war began, and I well remember feeling at that time profoundly convinced that in declaring war on Germany our country had performed the most noble deed in all its history.* [Applause.] *We have gone through a lot since then: terrible losses, many disasters, bitter disappointments, but I never felt more sure than now, on this fine autumn afternoon, that the course we took two years ago was absolutely right* – [cheers] – *and that our children will live to bless the day and to glorify the deed.* [Loud cheers.]' On 7 December, Lloyd George replaced Asquith as Prime Minister. Churchill did not receive a place in the new Government; several Conservatives, including Lord Curzon, had insisted upon his exclusion.

142

Churchill returned to London from the western front in May 1916. Asquith did not offer him a place in the Government. On 15 July he wrote to his brother: '*Is it not damnable that I should be denied all real scope to serve this country, in this tremendous hour? Though my life is full of comfort, pleasure & prosperity, I writhe hourly not to be able to get my teeth effectively into the Boche. . . . Jack my dear I am learning to hate.*'

**144
and
145** In July 1917, despite strong Conservative opposition, Lloyd George appointed Churchill Minister of Munitions. For over a year he supervised the production of guns, tanks, aeroplanes and munitions. These photographs show him at Beardmore's Gun Works in Glasgow on 8 October 1918. Any defeatism, he told a public meeting in Glasgow that day, *'should be stamped out . . . with all the vigour of public opinion'.*

146 Churchill in Lille, 29 October 1918, watching a march past of British troops who had liberated the town eleven days before. Eddie Marsh is standing behind him (in bowler hat). Two days later, on 30 October, Turkey surrendered, followed by Austria–Hungary on 3 November and Germany on 11 November – '*a drizzle of empires*', Churchill told Marsh, '*falling through the air*'.

147 On 10 January 1919 Churchill became Secretary of State for War. A month later, on 14 February he went to the Paris Peace Conference with Field Marshal Sir Henry Wilson (Chief of the Imperial General Staff) to urge upon the French and Americans the need for a military expedition against the Russian Bolsheviks. But they were insistent that no Allied invasion would take place. Churchill accepted their decision. On 19 February, after his return to London, he told an audience at the Mansion House: '*If Russia is to be saved, as I pray she may be saved, she must be saved by Russians. It must be by Russian manhood and Russian courage and Russian virtue that the rescue and regeneration of this once mighty nation and famous branch of the European family can alone be achieved. The aid which we can give to these Russian Armies – who we do not forget were called into the field originally during the German war to some extent by our inspiration and who are now engaged in fighting against the foul baboonery of Bolshevism – can be given by arms, munitions, equipment, and technical services raised upon a voluntary basis.*'

WINSTON'S BAG

HE HUNTS LIONS AND BRINGS HOME DECAYED CATS

148 Throughout 1919 Churchill tried to increase British arms supplies to the anti-Bolsheviks, and denounced Bolshevism in Parliament and in the Press. By the end of 1919 the War Office had sent over £100 million pounds of military supplies from Britain to Russia. But the anti-Bolshevik forces, despite British support, were unable to capture Petrograd or Moscow, and were finally defeated. Churchill's vociferous denunciation of the Bolsheviks provoked bitter comment; this cartoon, by the cartoonist Low, was published in the 'Star' on 21 January 1920.

149 In August 1919 Churchill went to Cologne, where he inspected the British Army of Occupation. Field-Marshal Sir Henry Wilson (Chief of the Imperial General Staff) is standing on Churchill's left, with Sir Archibald Sinclair (who had become Churchill's Military Secretary), between them.

150 and 151 Inspecting British forces, Cologne, August 1919.

152 Churchill and the Prince of Wales (later King Edward VIII) at a luncheon party in the House of Commons, 5 June 1919, to honour the three American airmen who had flown the Atlantic from the United States to Portugal. Six years earlier, after Churchill had met the Prince of Wales at Balmoral, he wrote to his wife (on 20 September 1913): '*He is so nice, & we have made rather friends. They are worried a little about him, as he has become very spartan – rising at 6 & eating hardly anything. He requires to fall in love with a pretty cat. . . .*'

153

Churchill and his wife arrive at Lincolns Inn on 7 October 1919, when he was summoned to give evidence to the Royal Commission on Awards to Inventors, which was enquiring into the origins of the tank.

154

Churchill reading his evidence about the origins of the tank. In its report the Royal Commission declared (on 17 November 1919): '*In the first place the Commission desire to record their view that it was primarily due to the receptivity, courage and driving force of the Rt. Hon Winston Spencer Churchill that the general idea of the use of such an instrument of warfare as the Tank was converted into a practical shape.*' The report continued: '*Mr Winston Churchill has very properly taken the view that all his thought and time belonged to the State and that he was not entitled to make any claim for an award, even had he wished to do so.*'

155 In 1919 and 1920 Churchill was Secretary of State for Air, as well as for War. Here, at the Hendon Air Display on 8 July 1920, he stands with Lady Sykes (Bonar Law's daughter), her husband Sir Frederick Sykes (Controller-General of Civil Aviation) and the Chief of the Air Staff, Sir Hugh Trenchard. Both as Secretary for Air, and as Colonial Secretary (1921–22) Churchill was a strong advocate of an independent Air Force; and supported plans for many pioneer air policies, including the Cairo to Karachi air service, the Air Force Administration of Iraq, the development of long-range flying, and the use of aerial bombing as an instrument of imperial policy.

156

Relaxation: Churchill playing Polo at Roehampton, June 1920. Because he had badly dislocated his shoulder in India in 1894, he had to play polo with a strap round his right arm; but he continued to play until he was fifty-one years old. His last game was in Malta in 1926.

157 On 15 February 1921 Churchill became Colonial Secretary. Three weeks later he set off for Cairo, where, in conference with his Middle East advisers, he set up two Arab kingdoms (in Transjordan and Iraq) and confirmed Britain's promise to the Jews of a 'National Home' in Palestine. On Sunday 20 March Churchill, his wife, T. E. Lawrence (his adviser on Arab affairs) and Gertrude Bell visited the Pyramids, and were photographed on camels. Churchill also set up his easel and spent part of the day painting the Pyramids.

158 From Cairo, Churchill went to Jerusalem, where, on 28 March 1921, he informed the Emir Abdullah (who was to become King of Transjordan) that Palestine was to remain a British Mandate open to Jewish settlement. Here Churchill is seen, with Lawrence and Abdullah, during a break in their talks. Churchill then visited the Jewish settlement at Rishon-le-Zion. On 14 June, after his return to England, he told the House of Commons: '*I was driven into a fertile and thriving country estate, where the scanty soil gave place to good crops and good cultivation, and then to vineyards and finally to the most beautiful, luxurious orange groves, all created in 20 or 30 years by the exertions of the Jewish community who live there. . . . I defy anybody, after seeing work of this kind, achieved by so much labour, effort and skill, to say that the British Government, having taken up the position it has, could cast it all aside and leave it to be rudely and brutally overturned by the incursion of a fanatical attack by the Arab population from outside.*'

160

In October 1922 Churchill was defeated in the General Election, and for the first time in twenty-two years was no longer a Member of Parliament. With the defeat of Lloyd George's Coalition, he was also excluded from the Cabinet. He began to write his war memoirs, entitled 'The World Crisis', for which he received over £40,000 as an advance. At the same time he bought Chartwell, an Elizabethan manor house near Westerham, in Kent, for less than £5,000. Chartwell remained his home until his death. Churchill greatly extended the house, and even built an island. Here he is seen at his fishpond.

159

Churchill leaving one of the Irish Treaty Conferences at 10 Downing Street on 26 May 1922. For nearly a year he took a major part, first in the Treaty negotiations, then in seeking to reconcile the Irish leaders from both north and south, and finally in persuading the House of Commons to accept the establishment of the Irish Free State in Southern Ireland. On 16 February 1922 he told the House of Commons: '*For generations we have been wandering and floundering in the Irish bog; but at last we think that in this Treaty we have set our feet upon a pathway, which has already become a causeway – narrow, but firm and far-reaching. Let us march along this causeway with determination and circumspection, without losing heart and without losing faith. If Britain continues to march forward along that path, the day may come – it may be distant, but it may not be so distant as we expect – when, turning round, Britain will find at her side Ireland united, a nation, and a friend.*'

161 Throughout 1923 and 1924 Churchill tried to return to Parliament. He was defeated at West Leicester, at the General Election in December 1923, and stood next for the Abbey Division of Westminster. This photograph shows him at his London home in Sussex Square, at work with his secretary, Miss Fisher, on 6 March 1924, during the Abbey election campaign.

162 Churchill and his wife receive a copy of Churchill's election address during the Abbey campaign. Churchill's main platform was an attack on Socialism. He described himself officially as an 'Independent anti-Socialist' candidate, and told the Press on 7 March that he represented '*all who believed in enterprise, self-reliance, and civil liberty, as opposed to the tyrannous barbarism of the Marxian system*'.

OUR OWN MUSSOLINI

163 This cartoon was published in the 'Weekly Westminster' on 15 March, during the Abbey campaign. Its caption was written by the historian Philip Guedalla: '*High up on the short waiting-list of England's Mussolinis stands the name of Winston Spencer Churchill. . . . In a wild vision of the distant future we seem to see him marching black-shirted upon Buckingham Palace with a victorious army of genteel but bellicose persons who have at last set their elegantly shod feet upon the coarse neck of Labour.*' The picture on the wall alludes to the British battleships sunk at the Dardanelles.

164 The Abbey by-election. Churchill's car overtakes Labour supporters on polling day, 20 March 1924. In a poll of over 22,000, he was defeated by only 43 votes by the official Conservative candidate.

165 Churchill doffs his hat after his defeat at the Abbey by-election. His wife turns to look at the camera.

THE FIGHT FOR THE FAVOURITE.

MR. LLOYD GEORGE. "HERE, I SAY, THIS IS MY MOUNT."
MR. WINSTON CHURCHILL. "NO, IT ISN'T. I THOUGHT OF IT FIRST."

166 Speaking at Liverpool on 8 May 1924, Churchill described Socialism as '*one of the most profound and mischievous delusions which can ever enter the brain of man*'. This cartoon appeared in 'Punch' on 4 June.

with recollections of a 1914 Recruiting poster.

The Recruiting Parade.

167 This cartoon by Low was published in the 'Star' on 7 October 1924. Lord Rothermere and Lord Beaverbrook (far right) are holding up the anti-Sosh banner. Two weeks earlier, on 23 September 1924 Churchill had been adopted as a 'Constitutional and Anti-Socialist' candidate by the Epping Conservatives, and on 26 September he had appealed to an audience of Scottish Conservatives for Conservative and Liberal unity in the face of Socialism. The policy of Ramsay MacDonald's Labour Government, Churchill declared, was: '*Our bread for the Bolshevik serpent; our aid for foreigners of every country; our favours for Socialists all over the world who have no country; but for our own daughter States across the oceans, on whom the future of the British island and nation depends, only the cold stones of indifference, aversion and neglect. That is the policy with which the Socialist Government confronts us, and against that policy we will strive to marshall the unconquerable might of Britain.*'

168
and
169
Churchill and his wife during the Epping election campaign. In his election address, issued
on 12 October 1924, he declared: '*Spellbound by the lure of Moscow, wire-pulled through
subterranean channels, Mr Ramsay MacDonald and his associates have attempted to make the
British nation accomplices in Bolshevist crimes.*' On 29 October he was elected by a majority
of near 10,000, in a total poll of 33,000. In 1925 he rejoined the Conservative Party, which he
had left twenty-one years earlier.

170 On 4 November 1924 the Conservative leader Stanley Baldwin replaced Ramsay Mac-Donald as Prime Minister; two days later he appointed Churchill as Chancellor of the Exchequer (although Churchill was still not a member of the Conservative Party). This photograph shows Churchill being driven to Buckingham Palace on 7 November to receive his seal of office from the King.

171 Churchill at Victoria Station, 7 January 1925, on his way to attend the Allied Financial Conference in Paris, With him is his political secretary, Lord Wodehouse (later Earl of Kimberley). Churchill tried to persuade the French to agree to a reduction in German reparations, and to persuade the Americans to reduce France's war debts. On 8 January he told the negotiators: '*Hope flies on wings, and Inter-Allied Conferences plod along dusty roads, but still the conviction exists that progress is being made towards the recognition of the unity and prosperity of Europe. . . .*'

172

Churchill leaving 11 Downing Street on 28 April 1925, on his way to the House of Commons to deliver his first budget speech, and to announce that Britain would return to the Gold Standard. In his budget, Churchill reduced income tax, increased death duties, and introduced pensions for widows and orphans. Stanley Baldwin told the Commons that Churchill's budget would bring *'hope and comfort to the aged, to the homes that are oppressed by sorrow'*. But the economist J. M. Keynes believed that the folly of a return to the Gold Standard would eventually obliterate all the benefits of the social legislation.

173 Churchill parking in Birdcage Walk, Westminster, 1925. As Chancellor of the Exchequer, he continually argued in favour of strict economy, warning the House of Commons on 7 August 1925: *'The day may come when the nation's whole scale of living must be reduced. If that day comes, Parliament must lay the burden equally on all classes.'* And he added: *'I am not invested with dictatorial powers. If I were I should be quite ready to dictate.'*

174

Churchill at 10 Downing Street on 3 May 1926, at the start of the General Strike. During the Strike he organized the printing of a Government newspaper, the 'British Gazette', and was a leading advocate of 'no surrender' to the strikers. On 19 May, when the Strike was over, the 'Daily Mail', after praising the courage of Stanley Baldwin and Lord Birkenhead declared: *'Nor can the services of Mr Winston Churchill be overlooked. His energy and initiative have never been more clearly shown in a great cause. His presence in the Cabinet at this juncture has been an undoubted source of strength.'* As soon as the strike was over, Churchill made great efforts to persuade the coal-owners to make concessions to the coal-miners; but his efforts were in vain.

175 Churchill and his son Randolph during their visit to Italy in January 1927. During his visit, Churchill told the Italian Press: *'If I had been an Italian, I am sure I should have been whole-heartedly with you in your triumphant struggle against the bestial appetites and passions of Leninism.'* Of Mussolini he said: *'I could not help being charmed, like so many other people have been, by his gentle and simple bearing and by his calm, detached poise in spite of so many burdens and dangers.'*

176 Their Italian visit over, Churchill and his son were the guests of the Duke of Westminster at Foucarmont, in the Forest of Eu. This photograph shows them about to set off for a wild boar hunt on 31 January 1927.

177 On holiday at Deauville, 1 August 1927.

178
Randolph
Churchill
skating with his
mother on the
lake at
Chartwell during
the 'Great Snow'
of 1927–28.

179
Chartwell under
snow.
Churchill's study
is the room
with the bow
window, on the
extreme left.

180
Churchi
putting th
finishing touche
to his snowman

181 Madame Chanel, Randolph Churchill (aged sixteen) and his father at the Duke of Westminster's boarhounds, Dampierre, France. During the inter-war years Churchill went
almost every year to France, where several of his friends had houses and estates. There he
hunted, painted, and wrote books. In England, he spent as much time as he could at Chartwell. From Chartwell, he wrote to his wife on 5 April 1928: '*I am becoming a Film fan, and
last week I went to see "The Last Command", a very fine anti-Bolshevik film, and "Wings"
which is all about aeroplane fighting and perfectly marvellous. I was so much impressed by it
that I went a second time. . . .*'

182

Churchill and his son at Dampierre. On 8 April 1928 Churchill wrote to his wife: *'Very satisfactory reports have arrived about Randolph. . . . There is no doubt he is developing fast, and in those directions wh will enable him to make his way in the world – by writing & speaking – in politics, at the bar, or in journalism. There are some vy strange & even formidable traits in his character. His mind is free & growing more powerful every day. It is quite startling to hear him argue. His present phase is rabid Agnosticism, & last night in argument with Grigg he more than defended his dismal position. The logical strength of his mind, the courage of his thought, & the brutal & sometimes repulsive character of his rejoinders impressed me vy forcibly. He is far more advanced than I was at his age, & quite out of the common – for good or ill.'*

184 Churchill on board the giant Short Brothers 'Calcutta' flying boat, moored on the Thames opposite the Houses of Parliament. Throughout his life he retained a keen interest in new inventions and means of transport. In 1924 he had published a pamphlet, entitled 'Shall We Commit Suicide', in which he had asked: *'Have we reached the end? . . . May there not be methods of using explosive energy incomparably more intense than anything heretofore discovered? Might not a bomb no bigger than an orange be found to possess a secret power to destroy a whole block of buildings – nay, to concentrate the force of a thousand tons of cordite and blast a township at a stroke? Could not explosives even of the existing type be guided automatically in flying machines by wireless or other rays, without a human pilot, in ceaseless procession upon a hostile city, arsenal, camp, or dockyard?'*

83

'hurchill on his way to deliver his fourth budget, 24 April 1928. With him (in top hat) is his 'arliamentary Private Secretary, Robert Boothby. Among the measures which Churchill itroduced was the first British tax on petrol, fixed at fourpence a gallon.

185 Churchill and his daughter Sarah photographed at Chartwell on 3 September 1928, laying the bricks for a new cottage on the estate. Sarah's fourteenth birthday was a month later. On the following day this photograph (minus Sarah) was published in the 'Daily Sketch' with the comment: *'Those who may be inclined to point out that he has not got his coat off should bear in mind that he took it off when he was helping to lay the foundations, and that, anyhow, he is wearing an old suit. He lays one brick a minute.'*

186

Churchill and his wife at 11 Downing Street, after he had driven up from Chartwell on 15 April 1929, to give his fifth budget. Behind them are Randolph, Robert Boothby (in top hat) and Sarah. One of his new measures was to remove the Preferential Duty on tea. Thus tea prices fell in 1929 (on the eve of the election), just as petrol prices had risen in 1928. He also abolished the Betting Tax, and reduced Publican's Licences. Before Churchill, only Walpole Pitt, Peel and Gladstone had introduced and carried five consecutive budgets; each was, or was to become, Prime Minister.

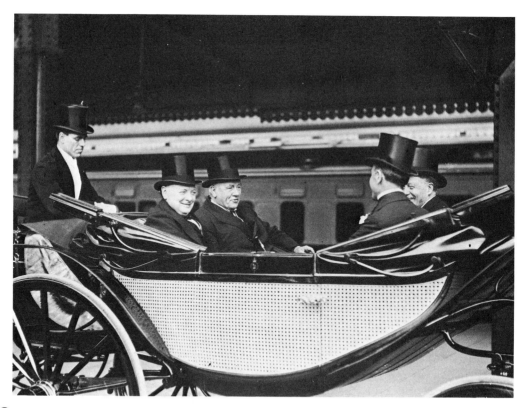

188 The General Election was held on 30 May 1929, and the Labour Party returned to power with more MPs (although less overall votes) than the Conservatives. This photograph shows Churchill and Lord Cushenden (Chancellor of the Duchy of Lancaster) leaving Windsor Station to hand in their seals of office to the King on 7 June.

187

Churchill as Chancellor of the Exchequer: a photograph issued on the front page of his election manifesto, 10 May 1929. In his manifesto Churchill denounced the Socialists who, he wrote, had planned during the General Strike '*to paralyse the life and industry of the whole Island, and if they had succeeded, they would have subverted the representative and parliamentary institutions under which we have lived and grown since the great Civil War of the 17th Century*'. This was a major theme of his election speeches. On 12 February he had told a mass meeting of the 'Anti-Socialist and Anti-Communist Union' in London: '*Socialism today is intellectually bankrupt and discredited, and has been proved on a gigantic scale and with perfect clearness to be fatal to the welfare of living nations. But we have seen with melancholy feelings how year after year a larger number of our own fellow-countrymen have allowed themselves to drift into an easy acceptance of Socialist doctrines, and let themselves be regimented under foreign made standards of Communist collectivism.*'

189 and 190 No longer a Minister, Churchill left England on 3 August 1929 for a three-month visit to Canada and the United States. These photographs were taken at Calgary. With him below are his son Randolph, his nephew John-George, and his brother Jack. On 21 September, while they were in Hollywood, Churchill persuaded Charlie Chaplin to do imitations of Napoleon, Uriah Heep, Henry Irving, and John Barrymore as Hamlet. Randolph Churchill noted in his diary: '*Papa & Charlie sat up till about 3. Papa wants him to act the young Napoleon and has promised to write the Scenario*'.

191
Churchill returned to England in November 1929. It was ten years before he held public office again. Much of that time he spent writing books: his memoirs 'My Early Life' (published in 1930); 'The World Crisis: The Eastern Front' (1931); 'Thoughts and Adventures' (1932); a life of his ancestor John Duke of Marlborough (1933); and 'Great Contemporaries' (1937, revised 1938). He did most of his writing at Chartwell, where this photograph was taken during a visit from Charlie Chaplin.

192 Churchill and Lloyd George at the Memorial Service for Lord Balfour, Westminster Abbey, 22 March 1930. Writing in the 'Strand' magazine in April 1931 Churchill reflected: '*Arthur Balfour did not mingle in the hurly-burly. He glided upon its surface. . . . His aversion from the Roman Catholic faith was dour and inveterate. Otherwise he seemed to have the personal qualification of a great Pope. . . . When they took him to the Front to see the war, he admired with bland interest through his pince-nez the bursting shells. Luckily none came near enough to make him jump, as they will make any man jump, if they have their chance. . . . [In December 1916] he passed from our Cabinet to the other, from the Prime Minister who was his champion to the Prime Minister who had been his most powerful critic, like a powerful graceful cat walking delicately and unsoiled across a rather muddy street.*'

193

Randolph Churchill about to leave Waterloo station for a lecture tour of the United States. Only nineteen years old, he was still an undergraduate at Oxford, and as a result of the tour, never took a university degree. But, as he wrote in his memoirs, 'Twenty-One Years': '*The idea of going off to America and teaching, rather than learning, appealed to me strongly, and I resolved to go. Everybody except my father thought I was crazy; he encouraged me to embark on the venture.*'

194 In 1930 Churchill was elected Chancellor of Bristol University. On his first visit to Bristol he was placed '*under arrest*' by the students, who had found him guilty '*of acquiring a new hat and a new chancellorship and with neglecting to supply forenoon coffee and biscuits to the students*'.

195

On 30 October 1930 at a meeting of Conservative MPs at Caxton Hall, a majority voted in favour of Baldwin's continued leadership of the Conservative Party. But Churchill had already begun to oppose Baldwin's policy of eventual self-government for India, and on 28 September had informed the Press that he would not even consider retiring from public life while the question of India's future was still undecided. On 1 October he wrote to Lord Burnham: *'I am deeply concerned about the folly and weakness which is going to throw India into hideous confusion.'*

196 Austen Chamberlain (with cigarette and eye glass), Sir Robert Horne and Churchill outside Caxton Hall, 30 October 1930. The meeting marked the beginning of five years' sustained and bitter opposition by Churchill to the Conservative Party's India policy.

197

Churchill waiting to speak at the first meeting of the Indian Empire Society, at Cannon Street, London on 12 December 1930. During his speech he denounced Conservative Party plans to give India Dominion Status, with the right to secede from the British Empire, telling the audience: '*The extremists who are, and will remain, the dominant force among the Indian political classes have in their turn moved their goal forward to absolute independence, and picture to themselves an early date when they will obtain complete control of the whole of Hindustan, when the British will be no more to them than any other European nation, when white people will be in India only upon sufferance, when debts and obligations of all kinds will be repudiated and when an army of white janissaries, officered if necessary from Germany, will be hired to secure the armed ascendancy of the Hindu. All these absurd and dangerous pretensions have so far been met in speech with nothing but soft deprecatory and placatory words by the British Government in India, or at home. . . . The truth is that Gandhi-ism and all it stands for will, sooner or later, have to be grappled with and finally crushed. It is no use trying to satisfy a tiger by feeding him with cat's-meat. . . . We have no intention of casting away that most truly bright and precious jewel in the crown of the King, which more than all our other Dominions and Dependencies constitutes the glory and strength of the British Empire. The loss of India would mark and consummate the downfall of the British Empire. That great organism would pass at a stroke out of life into history. From such a catastrophe there could be no recovery.*'

198 On 31 December 1931, while on a lecture tour in the United States, Churchill was knocked over by a taxi-cab in New York and badly injured. This photograph shows him leaving the Lennox Hill Hospital, New York.

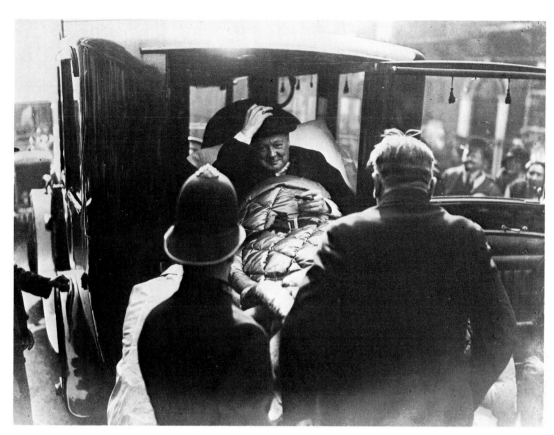

199 On 27 September 1932 Churchill was taken ill with paratyphoid. In this photograph he is seen leaving the Beaumont Street Nursing Home in London on 10 October. For six weeks he recuperated at Chartwell. Then, on 23 November, he returned to the House of Commons, and spoke with foreboding of the future of Europe, of the dangers of premature disarmament, and of the dangers of the Nazi movement: '*Do not delude yourselves. Do not let His Majesty's Government believe – I am sure they do not believe – that all that Germany is asking for is equal status. . . . All these bands of sturdy Teutonic youths, marching through the streets and roads of Germany, with the light of desire in their eyes to suffer for their Fatherland, are not looking for status. They are looking for weapons, and, when they have the weapons, believe me they will then ask for the return of lost territories and lost colonies, and when that demand is made it cannot fail to shake and possibly shatter to their foundations every one of the countries I have mentioned (Belgium, Poland, Rumania, Czechoslovakia and Yugoslavia).*' And Churchill continued: '. . . *I would now say, "Tell the truth to the British people." They are a tough people, a robust people. They may be a bit offended at the moment, but if you have told them exactly what is going on you have insured yourself against complaints and reproaches which are very unpleasant when they come home on the morrow of some disillusion. . . .*' Churchill then spoke of the policy which he believed should be pursued: '*I would follow any real path, not a sham or a blind alley, which led to lasting reconciliation between Germany and her neighbours. . . . Here is my general principle. The removal of the just grievances of the vanquished ought to precede the disarmament of the victors. . . . It would be far safer to reopen questions like those of the Dantzig Corridor and Transylvania, with all their delicacy and difficulty, in cold blood and in a calm atmosphere and while the victor nations still have ample superiority, than to wait and drift on, inch by inch and stage by stage, until once again vast combinations, equally matched, confront each other face to face.*'

Nazi Movement—Local Version

201 Lloyd George and Churchill in November 1934, at the Printers' Pension Corporation Festival Dinner, held at The Connaught Rooms in London. A year earlier, in August 1933, both of them – and also Austen Chamberlain – had been excluded by the BBC from taking part in a series of broadcast political talks. All three had protested about the ban, writing to the Chairman of the BBC, J. H. Whitley, on 23 August 1933: '. . . *we are the three senior Privy Councillors in the House of Commons. . . . Such a principle if applied in Parliament would reduce its debates to mere regimentations of machine-controlled opinion and would deny fair expression to independent and non-official news.*' The protest (which was sent from Chartwell) was in vain; the BBC persisted in its ban.

200

Churchill's continued denunciation of India self-government associated him, for the first time in his life, with the right-wing of the Conservative Party, to whom he appeared as a potential leader, and an alternative to Baldwin. On 30 March 1933 this cartoon appeared in the 'Daily Herald'. That same day Churchill told the House of Commons that: '*He would appeal particularly to the new members. Let them beware that in years to come they did not find themselves sitting by their own fireside when across the dark distances from India, to quote the phrase of John Morley, they would hear "the dull roar and scream of carnage and confusion" coming back to them. Then bitter would be their feelings of responsibility and agony when they felt that they themselves played a part in bringing about a situation of such frightful disaster.*' Of the people of India Churchill said: '*100,000,000 of human beings are here to greet the dawn, to toil upon the plains, to bow before the temples of inexorable gods. Because they are here you cannot abandon them. They are as much our children as any children can be. They are actually in the world as the result of what this nation and this Parliament have done. It is impossible that you should leave them to be diminished by the hideous process of diminution which keeps the population of China in check. It is impossible that you should hand them over to the oppressor and to the spoiler and disinterest yourself in their fortunes. By every law of God or man Parliament is responsible for them, and never could we hold an honourable name among the nations if we pretended that, by any sophistry of liberal doctrine or constitutional theory, we could give away our responsibility, so vital and great.*'

202 A photograph taken at the accession of Edward VIII, on 20 January 1936. Churchill is with a group of Privy Councillors (Sir Herbert Samuel is on the left. Churchill was anxious to return to the Cabinet, from which he had already been excluded for seven years. But on 21 February he wrote to his wife of how the new Prime Minister, Stanley Baldwin, '*desires above all things to avoid bringing me in. This I must now recognize. But his own position is much shaken, and the storm clouds gather.*' Six days later Clementine Churchill replied: '*My darling – I think Baldwin must be mad not to ask you to help him. Perhaps it is a case of "Those whom the Gods wish to Destroy. . . .".*' At the end of April, Churchill's name was much canvassed for the newly created post of Minister for Co-ordination of Defence, but Baldwin refused to bring him back. On 3 March, Churchill wrote to his wife: '*I do not mean to break my heart whatever happens. Destiny plays her part.*' If a post could be found for him, he added, '*I will work faithfully before God and man for PEACE, and not allow pride or excitement to sway my spirit.*'

203 Churchill on board the Admiralty yacht 'Enchantress' at Spithead, May 1936, when the new King, Edward VIII, reviewed the Fleet. Having failed to undermine Baldwin's Indian policy, or to dislodge him from the leadership of the Conservative Party, Churchill took up the new King's cause at the time of the abdication, and protested bitterly against Baldwin's part in the abdication crisis. On 5 December 1936 Churchill issued a public statement: *'I plead for time and patience. The nation must realise the character of the constitutional issue. There is no question of any conflict between the King and Parliament. Parliament has not been consulted in any way, nor allowed to express any opinion. The question is whether the King is to abdicate upon the advice of the Ministers of the day. No such advice has ever before been tendered to a Sovereign in Parliamentary times . . . If the King refuses to take the advice of his Ministers, they are, of course, free to resign. They have no right whatever to put pressure upon him to accept their advice by soliciting beforehand assurances from the Leader of the Opposition that he will not form an alternative administration in the event of their resignation, and thus confronting the King with an ultimatum. . . . Howsoever this matter may turn, it is pregnant with calamity and inseparable from inconvenience. But all the evil aspects will be aggravated beyond measure if the utmost chivalry is not shown, both by Ministers and by the British nation, toward a gifted and beloved King, torn between private and public obligations of love and duty.'* Two days later the House of Commons shouted Churchill down when he pleaded for delay on the King's behalf. Edward VIII abdicated on 9 December. Churchill's political reputation was at a low ebb. *'He has undermined in five minutes the patient reconstruction work of five years'* Harold Nicolson noted in his diary.

204 Churchill and his son after bathing at Chartwell, 1935. Churchill had himself supervised the building of the swimming pool on the estate.

205 Churchill walking in the grounds of Chartwell with his friend Ralph Wigram, a senior Foreign Office official who shared Churchill's fears of Nazi Germany. Wigram died suddenly at the age of forty, on 31 December 1936. On learning of Wigram's death Churchill wrote to Mrs Wigram (later Ava, Viscountess Waverley): '*I admired always so much his courage, integrity of purpose, high comprehending vision. He was one of those – how few – who guard the life of Britain. Now he is gone – and on the eve of this fateful year. Indeed it is a blow to England, and to all the best that England means. It is only a week or so that he rang me up to speak about the late King. I can hear his voice in my memory. And You? What must be your loss? But still you will have a right to dwell on all that you did for him. You shielded that bright steady flame that burned in the broken lamp. But for you it would long ago have been extinguished, and its light would not have guided us thus far upon our journey.*'

207 Churchill and Lord Halifax (the Foreign Secretary) in conversation in Whitehall, 29 March 1938. Hitler had annexed Austria seventeen days earlier, on 21 March. On 14 March, Churchill told the House of Commons: '*Europe is confronted with a programme of aggression, nicely calculated and timed, unfolding stage by stage, and there is only one choice open, not only to us but to other countries, either to submit like Austria, or else take effective measures while time remains to ward off the danger, and if it cannot be warded off to cope with it. . . . If we go on waiting upon events, how much shall we throw away of resources now available for our security and the maintenance of peace? How many friends will be alienated, how many potential allies shall we see go one by one down the grisly gulf? How many times will bluff succeed until behind bluff ever gathering forces have accumulated reality? . . . Where are we going to be two years hence, for instance, when the German Army will certainly be much larger than the French Army, and when all the small nations will have fled from Geneva to pay homage to the everwaxing powers of the Nazi system, and to make the best terms that they can for themselves?*'

206

Churchill at Chartwell, supervising the building of a new cottage on the estate, 25 February 1938. Although he had been out of office for over eight years, Churchill now emerged as the most vociferous advocate of rearmament, and international alliances, within the League of Nations, to deter German or Italian aggression. On 4 February 1938 he had declared, in an article in the 'Evening Standard': '*What is the alternative to the League of Nations and the maintenance of its authority, weakened as it now is? The alternative is sombre. It is for Britain and France, rich, powerful, heavily armed, to stand aside and allow Central and Eastern Europe to clatter into anarchy, or congeal into a Nazi domination. . . . This process would not be pleasant to any of the States now existing in Middle Europe. It would be accompanied by intense internal stresses such as destroyed the empire of the great Napoleon. It would be melancholy for the world. It seems very likely that the Western democracies would remain erect at the end of it. But what a cataract of misfortune would be opened upon these short-sighted governments and unfortunately peoples, who through mere incapacity to combine upon a broad international platform had left themselves the prey to measureless tribulation!*' On 16 February Hitler demanded – and obtained – the inclusion of Austrian Nazis in the Austrian Government.

**208
and
209**

Two photographs of Churchill leaving 10 Downing Street on 10 September 1938, during the Czech crisis. He was bitterly opposed to the Munich agreement signed by Hitler, Neville Chamberlain, Mussolini and Daladier which ceded large areas of Czechoslovakia to Germany. On 5 October he told the House of Commons: '*I do not grudge our loyal, brave people, who were ready to do their duty no matter what cost, who never flinched under the strain of last week – I do not grudge them the natural, spontaneous outburst of joy and relief when they learned that the hard ordeal would no longer be required of them at the moment; but they should know the truth. They should know that there has been gross neglect and deficiency in our defences; they should know that we have sustained a defeat without a war, the consequences of which will travel far with us along our road; they should know that we have passed an awful milestone in our history, when the whole equilibrium of Europe has been deranged, and that the terrible words have for the time being been pronounced against the Western democracies: "Thou art weighed in the balance and found wanting." And do not suppose that this is the end. This is only the beginning of the reckoning. This is only the first sip, the first foretaste of a bitter cup which will be proffered to us year by year unless by a supreme recovery of moral health and martial vigour, we arise again and take our stand for freedom as in the olden time.*'

**210
and
211** On 25 February 1939 the magazine 'Picture Post' sent a photographer to Chartwell, to photograph Churchill at work.

212
and In his study at Chartwell, 25 February 1939.
213

214 Churchill flies as a co-pilot, 16 April 1939, while visiting No 615 Auxiliary Air Force Squadron at Kenley. He had just been gazetted as the Squadron's Honorary Air Commodore. Nine days earlier, Italy had invaded Albania, and on 13 April Churchill had argued in the House of Commons in favour of compulsory national service, and a fuller use of national talent: '*The danger is now very near. A great part of Europe is to a very large extent mobilised. Millions of men are being prepared for war. Everywhere the frontier defences are manned. . . . How can we bear to continue to lead our comfortable, easy life here at home, unwilling even to pronounce the word "compulsion", unwilling even to take the necessary measure by which the armies that we have promised can alone be recruited and equipped? How can we continue – let me say it with particular frankness and sincerity – with less than the full force of the nation incorporated in the governing instrument? These very methods, which the Government owe it to the nation and to themselves to take, are not only indispensable to the duties that we have accepted but, by their very adoption, they may rescue our people and the people of many lands from the dark, bitter waters which are rising fast on every side.*' The House of Commons and the Government accepted Churchill's arguments. On 18 April his friend Brendan Bracken wrote to the American Financier Bernard Baruch: '*Winston has won his long fight. Our Government are now adopting the policy that he advised three years ago. No public man in our time has shown more foresight. And I believe that his long, lonely struggle to expose the dangers of the dictatorships will prove to be the best chapter in his crowded life.*'

215 Churchill addresses a lunch-time crowd at the Mansion House, London, on 24 April 1939, as part of the national drive for Territorial Army recruits. On his right is the Lord Mayor of London, Sir Frank Bowater. On 18 May Parliament passed a Bill for the introduction of compulsory national service. On the following day Churchill told an audience at the Corn Exchange in Cambridge: '*We have every reason to be contented with the reception which the Conscription Bill has received abroad. It could never have been intended to overawe Germany or Italy. In those countries they count their soldiers by the million; and Signor Mussolini says that he has eight million. Therefore the addition of two hundred thousand young men to our armed forces is no menace to the Dictator Powers. It is the effect upon our Allies and those countries to whom we have given guarantees that is important.*'

216 Leon Blum, the French Socialist leader (and former Prime Minister) visited Churchill at Chartwell on 10 May 1939. Nine days later, speaking at the Corn Exchange in Cambridge, Churchill declared, as an argument in favour of Compulsory National Service: '*The French do not easily understand that an island people who have not seen the watch fires of a hostile camp on their own soil for a thousand years have deep prejudices against militarism, and are historically attached to the voluntary system. They only know that they would have to stand for many terrible months against the German Army, and that we were not willing to put our prejudices aside, or depart from our normal system. They would not think it fair, and it would not have been fair.*'

MR. WINSTON CHURCHILL AND MR. ANTHONY EDEN
DEMAND A WHOLE-HEARTED ALLIANCE WITH RUSSIA.

217 During the Spring and Summer of 1939, Churchill was joined in his opposition to Government policy by Anthony Eden (who had resigned as Foreign Secretary in February 1938). Both believed that one way of deterring Hitler from aggression in Europe was by an immediate alliance between Britain, France and the Soviet Union. This cartoon was published in 'Punch' on 31 May 1939. But Neville Chamberlain distrusted Soviet intentions, and on 24 August 1939 the Soviet Union signed a non-aggression pact with Hitler, a secret clause of which envisaged the partition of Poland between Russia and Germany.

CALLING MR. CHURCHILL

218 and 219 Throughout the summer of 1939 there was a growing public demand for Churchill's inclusion in the Government. Strube's cartoon 'Calling Mr Churchill' was published in the 'Daily Express' on 6 July; Shepard's cartoon 'The Old Sea-Dog' appeared in 'Punch' six days later. In Strube's cartoon, Neville Chamberlain is sitting in the arm chair, and three Press Lords, Lord Kemsley, Lord Camrose and Lord Beaverbrook, are (left to right) calling for Churchill. Although he was not invited to join the Government, Churchill continued to speak, to write and to broadcast as a private citizen. On 2 August he warned the House of Commons of an imminent German attack on Poland. '*I may be wrong,*' he said, '*but I have not always been wrong.*' And on 8 August he broadcast to the people of the United States. '*If Herr Hitler does not make war,*' he said, '*there will be no war. No one else is going to make war. Britain and France are determined to shed no blood except in self-defence or in defence of their Allies.*'

THE OLD SEA-DOG

"Any telegram for me?"

220 A giant poster, paid for by an unknown Churchill supporter, which appeared in the Strand on 24 July 1939. Chamberlain refused to bring Churchill into his Government. But the French Government, led by Paul Reynaud, invited him, early in August, to examine the defence works of the Maginot Line.

221 For ten days in August, Churchill visited the French Maginot Line defences as the guest of the French Army. After visiting the Maginot Line, he went for a few days to the Chateau St George Motel, in Normandy – the house of Consuelo Balsan – where he painted and fished.

222
Churchill at St George
Motel; this and the pre-
vious photograph were
both taken on 22 August
1939, by the painter Paul
Maze, who later recalled:
'Winston was painting
that day. He suddenly
turned to me and said
*"This is the last picture we
shall paint in peace for a
very long time. . . ."* As
he worked he would now
and then make state-
ments as to the strength
of the German Army.
*"They are strong, I tell
you, they are strong,"* he
would say. Then his jaw
would clench his large
cigar, and I felt the determination of his will. *"Ah,"*
he would say, *"with it all,
we shall have him."* '

223 Churchill returned to England from France on the evening of 23 August 1939. This photograph was taken on his arrival at Croydon airport.

224 In the last week of August, Hitler began to threaten Poland. On 25 August Neville Chamberlain announced that if Poland were invaded, Britain would declare war in her defence. Parliament was summoned four days later on 29 August. Churchill and Eden (both of whom were still excluded from the Government) were photographed in Whitehall walking together to the House of Commons.

225 On 1 September 1939 Hitler invaded Poland. That same day, Chamberlain asked Churchill to join the Cabinet, as First Lord of the Admiralty. On 3 September Britain declared war on Germany. That afternoon Churchill told the House of Commons: '*Outside, the storms of war may blow and the lands may be lashed with the fury of its gales, but in our own hearts this Sunday morning there is peace. Our hands may be active, but our consciences are at rest. . . . This is not a question of fighting for Danzig or fighting for Poland. We are fighting to save the whole world from the pestilence of Nazi tyranny and in defence of all that is most sacred to man. This is no war for domination or imperial aggrandisement or material gain; no war to shut any country out of its sunlight and means of progress. It is a war . . . to establish, on impregnable rocks, the rights of the individual, and it is a war to establish and revive the stature of man.*' This photograph was taken on the morning of 4 September, Churchill's first full day at the Admiralty. His gas mask is with his two despatch boxes.

226 Churchill leaves the Admiralty for a meeting of the War Cabinet at 10 Downing Street on 5 September 1939.

227 Churchill arrives at 10 Downing Street from the Admiralty (in background), on the morning of 18 September 1939, after receiving news of the sinking of the aircraft carrier 'Courageous'. Over five hundred of her crew of 1,260 had been drowned.

228 Churchill making his first wartime broadcast, on 1 October 1939, after the defeat of Poland, and its partition between Hitler and Stalin. During the broadcast he said: *'Poland has been again overrun by two of the great Powers which held her in bondage for 150 years, but were unable to quench the spirit of the Polish nation. The heroic defence of Warsaw shows that the soul of Poland is indestructible, and that she will rise again like a rock, which may for a spell be submerged by a tidal wave, but which remains a rock.'* Later in his broadcast Churchill said: *'I cannot forecast to you the action of Russia. It is a riddle wrapped in a mystery inside an enigma: but perhaps there is a key. That key is Russian national interest. It cannot be in accordance with the interest or the safety of Russia that Germany should plant itself upon the shores of the Black Sea, or that it should overrun the Balkan States and subjugate the Slavonic peoples of South-Eastern Europe. That would be contrary to the historic life-interests of Russia.'*

230 A German cartoon, sent to Churchill at the end of October.

229

Churchill leaving the Admiralty on his way to a meeting of the War Council on 14 October 1939, shortly after learning that the battleship Royal Oak had been sunk while at anchor in Scapa Flow. A month later, on 12 November, he told the House of Commons: '*We do not at all underrate the power and malignity of our enemies. We are prepared to endure tribulation. But we made up our minds about all this ten weeks ago, and everything that has happened since has made us feel that we were right then and are still right now. No one in the British Islands supposed this was going to be a short or easy war. Nothing has ever impressed me so much as the calm, steady, businesslike resolution with which the masses of our wage-earning folk and ordinary people in our great cities faced what they imagined would be a fearful storm about to fall on them and their families at the very first moment. They all prepared themselves to have the worst happen to them at once, and they braced themselves for the ordeal. They did not see what else there was to do.*'

231 On 5 November 1939 Churchill visited Paris to discuss Anglo-French naval activity with the French Minister of Marine. While in Paris, several French Ministers spoke to him despondently of the war. General Spears, who was present, heard Churchill remark to one of them: '*We are quite capable of beating the Germans singlehanded.*' On his way back to England, Churchill visited the Commander-in-Chief of the British Expeditionary Force, Lord Gort, at his headquarters in France (the Chateau de Courcy, near Avesnes). Here he is seen with Gort, and the Chief of the General Staff, Lieutenant-General Pownall (who is filling his pipe). Churchill's aide-de-camp, Commander C. R. 'Tommy' Thompson can be seen reflected in the mirror. Thompson accompanied Churchill on nearly all his wartime journeys.

232
Lord Gort and Churchill at Avesnes, 5 November 1939.

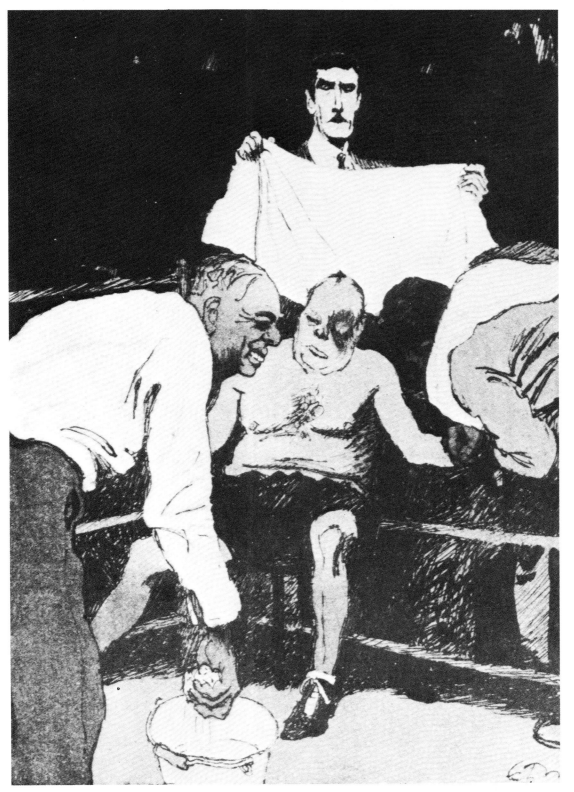

233 A German cartoon, published in 'Simplicissimus' (Munich) on 5 November 1939. Anthony Eden (who had returned as Secretary of State for the Dominions, but was not in the War Cabinet) is holding the towel; Leslie Hore-Belisha (Secretary of State for War) is wetting the sponge. The caption read: '*Churchill received several hard body-blows. Undoubtedly we have won the first round.*'

234 A photograph of the War Cabinet taken on 8 November 1939. In the front row are: Lord Halifax (Foreign Secretary), Sir John Simon (Chancellor of the Exchequer), Neville Chamberlain (Prime Minister), Sir Samuel Hoare (Lord Privy Seal), and Lord Chatfield (Minister for Co-ordination of Defence). Standing are Sir Kingsley Wood (Secretary of State for Air), Churchill, Leslie Hore-Belisha (Secretary of State for War) and Lord Hankey (Minister without Portfolio). The portrait on the wall is of the 3rd Marquess of Salisbury (Prime Minister at the time of the Boer War).

"Himmel! It's That Man Again"

235 A cartoon published in the 'Evening News' on 13 November 1939. On the previous day Churchill had told the House of Commons: *'The whole world is against Hitler and Hitlerism. Men of every race and clime feel that this monstrous apparition stands between them and the forward move which is their due, and for which the age is ripe. Even in Germany itself there are millions who stand aloof from the seething mass of criminality and corruption constituted by the Nazi Party machine. Let them take courage amid perplexities and perils, for it may well be that the final extinction of a baleful domination will pave the way to a broader solidarity of all the men in all the lands than we could ever have planned if we had not marched together through the fire.'*

236

Churchill at a meeting of the Admirality Board on 17 November 1939. In a series of Minutes he exorted his staff to action and vigilance. On 12 December he minuted: *'In view of the danger of surprise attacks at a time when the enemy may expect to find us off our ground, there must be no break or holiday period at Christmas or the New Year. The utmost vigilance must be practised at the Admiralty and in all naval ports.'*

237 On 14 February 1940 Churchill went to Plymouth to welcome the cruiser 'Exeter' on her return from sinking the Nazi pocket battleship 'Admiral Graf Spee' at the battle of the River Plate. Sixty of the 'Exeter's' officers and men had been killed in the action. The ship herself was finally sunk by the Japanese in the battle of the Straits of Sunda in 1942.

238 Churchill cheered by the officers and men of the 'Exeter'.

239 Churchill at the Guildhall, 23 February 1940, when the survivors of the 'Exeter' were given a lunch by the King and Queen. Neville Chamberlain is standing just behind Churchill (in top hat). Speaking at the luncheon, Churchill declared: '*. . . although mistakes and accidents will certainly occur, and sorrow will fall from time to time upon us, we hope that from Whitehall the sense of resolution and design at the centre will impart itself to all afloat, and will lighten the burden of their task and concert the vigour of their action.*'

240 On 28 March 1940 the Franco-British Supreme War Council met in London. Churchill was photographed leaving the luncheon in happy mood. The Council – at which Neville Chamberlain and Paul Reynaud were the principal speakers – decided to deprive Germany of Swedish iron ore by laying minefields along the Norwegian coast (inside Norwegian territorial waters) where the ore had to pass, and thus force the German ore ships into the open sea, where they could be hunted down.

241

Churchill photographed leaving the Admiralty – and knocking the ash off his cigar – on the morning of 4 April 1940, just after it had been announced that, while remaining First Lord of the Admiralty, he was also to be the head of a Committee made up of the three Service Ministers and the Army, Navy and Air Force Chiefs of Staff. Neville Chamberlain had instructed Churchill's Committee to make regular recommendations to the War Cabinet on the general conduct of the war. Commenting on this development, the Associated Press wrote: *The new appointment, in fact, makes Mr Churchill the country's war chief.*

242 Churchill was a leading advocate of British military and naval action to deprive Germany of Swedish iron ore. But the British minelaying along the Norwegian coast came too late; Hitler forestalled it by sending German troops into Denmark and Norway, and by the first week of May 1940 the position of the British forces – who had landed at several Norwegian ports, was precarious. This photograph shows Churchill in Horse Guards parade on the morning of 7 May 1940, about to enter the garden door of 10 Downing Street. That afternoon the House of Commons began to debate the efficiency of Chamberlain's conduct of the war, and the Norwegian expedition. Churchill sought to defend Chamberlain's policy, and the Navy's part in it, but over 80 Conservative MPs opposed the Government, thus challenging Chamberlain's leadership.

**243
and
244** Shaken by the severe criticisms of the Norwegian debate, Chamberlain decided to form a Coalition Government. But before he could do this, Hitler invaded France, Belgium, Holland and Luxemburg. This new danger was discussed by the Cabinet on the morning of 10 May 1940. These photographs show Sir Kingsley Wood, Churchill and Anthony Eden leaving the Cabinet meeting. Churchill's personal detective, Inspector Thompson, can be seen in the doorway, behind Eden.

245 Because of the German invasion of France, Belgium, Holland and Luxemburg, Neville Chamberlain decided that he must form an all-Party Government. But the Labour Party, led by Clement Attlee, refused to serve under him. During 10 May 1940 Chamberlain asked Lord Halifax if he was willing to try to form a Coalition, but Halifax declined. He then asked Churchill, who accepted. That same day Churchill became Prime Minister. In his memoirs he recalled: '. . . *as I went to bed at about 3 a.m., I was conscious of a profound sense of relief. At last I had the authority to give directions over the whole scene. I felt as if I were walking with destiny, and that all my past life had been but a preparation for this hour and for this trial.*' This photograph shows Churchill leaving the Admiralty for Buckingham Palace on 12 May to see the King, and to attend a meeting of the Privy Council at which the members of his Coalition took their oaths of office.

TWO-GUN WINSTON

246 As well as becoming Prime Minister, Churchill appointed himself Minister of Defence. This cartoon was published in the 'Daily Mail' on 13 May 1940.

247 Churchill crossing Horse Guards Parade on 20 May 1940, the morning after his first broadcast as Prime Minister. During his broadcast he had said: '*I speak to you for the first time as Prime Minister in a solemn hour for the life of our country, of our Empire, of our Allies, and, above all, of the cause of Freedom. . . . This is one of the most awe-striking periods in the long history of France and Britain. It is also beyond doubt the most sublime. Side by side, unaided except by their kith and kin in the great Dominions and by the wide Empires which rest beneath their shield – side by side, the British and French peoples have advanced to rescue not only Europe but mankind from the foulest and most soul-destroying tyranny which has ever darkened and stained the pages of history. Behind them – behind us – behind the Armies and Fleets of Britain and France – gather a group of shattered States and bludgeoned races: the Czechs, the Poles, the Norwegians, the Danes, the Dutch, the Belgians – upon all of whom the long night of barbarism will descend, unbroken even by a star of hope, unless we conquer, as conquer we must, as conquer we shall.*'

248
Churchill at his desk in 10 Downing Street.

249 Churchill and his wife arriving at Westminster Abbey on Sunday 26 May 1940, for National Prayers. Churchill is carrying his gas-mask.

250
Mrs Churchill at 10 Downing Street. This photograph was taken in September 1940.

251 and 252 During May and June of 1940 the Germans overran France, Belgium, Holland and Luxemburg. On 17 June France sued for peace. During August the Germans began to bomb London and the Channel ports, hoping to demoralize the British into asking for peace. Churchill urged defiance, and opposed all talk of surrender. On 28 August he visited Ramsgate. While in the town a German air raid began. These two photographs show Churchill on his way to the air raid shelter in the town's tunnels, and sitting in the shelter. In the top photograph, Inspector Thompson is carrying Churchill's gas mask, as well as his own.

253 The German air raids on London intensified at the beginning of September. Here Churchill is seen visiting bombed and fire-gutted buildings on 8 September. Three days later, on 11 September, he broadcast to the nation, speaking defiantly of *'a people who will not flinch or weary of the struggle – hard and protracted though it will be'*.

254 and 255 Churchill inspecting bomb damage in the City of London and at Battersea (above) on 10 September 1940. In his radio broadcast on the following day he declared: '*These cruel, wanton, indiscriminate bombings of London are, of course, a part of Hitler's invasion plans. He hopes, by killing large numbers of civilians, and women and children, that he will terrorize and cow the people of this mighty imperial city, and make them a burden and an anxiety to the Government and thus distract our attention unduly from the ferocious onslaught he is preparing. Little does he know the spirit of the British nation, or the tough fibre of the Londoners, whose forebears played a leading part in the establishment of Parliamentary institutions and who have been bred to value freedom far above their lives. This wicked man, the repository and embodiment of many forms of soul-destroying hatred, this monstrous product of former wrongs and shame, has now resolved to try to break our famous Island race by a process of indiscriminate slaughter and destruction. What he has done is to kindle a fire in British hearts, here and all over the world, which will glow long after all traces of the conflagration he has caused in London have been removed. He has lighted a fire which will burn with a steady and consuming flame until the last vestiges of Nazi tyranny have been burnt out of Europe, and until the Old World – and the New – can join hands to rebuild the temples of man's freedom and man's honour, upon foundations which will not soon or easily be overthrown.*'

256 On 3 October 1940 Churchill reconstructed his War Cabinet. Here he is seen leaving 10 Downing Street on the following day with the three Labour members: Ernest Bevin (Minister of Labour), Clement Attlee (Lord Privy Seal), and Arthur Greenwood (Minister without Portfolio). The other members of his new War Cabinet were: Sir John Anderson (President of the Council), Lord Halifax (Foreign Secretary) and Sir Kingsley Wood (Chancellor of the Exchequer).

258 Churchill's own office and bedroom in the underground War Room. Several of his wartime broadcasts were made from this desk. The map at the foot of his bed (normally covered by a curtain) showed in detail the defences of Britain in 1940 and 1941, when invasion seemed imminent.

257 Before the outbreak of war, a Cabinet War Room had been established underground in Whitehall. Here, on 3 September 1939, Neville Chamberlain made his first broadcast after war was declared on Germany, and here, during air raids, and air raid alerts, Churchill conferred with his Cabinet, his War Cabinet, and his Chiefs of Staff.

259 to 261 Churchill and his wife visit the bomb damaged City of London on 31 December 1940. With them (with glasses, and no hat in the bottom left photograph) is the Minister of Information Churchill's friend Brendan Bracken. Later that day Churchill wrote to President Roosevelt: '*They burned a large part of the City of London last night, and the scenes of widespread destruction here and in our provincial centres are shocking; but when I visited the still-burning ruins to-day the spirit of the Londoners was as high as in the first days of the indiscriminate bombing in September, four months ago.*'

262 Churchill watches the first American-built aeroplane arriving in Britain, as part of the Lend–Lease programme instituted by President Roosevelt. The Lend–Lease Act became law on 11 March 1941. Under it, Britain could 'loan' vital war materials for as long as the war might last. Through Lend–Lease, Britain was soon able to replenish her dwindling stocks of food, machine tools and even tobacco. By the end of the war the United States had provided Britain with half its tanks, most of its transport aircraft, a quarter of its ammunition and almost all its extra shipping. Churchill called Lend–Lease *'the most unsordid act in the history of any nation'*. On 22 June 1941 Hitler invaded the Soviet Union; from that moment, at Churchill's insistence, Britain herself sent what aid she could to Russia, despite her own grave shortages.

263
Although Japan remained neutral throughout 1940 and most of 1941, her troops continued their conquest of China and Indo-China. This Japanese cartoon, published early in 1941, expressed the official Japanese view.

264
Churchill at Bristol, 14 April 1941, two days after a heavy air raid on the city.

265 and 266 On the morning of 14 July 1941 Churchill reviewed the Civil Defence Services in Hyde Park. After the review, he lunched at County Hall, London and spoke on the progress of the war. During the course of his speech he declared: '*We live in a terrible epoch of the human story, but we believe there is a broad and sure justice running through its theme. It is time that the Germans should be made to suffer in their own homeland and cities something of the torment they have twice in our lifetime let loose upon their neighbours and upon the world. We have now intensified for a month past our systematic, scientific, methodical bombing on a large scale of the German cities, seaports, industries, and other military objectives. We believe it to be in our power to keep this process going, on a steadily rising tide, month after month, year after year, until the Nazi regime is either extirpated by us, or better still, torn to pieces by the German people themselves.*'

267 and 268 At the end of his speech on 14 July 1941 Churchill said: '*We do not expect to hit without being hit back, and we intend with every week that passes to hit harder. Prepare yourselves, then, my friends and comrades in the Battle of London, for this renewal of your exertions. We shall never turn from our purpose, however sombre the road, however grievous the cost, because we know that out of this time of trial and tribulation will be born a new freedom and glory for all mankind.*'

269
and
270
Churchill inspecting Czechoslovak forces in England, August 1941. In the bottom photograph, President Beneš is on the left.

271 Churchill, photographed during his luncheon with the exiled Czechoslovak leaders, August 1941.

273 On Sunday 10 August Roosevelt joined Churchill on board the 'Prince of Wales' for Divine Service. Later Churchill recalled: *'This service was felt by us all to be a deeply moving expression of the unity of faith of our two peoples, and none who took part in it will forget the spectacle presented that sunlit morning on the crowded quarterdeck – the symbolism of the Union Jack and the Stars and Stripes draped side by side on the pulpit; the American and British chaplains sharing in the reading of the prayers; the highest naval, military, and air officers of Britain and the United States grouped in one body behind the President and me; the close-packed ranks of British and American sailors, completely intermingled, sharing the same books and joining fervently together in the prayers and hymns familiar to both. I chose the hymns myself – "For Those in Peril on the Sea" and "Onward, Christian Soldiers". We ended with "O God, Our Help in Ages Past", which Macaulay reminds us the Ironsides had chanted as they bore John Hampden's body to the grave. Every word seemed to stir the heart. It was a great hour to live. Nearly half those who sang were soon to die.'*

272

On 9 August 1941, while the United States was still neutral, Churchill met Roosevelt on board the 'Augusta' in Placentia Bay, Newfoundland. It was their first wartime meeting. In this photograph, Roosevelt is being supported by his son Elliott; Churchill is handing Roosevelt a letter from King George V. During their meeting, Churchill and Roosevelt discussed the whole future conduct of the war.

274 On board the 'Prince of Wales', August 1941.

275 Churchill with the senior Service advisers who accompanied him on board the 'Prince of Wales'. From left to right: the First Sea Lord, Admiral Pound; the Chief of the Imperial General Staff, General Dill; Churchill; and the Vice-Chief of the Air Staff, Air Marshal Freeman.

276

Churchill with Lord Beaverbrook, on board the 'Prince of Wales'. Beaverbrook had been Minister of Aircraft Production in August 1940, during the Battle of Britain. Later Churchill wrote of him: '*All his remarkable qualities fitted the need. His personal buoyancy and vigour were a tonic. I was glad to be able sometimes to lean on him. He did not fail. . . . His personal force and genius, combined with so much persuasion and contrivance, swept aside many obstacles.*'

277
In Iceland, on his way back to Britain.

278

A photograph of Churchill having tea in a Royal Air Force mess, 25 September 1941. Over a year before, on 20 August 1940, he had told the House of Commons and later, in a broadcast, the whole nation: *'The gratitude of every home in our Island, in our Empire, and indeed throughout the world, except in the abodes of the guilty, goes out to the British airmen who, undaunted by odds, unwearied in their constant challenge and mortal danger, are turning the tide of the world war by their prowess and by their devotion. Never in the field of human conflict was so much owed by so many to so few.'*

279

Churchill at an aeroplane factory in Birmingham, 28 September 1941, watching a girl rivetter at work on a Spitfire. Two days later he told the House of Commons: *'Only the most strenuous exertions, a perfect unity of purpose, added to our traditional unrelenting tenacity, will enable us to act our part worthily in the prodigious world drama in which we are now plunged. Let us make sure these virtues are forthcoming.'*

280 Three days later, on 28 September, Churchill spoke to dock labourers while they were having their lunch. According to the official caption issued at the time he asked them: '*Are you managing to get plenty of food?*' to which they replied: '*Aye sir! we are doing grand, thank you.*'

281 Churchill arriving at the back door of 10 Downing Street on the morning of 8 December 1941, after learning that Japanese forces had attacked United States, British and Dutch territory in Asia and the Pacific. The war had become a 'World War', and the United States had become Britain's ally. In his memoirs Churchill recalled: '*No American will think it wrong of me if I proclaim that to have the United States at our side was to me the greatest joy. I could not foretell the course of events. I do not pretend to have measured accurately the martial might of Japan, but now at this very moment I knew the United States was in the war, up to the neck and in to the death. So we had won after all! . . . We had won the war. England would live; Britain would live; the Commonwealth of Nations and the Empire would live. How long the war would last or in what fashion it would end no man could tell, nor did I at this moment care. Once again in our long Island history we should emerge, however, mauled or mutilated, safe and victorious. We should not be wiped out. Our history would not come to an end. We might not even have to die as individuals. Hitler's fate was sealed. Mussolini's fate was sealed. As for the Japanese, they would be ground to powder. All the rest was merely the proper application of overwhelming force.*'

282 The Soviet Ambassador Ivan Maisky, Anthony Eden, the Soviet Foreign Minister, Vyaches-
lav Molotov, Churchill, and Commander Thompson walking in the garden of 10 Downing
Street, after the signature of the Anglo-Soviet Treaty, 26 May 1942. During his visit,
Molotov urged Churchill to open a 'second front' against Hitler in 1942. But Churchill
warned Molotov that Britain would have to have much greater air power before she could
launch a cross-Channel invasion.

283 On the evening of 10 August 1942 Churchill set off from Cairo to Moscow by air to tell Stalin in person that there could be no 'Second Front' in 1942. This photograph shows him on arrival at Moscow airport, on the morning of 13 August, listening to the band playing the Soviet national anthem. In his memoirs he wrote of his feelings on reaching Russia: '*I pondered on my mission to this sullen, sinister Bolshevik State I had once tried so hard to strangle at its birth, and which, until Hitler appeared, I had regarded as the mortal foe of civilised freedom. . . . We had always hated their wicked regime, and, till the German flail beat upon them, they would have watched us being swept out of existence with indifference and gleefully divided with Hitler our Empire in the East.*'

284 Churchill and Stalin in the Kremlin at a banquet given in Churchill's honour on 16 August 1942. Stalin signed this photograph for Churchill. After his initial, fierce anger at the postponement of a Second Front in Europe, Stalin showed a keen interest in the Anglo-American plans to drive the Germans out of North Africa.

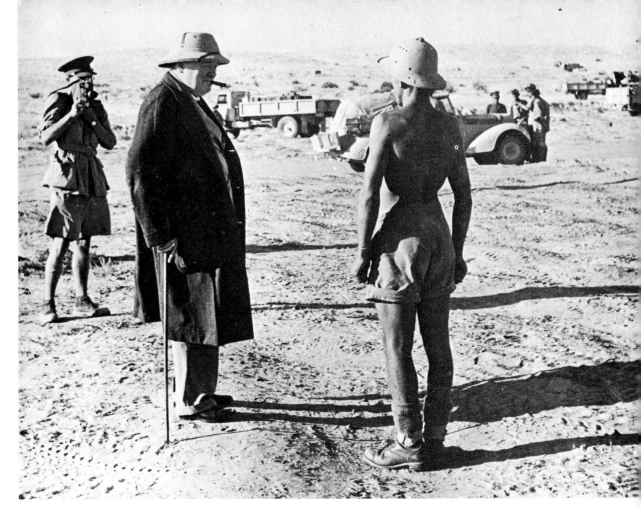

286

On 20 August Churchill visited the desert front west of Cairo, seven days after General Montgomery had taken command of the Eighth Army. On the following day he telegraphed to the War Cabinet: '. . . *I am satisfied that we have lively, confident, resolute men in command, working together as an admirable team under leaders of the highest military quality. Everything has been done and is being done that is possible, and it is now my duty to return home, as I have no part to play in the battle, which must be left to those in whom we place our trust.*'

5 Churchill in Cairo, after his visit to Moscow in August 1942. From Cairo, he urged his War Cabinet colleagues to do their utmost to help Russia in every possible way, telegraphing on 19 August: '*Everybody always finds it convenient to ease themselves at the expense of Russia, but grave issues depend upon preserving a good relationship with this tremendous army, now under dire distress.*'

287

On 13 January 1943 Churchill flew to North Africa from London, for further discussions with President Roosevelt and the British and American Chiefs of Staff. Churchill stayed in a hotel at Anfa, a suburb of Casablanca; here he is seen leaving his hotel with his Private Secretary, John Martin (carrying coat), Commander Thompson, Inspector Thompson, and his son Randolph, who was then serving as a Captain on the Tunisian front (and later parachuted into Yugoslavia as a member of the British Military Mission which served with Tito and his partisans behind the German lines).

288 General Giraud, Roosevelt, General de Gaulle and Churchill at Casablanca 24 January 1943, when Churchill and Roosevelt tried in vain to bring about a reconciliation between the two rival French leaders. In his memoirs Churchill recalled: '. . . *we forced them to shake hands in public before all the reporters and photographers. They did so, and the pictures of this event cannot be viewed even in the setting of these tragic times without a laugh.*'

289 Churchill with the Turkish President, Ismet Inönü, at Adana (in southern Turkey), 30 January 1943. Churchill handed Inönü a letter, at the end of which he wrote: '*I have not been in Turkey since 1909, when I met many of the brave men who laid the foundations of the modern Turkey. There is a long story of the friendly relations between Great Britain and Turkey. Across it is a terrible slash of the last war, when German intrigues and British and Turkish mistakes led to our being on opposite sides. We fought as brave and honourable opponents. But those days are done, and we and our American Allies are prepared to make vigorous exertions in order that we shall all be together and continue together to move forward into a world arrangement in which peaceful peoples will have a right to be let alone and in which all peoples will have a chance to help one another.*' Churchill tried to persuade Inönü to enter the war at once, as Britain's ally. But Turkey remained neutral until January 1945.

290 'Commando', the aeroplane in which Churchill had flown both to Russia and to Turkey. As a memento of these flights the aeroplane carried both the Hammer and Sickle, and the Crescent emblems. On 7 February 1943 Churchill flew in 'Commando' from North Africa to England. It was his last flight in her; later, with a different pilot and crew, she crashed with the loss of all on board.

Image annotations: *General Marshall U.S.A.* — *P.M.* — *B. L. Montgomery General Eighth Army* — *3·6·*

292 While in Algiers, Churchill finalised the plans for the invasion of Sicily and Italy with the British and American military leaders. This photograph, taken on 3 June 1943, was annotated by General Montgomery, who later recalled: '*Winston wanted me to say the Sicilian invasion would be all right. But I wouldn't.*' But it did in fact succeed. General George Marshall, the Chairman of the American Joint Chiefs of Staff Committee, is on the left.

291 On 11 May 1943 Churchill arrived in the United States for talks with Roosevelt; on 26 May he flew from the United States back to North Africa. Here he is seen in the Roman theatre at Carthage on 1 June, when he was given an ovation by the troops. With him is Lieutenant-General Anderson. In his memoirs Churchill recalled: '*The sense of victory was in the air. The whole of North Africa was cleared of the enemy. A quarter of a million prisoners were cooped in our cages. Everyone was very proud and delighted. There is no doubt that people like winning very much. I addressed many thousand soldiers at Carthage in the ruins of an immense amphitheatre. Certainly the hour and the setting lent themselves to oratory. I have no idea what I said, but the whole audience clapped and cheered as doubtless their predecessors of two thousand years ago had done as they watched gladiatorial combats.*'

293 Churchill returned to Britain in June 1943. On 9 August he arrived by sea in Canada for a conference at Quebec with Roosevelt, and the Allied Chiefs of Staff, at which the cross-Channel invasion was planned for May 1944. Here, during a journey to the Niagara Falls before the conference opened, Churchill stands at the rear of the train with his daughter Mary (and the ubiquitous Inspector Thompson). At the end of the conference, on 25 August, Churchill telegraphed to the War Cabinet: *'I am feeling rather tired, as the work of the Conference has been very heavy and many large and difficult questions have weighed upon us. I hope my colleagues will think it proper for me to take two or three days' rest. . . .'*

294

British mastery of the air was an indispensable part of the invasion plan. In this photograph, Churchill is seen with his friend Sir Archibald Sinclair (Secretary of State for Air), watching a flying demonstration.

295

Churchill travelling by train, dictating to a secretary.

296 On 27 November 1943 Churchill and Roosevelt went to Teheran for a discussion of war strategy with Stalin. The first meeting was held on 28 November. That night, at dinner, Churchill told Stalin: '*We are the trustees for the peace of the world. If we fail there will be perhaps a hundred years of chaos. . . . There is more than merely keeping the peace. The three Powers should guide the future of the world. I do not want to enforce any system on other nations. I ask for freedom and for the right of all nations to develop as they like.*'

297 On 30 November, while at Teheran, Churchill celebrated his sixty-ninth birthday. In this photograph, Stalin toasts Churchill. Eden is on Churchill's right; Marshal Voroshilov on his left; Churchill's daughter Sarah just behind Stalin; and Averell Harriman (Roosevelt's personal emissary to both Churchill and Stalin) on the far right (lighting a cigarette). During the course of the discussions at Teheran, Stalin suggested shooting 50,000 German officers and technicians as soon as the war was over. But Churchill declared: '*The British Parliament and public will never tolerate mass executions. Even if in war passion they allowed them to begin they would turn violently against those responsible after the first butchery had taken place. . . . I would rather be taken out into the garden here and now and be shot myself than sully my own and my country's honour by such infamy.*'

300 Although not fully recovered from his illness, and against the advice of his doctors, Churchill insisted on returning to Britain. On 14 January 1944 he flew from Marrakesh to Gibraltar, and on the following day sailed for Plymouth on board the battleship 'King George V'. Here he is seen on the bridge, with his daughter Sarah.

Exhausted by his work and travels, Churchill reached Tunis on 12 December 1943. To General Eisenhower, who met him at the airport, he said; '*I am afraid I shall have to stay with you a little longer than I had planned. I am completely at the end of my tether. . . .*' Churchill had contracted pneumonia. Later he recalled: '*The days passed in much discomfort. Fever flickered in and out. . . . The doctors tried to keep the work away from my bedside, but I defied them.*' These photographs show Churchill at Carthage on Christmas Day 1943, above with Generals Eisenhower and Alexander. Two days later he was flown from Tunis to Marrakesh, to recuperate fully from his illness. On the following day he telegraphed to Roosevelt: '*After travelling quite unaffected at 13,000 feet I arrived yesterday at our villa, when I am indeed in the lap of luxury, thanks to overflowing American hospitality. . . . I propose to stay here in the sunshine until I am quite strong again.*' While at Marrakesh, Churchill continued to press forward with plans for the cross-Channel invasion. But his illness was a serious one, and recuperation slow, as he himself later recorded: '*All my painting tackle had been sent out, but I could not face it. I could hardly walk at all. Even tottering from the motor-car to a picnic luncheon in lovely weather amid the foothills of the Atlas was limited to eighty or a hundred yards. I passed eighteen hours out of the twenty-four prone. I never remember such extreme fatigue and weakness in body. . . . I was utterly tired out.*'

301 and 302 Churchill and Eisenhower inspect United States machine gun squadrons 'somewhere in England', during the preparations for the cross-Channel invasion. Eisenhower had been appointed Supreme Commander-in-Chief of the Allied Expeditionary Force. All southern England, Churchill later recalled, '*became a vast military camp, filled with men, trained, instructed, and eager to come to grips with the Germans across the water*'.

303 On 5 June 1944 the Allied Armies in Italy entered Rome. On the following day, 6 June, the Allied Expeditionary Force landed in Normandy. The invasion of northern Europe had begun. This photograph shows Churchill leaving 10 Downing Street on the morning of the invasion. At midday he told the House of Commons: '*Nothing that equipment, science, or forethought could do has been neglected. . . .*' and to Stalin he telegraphed that afternoon: '*Everything has started well. The mines, obstacles, and land batteries have been largely overcome. . . . Infantry landings are proceeding rapidly, and many tanks and self-propelled guns are already ashore.*'

304 On 12 June 1944, six days after the Normandy landings, Churchill crossed to Normandy on the destroyer 'Kelvin'. While he was on board, the destroyer's guns bombed German positions inland. Here, Churchill is seen discussing with Commander 'Tommy' Thompson a suggestion made by General Montgomery (bottom right) as to how best to get out of the landing craft. The Chief of the Imperial General Staff, Sir Alan Brooke, watches (far left, in coat).

305

The dilemma solved, Churchill drives inland in a jeep, accompanied by General Montgomery. He was welcomed by troops unloading and guarding stores, and remained on French soil for seven hours.

306 On 10 July 1944 British troops entered Caen, the first German-held town of size and importance. Twelve days later, on 22 July, Churchill made his third visit to Normandy. Here he is seen, watching German planes being chased by British fighters. From left to right: Lieutenant-General O'Connor (commanding the 8th Corps), Churchill, Field Marshal Smuts, Montgomery and General Brooke.

307 Near Caen, on 22 July, Churchill talked to some of the troops who led the D-Day assault General Montgomery is on the right (in sweater). Recalling his two-day visit to the battle zone, Churchill wrote in his memoirs: '*The nights were very noisy, there being repeated raids by single aircraft, and more numerous alarms. By day I studied the whole process of the landing of supplies and troops, both at the piers, in which I had so long been interested, and on the beaches. On one occasion six tank landing-craft came to the beach in line. When their prows grounded their drawbridges fell forward and out came the tanks, three or four from each, and splashed ashore. In less than eight minutes by my stop-watch the tanks stood in column of route on the highroad ready to move into action. This was an impressive performance, and typical of the rate of discharge which had now been achieved. I was fascinated to see the D.U.K.W.s swimming through the harbour, waddling ashore, and then hurrying up the hill to the great dump where the lorries were waiting to take their supplies to the various units. Upon the wonderful efficiency of this system, now yielding results far greater than we had ever planned, depended the hopes of a speedy and victorious action.*'

308 Churchill at Caen, surveying the ruins; a photograph from General Montgomery's albums. General Dempsey (Commanding the Second Army) is standing between Churchill and Montgomery.

309 On 7 August 1944, during his third visit to Normandy, Churchill relaxes for a moment with one of Montgomery's dogs, 'Rommel'. His other dog was called 'Hitler'; both had been flown over from Portsmouth a short while before. Churchill has changed from his Naval to his Air Commodore's uniform.

310 General Alexander planned a major offensive north of Rome on 26 August 1944. Five days earlier, Churchill himself flew to Rome, for talks with the Italian leaders who – after Mussolini's flight to Northern Italy – had made peace with the Allies. On 23 August he was received by Pope Pius XII, recording in his memoirs: *'We had no lack of topics for conversation. The one that bulked the largest at this audience, as it had done with his predecessor eighteen years before, was the danger of Communism. I have always had the greatest dislike of it. . . .'* On 24 August Churchill flew to Alexander's headquarters at Siena. Here he is seen chatting to troops of the 66th Medium Regiment.

311 On 26 August Churchill flew from Siena to the battle headquarters of the Eighth Army, behind Monte Maggiore. At nine in the morning, only six hours after the attack had been launched, he and Alexander moved forward into the battle zone. This village street had been under German shell fire less than twenty minutes before Churchill arrived.

312 and 313

During the morning of 26 August 1944, Churchill reached the ruins of an old castle high above the front line. Watched by the Italian peasant who was living in a nearby hut, he watched the continuing battle. In his memoirs he recorded: *'The Germans were firing with rifles and machine-guns from thick scrub on the farther side of the valley, about five hundred yards away. Our front line was beneath us. The firing was desultory and intermittent. But this was the nearest I got to the enemy and the time I heard most bullets in the Second World War. After about half an hour we went back to our motor-cars and made our way to the river, keeping very carefully to our own wheel tracks or those of other vehicles. At the river we met the supporting columns of infantry, marching up to lend weight to our thin skirmish line, and by five o'clock we were home again at General Leese's headquarters, where the news from the whole of the Army front was marked punctually on the maps.'*

314 General Leese, Churchill and Alexander study the course of the battle, 26 August 1944.

315 Alexander and Churchill confer with Lieutenant-General Anders, the Commander-in-Chief of the Polish forces in Italy. The truck (with its right-hand drive and Arabic markings) had come from Egypt; the armchair from Italy; and the tent (with its swastika emblem, top right) had been captured from the Germans. Throughout 1944 Churchill tried to persuade the exiled Polish leaders and generals to accept eventual Russian control of eastern Poland, with territorial compensation for Poland in the west, from Germany. But the Poles were fearful of trusting Russia, or of making concessions to her. On 14 October Churchill told the Polish Prime Minister in exile, Mikolajczyk: '*I talked to General Anders the other day to whom I took a great liking. He entertains the hope that after the defeat of Germany the Russians will be beaten: this is crazy, you cannot beat the Russians. I beg you to settle upon the frontier question.*' Later in the discussion, when the Polish Prime Minister said he could not agree to give up any of eastern Poland, Churchill exclaimed: '*Unless you accept the frontier you are out of business forever. The Russians will sweep through your country and your people will be liquidated. . . . In your obstinacy you do not see what is at stake. . . . You will start another war in which 25 million lives will be lost.*' When one of the Poles present spoke of the desires of Polish public opinion, Churchill remarked: '*But what is it that your public opinion demands. The right to be crushed?*'

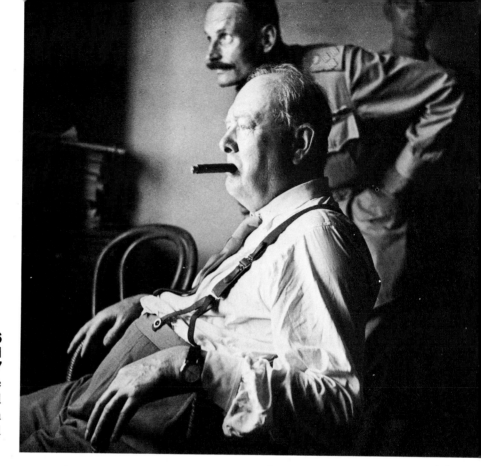

**316
and
317**

During his visit to the Italian front, Churchill watched Allied artillery in action, from a Forward Observation Post.

318 Paris was liberated from the Germans on 24 August 1944, while Churchill was in Italy. On 10 November he flew to Paris for political discussions with the French leaders, and on the following day he and de Gaulle watched the armistice day parade. Immediately behind Churchill (to his right) is Sir Alexander Cadogan, Permanent Under-Secretary of State for Foreign Affairs, who accompanied Churchill on most of his wartime journeys abroad, and who recorded in his diary that evening: *'Procession, which lasted a full hour, v. good. . . . Enormous, enthusiastic and good-humoured crowd who, most of the time, chanted Chur-chill!'* On 16 November, after he had returned to England, Churchill wrote to de Gaulle: *'I shall always recall as one of the proudest and most moving occasions of my life the wonderful reception which the people of Paris gave to their British guests on this our first visit to your capital after its liberation. I was also most grateful of the opportunity of seeing for myself something of the ardour and high quality of French troops, which are completing the liberation of their native soil. . . .'*

319 Throughout December, the situation in Greece caused Churchill much anxiety. He was much afraid that, with the Germans being driven out, the Greek Communists would seize control. By 17 December, civil war had broken out in Athens itself. On 22 December Churchill wrote to Field Marshal Smuts that *'if the powers of evil prevail in Greece, as is quite likely, we must be prepared for a quasi-Bolshevised Russian-led Balkan peninsula, and this may spread to Italy and Hungary'*. Churchill decided to go to Greece himself, and, abandoning his family Christmas, flew to Athens on 24 December, together with Anthony Eden. On 26 December he met Archbishop Damaskinos (with whom he is seen in this photograph) and persuaded the Archbishop to become Regent of Greece. To his wife, Churchill telegraphed on 26 December: *'The Conference at Greek Foreign Office was intensely dramatic. All those haggard Greek faces around the table, and the Archbishop with his enormous hat, making him, I should think, seven feet tall. . . . We have now left them together, as it was a Greek show. It may break up at any moment. At least we have done our best.'*

320

On 29 December Churchill returned from Athens to London; a month later, on 29 January he left London for the Soviet town of Yalta, in the Crimea, and for seven days, beginning on 4 February, discussed the future of Germany, of Poland, and of Eastern Europe, with Stalin and Roosevelt. On 8 February Churchill told the Conference: '*Do not let us underestimate the difficulties. Nations, comrades in arms, have in the past drifted apart within five or ten years of war. Thus toiling millions have followed a vicious circle, falling into the pit, and then by their sacrifices raising themselves up again. We now have a chance of avoiding the errors of previous generations and of making a sure peace. People cry out for peace and joy. Will the families be reunited? Will the warrior come home? Will the shattered dwellings be rebuilt? Will the toiler see his home? To defend one's country is glorious, but there are greater conquests before us. Before us lies the realisation of the dream of the poor—that they shall live in peace, protected by our invincible power from aggression and evil.*' This photograph shows Churchill and Roosevelt in private conclave at Yalta.

321
and
322
Churchill and Stalin arriving for one of the Yalta banquets.

323 Stalin and Churchill at Yalta. Proposing a toast to Stalin at dinner on 8 February 1945, Churchill said: '*I hope to see the future of Russia bright, prosperous, and happy. I will do anything to help, and I am sure so will the President. There was a time when the Marshal was not so kindly towards us, and I remember that I said a few rude things about him, but our common dangers and common loyalties have wiped all that out. The fire of war has burnt up the misunderstandings of the past. We feel we have a friend whom we can trust, and I hope he will continue to feel the same about us. I pray he may live to see his beloved Russia not only glorious in war, but also happy in peace.*'

324 'The Big Three' at Yalta. Roosevelt, who was already extremely ill, died two months later, on 12 April 1945. Five days later Churchill told the House of Commons: '. . . *at Yalta I noticed that the President was ailing. His captivating smile, his gay and charming manner, had not deserted him, but his face had a transparency, an air of purification, and often there was a far-away look in his eyes. When I took my leave of him in Alexandria harbour I must confess that I had an indefinable sense of fear that his health and his strength were on the ebb. But nothing altered his inflexible sense of duty. To the end he faced his innumerable tasks unflinching. . . . When death came suddenly upon him he had "finished his mail". That portion of his day's work was done. As the saying goes, he died in harness, and we may well say in battle harness, like his soldiers, sailors, and airmen, who side by side with ours are carrying on their task to the end all over the world. What an enviable death was his! He had brought his country through the worst of its perils and the heaviest of its toils. Victory had cast its sure and steady beam upon him. In the days of peace he had broadened and stabilised the foundations of American life and union. In war he had raised the strength, might, and glory of the great Republic to a height never attained by any nation in history.*'

325
and
326
On 7 March 1945, after six weeks of fierce and uninterrupted battles, the American First Army reached, and crossed, the Rhine. Two days later Churchill telegraphed to General Eisenhower: *'No one who studies war can fail to be inspired by the admirable speed and flexibility of the American armies . . . and the adaptiveness of commanders and their troops to the swiftly changing conditions of modern battles on the greatest scale.'* In mid-March General Montgomery planned to cross the upper Rhine with 80,000 Allied troops, and break into the industrial Ruhr. Churchill flew from London to Venlo, on the Meuse, on 23 March, in order to be in the battle zone at the time of the attack. The river was crossed at several points during 24 March, and Churchill throughout the day watched the attacks. These two photographs show him riding in an American armoured car on the western bank of the Rhine, and in the German town of Xanten.

327 Looking across the Rhine, 25 March 1945.

328 On board a United States landing craft, crossing the Rhine, 25 March 1945.

On 25 March 1945 Churchill and Montgomery went to see Eisenhower farther south. Churchill recorded in his memoirs: '*The Rhine – here about four hundred yards broad – flowed at our feet. There was a smooth, flat expanse of meadows on the enemy's side. The officers told us that the far bank was unoccupied so far as they knew, and we gazed and gaped at it for a while. . . . Then the Supreme Commander had to depart on other business, and Montgomery and I were about to follow his example when I saw a small launch come close by to moor. So I said to Montgomery, "Why don't we go across and have a look at the other side?" Somewhat to my surprise he answered, "Why not?" After he had made some inquiries we started across the river with three or four American commanders and half a dozen armed men. We landed in brilliant sunshine and perfect peace on the German shore, and walked about for half an hour or so unmolested.*'

329 Landing on the eastern bank of the Rhine, 25 March 1945.

330 Churchill on the Wesel bridge. After crossing back to the western bank of the Rhine on 25 March, Montgomery had suggested to Churchill that they visit the railway bridge at Wesel, where some action was still in progress. In his memoirs Churchill recalled: '*So we got into his car, and, accompanied by the Americans, who were delighted at the prospect, we went to the big iron-girder railway bridge, which was broken in the middle but whose twisted ironwork offered good perches. The Germans were replying to our fire, and their shells fell in salvos of four about a mile away. Presently they came nearer. Then one salvo came overhead and plunged in the water on our side of the bridge. The shells seemed to explode on impact with the bottom, and raised great fountains of spray about a hundred yards away. Several other shells fell among the motor-cars which were concealed not far behind us, and it was decided we ought to depart. I clambered down and joined my adventurous host for our two hours' drive back to his headquarters.*'

331 Churchill, General Brooke, and General Montgomery, picnic on the bank of the Rhine, 26 March 1945. Churchill has thrust his walking stick into the ground; it had been given to him as a wedding present in 1908 by King Edward VII.

332 Clement Attlee and Churchill leave Westminster Abbey, after the memorial service to Lloyd George, 11 April 1945. Lloyd George had died on 26 March 1945; two days later Churchill told the House of Commons: '*There was no man so gifted, so eloquent, so forceful, who knew the life of the people so well. His warm heart was stirred by the many perils which beset the cottage homes: the health of the bread-winner, the fate of his widow, the nourishment and upbringing of his children, the meagre and haphazard provision of medical treatment and sanatoria, and the lack of any organized accessible medical service of a kind worthy of the age, from which the mass of the wage earners and the poor suffered. All this excited his wrath. Pity and compassion lent their powerful wings. He knew the terror with which old age threatened the toiler – that after a life of exertion he could be no more than a burden at the fireside and in the family of a struggling son. When I first became Lloyd George's friend and active associate, now more than forty years ago, this deep love of the people, the profound knowledge of their lives and of the undue and needless pressures under which they lived, impressed itself indelibly upon my mind.*'

334 At three o'clock on the afternoon of 8 May, Churchill broadcast to the nation from 10 Downing Street. During the course of his speech he said: '*Today, perhaps, we shall think mostly of ourselves. To-morrow we shall pay a particular tribute to our Russian comrades, whose prowess in the field has been one of the grand contributions to the general victory. . . . We may allow ourselves a brief period of rejoicing; but let us not forget for a moment the toil and efforts that lie ahead. Japan, with all her treachery and greed, remains unsubdued. The injury she has inflicted on Great Britain, the United States, and other countries, and her detestable cruelties, call for justice and retribution. We must now devote all our strength and resources to the completion of our task, both at home and abroad. Advance, Britannia. Long live the cause of freedom. God save the King.*'

333

The German forces in Europe surrendered to the Allies on 7 May 1945. On the following day victory celebrations were held throughout Britain. This photograph shows Churchill on his way to the House of Commons, surrounded by an exhilarated crowd. A few minutes earlier, from the balcony of the Ministry of Health, he had declared: '*God bless you all. This is your victory. It is the victory of the cause of freedom in every land. In all our long history we have never seen a greater day than this. Everyone, man or woman, has done their best. Everyone has tried. Neither the long years, nor the dangers, nor the fierce attacks of the enemy, have in any way weakened the independent resolve of the British nation. God bless you all.*'

335 and 336 With the end of the war in Europe, the Labour Party insisted upon an end to the Coalition, and a return to Party politics. On 4 June 1945 Churchill made his first election broadcast. Speaking as Leader of the Conservative Party, he declared: '*My friends, I must tell you that a Socialist policy is abhorrent to the British ideas of freedom. Although it is now put forward in the main by people who have a good grounding in the Liberalism and Radicalism of the early part of this century, there can be no doubt that Socialism is inseparably interwoven with Totalitarianism and the abject worship of the State. It is not alone that property, in all its forms, is struck at, but that liberty, in all its forms, is challenged by the fundamental conceptions of Socialism. . . . No Socialist Government conducting the entire life and industry of the country could afford to allow free, sharp, or violently-worded expressions of public discontent. They would have to fall back on some form of Gestapo, no doubt very humanely directed in the first instance. And this would nip opinion in the bud; it would stop criticism as it reared its head, and it would gather all the power to the supreme party and the party leaders, rising like stately pinnacles above their vast bureaucracies of Civil servants, no longer servants and no longer civil. And where would the ordinary people simple folk – the common people, as they like to call them in America – where would they be, once this mighty organism had got them in its grip?*' This was Churchill's principal theme throughout the campaign; here he is seen speaking in public. With him in the car is Captain Margesson (a former Conservative Party Chief Whip).

337 Churchill and his wife touring Churchill's own constituency, Woodford, 26 May 1945. In his fourth and last, election broadcast, on 30 June, he said: *'This is the last of the broadcasts of this election. It ends the series which the B.B.C. have placed at the disposal of the politicians, and it may be the last time that I shall so address you through this medium as Prime Minister. That rests with you. I am convinced that I can help you through the dangers and difficulties of the next few years with more advantage than would fall to others, and I am ready, if desired, to try my best. I await your answer. It must be Aye or No. I await it not with pride or thirst for power – for what have I to gain or lose after all that has happened, and all you have done for me? But I await your answer with confidence. I have high confidence in the answer you will give.'*

338
Churchill addressing an audience of 20,000 people at Walthamstow, 4 July 1945. Three days later he left for a short holiday in the South of France. The election results would not be known until 26 July, as the votes of soldiers serving abroad had all to be counted.

339 On 15 July 1945 Churchill flew to Berlin for a final conference with Stalin at Potsdam. In this photograph he is shown shaking hands with the new President of the United States, Harry S. Truman. It was the first time they had met since Truman had become President. '*I called on him the morning after our arrival*', Churchill later wrote, '*and was impressed with his gay, precise, sparkling manner and obvious power of decision.*'

340 Visiting the ruins of Hitler's Chancellery, Berlin, 16 July 1945. Churchill's daughter Mary is at his side; his conference interpreter, Major Birse (who translated for him in his discussions with Stalin) is on his left (in military uniform, with jacket). *'In the square in front of the Chancellery . . .'* Churchill wrote in his memoirs, *'except for one old man who shook his head disapprovingly, they all began to cheer. My hate had died with their surrender. . . .'*

341 Leaving Hitler's underground bunker, Berlin, 16 July 1945. *'I went down to the bottom',* Churchill later recalled, *'and saw the room in which he and his mistress had committed suicide, and when we came up again they showed us the place where his body had been burned.'*

342 On 21 July 1945 Churchill took the salute at a Victory Parade in Berlin. Among those in the parade were troops of the 7th Armoured Division – 'The Desert Rats' – to whom Churchill spoke later that day, at the opening of the 'Winston Club' for British troops in Berlin. During his speech he said: '*This morning's parade brings back to my mind a great many moving incidents of these last long fierce years. Now you are here in Berlin, and I find you established in this great centre which, as a volcano, erupted smoke and fire all over Europe. Twice in our generation as in bygone times the German fury has been unleashed on her neighbours. . . . Now it is we who take our place in the occupation of this country. . . . I am unable to speak without emotion. Dear Desert Rats, may your glory ever shine. May your laurels never fade. May the memory of this glorious pilgrimage which you have made from Alamein to the Baltic and Berlin never die. A march – as far as my reading of history leads me to believe – unsurpassed in the whole story of war. May fathers long tell their children the tale. May you all feel that through following your great ancestors you have accomplished something which has done good to the whole world, which has raised the honour of your country and of which every man has the right to feel proud.*'

343 The saluting base. From left to right: Lord Cherwell (Churchill's scientific adviser and wartime confidant); Montgomery; Sir Alexander Cadogan (forehead only); Churchill; General
Ismay (Churchill's personal military secretary and adviser), Field Marshal Alexander and,
paper in hand, Churchill's doctor, Lord Moran.

344

Churchill left the Potsdam negotiations in mid-course, and returned to London to learn the results of the 1945 election, which were announced on 26 July. Labour won 393 seats, the Conservatives only 213. That night Churchill went to Buckingham Palace and resigned his position as Prime Minister. This photograph shows him on the way to the Palace. He was succeeded as Prime Minister by Clement Attlee. That same night, Sir Alexander Cadogan wrote in a private letter from Potsdam: *'The election will have come as a terrible blow to poor old Winston, and I am awfully sorry for the old boy. It certainly is a display of base ingratitude, and rather humiliating for our country.'* Churchill himself wrote to Cadogan on 5 August that the Labour victory would *'diminish our national stature at a time when we most need unity and strength'*.

345

In 1946 Churchill went to the United States, where he was again welcomed with enthusiasm, and received a host of honorary degrees from universities throughout the country. On 5 March 1946 he was at Westminster College, Fulton, Missouri, where he was introduced to the audience by President Truman. In a solemn speech, he warned of the twin dangers of War and Tyranny, spoke of the 'Iron Curtain' which had descended across Europe, and argued forcefully in favour of a 'special relationship' between Britain and the United States. During the course of his speech he declared: *'I repulse the idea that a new war is inevitable; still more that it is imminent. . . . I do not believe that Soviet Russia desires war. What they desire is the fruits of war and the indefinite expansion of their power and doctrines. But what we have to consider here to-day while time remains, is the permanent prevention of war and the establishment of conditions of freedom and democracy as rapidly as possible in all countries. . . .'* On 8 March Churchill went to Richmond, Virginia – he is seen here arriving at the station, followed by General Eisenhower, Mrs Churchill and Mrs Eisenhower. In his speech to the General Assembly of Virginia he said: *'Peace will not be preserved by pious sentiments expressed in terms of platitudes or by official grimaces and diplomatic correctitude, however desirable this may be from time to time. It will not be preserved by casting aside in dangerous years the panoply of warlike strength. There must be earnest thought. There must also be faithful perseverance and foresight. Greatheart must have his sword and armour to guard the pilgrims on their way. Above all, among the English-speaking peoples, there must be the union of hearts based upon conviction and common ideals. That is what I offer. That is what I seek.'*

347 Flying home from Marrakesh.

346

Throughout 1946 and 1947 Churchill was at work on his war memoirs, the first volume of which, 'The Gathering Storm', was published in 1948. At the end of 1947 he suffered from a severe attack of bronchitis, and went to Morocco to recuperate. Here he is seen painting, in Marrakesh, on 18 January 1948.

348

A persistent theme of Churchill's speeches while he was Leader of the Opposition (from 1945 to 1951) was the unity of Europe. On 7 May 1948 he told the Congress of Europe at the Hague: '*A high and a solemn responsibility rests upon us here this afternoon in this Congress of a Europe striving to be reborn. If we allow ourselves to be rent and disordered by pettiness and small disputes, if we fail in clarity of view or courage in action, a priceless occasion may be cast away for ever. But if we all pull together and pool the luck and the comradeship – and we shall need all the comradeship and not a little luck if we are to move together in this way – and firmly grasp the larger hopes of humanity, then it may be that we shall move into a happier sunlit age, when all the little children who are now growing up in this tormented world may find themselves not the victors nor the vanquished in the fleeting triumphs of one country over another in the bloody turmoil of destructive war, but the heirs of all the treasures of the past and the masters of all the science, the abundance and the glories of the future.*' This photograph shows Churchill at the end of his speech, overwhelmed by the response. From left to right are four of the leaders of the European movement: Dr Kerstens (Holland), Paul Ramadier (France), Dr Retinger (Secretary General of the Congress) and Denis de Rougemont.

349

An indefatigable speaker, Churchill led the Conservative attack on the Labour Government in the House of Commons, and spoke throughout Britain. This photograph was taken in Cambridge in June 1948. A month later, on 10 July, he told his constituents: '*Never under a socialist Government or while they follow the lines of Socialist restriction, wrong planning, wasteful management, and administrative incompetence will this country regain its sovereignty and independence.*'

351

At the General Election of 1950, the Labour Party was again returned to power, but with a majority of only five seats over all other parties. Another General Election was held on 25 October 1951. Here Churchill is seen going to cast his vote. The Conservatives were re-elected to power by a majority of only 17, and with less overall votes than Labour. Churchill became Prime Minister for the second time, holding office until 1955.

350

Churchill at Chartwell, 1950. It was at Chartwell that he painted, prepared his speeches, and finished his six-volume war memoirs, 'The Second World War'.

352 On 7 January 1953 Churchill visited Bermuda. Here he is seen leaving the aeroplane with his son-in-law, Christopher Soames, and his Principal Private Secretary, J. R. Colville. He had flown from the United States in President Eisenhower's personal aircraft.

June the 14th, 1954

353 On 14 June 1954 Churchill was installed at Windsor Castle as a Knight of the Garter, becoming 'Sir' Winston. But he later refused the Queen's offer of a Dukedom, not wanting to leave the House of Commons, or to lose the name 'Churchill'.

354 In June 1954 Churchill went to the United States for further talks with President Dwight D. Eisenhower. With Churchill and Eisenhower is the Vice-President, Richard M. Nixon. A year earlier, in June 1953, he had suffered a severe stroke, and had been unable for some time to attend to public affairs.

355

As Prime Minister from 1951 to 1955, Churchill remained a supporter of European unity. But the comprehensive unity of which he had spoken in the late 1940's proved impossible to secure in the early 1950's. Here he is at Chartwell on 23 August 1954, with the French Prime Minister, Pierre Mendès-France, after they had held emergency discussions on the breakdown of the European Defence Committee Conference at Brussels.

356 In March 1955 Churchill decided to resign, and on 4 April 1955, his last night as Prime Minister, he gave a dinner at 10 Downing Street for the Queen and Prince Philip. This photograph was taken as his guests left. Two days later, on 6 April 1955, he himself left 10 Downing Street.

357

Churchill at Chartwell; a photograph taken on 30 November 1955, his eighty-first birthday While in retirement, he worked on a four-volume 'History of the English Speaking Peoples which he had begun in the late 1930's, and which was published between 1956 and 1958 The book won him the Nobel Prize for Literature.

358 Relaxing at Roquebrune, in the South of France, with Field-Marshal Viscount Montgomery, 12 October 1957.

359 Churchill on his Golden Wedding Anniversary, 12 September 1958. With him are his son Randolph, Lady Churchill, and Randolph Churchill's daughter Arabella. This photograph was taken at The Villa Capponcina, Lord Beaverbrook's house on the Cap d'Ail, Nice.

360 Churchill painting in the South of France. For the last years of his life, painting was his principal relaxation.

361

While sailing as a guest on Aristotle Onassis' yacht 'Christina' in September 1960, Churchill was the guest of the Yugoslav leader, Marshal Tito, and landed briefly on Yugoslav soil.

362 Playing bezique at Chartwell in 1964, with the Hon. Mrs Anthony Henley, a close family friend.

363 Relaxing in a garden in the South of France.

Churchill died at his London home on 25 January 1965, at the age of ninety. After the lying in State at Westminster Hall, the funeral service was held at St Paul's Cathedral on 30 January. The funeral procession was watched by thousands of people in the streets of London, and by millions on television. Several years before, with typical foresight and thoroughness, Churchill himself had laid down in precise detail how the procession was to be made up – what route it was to take, which tunes the bands were to play, and which hymns were to be sung; and he had given this last great plan of action the code-name: *'Operation Hope Not'*.

364 Churchill's coffin being taken from St Paul's to Waterloo Station, as part of the final journey to Bladon churchyard near Blenheim Palace, where he was buried next to his father, mother, and brother.

List of Sources for the Photographs

1   Churchill Photograph Albums: Broadwater collection
2   Churchill Biography: Photographic collection
3   Churchill Photograph Albums: Broadwater collection
4   Churchill Photograph Albums: Broadwater collection
5   Churchill Biography: Photographic collection
6   Radio Times Hulton Picture Library: P 240
7   Radio Times Hulton Picture Library: P 600
8   Churchill Biography: Photographic collection
9   Churchill Photograph Albums: Broadwater collection
10   Churchill Photograph Albums: Broadwater collection
11   Churchill Photograph Albums: Broadwater collection
12   Churchill Biography: Photographic collection
13   Churchill Photograph Albums: Broadwater collection
14   Churchill Photograph Albums: Broadwater collection
15   Churchill Press Cutting Albums: *Illustrated Sporting and Dramatic News*, 25 November 1899
16   Longmans, Publishers
17   Churchill Photograph Albums: Broadwater collection
18   Radio Times Hulton Picture Library: 15291
19   Churchill Biography: Photographic collection
20   Churchill Press Cutting Albums: *The Saturday Herald*, 18 November 1899
21   Churchill Press Cutting Albums: *Daily News Weekly*, 25 November 1899
22   Edition Nels, Brussels
23   Churchill Press Cutting Albums: Pasted-in photograph
24   Churchill Press Cutting Albums: *Police News*, 6 January 1900
25   Churchill Photograph Albums: Broadwater collection
26   Churchill Photograph Albums: Broadwater collection
27   Churchill Photograph Albums: Broadwater collection
28   Churchill Photograph Albums: Broadwater collection
29   Churchill Photograph Albums: Broadwater collection
30   J. Bowers, Pretoria (provided by J. R. A. Bailey, Johannesburg)
31   Longmans, Publishers
32   Spy cartoon, Vanity Fair, 10 July 1900
33   Churchill Photograph Albums: Broadwater collection
34   Cardiff Naturalists Society
35   Churchill Photograph Albums: Broadwater collection
36   Churchill Press Cutting Albums: *Punch*, 10 September 1902
37   Churchill Photograph Albums: Broadwater collection
38   Therize Borry (provided by Paul Maze)
39   Radio Times Hulton Picture Library: P 4954
40   Churchill Press Cutting Albums: *Manchester Daily Despatch*, 19 March 1904
41   Churchill Press Cutting Albums: *Pall Mall Gazette*, 7 June 1904
42   Radio Times Hulton Picture Library: P 24523
43   Radio Times Hulton Picture Library: P 15777

44–50   Churchill Press Cutting Albums: original photographs by R. Banks
51   Churchill Photograph Albums: Broadwater collection
52   Churchill Papers: Chartwell Trust collection
53   Churchill Photograph Albums: Broadwater collection
54   Churchill Papers: Chartwell Trust collection
55   Churchill Papers: Chartwell Trust collection
56   Daily Mirror Picture Service
57   Churchill Press Cutting Albums: *Daily Mirror*, 11 May 1908
58   Bassano & Vandyk: G/B85A
59   Syndication International: DM 778 K
60   Churchill Photograph Album: Broadwater collection
61   Churchill Biography: Photographic collection
62   Die Woche (cutting sent by Mr and Mrs H Sornsen)
63   Barratt's Photo Press: P 71973
64   Churchill Press Cutting Albums: *Black & White*, 11 December 1909
65   Radio Times Hulton Picture Library: P 18993
66   Radio Times Hulton Picture Library: P 2547
67   Churchill Biography: Photographic collection
68   Churchill Photograph Albums: Broadwater collection
69   Churchill Press Cutting Albums: *Illustrated London News*, 10 April 1909
70   Churchill Press Cutting Albums: *Manchester Evening News*, 16 November 1909
71   Sport and General Press Agency: G 1408/13
72   Press Association: A 1738
73   Press Association: A 1286
74   Mrs Eva Reichmann (original at Blenheim Palace)
75   Radio Times Hulton Picture Library: P 15784
76   E. T. Reed
77   Baroness Spencer-Churchill photograph album
78   Churchill Biography: Photographic collection
79   Press Association: B 1214
80   Churchill Biography: Photographic collection
81   Press Association: A 1886
82   Press Association: B 1203
83   Radio Times Hulton Picture Library: P 13529
84   Radio Times Hulton Picture Library: P 16261
85   Churchill Photograph Albums: Broadwater collection
86   Chartwell Trust Papers; photograph by Campbell Gray: A 424
87   Radio Times Hulton Picture Library: P 2443
88   Churchill Press Cutting Albums: *Dover Express*, 27 April 1912
89   Press Association: C 1205
90   Press Association: C 1200
91   Radio Times Hulton Picture Library: P 15528
92   Radio Times Hulton Picture Library: P 15482
93   Radio Times Hulton Picture Library: P 13481
94   Mrs Constance Mainprice (photograph taken by Fleet Paymaster E. L. Mainprice)
95   Churchill Press Cutting Albums: *The Bystander*, 4 June 1913
96   Churchill Press Cutting Albums: *Punch*, 21 May 1913
97   Radio Times Hulton Picture Library: P 15765

98   Press Association: G 1204
99   Press Association: E 1327
100 Press Association: D 1237
101 Sport and General: 9261
102 Churchill Press Cutting Albums: *Ulk*, no 48, Berlin, 28 November 1913
103 Churchill Press Cutting Albums: *Birmingham Evening Despatch*, 1 December 1913
104 Churchill Photograph Albums: Broadwater collection
105 Churchill Photograph Albums: Broadwater collection
106 Radio Times Hulton Picture Library: P 15525
107 Churchill Press Cutting Albums: *The Bystander*, 28 January 1914
108 Radio Times Hulton Picture Library: Y 36686
109 Press Association: E 1218
110 Press Association: B 1207
111 Lady Patricia Kingsbury
112 Churchill Press Cutting Albums: *Punch*, 25 May 1914
113 Radio Times Hulton Picture Library: P 2444
114 Press Association: E 1207
115 Poy, 4 August 1914
116 Churchill Press Cutting Albums: *The Tatler*, 12 August 1914
117 Churchill Press Cutting Albums: *Everyman*, 21 August 1914
118 Churchill Press Cutting Albums: *Great Deeds of the War*, 12 December 1914
119 Syndication International: FF10
120 Peregrine S. Churchill
121 Poy, 30 November 1915
122 Press Association: F 1249
123 Harry Skinner
124 Churchill Press Cutting Albums: *Manchester Dispatch*, 19 February 1915
125 Churchill Press Cutting Albums: *Westminster Gazette*, 25 February 1915
126 Imperial War Museum: Q 13619
127 Radio Times Hulton Picture Library: 062913-P
128 Radio Times Hulton Picture Library: 062912-P
129 Churchill Press Cutting Albums: *The Bystander*, 2 June 1915
130 Imperial War Museum: Q 11428
131 London News Agency
132 Press Association: G 1351
133 Press Association: F 1217
134 Press Association: F 1218
135 Press Association: G 1244
136 Press Association: G 1245
137 Radio Times Hulton Picture Library: P 15774
138 Churchill Photograph Albums: Broadwater collection
139 Churchill Biography: Photographic collection
140 Major-General Sir Edmund Hakewill-Smith
141 European Picture Service
142 Chartwell Trust Papers: *London Magazine*, October 1916 (photograph by Dinham, Torquay)
143 Radio Times Hulton Picture Library: P 15782
144 Radio Times Hulton Picture Library: P 21862

145 Radio Times Hulton Picture Library: P 22055
146 Imperial War Museum: Q 11428
147 Associated Newspapers
148 Churchill Press Cutting Albums: *The Star*, 21 January 1920
149 Churchill Photograph Albums: Broadwater collection
150 Churchill Photograph Albums: Broadwater collection
151 K. C. Felce
152 Press Association: K 48
153 Radio Times Hulton Picture Library: 14112-P
154 Press Association: K 1304
155 Trenchard Photograph Albums
156 Churchill Photograph Albums: Broadwater collection
157 Churchill Photograph Albums: Broadwater collection
158 Churchill Photograph Albums: Broadwater collection
159 Press Association: N 1226
160 Churchill Photograph Albums: Broadwater collection
161 Press Association: P 1288
162 Syndication International: DM 799 T
163 Churchill Press Cutting Albums: *The Weekly Westminster*, 15 March 1924
164 Press Association: 102168–62
165 Press Association: 102168–15
166 Churchill Press Cutting Albums: *Punch*, 4 June 1924
167 Churchill Press Cutting Albums: *The Star*, 7 October 1924
168 Churchill Photograph Albums: Broadwater collection
169 Central Press Photos: Box 1525/1
170 Syndication International: DM 780 F
171 Syndication International: DM 780 G
172 Churchill Photograph Albums: Broadwater collection
173 Churchill Photograph Albums: Broadwater collection
174 Syndication International: DM 760 L
175 Associated Press: B 12811
176 Churchill Photograph Albums: Broadwater collection
177 Topical Press Agency: D 7630
178 Churchill Photograph Albums: Broadwater collection
179 Churchill Photograph Albums: Broadwater collection
180 Churchill Photograph Albums: Broadwater collection
181 Churchill Photograph Albums: Broadwater collection
182 Churchill Photograph Albums: Broadwater collection
183 Radio Times Hulton Picture Library: E 358P-P
184 Radio Times Hulton Picture Library: E 7361-P
185 Radio Times Hulton Picture Library: E 8410-P
186 United Press International, Planet News: LN 5210
187 Martin Gilbert Archive
188 Press Association: U 1203
189 Churchill Photograph Albums: Broadwater collection
190 Churchill Photograph Albums: Broadwater collection
191 Churchill Photograph Albums: Broadwater collection
192 Associated Press: 29740

193 Press Association: V 1384
194 Syndication International: DM 7807
195 Churchill Photograph Albums: Broadwater collection
196 Radio Times Hulton Picture Library: G 8535-P
197 Radio Times Hulton Picture Library: G 9496-P
198 Associated Press: 50307
199 Press Association: X 1215
200 Churchill Press Cutting Albums: *Daily Herald*, 30 March 1933
201 Associated Press: 106927
202 Syndication International: OP 708 E
203 Radio Times Hulton Picture Library: 54374 P
204 Ava, Viscountess Waverley
205 Ava, Viscountess Waverley
206 Radio Times Hulton Picture Library: P 239
207 Radio Times Hulton Picture Library: T 2899 P
208 Topix (Thomson Newspapers)
209 Associated Press: 192483
210 Radio Times Hulton Picture Library: P 5012
211 Radio Times Hulton Picture Library: P 241
212 Radio Times Hulton Picture Library: P 5779
213 Radio Times Hulton Picture Library: P 53031
214 Fox Photos: 218803
215 Radio Times Hulton Picture Library: V 2356-P
216 Associated Press: 208468
217 Churchill Press Cutting Albums: *Punch*, 31 May 1939
218 Churchill Press Cutting Albums: *Daily Express*, 6 July 1939
219 Churchill Press Cutting Albums: *Punch*, 12 July 1939
220 *Daily Mirror*, 25 July 1939
221 Paul Maze
222 Paul Maze
223 Associated Press: 214842
224 Churchill Press Cutting Albums: *The Tatler*, 6 September 1939
225 United Press International: 88814
226 Associated Press: 215679
227 Associated Press: 216223
228 Fox Photos: HP 46253
229 Radio Times Hulton Picture Library: V 6124-P
230 Churchill Press Cutting Albums: no newspaper source given
231 Imperial War Museum: O 190
232 Imperial War Museum: O 188
233 *Simplicissimus* (Munich), 5 November 1939
234 Syndication International: OP 708-F
235 Churchill Press Cutting Albums: *Evening Standard*, 13 November 1939
236 Sir Geoffrey Shakespeare
237 Central Press Photos: Box 5233
238 Radio Times Hulton Picture Library: W 720 P
239 Radio Times Hulton Picture Library: W 882 P
240 Associated Press: 223945

241 Associated Press: 224159
242 Radio Times Hulton Picture Library: W 2360 P
243 Radio Times Hulton Picture Library: W 2418 P
244 Radio Times Hulton Picture Library: W 2418 A-P
245 Associated Press: 225376
246 Churchill Press Cutting Albums: *Daily Mail*, 13 May 1940
247 Associated Press: 225592
248 Sir Cecil Beaton
249 Radio Times Hulton Picture Library: W 2628 P
250 Baroness Spencer-Churchill photograph album
251 Imperial War Museum: H 3516
252 Imperial War Museum: H 3504
253 Imperial War Museum: H 3977
254 Fox Photos: WE 1216
255 Central Press Photos
256 Associated Press: 230388
257 George Rance
258 George Rance
259 Radio Times Hulton Picture Library: W 5547 P
260 Radio Times Hulton Picture Library: W 5548 P
261 Radio Times Hulton Picture Library: W 5549 P
262 Acme News Pictures
263 Churchill Biography: Photographic collection
264 United Press International
265 Radio Times Hulton Picture Library: Y 1851 P
266 Radio Times Hulton Picture Library: Y 1855 P
267 Radio Times Hulton Picture Library: Y 1857 P
268 Radio Times Hulton Picture Library: Y 1858A P
269 Czechoslovak Army Film & Photo Service: No 38
270 Czechoslovak Army Film & Photo Service: No 33
271 Czechoslovak Army Film & Photo Service: No 48
272 Churchill Photograph Albums: Broadwater collection
273 Churchill Photograph Albums: Broadwater collection
274 Churchill Photograph Albums: Broadwater collection
275 Churchill Photograph Albums: Broadwater collection
276 Churchill Photograph Albums: Broadwater collection
277 A. Massen
278 Imperial War Museum: H 14201
279 Imperial War Museum: H 14266
280 Imperial War Museum: H 14259
281 Radio Times Hulton Picture Library: Y 2628 P
282 Camera Press: 7016–2
283 Winston S. Churchill MP: Private collection
284 Churchill Photograph Albums: Broadwater collection
285 Churchill Photograph Albums: Broadwater collection
286 Churchill Photograph Albums: Broadwater collection
287 Churchill Photograph Albums: Broadwater collection
288 Churchill Photograph Albums: Broadwater collection

289 Churchill Photograph Albums: Broadwater collection
290 Churchill Photograph Albums: Broadwater collection
291 Imperial War Museum: NA 3253
292 Field Marshal Viscount Montgomery's photograph albums
293 Imperial War Museum: H 31958
294 Imperial War Museum: H 33565
295 Imperial War Museum: H 10874
296 Churchill Photograph Albums: Broadwater collection
297 Churchill Photograph Albums: Broadwater collection
298 Churchill Photograph Albums: Broadwater collection
299 Churchill Photograph Albums: Broadwater collection
300 Churchill Photograph Albums: Broadwater collection
301 Imperial War Museum: EA 18275
302 Imperial War Museum: EA 18277
303 Fox Photos: 312060
304 Field Marshal Viscount Montgomery's photograph albums
305 Imperial War Museum: B 5359
306 Field Marshal Viscount Montgomery's photograph albums
307 Imperial War Museum: B 7888
308 Field Marshal Viscount Montgomery's photograph albums
309 Field Marshal Viscount Montgomery's photograph albums
310 Imperial War Museum: NA 17905
311 Field Marshal Earl Alexander of Tunis' photograph albums
312 Imperial War Museum: NA 18030
313 Imperial War Museum: NA 18044
314 Field Marshal Earl Alexander of Tunis' photograph albums
315 Field Marshal Earl Alexander of Tunis' photograph albums
316 Imperial War Museum: NA 17915
317 Imperial War Museum: NA 17923
318 Camera Press: 4588–9
319 A. Butterworth
320 Churchill Photograph Albums: Broadwater collection
321 Churchill Photograph Albums: Broadwater collection
322 Imperial War Museum: NAM 185
323 Churchill Photograph Albums: Broadwater collection
324 Churchill Photograph Albums: Broadwater collection
325 Imperial War Museum: BU 2271
326 Field Marshal Viscount Montgomery's photograph albums
327 Field Marshal Viscount Montgomery's photograph albums
328 Field Marshal Viscount Montgomery's photograph albums
329 Field Marshal Viscount Montgomery's photograph albums
330 Field Marshal Viscount Montgomery's photograph albums
331 Imperial War Museum: BU 2636
332 Press Association: 102168–38
333 Churchill Photograph Albums: Broadwater collection
334 Imperial War Museum: H 41846
335 Peter Woodard
336 Peter Woodard

337 Press Association: 102168-32
338 Central Press Photos: Box 5414
339 Field Marshal Viscount Montgomery's photograph albums
340 Imperial War Museum: BU 8954
341 Imperial War Museum: BU 8955
342 Field Marshal Earl Alexander of Tunis' photograph albums
343 Field Marshal Earl Alexander of Tunis' photograph albums
344 Associated Press: 280447
345 Charles T. Mayer
346 United Press International
347 Mr Harvey
348 Radio Times Hulton Picture Library: P 1233
349 D. Freeman
350 Time Incorporated and Miss Grace Hamblin
351 United Press International
352 Churchill Photograph Albums: Broadwater collection
353 Baroness Spencer-Churchill photograph album
354 Churchill Biography: Photographic collection
355 United Press International
356 United Press International
357 Vivienne, London; Camera Press 2589-31
358 Field Marshal Viscount Montgomery's photograph albums
359 United Press International
360 Churchill Biography: Photographic collection
361 Churchill papers: Chartwell Trust collection
362 Paris Match: No 825
363 Paul Maze
364 Topix (Thomson Newspapers)

List of Sources for the Quotations

H. H. Asquith papers (photograph numbers: 71, 73, 80, 82, 107, 127, 132, 137); Margot Asquith papers (121); Balfour papers (128, 140); Baruch papers (214); Cabinet papers, Public Record Office (84, 123, 131); Cadogan papers (318, 344); Jack Churchill papers (33, 120, 142); Lord Randolph Churchill papers, Blenheim Palace Archive, (4, 9); Randolph Churchill papers (189); Elgin papers (54); Fisher papers (87); Jellicoe papers (115); T. E. Lawrence papers (51); Leonie Leslie papers (31); Lloyd George papers (106); Londonderry papers (25); Pamela, Countess of Lytton papers (17, 27, 28); Marquess of Milford Haven papers (88); Venetia Montagu papers (119, 121); Mottistone papers (130); Countess Mountbatten of Burma papers (42); Harold Nicolson papers (205); Rosebery papers (36); Royal Archives (73, 75); Spears papers (138); Baroness Spencer-Churchill papers (56, 60, 67, 70, 77, 78, 85, 89, 99, 105, 112, 114, 138, 139, 141, 152, 181, 182); Quickswood papers (39); Ava, Viscountess Waverley papers (203).

All other quotations are from the Churchill papers (Chartwell Trust Collection), or from Churchill's own writings and speeches.

Biographical Index

compiled by the author

I have included only those individuals whom I have been able to identify in the photographs, and have not indexed those that appear in the cartoons, or Churchill himself. Anyone who is identified after the book has been published will be included in both the index and the captions of subsequent editions.

VERSION
2003

MICROSOFT
VISUAL BASIC .NET
STEP BY STEP

Microsoft®
.net™

Michael Halvorson

PUBLISHED BY
Microsoft Press
A Division of Microsoft Corporation
One Microsoft Way
Redmond, Washington 98052-6399

Library of Congress Cataloging-in-Publication Data
Halvorson, Michael.
    Microsoft Visual Basic .NET Step by Step: Version 2003 / Michael Halvorson.
        p. cm.
    Includes index.
    ISBN 0-7356-1905-0
    1. Microsoft Visual Basic. 2. Basic (Computer program language) 3. Microsoft
.NET. I. Title.

    QA76.73.B3H3385   2003
    005.2'768--dc21   2002045517

Printed and bound in the United States of America.

9   QWT   8 7 6

Distributed in Canada by H.B. Fenn and Company Ltd.

A CIP catalogue record for this book is available from the British Library.

Microsoft Press books are available through booksellers and distributors worldwide. For further information about international editions, contact your local Microsoft Corporation office or contact Microsoft Press International directly at fax (425) 936-7329. Visit our Web site at www.microsoft.com/mspress. Send comments to *mspinput@microsoft.com*.

Acquisitions Editor: Robin Van Steenburgh
Project Editor: Denise Bankaitis
Technical Editor: Julie Xiao

Body Part No. X09-45376

Table of Contents

Acknowledgments

This book is a weaving together of the ideas and innovations of many talented programmers, testers, writers, editors, and teachers. Although I am the author of record, this book reflects the expertise of a number of interesting people, both inside and outside of Microsoft Corporation. First I'd like to thank the developers of the Visual Basic .NET product for their comments and assistance. Several programmers and product managers offered early glimpses of the Visual Studio .NET software to me and explained the product's inner workings. In particular, Rob Howard, Dennis Angeline, Sam Spencer, Michael Pizzo, Mike Iem, Chris Dias, Omar Khan, Matt Stoecker, and Connie Sullivan deserve special mention. Thanks for creating a great development product for us to use and write about!

At Microsoft Press, I would like to acknowledge the contributions of a thoroughly awesome team of professionals. Thanks to Danielle Bird and Robin Van Steenburgh, acquisitions editors; Elizabeth Hansford, principal compositor; Katherine Erickson, compositor; Patty Masserman and Sandi Resnick, copy editors; Michael Kloepfer, electronic artist; Bill Meyers and Richard Shrout, indexers; and Bill Teel, publishing support specialist. Your efforts will help numerous readers navigate the complex features of Visual Basic .NET and write their first programs.

I would also like to thank several Microsoft Press editors who spent considerable time shepherding this book through its many stages of production. Dick Brown worked on the first version of this book as a project editor, and his editorial fingerprints are still on each page of the manuscript. Technical editor Robert Lyon tested the code in the book for Visual Basic .NET Version 2002, and his late-night efforts are still making a significant contribution, especially in the chapter on printing. Technical editor Julie Xiao did an expert job of testing the code for Visual Basic .NET Version 2003, and she also verified each of the step by step lessons, prepared the companion CD-ROM, and researched several critical issues related to the software. Project editor Denise Bankaitis coordinated the team that worked on the book, calmly managed each crisis that arose during the project, and kept each file and folder moving to its intended destination. Denise is an excellent editor and arbiter of style, and the book has benefited greatly from her caring hand.

Finally, I would like to thank my wife, Kim, and my sons, Henry and Felix, for their support and patience as this book has moved through two rapid editions in 2002 and 2003. For the missed trips to the park on behalf of Visual Basic .NET, I am truly sorry.

Introduction

Microsoft Visual Basic .NET Step by Step—Version 2003 is a comprehensive introduction to Visual Basic programming using the Microsoft Visual Basic .NET 2003 software. I've designed this course with a variety of skill levels in mind so that new programmers can learn software development fundamentals in the context of useful, real-world applications and experienced Visual Basic programmers can quickly master the essential tools and programming techniques offered in the Visual Basic .NET upgrade. Complementing this comprehensive approach is the book's structure—six topically organized parts, 22 chapters, and more than 65 step-by-step exercises and sample programs. By using this book, you'll quickly learn how to create professional-quality Visual Basic .NET applications for the Microsoft Windows operating system and a variety of Web browsers. You'll also have fun!

▶ **Important**   Visual Basic .NET 2003 is available in different editions and product configurations, including Standard Edition. It is also distributed as a component in the Microsoft Visual Studio .NET 2003 programming suite, which includes the Microsoft Visual C# .NET, Microsoft Visual C++ .NET, and Microsoft Visual J# .NET compilers and other .NET development tools. Visual Studio .NET 2003 is available in several different editions, including Professional Edition, Enterprise Developer Edition, Enterprise Architect Edition, and Academic Edition. I've written this book to be compatible with Visual Basic .NET 2003 Standard Edition, Visual Studio .NET 2003 Professional Edition, Visual Studio .NET 2003 Enterprise Developer Edition, and Visual Studio .NET 2003 Enterprise Architect Edition. Although Visual Basic .NET 2003 is quite similar to Visual Basic .NET 2002, there are a few important differences, so I recommend that you complete the exercises in this book using the Visual Basic .NET 2003 software.

Finding Your Best Starting Point in This Book

This book is designed to help you build skills in a number of essential areas. You can use this book if you're new to programming, switching from another programming language, or upgrading from Microsoft Visual Basic 6. Use the following table to find your best starting point in this book.

If you are	Follow these steps

New

To programming	1	Install the practice files as described in the section "Installing the Practice Files on Your Computer."
	2	Learn basic skills for using Microsoft Visual Basic .NET by working sequentially from Chapter 1 through Chapter 18.
	3	Complete Parts 5 and 6 as your level of interest or experience dictates.

If you are	Follow these steps

Switching

From Microsoft QuickBasic or an earlier version of the BASIC programming language	1	Install the practice files as described in the section "Installing the Practice Files on Your Computer."
	2	Complete Chapter 1 through Chapter 4, skim Chapter 5 through Chapter 7, and complete Parts 3 and 4 sequentially.
	3	For specific information about creating database and Internet programs, read Parts 5 and 6, respectively.

If you are	Follow these steps

Upgrading

From Microsoft Visual Basic 6	1	Install the practice files as described in the section "Installing the Practice Files on Your Computer."
	2	Read Chapter 1 through Chapter 4 carefully to learn the new features of the Visual Studio .NET development environment.
	3	Pay special attention to the "Upgrade Notes: What's New in Visual Basic .NET?" sidebars near the beginning of each chapter, which highlight the significant differences between Visual Basic 6 and Visual Basic .NET.
	4	Skim Chapter 5 through Chapter 7 to review the fundamentals of event-driven programming, using variables, and writing decision structures.
	5	Work sequentially from Chapter 8 through Chapter 22 to learn the new features of Visual Basic .NET.
	6	Read Appendix A: "Upgrading Visual Basic 6 Programs to Visual Basic .NET 2003" to learn how to convert Visual Basic 6 programs using the Visual Basic Upgrade Wizard.

If you are	Follow these steps
Referencing	
This book after working through the chapters	**1** Use the index to locate information about specific topics, and use the table of contents to locate information about general topics.
	2 Use the Upgrading Index to see a list of the new features in Visual Basic .NET and how Visual Basic 6 program code should be upgraded.
	3 Read the Quick Reference at the end of each chapter for a brief review of the major tasks in the chapter. The Quick Reference topics are listed in the same order as they're presented in the chapter.

Visual Basic 6 vs. Visual Basic .NET: New Features and Concepts

The following table lists the major new features in both Microsoft Visual Basic .NET 2002 and Microsoft Visual Basic .NET 2003 that are covered in this book. The table is designed to identify features that a typical Visual Basic 6 programmer will be interested in, and it shows the chapter in which you can find more information about the feature described. You can also use the Upgrading Index or the general index to find specific information about a feature or a task you want to learn.

To learn how to	See
Use the new integrated Visual Studio .NET development environment and programming tools	Chapter 1
Find an executive summary of improvements and new features in the Visual Basic .NET 2003 upgrade	Chapter 1
Use the new Windows Forms Toolbox controls, including *DateTimePicker* and *LinkLabel*	Chapters 2 and 3
Compile your program as debug builds and release builds	Chapter 2
Use the new *MainMenu* control and new dialog box controls	Chapter 4
Use methods in the new .NET Framework in program code	Chapter 5
Master the new variable types and math shortcut operators	Chapter 5
Understand changes in While loops and *Timer* controls	Chapter 7
Use the new debugging features in Visual Basic .NET	Chapter 8

To learn how to	See
Use the new Try...Catch syntax for building error handlers	Chapter 9
Learn the new syntax for declaring and calling procedures	Chapter 10
Use Visual Basic .NET collections	Chapter 11
Use new file and string processing methods in the *System.IO* namespace and *String* class	Chapter 12
Work with older ActiveX (COM) objects in Visual Basic .NET	Chapters 3 and 13
Use a *Process* component to manage a running application	Chapter 13
Deploy Visual Basic .NET applications and assemblies	Chapter 14
Use the *System.Drawing* namespace to create graphics and animation effects	Chapter 16
Use inheritance in programs	Chapter 17
Print graphics and text by using new methods, classes, and controls	Chapter 18
Use Server Explorer and Microsoft ADO.NET techniques to manage databases	Chapters 19 and 20
Create data adapters and datasets	Chapters 19 and 20
Use Web Forms controls to build interactive Web applications	Chapter 22
Use the new Web Forms Designer to build Web pages	Chapter 22
Use Microsoft ASP.NET for Internet programming	Chapter 22

About the Companion CD-ROM

The CD-ROM inside the back cover of this book contains a fully searchable electronic version of the book. This eBook allows you to view the book text on screen and to search the contents. For information on installing and using the eBook, see the Readme.txt file in the \eBook folder.

The CD-ROM also contains practice files that you'll use as you perform the exercises in the book. For example, when you're learning how to display database records with an ADO.NET dataset, you'll open one of the practice files—an academic database named Students.mdb—and then use ADO.NET commands to access the database. By using the practice files, you won't waste time creating all the samples used in the exercises. Instead, you can concentrate on learning how to master Visual Basic .NET 2003 programming techniques. With the files and the step-by-step instructions in the chapters, you'll also learn by doing, which is an easy and effective way to acquire and remember new skills.

▶ **Important**   Before you break the seal on the CD-ROM, be sure that this book matches your version of the software. This book is designed for use with Microsoft Visual Basic .NET 2003 and Microsoft Visual Studio .NET 2003 for the Microsoft Windows operating system. To find out what software you're running, you can check the product package, or you can start the software, open a project, and then click About Microsoft Visual Basic .NET on the Help menu at the top of the screen.

System Requirements

To compile and run all the practice files on this book's companion CD-ROM, you'll need the following configuration:

- Microsoft Windows 2000 Professional, Windows 2000 Server, Windows XP Home Edition, Windows XP Professional, Windows Server 2003 or later
- Microsoft Visual Basic .NET 2003, which can be one of the following editions:

  - Visual Basic .NET 2003 Standard
  - Visual Studio .NET 2003 Professional
  - Visual Studio .NET 2003 Enterprise Developer
  - Visual Studio .NET 2003 Enterprise Architect

  ▶ **Important**   A few features (such as the Setup Wizard, the Cab Project template, the Merge Module Project template, and the Web Setup Project template discussed in Chapter 14) aren't included in Visual Basic .NET 2003 Standard. Also, because Windows XP Home Edition doesn't include Microsoft Internet Information Services, you can't create local ASP.NET Web applications (discussed in Chapter 22) using Windows XP Home Edition.

This book and the practice files were tested using Visual Basic .NET 2003 Standard and Visual Studio .NET 2003 Professional. You might notice a few differences if you're using other editions of Visual Studio .NET 2003.

Installing the Practice Files on Your Computer

Installing the practice files on your hard disk requires approximately 5.5 MB of disk space. Follow these steps to install the practice files on your computer's hard disk so that you can use them with the exercises in this book.

1   Remove the CD-ROM from the package inside the back cover of this book, and insert it in your CD-ROM drive.

  ▶ **Important**   On many systems, Windows will automatically recognize that you've inserted a CD-ROM and will display a start window. If this happens, skip to step 4.

2   On the taskbar at the bottom of your screen, click the Start button, and then click Run.

The Run dialog box appears.

3   In the Open text box, type **d:\startcd**, and then click OK. Don't add spaces as you type. (If your CD-ROM drive is associated with a different drive letter, such as E, type that instead.)

A start window should appear.

4   Click Install Practice Files in the list of options on the left.

A Setup program appears.

5   Follow the directions on the screen.

The Setup program will copy the practice files from the CD-ROM to your hard drive and clear the Read-only flag on the files. For best results in using the practice files with this book, accept the preselected installation location, which by default is c:\vbnet03sbs. (If you change the installation location, you'll need to manually adjust the paths in a few practice files to locate essential components—such as artwork and database files—when you use them.)

6   When the files have been installed, remove the CD-ROM from your CD-ROM drive and replace it in the package inside the back cover of your book.

A folder named c:\vbnet03sbs has been created on your hard disk, and the practice files have been placed in that folder. You'll find one folder in c:\vbnet03sbs for each chapter in the book. If you have trouble running any of the practice files, refer to the text in the book that describes those files.

Using the Practice Files

Each chapter in this book explains when and how to use the practice files for that chapter. When it's time to use a practice file, the book will list instructions for how to open the file. The chapters are built around scenarios that simulate real programming projects so that you can easily apply the skills you learn to your own work.

Notice that Visual Basic .NET 2003 features a new file format for its projects and solutions. Accordingly, you won't be able to open the practice files for this book if you're using an older version of the Visual Basic or Visual Studio software. To check the version of Visual Basic or Visual Studio that you're using, click the About command on the Help menu.

For those of you who like to know all the details, here's a list of the Visual Basic projects included on the CD-ROM. Each project is located in its own folder and has several support files.

Project	Description
Chapter 1	
MusicTrivia	A simple trivia program that welcomes you to the programming course and displays a digital photo.
Chapter 2	
Lucky7	Your first program—a Lucky Seven Slot Machine game that simulates a Las Vegas one-armed bandit.
Chapter 3	
Birthday	A program that uses the *DateTimePicker* control to pick a date.
CheckBox	A program that demonstrates the *CheckBox* control and its properties.
Hello	A "Hello, world!" program that demonstrates the *Label* and *TextBox* controls.
Input Controls	The user interface for an electronic shopping program, assembled using several powerful input controls.
WebLink	A demonstration of the new Windows Forms *LinkLabel* control.
Chapter 4	
Dialog	Demonstrates how to use the Visual Basic .NET dialog box controls.
Menu	Shows how menus and commands are added to a form.
Chapter 5	
Advanced Math	Advanced use of operators for integer division, remainder division, exponentiation, and string concatenation.
Basic Math	Basic use of operators for addition, subtraction, multiplication, and division.
Constant Tester	Uses a constant to hold a fixed mathematical entity.
Data Types	A demonstration of different fundamental data types and their use with variables.
Framework Math	Demonstrates the .NET Framework classes with mathematical methods.
Input Box	Receives input with the *InputBox* function.
Variable Test	Declares and uses variables to store information.

Project	Description
Chapter 6	
Case Greeting	Uses the Case statement in a program to display an appropriate foreign-language welcome message.
Password Validation	Uses the And logical operator to check for logon password.
User Validation	Uses If...Then...Else to manage the logon process.
Chapter 7	
Celsius Conversion	Converts temperatures by using a Do loop.
Counter Variable	Uses an incremental counter as opposed to a loop to process data.
Digital Clock	A simple digital clock utility.
For Loop	Executing code with a For...Next loop.
For Loop Icons	Demonstrates using the counter in a loop to display icons.
Timed Password	A logon program with a password time-out feature.
Chapter 8	
Debug Test	A simulated debugging problem, designed to be solved using the Visual Studio .NET debugging tools.
Chapter 9	
Disk Drive Error	A program that crashes when a floppy disk drive is used incorrectly. (This project is used as the basis of a Visual Basic .NET error handler.)
Disk Drive Handler	A project with a completed error handler that demonstrates the Try...Catch syntax.
Chapter 10	
Final Track Wins	Uses a public variable to track the number of wins in the Lucky Seven Slot Machine project.
Module Test	Creating a new code module in a project.
Text Box Sub	A general-purpose Sub procedure that adds items to a list box.
Track Wins	A clean version of the Lucky Seven Slot Machine project from Chapter 2 (the basis of the Final Track Wins project).
Chapter 11	
Controls Collection	Uses a Visual Basic .NET collection to move objects on a form.
Dynamic Array	Computes the average temperature for any number of days by using a dynamic array.

Project	Description
Chapter 11	
continued	
Fixed Array	Computes the average weekly temperature by using a fixed-length array.
URL Collection	Demonstrates a user-defined collection containing a list of Web addresses (URLs) recently visited by the user.
Chapter 12	
Encrypt Text	Encrypts text files by shifting ASCII characters.
Quick Note	A simple note-taking utility.
Sort Text	A text file editor that demonstrates the Shell sort.
Text Browser	Displays the contents of a text file in a Visual Basic .NET program.
Xor Encryption	Encrypts text files by using the *Xor* operator.
Chapter 13	
Excel Automation	Calls Microsoft Excel 2002 from Visual Basic .NET to compute a loan payment.
Excel Sheet Tasks	Uses Automation to insert text and execute basic formatting in an Excel 2002 worksheet.
Start App	Starts and controls a Windows application process from within a Visual Basic .NET program.
Chapter 14	
Lucky Seven	Demonstrates how Visual Basic .NET applications are compiled and deployed using the Setup Wizard and other tools.
Chapter 15	
Add Controls	Demonstrates how controls are added to a Windows Form at runtime by using program code (not the Windows Forms Designer).
Anchor and Dock	Uses the *Anchor* and *Dock* properties of a form to align objects at runtime.
Desktop Bounds	Uses the *StartPosition* and *DesktopBounds* properties to position a Windows Form at runtime.
Lucky Seven	Lucky Seven Slot Machine project that's used as the basis of the Multiple Forms project. (Open this project when you start the chapter.)
Multiple Forms	A revision of the Lucky Seven Slot Machine project that uses a second form to display online Help.
Startup Form	Demonstrates how the startup (opening) form can be switched between Form1, Form2, and the Sub Main procedure.

Project	Description
Chapter 16	
Draw Shapes	Demonstrates a few of the new graphics methods in the *System.Drawing* namespace.
Moving Icon	Animates an icon on the form, moving it from the top of the form to the bottom each time that you click the Move Down button.
Transparent Form	Demonstrates how to change the transparency of a form.
Zoom In	Simulates zooming in, or magnifying, an object on a form (in this case, the planet Earth).
Chapter 17	
Class Inheritance	Demonstrates the inheritance feature of the Visual Basic .NET object-oriented programming model.
Form Inheritance	Uses the Visual Studio .NET Inheritance Picker to create a form that inherits its characteristics and functionality from another form.
Person Class	Demonstrates how new classes are created in a Visual Basic .NET project. The new class is called *Person*, an employee record with first name, last name, and date of birth fields. The class also contains a method that computes the current age of an employee.
Chapter 18	
Print Dialogs	Demonstrates how to create Print Preview and Page Setup dialog boxes.
Print File	A project that handles more sophisticated printing tasks, including printing a multipage text file with wrapping lines.
Print Graphics	Prints graphics from within a Visual Basic .NET program.
Print Text	Demonstrates how simple text is printed in a Visual Basic .NET program.
Chapter 19	
ADO Form	Demonstrates how ADO.NET is used to establish a connection to a Microsoft Access database and display information from it.
Chapter 20	
DataGrid Sample	Shows how the *DataGrid* control is used to display an entire record or collection of records on a form.

Project	Description
Chapter 21	
Explorer Objects	A project that demonstrates how a reference is made to the Microsoft Internet Controls library and how a COM wrapper is generated within a project. This exercise also instructs readers on how to use the Visual Studio .NET Object Browser tool.
Show HTML	Allows the user to pick one of several Web sites from a list box and then uses Microsoft Internet Explorer to display the selected Web site or HTML document.
Chapter 22	
WebCalculator	Demonstrates using Web Forms controls and ASP.NET to create a car loan calculator that runs in an Internet browser.
Appendix A	
AlarmVB6	A sample Visual Basic 6 program.
AlarmVB.NET	A Visual Basic .NET 2003 program that was upgraded from Visual Basic 6 using the Visual Basic Upgrade Wizard.

Uninstalling the Practice Files

Use the following steps to delete the practice files added to your hard drive by the Visual Basic .NET Step by Step—Version 2003 installation program.

1   Click Start, point to Settings, and then click Control Panel.
2   Double-click the Add/Remove Programs icon.
    The Add/Remove Programs window appears.
3   Select Visual Basic .NET 2003 SBS from the list, and then click Change/Remove.
    A confirmation message appears.
4   Click Yes.
    The practice files are uninstalled.
5   Close the Add/Remove Programs window.
6   Close the Control Panel window.

Conventions and Features in This Book

You can save time when you use this book by understanding, before you start the exercises, how I offer instructions and the elements I use to communicate information about Visual Basic .NET programming. Please take a moment to read the following list, which identifies stylistic issues and discusses helpful features of the book that you might want to use. A few conventions are especially useful for readers who plan to upgrade Visual Basic 6 applications to Visual Basic .NET 2003.

Conventions

- Hands-on exercises for you to follow are given in numbered lists of steps (1, 2, and so on). A round bullet (●) indicates an exercise that has only one step.
- Text that you need to type appears in boldface type.
- As you work through steps, you'll occasionally see tables with lists of properties that you'll type into Visual Studio. Text properties appear within quotes, but you don't need to type the quotes.
- A plus sign (+) between two key names means that you must press those keys at the same time. For example, "Press Alt+Tab" means that you hold down the Alt key while you press Tab.
- Elements labeled Note, Tip, or Important provide additional information or alternative methods for a step that you should read before continuing with the lesson.

Other Features of This Book

- You can learn special programming techniques, background information, or features related to the information being discussed by reading the shaded sidebars that appear throughout the chapters. These sidebars often highlight difficult terminology or suggest future areas for exploration.
- You can learn about options or techniques that build on what you learned in a chapter by trying the optional One Step Further exercise at the end of that chapter.
- You can get a quick reminder of how to perform the tasks you learned by reading the Quick Reference at the end of a chapter.

Upgrading Visual Basic 6 Programs

If you're upgrading from Visual Basic 6 to Visual Basic .NET 2003, you should be aware of three features in this book that are designed to help you evaluate and upgrade your existing projects quickly. Those features are

- The Upgrading Index, located before the comprehensive index, which lists in one place the major differences between Visual Basic 6 and Visual Basic .NET and provides page citations to information in the book about these differences.

- "Upgrade Notes" sidebars, near the beginning of each chapter, which provide a basic overview, or executive summary, of the features in Visual Basic .NET. Use these sidebars if you're interested in how Visual Basic .NET has changed in the context of an individual topic, such as variable declaration, Toolbox controls, or database programming.

- Appendix A, "Upgrading Visual Basic 6 Programs to Visual Basic .NET 2003," which is located immediately after Chapter 22. This appendix describes how to evaluate your existing Visual Basic 6 programs and how to upgrade them to Visual Basic .NET 2003 by using Internet resources and the Visual Basic Upgrade Wizard.

Corrections, Comments, and Help

Every effort has been made to ensure the accuracy of this book and the contents of the companion CD-ROM.

If you run into a problem, Microsoft Press provides corrections for its books through the World Wide Web at the following Web site:

http://www.microsoft.com/mspress/support/

If you have problems, comments, or ideas regarding this book or the companion CD-ROM, please send them to Microsoft Press.

Send e-mail to

mspinput@microsoft.com

Or send postal mail to

Microsoft Press
Attn: Microsoft Visual Basic .NET Step by Step—Version 2003 Editor
One Microsoft Way
Redmond, WA 98052-6399

Please note that support for the Visual Basic .NET software product itself is not offered through the preceding addresses.

Visual Basic .NET Software Support

For help using Visual Basic .NET in North America, you can call the Microsoft Professional Support for Developers line at 1-800-936-5800. This service is currently available 24 hours a day and is a charge-based service. (Your version of Visual Basic .NET or Visual Studio .NET might provide free phone support for a limited time.) You'll be connected to a live, trained Visual Studio .NET professional when you call the support number, not an endless series of phone recordings. Check your Visual Basic .NET product documentation for the details of your service agreement.

Visit the Microsoft Press World Wide Web Site

You're also invited to visit the Microsoft Press World Wide Web site at the following location:

http://www.microsoft.com/mspress/

You'll find descriptions for the complete line of Microsoft Press books (including others by Michael Halvorson), information about ordering titles, notice of special features and events, worldwide contact information, additional content for Microsoft Press books, and much more.

You can also find out the latest in Visual Basic software developments and news from Microsoft Corporation by visiting the following World Wide Web site:

http://www.microsoft.com/vbasic/

Get on line and check it out!

Getting Started with Microsoft Visual Basic .NET 2003

Opening and Running a Visual Basic .NET 2003 Program

In this chapter, you will learn how to:

- Start Microsoft Visual Studio .NET 2003.
- Use the Visual Studio development environment.
- Open and run a Microsoft Visual Basic program.
- Change a property setting.
- Move, resize, dock, and auto hide tool windows.
- Use online Help and exit Visual Studio.

Microsoft Visual Basic .NET 2003 is an important upgrade and enhancement of the popular Visual Basic development system and an iterative upgrade of the Visual Basic .NET 2002 software. This chapter introduces you to what's new in Visual Basic .NET and gives you the skills you will need to get up and running with the Visual Studio .NET 2003 development environment quickly and efficiently. You should read this chapter whether you are new to Visual Basic .NET programming or you have used previous versions of the Visual Basic compiler. The most important advantage of Visual Basic .NET is that it has been designed to make you even more productive in your daily development work—especially if you need to use information in databases or create solutions for the Internet—but an important additional benefit is that once you become comfortable with the development environment in Visual Studio, you can use the same tools to write programs for Microsoft Visual C++ .NET, Microsoft Visual C# .NET, Microsoft Visual J# .NET, and other third-party tools and compilers.

The first version of Visual Basic .NET (Visual Basic .NET 2002) was released in February 2002. The second release (Visual Basic .NET 2003) was generally available in March 2003. Visual Basic .NET 2003 contains several technical additions and performance enhancements, including the Visual J# .NET programming language, version 1.1 of the Microsoft .NET Framework, integration with Microsoft Windows Server 2003, and support for mobile computing through a compact version of the .NET Framework. Visual Basic .NET 2003 also offers a new and enhanced file format for projects and solutions, which means that older versions of Visual Basic and Visual Basic .NET won't be able to open Visual Basic .NET 2003 projects. However, Visual Basic .NET 2002 projects and solutions are automatically upgraded to Visual Basic .NET 2003 when they're opened the first time—there is, in other words, great compatibility between the products.

In this chapter, you'll learn how to start Visual Basic .NET 2003 and how to use the integrated development environment to open and run a simple program. You'll learn the essential Visual Studio menu commands and programming procedures; you'll open and run a simple Visual Basic program named MusicTrivia; you'll change a programming setting called a property; and you'll practice moving, sizing, docking, and auto hiding tool windows. You'll also learn how to get more information by using online Help and how to exit the development environment safely.

Upgrade Notes: What's New in Visual Basic .NET?

Upgrading from Visual Basic 6 to Visual Basic .NET involves a unique set of challenges, and the migration process continues to be an important topic even after the release of Visual Basic .NET 2003. For this reason, I begin each chapter in this book with a sidebar that highlights the general changes between Visual Basic 6 and Visual Basic .NET. Remember that you don't need *any* programming experience to learn Visual Basic .NET 2003 using this book. But if you have some Visual Basic 6 knowledge already or some Visual Basic 6 code that you need to upgrade, I want to give you a short executive summary of the differences. So to begin with, here is my list of Visual Basic .NET upgrade notes for this chapter:

- Visual Basic is now fully part of Visual Studio—it shares the Visual Studio development environment with Visual C++ .NET, Visual C# .NET, Visual J# .NET, and several other programming tools. Although Visual Basic .NET and Visual C++ .NET are still different programming languages, they share the same development environment.

- As part of its new development environment, Visual Studio offers a new Start Page pane, which shows recently used projects and lets you open new or existing source files. Additional links in the Start Page pane provide you with access to Visual Studio Web sites, profile information, and contacts in the Visual Studio development community.

- The Visual Studio development environment contains several new and modified programming tools. The Project window is now called Solution Explorer, and there is a context-sensitive help window called Dynamic Help. You'll find that the Toolbox has changed quite a bit— it's now subdivided into several functional categories, from Windows Forms to Web Forms to Data.

- Most of the programming tool windows have an auto hide feature to hide the tool as a tab when it isn't needed.

- Projects are now saved in a different way. You give your project a name *before* you create it. The project itself now is spread over several files and folders—even more than in Visual Basic 6. In Visual Basic 6, programs that were made up of multiple projects were called *project groups*; now they're called *solutions*.

The Visual Studio .NET Development Environment

Although the programming language you'll be learning in this book is Visual Basic, the development environment you'll be using to write programs is called the Microsoft Visual Studio .NET development environment. Visual Studio is a powerful and customizable programming workshop that contains all the tools you need to build robust programs for Windows quickly and efficiently. Most of the features in Visual Studio apply equally to Visual Basic .NET, Visual C++ .NET, Visual C# .NET, and Visual J# .NET. Use the following procedures to start Visual Studio now.

▶ **Important** If you haven't yet installed this book's practice files, work through "Finding Your Best Starting Point" and "About the CD-ROM and Practice Files" at the beginning of the book. Then return to this chapter.

Start Visual Studio .NET 2003

1   On the Windows taskbar, click the Start button, point to Programs, and then point to the Microsoft Visual Studio .NET 2003 folder. The icons in the Microsoft Visual Studio .NET 2003 folder appear in a list.

> ▶ **Note**   To perform the steps in this book, you must have one of the following Visual Studio .NET 2003 editions installed: Visual Basic .NET Standard, Visual Studio .NET Professional, Visual Studio .NET Enterprise Developer, or Visual Studio .NET Enterprise Architect. Also—don't try to use this book if you have an earlier version of the Visual Basic software; if that's your situation, you'll be better served by locating an earlier edition of my book, such as the first edition of *Microsoft Visual Basic .NET Step by Step* (which describes the Visual Basic .NET 2002 software) or *Microsoft Visual Basic Professional 6.0 Step by Step*, which describes the Visual Basic 6 software.

2   Click the Microsoft Visual Studio .NET 2003 program icon.

Visual Studio starts, and you see the development environment on the screen with its many menus, tools, and component windows. (These windows are sometimes called tool windows.) If this is a new installation of Visual Studio, you should see a Start Page with a set of links. (If you don't see the Start Page, click Show Start Page on the Help menu.)

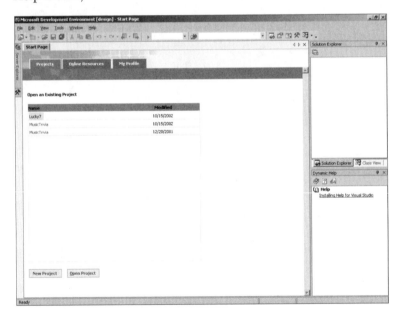

3 On the right side of the Start Page window, click the My Profile link.

Visual Studio displays the My Profile settings. The My Profile pane allows you to configure Visual Studio with your personal preferences. This is an important screen because Visual Studio can be used to build different types of programs (Visual Basic, Visual C++, and so on), so you want to identify yourself as a Visual Basic developer right away.

4 In the Profile drop-down list box, select Visual Basic Developer from the list of choices.

Visual Studio immediately configures the development environment for Visual Basic programming, displays the Toolbox, and makes adjustments to window characteristics and code formatting styles so that your programs will look like standard Visual Basic solutions.

5 In the At Startup drop-down list box, be sure that Show Start Page is selected.

Setting this option will ensure that the Start Page will appear each time you open Visual Studio.

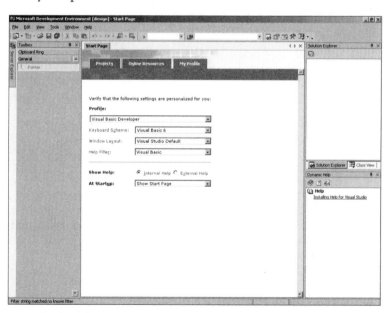

6 Investigate a few of the remaining settings—and notice that Visual Studio changed a few items on the list when you identified yourself as a Visual Basic programmer.

You can come back to My Profile at any time in the future to fine-tune your profile selections. They will mean more to you after you've written a few programs and have looked at some of the Visual Basic code your friends and coworkers have produced.

The first thing most developers do when they start Visual Studio is open an existing project—either a completed solution they want to work with again or an ongoing development project. Try opening an existing project now that I created for you—the MusicTrivia program.

Open a Visual Basic project

1   Click the Projects tab and then the Open Project button at the bottom of the Start Page.

The Open Project dialog box appears on the screen with several options. Even if you haven't used Visual Basic before, the Open Project dialog box will seem straightforward, like the familiar Open box in Microsoft Word or Microsoft Excel.

▶ **Tip**   In the Open Project dialog box, you'll see a number of shortcut icons along the left side of the window. The My Projects icon is particularly useful—it opens the Visual Studio Projects folder inside the My Documents folder on your system. By default, Visual Studio saves your projects in the Visual Studio Projects folder and gives each project its own folder. The folder VSMacros71 contains the macro files for Visual Studio .NET 2003 (which is also called Visual Studio version 7.1 in some parts of the software).

2   Browse to the folder c:\vbnet03sbs on your hard disk.

The folder c:\vbnet03sbs is the default location for this book's extensive sample file collection, and you'll find the files there if you followed the setup instructions in "About the CD-ROM and Practice Files" at the beginning of this book. If you didn't install the sample files, do so now using the CD-ROM included with this book.

3   Open the chap01\musictrivia folder, and then double-click the
MusicTrivia project file (MusicTrivia.vbproj).

Visual Studio loads the MusicTrivia form, properties, and program
code for the MusicTrivia project. The Start Page probably will still be
visible, but Solution Explorer in the upper right corner of the screen
will list some of the files in the project.

▶ **Tip**   If you don't see filename extensions in the Open Project dialog box,
the hide file extensions option might be turned on. You can change this
option in Windows Explorer. On the Tools menu in Windows Explorer, click
Folder Options. On the View tab of the Folder Options dialog box, you can
uncheck the Hide File Extensions For Known File Types check box.

Trouble?

If you see an error message indicating that the project you want to open
is in a newer file format, you might be trying to load Visual Basic .NET
2003 files into the older Visual Basic .NET 2002 software. (The Visual
Basic .NET 2002 software cannot open the Visual Basic .NET 2003
projects included on the companion CD-ROM.) To check which version of
Visual Studio .NET you're using, click the About command on the Help
menu.

Projects and Solutions

In Visual Studio, programs in development are typically called *projects* or *solutions* because they contain many individual components, not just one file. Visual
Basic .NET programs include a project file (.vbproj) and a solution file (.sln). A
project file contains information specific to a single programming task. A solution file contains information about one or more projects. Solution files are useful to manage multiple related projects and are similar to project group files
(.vbg) in Visual Basic 6. The samples included with this book typically have a
single project for each solution, so opening the project file (.vbproj) will have the
same effect as opening the solution file (.sln). But for a multi-project solution,
you will want to open the solution file. Visual Basic .NET 2003 offers a new file
format for its projects and solutions, but the same basic terminology still
applies.

The Visual Studio .NET Tools

At this point, you should take a few moments to study the development environment and identify some of the programming tools and windows that you'll be using as you complete this course. If you've written Visual Basic 6 programs before, you'll recognize many (but not all) of the development tools. (The Visual Basic .NET 2002 tools and the Visual Basic .NET 2003 tools are largely the same.) Collectively, these features are the components that you use to construct, organize, and test your Visual Basic programs. A few of the programming tools also help you learn more about the resources on your system, including the larger world of databases and Web site connections available to you. There are also several powerful online Help tools.

The *menu bar* provides access to most of the commands that control the development environment. Menus and commands work as they do in all Windows-based programs, and you can access them by using the keyboard or the mouse. Located below the menu bar is the *Standard toolbar*, a collection of buttons that serve as shortcuts for executing commands and controlling the Visual Studio development environment. If you've used Excel or Word, the toolbar should be a familiar concept. To activate a button on the toolbar, click the button using the mouse. Along the bottom of the screen is the Windows *taskbar*. You can use the taskbar to switch between various Visual Studio .NET components and to activate other Windows-based programs. You might also see taskbar icons for Microsoft Internet Explorer and other programs.

The following illustration shows some of the tools, windows, and other elements in the Visual Studio development environment. Don't worry that this illustration looks different from your current development environment view. You'll learn more about these elements as you step through the chapter.

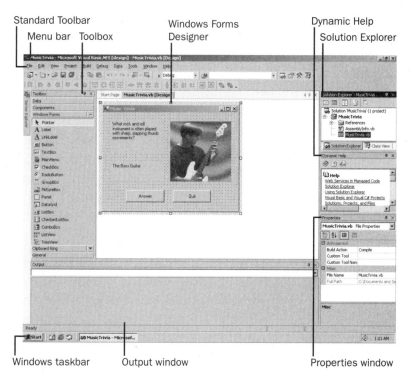

Standard Toolbar

Menu bar Toolbox

Windows Forms
Designer

Dynamic Help

Solution Explorer

Windows taskbar   Output window   Properties window

The main tools that you'll see in the Visual Studio development environment
are Solution Explorer (formerly called the Project Explorer), the Properties window, Dynamic Help, the Windows Forms Designer, the Toolbox, and the Output window. You might also see more specialized tools such as Server Explorer
and Class View, but these are often tabs along the margins of the development
environment or at the bottom of tool windows, or they aren't visible at all. If a
tool isn't visible and you want to see it, click the View menu and select the tool
you want to use. The View menu is now pretty full, so Microsoft moved some
of the lesser-used tools onto a submenu called (cleverly) Other Windows. Check
there if you don't see what you need.

The exact size and shape of the tools and windows depends on how your development environment has been configured. Visual Studio allows you to align and
attach, or *dock*, windows to make just the elements that you want visible. You
can also hide tools as tabs along the edge of the development environment to
move them out of the way until you need them again. Trying to sort out which
tools are important to you now and which you can learn about later is a difficult early challenge when you're first learning the busy Visual Studio interface.

Your development environment will probably look best if you set your monitor and Windows desktop settings so that they maximize your screen space, but even then things can get a little crowded. (For example, I'm using a desktop property setting of 1024 x 768 for some of the screen shots in this book—an attribute you can change by right-clicking the Windows desktop and clicking Properties.)

What Microsoft is doing with all this tool complexity is adding many new and useful features to the development environment, while providing clever mechanisms for dealing with the clutter. (These mechanisms include features such as docking, auto hiding, and a few other things that I describe later.) If you're just starting out with Visual Basic, the best way to resolve this feature tension is to hide the tools that you don't plan to use often and make room for the important ones. The crucial tools for Visual Basic programming—the ones you'll start using right away in this book—are Solution Explorer, Properties window, Windows Forms Designer, Toolbox, Dynamic Help, and the Output window. You won't use the Server Explorer, Class View window, Resource View window, Object Browser, or Debug windows until later in this book.

In the following exercises, you'll start experimenting with the crucial tools in the Visual Studio development environment. You'll also learn to hide the tools you won't use for a while.

The Windows Forms Designer

If you completed the last exercise, the MusicTrivia project will be loaded in the Visual Studio development environment. However, the user interface, or *form*, for the project might not yet be visible in Visual Studio. (More sophisticated projects might contain several forms, but this simple trivia program needs only one.) To make the form of the MusicTrivia project visible in the development environment, you display it by using Solution Explorer.

Display the Windows Forms Designer

1   Locate the Solution Explorer pane near the upper right corner of the Visual Studio development environment. If you don't see Solution Explorer (if it is hidden as a tab in a location that you cannot see or isn't currently visible), click Solution Explorer on the View menu to display it.

When the MusicTrivia project is loaded, Solution Explorer looks like this:

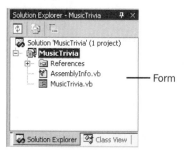

— Form

2   Click the MusicTrivia.vb form in the Solution Explorer window.

All form files, including this one, have a tiny form icon next to them so that you can easily identify them. When you click the form file, Visual Studio highlights it in Solution Explorer, and some information about the file appears in the Properties window (if you currently have it visible).

3   Click the View Designer button in Solution Explorer to display the program's user interface.

The MusicTrivia form is displayed in the Windows Forms Designer, as shown here:

Click this tab to display the Start Page

Click this tab to display the MusicTrivia form

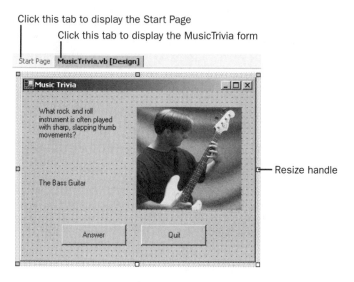

— Resize handle

Notice that a tab for the Start Page is still visible at the top of the Windows Forms Designer. You can click this tab to display the Start Page, change your profile settings, or open additional project files. To return to Windows Forms Designer view, click the tab labeled "MusicTrivia.vb [Design]" at the top of the MusicTrivia form.

Now try running a Visual Basic program with Visual Studio.

▶ **Tip**   If you don't see the Start Page and MusicTrivia.vb [Design] tabs, your development environment might be in MDI view instead of Tabbed Documents view. To change this option, click Options on the Tools menu. On the left side of the Options dialog box, click the Environment folder, and then click General. On the right, under Settings, click the Tabbed Documents radio button, and then click OK. The next time you start Visual Studio, the various windows that you open will have tabs, and you can switch between them with a simple button click.

Running a Visual Basic Program

MusicTrivia is a simple Visual Basic program designed to get you familiar with the programming tools in Visual Studio. The form you see now has been customized with five objects (two labels, a picture, and two buttons), and I've added three lines of program code to make the trivia program ask a simple question and display the appropriate answer. (The program "gives away" the answer now because it is currently in design mode, but the answer will be hidden when you run the program.) You'll learn more about creating objects and adding program code in the next chapter. For now, try running the program in the Visual Studio development environment.

Run the MusicTrivia program

1   Click the Start button on the Standard toolbar to run the Music-Trivia program in Visual Studio.

▶ **Tip**   You can also press F5 or click the Start command on the Debug menu to run a program in the Visual Studio development environment. Note that the placement of the Start command is different than it is in the Visual Basic 6 compiler.

Visual Studio loads and compiles the project into an *assembly* (a structured collection of modules, data, and manifest information for a program) and then runs the program in the development environment. An icon for the program also appears on the Windows taskbar.

During compilation, the Output window documents several of the loading and compiling steps and records any errors that occurred so that you can fix them. After a moment, you'll see the MusicTrivia form again, this time with the photograph and answer label hidden from view, as shown here:

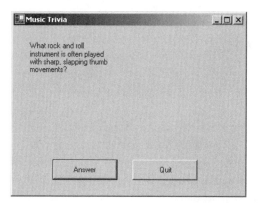

MusicTrivia now asks its important question: What rock and roll instrument is played with sharp, slapping thumb movements?

2   Click the Answer button to reveal the solution to the question.

When you do, the program displays the answer (The Bass Guitar) below the question and then displays a photograph of an obscure Seattle bass player demonstrating the technique. The test program works.

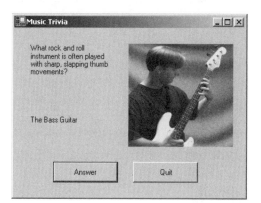

3   Click Quit to close the program.

The form closes, and the Visual Studio development environment becomes active again. Notice that the form looks a little different now in the development environment—a grid of alignment dots is visible on the surface of the form, the two labels are surrounded by some gray space, and resize handles surround the form. These features are visible only when a form is in design mode, and they'll help you design and align your user interface. The grid is also a quick giveaway if you're wondering whether a program is running in Visual Studio. (You'll practice using these features in the next chapter.)

The Properties Window

Use the Properties window to change the characteristics, or *property settings*, of the user interface elements on a form. A property setting is a quality of one of the objects in your user interface. For example, the trivia question the Music-Trivia program displays can be modified to appear in a different font or font size or with a different alignment. (With Visual Studio .NET, you can display text in any font installed on your system, just as you would in Excel or Word.) You can change property settings by using the Properties window while you're creating your user interface, or you can add program code via the Code Editor to change one or more property settings while your program is running.

The Properties window contains an Object drop-down list box that itemizes all the user interface elements (objects) on the form; the window also lists the property settings that can be changed for each object. (You can click one of two convenient buttons to view properties alphabetically or by category.) You'll practice changing the Font property of the first label in the MusicTrivia program now.

Change a property

1. Click the *Label1* object on the form. (*Label1* contains the text "What rock and roll instrument is played with short, slapping thumb movements?")

   To work with an object on a form, you must first select the object. When you select an object, resize handles surround it, and the property settings for the object are displayed in the Properties window.

2. Click the Properties Window button on the Standard toolbar.

   The Properties window is another tool that might or might not be visible in Visual Studio, depending on how it's been configured and used on your system. It usually appears below Solution Explorer on the right side of the development environment.

   You'll see a window similar to the following:

Font category

The Properties window lists all the property settings for the first label object (*Label1*) on the form. (In all, 46 properties are available to labels.) Property names are listed in the left column of the window, and the current setting for each property is listed in the right column. Because there are so many properties (including some that are rarely modified), Visual Studio organizes them into categories and displays them in outline view. If a category has a plus sign (+) next to it, you can click the collection title to display all the properties in that category. If a category has a minus sign (−) next to it, the properties are all visible, but you can hide the list under the category name by clicking the minus sign.

▶ **Tip**   The Properties window also has two handy buttons that you can use to further organize properties. The Alphabetic button lists all the properties in alphabetical order and puts them in just a few categories. (Click this button if you know the name of a property and want to locate it quickly.) The Categorized button breaks down the property list into many logical categories. (Click this button if you don't know much about the object you're customizing and would benefit from a more conceptual organization.) If you're new to Visual Studio and Visual Basic, I recommend that you use the Categorized configuration until you get familiar with the most common objects and properties.

3   Scroll in the Properties window list box until the *Font* property is visible.

The Properties window scrolls like a regular list box.

4   Click the *Font* property name (in the left column).

The current font (Microsoft Sans Serif) is partially displayed in the right column, and a button with three dots on it appears by the font name. This button is called an *ellipsis button* and means that a dialog box is available to customize the property setting.

5   Click the Font ellipsis button in the Properties window.

Visual Studio displays the Font dialog box, which allows you to specify new formatting characteristics for the text in the selected label on your form. The Font dialog box contains more than one formatting option; for each option you select, a different property setting will be modified.

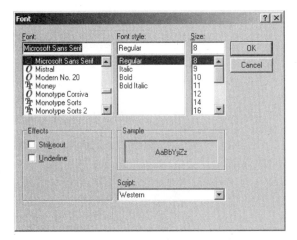

6   Change the size of the font from 8 point to 10 point, and then change the font style from Regular to Italic. Click OK to confirm your selections.

Visual Studio records your selections and adjusts the property settings accordingly. You can examine the changes that Visual Studio made by viewing your form in the Windows Forms Designer and by expanding the Font category in the Properties window.

Now change a property setting for the *Label2* object (the label that contains the text "The Bass Guitar").

7   In the Windows Forms Designer, click the second label object (*Label2*).

When you select the object, resize handles surround it.

8   Click the *Font* property again in the Properties window.

The *Label2* object has its own unique set of property settings—although the property names are the same as those of the *Label1* object, the values in the property settings are distinct and allow the *Label2* object to act independently on the playing field of the form.

9   Click the Font ellipsis button, set the font style to Bold, and then click OK.

10   Scroll to the *ForeColor* property in the Properties window, and then click it in the left column.

11   Click the ForeColor drop-down arrow in the right column, and then click a dark purple color on the Custom tab.

The text in the *Label2* object should now appear bold and in the color purple on the form.

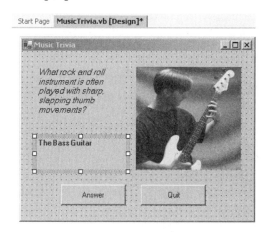

Congratulations! You've just learned how to set properties in a Visual Basic program using the Visual Studio Properties window—one of the important skills in becoming a Visual Basic programmer.

Thinking About Properties

In Visual Basic, each user interface element in a program (including the form itself) has a set of definable properties. You can set properties at design time by using the Properties window. Properties can also be referenced in code to do meaningful work while the program runs. (User interface elements that receive input often use properties to convey information to the program.) At first, you might find properties a difficult concept to grasp. Viewing them in terms of something from everyday life can help.

Consider this bicycle analogy: a bicycle is an object you use to ride from one place to another. Because a bicycle is a physical object, it has several inherent characteristics. It has a brand name, a color, gears, brakes, and wheels, and it's built in a particular style. (It might be a touring bike, a mountain bike, or a bicycle built for two.) In Visual Basic terminology, these characteristics are *properties* of the bicycle object. Most of the bicycle's properties would be defined while the bicycle was being built. But others (tires, travel speed, age, and options such as reflectors and mirrors) could be properties that change while the bicycle is used. As you work with Visual Basic, you'll find object properties of both types.

Moving and Resizing the Programming Tools

With numerous programming tools to contend with on the screen, the Visual Studio development environment can become a pretty busy place. To give you complete control over the shape and size of the elements in the development environment, Visual Studio lets you move, resize, dock, and auto hide most of the interface elements that you use to build programs.

To move one of the tool windows in Visual Studio, simply click the title bar and drag the object to a new location. If you align one window along the edge of another window, it will attach itself, or *dock*, to that window. Dockable windows are advantageous because they always remain visible. (They won't become hidden behind other windows.) If you want to see more of a docked window, simply drag one of its borders to view more content.

If you ever want to completely close a window, click the Close button in the upper right corner of the window. You can always open the window again later by clicking the appropriate command on the View menu.

If you want an option somewhere between docking and closing a window, you might try auto hiding a tool window to the side of the Visual Studio development environment by clicking the tiny Auto Hide pushpin button on the right side of the tool's title bar. This action removes the window from the docked position and places the title of the tool at the edge of the development environment in a tab that is quite unobtrusive. When you perform the auto hide action, you'll notice that the tool window will still be visible as long as you keep the mouse in the area of the window. When you move the mouse to another part of the development environment, the window will slide out of view.

To restore a window that has auto hide enabled, click the tool tab at the edge of the development environment or hold your mouse over the tab. (You can recognize a window that has auto hide enabled because the pushpin in its title bar is pointing sideways.) Holding the mouse over the title allows you to use the tools in what I call "peek-a-boo" mode—in other words, you can quickly display an auto hidden window by clicking its tab, check or set the information you need, and then move the mouse to make the window disappear. If you ever need the tool displayed permanently, click the Auto Hide pushpin button again so that the point of the pushpin faces down, and the window will remain visible.

Docking and auto hiding techniques definitely take some practice to master. Use the following exercises to hone your windows management skills and experiment with the features of the Visual Studio development environment along the way. After you complete the exercises here, feel free to configure the Visual Studio tools in a way that seems comfortable for you.

Moving and Resizing Tool Windows in Visual Studio

To move and resize one of the programming tool windows in Visual Studio, follow these steps. This exercise demonstrates how you manipulate the Properties window, but you can move around a different tool window if you want.

Move and resize the Properties window

1   Click the Properties Window button on the Standard toolbar if the Properties window isn't visible in the development environment.

    The Properties window is activated in the development environment, and its title bar is highlighted.

2   Double-click the Properties window title bar to display the window as a floating (nondocked) window.

You'll see a Properties window that looks like the following:

3   Using the Properties window title bar, drag the window to a new loca-
    tion in the development environment but don't allow it to be docked.

    Moving windows around the Visual Studio development environ-
    ment gives you some flexibility with the tools and your programming
    environment. Now resize the Properties window to see more of an
    object's property settings at once.

4   Move the mouse to the lower right corner of the Properties window
    until it becomes a resizing pointer.

    You resize windows in Visual Studio just as you resize other applica-
    tion windows in the Microsoft Windows operating system.

5   Drag the lower right border of the window down and to the right to
    enlarge the window.

    Your Properties window will now look bigger:

A bigger window lets you work more quickly and with more clarity of purpose. Feel free to move or resize a window when you need to see more of it.

Docking a Tool in Visual Studio

If a tool is floating over the development environment, you can return it to its original docked position by double-clicking the window's title bar. (Notice that this is the same technique that you used in the last exercise to expand a docked window—double-clicking a title bar works like a *toggle*, a state that switches back and forth between two standard positions.) You can also attach or dock a floating tool in a new place when it's in its floating, expanded position. You might want to do this if you need to make more room in Visual Studio for a particular programming task, such as creating a user interface with the Windows Forms Designer. Try docking the Properties window in a new location now.

Dock the Properties window

1   Verify that the Properties window (or another tool that you want to move) is floating over the Visual Studio development environment in an undocked position.

   If you completed the last exercise, the Properties window will be in an undocked position now.

2   Drag the title bar of the Properties window to the top, bottom, right, or left edge of the development environment (your choice!) until the border of the window snaps to the window edge you selected.

   This snapping behavior signifies that the window will be docked when you release the mouse button. Note that there are several valid docking locations for tool windows in Visual Studio, so you might want to try two or three different spots until you find one that looks right to you. (A window should be located in a place that's handy but not in the way of other needed tools.)

Docking the Properties window

3   Release the mouse button to dock the Properties window.

The window snaps into place in its new home.

> ▶ **Tip**   To prevent docking while you drag a window, hold down the Ctrl key while you drag. If you want the window you're dragging to be linked to another window by tabs, drag the window directly onto the title bar of the other window. When windows are linked together in this manner, a tab for each window will appear at the bottom of a shared window, and you can switch back and forth between windows by clicking the tabs. Tabbing windows provides an efficient way to use the space of one window for two or more purposes. (Solution Explorer and the Class View window are often tabbed together, for example.)

4   Try docking the Properties window several more times in different places to get the hang of how docking and tabbing works.

I guarantee that a few of these window procedures will seem confusing at first, but after a while they'll become routine for you. In general, you want to create window spaces that have enough room for the information you need to see and use while you work on your more important tasks in the Windows Forms Designer and Code Editor.

Hiding a Tool in Visual Studio

Visual Studio .NET includes a mechanism for hiding and displaying tools quickly, called *auto hide*. The auto hide feature is available for most tool windows. To hide a tool window, click the Auto Hide pushpin button on the right side of the title bar to conceal the window beneath a tool tab on the edge of the development environment, and click it again to restore the window to its docked position. You can also use the Auto Hide command on the Window menu to enable auto hide for a tool window. Note that the auto hide feature and pushpin button are available only for docked windows—you won't see the Auto Hide command or the pushpin for an active window floating on the top of the development environment.

Use the auto hide feature

1   Locate the Toolbox in the development environment (a window that's usually open on the left side of the Windows Forms Designer).

   The Toolbox contains many of the controls that you'll use to build Visual Basic applications. For example, I used the *Label*, *Button*, and *PictureBox* controls to create the objects you've seen in the Music-Trivia program. There are several different control collections in the Toolbox, and you can access them by clicking the tabs that you see within the Toolbox.

   If you don't see the Toolbox now, click Toolbox on the View menu. The following illustration shows you what it looks like.

Running a Program   1

2   Locate the Auto Hide pushpin button on the title bar of the Toolbox. The pushpin is currently in the "down," or "pushed in," position, meaning that the Toolbox is "pinned" open and auto hide is disabled.

3   Click the pushpin button in the Toolbox title bar, and keep the mouse pointer within the Toolbox.

The pushpin button changes direction (it now points to the left), indicating that the Toolbox is no longer pinned open and auto hide is enabled, and a tab appears on the left side of the development environment with the word Toolbox on it. You might also notice that the Windows Forms Designer shifted left. However, if your mouse pointer is still resting on the top of the Toolbox, nothing will have changed in the Toolbox itself—the designers of Visual Studio decided that it would be best if a window with auto hide enabled didn't disappear until you moved the mouse to another part of the Visual Studio development environment.

4   Move the mouse away from the Toolbox.

As soon as you move the mouse away, the Toolbox slides off the screen and is hidden beneath the small Toolbox tab. (You might also see a Server Explorer tab above the Toolbox tab—an indication that another tool has auto hide enabled. Indeed, depending on how Visual Studio is currently configured, you might now notice that there are other windows in the development environment with auto hide enabled.)

The benefit of enabling auto hide for windows is that they free up considerable work area in Visual Studio but are also quickly accessible.

5   Hold the mouse pointer over the Toolbox tab. (You can also click the Toolbox tab if you want.)

The Toolbox immediately slides back into view, and you can begin using Toolbox controls to build your user interface. (We'll do this in Chapter 2.)

6   Move the mouse away from the Toolbox, and the tool disappears again.

7   Finally, display the Toolbox again, and then click the pushpin button on the Toolbox title bar.

The Toolbox returns to its familiar docked position, and you can use it without worrying about it sliding away.

Spend some time moving, resizing, docking, and auto hiding tool windows in Visual Studio now, to create your version of the perfect work environment. As you work through this book, you'll want to adjust your window settings periodically to adapt your work area to the new tools you're using. When the need arises, come back to this section and practice your skills again.

Getting Help

Visual Studio .NET includes an online reference called "MSDN Library for Visual Studio .NET" that you can use to learn more about the Visual Studio development environment, the Visual Basic programming language, the resources in the .NET Framework, and the remaining tools in the Visual Studio .NET suite. Take a moment to explore your Help resources before moving to the next chapter, where you'll build your first program.

▶ **Tip** Visual Studio .NET online Help is provided by several MSDN Library CD-ROMs shipped with Visual Studio .NET. If you have plenty of disk space, you can install all the Visual Studio .NET documentation or a useful subset of Help materials (my recommendation), using the custom option during the MSDN Help Library setup.

You can access Help information in several ways.

To get Help information	Do this
About the task you're currently working on	Click the Dynamic Help tab in the development environment to see a list of Help topics related to the features you're using, or click Dynamic Help on the Visual Studio Help menu.
By topic or activity	On the Visual Studio Help menu, click Contents.
While working in the Code Editor	Click the keyword or program statement you're interested in, and then press F1.
While working in a dialog box	Click the Help button in the dialog box.
By searching for a specific keyword	On the Help menu, click Search and type the term you're looking for.
In a window separate from Visual Studio	On the Windows taskbar, click the Start button, point to Programs, point to Microsoft Visual Studio .NET 2003, and then click Microsoft Visual Studio .NET 2003 Documentation. Use the Contents, Index, and Search tabs to find information.
From Visual Studio Web sites and newsgroups	On the Visual Studio Start Page, click Online Resources, then Online Community, and then the Web site or newsgroup you're interested in.
About contacting Microsoft for product support	On the Help menu, click Technical Support.

In this section, you'll learn how to use the Dynamic Help feature in Visual Studio .NET. The goal of this tool is to anticipate the questions you'll ask based on the current context of your work in Visual Studio. I believe you'll find this searching mechanism vastly superior to the general search tools provided with Visual Basic 6 because Dynamic Help uses contextual logic to limit the material you see to the particular compiler or tool that you're using. (In other words, Dynamic Help doesn't bring up Visual C++, Visual C#, or Visual J# topics unless you're working with those tools.) A few of these search options can be set using the My Profile tab in the Visual Studio Start Page pane.

In this section, you'll also learn how to perform a full-text search of the Visual Studio Help system. Full-text search can be helpful when you want to search for specific keywords.

Because you just completed an exercise on auto hide with the Toolbox in Visual Studio, it is likely that the Dynamic Help system has been gathering information for you about the Toolbox and other recent commands you've issued in Visual Studio. Let's open Dynamic Help now and see.

Get help using Dynamic Help

1   Click the Dynamic Help tab in the development environment, or click Dynamic Help on the Visual Studio Help menu.

The Dynamic Help window appears, as shown here:

The Dynamic Help window is an integrated part of Visual Studio. The window can be moved, resized, docked, or auto hidden to suit your needs, and you can leave it open all the time or open it only when you need it.

2   Click a topic in the Dynamic Help window. It could be about the Toolbox or the Properties window.

The MusicTrivia form is hidden under the MusicTrivia.vb [Design] tab, and the Help topic appears in the main window of the development environment.

> ▶ **Tip**   If you didn't install the MSDN Library documentation on your system during setup, the Dynamic Help window won't display any topics. To install the documentation, insert the MSDN CD-ROM included with Visual Studio .NET 2003 and run MSDN setup.

3   Browse a few of the other Help topics in the Dynamic Help listing, and see how close these picks are to the actual activities you've been working on.

> ▶ **Tip**   You can adjust how Dynamic Help comes up with Help information by clicking the Options command on the Tools menu, opening the Environment folder, clicking the Dynamic Help topic, and identifying which topics you want Help to list and how many links there should be. These settings will help you further manage the amount of information Help offers you.

Do a full-text search in Help

1   On the Visual Studio Help menu, click Search.

The Search window appears in the development environment.

2   In the Look For drop-down list box, type **"windows forms designer" and controls** (include the quotes because the name contains spaces).

3   Check the Highlight Search Hits (In Topics) check box, and then click the Search button. (Expand the Help Search tool if the Highlight Search Hits check box isn't visible.)

The Search Results window appears with many topics that match your search criteria.

4   In the Search Results window, double-click a topic to see its contents.

The topic appears in the main window, and the text that you searched for is highlighted, as shown here:

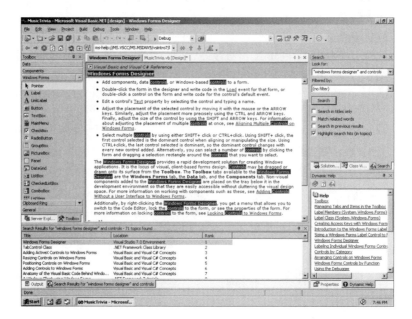

▶   **Tip**   The Help Contents and Index windows are also integrated into the Visual Studio development environment. You can open these help windows by clicking the Contents or Index command on the Help menu. Keep in mind that you don't have to use the Help features one at a time. (See the Help Information table earlier in this section for other Help suggestions.)

One Step Further: Exiting Visual Studio .NET

Each chapter in this book concludes with a section entitled "One Step Further" that enables you to practice an additional skill related to the topic at hand. After the "One Step Further" tutorial, I've compiled a Quick Reference table that reprises the important concepts discussed in each chapter.

When you're finished using Visual Studio for the day, save any projects that are open, and close the development environment. Give it a try.

Exit Visual Studio

1   Save any changes you've made to your program by clicking the Save All button on the Standard toolbar.

In contrast with Visual Basic 6, in Visual Studio .NET you give your program a name when you begin the project, not when you're ready to save it, so you won't need to provide any filename information now. As you'll learn, there are also many more folders for projects in Visual

Studio .NET than there were in Visual Basic 6. Each project fits in a folder of its own, and several subfolders are created below the main project folder to hold files as the program is built and compiled.

2 On the File menu, click the Exit command.

The Visual Studio .NET program exits. Time to move on to your first program in Chapter 2!

Lesson 1 Quick Reference

To	Do this
Start Visual Studio .NET	Click the Start button on the taskbar, point to Programs, point to the Microsoft Visual Studio .NET 2003 folder, and then click the Microsoft Visual Studio .NET 2003 program icon.
Open an existing project	Start Visual Studio .NET. Click the File menu, point to Open, and then click Project. *or* On the Start Page, click Open Project.
Run a program	Click the Start button on the Standard toolbar. *or* Press F5.
Set properties	Click the object on the form containing the properties you want to set, and then click the Properties Window button on the standard toolbar to display the Properties window (if it isn't open).
Display and resize a tool window	Double-click the window's title bar to display it as a floating window. Resize the window by dragging the edges of the window.
Move a tool window	Double-click the window's title bar to display it as a floating window, and then drag the title bar.
Dock a tool window	Double-click the title bar. *or* Drag the tool to the edge of another tool until it snaps into place.
Enable auto hide for a tool window	Click the Auto Hide pushpin button on the right side of the tool's title bar. The tool window hides behind a small tab at the edge of the development environment until you hold the mouse over it.
Disable auto hide for a tool window	Click the tool tab, and then click the Auto Hide pushpin button again.
Quit Visual Studio .NET	On the File menu, click Exit.

Writing Your First Program

In this chapter, you will learn how to:

■ Create the user interface for a new program.

■ Set the properties for each object in your user interface.

■ Write program code.

■ Save and run the program.

■ Build an executable file.

As you learned in Chapter 1, the Microsoft Visual Studio .NET development environment contains several powerful tools to help you run and manage your programs. Visual Studio also contains everything you need to build your own applications for Microsoft Windows from the ground up. In this chapter, you'll learn how to create a simple but attractive user interface with the controls in the Visual Studio Toolbox. Next you'll learn how to customize the operation of these controls with property settings. Then you'll see how to identify just what your program should do by writing program code. Finally, you'll learn how to save and run your new program (a Las Vegas–style slot machine) and how to compile it as an executable file.

Upgrade Notes: What's New in Visual Basic .NET?

If you're experienced with Microsoft Visual Basic 6, you'll notice some new features in Visual Basic .NET, including the following:

- The Visual Studio .NET development environment provides a few different menus and toolbars with which you can build your programs. For example, Visual Basic 6 included Format, Run, and Add-Ins menus, which aren't included in Visual Studio. Most of the commands have been relocated—you'll find many of the Run menu commands on the Debug menu.

- The *CommandButton* control is named the *Button* control in Visual Studio .NET, and many of its properties and methods have changed. For example, the *Caption* property is now named the *Text* property.

- Some of the properties and methods for the *Label* control are new or have changed. For example, the *Caption* property is now named the *Text* property, and the *TextAlign* property has more alignment options than the previous *Alignment* property.

- The *Image* control has been removed from Visual Studio .NET. To display pictures, use the *PictureBox* control.

- Visual Basic .NET code contains more compiler-generated statements than you saw in Visual Basic 6. In particular, Visual Basic .NET adds to the top of each form a block of code labeled "Windows Forms Designer generated code," which defines important form characteristics and shouldn't be modified. (Add your own program code below this code block.)

- Visual Studio .NET can create two types of executable files for your project, a *debug build* and a *release build*. Debug builds contain debugging information and are used when testing and debugging your program. Release builds are optimized and smaller and are used when you complete your program.

Lucky Seven: Your First Visual Basic .NET Program

The Windows-based application you're going to construct is Lucky Seven, a game program that simulates a lucky number slot machine. Lucky Seven has a simple user interface and can be created and compiled in just a few minutes using Visual Basic .NET. (If you'd like to run a completed version of Lucky before you start, you can find it in the c:\vbnet03sbs\chap02\lucky7 folder on your hard disk.) Here's what your program will look like when it's finished:

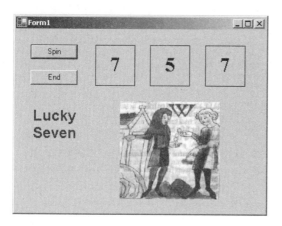

Programming Steps

The Lucky Seven user interface contains two buttons, three lucky number boxes, a digital photo depicting your winnings, and the label "Lucky Seven." I produced these elements by creating seven objects on the Lucky Seven form and then changing several properties for each object. After I designed the interface, I added program code for the Spin and End buttons to process the user's button clicks and produce the random numbers. To re-create Lucky Seven, you'll follow three essential programming steps in Visual Basic: create the user interface, set the properties, and write the program code. The following table summarizes the process for Lucky Seven.

Programming step	Number of items
1. Create the user interface.	7 objects
2. Set the properties.	12 properties
3. Write the program code.	2 objects

Creating the User Interface

In this exercise, you'll start building Lucky Seven by creating a new project and then using controls in the Toolbox to construct the user interface.

Create a new project

1   Start Visual Studio .NET 2003.

2   On the Visual Studio Start Page, click the New Project button.

▶ **Tip**   You can also start a new programming project by clicking the File menu, pointing to New, and then clicking Project.

The New Project dialog box appears.

Visual Studio can create operating system components and Web applications, in addition to the standard Windows application that you'll create in this chapter. The New Project dialog box lets you specify the type of program or component that you want to create, the language you'll use to create the program or component, and the name and location you'll use for the files.

3   In the list of Project Types, verify that the Visual Basic Projects folder is selected, and then, in the list of Templates, click the Windows Application icon.

Once these project settings are applied, Visual Studio will set up the development environment for Visual Basic .NET Windows application programming.

4   In the Name text box, type **MyLucky7**, and then specify the c:\vbnet03sbs\chap02 folder in the Location text box. (If you'd like, click the Browse button to specify the project location.)

Visual Studio assigns the name MyLucky7 to your program and prepares to create a new folder on your hard disk for the project named MyLucky7. The New Project dialog box should now look like this:

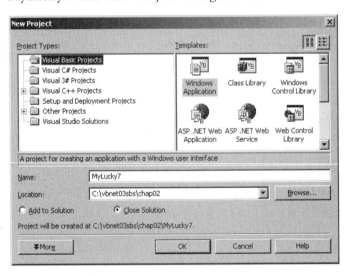

▶ **Tip** If your copy of Visual Basic .NET didn't come with some of the other tools in the Visual Studio .NET development suite (such as Microsoft Visual C++ .NET), you'll see a few differences when you work through the procedures in this book. For example, you might not have all the project types and templates shown in the previous illustration. I wrote this book with an installation of the Professional Edition of the Visual Studio .NET 2003 suite, which includes Visual C++ .NET, Microsoft Visual C# .NET, Microsoft Visual J# .NET, and other development tools. It isn't necessary that you have these extra tools—I won't be using Visual C++ .NET, Visual C# .NET, or Visual J# .NET in this book—but I wanted you to see an installation that would be typical in the workplace of a professional software developer.

5 Click OK to create the new project in Visual Studio.

Visual Studio cleans the slate for a new programming project and displays in the center of the screen a blank Windows form (typically called simply "form") you can use to build your user interface.

Now you'll enlarge the form, and then you'll create the two buttons in the interface.

Create the user interface

1 Position the mouse pointer over the lower right corner of the form until the mouse changes into a resizing pointer, and then drag to increase the size of the form to make room for the objects in your program.

As you resize the form, scroll bars might appear in the Windows Forms Designer to give you access to the entire form you're creating. Depending on your screen resolution and the Visual Studio tools you have open, there might not be enough room for you to see the entire form at once. Don't worry about this—your form can be small, or it can fill the entire screen, and the scroll bars will give you access to the entire form.

Size your form so that it is about the size of the form shown here:

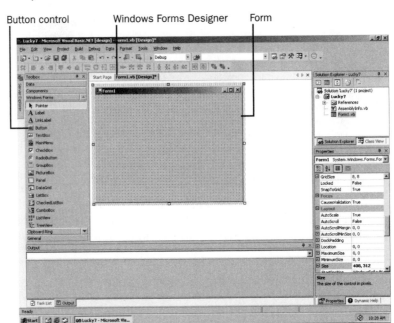

To see the entire form without obstruction, you can resize or close the other programming tools, as you learned in Chapter 1. (Return to Chapter 1 if you have questions about resizing windows or tools.)

Now you'll practice adding a button object on the form.

2   Click the *Button* control in the Toolbox.

3   Place the mouse pointer over the form.

The mouse pointer changes to crosshairs and a button icon. The crosshairs are designed to help you draw the rectangular shape of a button. When you hold down the left mouse button and drag, the button object takes shape and snaps to the grid formed by the intersection of dots on the form.

Try creating your first button now.

4   Move the mouse pointer close to the upper left corner of the form, hold down the left mouse button, and then drag down and to the right. Stop dragging, and release the mouse button when you've drawn a button similar to the one shown here:

Resize handle

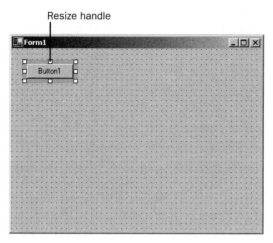

A button with resize handles appears on the form. The button is named *Button1*, the first button in the program. (You should make a mental note of this button name—you'll see it again when you write your program code.)

You can move buttons by dragging them with the mouse, and you can resize them by using the resize handles whenever Visual Basic is in *design mode* (whenever the Visual Studio programming environment is active). While a program is running, however, the user won't be able to move interface elements unless you've changed a special property in the program to allow this. You'll practice moving and resizing the button now.

Move and resize a button

1 Position the mouse pointer over the button so that it changes to a four-headed arrow, and then drag the button down and to the right.

   The button snaps to the grid when you release the mouse button. The form grid is designed to help you edit and align different user interface elements. You can change the size of the grid by clicking the Options command on the Tools menu, clicking the Windows Forms Designer folder, and then modifying the *GridSize* property.

2 Position the mouse pointer on the lower right corner of the button.

   When the mouse pointer rests on a resize handle of a selected object, it changes into a resizing pointer. You can use the resizing pointer to change the size of an object.

3   Enlarge the button by holding down the left mouse button and dragging the pointer down and to the right.

When you release the mouse button, the button changes size and snaps to the grid.

4   Use the resizing pointer to return the button to its original size, and then move the button back to its original location on the form.

Now you'll add a second button to the form, below the first button.

Add a second button

1   Click the *Button* control in the Toolbox.

2   Draw a button below the first button on the form. (For consistency, create a button of the same size.)

> ▶ **Tip**   To quickly add a control to your form, double-click the control in the Toolbox, and a default-size control will be added to your form.

3   Move or resize the button as necessary after you place it. If you make a mistake, feel free to delete the button and start over. (You can delete an object by selecting the object on the form and then pressing Delete.)

Now you'll add the labels used to display the numbers in the program. A *label* is a special user interface element designed to display text, numbers, or symbols when a program runs. When the user clicks the Lucky Seven program's Spin button, three random numbers appear in the label boxes. If one of the numbers is a 7, the user hits the jackpot.

Add the number labels

1   Click the *Label* control in the Toolbox.

2   Place the mouse pointer over the form.

The mouse pointer changes to crosshairs and a letter *A* icon.

3   Draw a small rectangular box like the one shown in the following illustration.

The label object you have created is named *Label1*, the first label in the program. Now you'll create two more labels, named *Label2* and *Label3*, on the form.

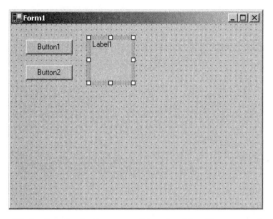

4   Click the *Label* control in the Toolbox, and then draw a label box to the right of the first label.

Make this label the same size as the first. The text "Label2" will appear in the label.

5   Click the *Label* control again, and add a third label to the form, to the right of the second label.

The text "Label3" appears in the label.

Now you'll use the *Label* control to add a descriptive label to your form. This will be the fourth and final label in the program.

6   Click the *Label* control in the Toolbox.

7   Draw a larger rectangle directly below the two buttons.

When you've finished, your four labels should look like those in the following illustration. (You can resize the label objects if they don't look quite right.)

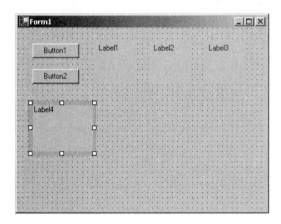

Now you'll add a *picture box* to the form to graphically display the payout you'll receive when you draw a 7 and hit the jackpot. A picture box is designed to display bitmaps, icons, digital photos, and other artwork in a program. One of the best uses for a picture box is to display a JPEG image file.

Add a picture

1   Click the *PictureBox* control in the Toolbox.

2   Using the *PictureBox* control, draw a large rectangular box directly beneath the three number labels.

When you've finished, your picture box object should look like this:

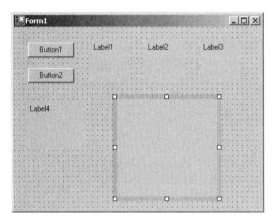

This object will be named *PictureBox1* in your program; you'll use this name later in the program code.

Now you're ready to customize your interface by setting a few properties.

Setting the Properties

As you discovered in Chapter 1, you can change properties by selecting objects on the form and changing their settings in the Properties window. You'll start by changing the property settings for the two buttons.

Set the button properties

1   Click the first button (*Button1*) on the form.

The button is selected and is surrounded by resize handles.

2   Double-click the Properties window title bar.

> ▶ **Tip**   If the Properties window isn't visible, click the Properties Window command on the View menu or press F4.

3   Resize the Properties window so that there is plenty of room to see the property names and their current settings.

Once you get used to setting properties, it's OK to use the Properties window without enlarging it, but making it bigger helps when you first try it out. The Properties window in the following illustration is a good size for setting properties:

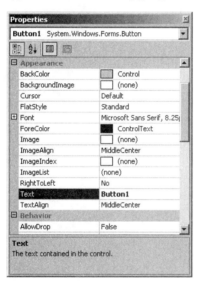

The Properties window lists the settings for the first button. These include settings for the background color, text, font height, and width of the button. Because there are so many properties, Visual Studio organizes them into categories and displays them in outline view. If you want to see the properties in a category, click the plus sign (+) next to the category title.

4   Scroll in the Properties window until you see the *Text* property, located in the Appearance category.

5   Double-click the *Text* property in the left column of the Properties window.

The current Text setting ("Button1") is highlighted in the Properties window.

6   Type **Spin,** and press Enter.

The *Text* property changes to "Spin" in the Properties window and on the button on the form. Now you'll change the *Text* property of the second button to "End". (You'll select the second button in a new way this time.)

7   Open the Object drop-down list box at the top of the Properties window.

A list of the interface objects in your program appears as follows:

The object drop-down list box lets you switch from one object to the next

8   Click Button2 System.Windows.Forms.Button (the second button) in the list box.

The property settings for the second button appear in the Properties window, and Visual Studio highlights Button2 on the form.

9   Double-click the current *Text* property ("Button2"), type **End,** and then press Enter.

The text of the second button changes to "End".

▶ **Tip** Using the Object drop-down list is a handy way to switch between objects in your program. You can also switch between objects on the form by clicking each object.

Now you'll set the properties for the labels in the program. The first three labels will hold the random numbers generated by the program and will have identical property settings. (You'll set most of them as a group.) The descriptive label settings will be slightly different.

Set the number label properties

1 Click the first number label (*Label1*), and then, holding down the Shift key, click the second and third number labels. (If the Properties window is in the way, move it to a new place.)

  A selection rectangle and resize handles appear around each label you click. When you've selected all three labels, release the Shift key. You'll change the *TextAlign*, *BorderStyle*, and *Font* properties now so that the numbers that appear in the labels will be centered, boxed, and identical in font and point size. (Each property is located in the Appearance category of the Properties window.)

  ▶ **Tip** When more than one object is selected, only those properties that can be changed as a group are displayed in the Properties window.

2 Click the *TextAlign* property in the Properties window, and then click the drop-down arrow that appears to the right.

  A graphical assortment of alignment options appears in the list box; these settings let you align text anywhere within the borders of the label object.

3 Click the center option (MiddleCenter).

  The *TextAlign* property for each of the selected labels changes to MiddleCenter.

  Now you'll change the *BorderStyle* property.

4 Click the *BorderStyle* property, and then click the drop-down arrow that appears to the right.

  A list of the valid property settings (None, FixedSingle, and Fixed3D) appears in the list box.

5 Click FixedSingle in the list box to add a thin border around each label.

  Now you'll change the font for the labels by changing settings for the *Font* property.

6   Click the *Font* property in the Properties window, and then click the ellipsis button (the button with three dots that's located next to the current font setting).

The Font dialog box appears, as shown here:

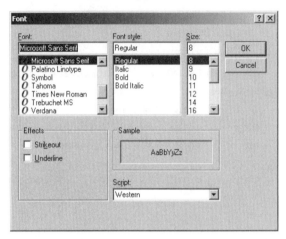

7   Change the font to Times New Roman, the font style to Bold, and the point size to 24, and then click OK.

The label text appears in the font, style, and size you specified.

Now you'll delete the text for the three labels so that the boxes will be empty when the program starts. (Your font selections will remain with the labels because they're stored as separate properties.) To complete this operation, you'll first need to select each of the labels individually.

8   Click a blank area on the form to remove the selection from the three labels, and then click the first label.

9   Double-click the *Text* property in the Properties window, press the Delete key, and then press Enter.

The text of the *Label1* object is deleted. You'll use program code to put a random "slot machine" number in this property later in this chapter.

10   Delete the text in the second and third labels on the form.

You've finished with the first three labels. Now you'll change the *Text*, *Font*, and *ForeColor* properties of the fourth label.

Set the descriptive label properties

1 Click the fourth label object (*Label4*) on the form.

2 Change the *Text* property in the Properties window to **Lucky Seven**.

3 Click the *Font* property, and then click the ellipsis button.

4 Use the Font dialog box to change the font to Arial, the font style to Bold, and the point size to 18. Click OK.

The font in the label box is updated. Notice that the text in the box wrapped to two lines. This is an important concept: the contents of an object must fit inside the object. If they don't, the contents will wrap or be truncated.

Now you'll change the foreground color of the text.

5 Click the *ForeColor* property in the Properties window, and then click the drop-down arrow in the second column.

Visual Studio displays a list box with Custom, Web, and System tabs for setting foreground colors (the color of your text) in the label object. The Custom tab contains many of the colors available in your system. The Web tab sets colors for Web pages and lets you pick colors using their common names. The System tab displays the current colors used for user interface elements in your system. (The list reflects the current settings on the Appearance tab of the Display Properties dialog box.)

6 Click the purple color on the Custom tab.

The text in the label box changes to purple.

Now you're ready to set the properties for the last object.

The Picture Box Properties

The picture box object will contain a picture of a person paying you money when you hit the jackpot (that is, when at least one 7 appears in the number labels on the form). This picture is a digitized image from an unpublished fourteenth-century German manuscript stored in JPEG format. You need to set the *SizeMode* property to accurately size the picture and set the *Image* property to specify the name of the JPEG file that you will load into the picture box. You also need to set the *Visible* property, which specifies the picture state at the beginning of the program.

Set the picture box properties

1   Click the picture box object on the form.

2   Click the *SizeMode* property in the Properties window (listed in the Behavior category), click the drop-down arrow, and then click StretchImage.

Setting *SizeMode* to StretchImage before you open a graphic causes Visual Studio to resize the graphic to the exact dimensions of the picture box. (Typically, you set this property before you set the *Image* property.)

3   Double-click the *Image* property in the Properties window, and then click the ellipsis button in the second column.

The Open dialog box appears.

4   In the dialog box, navigate to the c:\vbnet03sbs\chap02 folder.

The digital photo PayCoins.jpg appears in the list.

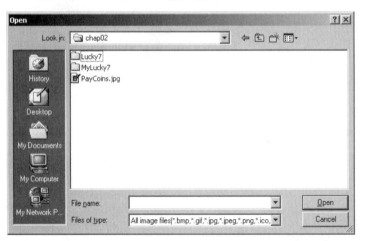

5   Select the file PayCoins.jpg in the dialog box, and then click Open.

The PayCoins photo is loaded into the picture box on the form. Because the photo is relatively small (24 KB), it opens quickly on the form.

Now you'll change the *Visible* property to False so that the image will be invisible when the program starts. (You'll use program code to make it visible later.)

6 Click the *Visible* property in the Behavior category of the Properties window. Click the Visible drop-down arrow.

The valid settings for the *Visible* property appear in a list box.

7 Click False to make the picture invisible when the program starts.

The *Visible* property is set to False. This affects the picture box when the program runs, but not now while you're designing it. Your completed form should look similar to this:

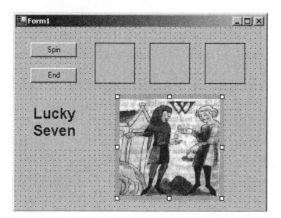

8 Double-click the title bar of the Properties window to return it to the docked position.

Writing the Code

Now you're ready to write the code for the Lucky Seven program. Because most of the objects you've created already "know" how to work when the program runs, they're ready to receive input from the user and process it automatically. The inherent functionality of objects is one of the great strengths of Visual Basic—once objects are placed on a form and their properties are set, they're ready to run without any additional programming. However, the "meat" of the Lucky Seven game—the code that actually calculates random numbers, displays them in boxes, and detects a jackpot—is still missing from the program. This computing logic can be built into the application only by using program statements—code that clearly spells out what the program should do each step of the way. Because the Spin and End buttons drive the program, you'll associate the code for the game with those buttons. You enter and edit Visual Basic program statements in the Code Editor.

Reading Properties in Tables

In this chapter, you've set the properties for the Lucky Seven program step by step. In future chapters, the instructions to set properties will be presented in table format unless a setting is especially tricky. Here are the properties you've set so far in the Lucky Seven program in table format, as they'd look later in the book. Settings you need to type in are shown in quotation marks. You shouldn't type the quotation marks.

Object	Property	Setting
Button1	Text	"Spin"
Button2	Text	"End"
Label1, Label2, Label3	BorderStyle	Fixed Single
	Font	Times New Roman, Bold, 24-point
	Text	(empty)
	TextAlign	MiddleCenter
Label4	Text	"Lucky Seven"
	Font	Arial, Bold, 18-point
	ForeColor	Purple
PictureBox1	Image	"c:\vbnet03sbs\chap02\paycoins.jpg"
	SizeMode	StretchImage
	Visible	False

In the following steps, you'll enter the program code for Lucky Seven in the Code Editor.

Use the Code Editor

1   Double-click the End button on the form.

After a few moments, the Code Editor appears in the center of the Visual Studio development environment, as shown on the following page.

Inside the Code Editor are program statements associated with the current form. Program statements that are used together to perform some action are typically grouped in a programming construct called a *procedure*. A common type of procedure is a Sub procedure, sometimes called a *subroutine*. Sub procedures include a *Sub* keyword in the first line and end with *End Sub*. Procedures typically get executed when certain events occur, such as when a button is clicked. When a procedure is associated with a particular object and an event, it is called an *event handler* or an *event procedure*.

Code Editor

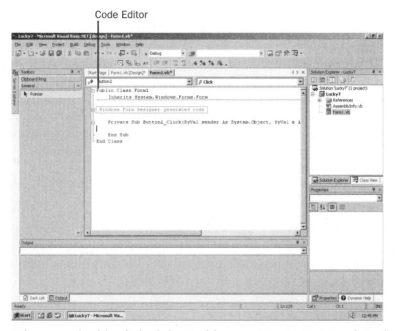

When you double-clicked the End button (*Button2*), Visual Studio automatically added the first and last lines of the End button event procedure, as the following code shows. (The first line was wrapped to stay within the book margins.) You'll notice other lines of code in the Code Editor, which Visual Studio has added to define important characteristics of the form. (You can recognize these statements by the words "Windows Form Designer generated code".) Ignore these statements for now, and don't modify them. You'll learn about this boilerplate code in later chapters.

```
Private Sub Button2_Click(ByVal sender As System.Object, _
    ByVal e As System.EventArgs) Handles Button2.Click


End Sub
```

The body of a procedure fits between these lines and is executed whenever a user activates the interface element associated with the procedure. In this case, the event is a mouse click, but as you'll see later in the book, it could also be a different type of event.

2   Type **End**, and then press the Down arrow key.

After you type the statement, the letters turn blue, indicating that Visual Basic recognizes it as a valid statement, or *keyword*, in the program.

Your First Program

2

You use the program statement *End* to stop your program and remove it from the screen. The Visual Basic programming language contains several hundred unique keywords such as this, complete with their associated operators and symbols. The spelling of and spacing between these items are critical to writing program code that will be accurately recognized by the Visual Basic compiler. As you enter these keywords and perform other edits, the Code Editor will handle many of the formatting details for you, including indents, spacing, and adding parentheses that you need.

▶ **Tip**   Another name for the exact spelling, order, and spacing of keywords in a program is *statement syntax*.

When you pressed the Down arrow key, the *End* statement was indented to set it apart from the *Private Sub* and *End Sub* statements. This indenting scheme is one of the programming conventions you'll see throughout this book to keep your programs clear and readable. The group of conventions regarding how program code is organized in a program is often referred to as *program style*.

Now that you've written the code associated with the End button, you'll write code for the Spin button. These programming statements will be a little more extensive and will give you a chance to learn more about program syntax and style. You'll study each of the program statements later in this book, so you don't need to know everything about them now. Just focus on the general structure of the program code and on typing the program statements exactly as they are printed. (Visual Basic is fussy about spelling and the order in which keywords and operators appear.)

Write code for the Spin button

1 Click the View Designer button in the Solution Explorer window to display your form again.

When the Code Editor is visible, you won't be able to see the form you're working on. The View Designer button is one mechanism you can use to display it again. (If more than one form is loaded in Solution Explorer, click the form you want to display first.)

▶ **Note**   To display the form again, you can also click the tab labeled "Form1.vb [Design]" at the top edge of the Code Editor. If you don't see tabs at the top of the Code Editor, enable Tabbed Documents view in the Options dialog box, as discussed in a Tip in Chapter 1.

2 Double-click the Spin button.

After a few moments, the Code Editor appears, and an event procedure associated with the *Button1* button appears near the *Button2* event procedure.

Although you changed the text of this button to "Spin", its name in the program is still *Button1*. (The name and the text of an interface element can be different to suit the needs of the programmer.) Each object can have several procedures associated with it, one for each event it recognizes. The click event is the one we're interested in now because users will click the Spin and End buttons when they operate the program.

3 Type the following program lines between the *Private Sub* and *End Sub* statements, pressing Enter after each line, indenting with Tab, and taking care to type the program statements exactly as they appear here. (The Code Editor will scroll to the left as you enter the longer lines.) If you make a mistake (usually identified by jagged underline), delete the incorrect statements and try again.

▶ **Tip** As you enter the program code, Visual Basic formats the text and displays different parts of the program in color to help you identify the various elements. When you begin to type a property, Visual Basic also displays the available properties for the object you're using in a list box, so you can double-click the property or keep typing to enter it yourself. If Visual Basic displays an error message, you might have misspelled a program statement. Check the line against the text in this book, make the necessary correction, and continue typing. (You can also delete a line and type it from scratch.) In addition, Visual Basic might also add code automatically when it's necessary. For example, when you type the following code, Visual Basic will automatically add the *End If* line. Readers of previous editions of this book have found this first typing exercise to be the toughest part of this chapter—"But Mr. Halvorson, I know I typed it just as written!"—so please give this program code your closest attention. I promise you, it works!

```
PictureBox1.Visible = False    ' hide picture
Label1.Text = CStr(Int(Rnd() * 10))    ' pick numbers
Label2.Text = CStr(Int(Rnd() * 10))
Label3.Text = CStr(Int(Rnd() * 10))
' if any caption is 7 display picture and beep
If (Label1.Text = "7") Or (Label2.Text = "7") _
Or (Label3.Text = "7") Then
    PictureBox1.Visible = True
    Beep()
End If
```

When you've finished, the Code Editor should look like this:

```
Start Page | Form1.vb [Design]* | Form1.vb*                          ◁ ▷ ×
✦ Button1                          ▼   ƒ Click                        ▼
⊟ Public Class Form1
       Inherits System.Windows.Forms.Form

⊞ | Windows Form Designer generated code |

⊟     Private Sub Button2_Click(ByVal sender As System.Object, ByVal e A
           End
       End Sub

⊟     Private Sub Button1_Click(ByVal sender As System.Object, ByVal e A
           PictureBox1.Visible = False      ' hide picture
           Label1.Text = CStr(Int(Rnd() * 10))      ' pick numbers
           Label2.Text = CStr(Int(Rnd() * 10))
           Label3.Text = CStr(Int(Rnd() * 10))
           ' if any caption is 7 display picture and beep
           If (Label1.Text = "7") Or (Label2.Text = "7") _
           Or (Label3.Text = "7") Then
               PictureBox1.Visible = True
               Beep()|
           End If
       End Sub
⌐End Class
◄                                                                    ►
```

4   Click the Save All command on the File menu to save your additions
to the program.

The Save All command saves everything in your project—the project
file, the form file, any code modules, and other related components
in your application. Note that if you want to save just the item you
are currently working on (the form, the code module, or something
else), you can use the Save command on the File menu. If you want
to save the current item with a different name, you can use the Save
As command.

A Look at the *Button1_Click* Procedure

The *Button1_Click* procedure is executed when the user clicks the Spin button
on the form. The procedure uses some pretty complicated statements, and,
because I haven't formally introduced them yet, it might look a little confusing.
However, if you take a closer look, you'll probably see a few things that look
familiar. Taking a peek at the contents of the procedures will give you a feel for
the type of program code you'll be creating later in this book. (If you'd rather
not have a look, feel free to skip to the next section, "Running Visual Basic
.NET Applications.")

The *Button1_Click* procedure performs three tasks: it hides the digital photo,
creates three random numbers for the number labels, and displays the photo
when the number 7 appears. Let's look at each of these steps individually.

Hiding the photo is accomplished with the following line:

```
PictureBox1.Visible = False      ' hide picture
```

This line is made up of two parts: a program statement and a comment. The program statement (`PictureBox1.Visible = False`) sets the *Visible* property of the picture box object (*PictureBox1*) to False (one of two possible settings). You might remember that you set this property to False once before by using the Properties window. You're doing it again now in the program code because the first task is a spin and you need to clear away a photo that might have been displayed in a previous game. Because the property will be changed at runtime and not at design time, you must set the property by using program code. This is a handy feature of Visual Basic, and I'll talk about it more in Chapter 3.

The second part of the first line (the part displayed in green type on your screen) is called a *comment*. Comments are explanatory notes included in program code following a single quotation mark ('). Programmers use comments to describe how important statements work in a program. These notes aren't processed by Visual Basic when the program runs; they exist only to document what the program does. You'll want to use comments often when you write Visual Basic programs to leave an easy-to-understand record of what you're doing.

The next three lines handle the random number computations. Does this concept sound strange? You can actually make Visual Basic generate unpredictable numbers within specific guidelines—in other words, you can create random numbers for lottery contests, dice games, or other statistical patterns. The *Rnd* function in each line creates a random number between 0 and 1 (a number with a decimal point and several decimal places), and the *Int* function returns the integer portion of the product of the random number and 10. This computation creates random numbers between 0 and 9 in the program—just what we need for this particular slot machine application.

```
Label1.Text = CStr(Int(Rnd() * 10))     ' pick numbers
```

We then need to jump through a little hoop in our code—we need to copy these random numbers into the three label boxes on the form, but before we do so the numbers need to be converted to text with the *CStr* (convert to string) function. Notice how *CStr*, *Int*, and *Rnd* are all connected together in the program statement—they work collectively to produce a result like a mathematical formula. After the computation and conversion, the values are then assigned to the *Text* properties of the first three labels on the form, and the assignment causes the numbers to be displayed in boldface, 24-point, Times New Roman type in the three number labels. The following illustration shows how Visual Basic evaluates one line of code step by step to generate the random number 7 and copy it to a label object. Visual Basic evaluates the expression just like a mathematician solving a mathematical formula.

Example:
```
Label1.Text = CStr(Int(Rnd() * 10))
```

Code	Result
"7"	
Rnd()	0.7055475
Rnd() * 10	7.055475
Int(Rnd() * 10)	7
CStr(Int(Rnd() * 10))	"7"
Label1.Text = CStr(Int(Rnd() * 10))	7

The last group of statements in the program checks whether any of the random numbers is 7. If one or more of them is, the program displays the medieval manuscript depiction of a payout, and a beep announces the winnings.

```
' if any caption is 7 display picture and beep
If (Label1.Text = "7") Or (Label2.Text = "7") _
Or (Label3.Text = "7") Then
    PictureBox1.Visible = True
    Beep()
End If
```

Each time the user clicks the Spin button, the *Button1_Click* procedure is called, and the program statements in the procedure are executed again. The complete Lucky7 program is located in the c:\vbnet03sbs\chap02\lucky7 folder.

Running Visual Basic .NET Applications

Congratulations! You're ready to run your first real program. To run a Visual Basic .NET program from the programming environment, you can click Start on the Debug menu, click the Start button on the Standard toolbar, or press F5. Try running your Lucky Seven program now. If Visual Basic displays an error message, you might still have a typing mistake or two in your program code. Try to fix it by comparing the printed version in this book with the one you typed, or load Lucky7 from your hard disk and run it.

Run the Lucky Seven program

1 Click the Start button on the Standard toolbar.

The Lucky Seven program compiles and runs in the programming environment. After a few seconds, the user interface appears, just as you designed it.

2 Click the Spin button.

The program picks three random numbers and displays them in the labels on the form, as follows:

Because a 7 appears in the first label box, the digital photo appears depicting your payoff, and the computer beeps. You win! (The sound you hear depends on your Sounds And Multimedia setting [or the Sounds And Devices setting] in Windows Control Panel—to make this game sound really cool, change the Default Beep sound to something more dynamic.)

3 Click the Spin button 15 or 16 more times, watching the results of the spins in the number boxes.

About half the time you spin, you hit the jackpot—pretty easy odds. (The actual odds are about 2.8 times out of 10; you're just lucky at first.) Later on you might want to make the game tougher by displaying the photo only when two or three 7s appear, or by creating a running total of winnings.

4   When you've finished experimenting with your new creation, click the End button.

The program stops, and the programming environment reappears on your screen.

> ▶ **Tip**   If you run this program again, you might notice that Lucky Seven displays exactly the same sequence of random numbers. There is nothing wrong here—the Visual Basic *Rnd* function was designed to display a repeating sequence of numbers at first so that you can properly test your code using output that can be reproduced again and again. To create truly "random" numbers, use the *Randomize* function in your code, as shown in the exercise at the end of this chapter.

Building an Executable File

Your First Program

Your last task in this chapter is to complete the development process and create an application for Windows, or an *executable file*. Windows applications created with Visual Basic have the filename extension .exe and can be run on any system that contains Microsoft Windows and the necessary support files. (Visual Basic installs these support files—including the dynamic link libraries and the .NET Framework files—automatically.) If you plan to distribute your applications, see Chapter 14. In that chapter, you'll learn more about optimizing your Visual Basic .NET applications and how to use *assemblies* to distribute solutions.

At this point, you need to know that Visual Studio has the ability to create two types of executable files for your project, a debug build and a release build. Debug builds are the default type in Visual Studio, and you'll use them often as you test and debug your program. Debug builds contain debugging information that makes them run slower, but the Visual Basic compiler is able to produce the builds quite quickly. When your project is complete, however, you want to compile your application using a release build, which includes numerous optimizations and doesn't contain unneeded debugging information.

> ▶ **Tip**   Although there are many similarities, Visual Basic .NET approaches compiling and distributing your applications in a different way than Visual Basic 6. For example, the Make Project.exe command on the Visual Basic 6 File menu has been replaced with the Build Solution command on the Build menu, and assemblies and manifests are now a feature of compilation and deployment. For additional details about this conceptual change, see Chapter 14.

Try creating a release build named MyLucky7.exe now.

Create an executable file

1   On the Build menu, click the Configuration Manager command.

The Configuration Manager dialog box appears. This dialog box lets you switch between debug builds and release builds, and it contains additional program settings such as the operating platform for which you are creating the application.

2   Click Release in the Active Solution Configuration list box, and then click Close.

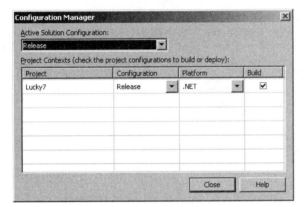

Your project will now be compiled and optimized as a release build.

▶   **Tip**   You can also specify the debug or release build type using the Solution Configurations drop-down list box on the Standard toolbar.

3   On the Build menu, click the Build Solution command.

The Build Solution command creates a bin folder in which your project is located (if the folder doesn't already exist) and compiles the source code in your project. The result is an executable file named MyLucky7.exe. To save you time, Visual Studio often creates these files while you develop your application; however, it's always a good idea to recompile your application manually with the Build Solution command when you reach an important milestone. In particular, you'll need to recompile if you switch from debug build to release build.

Try running this program now by using the Run command on the Start menu.

4   On the Windows taskbar, click the Start button, and then click Run. The Run dialog box appears.

5   Click the Browse button, and then navigate to the c:\vbnet03sbs\chap02\mylucky7\bin folder.

6   Click the MyLucky7.exe application icon, click Open, and then click OK.

7   The Lucky Seven program loads and runs in Windows—you've run the program outside the Visual Studio development environment.

8   Click Spin a few times to verify the operation of the game, and then click End.

> ▶ **Tip**   You can also run Windows applications, including compiled Visual Basic programs, by opening Windows Explorer and double-clicking the executable file. To create a shortcut icon for MyLucky7.exe on the Windows desktop, right click the Windows desktop, point to New, and then click Shortcut. When you're prompted for the location of your application file, click Browse, and select the MyLucky7.exe executable file. Click the OK, Next, and Finish buttons, and Windows will place an icon on the desktop that you can double-click to run your program.

9   On the File menu, click Exit to close Visual Studio and the MyLucky7 project.

The Visual Studio development environment closes. If you decide later that you want to make extensive changes to this program (more than the following changes), use the Configuration Manager command on the Build menu to change the build type from release build to debug build.

One Step Further: Adding to a Program

You can restart Visual Studio at any time and work on a programming project you've stored on disk. You'll restart Visual Studio now and add a special statement named *Randomize* to the Lucky Seven program.

Reload Lucky Seven

1   On the Windows taskbar, click the Start button, point to Programs, point to Microsoft Visual Studio .NET 2003, and then click the Microsoft Visual Studio .NET 2003 program icon.

A list of the most recent projects that you've worked on appears on the Visual Studio Start Page. Because you just finished working with Lucky Seven, MyLucky7 should be the first project on the list.

2 Click the MyLucky7 link to open the Lucky Seven project.

The Lucky Seven program opens, and the MyLucky7 form appears. (If you don't see the form, click Form1.vb in Solution Explorer, and then click the View Designer button.)

Now you'll add the *Randomize* statement to the *Form_Load* procedure, a special procedure that is associated with the form and that is executed each time the program is started.

3 Double-click the form (not one of the objects) to display the *Form_Load* procedure.

The *Form_Load* procedure appears in the Code Editor, as shown here:

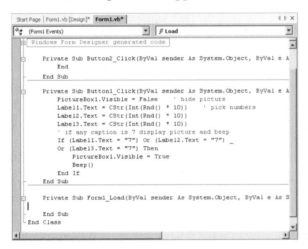

4 Type **Randomize**, and then press the Down arrow key.

The *Randomize* statement is added to the program and will be executed each time the program starts. *Randomize* uses the system clock to create a truly random starting point, or *seed*, for the *Rnd* statement used in the *Button1_Click* procedure. As I mentioned earlier, without the *Randomize* statement the Lucky Seven program produces the same string of random spins every time you restart the program. With *Randomize* in place, the program will spin randomly every time it runs. The numbers won't follow a recognizable pattern.

5 Run the new version of Lucky Seven, and then save the project. If you plan to use the new version a lot, you might want to create a new .exe file, too.

6 When you're finished, click Close Solution on the File menu.

The files associated with the Lucky Seven program are closed.

Lesson 2 Quick Reference

To	Do this
Create a user interface	Use Toolbox controls to place objects on your form, and then set the necessary properties. Resize the form and the objects as appropriate.
Move an object	Position the mouse over the object until you get the four-headed arrow, and then drag the object.
Resize an object	Click the object to select it, and then drag the resize handle attached to the part of the object you want to resize.
Delete an object	Click the object, and then press the Delete key.
Open the Code Editor	Double-click an object on the form (or the form itself). *or* Select a form or a module in the Solution Explorer, and then click the View Code button.
Write program code	Type Visual Basic program statements associated with the object you want to program in the Code Editor.
Save a program	On the File menu, click the Save All command. *or* Click the Save All button on the Standard toolbar.
Save a form file	Make sure the form is open, and then, on the File menu, click the Save command. *or* Click the Save button on the Standard toolbar.
Change the build type from debug build to release build	On the Build menu, click the Configuration Manager command. Click the build type you want (Debug or Release) in the Active Solution Configuration drop-down list box. *or* Select the build type from the Solution Configurations drop-down list box on the Standard toolbar.
Create an .exe file	On the Build menu, click the Build Solution command.
Reload a project	On the File menu, point to Open, and then click the Projects command. *or* On the File menu, point to Recent Projects, and then click the desired project. *or* Click the project in the recent projects list on the Visual Studio Start Page.

Working with Toolbox Controls

In this chapter, you will learn how to:

- Use *TextBox* and *Button* controls to create a "Hello World" program.

- Use the *DateTimePicker* control to display your birth date.

- Use *CheckBox*, *RadioButton*, *ListBox*, and *ComboBox* controls to process user input.

- Use a *LinkLabel* control to display a Web page on the Internet.

- Install ActiveX controls.

As you learned in Chapter 1 and Chapter 2, Microsoft Visual Studio .NET controls are the graphical tools you use to build the user interface of a Microsoft Visual Basic program. Controls are located in the Toolbox in the development environment, and you use them to create objects on a form with a simple series of mouse clicks and dragging motions. Windows Forms controls are specifically designed for building Microsoft Windows applications, and you'll find them organized on the Windows Forms tab of the Toolbox. (You used a few of these controls in the previous chapter.) You'll learn about other controls, including the tools you use to build Web Forms and database applications, later in the book.

In this chapter, you'll learn how to display information in a text box, work with date and time information on your system, process user input, and display a Web page within a Visual Basic .NET program. The exercises in this chapter will help you design your own Visual Basic applications and will teach you more about objects, properties, and program code. You'll also learn how to add older Microsoft ActiveX controls to the Toolbox so that you can extend the functionality of Visual Basic.

Upgrade Notes: What's New in Visual Basic .NET?

If you're experienced with Visual Basic 6, you'll notice some new features in Visual Basic .NET, including the following:

- A new control named *DateTimePicker* helps you prompt the user for date and time information. The new *LinkLabel* control is designed to display and manage Web links on a form.

- The *OptionButton* control has been replaced with a new *RadioButton* control.

- The *Frame* control has been replaced with a new *GroupBox* control.

- The *ListIndex* property in the *ListBox* control has been replaced with a property called *SelectedIndex*. The same change was made to the *ComboBox* control.

- There is no longer an *Image* control. You use the *PictureBox* control instead.

- Images are added to picture box objects by using the *System.Drawing.Image.FromFile* method (not the *LoadPicture* function).

- Web browsers and other applications are now started by using the *System.Diagnostics.Process.Start* method.

- ActiveX controls are added to the Toolbox in a new way and are "wrapped" by Visual Studio so that they can be used in Visual Basic .NET applications.

The Basic Use of Controls: The "Hello World" Program

A great tradition in introductory programming books is the "Hello World" program. Hello World is the name given to a short program that demonstrates how the simplest utility can be built and run in a given programming language. In the days of character-based programming, Hello World was usually a two-line or three-line program typed in a program editor and assembled with a stand-alone compiler. With the advent of graphical programming tools, however, the typical Hello World has grown into a complex program containing dozens of lines and requiring several programming tools for its construction. Fortunately, creating a Hello World program is still quite simple with Visual Basic .NET. You can construct a complete user interface by creating two objects, setting two properties, and entering one line of code. Give it a try.

Create a Hello World program

1 Start Visual Studio if it isn't already open.

2 On the File menu, point to New, and then click Project.

Visual Studio displays the New Project dialog box, which prompts you for the name and location of your project and the template that you want to use to open it. (Unlike previous versions of Visual Basic, you begin a project by specifying a name for your program.)

> ▶ **Note** Use the following instructions each time you want to create a new project on your hard disk.

3 Make sure the Visual Basic Projects folder is selected, and then click the Windows Application template.

These selections indicate that you'll be building a standalone Visual Basic Windows application.

4 Type **MyHello** in the Name text box, and then click the Browse button.

The Project Location dialog box opens. You use this dialog box to specify the location of your project and to create new folders for your projects if necessary. Although you can save your projects in any location that you want (the folder \My Documents\Visual Studio Projects is a common location), in this book I'll instruct you to save your projects in the c:\vbnet03sbs folder, the default location for your Step by Step practice files. If you ever want to remove all the files associated with this programming course, you'll know just where the files are, and you'll be able to remove them easily by deleting the entire folder.

> ▶ **Note** Throughout this book, I ask you to create sample projects with the My prefix, to distinguish your own work from the sample files I include on the companion CD-ROM.

5 Click the Desktop icon in the Project Location dialog box, double-click the My Computer icon, and then browse to the folder c:\vbnet03sbs\chap03.

6 Click the Open button to indicate that the MyHello project and its supporting files will be saved in the c:\vbnet03sbs\chap03 folder in a subfolder named MyHello.

3

Working with Controls

The New Project dialog box now looks like this:

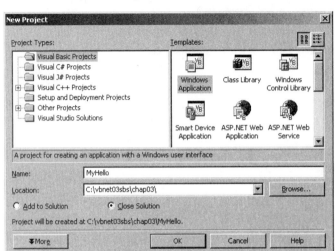

7   Click OK to create your new project.

The new project is created, and a blank form appears in the Windows Forms Designer, as shown in the following illustration. The two controls you'll use in this exercise, *Button* and *TextBox*, are labeled in the Toolbox. If your programming tools are configured differently now, take a few moments to organize them as shown in the illustration. (Chapter 1 describes how to configure the Visual Studio development environment if you need a refresher course.)

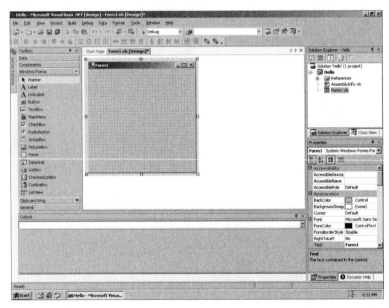

8 Click the *TextBox* control on the Windows Forms tab of the Toolbox.

9 Draw a text box similar to this:

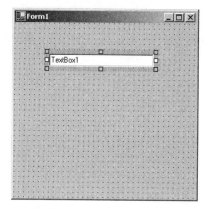

A *text box object* is used to display text on a form or to get user input while a Visual Basic program is running. How a text box works depends on how you set its properties and how you reference the text box in the program code. In this simple program, a text box object will be used to display the message "Hello, world!" when you click a button object on the form.

You'll add that button now.

10 Click the *Button* control in the Toolbox.

11 Draw a button below the text box on the form.

Your form should look like this:

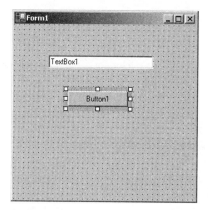

A *button object* is used to get the most basic input from a user. When a user clicks a button, he or she is requesting that the program perform a specific action immediately. In Visual Basic terms, the user is using the button to create an event that needs to be processed in the program. Typical buttons in a program are the OK button, which a user clicks to accept a list of options and to indicate that he or she is ready to proceed; the Cancel button, which a user clicks to discard a list of options; and the Quit button, which a user clicks to exit the program. In each case, you should use buttons in a recognizable way so that they work as expected when the user clicks them. A button's characteristics (like those of all objects) can be modified with property settings and references to the object in program code.

12 Set the following properties for the text box and button objects, using the Properties window. The setting "(empty)" for *TextBox1* means that you should delete the current setting and leave the property blank. Settings you need to type in are shown in quotation marks. You shouldn't type the quotation marks.

▶ **Tip**   For more information about setting properties, see the section "The Properties Window" in Chapter 1.

Object	Property	Setting
TextBox1	*Text*	(empty)
Button1	*Text*	"OK"

13 Double-click the OK button, and type the following program statement between the *Private Sub Button1_Click* and *End Sub* statements in the Code Editor:

```
TextBox1.Text = "Hello, world!"
```

▶ **Note**   After you type the *TextBox1* object name and a period, Visual Studio displays a list box containing all the valid properties for text box objects, to jog your memory if you've forgotten the complete list. You can select a property from the list by double-clicking it, or you can continue typing and enter it yourself. (I usually just keep on typing, unless I'm exploring new features.)

The statement you've entered changes the *Text* property of the text box to "Hello, world!" when the user clicks the button at runtime. (The equal sign (=) assigns everything between the quotation marks to the *Text* property of the *TextBox1* object.) This example changes a property at runtime—one of the most common uses of program code in a Visual Basic program. Your statement is in an *event procedure*—an instruction that's executed when the *Button1* object is clicked. It changes the property setting (and therefore the text box contents) immediately after the user clicks the button.

Now you're ready to run the Hello World program. (The complete Hello World program is located in the c:\vbnet03sbs\chap03\hello folder.)

Run the Hello World program

1 Click the Start button on the Standard toolbar.

The Hello World program compiles and after a few seconds runs in the Visual Studio development environment.

2 Click the OK button.

The program displays the greeting "Hello, world!" in the text box, as shown here:

When you clicked the OK button, the program code changed the *Text* property of the empty *TextBox1* text box to "Hello, world!" and displayed this text in the box. If you didn't get this result, repeat the steps in the previous section, and build the program again. You might have set a property incorrectly or made a typing mistake in the program code. (Syntax errors appear with a jagged underline in the Code Editor.)

3 Click the Close button in the upper right corner of the Hello World program window to stop the program.

▶ **Note** To stop a program running in Visual Studio, you can also click the Stop Debugging button on the Visual Studio Debug toolbar to close the program. (In Visual Basic 6, this button was named End.)

4 Click the Save All button on the Visual Studio Standard toolbar to save your changes.

Congratulations—you've joined the ranks of programmers who've written a Hello World program. Now let's try another control.

Using the *DateTimePicker* Control

Some Visual Basic controls display information, and others gather information from the user or process data behind the scenes. In this exercise, you'll work with the *DateTimePicker* control, which prompts the user for a date or time using a graphical calendar with scroll arrows. Although your use of the control will be rudimentary at this point, experimenting with *DateTimePicker* will give you an idea of how much Visual Basic controls can do for you automatically and how you process the information that comes from them.

The Birthday Program

The Birthday program uses a *DateTimePicker* control and a *Button* control to prompt the user for the date of his or her birthday and displays that informa-tion using a message box along with other information. Give it a try now.

Build the Birthday program

1   On the File menu, click Close Solution to close the MyHello project.
    The files associated with the Hello World program are closed.

2   On the File menu, point to New, and then click Project.
    The New Project dialog box appears.

3   Create a new Visual Basic Windows Application project named
    MyBirthday in the c:\vbnet03sbs\chap03 folder.
    The new project is created and a blank form appears in the Windows
    Forms Designer.

4   Click the *DateTimePicker* control in the Toolbox.

   ▶ **Note**   If you don't see the *DateTimePicker* in the Toolbox, it might be lower in the Toolbox list hidden from your view. To scroll down in the Tool-box list, click the down scroll arrow next to the Clipboard Ring tab. To scroll back up, click the up scroll arrow next to the Windows Forms tab.

5   Draw a date time picker object in the middle of the form, as shown
    in the following:

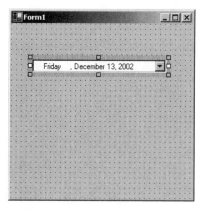

The date time picker object by default displays the current date, but you can adjust the date displayed by changing the object's *Value* property. Displaying the date is a handy design guide—it lets you size the date time picker object correctly when you're creating it.

6   Click the *Button* control in the Toolbox, and then add a button object below the date time picker.

You'll use this button to display your birth date and verify that the date time picker works correctly.

7   In the Properties window, change the *Text* property of the button object to **Show My Birthday**.

Now you'll add a few lines of program code to a procedure associated with the button object. This procedure is called an event procedure because it runs when an event, such as a mouse click, occurs in the object.

8   Double-click the button object on the form to display its default event procedure, and then type the following program statement between the *Private Sub* and *End Sub* statements in the *Button1_Click* event procedure:

```
MsgBox("Your birth date was " & DateTimePicker1.Text)
MsgBox("Day of the year: " & _
  DateTimePicker1.Value.DayOfYear.ToString())
MsgBox("Today is " & DateTimePicker1.Value.Now.ToString())
```

These program statements display three successive message boxes (small dialog boxes) with information from the date time picker object. The first line uses the *Text* property of the date time picker to display the birth date information you select when using the object at runtime. The *MsgBox* function displays the string value "Your birth date was" in addition to the textual value held in the date time picker's *Text* property. These two pieces of information are joined together by the string concatenation operator (&). You'll learn more about the *MsgBox* function and the string concatenation operator in Chapter 5.

The second and third lines collectively form one program statement and have been broken by the line continuation character (_) because the statement was a bit too long to print in this book. (See the following Note for an explanation of this useful convention for breaking longer lines.) The statement `DateTimePicker1.Value.DayOf-Year.ToString()` uses the date time picker object to calculate the day of the year in which you were born, counting from January 1. This is accomplished by the *DayOfYear* property and the *ToString* method, which converts the numeric result of the date calculation to a textual value that's more easily displayed by the *MsgBox* function.

> ▶ **Note**   Program lines can be more than 65,000 characters long in the Visual Studio Code Editor, but it's usually easiest to work with lines of 80 or fewer characters. You can divide long program statements among multiple lines by using a space and a line continuation character (_) at the end of each line in the statement, except the last line. (You cannot use a line continuation character to break a string that's in quotation marks, however.) I use the line continuation character in this exercise to break the second line of code into two parts.

Methods are special statements that perform an action or a service for a particular object, such as converting a number to a string or adding items to a list box. Methods differ from properties, which contain a value, and event procedures, which execute when a user manipulates an object. Methods can also be shared among objects, so when you learn how to use one method, you'll often be able to apply it to several circumstances. We'll discuss several important methods as you work through this book.

The fourth line in the program code uses the *Now* property to check your computer's system clock for the current date and time and displays that information in a message box after converting it to a string, or textual, value.

After you enter the code for the *Button1_Click* event procedure, the Code Editor should look similar to the following illustration:

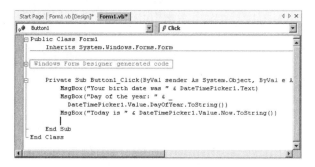

```
Start Page | Form1.vb [Design]* | Form1.vb*                           ◁ ▷ ×
Button1                          ▼   ƒ Click                             ▼
Public Class Form1
    Inherits System.Windows.Forms.Form

    Windows Form Designer generated code

    Private Sub Button1_Click(ByVal sender As System.Object, ByVal e A
        MsgBox("Your birth date was " & DateTimePicker1.Text)
        MsgBox("Day of the year: " & _
        DateTimePicker1.Value.DayOfYear.ToString())
        MsgBox("Today is " & DateTimePicker1.Value.Now.ToString())

    End Sub
End Class
```

▶ **Tip** The complete Birthday program is located in the
c:\vbnet03sbs\chap03\birthday folder.

9 Click the Save All button to save your changes to disk.

Now you're ready to run the Birthday program.

Run the Birthday program

1 Click the Start button on the Standard toolbar.

The Birthday program starts to run in the development environment. The current date is displayed in the date time picker.

2 Click the drop-down arrow in the date time picker to display the object in calendar view.

Your form will look like the following illustration. (You'll see a different date.)

3   Click the left scroll arrow to look at previous months on the calendar.

Notice that the text box portion of the object also changes as you scroll the date. The "today" value at the bottom of the calendar doesn't change, however.

Although you can scroll all the way back to your exact birthday, you might not have the patience to scroll month by month. To move to your birth year faster, select the year value in the date time picker text box and enter a new date.

4   Select the four-digit year in the date time picker text box.

When you select the date, the date time picker will close.

5   Type your birth year in place of the year that's currently selected, and then click the drop-down arrow again.

The calendar reappears in the year of your birth.

6   Click the scroll arrow again to locate the month in which you were born, and then click the exact day on which you were born.

If you didn't know the day of the week you were born on, now you can find out!

When you select the final date, the date time picker closes, and your birth date is displayed in the text box. Now click the button object to see how this information is made available to other objects on your form.

7   Click the Show My Birthday button.

Visual Basic executes your program code and displays a message box containing the day and date of your birth. Notice how the two dates match:

8   Click OK in the message box.

A second message box appears indicating which day of the year you were born on.

9   Click OK to display the final message box.

The current date and time are displayed—the program works!

You'll find the date time picker object to be quite capable—not only does it remember the new date or time information that you enter, but it also keeps track of the current date and time as well, and it can display this date and time information in a variety of useful formats.

▶ **Note**   To configure the date time picker object to display times instead of dates, set the object's *Format* property to Time.

10   Click OK to close the message box, and then click the Close button on the form.

You're finished using the *DateTimePicker* control for now.

A Word About Terminology

So far in this book I've used several different terms to describe items in a Visual Basic program. Although I haven't defined each of them formally, it's worth listing several of them now to clear up any confusion. Can you tell the difference yet?

Program statement   A program statement is a keyword in the code that does the work of the program. Visual Basic program statements create storage space for data, open files, perform calculations, and do several other important tasks. Most keywords are shown in blue type in the Code Editor.

Variable   A variable is a special container used to hold data temporarily in a program. The programmer creates variables using the *Dim* statement and uses these variables to store the results of a calculation, filenames, input, and so on. Numbers, names, and property values can be stored in variables.

Control   A control is a tool you use to create objects on a Visual Basic form. You select controls from the Toolbox and use them to draw objects on a form with the mouse. You use most controls to create user interface elements, such as buttons, picture boxes, and list boxes.

Object   An object is the name of a user interface element you create on a Visual Basic form with a control in the Toolbox. You can move, resize, and customize objects by using property settings. Objects have what is known as *inherent functionality*—they know how to operate and can respond to certain situations on their own. (A list box "knows" how to scroll, for example.) And objects are the members of *classes*, which serve as the blueprints for defining what objects do. You can program Visual Basic objects by using customized event procedures for different situations in a program. In Visual Basic, the form itself is also an object.

Property   A property is a value, or characteristic, held by an object. For example, a button object has a *Text* property to specify the text that appears on the button and an *Image* property to specify the path to an image file that should appear on the button face. In Visual Basic, properties can be set at design time by using the Properties window or at runtime by using statements in the program code. In code, the format for setting a property is

```
Object.Property = Value
```

where *Object* is the name of the object you're customizing, *Property* is the characteristic you want to change, and *Value* is the new property setting. For example,

```
Button1.Text = "Hello"
```

could be used in the program code to set the *Text* property of the *Button1* object to "Hello".

Event procedure   An event procedure is a block of code that's executed when an object is manipulated in a program. For example, when the *Button1* object is clicked, the *Button1_Click* event procedure is executed. Event procedures typically evaluate and set properties and use other program statements to perform the work of the program.

Method   A method is a special statement that performs an action or a service for a particular object in a program. In program code, the notation for using a method is

```
Object.Method(Value)
```

where *Object* is the name of the object you want to work with, *Method* is the action you want to perform, and *Value* is an optional argument to be used by the method. For example, the statement

```
ListBox1.Items.Add("Check")
```

uses the *Add* method to put the word *Check* in the *ListBox1* list box. Methods and properties are often identified by their position in a collection or object library, so don't be surprised if you see long references such as *System.Drawing.Image.FromFile*, which would be read as "the *FromFile* method, which is a member of the *Image* class, which is a member of the *System.Drawing* object library (or *namespace*)."

Controls for Gathering Input

Visual Basic provides several mechanisms for gathering input in a program. *Text boxes* accept typed input, *menus* present commands that can be clicked or chosen with the keyboard, and *dialog boxes* offer a variety of elements that can be chosen individually or selected in a group. In this exercise, you'll learn to use four important controls that will help you gather input in several different situations. You'll learn about the *RadioButton*, *CheckBox*, *ListBox*, and *ComboBox* controls. You'll explore each of these objects as you use a Visual Basic program called Input Controls, the user interface for a graphical ordering system. As you run the program, you'll get some hands-on experience with the input objects. In the next chapter, I'll discuss how these objects can be used along with menus in a full-fledged program.

As a simple experiment, try using the *CheckBox* control now to see how user input is processed on a form and in program code. Follow these steps:

Experiment with the *CheckBox* control

1   On the File menu, click Close Solution to close the Birthday project.

2   On the File menu, point to New, and then click Project.
    The New Project dialog box appears.

3   Create a new Visual Basic Windows Application project named **MyCheckBox** in the c:\vbnet03sbs\chap03 folder.
    The new project is created and a blank form appears in the Windows Forms Designer.

4   Click the *CheckBox* control in the Toolbox.

5   Draw two check box objects on the form, one above the other.
    Check boxes appear as objects on your form just as other objects do.

6   Click the *PictureBox* control, and draw two square picture box objects beneath the two check boxes.

7   Set the following properties for the check box and label objects:

Object	Property	Setting
CheckBox1	Checked	True
	Text	"Calculator"
CheckBox2	Text	"Copy machine"
PictureBox1	Image	c:\vbnet03sbs\chap03\calcultr.bmp
	SizeMode	StretchImage
PictureBox2	SizeMode	StretchImage

In this demonstration program, you'll use the check boxes to display and hide images of a calculator and a copy machine. The *Text* property of the check box object determines the contents of the check box label in the user interface. The *Checked* property lets you set a default value for the check box. Setting *Checked* to True will place a check mark in the box, and setting *Checked* to False (the default setting) will remove the check mark. I use the *SizeMode* properties in the picture boxes to size the images so that they stretch to fit in the picture box.

Your form should look like this:

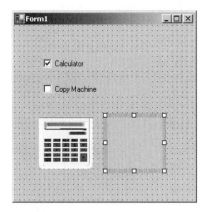

8   Double-click the first check box object to open the Code Editor for the *CheckBox1_CheckedChanged* event procedure, and then enter the following program code:

```
If CheckBox1.CheckState = 1 Then
    PictureBox1.Image = System.Drawing.Image.FromFile _
        ("c:\vbnet03sbs\chap03\calcultr.bmp")
    PictureBox1.Visible = True
Else
    PictureBox1.Visible = False
End If
```

The *CheckBox1_CheckedChanged* event procedure runs only if the user clicks in the first check box object. The event procedure uses an If..Then decision structure (described in Chapter 6) to check the current status, or state, of the first check box, and it displays a calculator picture from the c:\vbnet03sbs\chap03 folder if a check mark is in the box. The *CheckState* property holds a value of 1 if there's a check mark present and 0 if there's no check mark present. I use the *Visible* property to display the picture if a check mark is present or hide the picture if a check mark isn't present. Notice that I wrapped the long line that loads the image into the picture box object by using the line continuation (_) character.

9 Click the View Designer button in Solution Explorer to display the form again, and then double-click the second check box and add the following code to the *CheckBox2_CheckedChanged* event procedure:

```
If CheckBox2.CheckState = 1 Then
    PictureBox2.Image = System.Drawing.Image.FromFile _
      ("c:\vbnet03sbs\chap03\copymach.bmp")
    PictureBox2.Visible = True
Else
    PictureBox2.Visible = False
End If
```

This event procedure is almost identical to the one that you just entered; only the names of the image (copymach.bmp), the check box object (*CheckBox2*), and the picture box object (*PictureBox2*) are different.

▶ **Tip** The complete CheckBox program is located in the c:\vbnet03sbs\chap03\checkbox folder.

10 Click the Save All button on the Standard toolbar to save your changes.

Run the CheckBox program

1 Click the Start button on the Standard toolbar.

Visual Basic runs the program in the development environment. Because you placed a check mark in the first check box, the calculator image appears on the form.

2 Click the Copy machine check box.

Visual Basic displays the copy machine image, as shown here:

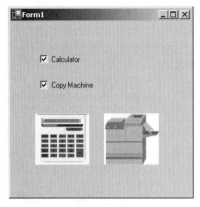

3   Experiment with different combinations of check boxes, clicking the boxes several times to test the program. The program logic you added with a few short lines of Visual Basic code manages the boxes perfectly. (You'll learn much more about program code in upcoming chapters.)

4   Click the Close button on the form to end the program.

The Input Controls Demo

Now that you've had a little experience with check boxes, run and examine the Input Controls demonstration program that I created to simulate an electronic ordering environment that makes more extensive use of check boxes, radio buttons, a list box, and a combo box. If you work in a business that does a lot of order entry, you might want to expand this program into a full-featured graphical order entry program. After you experiment with Input Controls, spend some time learning how the four input controls work in the program. They were created in a few short steps by using Visual Basic and the techniques you just learned.

Run the Input Controls program

1   On the File menu, point to Open, and then click Project.
     The Open Project dialog box appears.

2   Open the c:\vbnet03sbs\chap03\input controls folder, and then double-click the Input Controls project file (Input Controls.vbproj).
     The Input Controls project opens in the development environment.

3   If the project's form isn't visible, click the Form1.vb form in Solution
Explorer, and then click the View Designer button.

4   Move or close the windows that block your view of the form so that
you can see how the objects are laid out.

You'll see a form similar to this:

The Input Controls form contains radio button, check box, list box,
combo box, picture box, button, and label objects. These objects work
together to create a simple order entry program that demonstrates how
the Visual Basic input objects work. When the Input Controls program
is run, it loads images from the \vbnet03sbs\chap03\input controls
folder on drive C and displays them in the six picture boxes on the
form.

▶   **Note**   If you installed the practice files in a location other than the
default c:\vbnet03sbs folder, the statements in the program that load the
artwork from the disk will contain an incorrect path. (Each statement
begins with c:\vbnet03sbs\chap03\input controls, as you'll see soon.) If
this is the case, you can make the program work by renaming your practice files folder \vbnet03sbs or by changing the paths in the Code Editor
using the editing keys or the Find And Replace submenu on the Edit
menu.

5   Click the Start button on the Standard toolbar.

The program runs in the development environment.

6   Click the Laptop radio button in the Computer box.

The image of a laptop computer appears in the Products Ordered
area on the right side of the form. The user can click various options,

and the current choice is depicted in the order area on the right. In the Computer box, a group of *radio buttons* is used to gather input from the user. (Note: Radio buttons were called option buttons in Visual Basic 6.) Radio buttons force the user to choose one (and only one) item from a list of possibilities.

When radio buttons are placed inside a group box object on a form, the radio buttons are considered to be part of a group and only one option can be chosen. To create a group box, click the *GroupBox* control on the Windows Forms tab of the Toolbox, and then draw the control on your form. (The *GroupBox* control replaces the *Frame* control in Visual Basic 6.) You can give the group of radio buttons a title (as I have) by setting the *Text* property of the group box object. When you move a group box object on the form, the controls within it also move.

7 Click the Answering Machine, Calculator, and Copy Machine check boxes in the Office Equipment box.

Check boxes are used in a program so that the user can select more than one option at a time from a list. Click the Calculator check box again, and notice that the picture of the calculator disappears from the order area. Because each user interface element is live and responds to click events as they occur, order choices are reflected immediately. The code that completes these tasks is nearly identical to the code you entered earlier in the CheckBox program.

8 Click Satellite Dish in the Peripherals list box.

A picture of a satellite dish is added to the order area. A *list box* is used to get a user's single response from a list of choices. List boxes are created with the *ListBox* control, and might contain many items to choose from (scroll bars appear if the list of items is longer than the list box). Unlike radio buttons, a list box doesn't require a default selection. In a Visual Basic program, items can be added to, removed from, or sorted in a list box while the program is running. If you would like to see check marks next to the items in your list box, use the *CheckedListBox* control in the Toolbox instead of the *ListBox* control.

9 Now choose U.S. Dollars (sorry, no credit) from the payment list in the Payment Method combo box.

A *combo box*, or drop-down list box, is similar to a regular list box, but it takes up less space. (The "combo" in a combo box basically comes from a "combination" of an editable text box and a drop-down list.) Visual Basic automatically handles the opening, closing, and scrolling of the list box. All you do as a programmer is create the combo box using the *ComboBox* control in the Toolbox, set the *Text* property to provide directions or a default value, and then write code to add items to the combo box and to process the user's combo box selection. You'll see examples of each task in the program code for the Input Controls demonstration.

After you make your order selections, your screen should look something like this:

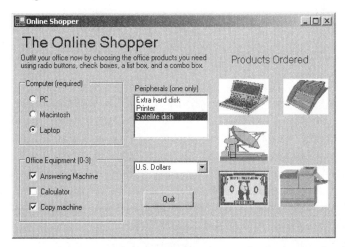

10 Practice making a few more changes to the order list in the program (try different computers, peripherals, and payment methods), and then click the Quit button in the program to exit.

The program closes when you click Quit, and the programming environment appears.

Looking at the Input Controls Program Code

Although you haven't had much formal experience with program code yet, it's worth taking a quick look at a few event procedures in Input Controls to see how the program processes input from the user interface elements. In these procedures, you'll see the *If...Then* and *Select Case* statements at work. You'll learn about these and other decision structures in Chapter 6. For now, concentrate on the *CheckState* property, which changes when a check box is selected, and the *SelectedIndex* property, which changes when a list box is selected.

Examine the check box code and the list box code

1   Be sure the program has stopped running, and then double-click the Answering Machine check box in the Office Equipment box to display the *CheckBox1_CheckedChanged* event procedure in the Code Editor. You'll see the following program code:

```
'If the CheckState property for a check box is 1, it has a mark in it
If CheckBox1.CheckState = 1 Then
    PictureBox2.Image = System.Drawing.Image.FromFile _
        ("c:\vbnet03sbs\chap03\input controls\answmach.bmp")
    PictureBox2.Visible = True
Else
    'If there is no mark, hide the image
    PictureBox2.Visible = False
End If
```

The first line of this event procedure is called a *comment*. Comments are displayed in green type and are simply notes written by the programmer to describe what's important or interesting about this particular piece of program code. (Comments are also occasionally generated by automated programming tools that compile programs or insert code snippets.) I wrote this comment to remind myself that the *CheckState* property contains a crucial value in this routine—a value of 1 if the first check box was checked.

The rest of the event procedure is nearly identical to the one you just wrote in the CheckBox program. If you scroll down in the Code Editor, you'll see a similar event procedure for the *CheckBox2* and *CheckBox3* objects.

2   At the top edge of the Code Editor, click the tab labeled "Form1.vb [Design]" to display the form again, and then double-click the Peripherals list box on the form.

The *ListBox1_SelectedIndexChanged* event procedure appears in the Code Editor. You'll see the following program statements:

```
'The item you picked (0-2) is held in the SelectedIndex property
Select Case ListBox1.SelectedIndex
    Case 0
        PictureBox3.Image = System.Drawing.Image.FromFile _
            ("c:\vbnet03sbs\chap03\input controls\harddisk.bmp")
    Case 1
        PictureBox3.Image = System.Drawing.Image.FromFile _
            ("c:\vbnet03sbs\chap03\input controls\printer.bmp")
    Case 2
        PictureBox3.Image = System.Drawing.Image.FromFile _
            ("c:\vbnet03sbs\chap03\input controls\satedish.bmp")
End Select
```

Here you see code that executes when the user clicks an item in the Peripherals list box in the program. In this case, the important keyword is *ListBox1.SelectedIndex*, which is read "the *SelectedIndex* property of the first list box object." After the user clicks an item in the list box, the *SelectedIndex* property returns a number that corresponds to the location of the item in the list box. (The first item is numbered 0, the second item is numbered 1, and so on.)

In the previous code, *SelectedIndex* is evaluated by the Select Case decision structure, and a different image is loaded depending on the value of the *SelectedIndex* property. If the value is 0, a picture of a hard disk is loaded; if the value is 1, a picture of a printer is loaded; if the value is 2, a picture of a satellite dish is loaded. You'll learn more about how the Select Case decision structure works in Chapter 6.

3 At the top edge of the Code Editor, click the Form1.vb [Design] tab to display the form again, and then double-click the form (not any of the objects) to display the code associated with the form itself.

The *Form1_Load* event procedure appears in the Code Editor. This is the procedure that's executed each time the Input Controls program starts, or *loads*. Programmers put program statements in this special procedure when they want them executed every time a form loads. (Your program can display more than one form, or none at all, but the default behavior is that Visual Basic loads and runs the *Form1_Load* event procedure each time the user runs the program.) Often, as in the Input Controls program, these statements define an aspect of the user interface that couldn't be created by using the controls in the Toolbox or the Properties window.

Here's what the *Form1_Load* event procedure looks like for this program:

```
'These program statements run when the form loads
PictureBox1.Image = System.Drawing.Image.FromFile _
   ("c:\vbnet03sbs\chap03\input controls\pcomputr.bmp")
'Add items to a list box like this:
ListBox1.Items.Add("Extra hard disk")
ListBox1.Items.Add("Printer")
ListBox1.Items.Add("Satellite dish")
'Combo boxes are also filled with the Add method:
ComboBox1.Items.Add("U.S. Dollars")
ComboBox1.Items.Add("Check")
ComboBox1.Items.Add("English Pounds")
```

Three lines in this event procedure are comments displayed in green type. The second line in the event procedure loads the personal computer image into the first picture box. (This line is broken in two using a space and the line continuation character, but the compiler still thinks of it as one line.) Loading an image establishes the default setting reflected in the Computer radio button group box. The next three lines add items to the Peripherals list box (*ListBox1*) in the program. The words in quotes will appear in the list box when it appears on the form. Below the list box program statements, the items in the Payment Method combo box (*ComboBox1*) are specified. The important keyword in both these groups is *Add*, which is a special function, or method, to add items to list box and combo box objects.

You're finished using the Input Controls program. Take a few minutes to examine any other parts of the program you're interested in, and then move on to the next exercise.

Using the *LinkLabel* Control

Providing access to the Web is now a standard feature of many Windows applications, and Visual Studio .NET makes adding this functionality easier than ever before. You can create sophisticated Web-aware applications by using Web Forms and other technologies in Visual Studio, or you can open a simple Web page using your computer's Web browser utilizing just a few lines of program code.

In this exercise, you'll learn to use the *LinkLabel* control to display text on a Visual Basic form that looks and acts just like an Internet link. When you combine the *LinkLabel* control with the *Process.Start* method, you can quickly open links on your form using Internet Explorer, Netscape Navigator, or another browser. Use the *LinkLabel* control now to connect to the Microsoft Press home page on the Internet.

▶ **Note**   To learn more about writing Web-aware Visual Basic .NET applications, read Chapter 21 and Chapter 22.

Create the WebLink program

1 On the File menu, click Close Solution to close the Input Controls project.

2 On the File menu, point to New, and then click Project.

The New Project dialog box appears.

3 Create a new Visual Basic Windows Application project named **MyWebLink** in the c:\vbnet03sbs\chap03 folder.

The new project is created, and a blank form appears in the Windows Forms Designer.

4 Click the *LinkLabel* control in the Toolbox, and draw a rectangular link label object on your form.

Link label objects look like label objects, except that all label text is displayed in blue underlined type on the form.

5 Set the *Text* property of the link label object to **www.microsoft.com/mspress/** (the Web site for Microsoft Press).

Your form will look like this:

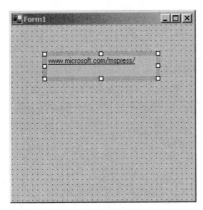

6 Click the form in the development environment to select it. (Click the form itself, not the link label object.)

This is the technique you use to view the properties of the default form or Form1 in the Properties window. Like other objects in your project, the form also has properties that you can set.

7   Set the *Text* property of the form object to **Web Link Test**.

The *Text* property for a form controls what appears on the form's title bar when the program runs. Although this isn't customization related exclusively to the Web, I thought you'd enjoy picking up that skill now, before we move on to other projects. (We'll customize the title bar in most of the programs we build.)

8   Double-click the link label object, and type the following program code in the *LinkLabel1_LinkClicked* event procedure:

```
' Change the color of the link by setting LinkVisited to True.
LinkLabel1.LinkVisited = True
' Use the Process.Start method to open the default browser
' using the Microsoft Press URL:
System.Diagnostics.Process.Start _
  ("http://www.microsoft.com/mspress/")
```

I've included comments in the program code to give you some practice entering them. As soon as you enter the single quote character ('), Visual Studio changes the color of the line to green, identifying the line as a comment. Comments are for documentation purposes only—they aren't evaluated or executed by the compiler.

The two program statements that aren't comments actually control how the link works. Setting the *LinkVisited* property to True gives the link that dimmer color of purple, which indicates in many browsers that the HTML document associated with the link has already been viewed. Although setting this property isn't necessary to display a Web page, it's good programming practice to provide the user with information that's consistent in other applications.

The second program statement (which was broken into two lines) runs the default Web browser (such as Internet Explorer) if the browser isn't already running. (If the browser is running, the URL just loads immediately.) The *Start* method in the *Process* class performs the important work, by starting a process or executable program session in memory for the browser. The *Process* class, which manages many other aspects of program execution, is a member of the *System.Diagnostics* object library, which Visual Basic .NET programmers called the *System.Diagnostics* namespace. By including an Internet address or a URL along with the *Start* method, I'm letting

Visual Basic know that I want to view a Web site, and Visual Basic is clever enough to know that the default system browser is the tool that would best display that URL, even though I didn't identify the browser by name.

An exciting feature of the *Process.Start* method is that it can be used to run other Windows applications, too. If I did want to identify a particular browser by name to open the URL, I could have specified one using the following syntax. (Here I'll request the Internet Explorer browser.)

```
System.Diagnostics.Process.Start("IExplore.exe", _
  "http://www.microsoft.com/mspress/")
```

Two arguments are used here with the *Start* method, separated by a comma. The exact location for the program named IExplore.exe on my system isn't specified, but Visual Basic will search the current system path for it when the program runs.

Or if I had wanted to run a different application with the *Start* method, such as the application Microsoft Word (and open the document c:\myletter.doc), I could have used the following syntax:

```
System.Diagnostics.Process.Start("Winword.exe", _
  "c:\myletter.doc")
```

As you can see, the *Start* method in the *Process* class is very useful, and we'll make use of it again in this book. Now that you've entered your code, save your project and run it. (If you experimented with the *Start* syntax as I showed you, restore the original code shown at the beginning of step 8.) The complete WebLink program is located in the c:\vbnet03sbs\chap03\weblink folder.

9   Click the Save All button on the Standard toolbar to save your changes.

Run the WebLink program

1   Click the Start button on the Standard toolbar to run the WebLink program.

The form opens and runs, showing its Web site link and handsome title bar text.

2   Click the link to open the Web site shown (*www.microsoft.com/mspress/*).

3

Working with Controls

Recall that it's only a happy coincidence that the link label *Text* property contains the same URL as the site you named in the program code. You may enter any text you like in the link label. You can also use the *Image* property for a link label to specify a picture to display in the background of the link label. The following figure shows what the Microsoft Press Web page looks like (in English) when the WebLink program displays it using Internet Explorer.

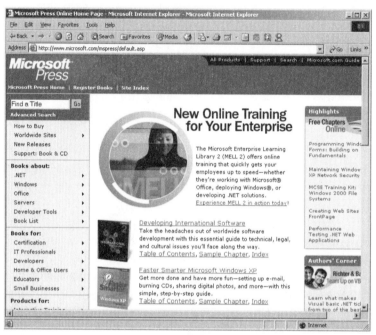

3   Display the form again. (Click the Web Link Test form icon on the Windows task bar if the form isn't visible.)

Notice that the link now appears in a dimmed style. Like a standard Web link, your link label communicates that it's been used (but is still active) by the color and intensity that it appears in.

4   Click the Close button on the form to quit the test utility.

You're finished writing code in this chapter.

One Step Further: Installing ActiveX Controls

Visual Studio .NET is a relatively new product, so many developers will find that the current list of Windows Forms controls isn't as extensive as the ActiveX controls that were available to Visual Basic 6 programmers. If you want to expand the collection of controls that you have access to in Visual Studio .NET, you can load and use older ActiveX (COM) components and controls. These customizable programming tools were provided by Visual Basic 6, Microsoft Visual C++ 6, Microsoft Office, and other third-party products. When you add older ActiveX controls to your Toolbox, Visual Studio displays them with the .NET controls, and you can use the ActiveX controls on your forms with few limitations. The only technical qualification is that Visual Studio must create a *wrapper* for the control, which makes the objects in the control usable in a .NET program. In most cases, Visual Studio .NET handles the creation of a control wrapper automatically when the ActiveX control is loaded.

▶ **Note**   ActiveX controls on your computer typically have an .ocx or .dll filename extension. These library files are routinely added to your system when you install a new application program, and you can reuse them in your own programs if you can figure out how to use the objects, methods, and properties that they provide, or expose. Visual Studio .NET "learns" about the presence of new ActiveX controls when they're cataloged in the Windows system registry.

The Microsoft *Chart* Control

You probably have numerous ActiveX controls on your system now, especially if you have a previous version of Visual Basic or Microsoft Office on your system. Try installing one of the ActiveX controls now, even if you're not sure how to use it yet. (You'll start putting ActiveX controls to work later in the book, so you should learn the installation technique now.) The control you'll open in this exercise is the Microsoft *Chart* control, which allows you to build charts on your forms. The Microsoft *Chart* control is included in several versions of Microsoft Office. If you don't have Office or this control, pick another one.

3

Working with Controls

Install the *Chart* control

1   If you still have the Code Editor open for the WebLink project, display the form.

2   Click the Toolbox, and open the tab to which you'd like to add an ActiveX control. For example, click the Windows Forms tab.

ActiveX controls are added to individual tabs in the Toolbox so that you can remember where they are. Once on a Toolbox tab, they look just like regular controls in Visual Studio .NET.

3   Click the Windows Forms tab again with the right mouse button, and then click Add/Remove Items on the pop-up menu.

The Customize Toolbox dialog box opens.

4   Click the COM Components tab in the Customize Toolbox dialog box.

You'll see a long list of ActiveX components and controls that's unique to your system. The components appear in alphabetical order.

5   Scroll to the Microsoft Office Chart 9.0 control or to another control that looks interesting, and then click the check box next to the control.

Your dialog box will look similar to the following illustration.

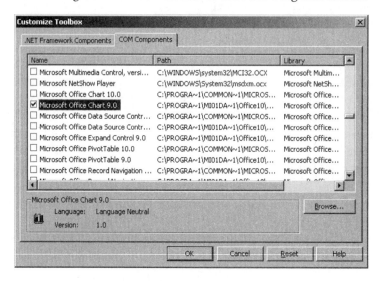

6   To add additional controls to the Toolbox, simply click check boxes next to the controls that you want.

> ▶   **Note**   Not all the components listed in the Customize Toolbox dialog box are designed to work in the Toolbox, so they might not work properly when you try to use them.

7   Click OK to add the selected ActiveX control (or controls) to this project's Toolbox.

   The control will appear at the bottom of the Toolbox list. The control will appear for this project only and won't appear in other projects.

8   Click the down scroll arrow in the Toolbox to see the newly added control, as shown here:

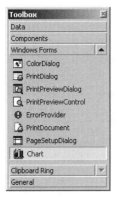

The Microsoft Office Chart ActiveX control is available in several different versions and is included with applications such as Office 2000 and Office XP. You'll find that most ActiveX controls work just like the standard controls in the Visual Basic .NET Toolbox. In fact, if you didn't know they were ActiveX controls, it would be difficult to tell them apart from the default controls in Visual Studio .NET. Each ActiveX control has adjustable property settings and methods that you can call just like the other controls you've used in this chapter.

Lesson 3 Quick Reference

To	Do this
Create a text box	Click the *TextBox* control, and draw the box.
Create a button	Click the *Button* control, and draw the button.
Change a property at runtime	Change the value of the property by using program code. For example: `Label1.Text = "Hello!"`
Create a radio button	Use the *RadioButton* control. To create multiple radio buttons, place more than one button object inside a box that you create by using the *GroupBox* control.
Create a check box	Click the *CheckBox* control, and draw a check box.
Create a list box	Click the *ListBox* control, and draw a list box.
Create a drop-down list box	Click the *ComboBox* control, and draw a drop-down list box.
Add items to a list box	Include statements with the *Add* method in the *Form1_Load* event procedure of your program. For example: `ListBox1.Items.Add "Printer"`
Display a Web page	Create a link to the Web page using the *LinkLabel* control, and then open the link in a browser using the *Process.Start* method in program code.
Install ActiveX controls	Right-click the Toolbox tab that you want to place the control in, and then click Add/Remove Items to display the Customize Toolbox dialog box. Click the COM Components tab, place a check mark next to the ActiveX control that you want to install, and then click OK.

Chapter

4

Working with Menus and Dialog Boxes

In this chapter, you will learn how to:

■ Add menus to your programs by using the *MainMenu* control.

■ Process menu choices by using program code.

■ Use the *OpenFileDialog* and *ColorDialog* controls to display special-purpose dialog boxes.

In Chapter 3, you used several Microsoft Visual Studio controls to gather input from the user while he or she was using a program. In this chapter, you'll learn to present choices to the user by using professional-looking menus and dialog boxes. A *menu* is located on the menu bar and contains a list of related commands. When you click a menu title, a list of the menu commands appears in a drop-down list. Most menu commands are executed immediately after they're clicked; for example, when the user clicks the Copy command on the Edit menu, information is copied to the Clipboard immediately. If a menu command is followed by an ellipsis (...), however, Microsoft Visual Basic displays a dialog box requesting more information before the command is carried out. In this chapter, you'll learn how to use the *MainMenu* control and two dialog box controls to add menus and standard dialog boxes to your programs.

Upgrade Notes: What's New in Visual Basic .NET?

If you're experienced with Visual Basic 6, you'll notice some new features in Visual Basic .NET, including the following:

■ Menus are no longer created using the Visual Basic 6 Menu Editor tool. Instead, you create a main menu object on your form using the *MainMenu* control, and then customize the object using property settings and the Menu Designer. However, menu choices are still processed with program code.

■ Standard dialog boxes are no longer created using the *CommonDialog* control. Instead, you use one of seven Windows Forms controls that add standard dialog boxes to your project. These controls are *OpenFileDialog*, *SaveFileDialog*, *FontDialog*, *ColorDialog*, *PrintDialog*, *PrintPreviewDialog*, and *PageSetupDialog*.

■ Forms now feature the *ShowDialog* method and the *DialogResult* property, making it easier to create custom forms that look and act like standard dialog boxes.

Adding Menus Using the *MainMenu* Control

The *MainMenu* control is a tool that adds menus to your programs and allows you to customize them with property settings in the Properties window. With the control, you can add new menus, modify and reorder existing menus, and delete old menus. You also can add special effects to your menus, such as access keys, check marks, and keyboard shortcuts. After you've added menus to your form, you can use event procedures to process the menu commands. In the following exercise, you'll use the *MainMenu* control to create a Clock menu containing commands that display the current date and time.

Create a menu

1   Start Visual Studio.

2   On the File menu, point to New, and then click Project.
    The New Project dialog box appears.

3   Create a new Visual Basic Windows Application project named **MyMenu** in the c:\vbnet03sbs\chap04 folder.

4   Click the *MainMenu* control on the Windows Forms tab of the Toolbox, and draw a menu control on your form.
    Don't worry about the location—Visual Studio will move the control and resize it automatically. Your screen will look like this:

Menu Designer

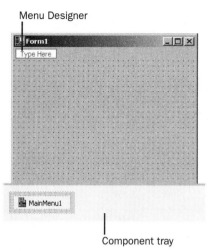

Component tray

The main menu object doesn't appear on your form, but below it. That's different from previous versions of Visual Basic, which in one way or another displayed all objects on the form itself—even ones that didn't have a visual representation when the program ran, such as the *Timer* control. But in Visual Studio .NET, non-visible objects such as menus and timers are displayed on a separate pane, named the *component tray*, in the development environment, and you can select them, set their properties, or delete them right from this pane.

In addition to the main menu object in the component tray, Visual Studio .NET displays a visual representation of the menu you created at the top of the form. The tag "Type Here" encourages you to click the tag and enter the title of your menu right now. After you enter the first menu title, you can enter submenu titles and other menu names by pressing the arrow keys and typing additional names. Best of all, you can come back to this in-line Menu Designer later and edit what you've done or add additional menu items—the main menu object is fully customizable and allows you to create an exciting menu-driven user interface like the ones you've seen in the best Microsoft Windows applications.

5   Click the Type Here tag, type **Clock**, and then press Enter.

The word "Clock" is entered as the name of your first menu, and two additional Type Here tags appear, allowing you to create submenu items below the new Clock menu or additional menu titles. The submenu item is currently selected.

▶ **Note**   If the menu disappears from the form, click MainMenu1 in the component tray, and the menu on the form should reappear.

6   Type **Date** to create a Date command for the Clock menu, and then press Enter.

Visual Studio adds the Date command to the menu and selects the next submenu item.

7   Type **Time** to create a Time command for the menu, and then press Enter.

You now have a Clock menu with two menu commands, Date and Time. You could continue to create additional menus or commands, but what you've done is sufficient for this example program. Your form will look like this:

8   Click the form to close the Menu Designer.

The Menu Designer closes, and your form appears in the development environment with the Clock menu. You're ready to start customizing the menu now.

Adding Access Keys to Menu Commands

Most applications allow you to access and execute menu commands using the keyboard. For example, in Visual Studio you can open the File menu by pressing the Alt key and then pressing the F key. Once the File menu is open, you can execute the Print command by pressing the P key. The key that you press in addition to the Alt key and the key that you press to execute a command in an open menu are called *access keys*. You can identify the access key in a menu item because it's underlined.

Visual Studio makes it easy to provide access key support. To add an access key to a menu item, activate the Menu Designer, and type an ampersand (&) before the appropriate letter in the menu name. When you open the menu at runtime (when the program is running), your program will automatically support the access key.

▶ **Note**   By default, Windows 2000, Windows XP, and Windows Server 2003 don't display the underline for access keys in a program until you press the Alt key for the first time. In Windows 2000, you can turn off this option on the Effects tab of the Display control panel. In Windows XP and Windows Server 2003, you can turn off this option using the Effects button on the Appearances tab of the Display control panel.

Try adding access keys to the Clock menu now.

Menu Conventions

By convention, each menu title and menu command in an application for Microsoft Windows has an initial capital letter. File and Edit are often the first two menu names on the menu bar, and Help is the last. Other common menu names are View, Format, and Window. No matter what menus and commands you use in your applications, take care to be clear and consistent with them. Menus and commands should be easy to use and should have as much in common with those in other Windows-based applications as possible. As you create menu items, use the following guidelines:

■ Use short, specific captions consisting of one or two words at most.

■ Assign each menu item an access key. Use the first letter of the item if possible.

■ Menu items at the same level must have a unique access key.

■ If a command is used as an on/off toggle, place a check mark next to the item when it's active. You can add a check mark by setting the *Checked* property of the menu command to True by using the Properties window.

■ Place an ellipsis (…) after a menu command that requires the user to enter more information before the command can be executed. The ellipsis indicates that you'll open a dialog box if the user selects this item.

Add access keys

1   Click the Clock menu name on the form, and then click it again.

A blinking text-editing cursor appears in the Clock menu name. The text-editing cursor allows you to edit your menu name or add the ampersand character (&) for an access key.

2   Press the Left Arrow key to move the text-editing cursor to the beginning of the Clock menu name.

The cursor blinks before the letter "C" in Clock.

3   Type & to define the letter "C" as the access key for the Clock menu.

An ampersand appears in the text box in front of the word Clock.

4   Click the Date command in the menu list, and then click Date a second time to display the text-editing cursor.

5   Type & before the letter "D".

The letter "D" is now defined as the access key for the Date command.

6   Click the Time command in the menu list, and then click the command a second time to display the text-editing cursor.

7   Type & before the letter "T".

The letter "T" is now defined as the access key for the Time command.

8   Press Enter.

Pressing Enter locks in your text-editing changes. Your form will look like this:

Now you'll practice using the Menu Designer to switch the order of the Date and Time commands on the Clock menu. Changing the order of menu items is an important skill because at times you'll think of a better way to define your menus.

Change the order of menu items

1 Click the Clock menu on the form to display its menu items.

Changing the order of menu items is very easy. You simply drag the menu item that you want to move to a new location on the menu. Try it now.

2 Drag the Time menu on top of the Date menu, and then release the mouse button.

Dragging one menu item on top of a second menu item means that you want to place the first menu item ahead of the second menu item on the menu. As quickly as that, Visual Studio moved the Time menu item ahead of the Date item.

You've finished creating the user interface for the Clock menu. Now you'll use the menu event procedures to process the user's menu selections in the program.

▶ **Note** To delete an unwanted menu item from a menu, click the unwanted item in the menu list, and then press the Delete key.

Processing Menu Choices

After menus and commands are configured using the main menu object, they also become new objects in your program. To make the menu objects do meaningful work, you need to write event procedures for them. Menu event procedures typically contain program statements that display or process information on the user interface form and modify one or more menu properties. If more information is needed from the user to process the selected command, an event procedure will often display a dialog box by using one of the Windows Forms dialog box controls or one of the input controls you used in Chapter 3.

In the following exercise, you'll add a label object to your form to display the output of the Time and Date commands on the Clock menu.

Add a label object to the form

1 Click the *Label* control in the Toolbox.

2 Draw a medium-sized label in the middle area of the form.

The label object appears on the form and will bear the name *Label1* in the program code.

3   Set the following properties for the label:

Object	Property	Setting
Label1	*BorderStyle*	FixedSingle
	Font	Microsoft Sans Serif,
	Text	Bold, 14-point
	TextAlign	(empty)
		MiddleCenter

Your form should look like this:

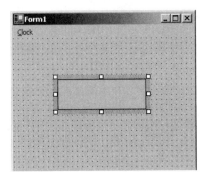

▶ **Note**   In the following exercises, you'll enter program code to process menu choices. It's OK if you're still a bit hazy on what program code does and how you use it—you'll learn much more about program statements in Chapter 5 through Chapter 7.

Now you'll add program statements to the Time and Date event procedures to process the menu commands.

Edit the menu event procedures

1   Click the Clock menu on the form to display its submenus.

2   Double-click the Time command in the menu to open an event procedure for the command in the Code Editor.

The *MenuItem3_Click* event procedure appears in the Code Editor. The name *MenuItem3_Click* means that Time was the third menu item you created in this project (following Clock and Date), and the *_Click* syntax means that this is the event procedure that runs when a user clicks the menu item. We'll keep this menu name for now, but I wanted to point out to you that it isn't really that intuitive to use. You can create your own names for objects that describe their function in the program a little more specifically by using the *Name* property. Although I don't bother with that extra step in the first few exercises, later in the chapter you'll create menu names to establish more understandable and professional programming practices.

3   Type the following program statement:

```
Label1.Text = TimeString
```

This program statement displays the current time (from the system clock) in the *Text* property of the *Label1* object, replacing the previous *Label1* text (if any). *TimeString* is a property that contains the current time formatted for display or printing; you can use *TimeString* at any time in your programs to display the time accurately down to the second. (*TimeString* is essentially a replacement for the older QuickBASIC *TIME$* statement.)

▶ **Note**   Visual Basic's *TimeString* property returns the current system time. You can set the system time by using the Date/Time icon in Windows Control Panel; you can change the system time format by using Control Panel's Regional Options (or Regional And Language Options) icon.

4   Press the Down Arrow key.

Visual Basic interprets the line and adjusts capitalization and spacing, if necessary. (Visual Basic checks each line for syntax errors as you enter it. You can enter a line by pressing Enter, Up Arrow, or Down Arrow.)

5   Click the View Designer button in Solution Explorer, and then double-click the Date command on the Clock menu.

The *MenuItem2_Click* event procedure appears in the Code Editor. This event procedure is executed when the user clicks the Date command on the Clock menu.

6   Type the following program statement:

```
Label1.Text = DateString
```

This program statement displays the current date (from the system clock) in the *Text* property of the *Label1* object, replacing the previous *Label1* text. The *DateString* property is also available for general use in your programs. Assign *DateString* to the *Text* property of an object whenever you want to display the current date on a form.

▶ **Note**   Visual Basic's *DateString* property returns the current system date. You can set the system date by using the Date/Time icon in Control Panel; you can change the system date format by using Control Panel's Regional Options (or Regional And Language Options) icon.

7   Press the Down Arrow key to enter the line.

Your screen should look like this:

You've finished entering the menu demonstration program. Now you'll save your changes to the project and prepare to run it.

8   Click the Save All button on the Standard toolbar.

▶   **Tip**   The complete Menu program is located in the c:\vbnet03sbs\chap04\menu folder.

Run the Menu program

1   Click the Start button on the Standard toolbar.

The Menu program runs in the development environment.

2   Click the Clock menu on the menu bar.

The Clock menu appears.

3   Click the Time command.

The current system time appears in the label box, as shown here:

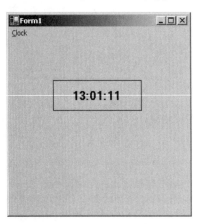

Now you'll try displaying the current date by using the access keys on the menu.

4   Press and release the Alt key.

The Clock menu on the menu bar is highlighted.

5   Press C to display the Clock menu.

The contents of the Clock menu appear.

6   Press D to display the current date.

The current date appears in the label box.

7   Click the Close button on the program's title bar to stop the program.

Congratulations! You've created a working program that makes use of menus and access keys. In the next exercise, you'll learn how to use menus to display standard dialog boxes.

System Clock Properties and Functions

You can use various properties and functions to retrieve chronological values from the system clock. You can use these values to create custom calendars, clocks, and alarms in your programs. The following table lists the most useful system clock functions. For more information, check the Visual Studio online Help.

Property or Function	Description
TimeString	This property returns the current time from the system clock.
DateString	This property returns the current date from the system clock.
Now	This property returns an encoded value representing the current date and time. This property is most useful as an argument for other system clock functions.
Hour (time)	This function returns the hour portion of the specified time (0 through 23).
Minute (time)	This function returns the minute portion of the specified time (0 through 59).
Second (time)	This function returns the second portion of the specified time (0 through 59).
Day (date)	This function returns a whole number representing the day of the month (1 through 31).
Month (date)	This function returns a whole number representing the month (1 through 12).
Year (date)	This function returns the year portion of the specified date.
Weekday (date)	This function returns a whole number representing the day of the week (1 is Sunday, 2 is Monday, and so on).

Menus and Dialog Boxes

4

Using Dialog Box Controls

Visual Studio contains seven standard dialog box controls on the Windows Forms tab of the Toolbox. These are provided ready-made so that you don't need to create your own custom dialog boxes for the most common tasks in Windows applications, such as opening files, saving files, and printing. In many cases, you'll still need to write the program code that connects these dialog boxes to your program, but the user interfaces are built for you and conform to the standards for common use among Windows applications. The seven standard dialog box controls available to you are listed in the following table. In many respects, they're parallel to the objects provided by the *CommonDialog* control in Visual Basic 6, with a few important exceptions. The *PrintPreviewControl* control isn't listed here, but you'll find it useful if you use the *PrintPreviewDialog* control.

Control Name	Purpose
OpenFileDialog	Gets the drive, folder name, and filename for an existing file
SaveFileDialog	Gets the drive, folder name, and filename for a new file
FontDialog	Lets the user choose a new font type and style
ColorDialog	Lets the user select a color from a palette
PrintDialog	Lets the user set printing options
PrintPreviewDialog	Displays a print preview dialog box as Microsoft Word does
PageSetupDialog	Lets the user control page setup options, such as margins, paper size, and layout

In the following exercises, you'll add a new menu to the Menu program and practice using the *OpenFileDialog* and *ColorDialog* controls. You may either use your existing Menu project or load the Menu project from the practice files folder if you didn't create it from scratch. (I've named the completed version Dialog, to preserve both projects on disk.)

Add *OpenFileDialog* and *ColorDialog* controls

1   If you didn't create the Menu project, click the File menu, point to Open, and then click Project, select the Menu project in the c:\vbnet03sbs\chap04\menu folder, and then click Open. If the form isn't open, double-click Form1.vb in Solution Explorer to display the form.

Start your upgrades to this program by adding two dialog box controls to the component tray that contains the main menu object. The *OpenFileDialog* control will let your program open bitmap files, and the *ColorDialog* control will enable your program to change the color of the clock output. Dialog box controls appear in the component tray because they don't appear on the form at runtime.

2   Click the *OpenFileDialog* control on the Windows Forms tab of the Toolbox, and then click the component tray containing the main menu object.

> ▶   **Note**   If you don't see the *OpenFileDialog* in the Toolbox, it might be lower in the Toolbox list hidden from your view. To scroll down in the Toolbox list, click the down scroll arrow next to the Clipboard Ring tab.

An open file dialog object appears in the component tray.

3   Click the *ColorDialog* control on the Windows Forms tab of the Toolbox, and then click the component tray below the form again.

The component tray now looks like this:

Just like the main menu object, the open file dialog and color dialog objects can be customized with property settings.

Now you'll create a picture box object by using the *PictureBox* control. As you've seen, the picture box object displays artwork on a form. This time, you'll display artwork in the picture box by using the open file dialog box.

Add a picture box object

1   Click the *PictureBox* control in the Toolbox.
2   Draw a picture box object on the form, below the label.
3   Use the Properties window to set the *SizeMode* property of the picture box to StretchImage.

Now you'll use the Menu Designer to add a File menu to the program.

Add a File menu

1   Click the Clock menu on the form, and then click the Type Here tag to the right of the menu.

Now you'll add to the program a File menu that includes Open, Close, and Exit commands.

2   Type **&File** to create a File menu with the letter "F" as an access key.

3   Press the Down Arrow key, and then type **&Open...** to create an Open... command with the letter "O" as an access key.

The Open command will be used to open Windows bitmaps. Because the command will display a dialog box, you added an ellipsis to the command name.

4   Press the Down Arrow key, and then type **&Close** to create a Close command with the letter "C" as an access key.

The Close command will be used to close bitmap files in your program.

5   Press the Down Arrow key, and then type **E&xit** to create an Exit command with the letter "x" as an access key.

The Exit command will be used to close the program. Notice that in this case, the second letter of the Exit command was used as an access key, which matches how Exit is used in most Windows applications (such as Microsoft Word).

6   Drag the File menu on top of the Clock menu to move it to the first position.

You can move entire menus, as well as menu commands, with the Menu Designer. It makes sense to have the File menu be the first menu in your program.

Your form should look like this:

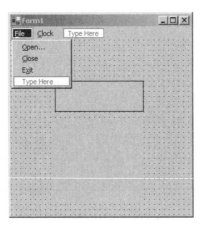

Changing the Object Names for Items on the File Menu

As I mentioned earlier in the chapter, you can change the name of objects on your form, including the names of menu item objects, by changing the *Name* property for each object that you want. The *Name* property doesn't change how an object looks at runtime, or what it displays for the user to see, but it does make objects more readable and recognizable in your program code. Practice changing the names of the objects on the new File menu now so that you can recognize them more clearly in your program code. In future chapters, you'll routinely change the names of the objects you use often.

Change the object names

1   Click the File menu item, open the Properties window, and change the *Name* property to **mnuFile**. (The *Name* property appears in the Design category and is enclosed by parentheses.)

Most programmers begin the names of their objects with a three-character extension that identifies what control or object library the object is related to or derived from. I've used *mnu* here to identify this object as a menu item, and I've used the word *File* to remind myself that the object is the File menu on the menu bar. In future chapters, you'll use other three-character extensions to identify different types of objects.

2   Click the Open…menu item, and change its *Name* property to **mnuOpenItem**.

3   Click the Close menu item, and change its *Name* property to **mnuCloseItem**.

4   Click the Exit menu item, and change its *Name* property to **mnuExitItem**.

5   Click the Save All button on the Standard toolbar to save your changes.

These names will make your program easier to understand, and you can name the other objects in your project now if you like. (Good candidates would be the label object, the picture box object, and the other menu items.) But as I indicated, naming objects is optional, and the three-character prefix I recommended for menus is just an industry convention that some Visual Basic programmers follow.

Disabling a Menu Command

In a typical application for Windows, not all menu commands are available at the same time. In a typical Edit menu, for example, the Paste command is available only when there is data on the Clipboard. You can disable a menu item by setting the *Enabled* property for the menu object to False. When a command is disabled, it appears in dimmed type on the menu bar.

In the following exercise, you'll disable the Close command on the File menu. (Close is a command that can be used only after a file has been opened in the program.) Later in the chapter, you'll include a statement in the Open command event procedure that enables the Close command at the proper time.

Disable the Close command

1   Click the Close command on the Menu program's File menu.

2   Open the Properties window, and set the *Enabled* property for the *mnuCloseItem* object to False.

Now you'll add a Text Color command to the Clock menu to demonstrate how the color dialog box works. The color dialog box returns a color setting to the program through the *Color* property. You'll use that property to change the color of the text in the *Label1* object.

Add the Text Color command to the Clock menu

1   Click the Clock menu, and then click the Type Here tag at the bottom of it.

2   Type **Text Co&lor...** to add a Text Color command to the menu with an access key of "l".

The command Text Color is added to the Clock menu. The command contains a trailing ellipsis to indicate that it will display a dialog box when the user clicks it. The access key chosen for this command is "l" because "T" is already used in the menu, for Time. Your access keys won't behave correctly if you use duplicate keys at the same level within a particular menu or duplicate keys at the menu bar level.

3   Use the Properties window to change the *Name* property of the Text Color command to **mnuTextColorItem**.

Event Procedures That Manage Common Dialog Boxes

To display a dialog box in a program, you need to type the dialog box name with the *ShowDialog* method in an event procedure associated with the menu command. If necessary, you must also set one or more dialog box properties by using program code before opening the dialog box. Finally, you need to use program code to respond to the user's dialog box selections after the dialog box has been manipulated and closed. In the following exercise, you'll type in the program code for the *mnuOpenItem_Click* event procedure, the routine that executes when the Open command is clicked. You'll set the *Filter* property in the *OpenFileDialog1* object to define the file type in the Open common dialog box. (You'll specify Windows bitmaps.) Then you'll use the *ShowDialog* method to display the open file dialog box. After the user has selected a file and closed this dialog box, you'll display the file he or she selects in a picture box by setting the *Image* property of the picture box object to the filename the user selected. Finally you'll enable the Close command so that the user can unload the picture if he or she wants.

Edit the Open command event procedure

1   Double-click the Open command on the Menu project's File menu.

The *mnuOpenItem_Click* event procedure appears in the Code Editor.

2   Type the following program statements in the event procedure, between the *Private Sub* and *End Sub* statements. Be sure to type each line exactly as it's printed here, and press the Down Arrow key after the last line.

```
OpenFileDialog1.Filter = "Bitmaps (*.bmp)|*.bmp"
If OpenFileDialog1.ShowDialog() = DialogResult.OK Then
    PictureBox1.Image = System.Drawing.Image.FromFile _
        (OpenFileDialog1.FileName)
    mnuCloseItem.Enabled = True
End If
```

Your screen should look like the illustration shown here:

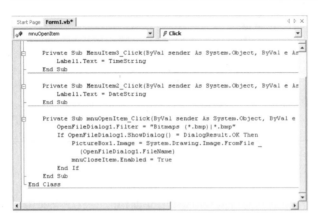

The first three statements in the event procedure refer to three different proper-ties of the open file dialog object. The first statement uses the *Filter* property to define a list of valid files. (In this case, the list has only one item: *.bmp.) This is important for the Open dialog box because a picture box object is designed for six types of files: bitmaps (.bmp files), Windows metafiles (.emf and .wmf files), icons (.ico files), Joint Photographic Experts Group format (.jpg and .jpeg files), Portable Network Graphics format (.png files), and Graphics Interchange For-mat (.gif files). (Attempting to display a .txt file in an image object would cause a runtime error, for example.) To add additional items to the *Filter* list, you can type a pipe symbol (|) between items. For example,

```
OpenFileDialog1.Filter = "Bitmaps (*.bmp)|*.bmp|Metafiles (*.wmf)|*.wmf"
```

allows both bitmaps and Windows metafiles to be chosen in the Open dialog box.

The second statement in the event procedure displays the Open dialog box in the program. *ShowDialog* is similar to the *Show* method in Visual Basic 6, but it can be used with any Windows Form. The *ShowDialog* method returns a result, named *DialogResult*, which indicates the button on the dialog box the user clicked. To determine whether the user clicked the Open button, an If…Then decision structure is used to check whether the returned result equals *DialogResult.OK*. If it does, a valid bmp file path should be stored in the *File-Name* property of the open file dialog object. (You'll learn more about the syntax of If…Then decision structures in Chapter 6.)

The third statement uses the filename selected in the dialog box by the user. When the user selects a drive, folder, and filename and then clicks Open, the complete path is passed to the program through the *OpenFileDialog1.FileName* property. The *System.Drawing.Image.FromFile* method, a method that loads electronic artwork, is then used to copy the specified Windows bitmap into the picture box object. (I wrapped this statement with the line continuation charac-ter because it was rather long.)

The fourth statement in the procedure enables the Close command on the File menu. Now that a file has been opened in the program, the Close command should be available so that users can close the file.

Now you'll type in the program code for the *mnuCloseItem_Click* event procedure, the routine that runs when the Close command on the File menu is clicked.

Edit the Close command event procedure

1 Display the form again, and then double-click the Close command on the File menu.

The event procedure for the Close command appears in the Code Editor.

2 Type the following program statements in the event procedure, between the *Private Sub* and *End Sub* statements:

```
PictureBox1.Image = Nothing
mnuCloseItem.Enabled = False
```

The first statement closes the open Windows bitmap by clearing the picture box object's *Image* property. The *Nothing* keyword is used here to disassociate the current bitmap object from the *Image* property—in other words, *Nothing* sets the property to zero, and the picture disappears. (You'll use *Nothing* later in this book to reset other object variables and properties, too.) The second statement dims the Close command on the File menu because there's no longer an open file. This program statement is the equivalent of using the Properties window to change the *Enabled* property from True to False.

Now you'll type in the program code for the *mnuExitItem_Click* event procedure, the routine that stops the program when the Exit command on the File menu is clicked.

Edit the Exit command event procedure

1 Display the form again, and then double-click the Exit command on the File menu.

The event procedure for the Exit command appears in the Code Editor.

2 Type the following program statement in the event procedure, between the *Private Sub* and *End Sub* statements:

```
End
```

The *End* statement stops the program when the user is finished. (It might look familiar by now.)

Menus and Dialog Boxes

Edit the Text Color command event procedure

1   Display the form again, and then double-click the new Text Color command on the Clock menu.

    The event procedure for the Text Color command appears in the Code Editor.

2   Type the following program statements in the event procedure:

```
ColorDialog1.ShowDialog()
Label1.ForeColor = ColorDialog1.Color
```

> ▶ **Note**   The Color dialog box can be used to set the color of any user interface element that supports color. Other possibilities include the form background color, the colors of shapes on the form, and the foreground and background colors of objects.

The first program statement uses the *ShowDialog* method to open the color dialog box. As you learned earlier in this chapter, *ShowDialog* is the method you use to open any form as a dialog box, including a form created by one of the standard dialog box controls that Visual Studio provides. The second statement in the event procedure assigns color that the user selected in the dialog box to the *Fore-Color* property of the *Label1* object. You might remember *Label1* from earlier in this chapter—it's the label box you used to display the current time and date on the form. You'll use the color returned from the color dialog box to set the color of the text in the label.

3   Click the Save All button on the Standard toolbar to save your changes.

Controlling Color Choices by Setting Color Dialog Box Properties

If you want to further customize the color dialog box, you can control just what color choices the dialog box presents to the user when the dialog box opens. You can adjust these color settings by using the Properties window, or by setting properties by using program code before you display the dialog box with the *ShowDialog* method. The following table describes the most useful properties of the *ColorDialog* control. Each property should be set with a value of True to enable the option or False to disable the option.

Property	Meaning
AllowFullOpen	Set to True to enable the Define Custom Colors button in the dialog box.
AnyColor	Set to True if the user can select any color shown in the dialog box.
FullOpen	Set to True if you want to display the Custom Colors area when the dialog box first opens.
ShowHelp	Set to True if you want to enable the Help button in the dialog box.
SolidColorOnly	Set to True if you want the user to select only solid colors (dithered colors will be disabled).

Now you'll run the Menu program and experiment with the menus and dialog boxes you've created. The complete program is located in the c:\vbnet03sbs\chap04\dialog folder.

Run the Menu program

1 Click the Start button on the Standard toolbar.

The program runs, and both the File and Clock menus appear on the menu bar.

2 On the form's File menu, click Open.

The Open dialog box appears. It looks great, doesn't it? Notice the Bitmaps (*.bmp) entry in the Files Of Type box. You defined this entry with the statement

```
OpenFileDialog1.Filter = "Bitmaps (*.bmp)|*.bmp"
```

in the *mnuOpenItem_Click* event procedure. The first part of the text in quotes—Bitmaps (*.bmp)—specifies which items are listed in the Files Of Type box. The second part—*.bmp—specifies the file-name extension of the files that are to be listed in the dialog box.

3 Open the c:\windows folder (or c:\winnt folder) on your hard disk, and browse through the long list of folders to get to the bitmap files.

A standard collection of bitmaps appears. Most of these files were included with Windows, and you might have added to the collection yourself.

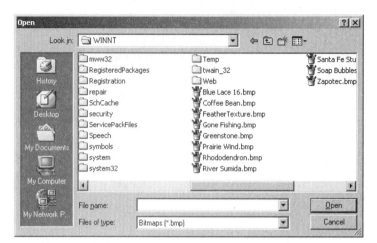

4   Select one of the bitmap files, and then click the Open button.

A picture of the bitmap appears in the picture box. (I've selected the FeatherTexture.bmp file.) Your form looks like this:

Now you'll practice using the Clock menu.

5   On the Clock menu, click the Time command.

The current time appears in the label box.

6   On the Clock menu, click the Text Color command.

The Color dialog box appears, as shown here:

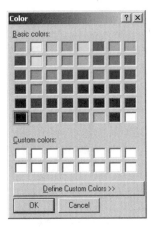

The Color dialog box contains elements that let you change the color of the clock text in your program. The current color setting, black, is selected.

7   Click the blue box, and then click the OK button.

The Color dialog box closes, and the color of the text in the clock label changes to blue, as shown here:

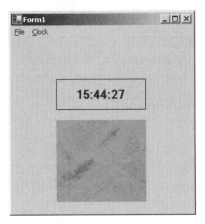

8   On the Clock menu, click the Date command.

The current date is displayed in blue type. Now that the text color has been set in the label, it will remain blue until the color is changed again or the program closes.

9   Click the File menu.

Notice that the Close command is now enabled. (You enabled it in the *mnuOpenItem_Click* event procedure by using the statement `mnuCloseItem.Enabled = True`.)

10 Press C (the access key for Close) to close the bitmap image.

The file closes, and the Windows bitmap is removed. (This is the *Nothing* keyword at work.)

11 Click the File menu.

The Close command is now dimmed because there's no bitmap in the picture box.

12 Click the Exit command.

The program closes, and the Visual Studio development environment appears.

Adding Nonstandard Dialog Boxes to Programs

What if you need to add a dialog box to your program that isn't provided by one of the seven dialog box controls in Visual Studio? No problem—but you'll need to do a little extra design work. As you'll learn in future chapters, a Visual Basic program can use more than one form to receive and display information. To create nonstandard dialog boxes, you'll need to add new forms to your program, add input and output objects, and process the dialog box clicks in your program code. (These techniques will be discussed in Chapter 15.) In the next chapter, you'll learn how to use two handy dialog boxes that are specifically designed for receiving text input (*InputBox*) and displaying text output (*MsgBox*). These dialog boxes will help bridge the gap between the dialog box controls and the dialog boxes that you need to create on your own.

That's it! You've learned several important commands and techniques for creating menus and dialog boxes in your programs. After you learn more about program code, you'll be able to put these skills to work in your own programs.

One Step Further:
Assigning Shortcut Keys to Menus

The *MainMenu* control also lets you assign *shortcut keys* to your menus. Shortcut keys are key combinations that a user can press to activate a command without using the menu bar. For example, on a typical Edit menu in an application for Windows (Microsoft Word), you can copy selected text to the Clipboard by pressing Ctrl+C. The *MainMenu* control's *Shortcut* property allows you to customize this setting. Try assigning two shortcut keys to the Clock menu in the Menu program now.

Assign shortcut keys to the Clock menu

1   Make sure that your program has stopped running and is in design mode.

You can modify a program only when it isn't running.

2   Click the Clock menu, and then click the Time command to high-light it.

Before you set the shortcut key for a menu command, you must select it. You assign a shortcut key by setting the *Shortcut* property for the command by using the Properties window. The main menu object provides many standard shortcut key settings for you auto-matically.

You'll assign Ctrl+T as the shortcut key for the Time command.

3   Open the Properties window, click the *Shortcut* property, click the drop-down arrow in the second column, scroll down the list of short-cut key settings, and then click CtrlT.

The Properties window will look like this:

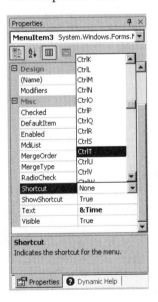

> ▶ **Tip**   Visual Basic normally displays the shortcut key combination in the menu when you run the program, to give users a hint about which keys to press. To hide shortcut key combinations from the user (if you're running out of space), set the *ShowShortcut* property to False. The shortcut key will still work, but users won't see a visual reminder for it.

4   Click the Date command, and then change its *Shortcut* property setting to CtrlD.

Now you'll run the program and try the shortcut keys.

5   Click the Start button on the Standard toolbar.

6   Press Ctrl+T to run the Time command.

The current time appears in the program.

7   Press Ctrl+D to run the Date command.

The current date appears in the program.

8   Click the Clock menu.

The shortcut keys are listed beside the Time and Date commands, as shown in the following illustration. Visual Basic adds these key combinations when you define the shortcuts by using the *Shortcut* property.

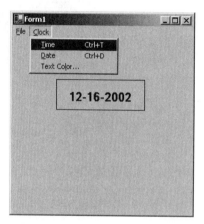

9   On the program's File menu, click the Exit command.

The program stops, and the development environment appears.

Lesson 4 Quick Reference

To	Do this
Create a menu item	Click the *MainMenu* control, and draw a menu on your form. Click the Type Here tag on your form, and type the name of the menu.
Add an access key to a menu item	Click the menu item twice to display the text-editing cursor, and then type an ampersand (&) before the letter you want to use as an access key.
Assign a shortcut key to a menu item	Set the *Shortcut* property of the menu item using the Properties window. A list of common shortcut keys is provided.
Change the order of menu items	Drag the menu item you want to move to a new location.
Use a standard dialog box in your program	Add one of the seven standard dialog box controls to your form, and then customize it with property settings and program code.
Display an open file dialog box	Add the *OpenFileDialog* control to your form. Display the dialog box with the *ShowDialog* method. The *FileName* property contains the name of the file selected.
Display a Color dialog box	Add the *ColorDialog* control to your form. Display the dialog box with the *ShowDialog* method. The *Color* property contains the color the user selected.
Disable a menu	Set the *Enabled* property of a menu item to False using the Properties window.
Enable a menu command by using program code	Use the program statement `mnuCloseItem.Enabled = True` but substitute your command name for *mnuCloseItem*.
Clear an image from a picture box	Use the program statement `PictureBox1.Image = Nothing`

Part

2

Programming Fundamentals

Visual Basic .NET Variables and Operators

In this chapter, you will learn how to:

- Use variables to store data in your programs.
- Get input by using the *InputBox* function.
- Display messages by using the *MsgBox* function.
- Work with different data types.
- Use mathematical operators and functions in formulas.
- Use the math methods in the *System.Math* class of the .NET Framework.
- Use variables and operators

In Part 1, you learned how to create the user interface of a Microsoft Visual Basic .NET program and how to build and run a program in the Microsoft Visual Studio development environment. In the next five chapters, you'll learn more about Visual Basic program code—the statements and keywords that form the core of a Visual Basic program. After you complete Part 2, you'll be ready for more advanced topics.

In this chapter, you'll learn how to use variables to store data temporarily in your program and how to use mathematical operators to perform tasks such as addition and multiplication. You'll also learn how to use mathematical functions to perform calculations involving numbers, and you'll use the *InputBox* and *MsgBox* functions to gather and present information by using dialog boxes. Finally, you'll get your first real look at using classes in the .NET Framework to perform useful work in a program.

Upgrade Notes: What's New in Visual Basic .NET?

If you're experienced with Visual Basic 6, you'll notice some new features in Visual Basic .NET, including the following:

■ To encourage better programming practices and cleaner program code, all Visual Basic .NET variables must be declared before they're used. The implicit declaration of variables (using variables without declaring them) is allowed only if you use the *Option Explicit Off* statement—a practice that's discouraged.

■ Visual Basic no longer supports the *Variant* data type. You should declare all variables using *Dim* and the keyword *As* to identify the type of data that they'll hold.

■ There are several new fundamental data types, and some of the older data types now support different ranges. For example, there's a 16-bit *Short* data type, a 32-bit *Integer* data type, and a 64-bit *Long* data type. The Visual Basic 6 *Currency* data type has been replaced with the *Decimal* data type.

■ Visual Basic .NET includes a new statement named *Option Strict*. When *Option Strict* is turned on, variables usually need to be the same type if they're added, compared, or combined. (Sometimes variables can be different types, as long as there won't be any data loss.) This means that type conversion is more important in Visual Basic .NET than in Visual Basic 6, and you'll need to become familiar with type conversion functions such as *CInt*, *CLng*, and *CType* to make different types of data compatible. As you upgrade your applications, you can use the *Option Strict Off* statement to continue combining data types as you did in Visual Basic 6 (permitting what's known as *automatic type coercion*), but this feature should be used sparingly and not relied on for future versions of Visual Basic .NET.

■ There are now shortcuts for mathematical operations with some arithmetic operators, such as addition (+), subtraction (-), and multiplication (*). These shortcuts allow you to write a formula such as X = X + 2 using the syntax X += 2.

■ Visual Basic .NET no longer provides built-in keywords (such as *Abs* or *Cos*) for mathematical operations. Instead, you must use the methods in the *System.Math* class library of the .NET Framework for mathematical functions. The functionality of these methods is similar to the familiar Visual Basic 6 functions, although a few names have changed (for example, *Sqr* is now *Sqrt*).

■ Visual Studio includes a *MessageBox* object, which is an alternative to the *MsgBox* function for displaying message boxes. To display a message box, you use the *MessageBox.Show* method.

The Anatomy of a Visual Basic Program Statement

As you learned in Chapter 2, a line of code in a Visual Basic program is called a *program statement*. A program statement is any combination of Visual Basic keywords, properties, functions, operators, and symbols that collectively create a valid instruction recognized by the Visual Basic compiler. A complete program statement can be a simple keyword, such as

```
End
```

which halts the execution of a Visual Basic program, or it can be a combination of elements, such as the following statement, which uses the *TimeString* property to assign the current system time to the *Text* property of the *Label1* object:

```
Label1.Text = TimeString
```

The rules of construction that must be used when you build a programming statement are called statement *syntax*. Visual Basic shares many of its syntax rules with earlier versions of the BASIC programming language and with other language compilers. The trick to writing good program statements is learning the syntax of the most useful language elements and then using those elements correctly to process the data in your program. Fortunately, Visual Basic does a lot of the toughest work for you, so the time you spend writing program code will be relatively short, and the results can be used again in future programs.

In the following chapters, you'll learn the most important Visual Basic keywords and program statements, as well as many of the objects, properties, and methods provided by Visual Studio controls and the .NET Framework. You'll find that these keywords and objects will complement nicely the programming skills you've already learned and will help you write powerful programs in the future. Variables and data types, the first topics, are critical features of nearly every program.

Using Variables to Store Information

A *variable* is a temporary storage location for data in your program. You can use one or many variables in your code, and they can contain words, numbers, dates, or properties. Variables are useful because they let you assign a short and easy-to-remember name to each piece of data you plan to work with. Variables can hold information entered by the user at runtime, the result of a specific calculation, or a piece of data you want to display on your form. In short, variables are handy containers that you can use to store and track almost any type of information.

Using variables in a Visual Basic .NET program requires some planning. Before you can use a variable, you must set aside memory in the computer for the variable's use. This process is a little like reserving a seat at the theater or a baseball game. I'll cover the process of making reservations for, or *declaring*, a variable in the next section.

Setting Aside Space for Variables: The *Dim* Statement

In Visual Basic .NET, you must explicitly declare your variables before using them. This is a change from earlier versions of Visual Basic, where (under certain circumstances) you could declare variables implicitly—in other words, simply by using them and without a *Dim* statement. This was a flexible but rather risky practice—it created the potential for variable confusion and misspelled variable names, which introduced potential bugs into the code that might (or might not) be discovered later.

To declare a variable in Visual Basic .NET, type the variable name after the *Dim* statement. (Dim stands for *dimension*.) This declaration reserves room in memory for the variable when the program runs, and it lets Visual Basic know what type of data it should expect to see later. Although this declaration can be done at any place in the program code (as long as the declaration happens before the variable is used), most programmers declare variables in one place at the top of their event procedures or code modules.

For example, the following statement creates space for a variable named *LastName* in a program that will hold a textual, or *string*, value:

```
Dim LastName As String
```

Note that in addition to identifying the variable by name, I've used the *As* keyword to give the variable a particular type, and I've identified the type by using the keyword *String*. (You'll learn about other data types later in this chapter.) A string variable contains textual information: words, letters, symbols—even numbers. I find myself using string variables a lot; they hold names, places, lines from a poem, the contents of a file, and many other "wordy" data. Why do you need to declare variables? Visual Basic wants you to identify the name and the type of your variables in advance so that the compiler can set aside the memory the program will need to store and process the information held in variables. Memory management might not seem like a big deal to you (after all, modern personal computers have lots of RAM and gigabytes of free hard disk space), but in some programs, memory usage can be consumed quickly, and it's a good practice to take memory allocation seriously even as you take your first steps as a programmer. As you'll soon see, different types of variables have different space requirements and size limitations.

▶ **Note**   In some earlier versions of Visual Basic, specific variable types (such as *String* or *Integer*) weren't required—information was simply held using a generic (and memory hungry) data type called *Variant*, which could hold data of any size or format. Variants are no longer supported in Visual Basic .NET. Although they were handy for beginning programmers, the way they were designed made them slow and inefficient, and they allowed variables to be converted from one type to another too easily—causing unexpected results.

After you declare a variable, you're free to assign information to it in your code by using the assignment operator (=). For example, the following program statement assigns the last name "Jefferson" to the *LastName* variable:

```
LastName = "Jefferson"
```

Note that I was careful to assign a textual value to the *LastName* variable because it's of the type *String*. I could also assign values with spaces, symbols, or numbers to the variable, such as

```
LastName = "1313 Mockingbird Lane"
```

but the variable would still be considered a string value. The number portion could only be used in a mathematical formula if it were first converted to an integer or a floating-point value using one of a handful of conversion functions I'll discuss later in this book.

After the *LastName* variable is assigned a value, it can be used in place of the name "Jefferson" in your code. For example, the assignment statement

```
Label1.Text = LastName
```

would display Jefferson in the first label (*Label1*) on your form.

▶ **Note**   If you really want to declare variables "the old way" in Visual Basic .NET, that is, without explicitly declaring them using the *Dim* statement, you can place the statement `Option Explicit Off` at the very top of your form or module's program code (before any event procedures), and it will defeat Visual Basic's default requirement that variables be declared before they're used. I don't recommend this statement as a permanent addition to your code, but you might find it useful temporarily as you convert older Visual Basic programs to Visual Studio .NET.

Using Variables in a Program

Variables can maintain the same value throughout a program, or they can change values several times, depending on your needs. The following exercise demonstrates how a variable named *LastName* can contain different text values and how the variable can be assigned to object properties.

Change the value of a variable

1   Start Visual Studio.

2   On the File menu, point to Open, and then click Project.

The Open Project dialog box appears.

3   Open the Variable Test project in the c:\vbnet03sbs\chap05\variable test folder.

4   If the project's form isn't visible, click Form1.vb in Solution Explorer, and then click the View Designer button.

The Variable Test form appears in the Windows Forms Designer. Variable Test is a *skeleton program*—it contains a form with labels and buttons for displaying output, but little program code. You'll add code in this exercise.

The Variable Test form looks like this:

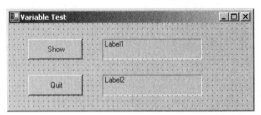

The form contains two labels and two buttons. You'll use variables to display information in each of the labels.

▶   **Note**   The label objects look like boxes because I set their *BorderStyle* properties to Fixed3D.

5   Double-click the Show button.

The *Button1_Click* event procedure appears in the Code Editor.

6   Type the following program statements to declare and use the *Last-Name* variable:

```
Dim LastName As String

LastName = "Luther"
Label1.Text = LastName

LastName = "Bodenstein von Karlstadt"
Label2.Text = LastName
```

The program statements are arranged in three groups. The first statement declares the *LastName* variable by using the *Dim* statement and the *String* type. The second and third lines assign the name "Luther" to the *LastName* variable and then display this name in the first label on the form. This example demonstrates one of the most common uses of variables in a program—transferring information to a property.

The fourth line assigns the name "Bodenstein von Karlstadt" to the *LastName* variable (in other words, it changes the contents of the variable). Notice that the second string is longer than the first and contains a few blank spaces. When you assign text strings to variables, or use them in other places, you need to enclose the text within quotation marks. (You don't need to do this with numbers.)

Finally, keep in mind another important characteristic of the variables being declared in this event procedure—they maintain their *scope*, or hold their value, only within the event procedure you're using them in. Later in this chapter, you'll learn how to declare variables so that they can be used in any of your form's event procedures.

7 Click the Form1.vb [Design] tab to display the form again.

8 Double-click the Quit button.

The *Button2_Click* event procedure appears in the Code Editor.

9 Type the following program statement to stop the program:

```
End
```

Your screen should look like this:

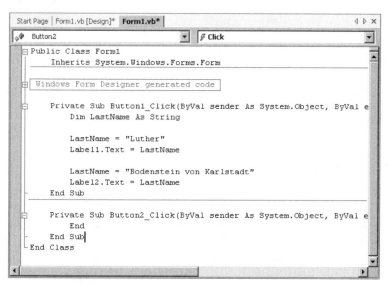

10 Click the Save All button to save your changes.

11 Click the Start button on the Standard toolbar to run the program.

The program runs in the development environment.

12 Click the Show button.

The program declares the variable, assigns two values to it, and copies each value to the appropriate label on the form. The program produces the following output:

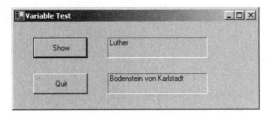

13 Click the Quit button to stop the program.

The program stops, and the development environment returns.

Variable Naming Conventions

Naming variables can be a little tricky because you need to use names that are short but intuitive and easy to remember. To avoid confusion, use the following conventions when naming variables:

Begin each variable name with a letter. With the exception of the underscore, this is a Visual Basic requirement. Variable names can contain only letters, numbers, and underscores.

Although variable names can be virtually any length, try to keep them under 33 characters to make them easier to read. (Variable names were limited to 255 characters in Visual Basic 6, but that's no longer a constraint.)

Make your variable names descriptive by combining one or more words when it makes sense to do so. For example, the variable name *SalesTaxRate* is much clearer than *Tax* or *Rate*.

Use a combination of uppercase and lowercase characters and numbers if you want. An accepted convention is to capitalize the first letter of each word in a variable; for example, *DateOfBirth*. However, some programmers prefer to use so-called *camel casing* (making the first letter of a variable name lowercase) to distinguish variable names from functions and module names (which usually do begin with uppercase letters). Examples of camel casing include *dateOfBirth*, *employeeName*, and *counter*.

Don't use Visual Basic keywords, objects, or properties as variable names. If you do, you'll get an error when you try to run your program.

(Optional) Begin each variable name with a two- or three-character abbreviation corresponding to the type of data that's stored in the variable. For example, use *strName* to show that the *Name* variable contains string data. Although you don't need to worry too much about this detail now, you should make a note of this convention for later—you'll see it in the Visual Studio online Help and in many of the advanced books about Visual Basic programming. (This convention and abbreviation scheme was originally created by Microsoft Distinguished Engineer Charles Simonyi and is sometimes called the Hungarian Naming Convention.)

Using a Variable to Store Input

One practical use for a variable is to hold information input from the user. Although you can often use an object such as a list box or a text box to retrieve this information, at times you might want to deal directly with the user and save the input in a variable rather than in a property. One way to retrieve input is to use the *InputBox* function to display a dialog box on the screen, and then use a variable to store the text the user types. You'll try this approach in the following example.

Get input by using *InputBox*

1   On the File menu, point to Open, and then click Project.
    The Open Project dialog box appears.

2   Open the Input Box project in the c:\vbnet03sbs\chap05\input box folder.
    The Input Box project opens in the development environment. Input Box is a skeleton program.

3   If the project's form isn't visible, click Form1.vb in Solution Explorer, and then click the View Designer button.
    The form contains one label and two buttons. You'll use the *Input-Box* function to get input from the user, and then you'll display the input in the label on the form.

4   Double-click the Input Box button.
    The *Button1_Click* event procedure appears in the Code Editor.

5   Type the following program statements to declare two variables and call the *InputBox* function:

```
Dim Prompt, FullName As String
Prompt = "Please enter your name."

FullName = InputBox(Prompt)
Label1.Text = FullName
```

This time, you're declaring two variables by using the *Dim* statement: *Prompt* and *FullName*. Both variables are declared using the *String* type. (You can declare as many variables as you want on the same line, as long as they're of the same type.) Note that in Visual Basic 6, this same syntax would have produced different results. *Dim* would create the *Prompt* variable using the *Variant* type (because no type was specified), and *Dim* would create the *FullName* variable using the *String* type. But this logical inconsistency has been fixed in Visual Basic .NET.

The second line in the event procedure assigns a text string to the *Prompt* variable. This message will be used as a text *argument* for the *InputBox* function. (An argument is a value or an expression passed to a procedure or a function.) The next line calls the *Input-Box* function and assigns the result of the call (the text string the user enters) to the *FullName* variable. *InputBox* is a special Visual Basic function that displays a dialog box on the screen and prompts the user for input. In addition to a prompt string, the *InputBox* function supports other arguments you might want to use occasionally. Consult the Visual Basic online Help for details.

After *InputBox* has returned a text string to the program, the fourth statement in the procedure places the user's name in the *Text* property of the *Label1* object, which displays it on the form.

▶ **Note**   In older versions of BASIC, the *InputBox* function was spelled with a $ character at the end to help programmers remember that the function returned information in the string ($) data type. String variables were also identified with the $ symbol on occasion. These days we don't use type character abbreviations. *String* ($), *Integer* (%), and the other type abbreviations are relics.

6   Save your changes.

Do you remember which toolbar button to click to save your project? See step 10 of the previous exercise if you've forgotten.

7   Click the Start button on the Standard toolbar to run the program.

The program runs in the development environment.

8   Click the Input Box button.

Visual Basic executes the *Button1_Click* event procedure, and the Input Box dialog box appears on your screen, as shown here:

9   Type your full name, and then click OK.

The *InputBox* function returns your name to the program and places it in the *FullName* variable. The program then uses the variable to display your name on the form, as shown here:

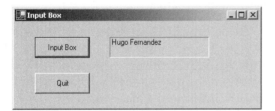

Use the *InputBox* function in your programs anytime you want to prompt the user for information. You can use this function in combination with the other input controls to regulate the flow of data into and out of a program. In the next exercise, you'll learn how to use a similar function to display text in a dialog box.

10   Click the Quit button on the form to stop the program.

The program stops, and the development environment returns.

What Is a Function?

InputBox is a special Visual Basic keyword known as a *function*. A function is a statement that performs meaningful work (such as prompting the user for information or calculating an equation) and then returns a result to the program. The value returned by a function can be assigned to a variable, as it was in the Input Box program, or it can be assigned to a property or another statement or function. Visual Basic functions often use one or more arguments to define their activities. For example, the *InputBox* function you just executed used the *Prompt* variable to display dialog box instructions for the user. When a function uses more than one argument, commas separate the arguments, and the whole group of arguments is enclosed in parentheses. The following statement shows a function call that has two arguments:

```
FullName = InputBox(Prompt, Title)
```

Using a Variable for Output

You can display the contents of a variable by assigning the variable to a property (such as the *Text* property of a label object) or by passing the variable as an argument to a dialog box function. One useful dialog box function for displaying output is the *MsgBox* function. When you call the *MsgBox* function, it displays a dialog box, sometimes called a *message box*, with various options that you can specify. Like *InputBox*, it takes one or more arguments as input, and the results of the function call can be assigned to a variable. The syntax for the *MsgBox* function is

```
ButtonClicked = MsgBox(Prompt, Buttons, Title)
```

where *Prompt* is the text to be displayed in the message box, *Buttons* is a number that specifies the buttons, icons, and other options to display for the message box, and *Title* is the text displayed in the message box title bar. The variable *ButtonClicked* is assigned the result returned by the function, which indicates which button the user clicked in the dialog box.

If you're just displaying a message using the *MsgBox* function, the *Button-Clicked* variable, the assignment operator (=), the *Buttons* argument, and the *Title* argument are optional. You'll be using the *Title* argument, but you won't be using the others in the following exercise; for more information about them (including the different buttons you can include in *MsgBox* and a few more options), search for *MsgBox* in Visual Basic online Help.

▶ **Note**   Visual Basic .NET provides both the *MsgBox* function and the *Message-Box* class for displaying text on a form using a dialog box. The *MessageBox* class is part of the *System.Windows.Forms* namespace, takes arguments much like *MsgBox*, and is displayed using the *Show* method. I'll use both *MsgBox* and *MessageBox* in this book.

Now you'll add a *MsgBox* function to the Input Box program to display the name the user enters in the Input Box dialog box.

Display a message by using *MsgBox*

1   If the Code Editor isn't visible, double-click the Input Box button on the Input Box form.

The *Button1_Click* event procedure appears in the Code Editor. (This is the code you entered in the last exercise.)

2   Select the following statement in the event procedure (the last line):

```
Label1.Text = FullName
```

This is the statement that displays the contents of the *FullName* variable in the label.

3 Press the Delete key to delete the line.

The statement is removed from the Code Editor.

4 Type the following line into the event procedure as a replacement:

```
MsgBox(FullName, , "Input Results")
```

This new statement will call the *MsgBox* function, display the contents of the *FullName* variable in the dialog box, and place the words *Input Results* in the title bar. (The optional *Buttons* argument and the *ButtonClicked* variable are irrelevant here and have been omitted.) Your event procedure should look like this:

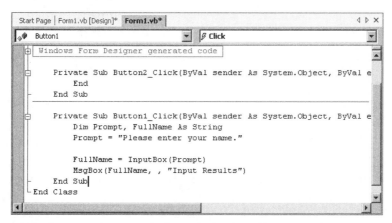

5 Click the Start button on the Standard toolbar.

6 Click the Input Box button, type your name in the input box, and then click OK.

Visual Basic stores the input in the program in the *FullName* variable and then displays it in a message box. Your screen should look similar to this:

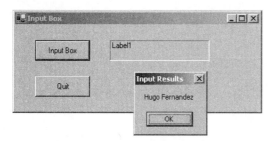

7   Click OK to close the message box. Then click Quit to close the program.

The program closes, and the development environment returns.

▶ **Note**   You might have noticed that when you run a Visual Basic program, Visual Studio .NET automatically saves your project before it starts the compiler and displays your opening form. This is a safety feature that should prevent data loss if something unexpected were to happen during the compilation.

Working with Specific Data Types

The *String* data type is useful for managing text in your programs, but what about numbers, dates, and other types of information? To allow for the efficient memory management of all types of data, Visual Basic provides several additional data types that you can use for your variables. Many of these are familiar data types from earlier versions of BASIC or Visual Basic, and some of the data types are new or have been changed in Visual Studio .NET to allow for the efficient processing of data in newer 64-bit computers.

The following table lists the fundamental (or elementary) data types in Visual Basic .NET. You'll gain a performance advantage in your programs if you choose the right data type for your variables—a size that's neither too big nor too small. In the next exercise, you'll see how several of these data types work.

▶ **Note**   Variable storage size is measured in bits. The amount of space required to store one standard (ASCII) keyboard character in memory is 8 bits, which equals 1 byte.

Data type	Size	Range	Sample usage
Short	16-bit	−32,768 through 32,767	`Dim Birds As Short` `Birds = 12500`
Integer	32-bit	−2,147,483,648 through 2,147,483,647	`Dim Insects As Integer` `Insects = 37500000`
Long	64-bit	−9,223,372,036,854,775,808 to 9,223,372,036,854,775,807	`Dim WorldPop As Long` `WorldPop = 4800000004`
Single	32-bit floating point	−3.4028235E38 through 3.4028235E38	`Dim Price As Single` `Price = 899.99`
Double	64-bit floating point	−1.79769313486231E308 through 1.79769313486231E308	`Dim Pi As Double`

Data type	Size	Range	Sample usage
Decimal	128-bit	values up to +/–79,228 × 10^{24}	`Dim Debt As Decimal` `Debt = 7600300.50`
Byte	8-bit	0–255 (no negative numbers)	`Dim RetKey As Byte` `RetKey = 13`
Char	16-bit	Any Unicode symbol in the range 0–65,535	`Dim UnicodeChar As Char` `UnicodeChar = "Ä"`
String	Usually 16-bits per character	0 to approximately 2 billion 16-bit Unicode characters	`Dim Dog As String` `Dog = "pointer"`
Boolean	16-bit	True or False (during conversions, 0 is converted to False, other values to True)	`Dim Flag as Boolean` `Flag = True`
Date	64-bit	January 1, 0001, through December 31, 9999	`Dim Birthday as Date` `Birthday = #3/1/1963#`

Object	32-bit	Any type can be stored in a variable of type *Object*	`Dim MyApp As Object`
			`MyApp = CreateObject _`
			`   ("Word.Application")`

Use fundamental data types in code

1   On the File menu, point to Open, and then click Project.

The Open Project dialog box appears.

2   Open the Data Types project in the c:\vbnet03sbs\chap05\data types folder.

3   If the project's form isn't visible, click Form1.vb in Solution Explorer, and then click the View Designer button.

Data Types is a complete Visual Basic program that demonstrates how several fundamental data types work. You'll run the program to see what the data types look like, and then you'll look at how the variables are declared and used in the program code. You'll also learn where to place variable declarations so that they're available to all the event procedures in your program.

4   Click the Start button on the Standard toolbar.

The following application window appears:

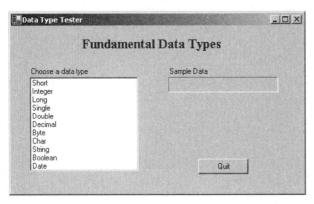

The Data Types program lets you experiment with 11 data types, including integer, single-precision floating point, and date. The program displays an example of each type when you click its name in the list box.

5   Click the Integer type in the list box.

The number 37,500,000 appears in the Sample Data box, as shown in the following illustration. Note that neither the *Short*, *Integer*, nor *Long* data type allows you to insert or display commas in them. To display commas, you'll need to use the *Format* function.

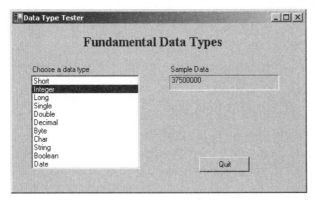

6   Click the Date type in the list box.

The date 3/1/1963 appears in the Sample Data box.

7   Click each data type in the list box to see how Visual Basic displays it in the Sample Data box.

8   Click the Quit button to stop the program.

Now you'll examine how the fundamental data types are declared at the top of the form and how they're used in the *ListBox1_SelectedIndexChanged* event procedure.

9 Double-click the form itself (not any objects on the form), and enlarge the Code Editor to see more of the program code. The Code Editor will look like this:

At the top of the Code Editor, you'll see a line that says "Windows Form Designer generated code". If you click the plus sign next to this line, you'll see statements that Visual Basic adds to your project so that the objects placed on the form contain the correct properties and the form loads correctly. In previous versions of Visual Basic, this "setup" code wasn't accessible, but now it exists in each form file so that you can examine the inner workings of your forms and fine-tune them if you want. (I don't recommend customizing the Windows Forms Designer generated code until you've completed this book and feel very comfortable with Visual Basic programming!)

Below the Windows Forms Designer generated code, you'll see the dozen or so program statements I added to declare 11 variables in your program—one for each of the fundamental data types in Visual Basic. (I didn't create an example for the *Object* type, but we'll experiment with that in later chapters.) By placing each *Dim* statement here, at the top of the form's code initialization area, I'm insuring that the variables will be valid, or will have *scope*, in all of the form's event procedures. That way, I can set the value of a variable in one event procedure and read it in another. Normally, variables are valid only in the event procedure in which they're declared. To make them valid across the form, you need to declare variables at the top of your form's code.

5

Variables and Operators

> ▶ **Note**   I've given each variable the same name as I did in the data types table earlier in the chapter so that you can see the examples I showed you in actual program code.

10 Scroll down in the Code Editor, and examine the *Form1_Load* event procedure.

You'll see the following statements that add items to the list box object in the program. (You might remember this syntax from Chapter 3—I used some similar statements there.)

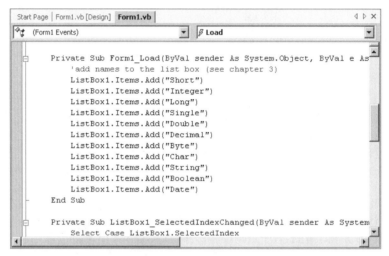

```vb
Start Page | Form1.vb [Design] | Form1.vb                                    ◁ ▷ ×
(Form1 Events)                        ▼  ƒ Load                              ▼

     Private Sub Form1_Load(ByVal sender As System.Object, ByVal e As
         'add names to the list box (see chapter 3)
         ListBox1.Items.Add("Short")
         ListBox1.Items.Add("Integer")
         ListBox1.Items.Add("Long")
         ListBox1.Items.Add("Single")
         ListBox1.Items.Add("Double")
         ListBox1.Items.Add("Decimal")
         ListBox1.Items.Add("Byte")
         ListBox1.Items.Add("Char")
         ListBox1.Items.Add("String")
         ListBox1.Items.Add("Boolean")
         ListBox1.Items.Add("Date")
     End Sub

     Private Sub ListBox1_SelectedIndexChanged(ByVal sender As System
         Select Case ListBox1.SelectedIndex
```

11 Scroll down and examine the *ListBox1_SelectedIndexChanged* event procedure.

The *ListBox1_SelectedIndexChanged* event procedure processes the selections you make in the list box and looks like this:

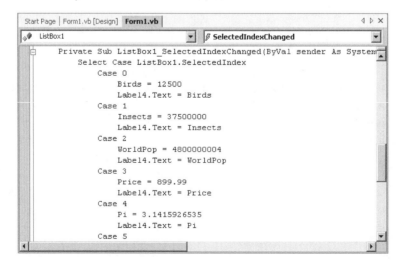

```vb
Start Page | Form1.vb [Design] | Form1.vb                                    ◁ ▷ ×
ListBox1                              ▼  ƒ SelectedIndexChanged              ▼

     Private Sub ListBox1_SelectedIndexChanged(ByVal sender As System
         Select Case ListBox1.SelectedIndex
             Case 0
                 Birds = 12500
                 Label14.Text = Birds
             Case 1
                 Insects = 37500000
                 Label14.Text = Insects
             Case 2
                 WorldPop = 4800000004
                 Label14.Text = WorldPop
             Case 3
                 Price = 899.99
                 Label14.Text = Price
             Case 4
                 Pi = 3.1415926535
                 Label14.Text = Pi
             Case 5
```

The heart of the event procedure is a Select Case decision structure. In the next chapter, we'll discuss how this group of program statements selects one choice from many. For now, notice how each section of the Select Case block assigns a sample value to one of the fundamental data type variables and then assigns the variable to the *Text* property of the *Label4* object on the form. I used code like this in Chapter 3 to process list box choices, and you can also use these techniques to work with list boxes and data types in your own programs.

▶ **Note**   If you have more than one form in your project, you need to declare variables in a slightly different way (and place) to give them scope throughout your program (that is, in each form that your project contains). The type of variable that you'll declare is a public, or global, variable, and it's declared in a *code module* (a special file that contains declarations and procedures not associated with a particular form.) For information about creating public variables in code modules, see Chapter 10.

12 Scroll through the *ListBox1_SelectedIndexChanged* event procedure, and examine each of the variable assignments closely.

Try changing the data in a few of the variable assignment statements and running the program again to see what the data looks like. In particular, you might try assigning values to variables that are outside their accepted range, as shown in the data types table presented earlier. If you make such an error, Visual Basic will add a jagged underline below the incorrect value in the Code Editor, and the program won't run until you change it. To learn more about your mistake, you can hold the mouse over the jagged underlined value and read a short tooltip error message about the problem.

13 If you made any changes you want to save to disk, click the Save All button on the Standard toolbar.

User-Defined Data Types

Visual Basic also lets you create your own data types. This feature is most useful when you're dealing with a group of data items that naturally fit together but fall into different data categories. You create a *user-defined type* (UDT) by using the *Structure* statement, and you declare variables associated with the new type by using the *Dim* statement. Be aware that the *Structure* statement cannot be located in an event procedure—it must be located at the top of the form, along with other variable declarations, or in a code module.

For example, the following declaration creates a user-defined data type named *Employee* that can store the name, date of birth, and hire date associated with a worker:

```
Structure Employee
    Dim Name As String
    Dim DateOfBirth As Date
    Dim HireDate As Date
End Structure
```

After you create a data type, you can use it in the program code for the form or module's event procedures. The following statements use the new *Employee* type. The first statement creates a variable named *ProductManager*, of the *Employee* type, and the second statement assigns the name "Erick Cody" to the *Name* component of the variable:

```
Dim ProductManager As Employee
ProductManager.Name = "Erick Cody"
```

This looks a little similar to setting a property, doesn't it? Visual Basic uses the same notation for the relationship between objects and properties as it uses for the relationship between user-defined data types and component variables.

Constants: Variables That Don't Change

If a variable in your program contains a value that never changes (such as π, a fixed mathematical entity), you might consider storing the value as a *constant* instead of as a variable. A constant is a meaningful name that takes the place of a number or a text string that doesn't change. Constants are useful because they increase the readability of program code, they can reduce programming mistakes, and they make global changes easier to accomplish later. Constants operate a lot like variables, but you can't modify their values at runtime. They are declared with the *Const* keyword, as shown in the following example:

```
Const Pi As Double = 3.14159265
```

This statement creates a constant named *Pi* that can be used in place of the value of π in the program code. To make a constant available to all the objects and event procedures in your form, place the statement at the top of your form along with other variable and structure declarations that will have scope in all of the form's event procedures. To make the constant available to all the forms and modules in a program (not just *Form1*), create the constant in a code module, with the *Public* keyword in front of it. For example:

```
Public Const Pi As Double = 3.14159265
```

The following exercise demonstrates how you can use a constant in an event procedure.

Use a constant in an event procedure

1   On the File menu, point to Open, and then click Project.

The Open Project dialog box appears.

2   Open the Constant Tester project in the c:\vbnet03sbs\chap05\constant tester folder.

3   If the project's form isn't visible, click Form1.vb in Solution Explorer, and then click the View Designer button.

The Constant Tester form appears in the Windows Forms Designer. Constant Tester is a skeleton program. The user interface is finished, but you need to type in the program code.

4   Double-click the Show Constant button on the form.

The *Button1_Click* event procedure appears in the Code Editor.

5   Type the following statements in the *Button1_Click* event procedure:

```
Const Pi As Double = 3.14159265
Label1.Text = Pi
```

> ▶ **Tip**   The location you choose for your declarations should be based on how you plan to use the constants or the variables. Programmers typically keep the scope for declarations as small as possible, while still making them available for code that needs to use them. For example, if a constant is needed only in a single event procedure, you should put the constant declaration within that event procedure. However, you could also place the declaration at the top of the form code, which would give all the event procedures in your form access to it.

6   Click the Start button on the Standard toolbar to run the program.

7   Click the Show Constant button.

The Pi constant appears in the label box, as shown here:

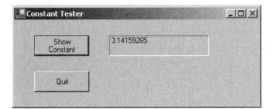

8   Click the Quit button to stop the program.

Constants are useful in program code, especially in involved mathematical formulas, such as Area = πr^2. The next section describes how you can use operators and variables to write similar formulas.

Working with Visual Basic Operators

A *formula* is a statement that combines numbers, variables, operators, and keywords to create a new value. Visual Basic contains several language elements designed for use in formulas. In this section, you'll practice working with mathematical *operators*, the symbols used to tie together the parts of a formula. With a few exceptions, the mathematical symbols you'll use are the ones you use in everyday life, and their operations are fairly intuitive. You'll see each demonstrated in the following exercises.

Visual Basic includes the following operators:

Operator	Description
+	Addition
–	Subtraction
*	Multiplication
/	Division
\	Integer (whole number) division
Mod	Remainder division
^	Exponentiation (raising to a power)
&	String concatenation (combination)

Basic Math: The +, –, *, and / Operators

The operators for addition, subtraction, multiplication, and division are pretty straightforward and can be used in any formula where numbers or numeric variables are used. The following exercise demonstrates how you can use them in a program.

Work with basic operators

1   On the File menu, point to Open, and then click Project.

2   Open the Basic Math project in the c:\vbnet03sbs\chap05\basic math folder.

3   If the project's form isn't visible, click Form1.vb in Solution Explorer, and then click the View Designer button.

The Basic Math form appears in the Windows Forms Designer. The Basic Math program demonstrates how the addition, subtraction, multiplication, and division operators work with numbers you type. It also demonstrates how you can use text box, radio button, and button objects to process user input in a program.

4   Click the Start button on the Standard toolbar.

The Basic Math program runs in the development environment. The program displays two text boxes in which you enter numeric values, a group of operator radio buttons, a box that displays results, and two button objects (Calculate and Quit).

5   Type **100** in the Variable 1 text box, and then press Tab.

The cursor moves to the second text box.

6   Type **17** in the Variable 2 text box.

You can now apply any of the mathematical operators to the values in the text boxes.

7   Click the Addition radio button, and then click the Calculate button.

The operator is applied to the two values, and the number 117 appears in the Result box, as shown here:

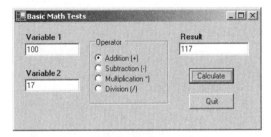

8   Practice using the subtraction, multiplication, and division operators with the two numbers in the variable boxes. (Click Calculate to calculate each formula.)

The results appear in the Result box. Feel free to experiment with different numbers in the variable text boxes. (Try a few numbers with decimal points if you like.) I used the *Double* data type to declare the variables, so you can use very large numbers if you like.

Now try the following test to see what happens:

9 Type **100** in the Variable 1 text box, type 0 in the Variable 2 text box, click the Division radio button, and then click Calculate.

Dividing by zero is a no-no in mathematical calculations, because it produces an infinite result. But Visual Basic is able to handle this calculation and displays a value of Infinity in the Result text box. Being able to handle some divide-by-zero conditions is a new feature that Visual Basic .NET automatically provides.

10 When you've finished contemplating this and other tests, click the Quit button.

The program stops, and the development environment returns.

Now take a look at the program code to see how the results were calculated. Basic Math uses a few of the standard input controls you experimented with in Chapter 3 and an event procedure that uses variables and operators to process the simple mathematical formulas. The program declares its variables at the top of the form so that they can be used in all of the Form1 event procedures.

Examine the Basic Math program code

1 Double-click the Calculate button on the form.

The Code Editor displays the *Button1_Click* event procedure. At the top of the form code, you'll see the following statement that declares two variables of type *Double*:

```
'Declare FirstNum and SecondNum variables
Dim FirstNum, SecondNum As Double
```

I used the *Double* type because I wanted a large, general purpose variable type that could handle many different numbers—integers, numbers with decimal points, very big numbers, small numbers, and so on. The variables are declared on the same line using the shortcut notation. Both *FirstNum* and *SecondNum* are of type *Double*, and they'll be used to hold the values input in the first and second text boxes, respectively.

2 Scroll down in the Code Editor to see the contents of the *Button1_Click* event procedure.

Your screen will look like this:

```
Start Page | Form1.vb [Design]  Form1.vb |                            ◁ ▷ ×
 ⚙ Button1                          ▼    ƒ Click                          ▼

         Private Sub Button1_Click(ByVal sender As System.Object, ByVal e
              'Assign text box values to variables
              FirstNum = TextBox1.Text
              SecondNum = TextBox2.Text

              'Determine checked button and calculate
              If RadioButton1.Checked = True Then
                   TextBox3.Text = FirstNum + SecondNum
              End If
              If RadioButton2.Checked = True Then
                   TextBox3.Text = FirstNum - SecondNum
              End If
              If RadioButton3.Checked = True Then
                   TextBox3.Text = FirstNum * SecondNum
              End If
              If RadioButton4.Checked = True Then
                   TextBox3.Text = FirstNum / SecondNum
              End If
         End Sub

     End Class
```

The first two statements in the event procedure transfer data entered into the text box objects into the *FirstNum* and *SecondNum* variables.

```
'Assign text box values to variables
FirstNum = TextBox1.Text
SecondNum = TextBox2.Text
```

The *TextBox* control handles the transfer with the *Text* property—a property that accepts text entered by the user and makes it available for use in the program. I'll make frequent use of the *TextBox* control in this book. When it's set to multiline and resized, it can display many lines of text—even a whole file!

After the text box values are assigned to the variables, the event procedure determines which radio button has been checked, calculates the mathematical formula, and displays the result in a third text box. The first radio button test looks like this:

```
'Determine checked button and calculate
If RadioButton1.Checked = True Then
    TextBox3.Text = FirstNum + SecondNum
End If
```

Variables and Operators

5

Remember from Chapter 3 that only one radio button object in a group box object can be selected at once. You can tell whether a radio button has been selected by evaluating the *Checked* property. If it's True, the button has been selected. If the *Checked* property is False, the button has not been selected. After this simple test, you're ready to compute the result and display it in the third text box object. That's all there is to using basic mathematical operators. (You'll learn more about the syntax of If...Then tests, or decision structures, in Chapter 6.)

You're done using the Basic Math program.

Using Advanced Operators: \, *Mod*, ^, and &

In addition to the four basic mathematical operators, Visual Basic includes four advanced operators, which perform integer division (\), remainder division (*Mod*), exponentiation (^), and string concatenation (&). These operators are useful in special-purpose mathematical formulas and text processing applications. The following utility (a slight modification of the Basic Math program) shows how you can use each of these operators in a program.

New Shortcut Operators

An interesting new feature of Visual Basic .NET is that you can use shortcut operators for mathematical and string operations that involve changing the value of an existing variable. For example, if you combine the "+" symbol with the "=" symbol, you can add to a variable without repeating the variable name twice in the formula. Thus, you can write the formula X = X + 6 using the syntax X += 6. The following table shows examples of these shortcut operators:

Operation	Long-form syntax	Shortcut syntax
Addition (+)	X = X +6	X += 6
Subtraction (-)	X = X − 6	X -= 6
Multiplication (*)	X = X * 6	X *= 6
Division (/)	X = X / 6	X /= 6
Integer division (\)	X = X \ 6	X \= 6
Exponentiation (^)	X = X ^ 6	X ^= 6
String concatenation (&)	X = X & "ABC"	X &= "ABC"

Work with advanced operators

1 On the File menu, point to Open, and then click Project.

The Open Project dialog box appears.

2 Open the Advanced Math project in the
c:\vbnet03sbs\chap05\advanced math folder.

3 If the project's form isn't visible, click Form1.vb in Solution Explorer,
and then click the View Designer button.

The Advanced Math form appears in the Windows Forms Designer.
The Advanced Math program is identical to the Basic Math program, with the exception of the operators shown in the radio buttons
and in the program.

4 Click the Start button on the Standard toolbar.

The program displays two text boxes in which you enter numeric
values, a group of operator radio buttons, a text box that displays
results, and two buttons.

5 Type **9** in the Variable 1 text box, and then press Tab.

6 Type **2** in the Variable 2 text box.

You can now apply any of the advanced operators to the values in
the text boxes.

7 Click the Integer Division radio button, and then click the Calculate
button.

The operator is applied to the two values, and the number 4 appears
in the Result box, as shown here:

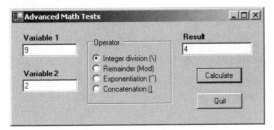

Integer division produces only the whole number result of the division operation. Although 9 divided by 2 equals 4.5, the integer division operation returns only the first part, an integer (the whole
number 4). You might find this result useful if you're working with
quantities that can't easily be divided into fractional components,
such as the number of adults that can fit in a car.

5

Variables and Operators

8   Click the Remainder radio button, and then click the Calculate button.

The number 1 appears in the Result box. Remainder division (modulus arithmetic) returns the remainder (the part left over that won't evenly divide) after two numbers are divided. Because 9 divided by 2 equals 4 with a remainder of 1 (2 × 4 + 1 = 9), the result produced by the *Mod* operator is 1. In addition to adding an early-seventies quality to your code, the *Mod* operator can help you track "leftovers" in your calculations, such as the amount of change left over after a financial transaction.

9   Click the Exponentiation radio button, and then click the Calculate button.

The number 81 appears in the Result box. The exponentiation operator ($\wedge$) raises a number to a specified power. For example, $9 \wedge 2$ equals 9^2, or 81. In a Visual Basic formula, 9^2 is written $9 \wedge 2$.

10   Click the Concatenation radio button, and then click the Calculate button.

The number 92 appears in the Result box. The string concatenation operator (&) combines two strings in a formula, but not through addition. The result is a combination of the "9" character and the "2" character. String concatenation can be performed on numeric variables—for example, if you're displaying the inning-by-inning score of a baseball game as they do in old-time score boxes—but concatenation is more commonly performed on string values or variables.

Because I declared the *FirstNum* and *SecondNum* variables as type *Double*, you can't combine words or letters using the program code as written. Try the following test, for example, which will cause an error and end the program.

11   Type **birth** in the Variable 1 text box, type **day** in the Variable 2 text box, verify that Concatenation is selected, and then click Calculate.

Visual Basic is unable to process the text values you entered; the program stops running, and an error message appears on the screen, as shown here:

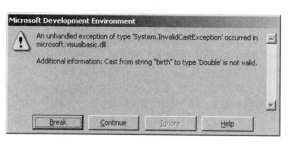

This type of error is called a *runtime error*—an error that surfaces not during the design and compilation of the program, but later, when the program is running and encounters a condition it doesn't know how to process. If this seems odd, you might imagine that Visual Basic is simply offering you a modern rendition of the robot plea "Does not compute!" from the best science fiction films of the 1950s. The updated computer-speak message "Cast from string ('birth') to Double is not valid" means that the words you entered in the text boxes ("birth" and "day") could not be assigned, or *cast*, by Visual Basic to variables of the type *Double*. *Double* types can only contain numbers. Period.

12 Click the Continue button in the Microsoft Development Environment dialog box.

If another Microsoft Development Environment dialog box is displayed indicating that no source code is available for the current location, click OK.

Your program ends and returns you to the development environment. The Break button, which you'll learn about in Chapter 8, allows you to use the debugging tools in Visual Studio to learn more about the defects, or *bugs*, in your program code.

Now take a look at the program code to see how variables were declared and how the advanced operators were used.

13 Scroll to the code at the top of the Code Editor. You'll see the following comment and program statement:

```
'Declare FirstNum and SecondNum variables
Dim FirstNum, SecondNum As Double
```

As you might recall from the previous exercise, *FirstNum* and *SecondNum* are the variables that hold numbers coming in from the *TextBox1* and *TextBox2* objects.

14 Change the data type from *Double* to *String* now so that you can properly test how the string concatenation (&) operator works.

15 Now scroll down in the Code Editor to see how the advanced operators are used in the program code. You'll see the following code:

```
'Assign text box values to variables
FirstNum = TextBox1.Text
SecondNum = TextBox2.Text

'Determine checked button and calculate
If RadioButton1.Checked = True Then
    TextBox3.Text = FirstNum \ SecondNum
End If
```

```
If RadioButton2.Checked = True Then
    TextBox3.Text = FirstNum Mod SecondNum
End If
If RadioButton3.Checked = True Then
    TextBox3.Text = FirstNum ^ SecondNum
End If
If RadioButton4.Checked = True Then
    TextBox3.Text = FirstNum & SecondNum
End If
```

Like the Basic Math program, this program loads data from the text boxes and places it in the *FirstNum* and *SecondNum* variables. The program then checks to see which radio button the user checked and computes the requested formula. In this event procedure, the integer division (\), remainder (*Mod*), exponentiation (^), and string concatenation (&) operators are used. Now that you've changed the data type of the variables to *String*, run the program again to see how the & operator works on text.

16 Click the Start button.

17 Type **birth** in the Variable 1 text box, type **day** in the Variable 2 text box, click Concatenation, and then click Calculate.

The program now concatenates the string values and doesn't produce a runtime error, as shown here:

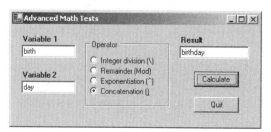

18 Click the Quit button to close the program.

You're finished working with the Advanced Math program.

> ▶   **Tip**   Runtime errors are difficult to avoid completely—even the most sophisticated application programs, such as Microsoft Word or Microsoft Excel, run into error conditions they can't handle sometimes, producing runtime errors, or *crashes*. Designing your programs to handle many different data types and operating conditions will help you produce solid, or *robust*, applications. In Chapter 9, you'll learn about another helpful tool for preventing runtime error crashes—the structured error handler.

Working with Math Methods in the .NET Framework

Now and then you'll want to do a little extra number crunching in your programs. You might need to round a number, calculate a complex mathematical expression, or introduce randomness into your programs. The math methods shown in the following table can help you work with numbers in your formulas. These methods are provided by the .NET Framework, a class library that lets you tap into the power of the Microsoft Windows operating system and accomplish many of the common programming tasks that you need to create your projects. The .NET Framework is a new feature of Visual Studio .NET that is shared by Microsoft Visual Basic, Microsoft Visual C++, Microsoft Visual C#, Microsoft Visual J#, and other tools in Visual Studio. It's an underlying interface that becomes part of the Windows operating system itself. The .NET Framework is organized into classes that you can include by name in your programming projects by using the *Imports* statement. The process is quite simple, and you'll experiment with how it works now by using a math method in the *System.Math* class of the .NET Framework.

The following table offers a partial list of the math methods in the *System.Math* class. The argument *n* in the table represents the number, variable, or expression you want the method to evaluate. If you use any of these methods, be sure that you put the statement

```
Imports System.Math
```

at the very top of your form code in the Code Editor.

Method	Purpose
Abs(n)	Returns the absolute value of *n*.
Atan(n)	Returns the arctangent, in radians, of *n*.
Cos(n)	Returns the cosine of the angle *n*. The angle *n* is expressed in radians.
Exp(n)	Returns the constant *e* raised to the power *n*.
Sign(n)	Returns −1 if *n* is less than 0, 0 if *n* is 0, and +1 if *n* is greater than 0.
Sin(n)	Returns the sine of the angle *n*. The angle *n* is expressed in radians.
Sqrt(n)	Returns the square root of *n*.
Tan(n)	Returns the tangent of the angle *n*. The angle *n* is expressed in radians.

Use the *System.Math* class to compute square roots

1 On the File menu, point to New, and then click Project.

The New Project dialog box appears.

2 Create a new Visual Basic Windows Application project named **My Framework Math** in the c:\vbnet03sbs\chap05 folder.

The new project is created, and a blank form appears in the Windows Forms Designer.

3 Click the *Button* control on the Windows Forms tab of the Toolbox, and create a button object at the top of your form.

4 Click the *TextBox* control in the Toolbox, and draw a text box below the button object.

5 Set the *Text* property of the button object to Square Root, and set the *Text* property of the text box object to blank (empty).

6 Double-click the button object to display the Code Editor.

7 At the very top of the Code Editor, above the *Public Class Form1* statement, type the following program statement:

```
Imports System.Math
```

The *Imports* statement adds a library of objects, properties, and methods to your project. This statement must be the first statement in your program—it must come even before the variables that you declare for the form and the *Public Class Form1* statement that Visual Basic automatically provides. The particular library you've chosen is the *System.Math* class, a collection of objects, properties, and methods provided by the .NET Framework for mathematical operations.

8 Move down in the Code Editor, and add the following code to the *Button1_Click* event procedure between the *Private Sub* and *End Sub* statements:

```
Dim Result As Double
Result = Sqrt(625)
TextBox1.Text = Result
```

These three statements declare a variable of the double type named *Result*, use the *Sqrt* method to compute the square root of 625, and assign the *Result* variable to the *Text* property of the text box object so that the answer will be displayed.

9 Click the Save All button on the Standard toolbar to save your changes.

10 Click the Start button on the Standard toolbar.

The Framework Math program runs in the development environment.

11 Click the Square Root button.

Visual Basic calculates the square root of 625 and displays the result (25) in the text box, as shown here. The *Sqrt* method works!

12 Click the Close button on the form to end the program.

To use a particular .NET Framework class in your program, include the *Imports* statement, and specify the appropriate class library. You can use this technique to use any class in the .NET Framework. You'll see several more examples of this skill as you work through the book.

Operator Precedence

In the past few exercises, you experimented with several mathematical operators and one string operator. Visual Basic lets you mix as many mathematical operators as you like in a formula, as long as each numeric variable and expression is separated from another by one operator. For example, this is an acceptable Visual Basic formula:

```
Total = 10 + 15 * 2 / 4 ^ 2
```

The formula processes several values and assigns the result to a variable named *Total*. But how is such an expression evaluated by Visual Basic? In other words, what sequence of mathematical operators does Visual Basic use when solving the formula? You might not have noticed, but the order of evaluation matters a great deal in this example.

Visual Basic solves this dilemma by establishing a specific *order of precedence* for mathematical operations. This list of rules tells Visual Basic which operator to use first, second, and so on when evaluating an expression that contains more than one operator. The following table lists the operators from first to last in the order in which they'll be evaluated. (Operators on the same level in this table are evaluated from left to right as they appear in an expression.)

Operators	Order of Preference
( )	Values within parentheses are always evaluated first.
^	Exponentiation (raising a number to a power) is second.
–	Negation (creating a negative number) is third.
* /	Multiplication and division are fourth.
\	Integer division is fifth.
Mod	Remainder division is sixth.
+ –	Addition and subtraction are last.

Given the order of precedence in this table, the expression

```
Total = 10 + 15 * 2 / 4 ^ 2
```

would be evaluated by Visual Basic in the following steps. (Boldface type is used to show each step in the order of evaluation and its result.)

```
Total = 10 + 15 * 2 / 4 ^ 2
Total = 10 + 15 * 2 / 16
Total = 10 + 30 / 16
Total = 10 + 1.875
Total = 11.875
```

One Step Further: Using Parentheses in a Formula

You can use one or more pairs of parentheses in a formula to clarify the order of precedence. For example, Visual Basic would calculate the formula

```
Number = (8 - 5 * 3) ^ 2
```

by determining the value within the parentheses (–7) before doing the exponentiation—even though exponentiation is higher in order of precedence than subtraction and multiplication, according to the preceding table. You can further refine the calculation by placing nested parentheses in the formula. For example,

```
Number = ((8 - 5) * 3) ^ 2
```

directs Visual Basic to calculate the difference in the inner set of parentheses first, perform the operation in the outer parentheses next, and then determine the exponentiation. The result produced by the two formulas is different: the first formula evaluates to 49 and the second to 81. Parentheses can change the result of a mathematical operation, as well as make it easier to read.

Lesson 5 Quick Reference

To	Do this
Declare a variable	Type *Dim* followed by the variable name, the *As* keyword, and the variable data type in the program code. To make the variable valid in all of the form's event procedures, place this statement at the top of the code for a form, before any event procedures. For example: ```Dim Country As String```
Change the value of a variable	Assign a new value with the assignment operator of (=). For example: ```Country = "Japan"```
Get input with a dialog box	Use the *InputBox* function, and assign the result to a variable. For example: ```UserName = InputBox("What is your name?")```

Display output in a dialog box	Use the *MsgBox* function. (The string to be displayed in the dialog box can be stored in a variable.) For example:
	
	```Forecast = "Rain, mainly on the plain."```
	```MsgBox(Forecast, , "Spain Weather Report")```

Create a constant	Type the *Const* keyword followed by the constant name, the assignment operator (=), the constant data type, and the fixed value. For example: ```Const JackBennysAge As Short = 39```
Create a formula	Link together numeric variables or values with one of the seven mathematical operators, and then assign the result to a variable or a property. For example: ```Result = 1 ^ 2 * 3 \ 4 'this equals 0```
Combine text strings	Use the string concatenation operator (*&*). For example: ```Msg = "Hello" & "," & " world!"```
Include a class library from the .NET Framework	Place an *Imports* statement at the very top of the form's code that identifies the class library. For example: ```Imports System.Math```
Make a call to a method from an included class library	Use the method name, and include any necessary arguments so that it can be used in a formula or a program statement. For example, to make a call to the *Sqrt* method in the *System.Math* class library: ```Hypotenuse = Sqrt(x ^ 2 + y ^ 2)```

Control the evaluation order in a formula	Use parentheses in the formula. For example:
	
	```Result = 1 + 2 ^ 3 \ 4 'this equals 3```
	```Result = (1 + 2) ^ (3 \ 4) 'this equals 1```

Using Decision Structures

In this chapter, you will learn how to:

- Write conditional expressions.

- Use an *If...Then* statement to branch to a set of program statements based on a varying condition.

- Short-circuit an *If...Then* statement.

- Use a *Select Case* statement to select one choice from many options in program code.

- Detect and manage mouse events.

In the past few chapters, you used several features of Microsoft Visual Basic .NET to process user input. You used menus, objects, and dialog boxes to display choices for the user, and you processed input by using properties and variables. In this chapter, you'll learn how to branch conditionally to a specific program code section based on input you receive from the user. You'll also learn how to evaluate one or more properties or variables by using conditional expressions and then execute one or more program statements based on the results.

Upgrade Notes: What's New in Visual Basic .NET?

If you're experienced with Visual Basic 6, you'll notice some new features in Visual Basic .NET, including the following:

- Visual Basic .NET includes two new logical operators named *AndAlso* and *OrElse*. In a conditional statement that contains multiple conditions, such as an If...Then structure, it might not be necessary to always evaluate all the conditions. Passing over conditions is some-times called *short-circuiting* and can be specified by using the *AndAlso* and *OrElse* operators.

Event-Driven Programming

The programs you've written so far in this book have displayed menus, objects, and dialog boxes on the screen, and these programs have encouraged users to manipulate the screen elements in whatever order they saw fit. The programs put the user in charge, waited patiently for a response, and then processed the input predictably. In programming circles, this methodology is known as *event-driven programming*. You build a program by creating a group of "intelligent" objects that know how to respond when the user interacts with them, and then you process the input by using event procedures associated with the objects. The following diagram shows how an event-driven program works in Visual Basic:

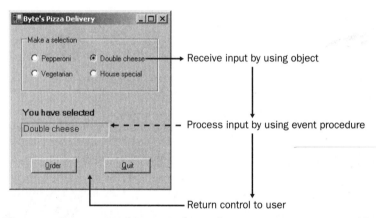

Program input can also come from the computer system itself. For example, your program might be notified when a piece of electronic mail arrives or when a specified period of time has elapsed on the system clock. The computer, not the user, triggers these events. Regardless of how an event is triggered, Visual Basic reacts by calling the event procedure associated with the object that recognized the event. So far, you've dealt primarily with the *Click*, *CheckedChanged*, and *SelectedIndexChanged* events. However, Visual Basic objects also can respond to several other types of events.

Events Supported by Visual Basic Objects

Each object in Visual Basic has a predefined set of events it can respond to. These events are listed when you select an object name in the Class Name drop-down list box at the top of the Code Editor and then click the Method Name drop-down list box. (Events are visually identified in Microsoft Visual Studio by a lightning bolt icon.) You can write an event procedure for any of these events, and if that event occurs in the program, Visual Basic will execute the event procedure that's associated with it. For example, a list box object supports more than 60 events, including *Click*, *DoubleClick*, *DragDrop*, *DragOver*, *GotFocus*, *KeyDown*, *KeyPress*, *KeyUp*, *LostFocus*, *MouseDown*, *MouseMove*, *MouseUp*, *MouseHover*, *TextChanged*, and *Validated*. You probably won't need to program for more than three or four of these events in your applications, but it's nice to know that you have so many choices when you create elements in your interface. The following illustration shows a partial listing of the events for a list box object in the Code Editor:

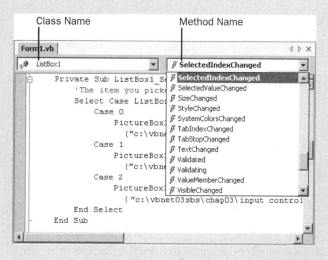

The event-driven nature of Visual Basic means that most of the computing done in your programs will be accomplished by event procedures. These event-specific blocks of code process input, calculate new values, display output, and handle other tasks. In the previous chapter, you learned how to use variables, operators, and mathematical formulas to perform calculations in your event procedures. In this chapter, you'll learn how to use *decision structures* to compare variables, properties, and values, and you'll learn how to execute one or more statements based on the results. In Chapter 7, you'll use *loops* to execute a group of statements over and over until a condition is met or while a specific condition is true. Together, these powerful flow-control structures will help you build your event procedures so that they can respond to almost any situation.

Using Conditional Expressions

One of the most useful tools for processing information in an event procedure is a *conditional expression*. A conditional expression is a part of a complete program statement that asks a True-or-False question about a property, a variable, or another piece of data in the program code. For example, the conditional expression

```
Price < 100
```

evaluates to True if the *Price* variable contains a value that is less than 100, and it evaluates to False if *Price* contains a value that is greater than or equal to 100. You can use the following comparison operators in a conditional expression.

Comparison operator	Meaning
=	Equal to
<>	Not equal to
>	Greater than
<	Less than
>=	Greater than or equal to
<=	Less than or equal to

▶ **Tip**   Expressions that can be evaluated as True or False are also known as *Boolean expressions*, and the True or False result can be assigned to a Boolean variable or property. You can assign Boolean values to certain object properties or Boolean variables that have been created by using the *Dim* statement and the *As Boolean* keywords.

The following table shows some conditional expressions and their results. In an exercise later in this chapter, you'll work with conditional expressions.

Conditional expression	Result
10 <> 20	True (10 is not equal to 20)
Score <20	True if *Score* is less than 20; otherwise, False
Score = Label1.Text	True if the *Text* property of the *Label1* object contains the same value as the *Score* variable; otherwise, False
TextBox1.Text = "Bill"	True if the word "Bill" is in the first text box; otherwise, False

If...Then Decision Structures

Conditional expressions used in a special block of statements called a *decision structure* control whether other statements in your program are executed and in what order they're executed. You can use an If...Then decision structure to evaluate a condition in the program and take a course of action based on the result. In its simplest form, an If...Then decision structure is written on a single line:

```
If condition Then statement
```

where *condition* is a conditional expression, and *statement* is a valid Visual Basic program statement. For example,

```
If Score >= 20 Then Label1.Text = "You win!"
```

is an If..Then decision structure that uses the conditional expression

```
Score >= 20
```

to determine whether the program should set the *Text* property of the *Label1* object to "You win!" If the *Score* variable contains a value that's greater than or equal to 20, Visual Basic sets the *Text* property; otherwise, it skips the assignment statement and executes the next line in the event procedure. This sort of comparison always results in a True or False value. A conditional expression never results in maybe.

Testing Several Conditions in an If...Then Decision Structure

Visual Basic also supports an If...Then decision structure that allows you to include several conditional expressions. This block of statements can be several lines long and contains the important keywords *ElseIf*, *Else*, and *End If*.

```
If condition1 Then
    statements executed if condition1 is True
ElseIf condition2 Then
    statements executed if condition2 is True
[Additional ElseIf clauses and statements can be placed here]
Else
    statements executed if none of the conditions is True
End If
```

In this structure, *condition1* is evaluated first. If this conditional expression is True, the block of statements below it is executed, one statement at a time. (You can include one or more program statements.) If the first condition isn't True, the second conditional expression (*condition2*) is evaluated. If the second condition is True, the second block of statements is executed. (You can add additional *ElseIf* conditions and statements if you have more conditions to evaluate.) If none of the conditional expressions is True, the statements below the *Else* keyword are executed. Finally, the whole structure is closed by the *End If* keywords.

The following code shows how a multiple-line If...Then structure could be used to determine the amount of tax due in a hypothetical progressive tax return. (The income and percentage numbers are from the United States Internal Revenue Service 2001 Tax Rate Schedule for single filing status.)

```
Dim AdjustedIncome, TaxDue As Double
AdjustedIncome = 32000

If AdjustedIncome <= 27050 Then          '15% tax bracket
    TaxDue = AdjustedIncome * 0.15
ElseIf AdjustedIncome <= 65550 Then      '28% tax bracket
    TaxDue = 4057.5 + ((AdjustedIncome - 27050) * 0.28)
ElseIf AdjustedIncome <= 136750 Then     '31% tax bracket
    TaxDue = 14837.5 + ((AdjustedIncome - 65550) * 0.31)
ElseIf AdjustedIncome <= 297350 Then     '36% tax bracket
    TaxDue = 36909.5 + ((AdjustedIncome - 136750) * 0.36)
Else                                     '39.6% tax bracket
    TaxDue = 94725.5 + ((AdjustedIncome - 297350) * 0.396)
End If
```

▶   **Important**   The order of the conditional expressions in your *If...Then* and *ElseIf* clauses is critical. What if you reversed the order of the conditional expressions in the tax computation example and listed the rates in the structure from highest to lowest? Taxpayers in the 15 percent, 28 percent, and 31 percent tax brackets would all be placed in the 36 percent tax bracket because they all would have an income that's less than or equal to 297,350. (Visual Basic stops at the first conditional expression that is True, even if others are also True.) Because all the conditional expressions in this example test the same variable, they need to be listed in ascending order to get the taxpayers to fall out at the right spots. Moral: when you use more than one conditional expression, consider the order carefully.

This useful decision structure tests the double-precision variable *AdjustedIncome* at the first income level and subsequent income levels until one of the conditional expressions evaluates to True, and then determines the taxpayer's income tax accordingly. With some simple modifications, it could be used to compute the tax owed by any taxpayer in a progressive tax system, such as the one in the United States. Provided that the tax rates are complete and up to date and that the value in the *AdjustedIncome* variable is correct, the program as written will give the correct tax owed for single U.S. taxpayers for 2001. If the tax rates change, it's a simple matter to update the conditional expressions. With an additional decision structure to determine taxpayers' filing status, the program readily extends itself to include all U.S. taxpayers. In the next exercise, you'll use an If...Then decision structure to validate users as they log in to a program. You might use similar program logic to write a network application that includes user validation.

Validate users by using If...Then

1 Start Visual Studio, and create a new Visual Basic Windows Application project named **My User Validation** in the c:\vbnet03sbs\chap06 folder.

   The new project is created, and a blank form appears in the Windows Forms Designer.

2 Use the *Button* control on the Windows Forms tab of the Toolbox to create a button object in the upper left of the form.

3 Set the *Text* property of the button to "Sign In".

4 Use the *PictureBox* control to create a large rectangular picture box object on the form below the button object.

   Your form should look like this:

5 Double-click the Sign In button.

   The *Button1_Click* event procedure appears in the Code Editor.

6 Type the following program statements in the event procedure:

```
Dim UserName As String
UserName = InputBox("Enter your first name.")
If UserName = "Henry" Then
    MsgBox("Welcome, Henry!  How are you today?")
    PictureBox1.Image = System.Drawing.Image.FromFile _
      ("c:\vbnet03sbs\chap06\henry photo.jpg")
ElseIf UserName = "Felix" Then
    MsgBox("Welcome, Felix!  Ready to play?")
    PictureBox1.Image = System.Drawing.Image.FromFile _
```

```
            ("c:\vbnet03sbs\chap06\felix photo.jpg")
Else
    MsgBox("Sorry, I don't recognize you.")
    End    'quit the program
End If
```

The space and the line continuation character (_) used after the
PictureBox1.Image properties break two long program statements
into four lines so that they can be printed in this book. If you choose,
you can type each of these long statements on one line; the Code Editor will scroll to the right.

> ▶ **Tip**   Program lines can be more than 65,000 characters long in the
> Visual Studio Code Editor, but it's usually easiest to work with lines of 80
> or fewer characters. You can divide long program statements among mul-
> tiple lines by using a space and a line continuation character (_) at the
> end of each line in the statement except the last line. (You cannot use a
> line continuation character to break a string that's in quotation marks,
> however.)

When you've finished, your screen should look like this:

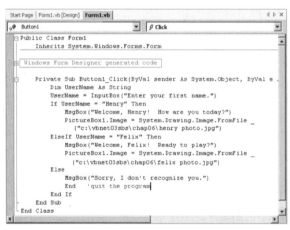

7   Click the Save All button on the Standard toolbar to save your
    changes.

8   Click the Start button on the Standard toolbar.

    The program runs in the development environment. A blank form
    appears on the screen, with a Sign In button in the upper left.

9   Click the Sign In button.

    The *InputBox* function in the *Button1_Click* event procedure dis-
    plays a dialog box that asks you to enter your first name.

10 Type **Henry**, and then click OK.

▶ **Note** The conditional checks in this program are case sensitive, so be sure to type "Henry" instead of "henry".

The If...Then decision structure compares the name you typed with the text "Henry" in the first conditional expression. The expression evaluates to True and the *If...Then* statement displays a welcome message by using the *MsgBox* function.

11 Click OK in the message box.

The message box closes, and a JPEG photo image appears in the picture box, as shown here:

The procedure used to load the picture is the same as I showed you in Chapter 3 and Chapter 4 of this book—I use the *System.Drawing.Image.FromFile* method, which is part of the *System.Drawing* namespace (or object library). This method is specially designed for loading pictures from files.

12 Click the Sign In button, type **Felix**, and then click OK.

This time the decision structure selects the *ElseIf* clause and admits Felix to the program. A welcome message is displayed on the screen again by the *MsgBox* function.

13 Click OK in the message box.

A JPEG photo image associated with this user is loaded into the picture box object, as shown on the following page.

14 Click the Sign In button, type **Sally**, and then click OK.

The *Else* clause in the decision structure is executed, and the following message appears in a message box:

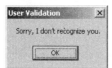

15 Click OK to close the message box.

The message box closes, and the program closes. Your code has prevented an unauthorized user from using the program. The complete User Validation program is available on disk in the c:\vbnet03sbs\chap06\user validation folder.

Using Logical Operators in Conditional Expressions

You can test more than one conditional expression in *If...Then* and *ElseIf* clauses if you want to include more than one selection criterion in your decision structure. The extra conditions are linked together by using one or more of the logical operators listed in the following table:

Logical operator	Meaning
And	If both conditional expressions are True, then the result is True.
Or	If either conditional expression is True, then the result is True.
Not	If the conditional expression is False, then the result is True. If the conditional expression is True, then the result is False.
Xor	If one and only one of the conditional expressions is True, then the result is True. If both are True or both are False, then the result is False. (*Xor* stands for exclusive *Or*.)

▶ **Tip**   When your program evaluates a complex expression that mixes different operator types, it evaluates mathematical operators first, comparison operators second, and logical operators third.

The following table lists some examples of the logical operators at work. In the expressions, it is assumed that the string variable *Vehicle* contains the value "Bike" and the integer variable *Price* contains the value 200.

Logical expression	Result
`Vehicle = "Bike" And Price < 300`	True (both conditions are True)
`Vehicle = "Car" Or Price < 500`	True (one condition is True)
`Not Price < 100`	True (condition is False)
`Vehicle = "Bike" Xor Price < 300`	False (both conditions are True)

In the following exercise, you'll modify the My User Validation program to prompt the user for a password during the validation process. An input box gets the password from the user, and you modify the *If...Then* and *ElseIf* clauses in the decision structure so that they use the *And* operator to verify the password.

Add password protection by using the *And* operator

1   Display the *Button1_Click* event procedure in the Code Editor.

2   Modify the *Dim* statement at the top of the event procedure so that it also declares a variable named *Pass* of the *String* type. Use this syntax:

```
Dim UserName, Pass As String
```

3   Insert the following statement between the *InputBox* statement and the *If...Then* statement in the procedure (between the second and third lines):

```
Pass = InputBox("Enter your password.")
```

4   Modify the *If...Then* statement to the following:

```
If UserName = "Henry" And Pass = "flower" Then
```

The statement now includes the *And* logical operator, which verifies the user name and password before Henry is admitted to the program.

5   Modify the *ElseIf* statement to the following:

```
ElseIf UserName = "Felix" And Pass = "sand" Then
```

The *And* logical operator adds a check for the "sand" password in Felix's account.

▶ **Tip**   The complete Password Validation application is available in the c:\vbnet03sbs\chap06\password validation folder.

6   Click the Start button on the Standard toolbar.

The program runs in the development environment.

7   Click the Sign In button, type **Henry**, and then click OK.

The program prompts you for a password.

8   Type **flower**, and then click OK.

The *And* conditional expression evaluates to True, and Henry is welcomed to the program.

9   Click OK to close the message box.

10   Click the Sign In button, type **Felix**, and then click OK.

The program prompts you for a password.

11   Type **sand**, and then click OK.

Felix is welcomed to the program—the passwords work!

12   Now try the Henry and Felix usernames with an incorrect or blank password.

You'll find that they don't work, the program ends, and the development environment returns.

> ▶ **Tip**   If you're writing a full-featured version of the Password Validation program, consider using a text box object on a form to receive the password input in the program. Text box objects support the *PasswordChar* property, which you can use to display a placeholder character such as an asterisk (*) as the user types, and the *MaxLength* property, which lets you limit the number of characters entered.

Short-Circuiting by Using *AndAlso* and *OrElse*

Visual Basic .NET offers two logical operators that you can use in your conditional statements, *AndAlso* and *OrElse*. These operators work the same way as *And* and *Or* respectively, but offer an important subtlety in the way they're evaluated that will be new to programmers experienced with earlier versions of Visual Basic.

Consider an *If* statement that has two conditions that are connected by an *AndAlso* operator. For the statements of the If structure to be executed, both conditions must evaluate to True. If the first condition evaluates to False, Visual Basic .NET will skip to the next line or *Else* statement immediately, without testing the second condition. This partial, or *short-circuiting*, evaluation of an *If* statement makes logical sense—why should Visual Basic continue to evaluate the *If* statement if both conditions cannot be True?

The *OrElse* operator works in a similar fashion. Consider an *If* statement that has two conditions that are connected by an *OrElse* operator. For the statements of the If structure to be executed, at least one condition must evaluate to True. If the first condition evaluates to True, Visual Basic .NET will begin to execute the statements in the If structure immediately, without testing the second condition.

Here's an example of the short-circuit situation in Visual Basic .NET, a simple routine that uses an *If* statement and an *AndAlso* operator to test two conditions and display the message *Inside If* if both conditions are True:

```
Dim Number As Integer = 0
If Number = 1 AndAlso MsgBox("Second condition test") Then
    MsgBox("Inside If")
Else
    MsgBox("Inside Else")
End If
```

The *MsgBox* function itself is used as the second conditional test, which is somewhat unusual, but the strange syntax is completely valid and gives us a perfect opportunity to see how short-circuiting works up close. The text *Second condition test* will appear in a message box only if the *Number* variable is set to 1; otherwise, the *AndAlso* operator short-circuits the *If* statement, and the second condition isn't evaluated. If you actually try this code, remember that it's for demonstration purposes only—you wouldn't want to use *MsgBox* with this syntax as a test because it doesn't really test anything. But by changing the *Number* variable from 0 to 1 and back, you can get a good idea of how the *AndAlso* statement and short-circuiting work.

Here's a second example of how short-circuiting functions in Visual Basic .NET when two conditions are evaluated using the *AndAlso* operator. This time, a more complex conditional test (7 / HumanAge <= 1) is used after the *AndAlso* operator to determine the "dog age" of a person:

```
Dim HumanAge As Integer
HumanAge = 7
'One year for a dog is seven years for a human
If HumanAge <> 0 AndAlso 7 / HumanAge <= 1 Then
    MsgBox("You are at least one dog year old")
Else
    MsgBox("You are less than one dog year old")
End If
```

This bare-bones routine tries to determine whether the value in the *HumanAge* integer variable is at least 7. It's part of a larger program that determines the so-called dog age of a person by dividing his or her current age by 7. (If you haven't heard the concept of "dog age" before, bear with me—following this logic, a 28-year-old person would be 4 dog years old.) The code uses two *If* statement conditions and can be used in a variety of different contexts—I used it in the *Click* event procedure for a button object. The first condition checks to see whether a non-zero number has been placed in the *HumanAge* variable—I've assumed momentarily that the user has enough sense to place a positive age into *HumanAge* because a negative number would produce incorrect results. The second condition checks to see whether the person is at least seven years old. If both conditions evaluate to True, the message *You are at least one dog year old* is displayed in a message box. If the person is less than seven, the message *You are less than one dog year old* is displayed. Now imagine that I've changed the value of the *HumanAge* variable from 7 to 0. What happens? The first *If* statement condition is evaluated as False by the Visual Basic .NET compiler, and that evaluation prevents the second condition from being evaluated, thus halting, or short-circuiting, the *If* statement and saving us from a nasty "divide by zero" error that could result if we divided 7 by 0 (the new value of the *HumanAge* variable). But although we get a benefit from the short-circuiting behavior in Visual Studio .NET, we don't have the same luck in Visual Basic 6. Setting the *HumanAge* variable to 0 in Visual Basic 6 produces a runtime error and crash because the entire *If* statement is evaluated, and division by zero isn't permitted in Visual Basic 6.

In summary, the *AndAlso* and *OrElse* operators in Visual Basic .NET open up a few new possibilities for Visual Basic programmers, including the potential to prevent runtime errors and other unexpected results. It's also possible to improve performance by placing conditions that are time-consuming to calculate at the end of the condition statement. Visual Basic .NET won't perform these expensive condition calculations unless it's necessary. However, you need to think carefully about all the possible conditions that your *If* statements might encounter as variable states change during program execution.

Select Case Decision Structures

Visual Basic also lets you control the execution of statements in your programs by using Select Case decision structures. You used Select Case structures in Chapter 3 and Chapter 5 of this book when you wrote event procedures to process list box and combo box choices. A Select Case structure is similar to an If...Then...ElseIf structure, but it's more efficient when the branching depends on one key variable, or *test case*. You can also use Select Case structures to make your program code more readable.

The syntax for a Select Case structure looks like this:

```
Select Case variable
    Case value1
        program statements executed if value1 matches variable
    Case value2
        program statements executed if value2 matches variable
    Case value3
        program statements executed if value3 matches variable
    ⋮
    Case Else
        program statements executed if no match is found
End Select
```

A Select Case structure begins with the *Select Case* keywords and ends with the *End Select* keywords. You replace *variable* with the variable, property, or other expression that is to be the key value, or test case, for the structure. You replace *value1*, *value2*, and *value3* with numbers, strings, or other values related to the test case being considered. If one of the values matches the variable, the statements below the *Case* clause are executed, and then Visual Basic jumps to the line after the *End Select* statement and picks up execution there. You can include any number of *Case* clauses in a Select Case structure, and you can include more than one value in a *Case* clause. If you list multiple values after a case, separate them with commas.

The following example shows how a Select Case structure could be used to print an appropriate message about a person's age in a program. Since the *Age* variable contains a value of 18, the string "You can vote now!" is assigned to the *Text* property of the label object.

```
Dim Age As Integer
Age = 18

Select Case Age
    Case 16
        Label1.Text = "You can drive now!"
    Case 18
        Label1.Text = "You can vote now!"
    Case 21
        Label1.Text = "You can drink wine with your meals."
    Case 65
        Label1.Text = "Time to retire and have fun!"
End Select
```

A Select Case structure also supports a *Case Else* clause that you can use to display a message if none of the preceding cases matches. Here's how *Case Else* would work in the following example—note that I've changed the value of *Age* to 25 to trigger the *Case Else* clause.

```
Dim Age As Integer
Age = 25

Select Case Age
    Case 16
        Label1.Text = "You can drive now!"
    Case 18
        Label1.Text = "You can vote now!"
    Case 21
        Label1.Text = "You can drink wine with your meals."
    Case 65
        Label1.Text = "Time to retire and have fun!"
    Case Else
        Label1.Text = "You're a great age! Enjoy it!"
End Select
```

Using Comparison Operators with a Select Case Structure

You can use comparison operators to include a range of test values in a Select Case structure. The Visual Basic comparison operators that can be used are =, <>, >, <, >=, and <=. To use the comparison operators, you need to include the *Is* keyword or the *To* keyword in the expression to identify the comparison you're making. The *Is* keyword instructs the compiler to compare the test variable to the expression listed after the *Is* keyword. The *To* keyword identifies a range of values. The following structure uses *Is*, *To*, and several comparison operators to test the *Age* variable and to display one of five messages:

```
Select Case Age
    Case Is < 13
        Label1.Text = "Enjoy your youth!"
    Case 13 To 19
        Label1.Text = "Enjoy your teens!"
    Case 21
        Label1.Text = "You can drink wine with your meals."
    Case Is > 100
        Label1.Text = "Looking good!"
    Case Else
        Label1.Text = "That's a nice age to be."
End Select
```

If the value of the *Age* variable is less than 13, the message "Enjoy your youth!" is displayed. For the ages 13 through 19, the message "Enjoy your teens!" is displayed, and so on.

A Select Case decision structure is usually much clearer than an If...Then structure and is more efficient when you're making three or more branching decisions based on one variable or property. However, when you're making two or fewer comparisons, or when you're working with several different values, you'll probably want to use an If...Then decision structure.

In the following exercise, you'll see how you can use a Select Case structure to process input from a list box. You'll use the *ListBox1.Text* and *ListBox1.SelectedIndexChanged* properties to collect the input, and then you'll use a Select Case structure to display a greeting in one of four languages.

Use a Select Case structure to process a list box

1 On the File menu, point to New, and then click Project.

The New Project dialog box appears.

2 Create a new Visual Basic Windows Application project named **My Case Greeting** in the c:\vbnet03sbs\chap06 folder.

The new project is created, and a blank form appears in the Windows Forms Designer.

3 Click the *Label* control on the Windows Forms tab of the Toolbox, and then draw a large label across the top of the form to display a title for the program.

4 Draw a small label just below the title label.

5 Click the *ListBox* control in the Toolbox, and then draw a list box below the two existing labels.

6 Draw two small labels below the list box to display program output.

7 Click the *Button* control in the Toolbox, and then draw a small button on the bottom of the form.

8 Click the Properties window button on the Standard toolbar, and then set the object properties as shown in the following table. You'll assign *Name* properties, too, because you have a number of objects to keep track of on your form.

Object	Property	Setting
Form1	*Text*	Case Greeting
Label1	*Font*	Times New Roman, Bold, 12-point
	Name	lblTitle
	Text	"International Welcome Program"
Label2	*Name*	lblTextBoxLabel
	Text	"Choose a country"

Object	Property	Setting
Label3	Font	10-point
	Name	lblCountry
	Text	(empty)
Label4	BorderStyle	Fixed3D
	ForeColor	Red
	Name	lblGreeting
	Text	(empty)
ListBox1	Name	lstCountryBox
Button1	Name	btnQuit
	Text	"Quit"

When you've finished setting properties, your form should look similar to this:

Now you'll enter the program code to initialize the list box.

9   Double-click the form.

The *Form1_Load* event procedure appears in the Code Editor.

10   Type the following program code to initialize the list box:

```
lstCountryBox.Items.Add("England")
lstCountryBox.Items.Add("Germany")
lstCountryBox.Items.Add("Mexico")
lstCountryBox.Items.Add("Italy")
```

These lines use the *Add* method of the list box object to add entries to the list box on your form.

11 Click the Form1.vb tab [Design] at the top of the Code Editor to
switch back to the Windows Forms Designer, and then double-click
the list box object on your form to edit its event procedure.
The *lstCountryBox_SelectedIndexChanged* event procedure appears
in the Code Editor.

12 Type the following lines to process the list box selection made by
the user:

```
lblCountry.Text = lstCountryBox.Text
Select Case lstCountryBox.SelectedIndex
    Case 0
        lblGreeting.Text = "Hello, programmer"
    Case 1
        lblGreeting.Text = "Hallo, programmierer"
    Case 2
        lblGreeting.Text = "Hola, programador"
    Case 3
        lblGreeting.Text = "Ciao, programmatore"
End Select
```

The first line copies the name of the selected list box item to the *Text*
property of the third label on the form (which you renamed *lblCoun-
try*). The most important property used in the statement is *lstCoun-
tryBox.Text*, which contains the exact text of the item selected in the
list box. The remaining statements are part of the Select Case decision structure. The structure uses the *lstCountryBox.SelectedIndex*
property as a test case variable and compares it to several values. The
SelectedIndex property always contains the number of the item
selected in the list box; the item at the top is 0 (zero), the second item
is 1, the next item is 2, and so on. Using *SelectedIndex*, the Select
Case structure can quickly identify the user's choice and display the
correct greeting on the form.

13 Display the form again, and double-click the Quit button (*btnQuit*).
The *btnQuit_Click* event procedure appears in the Code Editor.

14 Type **End** in the event procedure.

15 Click the Save All button on the Standard toolbar to save your changes.

Now run the program, and see how the *Select Case* statement works.
The complete Case Greeting project is located in the
c:\vbnet03sbs\chap06\case greeting folder.

16 Click the Start button on the Standard toolbar to run the program.

17 Click each of the country names in the Choose A Country list box.

The program displays a greeting for each of the countries listed. The following illustration shows the greeting for Italy:

18 Click the Quit button to stop the program.

The program stops, and the development environment returns.

You've finished working with If...Then and Select Case decision structures in this chapter. You'll have several additional opportunities to work with them in this book, however. If...Then and Select Case are two of the crucial decision-making mechanisms in the Visual Basic programming language, and you'll find that you use them in almost every program that you write.

One Step Further: Detecting Mouse Events

I began this chapter by discussing a few of the events that Visual Basic .NET programs can respond to, and as the chapter progressed, you learned how to manage different types of events using the If and Select Case decision structures. In this section, you'll add an event handler to the Case Greeting program that detects when the mouse pointer "hovers" over the country list box for a moment or two. You'll write the special routine, or *event handler*, by building a list box event procedure for the *MouseHover* event, one of several mouse-related activities that Visual Basic .NET can monitor and process. This event procedure will display the message "Please click the country name" if the user holds the mouse over the country list box for a moment or two but doesn't make a selection, perhaps because he or she doesn't know how to or has become engrossed in another task.

Add a mouse event handler

1 Open the Code Editor if it isn't already open.

2 At the top of the Code Editor, click the drop-down arrow in the Class Name list box, and then click the *lstCountryBox* object. (You can use the ToolTip feature to help identify elements in Visual Studio.)

3 Click the drop-down arrow in the Method Name list box, and then click the *MouseHover* event.

   Visual Basic opens the *lstCountryBox_MouseHover* event procedure in the Code Editor, as shown here:

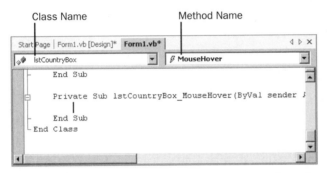

Each object on the form has one event procedure that opens automatically when you double-click the object on the form. You need to open the remaining event procedures by using the Method Name list box. When you build an event procedure to manage one of an object's events, it's called an *event handler*.

4 Type the following program statements in the *lstCountryBox_MouseHover* event procedure:

```
If lstCountryBox.SelectedIndex < 0 Or _
   lstCountryBox.SelectedIndex > 4 Then
     lblGreeting.Text = "Please click the country name"
End If
```

This *If* statement evaluates the *SelectedIndex* property of the list box object using two conditional statements and the *Or* operator. The event handler assumes that if there's a value between 1 and 4 in the *SelectedIndex* property, the user doesn't need help picking the country name (he or she has already selected a country!). But if the *SelectedIndex* property is outside that range, the event handler displays the message "Please click the country name" in the greeting label at the bottom of the form. This message appears when the user hovers the mouse over the list box and disappears when a country name is selected.

5   Click the Start button to run the program.

6   Hold the mouse over the country list box, and wait a few moments.

The message "Please click the country name" appears in red type in the label, as shown here:

7   Click a country name in the list box.

The translated greeting appears in the label, and the help message disappears.

8   Click the Quit button to stop the program.

You've learned how to process mouse events in a program!

Lesson 6 Quick Reference

To	Do this
Write a conditional expression	Use one of the following comparison operators between two values: =, <>, >, <, >=, or <=
Use an If...Then decision structure	Use the following syntax:

```
If condition1 Then
    Statements executed if condition1 True
ElseIf condition2 Then
    Statements executed if condition2 True
Else
    Statements executed if none are True
End If
```

Use a Select Case decision structure	Use the following syntax:

```
Select Case variable
Case value1
    Statements executed if value1 matches
Case value2
    Statements executed if value2 matches
Case Else
    Statements executed if none match
End Select
```

Make two comparisons in a conditional expression	Use a logical operator between comparisons (*And, Or, Not,* or *Xor*).
Short-circuit an *If...Then* statement	In Visual Basic .NET, *If...Then* statements can be short-circuited when the *AndAlso* and *OrElse* operators are used and two or more conditional expressions are given. Depending on the result of the first condition, Visual Basic .NET might not evaluate the additional conditions, and the statement is short-circuited.
Write an event handler	In the Code Editor, click an object name in the Class Name drop-down list box, and then click an event name in the Method Name drop-down list box. Add program statements to the event procedure (or event handler) that perform useful work when the event is executed.

6

Using Decision Structures

Chapter
7

Using Loops and Timers

In this chapter, you will learn how to:

■ Use a For...Next loop to execute statements a set number of times.

■ Display output in a multiline text box by using string concatenation.

■ Use a Do loop to execute statements until a specific condition is met.

■ Use a timer object to execute code at specific times.

■ Create your own digital clock and timed password utility.

In Chapter 6, you learned how to use the If...Then and Select Case decision structures to choose which statements to execute in a program. In this chapter, you'll learn how to execute a block of statements over and over again by using a *loop*. You'll use a For...Next loop to execute statements a set number of times, and you'll use a Do loop to execute statements until a conditional expression is met. You'll also learn how to display more than one line of text in a text box object by using the string concatenation (&) operator. Finally you'll learn how to use a timer object to execute code at specific intervals in your program.

Upgrade Notes: What's New in Visual Basic .NET?

If you're experienced with Microsoft Visual Basic 6, you'll notice some new features in Visual Basic .NET, including the following:

■ In Visual Basic 6, you could display text directly on your form by using the *Print* method, a holdover from the *Print* statement in GW-BASIC and Microsoft QuickBasic. In Visual Basic .NET, the *Print* method can be used only to send data to a file on disk. This chapter shows you an alternative method for displaying large amounts of text on a form—appending text to a multiline text box object by using the string concatenation operator (&).

- In Visual Basic 6, a While loop was specified with the following syntax: While...Wend. In Visual Basic .NET, the closing statement has changed to While...End While to parallel other similar structures.

- The *Timer* control in Visual Basic .NET is similar but not identical to the *Timer* control in Visual Basic 6. For example, the *Timer1_Timer* event procedure (which is executed at each pre-set timer interval) has been renamed *Timer1_Tick* in Microsoft Visual Studio .NET. In addition, you can no longer disable a timer by setting the *Interval* property to 0.

Writing For...Next Loops

With a For...Next loop, you can execute a specific group of program statements a set number of times in an event procedure or a code module. This approach can be useful if you're performing several related calculations, working with elements on the screen, or processing several pieces of user input. A For...Next loop is really just a shorthand way of writing out a long list of program statements. Because each group of statements in such a list would do essentially the same thing, Visual Basic lets you define just one group of statements and request that it be executed as many times as you want.

The syntax for a For...Next loop looks like this:

```
For variable = start To end
    statements to be repeated
Next [variable]
```

In this syntax statement, *For*, *To*, and *Next* are required keywords, and the equal to operator (=) also is required. You replace *variable* with the name of a numeric variable that keeps track of the current loop count (the variable after *Next* is optional), and you replace *start* and *end* with numeric values representing the starting and stopping points for the loop. (Note that you must declare *variable* before it's used in the For...Next statement.) The line or lines between the *For* and *Next* statements are the instructions that are repeated each time the loop is executed.

For example, the following For...Next loop sounds four beeps in rapid succession from the computer's speaker (although the result might be difficult to hear):

```
Dim i As Integer
For i = 1 To 4
    Beep()
Next i
```

This loop is the functional equivalent of writing the *Beep* statement four times in a procedure. The compiler treats it the same as

```
Beep()
Beep()
Beep()
Beep()
```

The variable used in the loop is *i*, a single letter that, by convention, stands for the first integer counter in a For...Next loop and is declared as an *Integer* type. Each time the loop is executed, the counter variable is incremented by one. (The first time through the loop, the variable contains a value of 1, the value of *start*; the last time through, it contains a value of 4, the value of *end*.) As you'll see in the following examples, you can use this counter variable to great advantage in your loops.

Displaying a Counter Variable in a *TextBox* Control

A counter variable is just like any other variable in an event procedure. It can be assigned to properties, used in calculations, or displayed in a program. One of the practical uses for a counter variable is to display output in a *TextBox* control. You used the *TextBox* control earlier in this book to display a single line of output, but in this chapter, you'll display many lines of text using a *TextBox* control. The trick to displaying more than one line is simply to set the *Multiline* property of the *TextBox* control to True and to set the *ScrollBars* property to Vertical. Using these simple settings, the one-line text box object becomes a multiline text box object with scroll bars for easy access.

Display information by using a For...Next loop

1   Start Visual Studio and create a new Visual Basic Windows Application project named **My For Loop** in the c:\vbnet03sbs\chap07 folder.

The new project is created, and a blank form appears in the Windows Forms Designer. Your first programming step is to add a *Button* control to the form, but this time you'll do it in a new way.

2   Double-click the *Button* control on the Windows Forms tab of the Toolbox.

Visual Studio places a button object in the upper left corner of the form. With the *Button* control and many others, double-clicking is a quick way to create a standard-sized object on the form. Now you can drag the button object to the place that you want, and customize it with property settings.

3 Drag the button object to the right and center it near the top of the form.

4 Open the Properties window, and then set the *Text* property of the button to Loop.

5 Double-click the *TextBox* control in the Toolbox.

Visual Studio creates a small text box object on the form.

6 Set the *Multiline* property of the text box object to True, and then set the *ScrollBars* property of the text box object to Vertical.

These settings prepare the text box for displaying more than one line of text.

7 Set the *Text* property of the text box object to blank (empty).

8 Move the text box below the button and enlarge it so that it takes up most of the form.

9 Double-click the *Loop* button on the form.

The *Button1_Click* event procedure appears in the Code Editor.

10 Type the following program statements in the procedure:

```
Dim i As Integer
Dim Wrap As String
Wrap = Chr(13) & Chr(10)
For i = 1 To 10
    TextBox1.Text = TextBox1.Text & "Line " & i & Wrap
Next i
```

This event procedure declares two variables, one of type *Integer* (*i*) and one of type *String* (*Wrap*), and then assigns the second variable a string value representing the carriage return character. (In programmer terms, a carriage return character is the equivalent of pressing the Enter key on the keyboard. I created a special variable for this character, which is made up of return and linefeed elements, to make using it less cumbersome.)

After the variable declaration and assignment, I use a For...Next loop to display Line *X* 10 times in the text box object, where *X* is the current value of the counter variable (in other words, Line 1 through Line 10). The string concatenation characters (&) join the component parts of each line together in the text box. First, the entire value of the text box, which is stored in the *Text* property, is added to the object so that previous lines aren't discarded when new ones are added. Next, the string "Line", the current line number, and the carriage return character (*Wrap*) are combined to display a new line and move the cursor to the left margin and down one line. The *Next* statement completes the loop.

Note that Visual Studio automatically adds the *Next* statement to the bottom of the loop when you type *For* to begin the loop. In this case, I edited the *Next* statement to include the *i* variable name—this is an optional syntax clarification that I like to use. (The variable name makes it clear which variable is being updated, especially in nested For...Next loops.)

11 Click the Save All button on the Standard toolbar to save your changes.

Now you're ready to run the program.

12 Click the Start button on the Standard toolbar.

13 Click the Loop button.

> ▶ **Tip** The complete For Loop program is available in the c:\vbnet03sbs\chap07\for loop folder.

The For...Next loop displays 10 lines in the text box, as shown here:

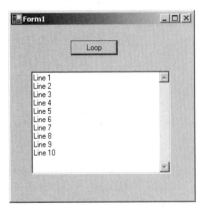

14 Click the Loop button again.

The For...Next loop displays another 10 lines on the form, and you can see any nonvisible lines by using the vertical scroll bar to scroll down. Each time the loop is repeated, it will add 10 more lines to the text box object.

> ▶ **Tip** Worried about running out of room in the text box object? It won't happen fast if you're displaying only simple text lines. A multiline text box object has a practical limit of 32 KB of text. (For even more space and formatting options, try the *RichTextBox* control.)

15 Click the Close button on the form to stop the program.

> ▶ **Tip**   If you need to execute a set of statements multiple times, a
> For...Next loop can considerably simplify your code and reduce the total
> number of statements that you need to type. In the previous example, a
> For...Next loop three lines long processed the equivalent of 10 program
> statements.

Creating Complex For...Next Loops

The counter variable in a For...Next loop can be a powerful tool in your programs. With a little imagination, you can use it to create several useful
sequences of numbers in your loops. To create a loop with a counter pattern
other than 1, 2, 3, 4, and so on, you can specify a different value for *start* in the
loop, and then use the *Step* keyword to increment the counter at different intervals. For example, the code

```
Dim i As Integer
Dim Wrap As String
Wrap = Chr(13) & Chr(10)

For i = 5 To 25 Step 5
    TextBox1.Text = TextBox1.Text & "Line " & i & Wrap
Next i
```

would display the following sequence of line numbers in a text box:

```
Line 5
Line 10
Line 15
Line 20
Line 25
```

You can also specify decimal values in a loop if you declare *i* as a single-precision or double-precision type. For example, the For...Next loop

```
Dim i As Single
Dim Wrap As String
Wrap = Chr(13) & Chr(10)

For i = 1 To 2.5 Step 0.5
    TextBox1.Text = TextBox1.Text & "Line " & i & Wrap
Next i
```

would display the following line numbers in a text box:

```
Line 1
Line 1.5
Line 2
Line 2.5
```

In addition to displaying the counter variable, you can use the counter to set properties, calculate values, or process files. The following exercise shows how you can use the counter to open Visual Basic icons that are stored on your hard disk in files that have numbers in their names. You'll find many files like this in the c:\program files\microsoft visual studio .net 2003\common7\graphics\icons\misc folder.

Open files by using a For...Next loop

1   On the File menu, point to New, and then click Project.

   The New Project dialog box appears.

2   Create a new Visual Basic Windows Application project named **My For Loop Icons** in the c:\vbnet03sbs\chap07 folder.

   The new project is created, and a blank form appears in the Windows Forms Designer.

3   Click the *PictureBox* control on the Windows Forms tab of the Toolbox, and then draw a medium-sized picture box object centered on the top half of the form.

4   Click the *Button* control in the Toolbox, and then draw a very wide button below the picture box (you'll put a longer than usual label on the button).

5   Set the following properties for the two objects:

Object	Property	Setting
PictureBox1	BorderStyle	Fixed3D
	SizeMode	StretchImage
Button1	Text	"Display four faces"

6   Double-click the Display Four Faces button on the form to display the event procedure for the button object.

   The *Button1_Click* event procedure appears in the Code Editor.

7   Type the following For...Next loop:

```
Dim i As Integer
For i = 1 To 4
    PictureBox1.Image = System.Drawing.Image.FromFile _
        ("c:\vbnet03sbs\chap07\face0" & i & ".ico")
    MsgBox("Click here for next face.")
Next
```

   ▶ **Tip**   The *FromFile* method in this event procedure is too long to fit on one line in this book, so I broke it into two lines by using a space and the line continuation character (_). You can use this character anywhere in your program code except within a string expression.

The loop uses the *FromFile* method to load four icon files from the c:\vbnet03sbs\chap07 folder on your hard disk. The filename is created by using the counter variable and the concatenation operator you used earlier in this chapter. The code

```
PictureBox1.Image = System.Drawing.Image.FromFile _
  ("c:\vbnet03sbs\chap07\face0" & i & ".ico")
```

combines a path, a filename, and the .ico extension to create four valid filenames of icons on your hard disk. In this example, you're loading face01.ico, face02.ico, face03.ico, and face04.ico into the picture box. This statement works because several files in the c:\vbnet03sbs\chap07 folder have the filename pattern face*xx*.ico. Recognizing the pattern lets you build a For...Next loop around the filenames.

▶ **Note**   The message box function (*MsgBox*) is used primarily to slow the action down and allow you to see what's happening in the For...Next loop. In a normal application, you probably wouldn't use such a function (but you're welcome to do so).

8   Click the Save All button on the toolbar to save your changes.

9   Click the Start button on the Standard toolbar to start the program, and then click the Display Four Faces button. (The complete For Loop Icons program is available in the c:\vbnet03sbs\chap07\for loop icons folder.)

The For...Next loop loads the first face into the picture box, and then displays this message box:

▶ **Note**   If Visual Basic displays an error message, check your program code for typos, and then verify that the icon files are in the path you specified in the program. If you installed the Step by Step practice files in a folder other than the default folder or if you moved your icon files after installation, the path in the event procedure might not be correct.

10 Click the OK button to display the next face.

Your screen will look like this:

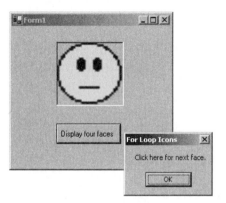

11 Click the OK button three more times to see the entire face collection.

You can repeat the sequence if you like.

12 When you're finished, click the Close button on the form to quit the program.

The program stops, and the development environment returns.

Opening Files Using a Counter That Has Greater Scope

Are there times when using a For...Next loop isn't that efficient or elegant? Sure. In fact, the preceding example, although useful as a demonstration, was a little hampered by the intrusive behavior of the message box, which opened four times in the For...Next loop and distracted the user from the form, where we want his or her attention to be. Is there a way we can do away with that intrusive message box?

One solution is to remove both the *MsgBox* function and the For...Next loop, and substitute in their place a counter variable that has greater scope throughout the form. As you learned in Chapter 5, you can declare a variable that has scope (or maintains its value) throughout the entire form by placing a *Dim* statement for the variable at the top of the form in the Code Editor—a special location above the event procedures and just below the Windows Forms Designer generated code section. In the following exercise, you'll use an *Integer* variable named *Counter* that will maintain its value between calls to the *Button1_Click* event procedure, and you'll use that variable to open the same icon files without using the *MsgBox* function to pause the action.

Use a global counter

1 In the Code Editor, locate the *Button1_Click* event procedure in the My For Loop Icons project.

2 Move the cursor above the *Button1_Click* event procedure, and directly below the Windows Forms Designer generated code section, declare an *Integer* variable named *Counter* using this syntax:

```
Dim Counter As Integer = 1
```

You've done something unusual here—in addition to declaring the variable *Counter*, you've also assigned the variable a value of 1. This is a new syntax option in Visual Studio .NET, and now and then you'll find it very handy to use. (Declaring and assigning at the same time isn't permitted in Visual Basic 6.)

3 Within the *Button1_Click* event procedure, change the code so that it precisely matches the following group of program statements. (Delete the statements that aren't here.)

```
PictureBox1.Image = System.Drawing.Image.FromFile _
  ("c:\vbnet03sbs\chap07\face0" & Counter & ".ico")
Counter += 1
If Counter = 5 Then Counter = 1
```

As you can see, I've deleted the declaration for the *i* integer, the *For* and *Next* statements, and the *MsgBox* function, and I've changed the way the *FromFile* method works. (I've replaced the *i* variable with the *Counter* variable.) I've also added two new statements that use the *Counter* variable. The first statement adds 1 to *Counter* (Counter += 1), and the second statement resets the *Counter* variable if the value has been incremented to 5. (Resetting the variable in this way will allow the list of icon files to cycle indefinitely.) The Counter += 1 syntax is a new shortcut feature in Visual Basic .NET—the functional equivalent of the statement

```
Counter = Counter + 1
```

4 Click the Start button to run the program.

> ▶ **Tip** The complete Counter Variable program is located in the c:\vbnet03sbs\chap07\counter variable folder.

The program runs in the development environment.

5 Click the Display Four Faces button several times. (Notice how the mood of the faces develops from glum to cheery.)

6   When you're finished, click the Close button on the form to stop the program.

As you can see, this solution is a little more elegant than the previous example I used because it allows the user to click just one button, not a form button and a message box button. The shortcoming of the interface in the first program wasn't the fault of the For...Next loop, however, but rather the limitation I'd imposed that the *Button1_Click* event procedure use only local variables (in other words, variables that were declared within the event procedure itself). Between button clicks, these local variables lost their value, and the only way I was able to increment the counter was to build a loop. Using an *Integer* variable with a greater scope, I was able to preserve the value of the *Counter* variable between clicks and use that numeric information to display files within the *Button1_Click* event procedure.

The *Exit For* Statement

Most For...Next loops run to completion without incident, but now and then you'll find it useful to end the computation of a For...Next loop if a particular "exit condition" comes up. Visual Basic allows for this possibility by providing the *Exit For* statement, a special statement that you use to terminate the execution of a For...Next loop early and move execution to the first statement after the loop.

For example, the following For...Next loop prompts the user for 10 names and displays them one by one in a text box unless the user enters the word "Done":

```
Dim i As Integer
Dim InpName As String
For i = 1 To 10
    InpName = InputBox("Enter your name or type Done to quit.")
```

```
        If InpName = "Done" Then Exit For
        TextBox1.Text = InpName
Next i
```

If the user does enter "Done", the *Exit For* statement terminates the loop, and execution picks up with the statement after *Next*.

Writing Do Loops

As an alternative to a For...Next loop, you can write a Do loop that executes a group of statements until a certain condition is True. Do loops are valuable because often you can't know in advance how many times a loop should repeat. For example, you might want to let the user enter names in a database until the user types the word "Done" in an input box. In that case, you can use a Do loop to cycle indefinitely until the text string "Done" is entered.

A Do loop has several formats, depending on where and how the loop condition is evaluated. The most common syntax is

```
Do While condition
    block of statements to be executed
Loop
```

For example, the following Do loop will prompt the user for input and display that input in a text box until the word "Done" is typed in the input box:

```
Dim InpName As String
Do While InpName <> "Done"
    InpName = InputBox("Enter your name or type Done to quit.")
    If InpName <> "Done" Then TextBox1.Text = InpName
Loop
```

The conditional statement in this loop is InpName <> "Done", which the Visual Basic compiler translates to mean "loop as long as the *InpName* variable doesn't contain the word *Done*." This brings up an interesting fact about Do loops: if the condition at the top of the loop isn't True when the *Do* statement is first evaluated, the Do loop is never executed. Here, if the *InpName* string variable did contain the value "Done" before the loop started (perhaps from an earlier assignment in the event procedure), Visual Basic would skip the loop altogether and continue with the line below the *Loop* keyword.

If you always want the loop to run at least once in a program, put the conditional test at the bottom of the loop. For example, the loop

```
Dim InpName As String
Do
    InpName = InputBox("Enter your name or type Done to quit.")
    If InpName <> "Done" Then TextBox1.Text = InpName
Loop While InpName <> "Done"
```

is essentially the same as the previous Do loop, but here the loop condition is tested after a name is received from the *InputBox* function. This has the advantage of updating the *InpName* variable before the conditional test in the loop so that a preexisting "Done" value won't cause the loop to be skipped. Testing the loop condition at the bottom ensures that your loop will be executed at least once, but often it will force you to add a few extra statements to process the data.

▶ **Note**   The previous code samples asked the user to type "Done" to quit. Note that the test of the entered text is case sensitive, which means that typing "done" or "DONE" doesn't end the program. You can do a case-insensitive test of the entered text by using the *StrComp* function. I'll discuss the *StrComp* function in Chapter 12.

Avoiding an Endless Loop

Because of the relentless nature of Do loops, it's very important to design your test conditions so that each loop has a true exit point. If a loop test never evaluates to False, the loop will execute endlessly, and your program might not respond to input. Consider the following example:

```
Dim Number as Double
Do
    Number = InputBox("Enter a number to square. Type -1 to quit.")
    Number = Number * Number
    TextBox1.Text = Number
Loop While Number >= 0
```

In this loop, the user enters number after number, and the program squares each number and displays it in the text box. Unfortunately, when the user has had enough, he or she can't quit because the advertised exit condition doesn't work. When the user enters -1, the program squares it, and the *Number* variable is assigned the value 1. (The problem can be fixed by setting a different exit condition.) Watching for endless loops is essential when you're writing Do loops. Fortunately, they're pretty easy to spot if you test your programs thoroughly.

▶ **Important**   Be sure that each loop has a legitimate exit condition.

The following exercise shows how you can use a Do loop to convert Fahrenheit temperatures to Celsius temperatures. The simple program prompts the user for input by using the *InputBox* function, converts the temperature, and displays the output in a message box.

Convert temperatures by using a Do loop

1   On the File menu, point to New, and then click Project.

The New Project dialog box appears.

2   Create a new Visual Basic Windows Application project named **My Celsius Conversion** in the c:\vbnet03sbs\chap07 folder.

The new project is created, and a blank form appears in the Windows Forms Designer. This time, you'll place all the code for your program in the *Form1_Load* event procedure so that Visual Basic immediately prompts you for the Fahrenheit temperature when you start the application. You'll use an *InputBox* function to request the Fahrenheit data, and you'll use a *MsgBox* function to display the converted value.

3   Double-click the form.

The *Form1_Load* event procedure appears in the Code Editor.

4   Type the following program statements in the *Form1_Load* event procedure:

```
Dim FTemp, Celsius As Single
Dim strFTemp As String
Dim Prompt As String = "Enter a Fahrenheit temperature."
Do
    strFTemp = InputBox(Prompt, "Fahrenheit to Celsius")
    If strFTemp <> "" Then
        FTemp = CSng(strFTemp)
        Celsius = Int((FTemp + 40) * 5 / 9 - 40)
        MsgBox(Celsius, , "Temperature in Celsius")
    End If
Loop While strFTemp <> ""
End
```

▶ **Tip**   Be sure to include the *End* statement at the bottom of the *Form1_Load* event procedure.

This code handles the calculations for the utility. The first line declares two single-precision variables, *FTemp* and *Celsius*, to hold the Fahrenheit and Celsius temperatures, respectively. The second line declares a string variable named *strFTemp* that holds a string version of the Fahrenheit temperature. The third line declares a string variable named *Prompt*, which will be used in the *InputBox* function, and assigns it an initial value. The Do loop repeatedly prompts the user for a Fahrenheit temperature, converts the number to Celsius, and then displays it on the screen by using the *MsgBox* function.

The value that the user enters in the input box is stored in the *strFTemp* variable. The *InputBox* function always returns a value of type string, even if the user enters in numbers. Because we want to perform mathematical calculations on the entered value, *strFTemp* must be converted to a number. The *CSng* function is used to convert a string into a *Single*. *CSng* is one of many conversion functions to convert a string to a different data type. The converted single value is then stored in the *FTemp* variable.

The loop executes until the user clicks the Cancel button or until the user presses Enter or clicks OK with no value in the input box. Clicking the Cancel button or entering no value returns an empty string (""). The loop checks for the empty string by using a While conditional test at the bottom of the loop. The program statement

```
Celsius = Int((FTemp + 40) * 5 / 9 - 40)
```

handles the conversion from Fahrenheit to Celsius in the program. This statement employs a standard conversion formula, but it uses the *Int* function to return to the Celsius variable a value that contains no decimal places. (Everything to the right of the decimal point is discarded.) This cutting sacrifices accuracy, but it helps you avoid long, unsightly numbers such as 21.11111, the Celsius value for 70 degrees Fahrenheit.

5 Click the Save All button on the toolbar to save your changes.

> ▶ **Tip** The complete Celsius Conversion program is available in the c:\vbnet03sbs\chap07\celsius conversion folder.

Now try running the program.

6 Click the Start button on the Standard toolbar.

The program starts, and the *InputBox* function prompts you for a Fahrenheit temperature.

7 Type **212**.

Your screen should look like this:

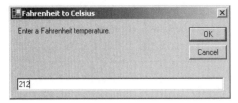

8   Click OK.

The temperature 212 degrees Fahrenheit is converted to 100 degrees Celsius, as shown in this message box:

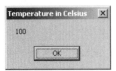

9   Click OK. Type **72** in the input box, and click OK.

The temperature 72 degrees Fahrenheit is converted to 22 degrees Celsius.

10   Click OK, and then quit the program by clicking Cancel in the input box.

The program quits, and the development environment returns.

Using the *Until* Keyword in Do Loops

The Do loops you've worked with so far have used the *While* keyword to execute a group of statements as long as the loop condition remains True. Visual Basic also lets you use the *Until* keyword in Do loops to cycle *until* a certain condition is True. You can use the *Until* keyword at the top or bottom of a Do loop to test a condition, just like the *While* keyword. For example, the following Do loop uses the *Until* keyword to loop repeatedly until the user enters the word "Done" in the input box:

```
Dim InpName As String
Do
    InpName = InputBox("Enter your name or type Done to quit.")
    If InpName <> "Done" Then TextBox1.Text = InpName
Loop Until InpName = "Done"
```

As you can see, a loop that uses the *Until* keyword is similar to a loop that uses the *While* keyword, except that the test condition usually contains the opposite operator—the = (equal to) operator versus the <> (not equal to) operator, in this case. If using the *Until* keyword makes sense to you, feel free to use it with test conditions in your Do loops.

The *Timer* Control

You can execute a group of statements at a specific time by using the *Timer* control. The *Timer* control is an invisible stopwatch that gives you access to the system clock in your programs. It can be used like an egg timer to count down from a preset time, to cause a delay in a program, or to repeat an action at prescribed intervals.

Although timer objects aren't visible at runtime, each timer is associated with an event procedure that runs every time the timer's preset *interval* has elapsed. You set a timer's interval by using the *Interval* property, and you activate a timer by setting the timer's *Enabled* property to True. Once a timer is enabled, it runs constantly—executing its event procedure at the prescribed interval—until the user stops the program or the timer is disabled.

Creating a Digital Clock Using a *Timer* Control

One of the most practical uses for a *Timer* control is creating a digital clock. In the following exercise, you'll create a simple digital clock that keeps track of the current time down to the second. In the example, you'll set the *Interval* property for the timer to 1000, directing Visual Basic to update the clock time every 1000 milliseconds, or once a second. Because the Microsoft Windows operating system is a multitasking environment and other programs will also require processing time, Visual Basic might not always get a chance to update the clock each second, but it will always catch up if it falls behind. To keep track of the time at other intervals (such as once every tenth of a second), simply adjust the number in the *Interval* property.

Create the Digital Clock program

1 On the File menu, point to New, and then click Project.

   The New Project dialog box appears.

2 Create a new Visual Basic Windows Application project named **My Digital Clock** in the c:\vbnet03sbs\chap07 folder.

   The new project is created, and a blank form appears in the Windows Forms Designer.

3 Resize the form to a small rectangular window (a window that's wider than it is tall).

   You don't want the clock to take up much room.

4   Double-click the *Timer* control on the Windows Forms tab of the Toolbox.

Visual Studio creates a small timer object in the component tray beneath your form, as shown here:

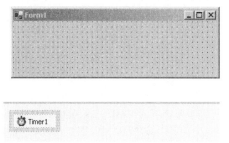

Recall from Chapter 4 that certain Visual Studio controls don't have a visual representation on the form, and when objects for these controls are created, they appear in the component tray beneath the form. (This was the case for the *MainMenu* control that you used in Chapter 4.) However, you can still select controls in this special pane and set properties for them, as you'll do for the timer object in this exercise.

5   Click the *Label* control in the Toolbox, and then draw a very large label object on the form—a label that's almost the size of the entire form itself.

You'll use the label to display the time in the clock, and you want to create a very big label to hold the 24-point type you'll be using.

6   Open the Properties window, and set the following properties for the form and two objects in your program.

Object	Property	Setting
Label1	*Text*	(empty)
	Font	Times New Roman, Bold, 24-point
	TextAlign	MiddleCenter
Timer1	*Enabled*	True
	Interval	1000
Form1	*Text*	"Digital Clock"

▶   **Tip**   If you'd like to put some artwork in the background of your clock, set the *BackgroundImage* property of the *Form1* object to the path of a graphics file.

Now you'll write the program code for the timer.

7 Double-click the timer object in the component tray.

The *Timer1_Tick* event procedure appears in the Code Editor. Experienced Visual Basic 6 programmers will notice that this event procedure has been renamed from *Timer1_Timer* to *Timer1_Tick*, clarifying what this event procedure does in the program (that is, the event procedure runs each time that the timer clock ticks).

8 Type the following statement:

```
Label1.Text = TimeString
```

This statement gets the current time from the system clock and assigns it to the *Text* property of the *Label1* object. (If you'd like to have the date displayed in the clock as well as the time, use the *System.DateTime.Now* property instead of the *TimeString* property.) Only one statement is required in this program because you set the *Interval* property for the timer by using the Properties window. The timer object handles the rest.

9 Click the Save All button on the toolbar to save your changes.

> ▶ **Tip** The complete Digital Clock program is available in the
> c:\vbnet03sbs\chap07\digital clock folder.

10 Click the Start button on the Standard toolbar to run the clock.

The clock appears, as shown in the following illustration. (Your time will be different, of course.)

If you used the *System.DateTime.Now* property, you'll see the date in the clock also, as shown here. (If your display wraps onto two lines, as this one does, you might want to enlarge the form a little.)

11 Watch the clock for a few moments.

Visual Basic updates the time every second.

12 Click the Close button in the title bar to stop the clock.

The Digital Clock program is so handy that you might want to compile it into an executable file and use it now and then on your computer. Feel free to customize it by using your own artwork, text, and colors.

One Step Further: Using a Timer Object to Set a Time Limit

Another interesting use of a timer object is to set it to wait for a given period of time and then either to enable or prohibit an action. This is once again a little like setting an egg timer in your program—you set the *Interval* property with the delay you want, and then you start the clock ticking by setting the *Enabled* property to True.

The following exercise shows how you can use this approach to set a time limit for entering a password. (The password for this program is "secret".) The program uses a timer to close its own program if a valid password isn't entered in 15 seconds. (Normally, a program like this would be part of a larger application.) You can also use this timer technique to display a welcome message or a copyright message on the screen or to repeat an event at a set interval, such as saving a file to disk every 10 minutes.

Set a password time limit

1 On the File menu, point to New, and then click Project.

The New Project dialog box appears.

2 Create a new Visual Basic Windows Application project named **My Timed Password** in the c:\vbnet03sbs\chap07 folder.

The new project is created, and a blank form appears in the Windows Forms Designer.

3 Resize the form to a small rectangular window about the size of an input box.

4 Click the *TextBox* control on the Windows Forms tab of the Toolbox, and then draw a text box for the password in the middle of the form.

5   Click the *Label* control in the Toolbox, and then draw a long label above the text box.

6   Click the *Button* control in the Toolbox, and then draw a button below the text box.

7   Double-click the *Timer* control in the Toolbox.

Visual Studio adds a timer object to the component tray below the form.

8   Set the properties in the following table for the program.

Object	Property	Setting
Label1	*Text*	"Enter your password within 15 seconds"
TextBox1	*PasswordChar*	"*"
	Text	(empty)
Button1	*Text*	"Try Password"
Timer1	*Enabled*	True
	Interval	15000
Form1	*Text*	"Password"

The *PasswordChar* setting will display asterisk (*) characters in the text box as the user enters a password. Setting the timer *Interval* property to 15000 will give the user 15 seconds to enter a password and click the Try Password button. Setting the *Enabled* property to True will start the timer running when the program starts. (You could also disable this property and then enable it in an event procedure if your timer wasn't needed until later in the program.)

Your form should look like this:

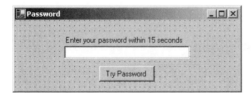

9   Double-click the timer object in the component tray, and then type the following statements in the *Timer1_Tick* event procedure:

```
MsgBox("Sorry, your time is up.")
End
```

The first statement displays a message indicating that the time has expired, and the second statement stops the program. Visual Basic executes this event procedure if the timer interval reaches 15 seconds and a valid password hasn't been entered.

10 Display the form, double-click the button object, and then type the following statements in the *Button1_Click* event procedure:

```
If TextBox1.Text = "secret" Then
    Timer1.Enabled = False
    MsgBox("Welcome to the system!")
    End
Else
    MsgBox("Sorry, friend, I don't know you.")
End If
```

This program code tests whether the password entered in the text box is "secret." If it is, the timer is disabled, a welcome message is displayed, and the program ends. (A more useful program would continue working rather than ending here.) If the password entered isn't a match, the user is notified with a message box and is given another chance to enter the password. But the user has only 15 seconds to do so!

11 Click the Save All button on the toolbar to save your changes.

▶   **Tip**   The complete Timed Password program is available in the c:\vbnet03sbs\chap07\timed password folder.

Test the Timed Password program

1 Click the Start button to run the program.

The program starts, and the 15-second clock starts ticking.

2 Type **open** in the text box.

The asterisk characters hide the text of your input, as shown here:

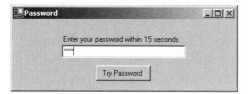

3 Click the Try Password button.

The following message box appears on the screen, noting your incorrect response:

4 Click OK, and then wait patiently until the sign-on period expires.

The program displays the time up message shown in this message box:

5 Click OK to end the program.

6 Run the program again, type **secret** (the correct password) in the text box, and then click Try Password.

7 The program displays this message:

8 Click OK to end the program.

The Visual Basic development environment appears.

As you can see, there are many practical uses for timer objects. As with For…Next loops and Do loops, you can use timer objects to repeat commands and procedures as many times as you need in a program.

Lesson 7 Quick Reference

To	Do this
Execute a group of program statements a set number of times	Insert the statements between *For* and *Next* statements in a loop. For example: ``` Dim i As Integer For i = 1 To 10 MsgBox("Press OK already!") Next i ```
Use a specific sequence of numbers with statements	Insert the statements in a For...Next loop, and use the *To* and *Step* keywords to define the sequence of numbers. For example: ``` Dim i As Integer For i = 2 To 8 Step 2 TextBox1.Text = TextBox1.Text & i Next i ```
Avoid an endless Do loop	Be sure the loop has a test condition that can evaluate to False.

Exit a For...Next loop prematurely	Use the *Exit For* statement. For example:
	
	``
	Dim InpName As String
	Dim i As Integer
	For i = 1 To 10
	    InpName = InputBox("Name?")
	    If InpName = "Trotsky" Then Exit For
	    TextBox1.Text = InpName
	Next i
	``

Execute a group of program statements until a specific condition is met	Insert the statements between *Do* and *Loop* statements. For example:
	
	``
	Dim Query As String = ""
	Do While Query <> "Yes"
	    Query = InputBox("Trotsky?")
	    If Query = "Yes" Then MsgBox("Hi")
	Loop
	``

Loop until a certain condition is True	Use a Do loop with the *Until* keyword. For example: ``` Dim GiveIn As String Do GiveIn = InputBox("Say 'Uncle'") Loop Until GiveIn = "Uncle" ```
Loop for a specific period of time in your program	Use the *Timer* control.

Debugging Visual Basic .NET Programs

In this chapter, you will learn how to:

■ Identify different types of errors in your programs.

■ Use Microsoft Visual Studio .NET debugging tools to set breakpoints and correct mistakes.

■ Use a Watch window to examine variables during program execution.

■ Use the Command window to change the value of variables and execute commands in Visual Studio.

In the past few chapters, you've had plenty of opportunity to make programming mistakes in your code. Unlike human conversation, which usually works well despite occasional grammatical mistakes and mispronunciations, communication between a software developer and the Microsoft Visual Basic compiler is successful only when the precise rules and regulations of the Visual Basic programming language are followed. In this chapter, you'll learn more about the software defects, or *bugs*, that stop Visual Basic programs from running. You'll learn about the different types of errors that turn up in programs and how to use the Visual Studio .NET debugging tools to detect and correct these defects. What you learn will be useful to you as you experiment with the programs in this book and when you write longer programs in the future.

Upgrade Notes: What's New in Visual Basic .NET?

If you're experienced with Visual Basic 6, you'll notice some new features in Visual Basic .NET, including the following:

■ Visual Basic .NET includes several new tools for finding and correcting errors. Many of the familiar Visual Basic 6 debugging commands are still a part of Visual Studio (Start, Break, End, Next, Step Into, Step Over), but there are also new debugging tools and commands, including a revised Debug toolbar, menu commands that manage processes and exceptions, and tools that support the debugging of multilanguage solutions.

■ Several new debugging windows have been added to the Visual Studio .NET user interface, including Autos, Command, Call Stack, Threads, Memory, Disassembly, and Registers. You won't use these tools for each debugging session, but you might find them useful in more sophisticated applications.

Finding and Correcting Errors

The defects you've encountered in your programs so far have probably been simple typing mistakes or syntax errors. But what if you discover a nastier problem in your program—one you can't find and correct by a simple review of the objects, properties, and statements you've used? The Visual Studio development environment contains several tools that will help you track down and fix errors in your programs. These tools won't stop you from making mistakes, but they'll often ease the pain when you encounter one.

Three Types of Errors

Three types of errors can occur in a Visual Basic program: syntax errors, runtime errors, and logic errors.

■ A *syntax error* (or *compiler error*) is a programming mistake (such as a misspelled property or keyword) that violates the rules of Visual Basic. Visual Basic points out several types of syntax errors in your programs while you type program statements and won't let you run a program until you fix each syntax error.

■ A *runtime error* is a mistake that causes a program to stop unexpectedly during execution. Runtime errors occur when an outside event or an undiscovered syntax error forces a program to stop while it's running. For instance, if you misspell a filename when you use the

System.Drawing.Image.FromFile method or if you try to read the diskette drive and it doesn't contain a disk, your code will generate a runtime error.

■ A *logic error* is a human error—a programming mistake that makes the program code produce the wrong results. Most debugging efforts are focused on tracking down logic errors introduced by the programmer.

If you encounter a syntax error, you often can solve the problem by using Visual Basic online Help to learn more about the error message, and you can fix the mistake by paying close attention to the exact syntax of the functions, objects, methods, and properties that you use. In the Code Editor, incorrect statements are underlined with a blue, jagged line, and you can learn more about the error by holding the mouse pointer over the statement. The following illustration shows the error message that appears in Visual Studio when I type the keyword *Case* incorrectly ("Csae" instead of "Case") and then hold the mouse pointer over the error. This error message is just like a ToolTip.

Syntax error identified by the Visual Basic compiler

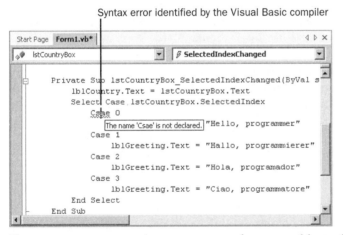

If you encounter a runtime error, you often can address the problem by correcting your typing. For example, if a bitmap loads incorrectly into a picture box object, the problem might simply be a misspelled path. However, many runtime errors require a more thorough solution—the *structured error handler*, which is a special block of program code that recognizes a runtime error when it happens, suppresses any error messages, and adjusts program conditions to handle the problem. I discuss the new syntax for structured error handlers in Chapter 9.

Identifying Logic Errors

Logic errors in your programs are often the most difficult to fix. They're the result of faulty reasoning and planning, not a misunderstanding about Visual Basic syntax. Consider the following If...Then decision structure, which evaluates two conditional expressions and then displays one of two messages based on the result:

```
If Age > 13 And Age < 20 Then
    TextBox2.Text = "You're a teenager"
Else
    TextBox2.Text = "You're not a teenager"
End If
```

Can you spot the problem with this decision structure? A teenager is a person who's between 13 and 19 years old, inclusive, but the structure fails to identify the person who's exactly 13. (For this age, the structure erroneously displays the message "You're not a teenager".) This type of mistake isn't a syntax error (because the statements follow the rules of Visual Basic); it's a mental mistake, or logic error. The correct decision structure contains a greater than or equal to operator (>=) in the first comparison after the If...Then statement, as shown here:

```
If Age >= 13 And Age < 20 Then
```

Believe it or not, this type of mistake is the most common problem in a Visual Basic program. Code that works most of the time—but not all of the time—is the hardest to test and to fix.

Debugging 101: Using Break Mode

One way to identify a logic error is to execute your program code one line at a time and examine the content of one or more variables or properties as they change. To do this, you can enter *break mode* while your program is running and then view your code in the Code Editor. Break mode gives you a close-up look at your program while the Visual Basic compiler is executing it. It's kind of like pulling up a chair behind the pilot and copilot and watching them fly the airplane. But in this case, you can touch the controls.

While you're debugging your application, you'll need to use the *Debug toolbar*, a special toolbar with buttons devoted entirely to tracking down errors. The following illustration shows this toolbar, which you can open by pointing to the Toolbars command on the View menu and then clicking Debug.

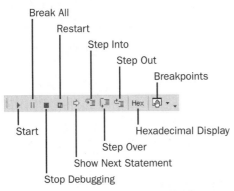

In the following exercise, you'll set a breakpoint and use break mode to find and correct the logic error you discovered earlier in the If...Then structure. (The error is part of an actual program.) To isolate the problem, you'll use the Step Into button on the Debug toolbar to execute program instructions one at a time, and you'll use the Autos window to examine the value of key program variables and properties. Pay close attention to this debugging strategy. You can use it to correct many types of glitches in your own programs.

Debug the Debug Test program

1   Start Visual Studio.

2   On the File menu, point to Open, and then click Project.

     The Open Project dialog box appears.

3   Open the Debug Test project in the c:\vbnet03sbs\chap08\debug test folder.

     The project opens in the development environment.

4   If the form isn't visible, display it now.

     The Debug Test program prompts the user for his or her age. When the user clicks the Test button, the program lets the user know whether he or she is a teenager. The program still has the problem with 13-year-olds that we identified earlier in the chapter, however. You'll open the Debug toolbar now, and set a breakpoint to find the problem.

5   If the Debug toolbar isn't visible, click the View menu, point to the Toolbars, and then click Debug.

     The Debug toolbar appears below the Standard toolbar.

6   Click the Start button on the Debug toolbar.

The program runs and displays the Debug Test form.

7   Remove the 0 from the age text box, type **14**, and then click the Test button.

The program displays the message "You're a teenager". So far, the program displays the correct result.

8   Type **13** in the age text box, and then click the Test button.

The program displays the message "You're not a teenager", as shown here:

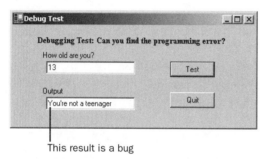

This result is a bug

This answer is incorrect, and you need to look at the program code to fix the problem.

9   Click the Quit button on the form, and then open the Code Editor.

10   Move the mouse pointer to the Margin Indicator bar (the gray bar just beyond the left margin of the Code Editor window), next to the statement `Age = TextBox1.Text` in the *Button1_Click* event procedure, and then click the bar to set a breakpoint.

The breakpoint immediately appears in red. A *breakpoint* is the place in your program where execution will stop so that you can use the Visual Studio development tools. See the following illustration for the breakpoint's location and shape:

Margin Indicator bar

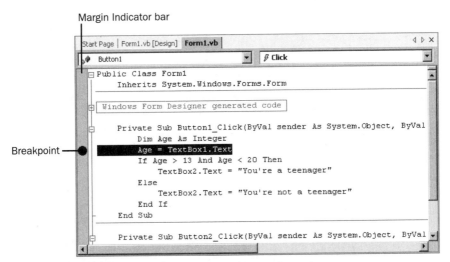

11 Click the Start button to run the program again.

The form appears just like before, and you can continue your tests.

12 Type **13** in the age text box, and then click Test.

Visual Basic opens the Code Editor again and displays the *Button1_Click* event procedure—the program code currently being executed by the compiler. The statement that you selected as a break-point is highlighted with yellow and an arrow appears in the Margin Indicator bar, as shown in the following illustration. Visual Studio is now in break mode, and you can tell because the text "[break]" appears in the Visual Studio title bar. In break mode you have an opportunity to see how the logic in your program is evaluated.

▶ **Note**   You can also enter break mode in a Visual Basic program by placing the *Stop* statement in your program code where you'd like to pause execution. This is an older, but still reliable, method for entering break mode in a Visual Basic program.

Break mode

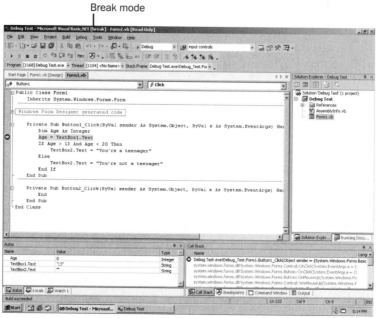

13 Place the mouse pointer over the *Age* variable in the Code Editor.

Visual Studio displays the message "Age = 0". While you're in break mode, you can display the value of variables or properties by simply holding the mouse over the value in the program code. *Age* currently holds a value of 0 because it hasn't yet been filled by the *TextBox1* text box—that statement is the next statement the compiler will evaluate.

▶ **Tip**   In break mode, you can examine the value of properties and variables but you cannot change the program code in the Code Editor—it's frozen and protected during program execution.

14 Click the Step Into button on the Debug toolbar to execute the next program statement.

The Step Into button executes the next program statement in the event procedure (the line that's currently highlighted); it allows you to see how the program state changes when just one more program statement is evaluated. If you hold the mouse pointer over the *Age* variable now, it will contain a value of 13.

15 From the Debug menu, point to Windows, and then click Autos.

The Debug Windows submenu gives you access to the entire set of debugging windows in Visual Studio. The Autos window is an automatic window that shows the state of variables and properties currently being used. As you can see in the following illustration, the

Age variable holds a value of 13, the *TextBox1.Text* property holds a string of 13, and the *TextBox2.Text* property is currently an empty string.

Breakpoint   Step Into button

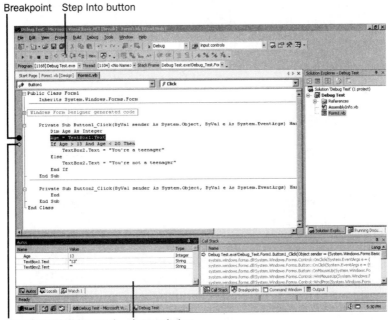

Next line to be executed   Autos window

16 Click the Step Into button twice more.

The *If* statement evaluates the conditional expression to False and moves to the *Else* statement in the decision structure. Here's our bug—the decision structure logic is somehow incorrect because a 13-year-old *is* a teenager.

17 Select the conditional test *Age > 13*, and then hold the mouse pointer over the selected text.

Visual Studio evaluates the condition and displays the message, "Age > 13 = False".

18 Select the conditional test *Age < 20*, and then hold the mouse pointer over the selected text.

Visual Studio displays the message "Age < 20 = True". The mouse pointer has given us an additional clue—only the first conditional test is producing an incorrect result! Because a 13-year-old is a teenager, Visual Basic should evaluate the test to True, but the *Age > 13* condition returns a False value. And this forces the *Else* clause in the decision structure to be executed. Do you recognize the problem?

The first comparison needs the >= operator to specifically test for this boundary case of 13. Stop debugging now, and fix this logic error.

19 Click the Stop Debugging button on the Debug toolbar.

20 In the Code Editor, add the = operator to the first condition in the *If* statement so that it reads

If Age >= 13 And Age < 20 Then

21 Run the program again and test your solution, paying particular attention to the numbers 12, 13, 19, and 20—the boundary, or "fringe," cases that are likely to cause problems.

Use the Step In button to watch the program flow around the crucial *If* statement, and use the Autos window to track the value of your variables as you complete the tests. When the form appears, enter a new value and try the test again. In addition, you might find that selecting certain expressions, such as the conditional tests, and holding the mouse over them gives you a better understanding of how they're being evaluated.

22 When you're finished experimenting with break mode, click the Stop Debugging button on the Debug toolbar to end the program.

Congratulations! You've successfully used break mode to find and correct a logic error in a program.

Tracking Variables by Using a Watch Window

The Autos window is useful for examining the state of certain variables and properties as they're evaluated by the compiler, but items in the Autos window *persist*, or maintain their values, only for the current statement (the statement highlighted in the debugger) and the previous statement (the statement just executed). When your program goes on to execute code that doesn't use the variables, they disappear from the Autos window.

To view the contents of variables and properties *throughout* the execution of a program, you need to use a *Watch window*, a special Visual Studio tool that tracks important values for you as long as you're working in break mode. In Visual Basic 6, you had access to one Watch window to examine variables as they changed. In Visual Studio .NET, you can open up to four Watch windows. These windows are numbered Watch 1, Watch 2, Watch 3, and Watch 4 on the Watch submenu, which you open by choosing the Windows command on the Debug menu. You can also add expressions, such as *Age >= 13*, to a Watch window.

8

Debugging Programs

Open a Watch window

1   Click the Start button to run the Debug Test program again.

> ▶ **Tip**   The Debug Test project is located in the
> c:\vbnet03sbs\chap08\debug test folder.

I'm assuming that the breakpoint you set on the line `Age =`
`TextBox1.Text` in the previous exercise is still present. If that breakpoint isn't set, stop the program now, and set the breakpoint by clicking in the Margin Indicator bar next to the statement, as shown in
step 10 of the previous exercise, and then start the program again.

2   Type **20** in the age text box, and then click Test.

The program stops at the breakpoint, and Visual Studio enters break
mode. To add variables, properties, or expressions to a Watch window, you need to be in break mode. Adding items is as simple as
selecting the values in the Code Editor, right clicking the selection,
and then clicking the Add Watch command.

3   Select the *Age* variable, right click it, and then click the Add Watch
command.

Visual Studio opens the Watch 1 window and adds the *Age* variable
to it. The value for the variable is currently 0, and the Type column
in the window identifies the *Age* variable as an *Integer* type.

4   Select the *TextBox2.Text* property, and then drag it to the empty row
in the Watch 1 window.

You can also drag items from the Code Editor into the Watch window. When you release the mouse button, Visual Studio adds the
property and displays its value (right now the property is an empty
string).

5   Select the expression *Age < 20*, and add it to the Watch window.

Age < 20 is a conditional expression, and you can use the Watch window to display its logical, or Boolean, value, much as you did by
holding the mouse over a condition earlier in this chapter. Your
Watch window will look like this:

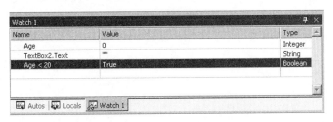

8

Debugging Programs

Now step through the program code to see how the values in the Watch 1 window change.

6   Click the Step Into button on the Debug toolbar.

> ▶   **Tip**   Instead of clicking the Step Into button on the Debug toolbar, you can press the F8 key on the keyboard.

The *Age* variable is set to 20, and the *Age < 20* condition evaluates to False. These values are displayed in red type in the Watch window because they've just been updated.

7   Click the Step Into button three more times.

The *Else* clause is executed in the decision structure, and the value of the *TextBox2.Text* property in the Watch window changes to "You're not a teenager". This conditional test is operating correctly. Because you're satisfied with this condition, you can remove the test from the Watch window.

8   Click the *Age < 20* row in the Watch window, and then press Delete.

Visual Studio removes the value from the Watch window. As you can see, adding and removing values from the Watch window is a speedy process.

Leave Visual Studio running in break mode for now. You'll continue using the *Age* variable in the next section.

Using the Command Window

So far, you've used the Visual Studio debugging tools that allow you to enter break mode, execute code one statement at a time, and examine the value of important variables, properties, and expressions in your program. Now you'll learn how to change the value of a variable and run other commands using the Command window, a dual-purpose tool in the Visual Studio development environment. When the Command window is in Immediate mode, you can use it to interact with the code in a Visual Basic program that you're debugging. When the Command window is in Command mode, you can use it to execute commands in Visual Studio, such as Save All or Print. If you execute more than one command, you can use the arrow keys to scroll through previous commands and see their results.

The following exercises demonstrate how the Command window works; they assume that you're currently debugging the Debug Test program and that the program is now in break mode.

Open the Command window in Immediate mode

1   From the Debug menu, point to Windows, and then click Immediate.

Visual Studio opens the Command window in Immediate mode, a special state that allows you to interact with a program in break mode. Because the Command window has two modes (Immediate and Command), it's important that you learn to recognize the different modes to avoid issuing the wrong commands. In Immediate mode, the window title bar contains the text "Command Window - Immediate".

> ▶ **Note**   If the Command window is in Command mode, you can switch to Immediate mode by typing the *immed* command. If the Command window is in Immediate mode, you can switch to Command mode by typing the *>cmd* command. (The > symbol is required.)

2   In the Command window, type **Age = 17**, and then press Enter.

You've just changed the value of a variable with the Command window. The value of the *Age* variable in the Watch window immediately changes to 17, and the next time the *If* statement is executed, the value in the *TextBox2.Text* property will change to "You're a teenager". Your Command window will look like this:

3   Type the following statement in the Command window, and then press Enter:

```
TextBox2.Text = "You're a great age!"
```

The *Text* property of the *TextBox2* object is immediately changed to "You're a great age!" In Immediate mode, the Command window lets you change the value of properties, as well as variables.

4   Click the Step Into button two times to display the Debug Test form again.

Notice that the *Text* property of the *TextBox2* object has been changed, as you directed, but the *Text* property of the *TextBox1* object still holds a value of 20 (not 17). This is because you changed the *Age* variable in the program, not the property that assigned a value to *Age*. Your screen will look like this:

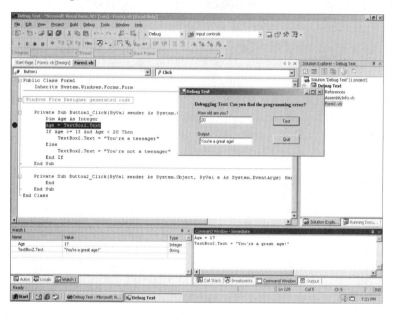

The Immediate mode of the Command window has many uses—it provides an excellent companion to the Watch window, and it can help you experiment with specific test cases that might otherwise be very difficult to enter into your program.

Switching to Command Mode in the Command Window

The Command window can also be used to run interface commands in the Visual Studio development environment. For example, the command *File.SaveAll* will save all the files in the current project. (The command is the equivalent of the Save All command on the File menu.) However, you must first switch to Command mode in the Command window before you can execute development environment commands. Practice using Command mode in the following exercise.

Run the *File.SaveAll* command

1   In the Command window, type **>cmd**, and then press Enter to switch to Command mode.

The Command window title bar changes to "Command Window", and the ">" prompt now appears in the window (a visual clue that the window is in Command mode).

2   Type **File.SaveAll** in the window, and then press Enter.

Visual Studio saves the current project, and the command prompt returns.

> ▶ **Tip**   Did you see all the commands that appeared when you typed the word "File" in the Command window? The Command window uses the statement completion feature to show you all the menu commands that match the letters you're typing. This is a powerful feature, and you can use it to discover most of the menu commands that you can execute using the Command window.

3   Click the Close button on the Command window; you're finished using it for now.

One Step Further: Removing Breakpoints

If you've been following the instructions in this chapter carefully, the Debug Test program will still be running and will have a breakpoint in it. Follow these steps to remove the breakpoint and end the program. You're finished debugging the Debug Test utility.

Remove a breakpoint

1   In the Code Editor, click the red circle associated with the breakpoint in the Margin Indicator bar.

The breakpoint disappears. That's all there is to it! Note that if you have more than one breakpoint in a program, you can remove them all by clicking the Clear All Breakpoints command on the Debug menu. Visual Studio saves breakpoints with your project, so it's important to know how to remove them; otherwise, they'll still be there in your program, even if you close Visual Studio and restart it!

2   Click the Stop Debugging button on the Debug toolbar.

The Debug Test program ends.

3   On the View menu, point to Toolbars, and then click Debug.

The Debug toolbar closes.

You've learned the fundamental techniques of debugging Visual Basic programs with Visual Studio .NET. Place a bookmark in this chapter so that you can return to it as you encounter problems later in the book. In the next chapter, you'll learn how to handle runtime errors using structured error handling techniques.

Lesson 8 Quick Reference

To	Do this
Display the Debug toolbar	From the View menu, point to Toolbars, and then click Debug.
Set a breakpoint	In the Code Editor, click in the Margin Indicator bar next to the statement where you want to stop program execution. When the compiler reaches the breakpoint, it will enter break mode. *or* Place a *Stop* statement in the program code where you want to enter break mode.
Execute one line of code in the Code Editor	Click the Step Into button on the Debug toolbar.
Examine a variable, a property, or an expression in the Code Editor	Select the value in the Code Editor, and then hold the mouse over it.
Use the Autos window to examine a variable on the current or previous line	In break mode, click the Debug menu, point to Windows, and then click Autos.
Add a variable, a property, or an expression to a Watch window	In break mode, select the value in the Code Editor, right click the value, and then click Add Watch.
Display a Watch window	In break mode, click the Debug menu, point to Windows, and then click Watch.
Open the Command window in Immediate mode	Click the Debug menu, point to Windows, and then click Immediate.
Switch between Command mode and Immediate mode in the Command window	To switch to Command mode in the Command window, type **>cmd**, and then press Enter. To switch to Immediate mode in the Command window, type **immed**, and then press Enter.
Remove a breakpoint	Click the breakpoint in the Margin Indicator bar of the Code Editor. *or* Click the Clear All Breakpoints command on the Debug menu.
Stop debugging	Click the Stop Debugging command on the Debug toolbar.

Chapter

9

Trapping Errors Using Structured Error Handling

In this chapter, you will learn how to:

- Manage runtime errors using the new Try...Catch error handler.
- Test specific error conditions using the *Catch When* statement.
- Use *Err.Number* and *Err.Description* properties to identify exceptions.
- Build nested Try...Catch statements.
- Use error handlers in combination with defensive programming techniques.
- Leave error handlers prematurely by using the Exit Try statement.

In Chapter 8, you learned how to recognize runtime errors in a Microsoft Visual Basic .NET program and how to locate logic errors and other defects in your program code by using the Microsoft Visual Studio .NET debugging tools. In this chapter, you'll learn how to build blocks of code that handle runtime errors, also referred to as *exceptions*, which occur as a result of normal operating conditions—for example, errors due to a disk not being in the drive or to an offline printer. These routines are called *structured error handlers* (or *structured exception handlers*), and you can use them to recognize runtime errors as they occur in a program, suppress unwanted error messages, and adjust program conditions so that your application can regain control and run again.

Visual Basic .NET includes the Try...Catch code block, a new syntax for handling errors. In this chapter, you'll learn how to trap runtime errors using Try...Catch code blocks, and you'll learn how to use the *Err.Number* and *Err.Description* properties to identify specific runtime errors. You'll also learn how to use multiple *Catch* statements to write more flexible error handlers, build nested Try...Catch code blocks, and use the *Exit Try* statement to exit a Try...Catch code block prematurely. The programming techniques you'll learn are similar to the *On Error Goto* syntax from earlier versions of Visual Basic and to the structured error handlers currently provided by the Java and C++ programming languages. The most seaworthy, or *robust*, Visual Basic programs make use of several error handlers to handle unforeseen circumstances and provide users with consistent and trouble-free computing experiences.

Upgrade Notes: What's New in Visual Basic .NET?

If you're experienced with Visual Basic 6, you'll notice some new features in Visual Basic .NET, including the following:

- The Try...Catch code block is a new mechanism for writing structured error handlers. Although you can still use Visual Basic 6 error-handling keywords, including *On Error Goto*, *Resume*, and *Resume Next*, the Try...Catch syntax avoids the potential complications of Goto constructions and offers a very efficient way to manage runtime errors.

- The *Catch When* statement allows you to test specific program conditions and handle more than one runtime error in a Try...Catch code block.

- The *Exit Try* statement offers a new way to exit structured error handlers.

- Visual Basic .NET continues to provide the *Err.Number* and *Err.Description* properties to identify runtime errors. In addition, you can use the new *Err.GetException* method to return information about the underlying error condition, or *exception*, that halted program execution.

Processing Errors Using Try...Catch

A runtime error, or *program crash*, is an unexpected problem in a Visual Basic program from which the program can't recover. You might have experienced your first program crash when Visual Basic couldn't load artwork from a file or in the previous chapter, when you intentionally introduced errors into your program code during debugging. A runtime error happens anytime Visual Basic executes a statement that for some reason can't be completed "as dialed" while the program is running. It's not that Visual Basic isn't smart enough to handle the glitch; it's just that Visual Basic hasn't been told what to do when something goes wrong.

Fortunately, you don't have to live with occasional errors that cause your programs to crash. You can write special Visual Basic routines, called structured error handlers, to respond to runtime errors. An error handler handles a runtime error by telling the program how to continue when one of its statements doesn't work. Error handlers are placed in the event procedures, in which there's a potential for trouble, or in generic functions or subprograms that handle errors for you systematically. (You'll learn more about writing functions and subprograms in Chapter 10.) As their name implies, error handlers handle, or *trap*, a problem by using the *Try...Catch* statement and a special error handling object named *Err*. The *Err* object has a *Number* property that identifies the error number and a *Description* property that allows you to print a description of the error. For example, if the runtime error is associated with loading a file from disk, your error handler might display a custom error message that identifies the problem and disables disk operations until the user fixes the problem.

When to Use Error Handlers

You can use error handlers in any situation in which an expected or unexpected action might result in an error that stops program execution. Typically, error handlers are used to process external events that influence a program—for example, events caused by a failed network or Internet connection, a disk not being in the floppy drive, or an offline printer. The following table lists potential problems that can be addressed by error handlers.

Problem	Description
Network/Internet problems	Network servers, modems, or resources that fail, or *go down*, unexpectedly.
Disk drive problems	Unformatted or incorrectly formatted disks, disks that aren't properly inserted, bad disk sectors, disks that are full, problems with a CD-ROM drive, and so on.
Path problems	A path to a necessary file is missing or incorrect.
Printer problems	Printers that are off line, out of paper, out of memory, or otherwise unavailable.
Software not installed	A file or component that your application relies on is not installed on the user's computer, or there's an operating system incompatibility.
Permissions problems	The user doesn't have the appropriate permissions to perform a task.
Overflow errors	An activity that exceeds the allocated storage space.

Problem	Description
Out-of-memory errors	Application or resource space that's not available in Microsoft Windows.
Clipboard problems	Problems with data transfer or the Windows Clipboard.
Logic errors	Syntax or logic errors undetected by the compiler and previous tests (such as an incorrectly spelled filename).

Setting the Trap: The *Try...Catch* Statement

The code block used to handle a runtime error is called Try...Catch. You place the *Try* statement in an event procedure right before the statement you're worried about, and the *Catch* statement follows immediately with a list of the statements that you want to run if a runtime error actually occurs. A number of optional statements, such as *Catch When, Finally, Exit Try*, and nested Try...Catch code blocks can also be included, as the examples in this chapter will demonstrate. However, the basic syntax for a Try...Catch exception handler is simply the following.

The *Try* statement identifies the beginning of an error handler

```
Try
    Statements that might produce a runtime error
Catch
    Statements to run if a runtime error occurs
Finally
    Optional statements to run whether an error occurs or not
End Try
```

in which *Try, Catch*, and *End Try* are required keywords, and *Finally* and the statements that follow are optional. Note that programmers sometimes call the statements between the *Try* and *Catch* keywords *protected code* because any runtime errors resulting from these statements won't cause the program to crash. (Instead, Visual Basic executes the error handling statements in the Catch code block.)

Path and Disk Drive Errors

The following example demonstrates a common runtime error situation—a problem with a path or floppy disk drive. To complete this exercise, you'll load a sample Visual Basic project that I created to show how artwork files are opened in a picture box object on a Windows Form. To prepare for the exercise, insert a floppy disk into drive A, and copy the file fileopen.bmp to it. (You can find a copy of this file, along with the Disk Drive Error project, in the c:\vbnet03sbs\chap09\disk drive error folder.) You'll use the disk throughout the chapter to force runtime errors and recover from them.

Experiment with disk drive errors

1   Insert a blank floppy disk in drive A (your primary floppy drive), and copy the file fileopen.bmp to it.

You'll find the fileopen.bmp file in the c:\vbnet03sbs\chap09\disk drive error folder. Use Windows Explorer or another tool to copy the file.

2   Start Visual Studio, and open the Disk Drive Error project in the c:\vbnet03sbs\chap09\disk drive error folder.

The Disk Drive Error project opens in the development environment.

3   If the project's form isn't visible, display it now.

The Disk Drive Error project is a skeleton program that displays the fileopen.bmp file in a picture box when the user clicks the Check Drive button. I designed the project as a convenient way to create and trap runtime errors, and you can use it throughout this chapter to build error handlers using the Try...Catch code block.

4   Double-click the Check Drive button on the form to display the *Button1_Click* event procedure.

You'll see the following line of program code between the *Private Sub* and *End Sub* statements:

```
PictureBox1.Image = _
   System.Drawing.Bitmap.FromFile("a:\fileopen.bmp")
```

As you've learned in earlier chapters, the *FromFile* method opens the specified file. This particular use of *FromFile* opens the fileopen.bmp file on drive A and displays it in a picture box. However, if the disk isn't fully inserted or if there's a problem with the file path, the statement will produce a "File Not Found" error in Visual Basic. This is the runtime error we want to trap.

5   With your floppy disk still in drive A, click the Start button to run the program.

The form for the project appears, as shown here:

6   Click the Check Drive button on the form.

The program loads the fileopen.bmp file from the floppy disk and displays it in the picture box, as shown here:

The *SizeMode* property of the picture box object is set to Stretch-Image, so the file fills the entire picture box object. Now see what happens when the floppy disk isn't in the disk drive when the program attempts to load the file.

7   Remove the floppy disk from the drive.

8   Click the Check Drive button on the form.

The program can't find the file, and Visual Basic issues a runtime error, or *unhandled exception*, which causes the program to crash. You'll see the following dialog box:

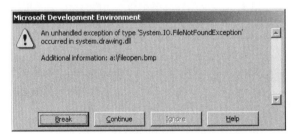

9   Click the Continue button to close the program.

The development environment returns.

Writing a Disk Drive Error Handler

The problem with the Disk Drive Error program isn't that it somehow defies the inherent capabilities of Visual Basic to process errors—we just haven't specified what Visual Basic should do when it encounters an exception that it doesn't know how to handle. The solution to this problem is to write a Try...Catch code block that recognizes the error and tells Visual Basic what to do about it. You'll add this error handler now.

Use Try...Catch to trap the error

1   Display the *Button1_Click* event procedure if it isn't visible in the Code Editor.

    You need to add an error handler to the event procedure that's caus-ing the problems. As you'll see in this example, you actually build the Try...Catch code block around the code that's the potential source of trouble, protecting the rest of the program from the runtime errors it might produce.

2   Modify the event procedure so that the existing *FromFile* statement fits between *Try* and *Catch* statements, as shown in the following code block:

```
Try
    PictureBox1.Image = _
        System.Drawing.Bitmap.FromFile("a:\fileopen.bmp")
Catch
    MsgBox("Please insert the disk in drive A!")
End Try
```

You don't need to retype the *FromFile* statement—just type the *Try*, *Catch*, *MsgBox*, and *End Try* statements above and below it.

This program code demonstrates the most basic use of a Try...Catch code block. It places the problematic *FromFile* statement in a Try code block so that if the program code produces an error, the state-ments in the Catch code block will be executed. The Catch code block simply displays a message box asking the user to insert the required disk in drive A so that the program can continue. This Try...Catch code block contains no *Finally* statement, so the error handler ends with the keywords *End Try*.

9

Trapping Errors

3   Make sure the floppy disk is removed from drive A, and then click the Start button to run the program.

4   Click the Check Drive button.

Instead of stopping program execution, Visual Basic invokes the Catch code block, which displays the following message box:

5   Click OK, and then click the Check Drive button again.

The program displays the message box again, asking you to insert the disk properly in drive A. Each time there's a problem loading the file, this message box will appear.

6   Insert the disk in drive A, click OK, and then click the Check Drive button again.

The file appears in the picture box, as expected. The error handler has completed its work effectively—rather than the program crashing inadvertently, it's told you how to correct your mistake, and you can now continue working with the application.

7   Click the Close button on the form to stop the program.

It's time to learn some of the variations of the Try...Catch error handler.

Using the *Finally* Clause to Perform Cleanup Tasks

As the syntax description for Try...Catch noted earlier in the chapter, you can use the optional *Finally* clause with Try...Catch to execute a block of statements regardless of how the compiler executes the Try or Catch blocks. In other words, whether or not the *Try* statements produced a runtime error, there might be some code that you need to run each time an error handler is finished. For example, you might want to update variables or properties, display the results of a computation using a message box or other mechanism, or perform "cleanup" operations by clearing variables or disabling unneeded objects on a form.

The following exercise demonstrates how the *Finally* clause works, by displaying a second message box whether or not the *FromFile* method produces a runtime error.

Use *Finally* to display a message box

1   Display the *Button1_Click* event procedure, and then edit the Try...Catch code block so that it contains two additional lines of code above the *End Try* statement. The complete error handler should look like this:

```
Try
    PictureBox1.Image = _
      System.Drawing.Bitmap.FromFile("a:\fileopen.bmp")
Catch
    MsgBox("Please insert the disk in drive A!")
Finally
    MsgBox("Error handler complete")
End Try
```

The *Finally* statement indicates to the compiler that a final block of code should be executed whether or not a runtime error is processed. To help you learn exactly how this feature works, I've inserted a *MsgBox* function to display a test message below the *Finally* statement. Although this simple use of *Finally* is helpful for testing purposes, in a real program you'll probably want to use the Finally code block to update important variables or properties, display data, or perform other cleanup operations.

2   Remove the floppy disk from drive A, and then click the Start button to run the program.

3   Click the Check Drive button.

The error handler displays a dialog box asking you to insert the disk in drive A.

4   Click OK.

The program executes the *Finally* clause in the error handler, and the following message box appears:

5   Click OK, insert the disk in drive A, and then click the Check Drive button again.

The file appears in the picture box as expected. In addition, the *Finally* clause is executed, and the "Error handler complete" message box appears again. As I noted earlier, *Finally* statements are executed at the end of a Try...Catch block whether or not there's an error.

6   Click OK, and then click the Close button on the form to stop the program.

More Complex Try...Catch Error Handlers

As your programs become more sophisticated, you might find it useful to write more complex Try...Catch error handlers that manage a variety of runtime errors and unusual error-handling situations. Try...Catch provides for this complexity by

- Permitting multiple lines of code in each Try, Catch, or Finally code block.
- Offering the Catch When syntax, which tests specific error conditions.
- Allowing nested Try...Catch code blocks, which can be used to build sophisticated and robust error handlers.

In addition, a special error-handling object named *Err* allows you to identify and process specific runtime errors and conditions in your program. You'll investigate each of these error-handling features in the following section.

The *Err* Object

Err is a special Visual Basic object that's assigned detailed error-handling information each time a runtime error occurs. The most useful *Err* properties for identifying runtime errors are *Err.Number* and *Err.Description*. *Err.Number* contains the number of the most recent runtime error, and *Err.Description* contains a short error message that matches the runtime error number. By using the *Err.Number* and *Err.Description* properties together in an error handler, you can recognize specific errors and respond to them, and you can give the user helpful information about how he or she should respond.

The *Err.Number* and *Err.Description* properties contain information about the most recent runtime error.

You can clear the *Err* object by using the *Err.Clear* method (which discards previous error information), but if you use the *Err* object within a Catch code block, clearing the *Err* object isn't usually necessary because Catch blocks are entered only when a runtime error has just occurred in a neighboring Try code block.

The following table lists many of the runtime errors that Visual Basic applications can encounter. (For more information on a particular error, search the Visual Studio online Help.) In addition to these error codes, you'll find that some Visual Basic libraries and other components (such as database and system components) provide their own unique error messages, which often can be discovered by using the online Help. Note that despite the error message descriptions, some errors don't appear as you might expect them to, so you'll need to specifically test the error numbers (when possible) by observing how the *Err.Number* property changes during program execution. Unused error numbers in the range 1–1000 are reserved for future use by Visual Basic .NET.

Error number	Default error message
5	Procedure call or argument is not valid
6	Overflow
7	Out of memory
9	Subscript out of range
11	Division by zero
13	Type mismatch
48	Error in loading DLL
51	Internal error
52	Bad file name or number
53	File not found
55	File already open
57	Device I/O error
58	File already exists
61	Disk full
62	Input past end of file
67	Too many files
68	Device unavailable
70	Permission denied
71	Disk not ready
74	Can't rename with different drive
75	Path/File access error
76	Path not found
91	Object variable or With block variable not set
321	File format is not valid
322	Cannot create necessary temporary file
380	Property value is not valid

Error number	Default error message
381	Property array index is not valid
422	Property not found
423	Property or method not found
424	Object required
429	Cannot create Microsoft ActiveX component
430	Class does not support Automation or does not support expected interface
438	Object does not support this property or method
440	Automation error
460	Clipboard format is not valid
461	Method or data member not found
462	The remote server machine does not exist or is unavailable
463	Class not registered on local machine
481	Picture is not valid
482	Printer error

The following exercise uses the *Err.Number* and *Err.Description* properties in a Try...Catch error handler to test for more than one runtime error condition. This capability is made possible by the *Catch When* syntax, which allows you to test for specific error conditions in a Try...Catch code block.

Test for multiple runtime error conditions

1   In the *Button1_Click* event procedure, edit the Try...Catch error handler so that it looks like the following code block. (The original *FromFile* statement is the same as the code you used in the previous exercises, but the *Catch* statements are all new.)

```
Try
    PictureBox1.Image = _
        System.Drawing.Bitmap.FromFile("a:\fileopen.bmp")
Catch When Err.Number = 53 'if File Not Found error
    MsgBox("Check pathname and disk drive")
Catch When Err.Number = 7  'if Out Of Memory error
    MsgBox("Is this really a bitmap?", , Err.Description)
Catch
    MsgBox("Problem loading file", , Err.Description)
End Try
```

The *Catch When* syntax is used twice in the error handler, and each time it's used with the *Err.Number* property to test whether the Try code block produced a particular type of runtime error. If the *Err.Number* property contains the number 53, the File Not Found runtime error has occurred during the file open procedure, and the message "Check pathname and disk drive" is displayed in a message box. If the *Err.Number* property contains the number 7, an Out of Memory error has occurred—probably the result of loading a file that doesn't actually contain artwork. (I get this error if I accidentally try to open a Microsoft Word document in a picture box object using the *FromFile* method.)

The final *Catch* statement handles all other runtime errors that could potentially occur during a file-opening process—it's a general "catch-all" code block that prints a general error message inside a message box and a specific error message from the *Err.Description* property in the title bar of the message box.

2   Click the Start button to run the program.

3   Remove the floppy disk from drive A.

4   Click the Check Drive button.

The error handler displays the error message "Check pathname and disk drive" in a message box. The first *Check When* statement works.

5   Click OK, and then click the Close button on the form to end the program.

6   Insert the floppy disk again, and then use Windows Explorer or another tool to copy a second file to the disk that isn't an artwork file. For example, copy a Word document or an Excel spreadsheet to the disk.

You won't open this file in Word or Excel—it's only for testing purposes.

7   In the Code Editor, change the name of the fileopen.bmp file in the *FromFile* program statement to the name of the file you just copied to the disk in drive A.

Using a file with a different format will give you an opportunity to test a second type of runtime error—an Out of Memory exception, which occurs when Visual Basic attempts to load a file that isn't a graphic or has too much information for a picture box.

8   Run the program again, and click the Check Drive button.

The error handler displays the following error message:

9 Click OK, and then click the Close button on the form to stop the program.

10 Change the filename back to fileopen.bmp in the *FromFile* method. (You'll use it in the next exercise.)

The *Catch When* statement is very powerful. In combination with the *Err.Number* and *Err.Description* properties, *Catch When* allows you to write sophisticated error handlers that recognize and respond to several types of exceptions.

Raising Your Own Errors

For testing purposes and other specialized uses, you can artificially generate your own runtime errors in a program, a technique called *throwing*, or *raising*, exceptions. To accomplish this, you use the *Err.Raise* method with one of the error numbers in the table presented earlier. For example, the following syntax uses the *Raise* method to produce a Disk Full runtime error and then handles the error using a *Catch When* statement:

```
Try
    Err.Raise(61) 'raise Disk Full error
Catch When Err.Number = 61
    MsgBox("Error: Disk is full")
End Try
```

When you learn how to write your own procedures, this technique will allow you to generate your own errors and return them to the calling routine.

Specifying a Retry Period

Another strategy you can use in an error handler is to try an operation a few times and then disable it if the problem isn't resolved. For example, in the following exercise, a Try...Catch block employs a counter variable named *Retries* to track the number of times the message "Please insert the disk in drive A!" is displayed, and after the second time, the error handler disables the Check Drive button. The trick to this technique is declaring the *Retries* variable at the top of the form's program code so that it has scope throughout all of the form's event procedures. The *Retries* variable is then incremented and tested in the Catch code block. The number of retries can be modified by simply changing the "2" in the statement, as shown here:

```
If Retries <= 2
```

Use a variable to track runtime errors

1 In the Code Editor, scroll to the top of the form's program code, and directly below the tag "Windows Form Designer generated code", type the following variable declaration:

```
Dim Retries As Short = 0
```

Retries is declared as a *Short* integer variable because it won't contain very big numbers. It's assigned an initial value of 0 so that it resets properly each time the program runs.

2 In the *Button1_Click* event procedure, edit the Try...Catch error handler so that it looks like the following code block:

```
Try
    PictureBox1.Image = _
      System.Drawing.Bitmap.FromFile("a:\fileopen.bmp")
Catch
    Retries += 1
    If Retries <= 2 Then
        MsgBox("Please insert the disk in drive A!")
    Else
        MsgBox("File Load feature disabled")
        Button1.Enabled = False
    End If
End Try
```

The Try block tests the same file-opening procedure, but this time, if an error occurs, the Catch block increments the *Retries* variable and tests the variable to be sure that it's less than or equal to 2. The number 2 can be changed to allow any number of retries—currently it allows only two runtime errors. After two errors, the *Else* clause is executed, and a message box appears indicating that the file-loading feature has been disabled. The Check Drive button is then disabled— in other words, grayed out and rendered unusable for the remainder of the program.

3 Click the Start button to run the program.

▶ **Tip** The complete Disk Drive Handler program is located in the c:\vbnet03sbs\chap09\disk drive handler folder.

4 Remove the floppy disk from drive A.

5 Click the Check Drive button.

The error handler displays the error message "Please insert the disk in drive A!" in a message box, as shown here. Behind the scenes, the *Retries* variable is also incremented to 1.

9

Trapping Errors

6 Click OK, and then click the Check Drive button again.

The *Retries* variable is set to 2, and the message "Please insert the disk in drive A!" appears again.

7 Click OK, and then click the Check Drive button a third time.

The *Retries* variable is incremented to 3, and the *Else* clause is executed. The message "File Load feature disabled" appears, as shown here:

8 Click OK in the message box.

The Check Drive button is disabled on the form, as shown here:

Disabled Check Drive button

The error handler has responded to the disk drive problem by allowing the user a few tries to fix the problem, and then it has disabled the problematic button. This disabling action will stop future runtime errors, although the program might no longer function exactly as it was originally designed.

9 Click the Close button to stop the program.

Using Nested Try...Catch Blocks

You can also use nested Try...Catch code blocks in your error handlers. For example, the following disk drive error handler uses a second Try...Catch block to retry the file open operation a single time if the first attempt fails and generates a runtime error:

```
Try
    PictureBox1.Image = _
      System.Drawing.Bitmap.FromFile("a:\fileopen.bmp")
Catch
    MsgBox("Insert the disk in drive A, then click OK!")
    Try
        PictureBox1.Image = _
          System.Drawing.Bitmap.FromFile("a:\fileopen.bmp")
    Catch
        MsgBox("File Load feature disabled")
        Button1.Enabled = False
    End Try
End Try
```

If the user inserts the disk in the drive as a result of the message prompt, the second Try block will open the file without error. However, if a file-related runtime error still appears, the second Catch block displays a message saying that the file load feature is being disabled, and the button is disabled.

In general, nested Try...Catch error handlers work well as long as you don't have too many tests or retries to manage. If you do need to retry a problematic operation many times, use a variable to track your retries, or develop a function containing an error handler that can be called repeatedly from your event procedures. (See the next chapter for more information about creating functions.)

Comparing Error Handlers with Defensive Programming Techniques

Error handlers aren't the only mechanism for protecting a program against runtime errors. For example, the following program code uses the *File.Exists* method in the *System.IO* namespace of the .NET Framework class library to check whether a file exists on disk before it's opened:

```
If File.Exists("a:\fileopen.bmp") Then
    PictureBox1.Image = _
      System.Drawing.Bitmap.FromFile("a:\fileopen.bmp")
Else
    MsgBox("Cannot find fileopen.bmp on drive A.")
End If
```

This *If...Then* statement isn't an actual error handler because it doesn't prevent a runtime error from halting a program. Instead, it's a validation technique that some programmers call *defensive programming*. It uses a handy method in the .NET Framework class library to verify the intended file operation *before* it's actually attempted in the program code. And in this particular case, testing to see whether the file exists with the .NET Framework method is actually faster than waiting for Visual Basic to issue an exception and recover from a runtime error using an error handler.

▶ **Note**   To get this particular program logic to work, the following statement must be included at the very top of the form's program code to make reference to the .NET Framework class library that's being invoked:

```
Imports System.IO
```

For more information about utilizing the *Imports* statement to use the objects, properties, and methods in the .NET Framework class libraries, see Chapter 5.

When should you use defensive programming techniques, and when should you use error handlers? The answer depends on how often you think a problem will occur with the statements that you plan to use. If an exception or runtime error will occur relatively rarely, say less than 25 percent of the time a particular piece of code is executed, using an error handler is probably the most efficient way to go. Error handlers are also essential if you have more than one condition to test and if you want to provide the user with numerous options for responding to the error. However, if there's a real likelihood that a piece of code will produce a runtime error more than 25 percent of the time, defensive programming logic is usually the most efficient way to manage potential problems. As I mentioned earlier when discussing the If...Then code block, the *File.Exists* method is actually faster than using a Try...Catch error handler, so it also makes sense to use a defensive programming technique if there are performance issues involved. In the end, it probably makes the most sense to use a combination of defensive programming and structured error handling techniques in your code.

One Step Further: The *Exit Try* Statement

You've learned a lot about error handlers in this chapter; now you're ready to put them to work in your own programs. But before you move on to the next chapter, here's one more syntax option for Try...Catch code blocks that you might find useful—the *Exit Try* statement. *Exit Try* is a quick and slightly abrupt technique for exiting a Try...Catch code block prematurely; if you've written Visual Basic programs before, you might notice its similarity to the *Exit*

For and *Exit Sub* statements, which allow you to leave a structured routine early. Using the *Exit Try* syntax, you can jump completely out of the current Try or Catch code block. If there's a Finally code block, this code will be executed, but *Exit Try* lets you jump over any remaining *Try* or *Catch* statements you don't want to execute.

The following sample routine shows how the *Exit Try* statement works. It first checks to see whether the *Enabled* property of the *PictureBox1* object is set to False, a flag that might indicate that the picture box isn't yet ready to receive input. If the picture box isn't yet enabled, the *Exit Try* statement skips to the end of the Catch code block, and the file load operation isn't attempted.

```
Try
    If PictureBox1.Enabled = False Then Exit Try
    PictureBox1.Image = _
      System.Drawing.Bitmap.FromFile("a:\fileopen.bmp")
Catch
    Retries += 1
    If Retries <= 2 Then
        MsgBox("Please insert the disk in drive A!")
    Else
        MsgBox("File Load feature disabled")
        Button1.Enabled = False
    End If
End Try
```

The example builds on the last error handler you experimented with in this chapter (the Disk Drive Handler project). If you'd like to test the *Exit Try* statement in the context of that program, load the Disk Drive Handler project again, and enter the *If* statement that contains the *Exit Try* in the Code Editor. You'll also need to use the Properties window to disable the picture box object on the form (in other words, set its *Enabled* property to False).

Congratulations! You've learned a number of important fundamental programming techniques in Visual Basic .NET, including how to write error handlers. Now you're ready to move on to more advanced programming topics.

9

Trapping Errors

Lesson 9 Quick Reference

To	Do this
Detect and process runtime errors	Build an error handler by using one or more Try...Catch code blocks. For example, the following error handler code tests for path or disk drive problems: ```\nTry\n PictureBox1.Image = _\n System.Drawing.Bitmap.FromFile _\n ("a:\fileopen.bmp")\nCatch\n MsgBox("Check path or insert disk")\nFinally\n MsgBox("Error handler complete")\nEnd Try\n```
Test for specific error conditions in an event handler	Use the *Catch When* syntax and the *Err.Number* property. For example: ```\nTry\n PictureBox1.Image = _\n System.Drawing.Bitmap.FromFile _\n ("a:\fileopen.bmp")\nCatch When Err.Number = 53 'if File Not Found\n MsgBox("Check pathname and disk drive")\nCatch When Err.Number = 7 'if Out Of Memory\n MsgBox("Is this really a bitmap?", , _\n Err.Description)\nCatch\n MsgBox("Problem loading file", , _\n Err.Description)\nEnd Try\n```
Create your own errors in a program	Use the *Err.Raise* method. For example, the following code generates a Disk Full error and handles it: ```\nTry\n Err.Raise(61) 'raise Disk Full error\nCatch When Err.Number = 61\n MsgBox("Error: Disk is full")\nEnd Try\n```

To	Do this
Write nested Try...Catch error handlers	Place one Try...Catch code block within another. For example:

```
Try
    PictureBox1.Image = _
      System.Drawing.Bitmap.FromFile _
      ("a:\fileopen.bmp")
Catch
    MsgBox("Insert the disk in drive A!")
    Try
        PictureBox1.Image = _
          System.Drawing.Bitmap.FromFile _
          ("a:\fileopen.bmp")
    Catch
        MsgBox("File Load feature disabled")
        Button1.Enabled = False
    End Try
End Try
```

To	Do this
Exit the current Try or Catch code block	Use the *Exit Try* statement in the Try or Catch code block. For example:

```
If PictureBox1.Enabled = False Then Exit Try
```

Managing Corporate Data

Using Modules and Procedures

In this chapter, you will learn how to:

■ Create standard modules.

■ Declare and use public variables that have a global scope.

■ Create user-defined functions and Sub procedures, known collectively as procedures.

■ Call user-defined procedures.

After studying the programs and completing the exercises in Chapters 1 through 9, you can safely call yourself an intermediate Visual Basic programmer. You've learned the basics of programming in Microsoft Visual Basic .NET, and you have the skills necessary to create a variety of useful utilities. In Part 3 of this book, you'll learn what it takes to write more complex programs in Visual Basic. You'll start by learning how to create *standard modules*.

A standard module is a separate container in a program that contains global, or *public*, variables and Function and Sub procedures. In this chapter, you'll learn how to declare and use public variables. You'll also learn how to create your own procedures and how to call them. The skills you'll learn will be especially applicable to larger programming projects and team development efforts.

Upgrade Notes: What's New in Visual Basic .NET?

If you're experienced with Visual Basic 6, you'll notice some new features in Visual Basic .NET, including the following:

- Standard modules are still supported in Visual Basic .NET, but there are now *Module* and *End Module* keywords that wrap the module content within the Code Editor. Public variables are declared in standard modules as they were in Visual Basic 6.

- Visual Basic .NET continues to support the *Function* and *Sub* keywords, allowing you to create your own procedures. However, the syntax for declaring and calling procedures has changed a little.

- If you're using the default Option Explicit setting to control variable declaration, a specific type declaration is also recommended for functions when you declare them. It's also recommended that you specifically declare all types in your procedure argument lists. If you don't assign a type using the *As* keyword, Visual Basic will use the default *Object* type for the parameter, a data type that's often less efficient than a specific data type.

- Visual Basic .NET has changed the way that arguments are passed to procedures. In Visual Basic 6, the default mechanism for passing arguments was by reference (*ByRef*), meaning that changes to arguments in the procedure were passed back to the calling routine. In Visual Basic .NET, the default way to pass arguments is by value (*ByVal*), meaning that changes to arguments within a procedure aren't passed back to the calling routine. You can explicitly specify the behavior for argument passing by using the *ByRef* and *ByVal* keyword in your argument declarations. If necessary, you can specify *ByRef* to achieve the same functionality you have in Visual Basic 6.

- When you call procedures in Visual Basic .NET, parentheses are now required around all argument lists. The Microsoft Visual Studio development environment will add these for you—even if your procedures don't require any arguments. (If no arguments are required, parentheses will be inserted.)

- Programmers now have the option of using the *Return* statement to send the result of a function calculation back to the calling routine. The older method—assigning a value to the function name—is also supported.

Working with Standard Modules

As you write longer programs, you're likely to have several forms and event procedures that use some of the same variables and routines. By default, variables are *local* to an event procedure, meaning that they can be read or changed only in the event procedure in which they were created. You can also declare variables at the top of a form's program code and give the variables a greater scope throughout the form. However, if you create multiple forms in a project, the variables declared at the top of a form will be valid only in the form in which they were declared. Likewise, event procedures are by default declared as private and are only local to the form in which they are created. For example, you can't call the *Button1_Click* event procedure from a second form named Form2 if the event procedure is declared to be private to Form1.

▶   **Note**   You'll learn how to add additional forms to your project in Chapter 15.

To share variables and procedures among all the forms and event procedures in a project, you can declare them in one or more *standard modules* for that project. A standard module, or code module, is a special file that has the file-name extension .vb and contains variables and procedures that can be used anywhere in the program. (Note that in previous versions of Visual Basic, modules had the file extension .bas.) Just like forms, standard modules are listed separately in Solution Explorer, and a standard module can be saved to disk by using the Save Module1 As command on the File menu. Unlike forms, however, standard modules contain only code and don't have a user interface.

Creating a Standard Module

To create a new standard module in a program, you click the Add New Item button on the Standard toolbar, or you click the Add New Item command on the Project menu. A dialog box opens that allows you to select the Module template and prompts you for the name of the module. A new, blank module then appears in the Code Editor. The first standard module in a program is named Module1.vb by default, but you can change the name by right-clicking the module in Solution Explorer or with the Save Module1.vb As command on the File menu. Try creating an empty standard module in a project now.

Create and save a standard module

1   Start Visual Studio, and create a new Visual Basic Windows Application project named **My Module Test** in the c:\vbnet03sbs\chap10 folder.

   The new project is created, and a blank form appears in the Windows Forms Designer.

2   Click the Add New Item command on the Project menu.

The Add New Item dialog box appears.

3   Select the Module template.

The default name of Module1.vb appears in the Name text box.

> ► **Tip**   The Add New Item dialog box has multiple containers that you can use in your projects. Each of these containers has different characteristics and includes starter code to help you use them. The containers you'll primarily use are modules, Windows Forms, and classes. Modules are containers in which you can place general-purpose procedures and variable declarations that are available throughout your project. You already have experience using Windows Forms because each new project includes a form. You'll learn more about forms in Chapter 15. Classes are a way to design your own objects with properties, methods, and events. You'll learn more about classes in Chapter 17.

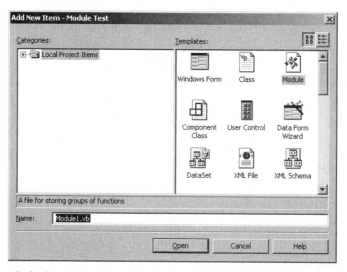

4   Click the Open button.

Visual Basic adds a standard module named Module1 to your project. The module appears in the Code Editor, as shown here:

Method Name

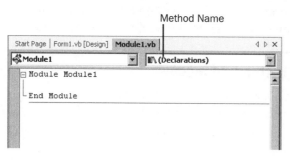

The Method Name list box indicates that the general declarations section of the standard module is open. Variables and procedures declared here will be available to the entire project. (You'll try declaring variables and procedures later.)

5   Double-click the Solution Explorer title bar to see the entire Solution Explorer window, and then select Module1.vb.

Solution Explorer appears, as shown here:

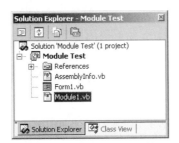

Solution Explorer lists the standard module you added to the program in the list of components for the project. The name Module1 identifies the default filename of the module. (Visual Studio created the file on disk when you first created the new module.) You'll change this filename in the following steps.

6   Double-click the Properties window title bar to see the window full size.

The Properties window displays the properties for Module1.vb, as shown here:

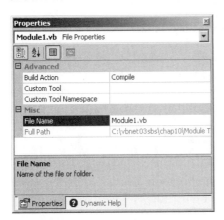

Because a standard module contains just code, it has only a few properties. Its most significant property is *File Name*. The *File Name* property lets you create a custom filename for the module that describes its purpose. It makes sense to give this identifying label some thought because later on you might want to incorporate your module into another solution. The remaining properties for the module are useful for more sophisticated projects—you don't need to worry about them now.

7   Change the *File Name* property to **Math Functions.vb** or another filename that sounds impressive, and then press Enter. (I'm granting you considerable leeway here because this project is simply for testing purposes—you won't actually create math functions or any other "content" for the module.)

The filename for your standard module is updated in the Properties window, Solution Explorer, the Code Editor, and on disk.

8   Return the Properties window and Solution Explorer to their regular docked positions by double-clicking their title bars.

As you can see, working with standard modules in a project is a lot like working with forms. In the next exercise, you'll add a public variable to a standard module.

▶ **Tip**   To remove a standard module from a project, click the module in Solution Explorer, and then click the Exclude From Project command on the Project menu. Exclude From Project doesn't delete the module from your hard disk, but it does remove the link between the specified module and the current project. You can reverse the effects of this command by clicking the Add Existing Item command on the File menu, selecting the file that you want to add to the project, and then clicking Open.

Working with Public Variables

Declaring a global, or public, variable in a standard module is simple—you type the keyword *Public* followed by the variable name and a type declaration. After you declare the variable, you can read it, change it, or display it in any procedure in your program. For example, the program statement

```
Public RunningTotal As Integer
```

declares a public variable named *RunningTotal* of type *Integer*.

The following exercises demonstrate how you can use a public variable named *Wins* in a standard module. You'll revisit Lucky Seven, the first program you wrote in this book, and you'll use the *Wins* variable to record how many spins you win as the slot machine runs.

▶ **Note**   Lucky Seven is the slot machine program from Chapter 2.

Revisit the Lucky Seven project

1   Click the Save All button on the Standard toolbar to save your changes, and then click the Close Solution command on the File menu.

The Close Solution command clears the current solution and projects from the development environment.

2   Open the Track Wins project in the c:\vbnet03sbs\chap10\track wins folder.

The project opens in the development environment.

3   If the form isn't visible, display it now.

You'll see the following user interface:

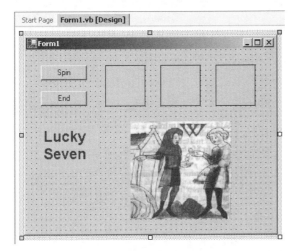

The Track Wins solution is the same slot machine program you created in Chapter 2. It allows the user to click a spin button to display "random" numbers in three number boxes, and if the number 7 appears in one of the boxes, the computer beeps and displays a bitmap showing an enticing, though quite dated, cash payout. I've simply renamed the Lucky7 solution in this chapter so that you won't modify the original version.

4   Click the Start button on the Standard toolbar to run the program.

5   Click the Spin button six or seven times, and then click the End button.

You win the first five spins (a 7 appears each time), and then your luck goes sour. As you might recall, the program uses the *Rnd* function to generate three random numbers each time you click the Spin button. If one of the numbers is a 7, the event procedure for the Spin button (*Button1_Click*) displays a cash payout picture and sounds a beep.

Now you'll edit the form, and add a standard module to enhance the program.

Add a standard module

1   Display the form in the Track Wins project.

2   Click the *Label* control in the Toolbox, and then create a new rectangular label below the Lucky Seven label.

3   Set the properties shown in the following table for the new label and the form. To help identify the new label in the program code, you'll change the new label object's name to lblWins.

Object	Property	Setting
Label5	*Font*	Arial, Bold Italic, 12-point
	ForeColor	Green (on Custom tab)
	Name	lblWins
	Text	"Wins: 0"
	TextAlign	MiddleCenter
Form1	*Text*	"Lucky Seven"

When you've finished, your form should look similar to this:

Now you'll add a new standard module to the project.

4   Click the Add New Item command on the Project menu, select the Module template, and then click Open.

A module named Module1.vb appears in the Code Editor.

5   Move the cursor to the blank line between the *Module Module1* and *End Module* statements, type **Public Wins As Short**, and then press Enter.

This program statement declares a public variable of the *Short* integer type in your program. It's identical to a normal variable declaration you might make in your program code, except the *Public* keyword has been substituted for the *Dim* keyword. When your program runs, each event procedure in the program will have access to this variable. Your standard module should look like this:

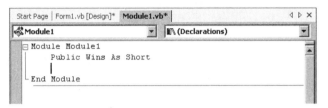

6   In Solution Explorer, click Form1.vb, click the View Designer button, and then double-click the Spin button.

The *Button1_Click* event procedure for the Spin button appears in the Code Editor.

7   Type the following statements below the *Beep()* statement in the event procedure:

```
Wins = Wins + 1
lblWins.Text = "Wins: " & Wins
```

This is the part of the program code that increments the *Wins* public variable if a 7 appears during a spin. The second statement uses the concatenation operator (&) to assign a string to the *lblWins* object in the format *Wins: X*, in which *X* is the number of wins. The completed event procedure should look like this:

```
Start Page | Form1.vb [Design]* | Module1.vb* | Form1.vb*

Button1                                    Click

    Private Sub Button1_Click(ByVal sender As System.Object, By
        PictureBox1.Visible = False      ' hide picture
        Label1.Text = CStr(Int(Rnd() * 10))      ' pick numbers
        Label2.Text = CStr(Int(Rnd() * 10))
        Label3.Text = CStr(Int(Rnd() * 10))
        ' if any caption is 7 display picture and beep
        If (Label1.Text = "7") Or (Label2.Text = "7") _
        Or (Label3.Text = "7") Then
            PictureBox1.Visible = True
            Beep()
            Wins = Wins + 1
            lblWins.Text = "Wins: " & Wins
        End If
    End Sub
End Class
```

8   Click the Save All button on the Standard toolbar to save all your changes to disk.

▶ **Note**   The complete program is named Final Track Wins and is located in the c:\vbnet03sbschap10\final track wins folder.

Save All saves your module changes as well as the changes on your form and in your event procedures.

9   Click the Start button to run the program.

10   Click the Spin button 10 times.

The Wins label keeps track of your jackpots. Each time you win, it increments the total by 1. After 10 spins, you'll have won six times, as shown here:

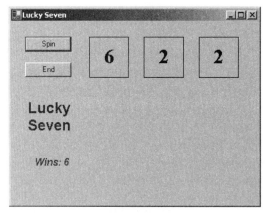

11   Click End to quit the program.

Public Variables vs. Form Variables

In the preceding exercise, you used a public variable to track the number of wins in the slot machine program. Alternatively, you could have declared the *Wins* variable within the form at the top of the form's program code. Both techniques would produce the same result because both a public variable and a variable declared in the general declarations area of a form have scope throughout the entire form. Public variables are unique, however, in that they maintain their values in *all* the forms and standard modules you use in a project, in other words, in all the components that share the same project *namespace*. The project namespace keyword is set automatically when you first save your project, and you can view or change the namespace text by selecting the project in Solution Explorer, clicking the Properties command on the Project menu, and then examining or changing the text in the Root Namespace text box.

The public variable *Wins* was useful in the previous procedure because it maintained its value through 10 calls to the *Button1_Click* event procedure. If you had declared *Wins* locally in the *Button1_Click* event procedure, the variable would have reset each time, just as the trip odometer in your car does when you reset it. Using a public variable in a standard module lets you avoid "hitting the reset." Public variables can be likened to the main odometer in your car.

Creating Procedures

Procedures are a way to group a set of related statements to perform a task. In Visual Basic .NET, there are primarily two types of procedures: Function procedures and Sub procedures. *Function procedures* are called by name from event procedures or other procedures. They can receive arguments, and they always return a value in the function name. They're typically used for calculations.

Sub procedures are called by name from event procedures or other procedures. They can receive arguments, and they also can return values. Unlike functions, however, Sub procedures don't return values associated with their particular Sub procedure names (although they can return values through the arguments). Sub procedures are typically used to receive or process input, display output, or set properties.

Function procedures and Sub procedures can be defined in a form's program code, but for many users it's most useful to create procedures in a standard module so that they have scope throughout the entire project. This is especially true for procedures that might be called *general-purpose procedures*—blocks of code that are flexible and useful enough to serve in a variety of programming contexts.

For example, imagine a program that has three mechanisms for printing a bitmap: a menu command named Print, a Print toolbar button, and a drag-and-drop printer icon. You could place the same printing statements in each of the three event procedures, or you could handle printing requests from all three sources by using one procedure in a standard module. General-purpose procedures save you typing time, reduce the possibility of errors, make programs smaller and easier to handle, and make event procedures easier to read.

Advantages of General-Purpose Procedures

General-purpose procedures provide the following benefits:

- Enable you to associate an often-used group of program statements with a familiar name.

- Eliminate repeated lines. You can define a procedure once and have your program execute it any number of times.

- Make programs easier to read. A program divided into a collection of small parts is easier to take apart and understand than is a program made up of one large part.

- Simplify program development. Programs separated into logical units are easier to design, write, and debug. Plus, if you're writing a program in a group setting, you can exchange procedures and modules instead of entire programs.

- Can be reused in other projects and solutions. You can easily incorporate standard-module procedures into other programming projects.

- Extend the Visual Basic language. Procedures often can perform tasks that can't be accomplished by individual Visual Basic keywords.

Writing Function Procedures

A *Function procedure* is a group of statements located between a *Function* statement and an *End Function* statement. The statements in the function do the meaningful work—typically processing text, handling input, or calculating a numeric value. You execute, or *call*, a function in a program by placing the function name in a program statement along with any required arguments. *Arguments* are the data used to make functions work, and they must be included between parentheses and separated by commas. Basically, using a Function procedure is exactly like using a built-in function or method such as *Int*, *Rnd*, or *FromFile*.

▶ **Tip**   Functions declared in standard modules are public by default. This allows their use in any event procedure.

Function Syntax

The basic syntax of a function is as follows:

```
Function FunctionName([arguments]) As Type
    function statements
```

```
    [Return value]
End Function
```

The following syntax items are important:

- *FunctionName* is the name of the function you're creating.

- *As Type* is a pair of keywords that specifies the function return type. (In Visual Basic 6, a specific type declaration was optional, but it's strongly recommended in Visual Basic .NET.)

- *arguments* is a list of optional arguments (separated by commas) to be used in the function. Each argument should also be declared as a specific type. (Visual Basic adds the *ByVal* keyword by default to each argument, indicating that a copy of the data is passed to the function through this argument but that any changes to the arguments won't be returned to the calling routine.)

- *function statements* is a block of statements that accomplishes the work of the function. The first statements in a function typically declare local variables that will be used in the function, and the remaining statements perform the work of the function.

- *Return* is a new statement in Visual Basic .NET—it allows you to indicate when in the function code block you want to return a value to the calling program and what that value is. Once a *Return* statement is executed, the function is exited, so if there are any function statements after the *Return* statement, these won't be executed. (Alternatively, you can use the Visual Basic 6 syntax and return a value to the calling routine by assigning the value to *FunctionName*.)

Brackets ([]) enclose optional syntax items. Visual Basic requires those syntax items not enclosed by brackets.

Functions always return a value to the calling procedure in the function's name (*FunctionName*). For this reason, the last statement in a function is often an assignment statement that places the final calculation of the function in *FunctionName*. For example, the Function procedure *TotalTax* computes the state and city taxes for an item and then assigns the result to the *TotalTax* name, as shown here:

```
Function TotalTax(ByVal Cost as Single) As Single
    Dim StateTax, CityTax As Single
    StateTax = Cost * 0.05   'State tax is 5%
    CityTax = Cost * 0.015   'City tax is 1.5%
    TotalTax = StateTax + CityTax
End Function
```

Alternatively, you can use the new Visual Basic .NET syntax and return a value to the calling procedure by using the *Return* statement, as shown in the following function declaration:

```
Function TotalTax(ByVal Cost as Single) As Single
    Dim StateTax, CityTax As Single
    StateTax = Cost * 0.05   'State tax is 5%
    CityTax = Cost * 0.015   'City tax is 1.5%
    Return StateTax + CityTax
End Function
```

I'll use the Return syntax most often in this book, but you're free to use either mechanism for returning data from a function.

Calling a Function Procedure

To call the *TotalTax* function in an event procedure, you'd use a statement similar to the following:

```
lblTaxes.Text = TotalTax(500)
```

This statement computes the total taxes required for a $500 item and then assigns the result to the *Text* property of the *lblTaxes* object. The *TotalTax* function can also take a variable as an argument, as shown in the following statements:

```
Dim TotalCost, SalesPrice As Single
SalesPrice = 500
TotalCost = SalesPrice + TotalTax(SalesPrice)
```

The last statement uses the *TotalTax* function to determine the taxes for the number in the *SalesPrice* variable and then adds the computed tax to *SalesPrice* to get the total cost of an item. See how much clearer the code is when a function is used?

Using a Function to Perform a Calculation

In the following exercise, you'll add a function to the Lucky Seven program to calculate the win rate in the game; in other words, the percentage of spins in which one or more 7s appear. To do this, you'll add a function named *HitRate* and a public variable named *Spins* to the standard module. Then you'll call the *HitRate* function every time the Spin button is clicked. You'll display the results in a new label you'll create on the form.

Create a win rate function

1   Display the form for the Lucky Seven program.

The user interface for the slot machine game appears.

2   Use the *Label* control to create a new label below the Wins label. Set
the following properties for the label:

Object	Property	Setting
Label5	*Font*	Arial, Bold Italic, 12-point
	ForeColor	Red (on Custom tab)
	Name	lblRate
	Text	"0.0%"
	TextAlign	MiddleCenter

Your form should look similar to this:

3   In Solution Explorer, click the Module1.vb module, and then click
the View Code button.

The Module1 standard module appears in the Code Editor.

4   Type the following public variable declaration below the `Public Wins`
`As Short` statement:

`Public Spins As Short`

The standard module now includes two public variables (*Wins* and
Spins) that will be available to all the procedures in the project.
You'll use *Spins* as a counter to keep track of the number of spins
you make.

5 Insert a blank line in the module, and then type the following function declaration:

```
Function HitRate(ByVal Hits As Short, ByVal Tries As Short) As String
    Dim Percent As Single
    Percent = Hits / Tries
    Return Format(Percent, "0.0%")
End Function
```

After you type the first line of the function code, Visual Basic automatically adds an *End Function* statement. After you type the remainder of the function's code, your screen should look identical to this:

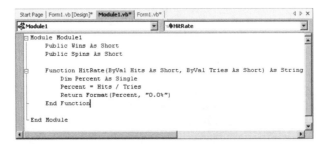

The *HitRate* function determines the percentage of wins by dividing the *Hits* argument by the *Tries* argument and then adjusting the appearance of the result by using the *Format* function. The *HitRate* function is declared as a string because the *Format* function returns a string value. The *Hits* argument and *Tries* argument are placeholders for the two short integer variables that will be passed to the function during the function call. The *HitRate* function is general-purpose enough to be used with any integer numbers or variables, not only with *Wins* and *Spins*.

6 Display the form again, and then double-click the Spin button on the Lucky Seven form to bring up the *Button1_Click* event procedure.

7 Below the fourth line of the event procedure (`Label3.Text = CStr(Int(Rnd() * 10))`), type the following statement:

```
Spins = Spins + 1
```

This statement increments the *Spins* variable each time the user clicks Spin, and new numbers are placed in the spin windows.

8 Scroll down in the Code Editor, and then type the following statement as the last line in the *Button1_Click* event procedure, between the *End If* and *End Sub* statements:

```
lblRate.Text = HitRate(Wins, Spins)
```

As you type the *HitRate* function, notice how Visual Studio automatically displays the names and types of the arguments for the *HitRate* function you just built (a nice touch).

The purpose of this statement is to call the *HitRate* function by using the *Wins* and *Spins* variables as arguments. The result returned is a percentage in string format, and this value is assigned to the *Text* property of the *lblRate* label on the form after each spin. That's all there is to it!

9   Click the Save All button to save your project files.

Now you'll run the program.

Run the Lucky Seven program

1   Click the Start button to run the modified Lucky Seven program.

▶   **Note**   The complete Final Track Wins program is located in the c:\vbnet03sbs\chap10\final track wins folder.

2   Click the Spin button 10 times.

The first five times you click Spin, the win rate stays at 100.0%. You're hitting the jackpot every time. As you continue to click, however, the win rate adjusts to 83.3%, 71.4%, 75.0% (another win), 66.7%, and 60.0% (a total of 6 for 10). After 10 spins, your screen looks like this:

If you continue to spin, you'll notice that the win rate drops to about 28%. The *HitRate* function shows you that you were really pretty lucky when you started spinning, but after a while reality set in.

3   When you're finished with the program, click the End button.

The program stops, and the development environment returns.

> ▶ **Tip**   To revise this program so that it displays a random series of spins each time you run it, put a *Randomize* statement in the *Form_Load* event procedure. For instructions, see the section in Chapter 2 entitled "One Step Further: Adding to a Program."

Writing Sub Procedures

A *Sub procedure* is similar to a Function procedure, except that a Sub procedure doesn't return a value associated with its name. Sub procedures are typically used to get input from the user, display or print information, or manipulate several properties associated with a condition. Sub procedures are also used to process and return several variables during a procedure call. Like functions, Sub procedures can return one or more values to the calling program through their argument lists.

Sub Procedure Syntax

The basic syntax for a Sub procedure is

```
Sub ProcedureName([arguments])
    procedure statements
End Sub
```

The following syntax items are important:

- *ProcedureName* is the name of the Sub procedure you're creating.
- *arguments* is a list of optional arguments (separated by commas if there's more than one) to be used in the Sub procedure. Each argument should also be declared as a specific type. (Visual Studio adds the *ByVal* keyword by default to each argument, indicating that a copy of the data is passed to the function through this argument but that any changes to the arguments won't be returned to the calling routine.)
- *procedure statements* is a block of statements that accomplishes the work of the procedure.

In the Sub procedure call, the number and type of arguments sent to the procedure must match the number and type of arguments in the Sub procedure declaration, and the entire group must be enclosed in parentheses. If variables passed to a Sub procedure are modified during the procedure, the updated variables aren't returned to the program unless the procedure defined the arguments by using the *ByRef* keyword. By default, Sub procedures declared in a standard module are public, so they can be called by any event procedure in a project.

▶ **Important**   In Visual Basic .NET, all calls to a Sub procedure must include parentheses after the procedure name. A set of empty parentheses is required if there are no arguments being passed to the procedure. This is a change from previous versions of Visual Basic, in which parentheses were required only when an argument was being passed by value to a Sub procedure. You'll learn more about passing variables by reference and by value later in this chapter.

For example, the following Sub procedure receives a string argument representing a person's name and uses a text box to wish that person happy birthday. If this Sub procedure is declared in a standard module, it can be called from any event procedure in the program.

```
Sub BirthdayGreeting (ByVal Person As String)
    Dim Msg As String
    If Person <> "" Then
        Msg = "Happy birthday " & Person & "!"
    Else
        Msg = "Name not specified."
    End If
    MsgBox(Msg, , "Best Wishes")
End Sub
```

The *BirthdayGreeting* procedure receives the name to be greeted by using the *Person* argument, a string variable received by value during the procedure call. If the value of *Person* isn't empty, or *null*, the specified name is used to build a message string that will be displayed with a *MsgBox* function. If the argument is null, the procedure displays the message "Name not specified."

Calling a Sub Procedure

To call a Sub procedure in a program, you specify the name of the procedure, and then list the arguments required by the Sub procedure. For example, to call the *BirthdayGreeting* procedure, you could type the following statement:

```
BirthdayGreeting("Robert")
```

In this example, the *BirthdayGreeting* procedure would insert the name "Robert" into a message string, and the routine would display the following message box:

The space-saving advantages of a procedure become clear when you call the procedure many times using a variable, as shown in the example below:

```
Dim NewName As String
Do
    NewName = InputBox("Enter a name for greeting.", "Birthday List")
    BirthdayGreeting(NewName)
Loop Until NewName = ""
```

Here the user's allowed to enter as many names for birthday greetings as he or she likes. The next exercise gives you a chance to practice using a Sub procedure to handle another type of input in a program.

Using a Sub Procedure to Manage Input

Sub procedures are often used to handle input in a program when information comes from two or more sources and needs to be in the same format. In the following exercise, you'll create a Sub procedure named *AddName* that prompts the user for input and formats the text so that it can be displayed on multiple lines in a text box. The procedure will save you programming time because you'll use it in two event procedures, each associated with a different text box. Because the procedure will be declared in a standard module, you need to type it in only one place.

Create a text box Sub procedure

1   On the File menu, click the Close Solution command.

     Visual Studio closes the current project (the Lucky Seven slot machine).

2   Create a new Visual Basic Windows Application project named **My Text Box Sub** in the c:\vbnet03sbs\chap10 folder.

     The new project is created, and a blank form appears in the Windows Forms Designer.

3   Use the *TextBox* control to create two text boxes, side by side, in the middle of the form.

     You'll use these text boxes to hold the names of employees you'll be assigning to two departments. You get to make your own personnel decisions today.

4   Use the *Label* control to create two labels above the text boxes.

     These labels will hold the names of the departments.

5 Use the *Button* control to create three buttons, a button under each text box and a button at the bottom of the form.

You'll use the first two buttons to add employees to their departments. You'll use the last button to quit the program.

6 Set the properties shown in the following table for the objects on the form.

Because the text boxes will contain more than one line, you'll set their *Multiline* properties to True and their *ScrollBars* properties to Vertical. These settings are typically used when multiple lines are displayed in text boxes. You'll also set their *TabStop* properties to False and their *ReadOnly* properties to True so that the information can't be modified.

Object	Property	Setting
TextBox1	Multiline	True
	Name	txtSales
	ReadOnly	True
	ScrollBars	Vertical
	TabStop	False
	Text	(empty)
TextBox2	Multiline	True
	Name	txtMkt
	ReadOnly	True
	ScrollBars	Vertical
	TabStop	False
	Text	(empty)
Label1	Font	Bold
	Name	lblSales
	Text	"Sales"
Label2	Font	Bold
	Name	lblMkt
	Text	"Marketing"
Button1	Name	btnSales
	Text	"Add Name"
Button2	Name	btnMkt
	Text	"Add Name"
Button3	Name	btnQuit
	Text	"Quit"
Form1	Text	"Assign Department Teams"

10

Modules and Procedures

7   Resize and position the objects so that your form looks similar to this:

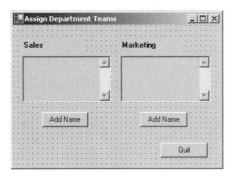

Now you'll add a standard module and create the general-purpose *AddName* Sub procedure.

8   On the Project menu, click the Add New Item command, select the Module template, and then click Open.

A new standard module appears in the Code Editor.

9   Type the following *AddName* procedure between the *Module Module1* and *End Module* statements:

```
Sub AddName(ByVal Team As String, ByRef ReturnString As String)
    Dim Prompt, Nm, WrapCharacter As String
    Prompt = "Enter a " & Team & " employee."
    Nm = InputBox(Prompt, "Input Box")
    WrapCharacter = Chr(13) + Chr(10)
    ReturnString = Nm & WrapCharacter
End Sub
```

This general-purpose Sub procedure uses the *InputBox* function to prompt the user for an employee name. It receives two arguments during the procedure call: *Team*, a string containing the department name; and *ReturnString*, an empty string variable that will contain the formatted employee name. *ReturnString* is declared with the *ByRef* keyword so that any changes made to this argument in the procedure will be passed back to the calling routine through the argument.

Before the employee name is returned, carriage return and linefeed characters are appended to the string so that each name in the text box will appear on its own line. This is a general technique that you can use in any string to create a new line.

Your Code Editor should look like this:

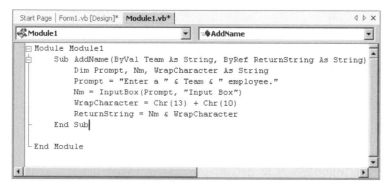

10 Display the form again, and then double-click the first Add Name button on the form (the button below the Sales text box). Type the following statements in the *btnSales_Click* event procedure:

```
Dim SalesPosition As String
AddName("Sales", SalesPosition)
txtSales.Text = txtSales.Text & SalesPosition
```

The call to the *AddName* Sub procedure includes one argument passed by value (*"Sales"*) and one argument passed by reference (*SalesPosition*). The last line uses the argument passed by reference to add text to the *txtSales* text box. The concatenation operator (&) adds the new name to the end of the text in the text box.

11 Open the Class Name drop-down list box in the Code Editor and click the *btnMkt* object, and then open the Method Name drop-down list box and click the Click event.

The *btnMkt_Click* event procedure appears in the Code Editor.

12 Type the following statements in the event procedure:

```
Dim MktPosition As String
AddName("Marketing", MktPosition)
txtMkt.Text = txtMkt.Text & MktPosition
```

This event procedure is identical to *btnSales_Click*, except that it sends *"Marketing"* to the *AddName* procedure and updates the *txtMkt* text box. The name of the local return variable (*MktPosition*) was renamed to make it more intuitive.

13 Open the Class Name drop-down list box and click the *btnQuit* object, and then open the Method Name drop-down list box and click the Click event.

The *btnQuit_Click* event procedure appears in the Code Editor.

14 Type **End** in the *btnQuit_Click* event procedure.

15 Click the Save All button on the Standard toolbar.

That's it! Now you'll run the Text Box Sub program.

Run the Text Box Sub program

1 Click the Start button on the Standard toolbar to run the program.

▶ **Note** The complete Text Box Sub program is located in the c:\vbnet03sbs\chap10\text box sub folder.

2 Click the Add Name button under the Sales text box, and then type **Maria Palermo** in the input box. (Feel free to type a different name.) Your input box should look like this:

3 Click the OK button to add the name to the Sales text box.

The name appears in the text box.

4 Click the Add Name button under the Marketing text box, type **Abraham Asante** in the Marketing input box, and then press Enter.

The name appears in the Marketing text box. Your screen should look like this:

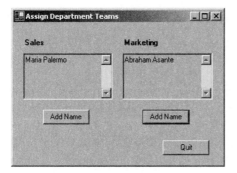

5 Enter a few more names in each of the text boxes. This is your chance to create your own dream departments.

Each name should appear on its own line in the text boxes. The text boxes don't scroll automatically, so you won't see every name you've entered if you enter more names than can fit in a text box. You can use the scroll bars to access names that aren't visible.

6 When you've finished, click the Quit button to stop the program.

One Step Further: Passing Arguments by Value and by Reference

In the discussion of Function and Sub procedures, you learned that arguments are passed to procedures by value or by reference. Using the *ByVal* keyword indicates that variables should be passed to a procedure by value (the default). Any changes made to a variable passed in by value aren't passed back to the calling procedure. However, as you learned in the Text Box Sub program, using the *ByRef* keyword indicates that variables should be passed to a procedure by reference, meaning that any changes made to the variable in the procedure are passed back to the calling routine. Passing by reference can have significant advantages, as long as you're careful not to change a variable unintentionally in a procedure. For example, consider the following Sub procedure declaration and call:

```
Sub CostPlusInterest(ByRef Cost As Single, ByRef Total As Single)
    Cost = Cost * 1.05   'add 5% to cost...
    Total = Int(Cost)    'then make integer and return
End Sub
.
.
.
```

```
Dim Price, TotalPrice As Single
Price = 100
TotalPrice = 0
CostPlusInterest(Price, TotalPrice)
MsgBox(Price & " at 5% interest is " & TotalPrice)
```

In this example, the programmer passes two single-precision variables by reference to the *CostPlusInterest* procedure: *Price* and *TotalPrice*. The programmer plans to use the updated *TotalPrice* variable in the subsequent *MsgBox* call but has unfortunately forgotten that the *Price* variable was also updated in an intermediate step in the *CostPlusInterest* procedure. (Because *Price* was passed by reference, changes to *Cost* automatically result in the same changes to *Price*.) This produces the following erroneous result when the program is run:

However, the programmer probably wanted to show the following message:

Which to Use: ByVal or ByRef?

So how should the preceding bug with the *CostPlusInterest* procedure be fixed? The easiest way is to declare the *Cost* argument by using the *ByVal* keyword, as shown in the following program statement:

```
Sub CostPlusInterest(ByVal Cost As Single, ByRef Total As Single)
```

Declaring *Cost* by using *ByVal* allows you to safely modify *Cost* in the *CostPlusInterest* procedure without sending the changes back to the calling procedure. Keeping *Total* declared by using *ByRef* allows you to modify the variable that's being passed, and only those changes will be passed back to the calling procedure. In general, if you use *ByRef* only when it's needed, your programs will be freer of defects.

Here are some guidelines on when to use *ByVal* and when to use *ByRef*:

- Use *ByVal* when you don't want a procedure to modify a variable that's passed to the procedure through an argument.
- Use *ByRef* when you want to allow a procedure to modify a variable that's passed to the procedure.
- When in doubt, use the *ByVal* keyword.

Lesson 10 Quick Reference

To	Do this
Create a new module	Click the Add New Item button on the Standard toolbar, and then select the Module template. *or* Click the Add New Item command on the Project menu, and then select the Module template.
Save a module with a new name	Select the module in Solution Explorer, click the Save Module1.vb As command on the File menu, and then specify a new name.
Remove a module from a program	Select the module in Solution Explorer, and then click the Exclude From Project command on the Project menu.
Add an existing module to a project	On the Project menu, click the Add Existing Item command.
Create a public variable	Declare the variable by using the *Public* keyword in a standard module within the *Module* and *End Module* keywords. For example: `Public TotalSales As Integer`

Create a public function	Place the function statements between the *Function* and *End Function* keywords in a standard module. Functions are public by default. For example:
	`Function HitRate(ByVal Hits As Short, ByVal _`
	`   Tries As Short) As String`
	`      Dim Percent As Single`
	`      Percent = Hits / Tries`
	`      Return Format(Percent, "0.0%")`
	`End Function`

Call a Function procedure	Type the function name and any necessary arguments in a program statement, and assign it to a variable or property of the appropriate return type. For example: `lblRate.Text = HitRate(Wins, Spins)`

Modules and Procedures

10

To	Do this
Create a public Sub procedure	Place the procedure statements between the *Sub* and *End Sub* keywords in a standard module. Sub procedures are public by default. For example:

```
Sub CostPlusInterest(ByVal Cost As Single, _
  ByRef Total As Single)
    Cost = Cost * 1.05
    Total = Int(Cost)
End Sub
```

To	Do this
Call a Sub procedure	Type the procedure name and any necessary arguments in a program statement. For example:

```
CostPlusInterest(Price, TotalPrice)
```

To	Do this
Pass an argument by value	Use the *ByVal* keyword in the procedure declaration. For example:

```
Sub GreetPerson(ByVal Name As String)
```

To	Do this
Pass an argument by reference	Use the *ByRef* keyword in the procedure declaration. For example:

```
Sub GreetPerson(ByRef Name As String)
```

Using Arrays and Collections to Manage Data

In this chapter, you will learn how to:

- Organize information in fixed-length and dynamic arrays.
- Preserve array data when you redimension arrays.
- Manipulate the *Controls* collection on a form.
- Use a For Each...Next loop to cycle through objects in a collection.
- Create your own collections for managing string data.

Managing information in a Microsoft Visual Basic .NET application is an important task, and as your programs become more substantial, you'll need additional tools to store and process data. In this chapter, you'll learn how to organize variables and other information into useful containers called *arrays*. Arrays streamline the data management process when you have several dozen or more items to manage, and they provide a solid introduction to the database programming techniques you'll learn later in the book. You'll also learn how to use groups of objects called *collections* in a Visual Basic program to manage information, and you'll learn how to process collections using the special loop For Each...Next. Considered together, arrays and collections are excellent tools for managing large amounts of information in a program.

11

Arrays and Collections

Upgrade Notes: What's New in Visual Basic .NET?

If you're experienced with Visual Basic 6, you'll notice some new features in Visual Basic .NET, including the following:

- Arrays in Visual Basic .NET are now always zero-based, meaning that the lowest array element is always 0. In Visual Basic 6, the *Option Base* statement allowed programmers to set the base of arrays to either 0 or 1. *Option Base* is no longer supported.

- Because arrays are now always zero-based, arrays can no longer be declared using the *To* keyword with specific lower and upper bounds. Another side effect of zero-bound arrays is that the *LBound* statement always returns a value of 0 because the lower bound for an array is always 0. (The *UBound* statement, however, continues to return the highest index in an array, which is the number of elements minus 1.)

- Arrays can now be declared and assigned data using the same program statement. For example, the syntax to declare an array named *myList()* and add four elements to it would be

```
Dim myList() as Integer = {5, 10, 15, 20}
```

- The *ReDim* statement is still valid in Visual Basic .NET, although it cannot be used to change the number of dimensions in an existing array. Also, you can't use the *ReDim* statement in the initial declaration.

- Visual Basic no longer has a single *Collection* data type. Instead, the functionality for collections is provided through the *System.Collections* namespace of the Microsoft .NET Framework class library. Using *System.Collections*, you can access several useful collection types, such as *Stack*, *Queue*, *Dictionary*, and *Hashtable*.

- Visual Basic no longer supports *control arrays* (collections of controls that share the same name and are processed as a group), and you cannot group controls by using the Clipboard as you could in Visual Basic 6. However, you can continue to store controls in an array if the array is declared in the object type.

Working with Arrays of Variables

In this section, you'll learn about *arrays*, a method for storing large amounts of information during program execution. Arrays are a powerful and time-tested mechanism for storing data in a program—the developers of BASIC, Pascal, C, and other popular programming languages incorporated arrays into the earliest versions of these products to refer to a group of values using one name and to process those values individually or collectively.

Arrays are useful because they help you track large amounts of data in ways that would be impractical using traditional variables. For example, imagine creating a nine-inning baseball scoreboard in a program. To save the scores for each inning of the game, you might be tempted to create two groups of 9 variables (a total of 18 variables) in the program. You'd probably name them something like *Inning1HomeTeam*, *Inning1VisitingTeam*, and so on, to keep them straight. Working with these variables individually would take considerable time and space in your program. Fortunately, Visual Basic lets you organize groups of similar variables into an array that has one common name and an easy-to-use index. For example, you could create a two-dimensional (2-by-9) array named *Scoreboard* to contain the scores for the baseball game. Let's see how this works.

Creating an Array

You create, or *declare*, arrays in program code just as you declare variables. As usual, the place in which you declare the array determines where it can be used, or its *scope*. If an array is declared locally in a procedure, it can be used only in that procedure. If an array is declared at the top of a form, it can be used throughout the form. If an array is declared publicly in a standard module, it can be used anywhere in the project. When you declare an array, you typically include the following information in your declaration statement.

Information in an array declaration statement	Description
Array name	The name you'll use to represent your array in the program. In general, array names follow the same rules as variable names. (See Chapter 5 for more information about variables.)
Data type	The type of data you'll store in the array. In most cases, all the variables in an array will be of the same type. You can specify one of the fundamental data types, or, if you're not yet sure which type of data will be stored in the array or whether you'll store more than one type, you can specify the *Object* type.
Number of dimensions	The number of dimensions your array will contain. Most arrays are one-dimensional (a list of values) or two-dimensional (a table of values), but you can specify additional dimensions if you're working with a complex mathematical model, such as a three-dimensional shape.
Number of elements	The number of elements your array will contain. The elements in your array correspond directly to the array index. In Visual Basic .NET, the first array index is always 0 (zero).

▶ **Tip**   Arrays that contain a set number of elements are called *fixed-size arrays*.
Arrays that contain a variable number of elements (arrays that can expand during the execution of the program) are called *dynamic arrays*.

Declaring a Fixed-Size Array

The basic syntax for a public fixed-size array is

```
Dim ArrayName(Dim1Index, Dim2Index, ...) As DataType
```

The following arguments are important:

- *Dim* is the keyword that declares the array. Use *Public* instead if you place the array in a standard module.
- *ArrayName* is the variable name of the array.
- *Dim1Index* is the upper bound of the first dimension of the array, which is the number of elements minus 1.
- *Dim2Index* is the upper bound of the second dimension of the array, which is the number of elements minus 1. (Additional dimensions can be included if they're separated by commas.)
- *DataType* is a keyword corresponding to the type of data that will be included in the array.

For example, to declare a one-dimensional string array named *Employees* that has room for 10 employee names (numbered 0 through 9), you would type the following in an event procedure:

```
Dim Employees(9) As String
```

In a standard module, the same array declaration would look like this:

```
Public Employees(9) As String
```

When you create the array, Visual Basic sets aside room for it in memory. The following illustration shows conceptually how the array is organized. The 10 array elements are numbered 0 through 9 rather than 1 through 10 because array indexes always start with 0. (The *Option Base* statement in Visual Basic 6, which allowed you to index arrays beginning with the number 1, is no longer supported.)

Employees

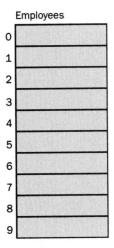

To declare a public two-dimensional array named *Scoreboard* that has room for two rows and nine columns of short integer data, you would type this statement in an event procedure or at the top of the form:

```
Dim Scoreboard(1, 8) As Short
```

When you declare a two-dimensional array, Visual Basic sets aside room for it in memory. You can then use the array in your program as if it were a table of values, as shown in the following illustration. (In this case, the array elements are numbered 0 through 1 and 0 through 8.)

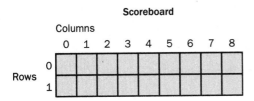

Working with Array Elements

After you've declared an array by using the *Dim* or *Public* keyword, you're ready to use the array in the program. To refer to an element of an array, you use the array name and an array index enclosed in parentheses. The index must be an integer or an expression that results in an integer. For example, the index could be a number such as 5, an integer variable such as *num*, or an expression such as "num – 1". (The counter variable of a For...Next loop is often used.) The following statement would assign the value "Leslie" to the element with an index of 5 in the *Employees* array example in the previous section:

```
Employees(5) = "Leslie"
```

This would produce the following result in our *Employees* array:

Employees

0	
1	
2	
3	
4	
5	Leslie
6	
7	
8	
9	

Similarly, the following statement would assign the number 4 to row 0, column 2 (the top of the third inning) in the *Scoreboard* array example in the previous section:

```
Scoreboard(0, 2) = 4
```

This would produce the following result in our *Scoreboard* array:

Scoreboard

Columns

	0	1	2	3	4	5	6	7	8
0			4						
1									

Rows

You can use these indexing techniques to assign or retrieve any array element.

Creating a Fixed-Size Array to Hold Temperatures

The following exercise uses a one-dimensional array named *Temperatures* to record the daily high temperatures for a seven-day week. The program demonstrates how you can use an array to store and process a group of related values on a form. The *Temperatures* array variable is declared at the top of the form, and then temperatures are assigned to the array by using an *InputBox* function and a For...Next loop, which you learned about in Chapter 7. The loop counter is used to reference each element in the array. The array contents are then displayed on the form by using a For...Next loop and a text box object. The average high temperature is also calculated and displayed.

The *LBound* and *UBound* Functions

To simplify working with the array, the Fixed Array program uses the *UBound* function to check for the upper bound, or top index value, of the array. *UBound* is an older BASIC and Visual Basic keyword that's still quite useful; it allows you to process arrays without referring to the declaration statements that defined exactly how many values the array would hold. The closely related *LBound* function, which checks the lower bound of an array, is still valid in Visual Basic .NET, but because all Visual Basic .NET arrays now have a lower bound of zero (0), the function simply returns a value of 0. The *UBound* and *LBound* functions have the syntax

```
LBound(ArrayName)
UBound(ArrayName)
```

where *ArrayName* is the name of an array that's been declared in the project.

Use a fixed-size array

1 Start Microsoft Visual Studio, and create a new Visual Basic Windows Application project named **My Fixed Array** in the c:\vbnet03sbs\chap11 folder.

2 Draw a text box object on the form.

3 Set the *Multiline* property of the *TextBox1* object to True so that you can resize the object.

4 Resize the text box object so that it fills up most of the form.

5 Draw two wide button objects on the form below the text box object, oriented one beside the other.

6 Set the following properties for the form and its objects:

Object	Property	Setting
TextBox1	ScrollBars	Vertical
	Text	(empty)
Button1	Text	"Enter Temps"
Button2	Text	"Display Temps"
Form1	Text	"Fixed Array Temps"

11

Arrays and Collections

Your form should look like this:

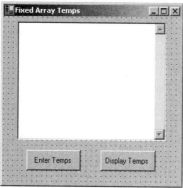

7   Click the View Code button in Solution Explorer to display the Code Editor.

8   Scroll to the top of the form's program code, and directly below the tag "Windows Form Designer generated code", type the following array declaration:

```
Dim Temperatures(6) As Single
```

This statement creates an array named *Temperatures* (of the type *Single*) that contains seven elements numbered 0 through 6. Because the array has been declared at the top of the form, it will be available in all the event procedures in the form.

9   Display the form again, and then double-click the Enter Temps button (*Button1*).

The *Button1_Click* event procedure appears in the Code Editor.

10   Type the following program statements to prompt the user for temperatures and to load the input into the array:

```
Dim Prompt, Title As String
Dim i As Short
Prompt = "Enter the day's high temperature."
For i = 0 To UBound(Temperatures)
    Title = "Day " & (i + 1)
    Temperatures(i) = InputBox(Prompt, Title)
Next
```

The For...Next loop uses the short integer counter variable *i* as an array index to load temperatures into array elements 0 through 6. Rather than using the simplified For loop syntax

```
For i = 0 to 6
```

to process the array, I chose a slightly more complex syntax involving the *UBound* function for future flexibility. The For loop construction

```
For i = 0 To UBound(Temperatures)
```

determines the upper bound of the array by using the *UBound* statement. This technique is flexible; if the array is expanded or reduced later, the For loop will automatically adjust itself to the new array size.

To fill the array with temperatures, the event procedure uses an *InputBox* function, which displays the current day using the For loop counter.

11 Display the form again, and then double-click the Display Temps button (*Button2*).

12 Type the following statements in the *Button2_Click* event procedure:

```
Dim Result As String
Dim i As Short
Dim Total As Single = 0
Result = "High temperatures for the week:" & vbCrLf & vbCrLf
For i = 0 To UBound(Temperatures)
    Result = Result & "Day " & (i + 1) & vbTab & _
        Temperatures(i) & vbCrLf
    Total = Total + Temperatures(i)
Next
Result = Result & vbCrLf & _
  "Average temperature:  " & Format(Total / 7, "0.0")
TextBox1.Text = Result
```

This event procedure uses a For...Next loop to cycle through the elements in the array, and it adds each element in the array to a string variable named *Result*, which is declared at the top of the event procedure. I've used several literal strings, constants, and string concatenation operators (&) to pad and format the string by using carriage returns (*vbCrLf*), tab characters (*vbTab*), and headings. The *vbCrLf* constant, used here for the first time, contains the carriage return and linefeed characters and is an efficient way to create new lines. The *vbTab* constant is also used here for the first time to put some distance between the day and temperature values in the *Result* string. At the end of the event procedure, an average for the temperatures is determined, and the final string is assigned to the *Text* property of the text box object, as shown in this statement:

```
TextBox1.Text = Result
```

13 Click the Save All button on the Standard toolbar to save the project.

14 Click the Start button to run the program.

▶ **Note**   The complete Fixed Array program is located in the
c:\vbnet03sbs\chap11\fixed array folder.

15 Click the Enter Temps button, and then enter seven different temperatures as you're prompted to by the *InputBox* function. (How about
the temperatures during your last vacation?)

The *InputBox* function dialog box looks like this:

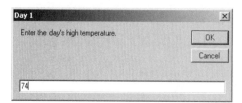

16 After you've entered the temperatures, click the Display Temps button.
Visual Basic displays each of the temperatures in the text box and prints
an average at the bottom. Your screen should look similar to this:

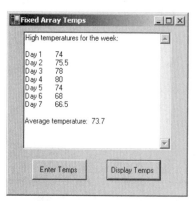

17 Click the Close button on the form to end the program.

Creating a Dynamic Array

As you can see, arrays are quite handy for working with lists of numbers, especially if you process them by using For...Next loops. But what if you're not sure
how much array space you'll need before you run your program? For example,
what if you want to let the user choose how many temperatures are entered into
the Fixed Array program?

Visual Basic handles this problem efficiently with a special elastic container
called a *dynamic array*. Dynamic arrays are dimensioned at runtime, either
when the user specifies the size of the array or when logic you add to the

program determines an array size based on specific conditions. Dimensioning a dynamic array takes several steps because although the size of the array isn't specified until the program is running, you need to make "reservations" for the array at design time. To create a dynamic array, you follow these basic steps:

- Specify the name and type of the array in the program at design time, omitting the number of elements in the array. For example, to create a dynamic array named *Temperatures*, you type

```
Dim Temperatures() As Single
```

- Add code to determine the number of elements that should be in the array at runtime. You can prompt the user by using an *InputBox* function or a text box object, or you can calculate the storage needs of the program by using properties or other logic. For example, the following statements get the array size from the user and assign it to the *Days* short integer variable:

```
Dim Days As Short
Days = InputBox("How many days?", "Create Array")
```

- Use the variable in a *ReDim* statement to dimension the array (subtract one because arrays are zero-based). For example, the following statement sets the size of the *Temperatures* array at runtime by using the *Days* variable:

```
ReDim Temperatures(Days - 1)
```

- The only important qualification with *ReDim* is that you don't try to change the number of dimensions in an array that you've previously declared.

- Use the *UBound* function to determine the upper bound in a For...Next loop, and process the array elements as necessary, as shown here:

```
For i = 0 to UBound(Temperatures)
    Temperatures(i) = InputBox(Prompt, Title)
Next
```

In the following exercise, you'll use these steps to revise the Fixed Array program so that it can process any number of temperatures by using a dynamic array.

Use a dynamic array to hold temperatures

1   Open the Code Editor to display the program code for the Fixed Array project.

2   Scroll to the top of the form's code, in which you originally declared the *Temperatures* fixed array.

3   Remove the number 6 from the *Temperatures* array declaration so that the array is now a dynamic array.

The statement should look like the following:

```
Dim Temperatures() As Single
```

4   Add the following variable declaration just below the *Temperatures* array declaration:

```
Dim Days As Integer
```

The integer variable *Days* will be used to receive input from the user and to dimension the dynamic array at runtime.

5   Scroll down in the Code Editor to display the *Button1_Click* event procedure, and modify the code so that it looks like the following. (The changed or added elements appear in bold text.)

```
Dim Prompt, Title As String
Dim i As Short
Prompt = "Enter the day's high temperature."
Days = InputBox("How many days?", "Create Array")
If Days > 0 Then ReDim Temperatures(Days - 1)
For i = 0 To UBound(Temperatures)
    Title = "Day " & (i + 1)
    Temperatures(i) = InputBox(Prompt, Title)
Next
```

The fourth and fifth lines prompt the user for the number of temperatures he or she wants to save, and then the input is used to dimension a dynamic array. The *If...Then* statement is used to verify that the number of days is greater than 0. (Dimensioning an array with a number less than 0 will generate errors.) Because index 0 of the array is used to store the temperature for the first day, the *Days* variable is decremented by 1 when dimensioning the array. The *Days* variable isn't needed to determine the upper bound of the For...Next loop—as in the previous example, the *UBound* function is used instead.

6   Scroll down in the Code Editor to display the *Button2_Click* event procedure. Modify the code so that it looks like the following routine. (The changed elements appear in bold.)

```
Dim Result As String
Dim i As Short
Dim Total As Single = 0
Result = "High temperatures:" & vbCrLf & vbCrLf
For i = 0 To UBound(Temperatures)
    Result = Result & "Day " & (i + 1) & vbTab & _
        Temperatures(i) & vbCrLf
    Total = Total + Temperatures(i)
Next
```

```
Result = Result & vbCrLf & _
    "Average temperature:  " & Format(Total / Days, "0.0")
TextBox1.Text = Result
```

The variable *Days* replaces the number 7 in the average temperature calculation at the bottom of the event procedure. I also edited the "High temperatures" heading that will be displayed in the text box.

7   Save your changes to disk.

▶   **Note**   On the companion CD-ROM, I gave this project a separate name to keep it distinct from the Fixed Array project. The complete Dynamic Array program is located in the c:\vbnet03sbs\chap11\dynamic array folder.

8   Click the Start button to run the program.

9   Click the Enter Temps button.

10   Type 5 when you're prompted for the number of days you want to record, and then click OK.

11   Enter five temperatures as you're prompted to do so.

12   When you've finished entering temperatures, click the Display Temps button.

The program displays the five temperatures on the form along with their average. Your screen should look similar to this:

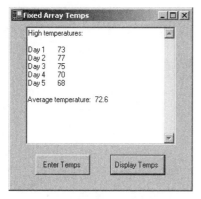

13   Click the Close button on the form to end the program.

Preserving Array Contents by Using *ReDim Preserve*

In the previous exercise, you used the *ReDim* statement to specify the size of a dynamic array at runtime. However, there's one potential shortcoming associated with the *ReDim* statement: if you redimension an array that already has data in it, all the existing data will be irretrievably lost. After the *ReDim* statement is executed, the contents of a dynamic array are set to their default value, such as zero or *null*. Depending on your outlook, this can be considered a useful feature for emptying the contents of arrays, or it can be an irksome feature that requires a workaround.

Fortunately, Visual Basic .NET provides the same useful feature that Visual Basic 6 provided for array redimensioning: the *Preserve* keyword, which you use to preserve the data in an array as you change its dimensions. The syntax for the *Preserve* keyword is as follows:

```
ReDim Preserve ArrayName(Dim1Elements, Dim2Elements, ...)
```

In such a redimension statement, the array must continue to have the same number of dimensions and contain the same type of data. In addition, there's a caveat that you can resize only the last array dimension. For example, if your array has two or more dimensions, you can change the size of only the last dimension and still preserve the contents of the array. (Single-dimension arrays automatically pass this test, so you can freely expand the size of dynamic arrays using the *Preserve* keyword.)

The following examples show how you can use *Preserve* to increase the size of the last dimension in a dynamic array without erasing any existing data contained in the array.

If you originally declared a dynamic string array named *Philosophers* by using the following syntax:

```
Dim Philosophers() As String
```

redimension the array, and add data to it by using code similar to the following:

```
ReDim Philosophers(200)
Philosophers(200) = "Steve Harrison"
```

You can expand the size of the *Philosophers* array to 301 elements (0–300), and preserve the existing contents, by using the following syntax:

```
ReDim Preserve Philosophers(300)
```

A more complex example involving a three-dimensional array makes use of similar syntax. Imagine that you want to make use of a three-dimensional single-precision floating-point array, named *myCube*, in your program. You could declare the *myCube* array by using the following syntax:

```
Dim myCube(,,) As Single
```

You could then redimension the array and add data to it by using the following code:

```
ReDim myCube(25, 25, 25)
myCube(10, 1, 1) = 150.46
```

after which you could expand the size of the third dimension in the array (while preserving the array's contents) by using this syntax:

```
ReDim Preserve myCube(25, 25, 50)
```

In this example, however, only the third dimension can be expanded—the first and second dimensions cannot be changed if you redimension the array by using the *Preserve* keyword. Attempting to change the size of the first or second dimension in this example will produce a runtime error when the *ReDim Preserve* statement is executed.

Experiment a little with *ReDim Preserve*, and see how you can use it to make your own arrays flexible and robust.

You're finished working with arrays for now. In the rest of this chapter, you'll learn about collections.

Working with Object Collections

In previous sections, you learned about using arrays to store information during program execution. In this section, you'll learn about collections, a complementary method to manipulate control objects and other data in a Visual Basic program. You already know that objects on a form are stored together in the same file. But did you also know that Visual Basic considers the objects to be members of the same group? In Visual Basic terminology, the entire set of objects on a form is called the *Controls collection*. The *Controls* collection is created automatically when you open a new form, and when you add objects to the form, they automatically become part of the collection. In fact, Visual Basic maintains several standard collections of objects that you can use when you write your programs. In the rest of this chapter, you'll learn the basic skills you need to work with any collection you encounter.

Each collection in a program has its own name so that you can reference it as a distinct unit in the program code. For example, as you just learned, the collection containing all the objects on a form is called the *Controls* collection. If you have more than one form in a project, you can create public variables associated with the form names and use those variables to differentiate one *Controls* collection from another. (You'll learn more about using public variables to store form data in Chapter 15.) You can even add controls programmatically to the *Controls* collection in a form.

In addition to letting you work with objects and collections in your own programs, Visual Studio lets you browse your system for other application objects

11

Arrays and Collections

and use them in your programs. We'll pick up this topic again in Chapter 13 when you learn how to use the Visual Studio Object Browser.

Referencing Objects in a Collection

You can reference the objects in a collection, or the individual members of the collection, by specifying the *index position* of the object in the group. Visual Basic stores collection objects in the reverse order of that in which they were created, so you can use an object's "birth order" to reference the object individually, or you can use a loop to step through several objects. For example, to identify the last object created on a form, you would specify the 0 (zero) index, as shown in this example:

```
Controls(0).Text = "Business"
```

This statement sets the *Text* property of the last object on the form to "Business". (The second-to-the-last object created has an index of 1, the third-to-the-last object created has an index of 2, and so on.) Considering this logic, it's important that you don't always associate a particular object on the form with an index value—if a new object is added to the collection, the new object will take the 0 index spot, and the remaining object indexes will be incremented by 1.

The following For...Next loop displays the names of the last four controls added to a form by using a message box:

```
Dim i As Integer
For i = 0 To 3
    MsgBox(Controls(i).Name)
Next i
```

Note that I've directed this loop to cycle from 0 to 3 because the last control object added to a form is in the "0" position. In the following section, you'll learn a more efficient method for writing such a loop.

Writing For Each...Next Loops

Although you can reference the members of a collection individually, the most useful way to work with objects in a collection is to process them as a group. In fact, the reason collections exist is so that you can process groups of objects efficiently. For example, you might want to display, move, sort, rename, or resize an entire collection of objects at once.

To handle one of these tasks, you can use a special loop called For Each...Next to cycle through objects in a collection one at a time. A For Each...Next loop is similar to a For...Next loop. When a For Each...Next loop is used with the *Controls* collection, it looks like this:

```
Dim CtrlVar As Control
...
For Each CtrlVar In Controls
    process object
Next CtrlVar
```

The *CtrlVar* variable is declared as a *Control* type and represents the current object in the collection. *Controls* (note the "s") is the collection class I introduced earlier that represents all the control objects on the current form. The body of the loop is used to process the individual objects of the collection. For example, you might want to change the *Enabled*, *Left*, *Top*, *Text*, or *Visible* properties of the objects in the collection, or you might want to list the name of each object in a list box.

The *CtrlVar* variable represents the current object in a For Each...Next loop.

Experimenting with Objects in the *Controls* Collection

In the following exercises, you'll use program code to manipulate the objects on a form using the *Controls* collection. The project you create will have three button objects, and you'll create event procedures that change the *Text* properties of each object, move objects to the right, and give one object in the group special treatment. The program will use three For Each...Next loops to manipulate the objects each time the user clicks one of the buttons.

Use a For Each...Next loop to change *Text* properties

1   Click the Close Solution command on the File menu to close the current project.
2   Create a new Visual Basic Windows Application project named **My Controls Collection** in the c:\vbnet03sbs\chap11 folder.
3   Use the *Button* control to draw three button objects on the left side of the form, as shown here:

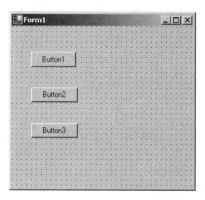

4   Use the Properties window to set the *Name* property of the third button object (*Button3*) to btnMoveObjects.

5   Double-click the first button object (*Button1*) on the form.

The *Button1_Click* event procedure appears in the Code Editor.

6   Type the following program statements:

```
For Each ctrl In Controls
    ctrl.Text = "Click Me!"
Next
```

This For Each...Next loop steps through the *Controls* collection on the form one control at a time and sets each control's *Text* property to "Click Me!" The loop uses *ctrl* as an object variable in the loop, which you'll declare in the following step.

7   Scroll to the top of the form's program code, and directly below the tag "Windows Form Designer generated code", type the following comment and variable declaration:

```
'Declare a variable of type Control to represent form controls
Dim ctrl As Control
```

This global variable declaration creates a variable in the *Control* class type that will represent the current form's controls in the program. You're declaring this variable in the general declarations area of the form so that it will be valid throughout all of the form's event procedures. Now you're ready to run the program and change the *Text* property for each button on the form.

8   Click the Start button on the Standard toolbar to run the program.

9   Click the first button on the form (*Button1*).

The *Button1_Click* event procedure changes the *Text* property for each control in the *Controls* collection. Your form will look like this:

10 Click the Close button on the form.

The program ends.

Now you're ready to try a different experiment with the *Controls* collection. Use the *Left* property to move each control in the *Controls* collection to the right.

Use a For Each...Next loop to move controls

1 Display the form again, and then double-click the second button object (*Button2*).

Type the following program code in the *Button2_Click* event procedure:

```
For Each ctrl In Controls
    ctrl.Left = ctrl.Left + 25
Next
```

Each time the user clicks the second button, this For Each...Next loop steps through the objects in the *Controls* collection one by one and moves them 25 pixels to the right. (To move objects 25 pixels to the left, you would subtract 25 instead.) A *pixel* is a device-independent measuring unit that allows you to precisely place objects on a form.

▶ **Tip** In Visual Basic 6, twips instead of pixels were usually used to specify measurements. For information about converting existing Visual Basic 6 code from twip measurements to pixel measurements, search for the topic "ScaleMode Is Not Supported" in the Visual Studio online Help.

2 As in the previous event procedure you typed, the *ctrl* variable is a "stand-in" for the current object in the collection and contains the same property settings as the object it represents. In this loop, you adjust the *Left* property, which determines an object's position relative to the left side of the form.

3 Click the Start button on the Standard toolbar.

The program runs, and three buttons appear on the left side of the form.

4 Click the second button several times.

Arrays and Collections

11

Each time you click the button, the objects on the form move to the right. Your screen will look like this after five clicks:

5   Click the Close button on the form to stop the program.

Moving all the objects on a form isn't a requirement, of course. Visual Basic allows you to process collection members individually if you want to. In the next exercise, you'll learn how to keep the third button object in one place while the other two buttons move to the right.

Using the *Name* Property in a For Each...Next Loop

If you want to process one or more members of a collection differently than you process the others, you can use the *Name* property, which uniquely identifies each object on the form. You've set the *Name* property periodically in this book to make your program code more readable, but *Name* also can be used programmatically to identify specific objects in your program.

To use the *Name* property in this way, single out the objects that you want to give special treatment to, and then note their *Name* properties. As you loop through the objects on the form using a For Each...Next loop, use one or more *If* statements to test for the important *Name* properties, and handle those objects differently. For example, let's say you wanted to construct a For Each...Next loop that moved one object slower across the form than the other objects. You could use an *If...Then* statement to spot the *Name* property of the slower object, and then move that object a shorter distance by not incrementing its *Left* property as much as you would for the other objects.

▶   **Tip**   If you plan to give several objects special treatment in a For Each...Next loop, you can use *ElseIf* statements with the *If...Then* statement, or you can use a Select Case decision structure.

In the following exercise, you'll test the *Name* property of the third button object (*btnMoveObjects*) to give that button special treatment in a For Each...Next loop. The end result will be an event procedure that moves the top two buttons to the right but keeps the bottom button stationary.

▶ **Tip** In addition to the *Name* property, most objects support the *Tag* property. Similar to the *Name* property, the *Tag* property is a location in which you can store string data about the object. The *Tag* property is empty by default, but you can assign information to it and test it to uniquely identify objects in your program that you want to process differently.

Use the *Name* property to give a control in the *Controls* collection special treatment

1 Display the form, and then double-click the third button object.

The *btnMoveObjects_Click* event procedure appears in the Code Editor. Remember that you changed the *Name* property of this object from Button1 to btnMoveObjects in an earlier exercise.

2 Type the following program code in the event procedure:

```
For Each ctrl In Controls
    If ctrl.Name <> "btnMoveObjects" Then
        ctrl.Left = ctrl.Left + 25
    End If
Next
```

The new feature of this For Each...Next loop is the *If...Then* statement that checks each collection member to see whether it has a *Name* property called btnMoveObjects. If the loop encounters this marker, it passes over the object without moving it. Note that, as in the previous examples, the *ctrl* variable was declared at the top of the form as a variable of the *Control* type with scope throughout the form.

3 Click the Save All button on the Standard toolbar.

4 Click the Start button.

▶ **Note** The complete Controls Collection program is located in the c:\vbnet03sbs\chap11\controls collection folder.

The program runs, and the three interface objects appear on the form.

5 Click the third button object six or seven times.

Arrays and Collections

As you click the button, the objects on the form move across the screen. The third button stays in the same place, however, as shown here:

Giving one object in a collection special treatment can be very useful. In this case, using the *Name* property in the For Each...Next loop improved the readability of the program code, suggesting numerous potential uses for a game or graphics program. As you use other types of collections in Visual Basic, be sure to keep the *Name* property in mind.

6 Click the Close button on the form to stop the program.

Creating Your Own Collections

Visual Basic allows you to create your own collections to track data in a program and manipulate it systematically. Although collections are often created to hold objects, such as user interface controls, you can also use collections to store numeric or string values while a program is running. In this way, collections nicely complement the capabilities of arrays, which you learned about at the beginning of this chapter.

New collections are declared as variables are in a program, and the location in which you declare them determines their *scope*, or the extent to which their assigned values persist. Because collections are so useful, I usually declare them at the top of a form or in a standard module. New collection declarations require the syntax

```
Dim CollectionName As New Collection()
```

where *CollectionName* is the name of your collection. If you place the collection declaration in a standard module, use the *Public* keyword instead of the *Dim* keyword. After you create a collection, you can add members to it by using the *Add* method, and you can examine the individual members using a For Each...Next loop.

The following exercise shows you how to create a collection to hold string data representing the Internet addresses (uniform resource locators, or URLs) you've recently used. To make a connection to the Web, the program will use the Visual Basic *System.Diagnostics.Process.Start* method and your default Web browser, a technique that I first introduced in Chapter 3.

Track Internet addresses by using a new collection

1   Click the Close Solution command on the File menu.

The current project closes.

2   Create a new Visual Basic Windows Application project named **My URL Collection** in the c:\vbnet03sbs\chap11 folder.

3   Draw a wide text box object at the top of the form, centered within the form.

4   Draw two wide button objects on the form below the text box object, one button below the other.

5   Set the following properties for the form and its objects:

Object	Property	Setting
TextBox1	*Text*	"http://www.microsoft.com/mspress"
Button1	*Text*	"Visit Site"
Button2	*Text*	"List all sites visited"
Form1	*Text*	"URL Collection"

6   Your form should look like this:

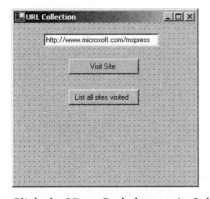

7   Click the View Code button in Solution Explorer to display the Code Editor.

Arrays and Collections

8 Scroll to the top of the form's program code, and directly below the tag "Windows Form Designer generated code", type the following variable declaration:

```
Dim URLsVisited As New Collection()
```

This statement creates a new collection and assigns it the variable name *URLsVisited*. Because you're placing the declaration at the top of the form, the collection will have scope throughout all of the form's event procedures.

9 Display the form again, double-click the Visit Site button, and then type the following code in the *Button1_Click* event procedure:

```
URLsVisited.Add(TextBox1.Text)
System.Diagnostics.Process.Start(TextBox1.Text)
```

This program code uses the *Add* method to fill up, or populate, the collection with members. When the user clicks the *Button1* object, the program assumes that a valid Internet address has been placed in the *TextBox1* object. Every time that the *Button1* object is clicked, the current URL in *TextBox1* is copied to the *URLsVisited* collection as a string. Next, *the System.Diagnostics.Process.Start* method is called with URL as a parameter. Because the parameter is a URL, the *Start* method will attempt to open the URL by using the default Web browser on the system. (If the URL is invalid or an Internet connection cannot be established, the Web browser will handle the error.)

▶ **Note** The only URLs this program adds to the *URLsVisited* collection are those you've specified in the *TextBox1* object. If you browse to additional Web sites by using your Web browser, those sites won't be added to the collection. (To learn a more sophisticated way of tracking Web sites by using the Internet Explorer object model, see Chapter 21.)

10 Display the form again, and then double-click the List All Sites Visited button.

11 Type the following program code using the Code Editor:

```
Dim URLName, AllURLs As String
For Each URLName In URLsVisited
    AllURLs = AllURLs & URLName & vbCrLf
Next URLName
MsgBox(AllURLs, MsgBoxStyle.Information, "Web sites visited")
```

This event procedure prints the entire collection using a For Each...Next loop and a *MsgBox* function. The routine declares a string variable named *URLName* to hold each member of the collection as it's processed, and the value is added to a string named *AllURLs* by using the concatenation operator (&) and the *vbCrLf* string constant.

Finally, the *AllURLs* string, which represents the entire contents of the *URLsVisited* collection, is displayed in a message box. I added the *MsgBoxStyle.Information* argument in the *MsgBox* function to emphasize that the text being displayed is general information and not a warning. (*MsgBoxStyle.Information* is also a built-in Visual Basic constant.)

12 Click the Save All button to save your changes.

▶ **Note**   To run the URL Collection program, your computer must establish a connection to the Internet and be equipped with a Web browser, such as Microsoft Internet Explorer or Netscape Navigator.

Run the URL Collection program

1 Click the Start button to run the program.

▶ **Note**   The complete URL Collection program is located in the c:\vbnet03sbs\chap11\url collection folder.

The utility features a default Web site in the URL textbox, so it isn't necessary to type your own Internet address at first.

2 Click the Visit Site button.

Visual Basic adds the Microsoft Press Web site (*http://www.microsoft.com/mspress*) to the *URLsVisited* collection and then opens the default Web browser on your system and loads the requested Web page, as shown here. Examine the content of this Web site if you're interested.

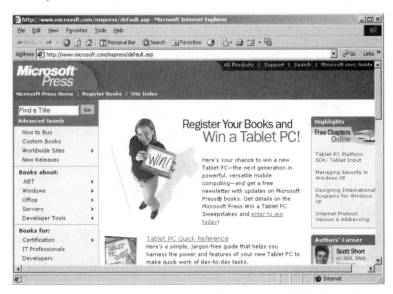

3   Click the form again. (You might need to click the icon on the Windows taskbar.)

4   Click the List All Sites Visited button.

Visual Basic executes the event procedure for the *Button2* object. You'll see a message box that looks like this:

5   Click OK in the message box, type a different Web site in the form's text box, and then click the Visit Site button.

You might want to visit the Microsoft Visual Basic Web site to learn more about Visual Basic .NET (at *http://msdn.microsoft.com/vbasic/*).

6   Visit a few more Web sites using the URL Collection form, and then click the List All Sites Visited button.

Each time you click the List All Sites Visited button, the *MsgBox* function expands to show the growing URL history list, as shown here:

If you visit more than a few dozen Web sites, you'll need to replace the *MsgBox* function with a multiline text box on the form. (Can you figure out how to write the code?)

7   When you're finished, click the Close button on the form, and then close your Web browser.

Congratulations! You've learned how to use the *Controls* collection and create new collections, and you've learned how to process them by using a For Each...Next loop. These skills will be useful whenever you work with collections.

One Step Further: Visual Basic for Applications Collections

If you decide to write Visual Basic macros for Microsoft Office applications in the future, you'll find that collections play a big role in the object models of

Microsoft Word, Microsoft Excel, Microsoft Access, Microsoft PowerPoint, and several other applications that support the Visual Basic for Applications programming language. In Word, for example, all the open documents in the word processor are stored in the *Documents* collection, and each paragraph in the current document is stored in the *Paragraphs* collection. You can manipulate these collections with the For Each...Next loop just as you did other collections in the preceding exercises.

For example, the following sample code comes from a Word 2002 macro that uses a For Each...Next loop to check each open document in the *Documents* collection for a file named *MyLetter.doc*. If the file is found in the collection, the macro saves the file by using the *Save* method. If the file isn't found in the collection, the macro attempts to open the file from the My Documents folder on drive C.

```
Dim aDoc As Object
Dim docFound As Boolean
Dim docLocation As String
docFound = False
docLocation = "c:\my documents\myletter.doc"
For Each aDoc In Documents
    If InStr(1, aDoc.Name, "myletter.doc", 1) Then
        docFound = True
        aDoc.Save
        Exit For
    End If
Next aDoc
If docFound = False Then
    Documents.Open FileName:=docLocation
End If
```

> ▶ **Tip** I've included this sample Word 2002 macro to show you how you can use collections in Visual Basic for Applications, but the source code is designed for Word, not the Visual Basic compiler. To try it, you'll need to start Word, click the Macros command on the Macro submenu of the Tools menu, create a new name for the macro, and then enter the code using Word's special macro editor. (If you're not in Word, the *Documents* collection won't have any meaning to the compiler.)

The macro begins by declaring three variables. The *aDoc* object variable will represent the current collection element in the For Each...Next loop. The Boolean variable *docFound* will be assigned a Boolean value of True if the document is found in the *Documents* collection. The string variable *docLocation* will contain the path of the MyLetter.doc file on disk. (This routine assumes that the MyLetter.doc file is in the My Documents folder on drive C.)

The For Each...Next loop cycles through each document in the *Documents* collection searching for the MyLetter file. If the file is detected by the *InStr* function (which detects one string in another), the file is saved. If the file isn't found, the macro attempts to open it by using the *Open* method of the *Documents* object.

Also note the *Exit For* statement, which I use to exit the For Each...Next loop when the MyLetter file has been found and saved. *Exit For* is a special program statement you can use to exit a For...Next loop or For Each...Next loop when continuing will cause unwanted results. In our example, if the MyLetter.doc file has been located in the collection, continuing the search would be fruitless. Here, the *Exit For* statement affords a graceful way to stop the loop as soon as its task is completed.

Lesson 11 Quick Reference

To	Do this
Create an array	Dimension the array by using the *Dim* keyword. For example: `Dim Employees(9) As String`
Create a public array	Dimension the array by using the *Public* keyword in a standard module. For example: `Public Employees(9) As String`
Assign a value to an array	Specify the array name, the index of the array element, and the value. For example: `Employees(5) = "Leslie"`
Format text strings with carriage return and tab characters	Use the *vbCrLf* and *vbTab* constants within your program code. (To add these values to strings, use the & operator.)
Create a dynamic array	Specify the name and type of the array at design time, but omit the number of elements. (If the array has multiple dimensions, insert commas between the dimensions but no numbers.) While your program is running, specify the size of the array by using the *ReDim* statement. For example: `ReDim Temperatures(10)`

Process the elements in an array	Write a For...Next loop that uses the loop counter variable to address each element in the array. For example:
	
	`Dim i As Short`
	`Dim Total As Single`
	`For i = 0 To UBound(Temperatures)`
	`  Total = Total + Temperatures(i)`
	`Next`

To	Do this
Redimension an array while preserving the data in it	Use the *Preserve* keyword in your *ReDim* statement. For example: `ReDim Preserve myCube(25, 25, 50)`

Process objects in a collection	Write a For Each...Next loop that addresses each member of the collection individually. For example:
	`Dim ctrl As Control`
	`For Each ctrl In Controls`
	`  ctrl.Text = "Click Me!"`
	`Next`

Move objects in the *Controls* collection from left to right across the screen	Modify the *Control.Left* property of each collection object in a For Each...Next loop. For example:
	`Dim ctrl As Control`
	`For Each ctrl In Controls`
	`  Ctrl.Left = Ctrl.Left + 25`
	`Next Ctrl`

Give special treatment to an object in a collection	Test the *Name* property of the objects in the collection by using a For Each...Next loop. For example:
	`Dim ctrl As Control`
	`For Each ctrl In Controls`
	`  If ctrl.Name <> "btnMoveObjects" Then`
	`    ctrl.Left = ctrl.Left + 25`
	`  End If`
	`Next`

Create a new collection and add members to it	Declare a variable by using the New Collection syntax. Use the *Add* method to add members. For example:
	`Dim URLsVisited As New Collection()`
	`URLsVisited.Add(TextBox1.Text)`

Exploring Text Files and String Processing

In this chapter, you will learn how to:

- Display a text file by using a text box object.

- Save notes in a text file.

- Use string processing techniques to sort and encrypt text files.

Managing electronic documents is an important function in any modern business, and Microsoft Visual Basic .NET provides numerous mechanisms for working with different document types and manipulating the information in them. The most basic document type is the *text file*, which is made up of non-formatted words and paragraphs, letters, numbers, and a variety of special-purpose characters and symbols. In this chapter, you'll learn how to work with information stored in text files on your system. You'll learn how to open a text file and display its contents by using a text box object, and you'll learn how to create a new text file on disk. You'll also learn more about managing strings in your programs, and you'll use methods in the .NET Framework *String* class to combine, sort, encrypt, and display words, lines, and entire text files.

Upgrade Notes: What's New in Visual Basic .NET?

If you're experienced with Visual Basic 6, you'll notice some new features in Visual Basic .NET, including the following:

- In Visual Basic 6, you opened and manipulated text files by using the *Open*, *Line Input #*, *Print #*, *EOF*, and *Close* keywords. In Visual Basic .NET, there's a new set of functions that manage text file operations. These functions are provided by the *FileSystem* object in the *Microsoft.VisualBasic* namespace and include *FileOpen*, *LineInput*, *PrintLine*, and *FileClose*.

- In addition to the built-in Visual Basic .NET functions just mentioned, you can use the objects in the *System.IO* namespace to open and manipulate files, browse drives and folders, copy and delete files, process text streams, and complete other file-management tasks. The objects in the *System.IO* namespace aren't a replacement for the preceding built-in Visual Basic .NET functions, but they do complement them.

- In terms of string processing, several of the older Visual Basic text functions have been supplemented by new methods in the .NET Framework *String* class. For example, the new *SubString* method provides functionality similar to the Visual Basic *Mid* function, and the *ToUpper* method is similar to the Visual Basic *UCase* function. You can use either method to manipulate text strings, but the newer .NET Framework methods are recommended.

Displaying Text Files by Using a Text Box Object

The simplest way to display a text file in a program is to use a text box object. You can create text box objects in a variety of sizes. If the contents of the text file don't fit neatly in the text box, you can also add scroll bars to the text box so that the user can examine the entire file. To load the contents of a text file into a text box, you need to use four functions. These functions are described in the following table and will be demonstrated in the first exercise in this chapter. As I noted earlier, several of these functions replace older keywords in the Visual Basic language.

Function	Description
FileOpen	Opens a text file for input or output
LineInput	Reads a line of input from the text file
EOF	Checks for the end of the text file
FileClose	Closes the text file

Opening a Text File for Input

A *text file* consists of one or more lines of numbers, words, or characters. Text files are distinct from *document files*, which contain formatting codes, and from *executable files*, which contain instructions for the operating system. Typical text files on your system will be identified by Microsoft Windows Explorer as "Text Documents" or will have the extension .txt, .ini, .log, or .inf. Because text files contain only ordinary, recognizable characters, you can display them easily by using text box objects.

You can let the user choose which text file to open in a program by using an *OpenFileDialog* control to prompt the user for the file's path. The *OpenFile-Dialog* control contains the *Filter* property, which controls which type of files are displayed, the *ShowDialog* method, which displays the Open dialog box, and the *FileName* property, which returns the path specified by the user. The *OpenFileDialog* control doesn't open the file; it just gets the path.

The *FileOpen* Function

After you get the path from the user, you open the file in the program by using the *FileOpen* function. The abbreviated syntax for the *FileOpen* function is

```
FileOpen(filenumber, pathname, mode)
```

You can find the complete list of arguments in the Visual Basic online Help. These are the most important:

- *filenumber* is an integer from 1 through 255.
- *pathname* is a valid Microsoft Windows path.
- *mode* is a keyword indicating how the file will be used. (You'll use the *OpenMode.Input* and *OpenMode.Output* modes in this chapter.)

The file number will be associated with the file when it's opened. You then use this file number in your code whenever you need to refer to the open file. Aside from this association, there's nothing special about file numbers; Visual Basic simply uses them to keep track of the different files you open in your program.

A typical *FileOpen* function using an *OpenFileDialog* object looks like this:

```
FileOpen(1, OpenFileDialog1.FileName, OpenMode.Input)
```

Text Files and String Processing   12

Here the *OpenFileDialog1.FileName* property represents the path, *OpenMode.Input* is the mode, and 1 is the file number.

▶ **Tip** Text files that are opened by using this syntax are called sequential files because you must work with their contents in sequential order. In contrast, you can access the information in a database file in any order. (You'll learn more about databases in Chapter 19.)

The following exercise demonstrates how you can use an *OpenFileDialog* control and the *FileOpen* function to open a text file. The exercise also demonstrates how you can use the *LineInput* and *EOF* functions to display the contents of a text file in a text box and how you can use the *FileClose* function to close a file.

▶ **Tip** For more information about using controls on the Windows Forms tab of the Toolbox to create standard dialog boxes, see Chapter 4.

Run the Text Browser program

1 Start Microsoft Visual Studio, and open the Text Browser project in the c:\vbnet03sbs\chap12\text browser folder.

The project opens in the development environment.

2 If the project's form isn't visible, display it now.

The Text Browser form appears, as shown here:

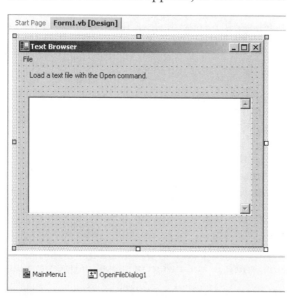

The form contains a large text box object that has scroll bars. It also contains a main menu object (with Open, Close, and Exit commands), a file open dialog object, and a label providing operating instructions. I also created the property settings shown in the following table. (Note especially the text box settings.)

Object	Property	Setting
txtNote	*Enabled*	False
	Multiline	True
	Name	txtNote
	ScrollBars	Both
	Text	(empty)
mnuOpenItem	*Name*	mnuOpenItem
mnuCloseItem	*Enabled*	False
	Name	mnuCloseItem
lblNote	*Text*	"Load a text file with the Open command."
	Name	lblNote
Form1	*Text*	"Text Browser"

3   Click the Start button on the Standard toolbar.

The Text Browser program runs.

4   On the Text Browser File menu, click the Open command.

The Open dialog box appears.

5   Open the c:\vbnet03sbs\chap12\text browser folder.

The contents of the Text Browser folder are shown here:

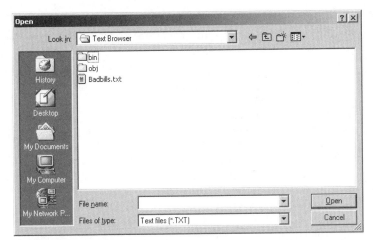

6   Double-click the filename Badbills.txt.

Badbills, a text file containing an article written in 1951 about the dangers of counterfeit money, appears in the text box, as shown here:

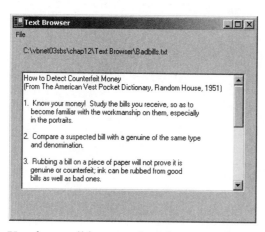

7 Use the scroll bars to view the entire document. Memorize number 5.

8 When you've finished, click the Close command on the File menu to close the file, and then click the Exit command to quit the program. The program stops, and the development environment returns.

Now you'll take a look at two important event procedures in the program.

Examine the Text Browser program code

1 On the Text Browser form File menu, double-click the Open command. The *mnuOpenItem_Click* event procedure appears in the Code Editor.

2 Resize the Code Editor to see more of the program code, if necessary. The *mnuOpenItem_Click* event procedure contains the following program code:

```
Dim AllText, LineOfText As String
OpenFileDialog1.Filter = "Text files (*.TXT)|*.TXT"
OpenFileDialog1.ShowDialog() 'display Open dialog box
If OpenFileDialog1.FileName <> "" Then
    Try 'open file and trap any errors using handler
        FileOpen(1, OpenFileDialog1.FileName, OpenMode.Input)
        Do Until EOF(1) 'read lines from file
            LineOfText = LineInput(1)
            'add each line to the AllText variable
            AllText = AllText & LineOfText & vbCrLf
        Loop
        lblNote.Text = OpenFileDialog1.FileName  'update label
        txtNote.Text = AllText 'display file
        txtNote.Select(1, 0)   'remove text selection
        txtNote.Enabled = True 'allow text cursor
```

```
        mnuCloseItem.Enabled = True   'enable Close command
        mnuOpenItem.Enabled = False   'disable Open command
    Catch
        MsgBox("Error opening file.")
    Finally
        FileClose(1) 'close file
    End Try
End If
```

This event procedure performs the following actions:

- Declares variables and assigns a value to the *Filter* property of the open file dialog object.
- Prompts the user for a path by using the *OpenFileDialog1* object.
- Traps errors by using a Try...Catch code block.
- Opens the specified file for input by using the *FileOpen* function.
- Uses the *LineInput* function to copy one line at a time from the file into a string named *AllText*.
- Copies lines until the end of the file is reached (EOF) or until there's no more room in the string. The *AllText* string has room for a very large file, but if an error occurs during the copying process, the *Catch* clause will display the error.
- Displays the *AllText* string in the text box, removes any selection, and enables the scroll bars and text cursor.
- Updates the File menu commands and closes the file by using the *FileClose* function.

Take a moment to see how the statements in the *mnuOpenItem_Click* event procedure work—especially the *FileOpen*, *LineInput*, *EOF*, and *FileClose* functions. For more information about these statements and functions, highlight the keyword you're interested in, and press F1 to see a discussion of it in the Visual Basic online Help. The error handler in the procedure displays a message and aborts the loading process if an error occurs.

3   Display the *mnuCloseItem_Click* event procedure, which is executed when the Close menu command is clicked.

The *mnuCloseItem_Click* event procedure looks like this:

```
txtNote.Text = ""                'clear text box
lblNote.Text = "Load a text file with the Open command."
mnuCloseItem.Enabled = False  'disable Close command
mnuOpenItem.Enabled = True    'enable Open command
```

The procedure clears the text box, updates the *lblNote* label, disables the Close command, and enables the Open command.

Now you can use this simple program as a template for more advanced utilities that process text files. In the next section, you'll learn how to type your own text into a text box and how to save the text in the text box to a file on disk.

Using the *StreamReader* Class to Open Text Files

In addition to the Visual Basic commands that open and display text files, the new *StreamReader* class in the .NET Framework library allows you to open and display text files in your programs. In this book, I'll use both the built-in Visual Basic functions and the *StreamReader* class to work with text files.

To use the *StreamReader* class, you add the following *Imports* statement to the top of your code, which provides access to the *StreamReader* class:

```
Imports System.IO
```

Then, if your program contains a text box object, you can display a text file inside the text box by using the following program code. (The text file opened in this example is Readme.txt, and the code assumes an object named *TextBox1* has been created on your form.)

```
Dim StreamToDisplay As StreamReader
StreamToDisplay = New StreamReader("c:\vbnet03sbs\chap14\readme.txt")
TextBox1.Text = StreamToDisplay.ReadToEnd
StreamToDisplay.Close()
TextBox1.Select(0, 0)
```

StreamReader is a .NET Framework alternative to opening a text file by using the Visual Basic *FileOpen* function. In this StreamReader example, I declare a variable named *StreamToDisplay* of the type *StreamReader* to hold the contents of the text file, and then I specify a valid path for the file I want to open. Next, I read the contents of the text file into the *StreamToDisplay* variable by using the *ReadToEnd* method, which retrieves all the text in the file from the current location (the beginning of the text file) to the end of the text file and assigns it to the *Text* property of the text box object. The final statements close the text file and use the *Select* method to remove the selection in the text box.

You'll use this *StreamReader* syntax in Chapter 15 as an alternative to using the built-in Visual Basic file functions.

Creating a New Text File on Disk

To create a new text file on disk by using Visual Basic, you'll use many of the functions and keywords you used in the last example. Creating new files on disk and saving data to them will be useful if you plan to generate custom reports or logs, save important calculations or values, or create a special-purpose word processor or text editor. Here's an overview of the steps you'll need to follow in the program:

1 Get input from the user or perform mathematical calculations, or do both.

2 Assign the results of your processing to one or more variables. For example, you could assign the contents of a text box to a string variable named *InputForFile*.

3 Prompt the user for a path by using a *SaveFileDialog* control. You use the *ShowDialog* method to display the dialog box.

4 Use the path received in the dialog box to open the file for output.

5 Use the *PrintLine* function to save one or more values to the open file.

6 Close the file when you've finished by using the *FileClose* function.

The following exercise demonstrates how you can use *TextBox* and *SaveFile-Dialog* controls to create a simple note-taking utility. The program uses the *File-Open* function to open a file, the *PrintLine* function to store string data in it, and the *FileClose* function to close the file. You can use this tool to take notes at home or at work and then to stamp them with the current date.

Run the Quick Note program

1 Click the Close Solution command on the File menu.

2 Open the Quick Note project in the c:\vbnet03sbs\chap12\quick note folder.

   The project opens in the development environment.

3 If the project's form isn't visible, display it now.

   The Quick Note form appears, as shown in the following illustration. It looks similar to the Text Browser form. However, I replaced the *OpenFileDialog* control with the *SaveFileDialog* control on the form. The File menu also contains different commands, including Save As, Insert Date, and Exit.

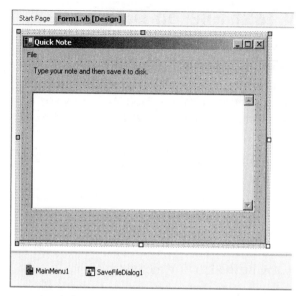

I set the following properties in the project:

Object	Property	Setting
txtNote	*Multiline*	True
	Name	txtNote
	ScrollBars	Both
	Text	(empty)
lblNote	*Text*	"Type your note and then save it to disk."
Form1	*Text*	"Quick Note"

4   Click the Start button on the toolbar.

5   Type the following text, or some text of your own, in the text box:

How to Detect Counterfeit Coins

   1   Drop coins on a hard surface. Genuine coins have a bell-like ring; most counterfeit coins sound dull.

   2   Feel all coins. Most counterfeit coins feel greasy.

   3   Cut edges of questionable coins. Genuine coins are not easily cut.

When you've finished, your screen should look similar to this:

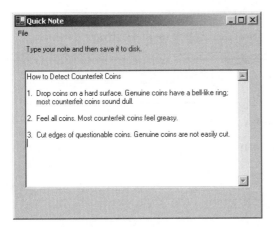

▶ **Tip** To paste text from the Windows Clipboard into the text box, press
Ctrl+V or Shift+Ins. To copy text from the text box to the Windows Clipboard, select the text, and then press Ctrl+C.

Now try using the commands on the File menu.

6 On the File menu, click the Insert Date command.

The current date appears as the first line in the text box, as shown
here:

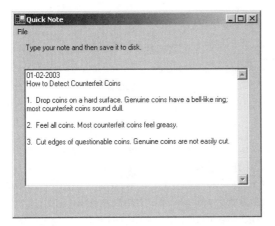

The Insert Date command provides a handy way to include the current date in a file. This is useful if you're creating a diary or a logbook.

7 On the File menu, click the Save As command.

8 In the Save As dialog box, open the c:\vbnet03sbs\chap12\quick note
folder if it isn't already open. Then type **Badcoins.txt** in the File
Name text box, and click Save.

The text of your document is saved in the new text file Badcoins.txt.

9   On the File menu, click the Exit command.

The program stops, and the development environment returns.

Now you'll take a look at the event procedures in the program.

Examine the Quick Note program code

1   On the Quick Note form File menu, double-click the Insert Date command.

The *mnuInsertDateItem_Click* event procedure appears in the Code Editor. You'll see the following program code:

```
txtNote.Text = DateString & vbCrLf & txtNote.Text
txtNote.Select(1, 0) 'remove selection
```

This event procedure adds the current date to the text box by linking together, or *concatenating*, the current date (generated by the *Date-String* property), a carriage return (added by the *vbCrLf* constant), and the *Text* property. You could use a similar technique to add the current time or any other information to the text in the text box.

2   Take a moment to see how the concatenation statements work, and then examine the *mnuSaveAsItem_Click* event procedure in the Code Editor.

You'll see the following program code:

```
SaveFileDialog1.Filter = "Text files (*.txt)|*.txt"
SaveFileDialog1.ShowDialog()
If SaveFileDialog1.FileName <> "" Then
    FileOpen(1, SaveFileDialog1.FileName, OpenMode.Output)
    PrintLine(1, txtNote.Text)  'copy text to disk
    FileClose(1)
End If
```

This block of statements uses a save file dialog object to display a Save As dialog box, checks to see whether the user selected a file, opens the file for output as file number 1, writes the value in the *txtNote.Text* property to disk by using the *PrintLine* function, and then closes the text file. Note especially the statement

```
PrintLine(1, txtNote.Text)  'copy text to disk
```

which assigns the entire contents of the text box to the open file. *PrintLine* is similar to the older Visual Basic *Print* and *Print #* statements; it directs output to the specified file rather than to the screen or the printer. The important point to note here is that the entire file is stored in the *txtNote.Text* property.

3   Review the *FileOpen*, *PrintLine*, and *FileClose* functions, and then
close the program by using the Close Solution command on the
File menu.

You've finished with the Quick Note program.

Processing Text Strings with Program Code

As you learned in the preceding exercises, you can quickly open, edit, and save
text files to disk with the *TextBox* control and a handful of well-chosen program statements. Visual Basic also provides a number of powerful statements
and functions specifically designed for processing the textual elements in your
programs. In this section, you'll learn how to extract useful information from a
text string, copy a list of strings into an array, and sort a list of strings.

An extremely useful skill to develop when working with textual elements is the
ability to sort a list of strings. The basic concepts in sorting are simple. You
draw up a list of items to sort, and then compare the items one by one until the
list is sorted in ascending or descending alphabetical order. In Visual Basic, you
compare one item with another by using the same relational operators that you
use to compare numeric values. The tricky part (which sometimes provokes
long-winded discussion among computer scientists) is the specific sorting algorithm you use to compare elements in a list. We won't get into the advantages
and disadvantages of different sorting algorithms in this chapter. (The bone of
contention is usually speed, which makes a difference only when several thousand items are sorted.) Instead, we'll explore how the basic string comparisons
are made in a sort. Along the way, you'll learn the skills necessary to sort your
own text boxes, list boxes, files, and databases.

Processing Strings by Using Methods and Keywords

The most common task you've accomplished so far with strings is concatenating them by using the concatenation operator (*&*). For example, the following
program statement concatenates three literal string expressions and assigns the
result "Bring on the circus!" to the string variable *Slogan*:

```
Dim Slogan As String
Slogan = "Bring" & " on the " & "circus!"
```

You can also concatenate and manipulate strings by using methods in the *String*
class of the .NET Framework library. For example, the *String.Concat* method
allows equivalent string concatenation by using this syntax:

```
Dim Slogan As String
Slogan = String.Concat("Bring", " on the ", "circus!")
```

Accordingly, Visual Basic .NET features two methods for string concatenation and many other string-processing tasks—you can use operators and functions from earlier versions of Visual Basic (*Mid*, *UCase*, *LCase*, and so on), or you can use newer methods from the .NET Framework (*Substring*, *ToUpper*, *ToLower*, and so on). There's no real "penalty" for using either string-processing technique. In the rest of this chapter, I'll introduce several useful string-processing functions from the .NET Framework *String* class, but I'll occasionally use the older string-processing functions, too. You can use either string-processing method or a combination of both.

The following table lists several of the .NET Framework methods that appear in subsequent exercises and their close equivalents in the Visual Basic .NET programming language. The fourth column in the table provides sample code for the methods in the *String* class of the .NET Framework.

.NET Framework method	Visual Basic function	Description	.NET Framework example

ToUpper	*UCase*	Changes letters in a string to upper-case.	```Dim Name, NewName As String```
			 ```Name = "Kim"```
			 ```NewName = Name.ToUpper```
			 ```'NewName = "KIM"```

ToLower	*LCase*	Changes letters in a string to lower-case.	```Dim Name, NewName As String```
			 ```Name = "Kim"```
			 ```NewName = Name.ToLower```
			 ```'NewName = "kim"```

Length	*Len*	Determines the number of characters in a string.	```Dim River As String```
			 ```Dim Size As Short```
			 ```River = "Mississippi"```
			 ```Size = River.Length```
			 ```'Size = 11```

Substring	*Mid*	Returns a fixed number of characters in a string from a given starting point. (Note: The first element in a string has an index of 0.)	```Dim Cols, Middle As String```
			 ```Cols = "First Second Third"```
			 ```Middle = Cols.SubString(6, 6)```
			 ```'Middle = "Second"```

IndexOf	*InStr*	Finds the starting point of one string within a larger string.	```Dim Name As String```
			 ```Dim Start As Short```
			 ```Name = "Abraham"```
			 ```Start = Name.IndexOf("h")```
			 ```'Start = 4```

.NET Framework method	Visual Basic function	Description	.NET Framework example

Trim	*Trim*	Removes leading and following spaces from a string.	`Dim Spacey, Trimmed As String`
			`Spacey = "   Hello   "`
			`Trimmed = Spacey.Trim`
			`'Trimmed = "Hello"`

Remove		Removes characters from the middle of a string.	`Dim RawStr, CleanStr As String`
			`RawStr = "Hello333 there!"`
			`CleanStr = RawStr.Remove(5, 3)`
			`'CleanStr = "Hello there!"`

Insert		Adds characters to the middle of a string.	`Dim Oldstr, Newstr As String`
			`Oldstr = "Hi Felix"`
			`Newstr = Oldstr.Insert(3, "there ")`
			`'Newstr = "Hi there Felix"`

StrComp		Compares strings and disregards case differences.	`Dim str1 As String = "Soccer"`
			`Dim str2 As String = "SOCCER"`
			`Dim Match As Short`
			`Match = StrComp(str1, _`
			`    str2, CompareMethod.Text)`
			`'Match = 0 [strings match]`

Sorting Text

Before Visual Basic can compare one character with another in a sort, it must convert each character into a number by using a translation table called the *ASCII character set* (also called the ANSI character set). ASCII is an acronym standing for American Standard Code for Information Interchange. Most of the basic symbols that you can display on your computer have different ASCII codes. These codes include the basic set of "typewriter" characters (codes 32 through 127) and special "control" characters, such as tab, linefeed, and carriage return (codes 0 through 31). For example, the lowercase letter *a* corresponds to the ASCII code 97, and the uppercase letter *A* corresponds to the ASCII code 65. This explains why Visual Basic treats these two characters quite differently when sorting or performing other comparisons.

In the 1980s, IBM extended ASCII with codes 128–255 that contained accented characters, Greek characters, graphic characters, and miscellaneous symbols. ASCII and these additional characters are typically known as the *IBM extended character set*.

▶ **Tip**   To see a table of the codes in the ASCII character set, search for "ASCII character codes" in the Visual Basic online Help.

The ASCII character set is still the most important numeric code for beginning programmers to learn, but it isn't the only character set. As the market for computers and application software has become more global in nature, a more comprehensive standard for character representation called Unicode has emerged. Unicode can hold up to 65,536 symbols—plenty of space to represent the traditional symbols in the ASCII character set and numerous international symbols as well. (As of this writing, about 45,000 characters are defined.) A standards body maintains the Unicode character set and adds symbols to it periodically. Microsoft Windows NT, Windows 2000, Windows XP, Windows Server 2003, and Visual Basic .NET have been specifically designed to manage ASCII and Unicode character sets. (For more information about the relationship between Unicode, ASCII, and Visual Basic .NET data types, see Chapter 5.)

In the following sections, you'll learn more about using the ASCII character set to process strings in your programs. As your applications become more sophisticated and you start planning for the global distribution of your software, you'll need to learn more about Unicode and other international settings.

Working with ASCII Codes

To determine the ASCII code of a particular letter, you can use the Visual Basic *Asc* function. For example, the following program statement assigns the number 122 (the ASCII code for the lowercase letter *z*) to the *AscCode* short integer variable:

```
Dim AscCode As Short
AscCode = Asc("z")
```

Conversely, you can convert an ASCII code to a letter with the *Chr* function. For example, this program statement assigns the letter *z* to the letter character variable:

```
Dim letter As Char
letter = Chr(122)
```

The same result could also be achieved if you used the *AscCode* variable just declared, as shown here:

```
letter = Chr(AscCode)
```

How can you compare one text string or ASCII code with another? You simply use one of the six relational operators Visual Basic supplies for working with textual and numeric elements. These relational operators are shown in the following table:

Operator	Meaning
<>	Not equal
=	Equal
<	Less than
>	Greater than
<=	Less than or equal to
>=	Greater than or equal to

A character is "greater than" another character if its ASCII code is higher. For example, the ASCII value of the letter "B" is greater than the ASCII value of the letter "A", so the expression

```
"A" < "B"
```

is true, and the expression

```
"A" > "B"
```

is false.

When comparing two strings that each contain more than one character, Visual Basic begins by comparing the first character in the first string with the first character in the second string and then proceeds through the strings character by character until it finds a difference. For example, the strings Mike and Michael are the same up to the third characters ("k" and "c"). Because the ASCII value of "k" is greater than that of "c", the expression

```
"Mike" > "Michael"
```

is true.

If no differences are found between the strings, they are equal. If two strings are equal through several characters but one of the strings continues and the other one ends, the longer string is greater than the shorter string. For example, the expression

```
"AAAAA" > "AAA"
```

is true.

Sorting Strings in a Text Box

The following exercise demonstrates how you can use relational operators and several string methods and functions to sort lines of text in a text box. The program is a revision of the Quick Note utility and features an Open command that allows you to open an existing file and a Close command that closes the file. There's also a Sort Text command on the File menu you use to sort the text currently displayed in the text box.

Because the entire contents of a text box are stored in one string, the program must first break that long string into smaller individual strings. These strings can then be sorted by using the *ShellSort* Sub procedure, a sorting routine based on an algorithm created by Donald Shell in 1959. To simplify these tasks, I created a standard module that defines a dynamic string array to hold each of the lines in the text box. I also placed the *ShellSort* Sub procedure in the standard module so that I could call it from any event procedure in the project. (For more about standard modules, see Chapter 10.)

One interesting part of this program is the routine that determines the number of lines in the text box object. No existing Visual Basic function computes this value automatically. I wanted the program to be able to sort a text box of any size line by line. To accomplish this, I created the code that follows. It uses the *Substring* method to examine one letter at a time in the text box object and then uses the *Chr* function to search for the carriage return character (which is ASCII code 13) at the end of each line. (Note in particular how the *Substring* method is used as part of the *Text* property of the *txtNote* object—the *String* class automatically provides this method, and many others, for any properties or variables that are declared in the *String* type.)

```
Dim ln, curline, letter As String
Dim i, charsInFile, lineCount As Short

'determine number of lines in text box object (txtNote)
lineCount = 0 'this variable holds total number of lines
charsInFile = txtNote.Text.Length 'get total characters
For i = 0 To charsInFile - 1 'move one char at a time
    letter = txtNote.Text.Substring(i, 1) 'get letter
    If letter = Chr(13) Then 'if carriage ret found
        lineCount += 1 'go to next line (add to count)
        i += 1 'skip linefeed char (always follows cr)
    End If
Next i
```

The total number of lines in the text box is assigned to the *lineCount* short integer variable. I use this value a little later to dimension a dynamic array in the program to hold each individual text string. The resulting array of strings then gets passed to the *ShellSort* Sub procedure for sorting, and *ShellSort* returns the string array in alphabetical order. Once the string array is sorted, I can simply copy it back to the text box by using a For loop.

Run the Sort Text program

1   Open the Sort Text project located in the c:\vbnet03sbs\chap12\sort text folder.

2   Click the Start button to run the program.

3   Type the following text, or some text of your own, in the text box:

- Zebra
- Gorilla
- Moon
- Banana
- Apple
- Turtle

Be sure to press Enter after you type "Turtle", or a last line of your own, so that Visual Basic will calculate the number of lines correctly.

4   On the File menu, click the Sort Text command.

The text you typed is sorted and redisplayed in the text box as follows:

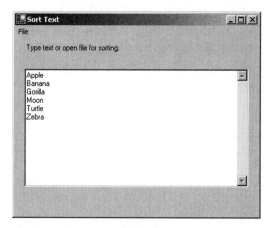

5   On the File menu, click the Open command, and open the file abc.txt in the c:\vbnet03sbs\chap12 folder, as shown on the following page.

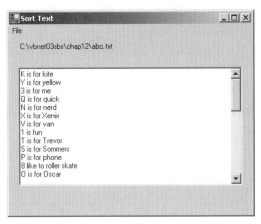

The abc.txt file contains 36 lines of text. Each line begins with either a letter or a number (1–10).

6   On the File menu, click the Sort Text command to sort the contents of the abc.txt file.

The Sort Text program sorts the file in ascending order and displays the sorted list of lines in the text box, as shown here:

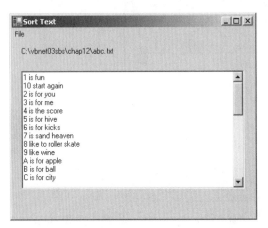

7   Scroll through the file to see the results of the alphabetical sort.

Notice that although the alphabetical portion of the sort ran perfectly, the sort did produce a strange result for one of the numeric entries—the line beginning with the number 10 appears second in the list rather than tenth. What's happening here is that Visual Basic is reading the 1 and the 0 in the number 10 as two independent characters, not as a number. Because we're comparing the ASCII codes of these strings from left to right, the program produces a purely alphabetical sort. If you want to sort numbers with this program, you'll need to store the numbers in numeric variables and compare them as numbers instead of strings.

Examine the Sort Text program code

1 On the Sort Text program File menu, click the Exit command to stop the program.

2 Open the Code Editor, and display the code for the *mnuSortTextItem_Click* event procedure.

We've already discussed the first routine in this event procedure, which counts the number of lines in the text box by using the *Substring* method to search for carriage return codes. The remainder of the event procedure dimensions a string array, copies each line of text into the array, calls a procedure to sort the array, and displays the reordered list in the text box.

The entire *mnuSortTextItem_Click* event procedure looks like this:

```
Dim ln, curline, letter As String
Dim i, charsInFile, lineCount As Short

'determine number of lines in text box object (txtNote)
lineCount = 0 'this variable holds total number of lines
charsInFile = txtNote.Text.Length 'get total characters
For i = 0 To charsInFile - 1 'move one char at a time
    letter = txtNote.Text.Substring(i, 1) 'get letter
    If letter = Chr(13) Then 'if carriage ret found
        lineCount += 1 'go to next line (add to count)
        i += 1 'skip linefeed char (always follows cr)
    End If
Next i

'build an array to hold the text in the text box
ReDim strArray(lineCount) 'create array of proper size
curline = 1
ln = "" 'use ln to build lines one character at a time
For i = 0 To charsInFile - 1 'loop through text again
    letter = txtNote.Text.Substring(i, 1) 'get letter
    If letter = Chr(13) Then 'if carriage return found
        curline = curline + 1 'increment line count
        i += 1 'skip linefeed char
        ln = "" 'clear line and go to next
    Else
        ln = ln & letter 'add letter to line
        strArray(curline) = ln 'and put in array
    End If
```

```
Next i

'sort array
ShellSort(strArray, lineCount)

'then display sorted array in text box
txtNote.Text = ""
curline = 1
For i = 1 To lineCount
    txtNote.Text = txtNote.Text & _
      strArray(curline) & vbCrLf
    curline += 1
Next i
txtNote.Select(1, 0)    'remove text selection
```

The array *strArray* was declared in a standard module (Module1.vb) that's also part of this program. By using the *ReDim* statement, I am dimensioning *strArray* as a dynamic array with the *lineCount* variable. This statement creates an array that has the same number of elements as the text box has lines of text (a requirement for the *ShellSort* Sub procedure). Using a For loop and the *ln* variable, I scan through the text box again, looking for carriage return characters and copying each complete line found to *strArray*. After the array is full of text, I call the *ShellSort* procedure I created previously in the Module1.vb standard module.

3   Display the code for the Module1.vb standard module in the Code Editor.

This module declares the public array variable *strArray* and then defines the content of the *ShellSort* procedure. The *ShellSort* procedure uses the <= relational operator to compare array elements and swap any that are out of order. The procedure looks like this:

```
Sub ShellSort(ByRef sort() As String, ByVal numOfElements As Short)
    Dim temp As String
    Dim i, j, span As Short
    'The ShellSort procedure sorts the elements of sort()
    'array in descending order and returns it to the calling
    'procedure.

    span = numOfElements \ 2
    Do While span > 0
        For i = span To numOfElements - 1

            For j = (i - span + 1) To 1 Step -span
                If sort(j) <= sort(j + span) Then Exit For
                'swap array elements that are out of order
                temp = sort(j)
```

```
                    sort(j) = sort(j + span)
                    sort(j + span) = temp
               Next j
          Next i
          span = span \ 2
     Loop
End Sub
```

The method of the sort is to continually divide the main list of elements into sublists that are smaller by half. The sort then compares the tops and the bottoms of the sublists to see whether the elements are out of order. If the top and bottom are out of order, they're exchanged. The end result is an array named *sort()* that's sorted alphabetically in descending order. To change the direction of the sort, simply reverse the relational operator (change <= to >=).

Let's move on to another variation of the Quick Note program that tackles basic encryption string processing.

Protecting Text with Encryption

Now that you've had some experience with ASCII codes, you can begin to write simple encryption routines that shift the ASCII codes in your documents and "scramble" the text to hide it from intruding eyes. This process, known as *encryption*, mathematically alters the characters in a file, making them unreadable to the casual observer. Of course, to use encryption successfully, you also need to be able to reverse the process—otherwise, you'll simply be *trashing* your files rather than protecting them. And you'll want to create an encryption scheme that can't be easily recognized, a complicated process that's only begun by the sample programs in this chapter.

The following exercises show you how to encrypt and decrypt text strings safely. You'll run the Encrypt Text program now to see a simple encryption scheme in action.

Encrypt text by changing ASCII codes

1   Close the Sort Text solution, and open the Encrypt Text project located in the c:\vbnet03sbs\chap12\encrypt text folder.

2   Click the Start button to run the program.

3   Type the following text, or some text of your own, in the text box:

Here at last, my friend, you have the little book long since expected and promised, a little book on vast matters, namely, "On my own ignorance and that of many others."

Francesco Petrarca, c. 1368

4   On the File menu, click the Save Encrypted File As command, and save the file in the c:\vbnet03sbs\chap12 folder with the name **padua.txt**.

As you save the text file, the program scrambles the ASCII code and displays the results in the text box shown below.

If you open this file in Microsoft Word or another text editor, you'll see the same result—the characters in the file have been encrypted to prevent unauthorized reading.

5   To restore the file to its original form, choose the Open Encrypted File command on the File menu, and open the padua.txt file in the c:\vbnet03sbs\chap12 folder.

The file appears again in its original form, as shown here:

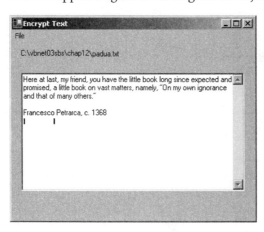

You might see one or two additional characters or symbols at the bottom of the text box window, depending on the number of carriage return and/or linefeed characters you placed at the end of the document.

6 On the File menu, click the Exit command to end the program.

Examine the Encrypt program code

1 Open the *mnuSaveAsItem_Click* event procedure in the Code Editor to see the program code that produces the encryption you observed when you ran the program.

Although the effect you saw might have looked mysterious, it was a very straightforward encryption scheme. Using the *Asc* and *Chr* functions and a For loop, I simply added one number to the ASCII code for each character in the text box and then saved the encrypted string to the specified text file.

The entire event procedure is listed here—in particular, note the items formatted with bold:

```
Dim Encrypt As String = ""
Dim letter As Char
Dim i, charsInFile As Short

SaveFileDialog1.Filter = "Text files (*.txt)|*.txt"
SaveFileDialog1.ShowDialog()
If SaveFileDialog1.FileName <> "" Then
    'save text with encryption scheme (ASCII code + 1)
    charsInFile = txtNote.Text.Length
    For i = 0 To charsInFile - 1
        letter = txtNote.Text.Substring(i, 1)
        'determine ASCII code and add one to it
        Encrypt = Encrypt & Chr(Asc(letter) + 1)
    Next
    FileOpen(1, SaveFileDialog1.FileName, OpenMode.Output)
    PrintLine(1, Encrypt) 'copy text to disk
    FileClose(1)
    txtNote.Text = Encrypt
    txtNote.Select(1, 0)   'remove text selection
    mnuCloseItem.Enabled = True
End If
```

Note especially the statement

```
Encrypt = Encrypt & Chr(Asc(letter) + 1)
```

which determines the ASCII code of the current letter, adds 1 to it, converts the ASCII code back to a letter, and adds it to the *Encrypt* string.

2   Now display the *mnuOpenItem_Click* event procedure in the Code Editor to see how the program reverses the encryption.

This program code is nearly identical to that of the Save Encrypted File As command, but rather than adding 1 to the ASCII code for each letter, it subtracts 1. Here's the complete *mnuOpenItem_Click* event procedure, with important statements in bold:

```
Dim AllText, LineOfText As String
Dim i, charsInFile As Short
Dim letter As Char
Dim Decrypt As String = ""

OpenFileDialog1.Filter = "Text files (*.TXT)|*.TXT"
OpenFileDialog1.ShowDialog() 'display Open dialog box
If OpenFileDialog1.FileName <> "" Then
    Try 'open file and trap any errors using handler
        FileOpen(1, OpenFileDialog1.FileName, OpenMode.Input)
        Do Until EOF(1) 'read lines from file
            LineOfText = LineInput(1)
            'add each line to the AllText variable
            AllText = AllText & LineOfText & vbCrLf
        Loop

        'now, decrypt string by subtracting one from ASCII code
        charsInFile = AllText.Length 'get length of string
        For i = 0 To charsInFile - 1 'loop once for each char
            letter = AllText.Substring(i, 1) 'get character
            Decrypt = Decrypt & Chr(Asc(letter) - 1) 'subtract 1
        Next i 'and build new string
        txtNote.Text = Decrypt 'then display converted string
        lblNote.Text = OpenFileDialog1.FileName
        txtNote.Select(1, 0)    'remove text selection
        txtNote.Enabled = True 'allow text cursor
        mnuCloseItem.Enabled = True   'enable Close command
        mnuOpenItem.Enabled = False   'disable Open command
    Catch
        MsgBox("Error opening file. It might be too big.")
    Finally
        FileClose(1) 'close file
    End Try
End If
```

This type of simple encryption might be all you need to conceal the information in your text files. However, files encrypted in this way can easily be decoded. By searching for possible equivalents of common characters such as the space character, determining the ASCII shift required to restore the common character, and running the conversion for the entire text file, a person experienced in encryption could readily decipher the file's content. Also, this sort of encryption doesn't prevent a malicious user from physically tampering with the file—for example, simply by deleting it if it's unprotected on your system or by modifying it in significant ways. But if you just want to hide information quickly, this simple encryption scheme should do the trick.

One Step Further: Using the *Xor* Operator

The preceding encryption scheme is quite safe for text files because it shifts the ASCII character code value up by just one. However, you'll want to be careful about shifting ASCII codes more than a few characters if you store the result as text in a text file. Keep in mind that dramatic shifts in ASCII codes (such as adding 500 to each character code) won't produce actual ASCII characters that can be decrypted later. For example, adding 500 to the ASCII code for the letter "A" (65) would give a result of 565. This value couldn't be translated into a character by the *Chr* function and would generate an error.

A safe way around this problem is to convert the letters in your file to numbers when you encrypt the file so that you can reverse the encryption no matter how large (or small) the numbers get. If you followed this line of thought, you could then apply mathematical functions—multiplication, logarithms, and so on—to the numbers as long as you knew how to reverse the results.

One of the best tools for encrypting numeric values is already built into Visual Basic. This tool is the *Xor operator*, which performs the "exclusive or" operation, a function carried out on the bits that make up the number itself. The *Xor* operator can be observed by using a simple *MsgBox* function. For example, the program statement

```
MsgBox(Asc("A") Xor 50)
```

would display a numeric result of 115 in a message box when the Visual Basic compiler executes it. Likewise, the program statement

```
MsgBox(115 Xor 50)
```

would display a result of 65 in a message box, the ASCII code for the letter "A" (our original value). In other words, the *Xor* operator produces a result that can be reversed—if the original Xor code is used again on the result of the first operation. This interesting behavior of the *Xor* function is used in many popular encryption algorithms. It can make your secret files much more difficult to decode.

Run the Xor Encryption program now to see how the *Xor* operator works in the note-taking utility you've been building.

Encrypt text with the *Xor* operator

1   Close the Encrypt Text solution, and then open the Xor Encryption project in the c:\vbnet03sbs\chap12\xor encryption folder.

2   Click the Start button to run the program.

3   Type the following text (or some of your own) for the encrypted text file:

Rothair's Edict (Lombard Italy, c. 643) 296. On Stealing Grapes. He who takes more than three grapes from another man's vine shall pay six soldi as compensation. He who takes less than three shall bear no guilt.

4   On the File menu, click the Save Encrypted File As command, and save the file in the c:\vbnet03sbs\chap12 folder with the name **old-laws.txt**.

The program prompts you for a secret encryption code (a number) that will be used to encrypt the file and decrypt it later. (Take note—you'll need to remember this code to decode the file.)

5   Type 500, or another numeric code, and then press Enter, as shown here:

Visual Basic encrypts the text by using the *Xor* operator and stores it on disk as a series of numbers. You won't see any change on your screen, but rest assured that the program created an encrypted file on disk. (You can verify this with a word processor or a text editor.)

6   Click the Close command on the program's File menu to clear the text in the text box.

Now you'll restore the encrypted file.

7   On the File menu, click the Open Encrypted File command.

8   Open the c:\vbnet03sbs\chap12 folder, and then double-click the old-laws.txt file.

9 Type 500 in the encryption code dialog box when it appears, and click OK. (If you specified a different encryption code, enter that instead.)

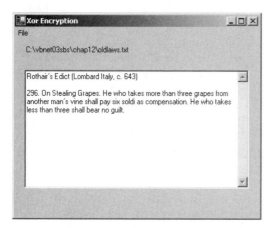

The program opens the file and restores the text by using the *Xor* operator and the encryption code you specified.

10 On the File menu, click the Exit command to end the program.

Examining the Encryption Code

The *Xor* operator is used in both the *mnuSaveAsItem_Click* and the *mnuOpenItem_Click* event procedures. By now, these generic menu processing routines will be fairly familiar to you. The *mnuSaveAsItem_Click* event procedure consists of these program statements (important lines in bold):

```
Dim letter As Char
Dim strCode As String
Dim i, charsInFile, Code As Short

SaveFileDialog1.Filter = "Text files (*.txt)|*.txt"
SaveFileDialog1.ShowDialog()
If SaveFileDialog1.FileName <> "" Then
    strCode = InputBox("Enter Encryption Code")
    If strCode = "" Then Exit Sub 'if cancel clicked
    'save text with encryption scheme
    Code = CShort(strCode)
    charsInFile = txtNote.Text.Length
    FileOpen(1, SaveFileDialog1.FileName, OpenMode.Output)
    For i = 0 To charsInFile - 1
        letter = txtNote.Text.Substring(i, 1)
        'convert to number w/ Asc, then use Xor to encrypt
        Print(1, Asc(letter) Xor Code) 'and save in file
```

```
        Next
        FileClose(1)
        mnuCloseItem.Enabled = True
End If
```

In the *Print* function, used here for the first time, the *Xor* operator is used to convert each letter in the text box to a numeric code, which is then saved to disk one number at time. (So far in this chapter I've used the *PrintLine* function, which copies an entire line to a file, but in this case, it's more useful to copy the numbers one at a time.)

The final result of this encryption is no longer textual, but numeric—guaranteed to bewilder even the nosiest snooper. For example, the following illustration shows the encrypted file produced by the preceding encryption routine, displayed in Windows Notepad. (I've enabled Word Wrap so that you can see all the code.)

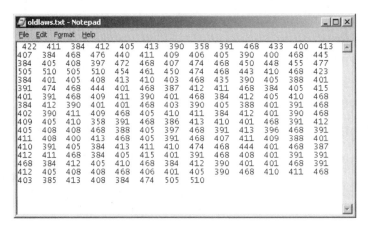

The *mnuOpenItem_Click* event procedure contains the following program statements. (Again, pay particular attention to the lines formatted with bold type.)

```
Dim ch As Char
Dim strCode As String
Dim Code, Number As Short
Dim Decrypt As String = ""

OpenFileDialog1.Filter = "Text files (*.TXT)|*.TXT"
OpenFileDialog1.ShowDialog() 'display Open dialog box
If OpenFileDialog1.FileName <> "" Then
    Try 'open file and trap any errors using handler
        strCode = InputBox("Enter Encryption Code")
        If strCode = "" Then Exit Sub 'if cancel clicked
```

```
            Code = CShort(strCode)
            FileOpen(1, OpenFileDialog1.FileName, OpenMode.Input)
            Do Until EOF(1) 'read lines from file
                Input(1, Number) 'read encrypted numbers
                ch = Chr(Number Xor Code) 'convert with Xor
                Decrypt = Decrypt & ch 'and build string
            Loop
            txtNote.Text = Decrypt 'then display converted string
            lblNote.Text = OpenFileDialog1.FileName
            txtNote.Select(1, 0)    'remove text selection
            txtNote.Enabled = True 'allow text cursor
            mnuCloseItem.Enabled = True   'enable Close command
            mnuOpenItem.Enabled = False  'disable Open command
        Catch
            MsgBox("Error opening file.")
        Finally
            FileClose(1) 'close file
        End Try
    End If
```

When the user clicks the Open Encrypted File command, this event procedure opens the encrypted file, prompts the user for an encryption code, and displays the translated file in the text box object. The *Input* function, introduced here for the first time, reads one number at a time from the encrypted file and stores it in the *Number* short integer variable. (*Input* is closely related to *LineInput*, but the *Input* function reads just one character from a file, not an entire line.) The *Number* variable is then combined with the *Code* variable by using the *Xor* operator, and the result is converted to a character by using the *Chr* function. These characters (stored in the *ch* variable of type *Char*) are then concatenated with the *Decrypt* string variable, which eventually contains the entire decrypted text file, as shown here:

```
ch = Chr(Number Xor Code) 'convert with Xor
Decrypt = Decrypt & ch 'and build string
```

Encryption techniques like this are useful, and they can also be very instructional. Because encryption relies so much on string processing techniques, it's a good way to practice a fundamental and important Visual Basic programming skill. Just be sure not to lose your encryption key!

Text Files and String Processing   **12**

Lesson 12 Quick Reference

To	Do this
Open a text file	Use the *FileOpen* function. For example: ```FileOpen(1, OpenFileDialog1.FileName, _\n OpenMode.Input)```
Get a line of input from a text file	Use the *LineInput* function. For example: ```Dim LineOfText As String\nLineOfText = LineInput(1)```
Check for the end of a file	Use the *EOF* function. For example: ```Dim LineOfText, AllText As String\nDo Until EOF(1)\n LineOfText = LineInput(1)\n AllText = AllText & LineOfText & _\n vbCrLf\nLoop```
Close an open file	Use the *FileClose* function. For example: ```FileClose(1)```
Display a text file	Use the *LineInput* function to copy text from an open file to a string variable, and then assign the string variable to a text box object. For example: ```Dim AllText, LineOfText As String\nDo Until EOF(1) 'read lines from file\n LineOfText = LineInput(1)\n AllText = AllText & LineOfText & _\n vbCrLf\nLoop\ntxtNote.Text = AllText 'display file```
Display an Open dialog box	Add an *OpenFileDialog* control to your form, and then use the *ShowDialog* method of the open file dialog object. For example: ```OpenFileDialog1.ShowDialog()```
Create a new text file	Use the *FileOpen* function. For example: ```FileOpen(1, SaveFileDialog1.FileName, _\n OpenMode.Output)```
Display a Save As dialog box	Add a *SaveFileDialog* control to your form, and then use the *ShowDialog* method of the save file dialog object. For example: ```SaveFileDialog1.ShowDialog()```

To	Do this
Save text to a file	Use the *Print* or *PrintLine* function. For example:

```
PrintLine(1, txtNote.Text)
```

To	Do this
Convert text characters to ASCII codes	Use the *Asc* function. For example:

```
Dim Code As Short
Code = Asc("A")   'Code equals 65
```

Convert ASCII codes to text characters	Use the *Chr* function. For example:

```
Dim Letter As Char
Letter = Chr(65)   'Letter equals "A"
```

Extract characters from the middle of a string	Use the *Substring* method or the *Mid* function. For example:

```
Dim Cols, Middle As String
Cols = "First Second Third"
Middle = Cols.SubString(6, 6)
'Middle = "Second"
```

Encrypt text	Use the *Xor* operator and a user-defined encryption code. For example, this code block uses *Xor* and a user code to encrypt the text in the *txtNote* text box and to save it in the encrypt.txt file as a series of numbers:

```
strCode = InputBox("Enter Encryption Code")
Code = CShort(strCode)
charsInFile = txtNote.Text.Length
FileOpen(1, SaveFileDialog1.FileName, _
  OpenMode.Output)
For i = 0 To charsInFile - 1
    letter = txtNote.Text.Substring(i, 1)
    Print(1, Asc(letter) Xor Code)
Next
FileClose(1)
```

Decrypt text	Request the code the user chose to encrypt the text, and use *Xor* to decrypt the text. For example, this code block uses *Xor* and a user code to reverse the encryption created in the preceding example:

```
strCode = InputBox("Enter Encryption Code")
Code = CShort(strCode)
FileOpen(1, OpenFileDialog1.FileName, _
  OpenMode.Input)
Do Until EOF(1)
    Input(1, Number)
    ch = Chr(Number Xor Code)
    Decrypt = Decrypt & ch
Loop
txtNote.Text = Decrypt
```

12

Text Files and String Processing

Automating Microsoft Office Applications and Managing Processes

In this chapter, you will learn how to:

■ Use the Object Browser to examine objects.

■ Use Microsoft Excel to compute mortgage payments.

■ Manipulate an Excel worksheet from Microsoft Visual Basic .NET.

■ Start and stop Microsoft Windows applications using the *Process* component.

In this chapter, you'll learn how to control Microsoft Office XP applications from Visual Basic .NET. You'll use the Microsoft Visual Studio Object Browser to examine the exposed objects in Windows-based programs, and you'll learn how to incorporate the functionality of Office applications on your system into your Visual Basic programs. In particular, you'll use Microsoft Excel 2002 to create two Automation solutions—you'll build a mortgage payment calculator that uses Excel's *Pmt* function, and you'll open a worksheet object in Excel and perform several worksheet-manipulation commands. Finally you'll learn how to start and stop Windows applications from within a Visual Basic program by using the *Process* component and the *Start* and *CloseMainWindow* methods. You experimented with the *Start* method briefly in Chapter 3 and Chapter 11.

Upgrade Notes: What's New in Visual Basic .NET?

If you're experienced with Visual Basic 6, you'll notice some new features in Visual Basic .NET, including the following:

- In Visual Basic 6, you could use the OLE *Container* control to add application objects to your Visual Basic forms. The OLE *Container* control is no longer included in the Toolbox.

- Visual Basic 6 featured ActiveX controls that were based on Component Object Model (COM) technology. In Visual Basic .NET, controls are no longer designed to COM specifications. However, you can still use COM components and applications in Visual Basic .NET programs by adding a reference to the components on the COM tab of the Add Reference dialog box. When you select a COM component, Visual Studio automatically generates a "wrapper" with the necessary types and classes for you.

- Microsoft Office XP applications and components (which continue to conform to COM specifications) can still be controlled in Visual Basic .NET applications through Automation, a popular method for accessing the objects of another application. However, in Visual Basic .NET, application objects shouldn't be assigned at run time, but rather should be assigned at compile time. (In other words, early binding is preferred to late binding when Automation is used.)

- In Visual Basic 6, programmers often used the *Shell* function to start Windows applications from within a program. In Visual Basic .NET, the task of starting and stopping applications is more easily handled by the *Process* component on the Components tab of the Toolbox.

Programming Application Objects by Using Automation

Automation is a technology based on the COM interoperability standard, an important guideline for designing applications and components that can be used together—even without an understanding of how the underlying components work. The goal of Automation is to use one application's features from within another application. Windows-based applications that fully support Automation make available, or *expose*, their application features as a collection of objects with associated properties and methods. The Windows-based applications that expose their objects are called *object*, or *server*, applications, and the programs that use the objects are called *controlling*, or *client*, applications.

Although Visual Studio .NET controls are no longer designed in accordance with COM specifications, you can still use COM components in Visual Basic .NET programs if you follow a few simple guidelines.

Currently, the following Microsoft applications can be used as either object or controlling applications:

- Microsoft Visual Studio .NET, Microsoft Visual Basic 6
- Microsoft Word 2002, Microsoft Word 2000, Microsoft Word 97
- Microsoft Excel 2002, Microsoft Excel 2000, Microsoft Excel 97, Microsoft Excel 95, Microsoft Excel 5.0
- Microsoft PowerPoint 2002, Microsoft PowerPoint 2000, Microsoft PowerPoint 97
- Microsoft Project 2000, Microsoft Project 97, Microsoft Project 95
- Microsoft Outlook 2002, Microsoft Outlook 2000, Microsoft Outlook 97/98

> ▶ **Tip**   Microsoft is currently licensing the Visual Basic for Applications programming language, so you'll find non-Microsoft applications for Windows that support Automation and Visual Basic programming techniques. Future versions of Microsoft Office will also support Automation.

Using Automation in Visual Basic

In Visual Basic .NET, you can create both object and controlling applications that support Automation. Creating an application that supports Automation is beyond the scope of this chapter. However, creating controlling applications that use the features of Automation is a straightforward process in all editions of Visual Basic and will be discussed in this chapter.

> ▶ **Note**   The applications in Microsoft Office XP (Excel 2002, Word 2002, Access 2002, PowerPoint 2002, and Outlook 2002) are all capable of exposing their functionality through Automation. Because the features and objects each of these applications provides are unique, you'll need to review the product documentation or online Help for each program before you move beyond the examples I show you here. If you have Microsoft Office installed on your system now, you can use the Visual Basic Object Browser to explore the available objects, properties, and methods.

In the next few sections, you'll learn how to write Visual Basic programs that work with Excel 2002. As you work through the exercises, note that the objects, properties, and methods exposed by an application typically correspond to the menu commands and dialog box options provided by the application. You can use these basic skills to automate the objects in Word, Outlook, PowerPoint, and the other applications and components that support COM standards.

The Visual Studio Object Browser

The Visual Studio Object Browser is a viewing utility that has the following two uses:

- It can display the objects, properties, and methods used by the program you're working on in the Visual Studio development environment.
- It can display the objects, properties, and methods available to you from applications that support Automation installed on your system.

In the following exercise, you'll use the Object Browser to view the Automation objects that Excel 2002 exposes.

Use the Object Browser to view Excel objects

1   Start Visual Studio, and create a new Visual Basic Windows Application project named **My Excel Automation** in the c:\vbnet03sbs\chap13 folder.

A new project appears in the development environment.

2   On the Project menu, click the Add Reference command.

The Add Reference dialog box appears, as shown here:

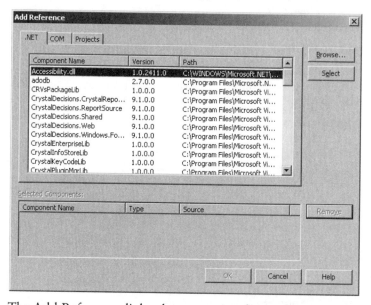

The Add Reference dialog box contains three tabs representing the available objects on your system: .NET, COM, and Projects. The .NET tab contains objects that conform to the .NET specifications, including Crystal Reports components, objects exposed by the Visual Studio .NET development environment, and various system objects.

The COM tab contains Component Object Model applications and components, including Microsoft Office application objects. The Projects tab contains objects exposed by your own Visual Basic projects that you can incorporate. Adding references to your project won't make your compiled program any bigger. However, the more references you have, the longer it will take Visual Basic to load and compile the program. Therefore, Visual Basic adds references to Automation object libraries only if you ask it to.

3 Click the COM tab in the Add Reference dialog box.

A list box displays the COM components recorded in your computer's system registry. This list will vary from computer to computer.

4 Scroll down the alphabetical list, and click the reference entitled Microsoft Excel 10.0 Object Library.

The list is usually quite long, and you'll need to scroll considerably to get through it—especially when you encounter the catalog of Microsoft object libraries.

▶ **Note** The illustrations show the Excel 10.0 Object Library included in Excel 2002 (in other words, Office XP). If you don't have a version of Excel, use the Object Browser to examine other application objects on your system.

5 After you click the Microsoft Excel 10.0 Object Library, click the Select button.

Your screen should look like this:

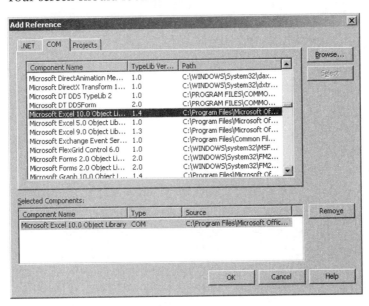

6   Click OK to close the dialog box and add the reference to your project.

You might see the following dialog box at this point:

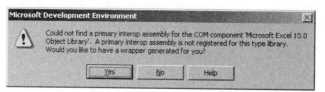

Because COM components are no longer native to the Visual Studio development environment, Visual Studio requires either that a *primary interoperability assembly* reference be included with the project or that a local "wrapper" containing the same class declarations be generated within the project by Visual Studio. Most COM applications and components will require a wrapper for any new library references you make.

7   If you see the primary interoperability assembly dialog box, click Yes to allow Visual Studio to create the needed class wrapper automatically for you.

The types associated with the wrapper are added to the project in Solution Explorer. Now you're ready to use the Object Browser.

8   On the View menu, click the Object Browser command. (The keyboard shortcut to display the Object Browser is F2.)

The Object Browser appears, as shown here:

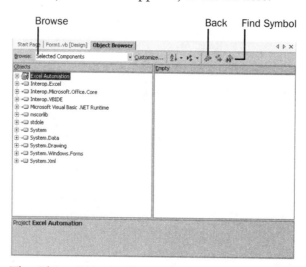

The Object Browser lists references and components in a tree hierarchy; the object hierarchy is shown in the left pane of the Object

Browser, and individual members are shown in the right pane. At the bottom of the Object Browser is a pane that contains syntax information, when available, for the selected object.

The Object Browser also offers a few useful tools for locating the information you want to find. The Browse drop-down list box lets you display the individual object libraries and components in your project. There's also a Find Symbol button that you can use to search for individual objects, properties, methods, and events in the occasionally vast object library listings. A Back button allows you to review earlier object listings.

9   Click the plus sign (+) next to the Interop.Excel object library, and then click the plus sign next to Excel.

A list of the Automation objects exposed by Excel fills the Objects pane.

10   If necessary, scroll down the list in the Objects pane, and then click the Application object.

A list of the methods, properties, and events associated with the *Application* object appears in the Members pane. These are some of the properties, methods, and events Excel provides for manipulating information in worksheets.

11   Scroll down in the Members pane, and click the Quit method.

Your screen will look like this:

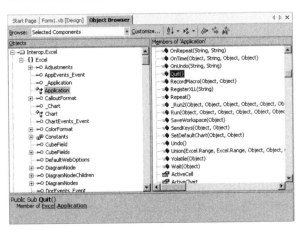

The syntax for the *Quit* method appears at the bottom of the Object Browser. This method closes the Excel application when you're done using it. It's a standard feature of most Office Automation sessions. The method syntax shows you the basic arguments for the method (none in this case) and the parent objects for the method (*Excel.Application*).

12 Continue to examine the Excel object library and the other object libraries associated with your Visual Basic application, if you like.

13 When you're finished, close the Object Browser.

You've finished exploring objects for the time being. Now it's time to put a few Excel Automation commands to work.

Automating Excel from Visual Basic

To use Excel commands in a Visual Basic program, you need to complete the following programming steps. Because these steps apply to other applications, you can use these guidelines to incorporate into your own programs the functionality of most applications that support Automation.

Step 1   Add references to the necessary object libraries to your project by using the Visual Studio Add Reference command.

Step 2   Write your Visual Basic program. In the event procedure in which you plan to use Automation, use the *Dim* statement to declare the Automation object type. Then use the *CType* and *CreateObject* functions to create an instance of that object, as shown here:

```
Dim xlApp As Excel.Application
xlApp = CType(CreateObject("Excel.Application"), Excel.Application)
```

In Visual Basic 6, you were allowed to create a variable of type *Object* for the application and then assign it a specific application type at run time. This variable assignment technique, called *late binding*, isn't recommended in Visual Basic .NET code. Variables that hold Automation objects should be assigned a type at design time so that they're bound to the data during compilation (so-called *early binding*), as I've demonstrated here. The *CType* function is the mechanism that returns the specific application type to the application variable at compilation.

Step 3   Use the methods and properties of the Automation object in the event procedure, consulting the Object Browser schematics or the application documentation for the proper syntax. The following sample code uses the Excel *WorksheetFunction.Pmt* method:

```
Dim LoanPayment As Single
LoanPayment = xlApp.WorksheetFunction.Pmt _
   (txtInterest.Text / 12, txtMonths.Text, txtPrincipal.Text)
MsgBox("The monthly payment is " & _
   Format(Abs(LoanPayment), "$#.##"), , "Mortgage")
```

Step 4   When you've finished using the application, issue a specific command to quit the application (unless you want to keep it running). For example:

```
xlApp.Quit()
```

This *Quit* command is the same method you just learned about using in the Visual Studio Object Browser.

In the following exercise, you'll create a Visual Basic application that uses the Excel *Pmt* method to compute loan payments for a home mortgage. The arguments for *Pmt* will be drawn from three text box objects on your form. The program will be built entirely in Visual Basic by using the functionality of Excel through Automation.

▶ **Note**   The following steps require that you have Excel 2002 installed on your system. You might be able to adapt this program code if you have an earlier version of Excel, but in my experience this is a non-trivial process. For this reason, I don't recommend Automation for programs that will be widely distributed—especially among users with different versions of Office.

Build a mortgage payment calculator

1   Display the form in the development environment, if it isn't visible.

2   At the top of the form, use the *Label* control to draw a large label object for your program's title.

3   Below the label, use the *TextBox* control to draw three text box objects on the right side of the form.

The text box objects will allow you to enter arguments for the *Pmt* function.

4   Using the *Label* control, draw a label object next to each of the text box objects.

The labels you've created will identify the *Pmt* function arguments to help you type them in the right place.

5   Use the *Button* control to draw a button object at the bottom of the form.

6   Set the following properties for the objects on your form:

Object	Property	Setting
Label1	*Font*	Microsoft Sans Serif, Bold, 11 point
	Text	"Calculate Payments Using Excel"
	TextAlign	MiddleCenter
TextBox1	*Name*	txtInterest
	Text	(empty)
TextBox2	*Name*	txtMonths
	Text	(empty)
TextBox3	*Name*	txtPrincipal
	Text	(empty)
Label2	*Text*	Interest
Label3	*Text*	Months
Label4	*Text*	Principal
Button1	*Name*	btnCalculate
	Text	Calculate
Form1	*Text*	Mortgage

Your form should look like this:

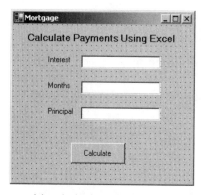

7   Double-click the Calculate button to display the *btnCalculate_Click* event procedure in the Code Editor.

8   Type the following program code to issue Excel commands via Automation and calculate the home mortgage payment:

```
Dim xlApp As Excel.Application
Dim LoanPayment As Single
xlApp = CType(CreateObject("Excel.Application"), Excel.Application)
LoanPayment = xlApp.WorksheetFunction.Pmt _
  (txtInterest.Text / 12, txtMonths.Text, txtPrincipal.Text)
MsgBox("The monthly payment is " & _
  Format(Abs(LoanPayment), "$#.##"), , "Mortgage")
xlApp.Quit()
```

This event procedure declares a variable named *xlApp* of the *Excel.Application* type, which is valid in the project now that you've made a reference to the Microsoft Excel 10.0 object library.

▶ **Note** If you see the type *Excel.Application* with a jagged blue underline in the Code Editor, it's probably because you forgot to add the reference or simply started typing this code without working through the Object Browser exercise. Go back and make the library reference now by using the Add Reference command on the Project menu.

The routine then assigns a type to the *xlApp* variable by using the *CreateObject* and *CType* functions and puts the variable to work by calling the Excel *WorksheetFunction.Pmt* method. The three arguments for the *Pmt* method are drawn from the three text box objects on the form. Because the *Pmt* function returns a negative number for payments, I've used the *Abs* (absolute value) function from the .NET Framework *System.Math* class to display the number as a positive floating-point value. (In Excel, loan payments are typically displayed as negative numbers, or debits, but on a Visual Basic form, payments usually look best as positive values.) Note that if one of the required arguments for the *Pmt* function is missing, the event procedure will produce a runtime error message. (Can you see how this shortcoming might be fixed by using a decision structure or an error handler?)

Finally, the routine displays the mortgage payment by using a message box and closes the Excel application by using the *Quit* method. In this example, the Excel application is never displayed, so the user won't even know it's been loaded.

9 Scroll to the top of the form's code in the Code Editor, and then type the following program statement:

```
Imports System.Math
```

This declaration will incorporate the *System.Math* class library in the project and provide access to the *Abs* function you specified. (After you make this reference, the *Abs* method will no longer have a jagged blue underline, whose presence is a visual clue that an object, a method, or a property is currently undefined.)

You'll run the program now to see how Excel Automation works.

Run the Excel Automation program

1   Click the Start button on the Standard toolbar.

▶ **Note**   The complete Excel Automation program is located in the c:\vbnet03sbs\chap13\excel automation folder.

The mortgage payment calculator appears.

2   Type **0.09** in the Interest text box.

3   Type **360** in the Months text box.

4   Type **150000** in the Principal text box.

Your form should look like this:

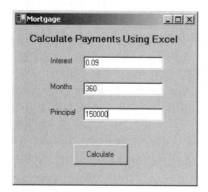

5   Click the Calculate button.

The program uses Excel to calculate the mortgage payment for a $150,000 loan at 9 percent interest over 360 months (30 years). As shown in the following illustration, a message box displays the result of $1206.93. (Remember that if this were a home mortgage payment, this amount would represent principal and interest only—not taxes, insurance, or other items that are typically included!)

6   Click the OK button in the message box, and then make a few more mortgage payment calculations using different values.

7   When you're finished, click the Close button on the form's title bar.

Now let's try an Excel Automation exercise that makes more detailed use of a visible Excel worksheet.

Manipulate Excel worksheets

1   Click the Close Solution command on the File menu, and then create a new Visual Basic Windows Application project named **My Excel Sheet Tasks** in the c:\vbnet03sbs\chap13 folder.

In this exercise, you'll issue Excel Automation commands that insert numbers and labels in worksheet cells, apply character formatting, insert a *Sum* function, and save the worksheet to disk. By using these basic skills, you can generate extensive Excel worksheets from within your Visual Basic applications.

2   On the Project menu, click the Add Reference command.

The Add Reference dialog box appears.

3   Click the COM tab, click the Microsoft Excel 10.0 Object Library in the component list, click the Select button, and click OK. If you see the primary interoperability assembly dialog box, click Yes.

4   Using the *Button* control, add a large button object to the form.

5   Use the Properties window to set the *Text* property of the button object to Create Worksheet, and then set the *Text* property of the form to Excel Worksheet Builder.

These are the only properties you'll set for this demonstration program—most of the work will be accomplished in Microsoft Excel.

6   Double-click the Create Worksheet button to open the *Button1_Click* event procedure in the Code Editor.

7   Type the following program statements:

```
' Declare Excel object variables and create types
Dim xlApp As Excel.Application
Dim xlBook As Excel.Workbook
Dim xlSheet As Excel.Worksheet
xlApp = CType(CreateObject("Excel.Application"), Excel.Application)
xlBook = CType(xlApp.Workbooks.Add, Excel.Workbook)
xlSheet = CType(xlBook.Worksheets(1), Excel.Worksheet)

' Insert data
xlSheet.Cells(1, 2) = 5000
xlSheet.Cells(2, 2) = 75
xlSheet.Cells(3, 1) = "Total"
' Insert a Sum formula in cell B3
xlSheet.Range("B3").Formula = "=Sum(R1C2:R2C2)"
' Format cell B3 with bold
```

```
xlSheet.Range("B3").Font.Bold = True
' Display the sheet
xlSheet.Application.Visible = True
' Save the sheet to c:\vbnet03sbs\chap13 folder
xlSheet.SaveAs("C:\vbnet03sbs\chap13\myexcelsheet.xls")
' Leave Excel running and sheet open
```

The program code for this event procedure is a little longer than the last Excel Automation sample—it could be much longer still if you choose to add numerous values and formatting options to the worksheet. Of particular interest are the first three variable declarations and *CreateObject* statements. Because I'm actually manipulating an Excel worksheet, not just running Excel commands, I need to create three Excel variables and assign them the proper types from the Microsoft Excel 10.0 object library. The first variable declaration references the *Excel.Application* type, the second variable declaration references the *Excel.Workbook* type (which relies on *Excel.Application*), and the third variable declaration references the *Excel.Worksheet* type (which relies on *Excel.Workbook*). Take note of these important variable and type declarations for your future work with Excel.

The remainder of the event procedure loads values into Excel cells. (Note the difference between how numeric and string values are entered.) A formula is then entered in cell B3 that uses a *Sum* function to total cells B1 and B2, and the result is formatted with bold type. At this point, the event procedure displays the active worksheet, and the worksheet is saved to disk in the c:\vbnet03sbs\chap13 folder. (If the file already exists, a dialog box will appear asking whether you want to overwrite the file, which you may do.) At this point, the event procedure ends, and the Excel application remains open and visible, inviting the user to complete additional Excel tasks. (Note that the Visual Basic program, too, continues running.) We could also have closed the program by using the *Quit* method, as we did in the first Excel Automation sample.

8   Click the Save All button on the Standard toolbar to save the project and its reference to disk.

13

Automating Applications

Run the Excel Sheet Tasks program

1   Click the Start button on the Standard toolbar.

▶ **Note**   The complete Excel Sheet Tasks program is located in the c:\vbnet03sbs\chap13\excel sheet tasks folder.

The simple form for your project appears, as shown here:

2   Click the Create Worksheet button.

Visual Basic starts Excel and quickly performs the Automation tasks you requested. After the *Visible* property is set to True, an Excel worksheet appears on your screen, as shown here:

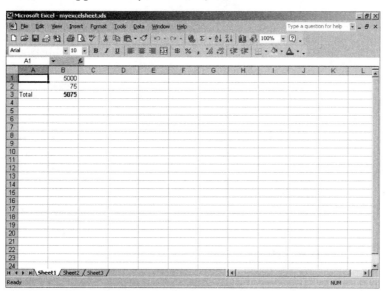

Note the position and content of the cells in columns A and B—the Automation commands have completed their work, and the *Sum* function produced the correct result in cell B3 (5000 + 75 = 5075). The current filename also appears on the Excel title bar (myexcelsheet.xls).

3   Continue to manipulate the Excel worksheet if you like, and then close the application. Note that the program you've written will work whether the Excel application is open or not.

4   Click the Close button on your Visual Basic program to stop it, too.

That's it! You've learned the essential skills to automate the Excel application. The Object Browser will teach you more about the details of the application objects if you choose to explore Automation on your own.

One Step Further: Starting and Stopping Windows Applications by Using the *Process* Component

In Chapter 3 and Chapter 11, you used the *Process.Start* method to start the default Internet browser on your system and view a Web page. The *Process.Start* method can be used to start any Windows application on your system that's registered in the system registry. You don't need to specify a path when you use the *Process.Start* method as long as the application or file extension you specify is recognized by the system, and the *Process.Start* method doesn't rely on Automation to do its work. For example, the following *Process.Start* command starts the Notepad application:

```
System.Diagnostics.Process.Start("notepad.exe")
```

The only problem with the technique I've demonstrated so far is that once the Notepad application is running, there's no easy way to control it—Visual Basic has started the Windows application, but it can't stop it. The solution to this shortcoming is to use one of the Visual Studio features more closely associated with Windows process control. In particular, you can start your applications, or *processes,* by using the *Process* component on the Components tab of the Visual Studio Toolbox. In the following exercise, you'll learn how to use the *Process* component to start and stop a Notepad application from within a Visual Basic program. You can use this basic technique to start and stop any Windows application program.

Control Notepad process execution

1   Click the Close Solution command on the File menu, and then create a new Visual Basic Windows Application project named **My Start App** in the c:\vbnet03sbs\chap13 folder.

2   Display the project's form, and then add two button objects to the form by using the *Button* control.

3 Set the *Text* property for the *Button1* object to "Start Notepad", and set the *Text* property for the *Button2* object to "Stop Notepad". Set the form's *Text* property to "Process Start Examples".

Now you'll add a *Process* component to the project, an invisible component that Visual Basic will use to keep track of the Notepad application while it runs.

4 Click the Components tab in the Visual Studio Toolbox.

The tab looks like this:

 ——— Process component

So far, you've used only the Windows Forms tab of the Toolbox, but the Components tab also is very useful. It contains .NET components that monitor events within the operating system and within the Visual Studio development environment.

5 Double-click the Process component on the Components tab of the Toolbox.

The *Process* component is added to the component tray below the form, just like other non-visible Toolbox controls. This component has no visible user interface; it just represents an application that's launched by your project.

6 Click the *Process1* object, and then use the Properties window to set the object's *Name* property to noteProcess.

7 In the Properties window, click the plus sign (+) next to the StartInfo category to open it, and then set the *FileName* property to notepad.exe.

You'll use the object name *noteProcess* in your program code when you want to start, stop, or monitor the Notepad application. The *FileName* property sets the application name to notepad.exe, which the system registry can find if the Notepad application has been installed correctly. (Change this name if you want to run another application, such as winword.exe or excel.exe.)

Automating Applications   13

▶   **Note**   To pass command-line arguments to the application you're starting, set the *Arguments* property in the StartInfo category.

Your form now looks like this:

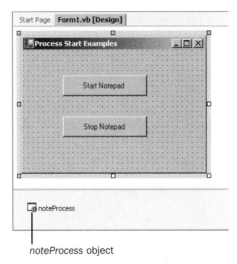

noteProcess object

8   Double-click the Start Notepad button on the form, and then type
the following program statement in the Code Editor:

```
noteProcess.Start()
```

Because you've already specified the application name by using the
Process component, you don't need to specify it again here. The
noteProcess object name carries the required information.

9   Display the form again, and then double-click the Stop Notepad
button.

10   Type the following program statement in the Code Editor:

```
noteProcess.CloseMainWindow()
```

The *CloseMainWindow* method is the equivalent of clicking the
Close button on Notepad's title bar. If the user has an unsaved file in
the application, he or she will be prompted to save the file before the
application closes. (Alternatively, you could close the application
using the *Kill* method, but that technique wouldn't allow the changes
to be saved.)

11   Scroll to the top of the form's program code, and then type the following class references:

```
Imports System.Threading
Imports System.Diagnostics
```

These *System* classes are useful when you manipulate processes in
your program code, although they're not required if you use only the

Start and *CloseMainWindow* methods as I do here. (I'm including them to identify the Framework classes you might want to investigate further down the road.)

12 Click the Save All button on the toolbar, and then run the program.

> ▶ **Note** The complete Start App program is located in the
> c:\vbnet03sbs\chap13\start app folder.

The following form appears:

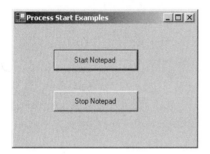

13 Click the Start Notepad button.

Your program starts the Notepad process, and the Notepad application opens in a window, as shown here:

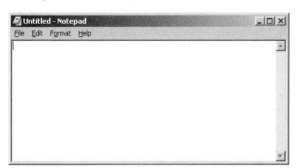

14 Display the form again, and then click the Stop Notepad button.

Visual Basic uses the *CloseMainWindow* method to quit the Notepad application.

Continue to start and stop Notepad as much as you like—your Visual Basic program can now track the application processes you start because it's assigned them to the *noteProcess* object. By using the Visual Basic online Help, you can learn more about processes and the other techniques you can employ to make even greater use of them.

15 When you're finished, click the Close button on the form to close the program.

Lesson 13 Quick Reference

To	Do this
Add a reference in your project to a component or an application that supports Automation	On the Project menu, click the Add Reference command. Click the COM tab, click the object library you want, click the Select button, and then click OK.
View objects that are available for use in your project	On the View menu, click the Object Browser command. Select the objects you want to examine by using the hierarchical tree structure in the Objects pane.

Create an Automation object in a program	Use the *Dim* statement and the *CType* and *CreateObject* functions. For example:
	
	```Dim xlApp As Excel.Application```
	```xlApp = CType(CreateObject _```
	``` ("Excel.Application"), Excel.Application)```

Access application features by using Automation	Create an Automation object, and then reference the methods or properties of the object. For example: ```xlApp.Quit()```

Start and stop applications from within Visual Basic	Add a *Process* component to your form by double-clicking the *Process* item on the Components tab of the Toolbox. Set the *Name* and *Filename* properties for the process object, and then use the following program statements in your program code to start and stop the process, respectively:
	
	```Objectname.Start()```
	```Objectname.CloseMainWindow()```

Chapter

14

Deploying Visual Basic .NET Applications

In this chapter, you will learn how to:

■ Add a deployment project to your solution.

■ Run the Setup Wizard to create a setup program for your application.

■ Customize your setup program by using properties and build settings.

■ Test installing and uninstalling your application.

When your Microsoft Visual Basic .NET application is finished, you might want to distribute it to other computer users in your workgroup, share it with friends on the Internet, or sell it to paying customers. Microsoft Visual Studio .NET helps you distribute your Visual Basic applications by providing several options for *deployment*—that is, installing the application on one or more computer systems. In this chapter, you'll learn how to deploy Visual Basic applications by adding a deployment project to your solution, and you'll run the Setup Wizard to create the installation files that you need. In addition, you'll learn how to customize your installation by using property settings and adjusting the deployment options in your build configuration.

Building a deployment project is a complex process, and you'll find that each edition of Visual Basic .NET offers a slightly different assortment of installation options. For example, Visual Basic .NET Standard doesn't include the Setup Wizard to automate a typical deployment. Visual Studio .NET Professional and advanced editions contain additional installation templates plus the ability to deploy solutions on the Web and create cabinet files. As you work through this chapter, you might see a few settings or options that aren't available in your edition of Visual Basic .NET.

14

Deploying Applications

Upgrade Notes: What's New in Visual Basic .NET?

If you're experienced with Visual Basic 6, you'll notice some new features in Visual Basic .NET, including the following:

- In Visual Basic 6, you deployed applications by using the Package and Deployment Wizard. In Visual Studio .NET, you deploy applications by adding a deployment project to the solution you want to distribute and configuring the deployment project for the type of installation that you want to perform.

- Visual Basic 6 applications typically relied on COM (Component Object Model) components, and over time we've realized that COM components can be problematic to install, register, and uninstall. Visual Studio addresses this problem by installing the .NET Framework class libraries on client computers (if necessary), packing applications in assemblies, and eliminating most COM dynamic-link libraries (DLLs).

- Visual Basic .NET applications can now be installed without interacting with the computer's system registry (the so-called XCOPY installation), but in practice I recommend that you install and uninstall Visual Basic .NET applications by using the Visual Studio deployment tools and the Windows Installer.

Planning a Deployment

In the early days of personal computer programming, creating an application that could be installed successfully on another computer was often as simple as compiling an .exe file for your project and copying it to a floppy disk. As application programs have become more sophisticated, however, the number of files needed for a typical installation has grown from a handful of files to several hundred or more. Although the Microsoft Windows operating system has helped to reduce the overall scope of application development (by providing common application services such as printing, Clipboard functionality, memory management, and user interface support), Windows applications have historically required sophisticated setup programs to copy the correct dynamic-link libraries (DLLs) and support files to the host computer and to register the application appropriately with the operating system.

At one time or another, most computer users have experienced the "dark side" of installing Windows programs—an application is successfully installed but it won't run, or the new program creates a DLL conflict with another program that was running fine until the new one came along. An equally irritating problem is the newly installed program that can't be uninstalled, either because the uninstall program no longer works or because the uninstall process leaves DLLs, registry entries, and other support files scattered throughout the file system. These shortcomings—known as "DLL Hell" by some of the more tortured users and developers—are a major limitation of COM components and traditional setup programs, including (potentially) those created by the Visual Basic 6 programming system.

Visual Studio .NET was designed, in part, to address the installation shortcomings of Visual Basic and Microsoft Visual C++ applications, especially those that rely on COM components. In Visual Studio .NET, it's possible to simplify the installation process because Visual Studio applications rely on .NET Framework class libraries for much of their functionality instead of on COM components and numerous function calls to the Windows API (application programming interface). In addition, Visual Studio applications are compiled as *assemblies*, deployment units consisting of one or more files necessary for the program to run.

Assemblies contain four elements: Microsoft intermediate language (MSIL) code, metadata, a manifest, and supporting files and resources. *MSIL code* is your program code compiled into a language that the common language runtime understands. *Metadata* is information about the types, methods, and other elements defined and referenced in your code. A *manifest* includes name and version information, a list of files in the assembly, security information, and other information about the assembly. The following illustration shows a diagram of a single file assembly we'll look at in this chapter:

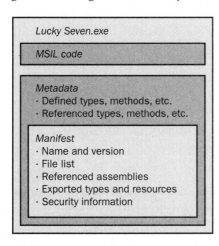

Assemblies are so comprehensive and self-describing that Visual Studio .NET applications don't need to be formally registered with the operating system to run. This means that a Visual Basic .NET application can be installed by simply copying the assembly for an application to a new computer that has the .NET Framework installed—a process called *XCOPY installation*, after the MS-DOS XCOPY command that copies a complete directory (folder) structure from one location to another. In practice, however, it isn't practical to deploy Visual Basic .NET applications by using a simple copy procedure such as XCOPY (via the command prompt) or Windows Explorer. For commercial applications, an installation program with a graphical user interface is usually preferred, and it's often desirable to register the program with the operating system so that it can be uninstalled later by using Add/Remove Programs in Control Panel. The flexibility of installed Visual Basic .NET applications is impressive. For example, Visual Basic .NET versions 2002 and 2003 can be installed side by side on a single computer (each with its own version of the .NET Framework), and each version runs independently without conflict.

To manage the installation process, Visual Studio .NET allows developers to add a *deployment project* to their solutions, which automatically creates a setup program for the application. This deployment project can be customized to allow for different methods of installation, such as CD-ROMs and Web servers. Best of all, you can add a deployment project to your solution at any time during the development process—at the beginning, when you're just defining your solution; at the end, when you're ready to distribute your solution; or in the middle, when you're having difficulty with some code and want to do something else for a few hours.

Different Ways to Deploy an Application

As you think about distributing your solution, consider the different methods that you can use to deploy your application. You can

- Install the application on your own computer and register it in the Windows system registry.
- Create an installation program that allows your application to be installed from a local network or from the Internet.
- Deploy your application using one or more CD-ROMs.
- Deploy your application using cabinet files (.cab), a technique that can be used to download files by using a Web browser.

In Visual Studio, you can quickly create a deployment project by running the Setup Wizard. You can customize the deployment project by setting various properties. If you deploy by using CD-ROMs, your computer will need a writable CD-ROM drive, often called a CD burner, and you'll need to copy the deployment files to the CD-ROMs. The .NET Framework is required on each system that runs Visual Basic .NET applications. The .NET Framework is available as a single redistributable file (Dotnetfx.exe) on the Visual Studio .NET Windows Component Update CD-ROM. In Visual Basic .NET 2003, a compact version of the .NET Framework is available for use with mobile computing devices. The .NET Framework will also be available as a download from the Microsoft Web site. The default Dotnetfx.exe is quite large (more than 20 MB), and when installed, the standard .NET Framework is approximately 30 MB. However, Microsoft has committed to distributing the .NET Framework along with Windows Server 2003 and future operating systems. If the target computer already has the .NET Framework installed, you could just copy the application and any required files to the computer, and the application should run properly. However, to create a complete setup program, the deployment files must include the .NET Framework redistributable.

▶ **Note**   Some of the deployment files that Visual Studio creates are too large to fit on floppy disks. It's possible to partition a large Windows installer file into smaller cabinet files, but some of the supporting files are still too large. If you're interested in deploying to floppy disks, you should create a test deployment project to verify that the deployment files will fit on 1.4 MB floppy disks.

Creating a Deployment Project

Now let's get some practice creating an actual deployment project and setup program for a Visual Basic application you've created in this book. The setup program you create will be designed for deployment on your own system, and you'll have the application and its Readme file install in the c:\program files\microsoft press\lucky seven folder. The setup program will add an application shortcut to the user's Programs list on the Start menu. In addition, the setup program will register the Lucky Seven application in the Windows system registry, and at the end of the chapter, you'll see how Add/Remove Programs in Control Panel can uninstall this application. This deployment can also be copied to a CD-ROM and used for CD installation.

▶ **Important**   The following steps use the Setup Wizard in the Setup and Deployment Projects folder of the New Project dialog box. If your edition of Visual Basic .NET doesn't include the Setup Wizard, you won't be able to perform these steps. You can, however, use the Setup Project template instead to create a deployment project manually. Skip to the section "Create a deployment project by using the Setup Project template" later in this chapter for the important steps you need to follow if you don't have the Setup Wizard.

Create a deployment project by using the Setup Wizard

1   Start Visual Studio, and open the Lucky Seven project in the c:\vbnet03sbs\chap14\lucky seven folder.

The Lucky Seven solution is identical to the Track Wins program you created in Chapter 10. It's a slot machine game that displays a bitmap if the number 7 appears one or more times on the form when you click the Spin button.

2   On the File menu, click New, and then click Project.

Visual Studio opens the New Project dialog box.

Now you'll add a deployment project to the solution that will automatically create a setup program for this application. Although most of the solutions you've created in this book have contained only one project, solutions that include a setup program have a minimum of two projects. (As you'll see, you use Solution Explorer to manage these projects.)

3   Click the Setup and Deployment Projects folder.

This option presents four templates and a wizard that you can use to create the deployment project. The New Project dialog box will look like this:

The four templates are designed to configure many of the settings in the deployment project for you. The Cab Project template configures the deployment project to create one or more cabinet files for the project. (You determine the size of the files.) Choose this option if you want to have users download the solution from the Internet (recommended for older browsers that can't accommodate a full Web setup). The Merge Module Project template is designed to create a general-purpose deployment project that can be used for several different Visual Basic applications. (It creates a .msm file that can be merged into other solutions.) The Setup Project template creates a setup program that uses the Windows Installer for installation. The Web Setup Project creates a setup program that uses the Windows Installer and a Web server for installation over the Internet.

Perhaps the most useful item in the Templates pane of the New Project dialog box is the Setup Wizard, which is a wizard that builds a deployment project based on how you answer several questions about installation media, Web preferences, and so on. You can use the Setup Wizard to create a cabinet project, a merge module project, a Windows Installer project, or a Windows Installer project for the Web.

▶   **Tip**   If you click the More button in the New Project dialog box, you can also specify a separate name and folder for the solution you're creating. This isn't required, but it is a useful way to isolate the deployment files that you're creating.

4   Click the Setup Wizard icon.

5   Type **Lucky** in the Name text box, and specify **c:\vbnet03sbs\chap14** in the Location text box.

6   Click the Add To Solution option button, and then click OK.

The Add To Solution option button is important here—if you don't click it, Visual Studio will close the Lucky Seven solution before it opens the deployment project, and you'll miss the benefits of combining the application with the setup files.

When you click OK, Visual Studio starts the Setup Wizard, which you'll complete in the following exercise.

Run the Setup Wizard

1   Read the first dialog box displayed by the Setup Wizard.

Your screen will look like this:

The purpose of the Setup Wizard is to customize the new deployment project and create an installation program for your solution. The Setup Wizard cannot control every installation feature, but it configures a basic deployment project that can be used in a variety of different contexts.

2   Click Next to display the Choose A Project Type dialog box. Your screen will look like this:

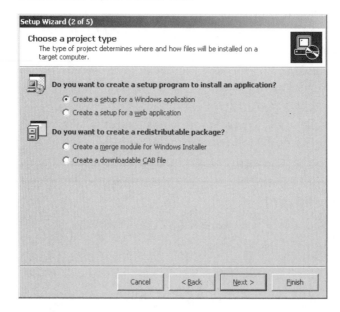

The Choose A Project Type dialog box lets you control how your solution will be distributed. The options map closely to the deployment templates you saw earlier in the New Project dialog box. In this exercise, you'll accept the default deployment type—Create A Setup For A Windows Application.

3 Click Next to display the Choose Project Outputs To Include dialog box.

You use this dialog box to identify the files that you want to include on the systems that will run your application. The Primary Output option is usually mandatory—by selecting it, you include the .exe file for your project or .dll if you're creating a dynamic-link library. The other options allow you to include information that might be useful in internationally deployed applications (Localized Resources) and in programs that might require further debugging (Debug Symbols) or development work (Content Files/Source Files).

4 Click the Primary Output option.

Your screen will look like this:

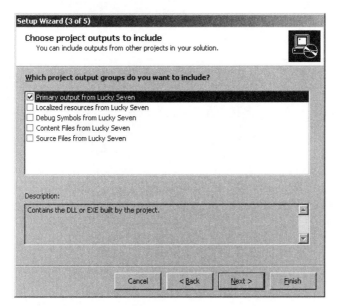

5 Click Next to display the Choose Files To Include dialog box.

In this dialog box, you pick additional files that you want to include with your deployment project, such as a Readme.txt file, troubleshooting tips, marketing information, and so on.

6 Click the Add button to add a Readme.txt file to this solution.

I created a simple Readme.txt file in the c:\vbnet03sbs\chap14 folder with which you can practice.

7   Browse to the c:\vbnet03sbs\chap14 folder, select the Readme.txt file, and then click Open.

Your screen will look like this:

8   Click the Next button to display the Create Project dialog box.

A summary of your deployment selections is listed, as shown here:

If you want to change any selections you've made, click the Back button and make your adjustments, and then click Next until this dialog box is visible again.

9 Click Finish to create the deployment project for the Lucky Seven application.

Visual Studio adds a deployment project named Lucky to the solution, and it appears as another component in Solution Explorer. The File System Editor also appears, as shown here:

File System Editor

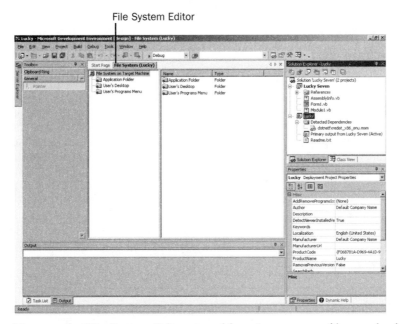

You use the File System Editor to add project output, files, and other items to a deployment project and to determine where they'll be placed on the computer receiving the installation. The File System Editor displays a standard set of folders that correspond to the standard folder structure on the setup computer. You can customize this folder list and add special folders if you want. You can also create application shortcuts by using the File System Editor.

Take a moment to examine the contents of the Lucky deployment project in Solution Explorer. You'll see the .NET Framework dependency in the Detected Dependencies folder, a placeholder for the .exe file (called Primary Output), and the Readme.txt file you included.

14

Deploying Applications

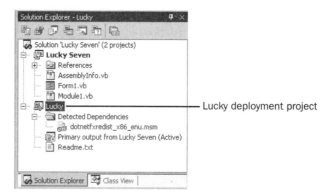

Lucky deployment project

▶   **Tip**   Although the .NET Framework is listed as a dependency, you can't include it within the installation files. If you try to include the .NET Framework by changing the *Exclude* property for the dependency to False, an error will be displayed when you build the solution. Earlier betas of Visual Studio .NET 2002 did allow you to include the .NET Framework. This change was made because including the .NET Framework within the installation files doesn't allow the .NET Framework to be separately updated when fixes and new versions are released. Visual Studio .NET 2003 doesn't allow you to include the .NET Framework component in your application installation, either—your user must install the .NET Framework first, before he or she installs an application built by Visual Basic .NET.

10   Skip to the "Customizing Your Deployment Options" section later in this chapter.

The following section describes how to create the Lucky deployment project without using the Setup Wizard. If you've already created the deployment project, you can skip to the "Customizing Your Deployment Options" section to learn how to customize your deployment project.

Create a deployment project by using the Setup Project template

1   Start Visual Studio, and open the Lucky Seven project in the c:\vbnet03sbs\chap14\lucky seven folder.

2   On the File menu, click New, and then click Project.

Visual Studio opens the New Project dialog box.

Now you'll add a deployment project to the solution that will automatically create a setup program for this application.

3 Click the Setup and Deployment Projects folder.

This option presents the Setup Project template, which can be used to create a Windows Installer setup program. The New Project dialog box will look like this:

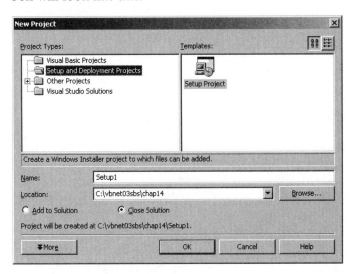

4 Click the Setup Project icon.

5 Type **Lucky** in the Name text box, and specify **c:\vbnet03sbs\chap14** in the Location text box.

6 Click the Add To Solution option button, and then click OK to create the deployment project for the Lucky Seven application.

Visual Studio adds a deployment project named Lucky to the solution, and it appears as another component in Solution Explorer. The File System Editor also appears, letting you add project output, files, and other items to a deployment project and determine where they'll be placed on the computer receiving the installation.

Now you'll need to add the Lucky Seven.exe file (called Primary Output) to the Lucky deployment project.

7 Make sure the Lucky deployment project is selected in Solution Explorer.

8 On the Project menu, click Add, and then click Project Output.

The Add Project Output Group dialog box appears, as shown here:

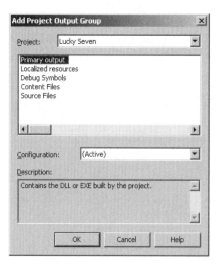

You use this dialog box to identify the files that you want to include on the systems that will run your application. The Primary Output option is usually mandatory—by selecting it you include the .exe file for your project or .dll if you're creating a dynamic-link library.

9   Click the Primary Output item, and then click OK.

A Primary Output component is added to the Lucky project in Solution Explorer. In addition, the .NET Framework dependency is added to the Detected Dependencies folder in Solution Explorer.

10   With the Lucky project still selected in Solution Explorer, click the Project menu, click Add, and then click File to display the Add Files dialog box.

In this dialog box, you pick additional files that you want to include with your deployment project, such as a Readme.txt file, troubleshooting tips, marketing information, and so on.

I created a simple Readme.txt file in the c:\vbnet03sbs\chap14 folder with which you can practice.

11   Browse to the c:\vbnet03sbs\chap14 folder, select the Readme.txt file, and then click Open.

The Readme.txt file is added to the Lucky project in Solution Explorer. Solution Explorer, along with the open File System Editor, is shown here:

File System Editor

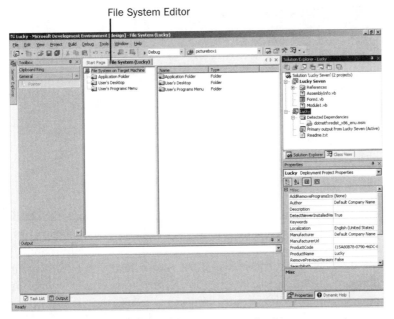

You'll now learn how to customize your deployment project.

Customizing Your Deployment Options

Your deployment project is basically ready to go now—the next time that you build your solution, the necessary setup program will be generated in the c:\vbnet03sbs\chap14\lucky folder and stored in an .msi (Windows Installer) file, which you can use to deploy your application. However, there are still a few customization options that you might want to set to fine-tune your program deployment. In this section, I'll discuss how you use the Configuration Manager to modify your build settings, how to create a shortcut to your application, and how you can change useful property settings, such as the company name and version information your setup program displays.

Configure build settings

1   Click the Configuration Manager command on the Build menu.

   You'll see this dialog box:

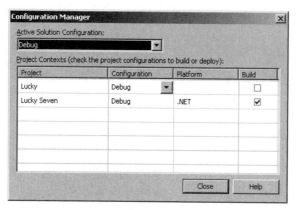

The Configuration Manager dialog box shows the current build mode for the projects in your solution. The Lucky Seven project and the Lucky deployment project are probably set to debug build, meaning that the compiler will generate files containing additional information for debugging and testing. When you're preparing your final projects for distribution, it's important to use the Configuration Manager dialog box to set all projects for release build.

2   Click the Active Solution Configuration drop-down list box, and then select Release.

3   Click the Configuration option for the Lucky project, and then click Release.

4   Click the Configuration option for the Lucky Seven project, and then click Release.

The Configuration Manager now shows that both projects are set for release builds. If you need to switch back to a debug build later, you should be able to just select Debug in the Active Solution Configuration drop-down list box.

5   Add check marks to the Build check boxes for both the Lucky project and the Lucky Seven project.

> ▶ **Tip**   If you remove the check mark from the Build check box in Configuration Manager, Visual Studio won't compile that project when either the Build Solution command on the Build menu or the Start command on the Debug menu is selected. Although you won't want to remove the check mark for your final builds, removing it can be useful while you work on a solution because building the deployment project can be time consuming, and the check mark isn't necessary if you're just working on the application project.

6   Click the Close button.

Next you'll use the File System Editor to create a shortcut to the Lucky Seven application so that users can easily start it.

Create an application shortcut

1   Select the Application Folder in the left pane of the File System Editor.

> ▶ **Tip**   If the File System Editor isn't visible, you can open it by first selecting the Lucky deployment project in Solution Explorer. Next click the View menu, click Editor, and then click File System.

2   In the right pane, right click Primary Output From Lucky Seven, and then select Create Shortcut To Primary Output From Lucky Seven.

   A shortcut icon appears with its name selected so that it can be renamed.

3   Rename the shortcut **Lucky Seven,** and then press Enter.

4   Drag the Lucky Seven shortcut into the User's Programs Menu folder in the left pane.

   The contents of the User's Programs Menu folder will look like this:

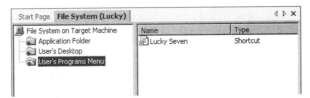

   When this application is installed, a shortcut will be added to the user's Programs menu, which can be accessed from the Start button on the Windows taskbar.

Now you'll set the company name and version information for your setup program.

Set company name and version information

1   Select the Lucky deployment project in Solution Explorer.

2   Open the Properties window, and enlarge it so that it's big enough to show several of the deployment project properties and settings.

   The Lucky deployment project properties fill the Properties window because Lucky is the project that's currently selected in Solution Explorer. The properties aren't related to visible objects in the project but rather are optional settings related to how the application is installed on a new computer. The *Author* and *Manufacturer* properties are usually set to the name of the company producing the software, and this value is also used to construct the default path for your program on disk. (For an example of this pattern, see the c:\program files folder.) Once the application is installed, the *Author* property is also displayed in the Contact field of the Support Info dialog box, which you can access for individual applications through Add/Remove Programs in Control Panel.

The *Title* property contains the name of the setup program, and the *Version* property allows you to specify version information for your setup program. A few properties, such as *Product Code* and *Package Code*, contain unique alphanumeric codes generated by Visual Studio that you can use to identify individual releases of your setup program. (Note that these property settings apply to the setup program and not the Lucky Seven application.)

3 Change the *Author* and *Manufacturer* properties to **Microsoft Press** by using the Properties window.

4 Change the *Version* property to **1.5.0** by using the Properties window.

When you change the *Version* property and press Enter, Visual Studio displays a dialog box asking whether you want to generate new ProductCode and PackageCode numbers.

5 Click Yes to create new code numbers.

6 Spend a few moments examining the remaining property settings, and then return the Properties window to its normal size.

Now you'll open the Property Pages dialog box to see where the media-related property settings are located.

Set deployment property pages

1 Select the Lucky deployment project in Solution Explorer.

2 Click the Properties command on the Project menu.

The Property Pages dialog box opens for the Lucky deployment project, as shown here:

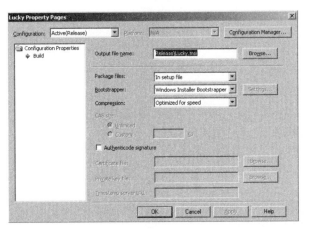

This dialog box gives you an opportunity to rethink a few of the decisions you made in the Setup Wizard (if you used the Setup Wizard) and to customize a few additional settings that weren't available in the wizard. I'll walk you through several of the settings in this dialog box now.

The Output File Name setting controls the name of the file your installation files are packaged into. This is usually one large file with an extension of .msi (Windows Installer) and a few supporting files, such as Setup.ini and Setup.exe. These supporting files are added based on additional deployment project options that will be discussed. The users installing your program can launch the .msi file directly or through a Setup.exe program. When they do so, the installation process copies the .exe application file and any associated files to the default folder for the application.

3 Click the Package Files drop-down list box.

This list box contains three options: As Loose Uncompressed Files, In Setup File, and In Cabinet File(s). In Setup File is currently selected because that's the option you selected when you ran the Setup Wizard earlier; this option creates one large .msi file in the specified folder. The As Loose Uncompressed Files option will create uncompressed files in the same folder as the .msi file. The In Cabinet File(s) option creates one or more .cab files to hold the application and places them in the same folder as the .msi file.

4 Select the In Cabinet File(s) option.

When you select this option, the CAB Size options become available. If you click the Custom option button, you can specify the maximum size of each cabinet file in the Custom text box.

14

Deploying Applications

5 Click the Package Files drop-down list box again, and then select In Setup File.

In this exercise, you'll create a single installation file that contains all the support files you need.

6 Click the Bootstrapper drop-down list box.

The Bootstrapper list box determines whether a bootstrapping program will be included in the setup program you're creating. A bootstrapping program includes the files needed to install Microsoft Windows Installer 2.0 on the target computer if it isn't already installed. This version of the installer is the default version included with Visual Studio .NET, Microsoft Windows XP, and Microsoft Windows Server 2003, but in case your users don't have one of these products, it's a good idea to include the bootstrapping programs along with your application. In the list box, you can choose a Windows-based or Web-based bootstrapping program. If you select Web Bootstrapper, the Web Bootstrapper Settings dialog box appears, in which you can specify the Web location for the bootstrapping files.

7 Click the Windows Installer Bootstrapper option.

8 Click the Compression drop-down list box.

The options in this list describe how your files will be packaged in the setup program. Optimized For Size is the most common option for developers who are trying to squeeze their installations into cabinet files. Optimized For Speed is the best choice if you have plenty of media space (in other words, a CD-ROM) but you want things to move along as quickly as possible.

9 Click the Optimized For Size option.

You'll try to minimize the size of your single installation file because the file will remain on your own system during the installation tests.

The final option in the Property Pages dialog box relates to the inclusion of an *Authenticode Signature* in your project. An Authenticode Signature is a digital document (an .spc file) that identifies you as the manufacturer of this software product. Such a file verifies that you're a "reputable" software vendor and are trustworthy to the extent that you can be located down the road if problems occur with your application. Although the creation and use of Authenticode Signatures are beyond the scope of this book—I won't enable it—this is an option you should investigate if you're planning a commercial release of your Visual Basic application. An Authenticode Signature allows your program to register as a "trusted source" in the end user's operating system.

10 Click OK to save your changes in the Property Pages dialog box. Visual Studio records your selections and is ready to compile the projects.

Building a Deployment Project and Testing Setup

When you're finished adding and customizing your deployment project, you're ready to build the solution and test the setup program. Here are the steps you should follow:

1 **Build the solution by using the Build Solution command on the Build menu.** This command will compile the entire solution, including the final version of the application and the deployment project you've included in the solution.

2 **Run the setup program to install the application.** Test the setup program and the installation process. In this exercise, you'll launch the setup program by double-clicking the Setup.exe file you build.

3 **Test the installation and examine the installed files.** Verify that the installed application works and that the expected files (such as Readme.txt) were installed in the proper folder.

The following exercises demonstrate this process for the Lucky Seven application and the Lucky deployment project.

Build the project

1 Click Build Solution on the Build menu.

Visual Studio compiles both the Lucky Seven and the Lucky projects and creates an .msi file in the c:\vbnet03sbs\chap14\lucky\release folder. The build process takes longer than normal because Visual Studio must package files required to deploy your application.

During longer compilations, a progress bar and a repeating compilation pattern are displayed on the Visual Studio status bar, indicating that the build process is under way. Staring at this box can be soothing.

If the compilation finishes with no errors, the words "Build Succeeded" appear on the left side of the status bar.

2   Click the Start button on the taskbar, click Programs, click Accessories, and then click Windows Explorer.

You'll use Windows Explorer to locate and identify the files that were created during the build process.

3   Browse to the c:\vbnet03sbs\chap14\lucky\release folder, and then click the Lucky.msi file once to select it.

You'll see the following list of files:

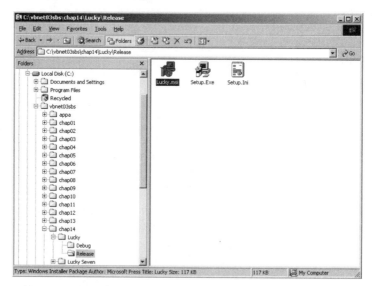

When you specify a release build in the Configuration Manager, Visual Studio places the compiled files in a Release folder. You specified this particular location and name for the files in the Lucky Property Pages dialog box. In this case, Visual Studio created a setup file (Setup.exe), an installation package for the Windows Installer (Lucky.msi), and a configuration settings file (Setup.ini).

Because you selected the Lucky.msi file, Windows Explorer displays the file type, author, and file size information for the file in the status bar. The Microsoft Press author name reflects a setting you made by using the Properties window earlier in this chapter. Lucky.msi contains the LuckySeven.exe file, the Readme.txt file, and setup program information.

▶ **Tip**   To create an actual installation CD-ROM for your application, you would copy the entire contents of the Release folder to a writable CD-ROM at this point. If the target computers don't include the .NET Framework, you should also copy the .NET Framework redistributable file (Dotnetfx.exe), which the user will have to install separately. You need a CD-RW drive to do this; check your computer documentation to see whether you have this capability, which is called "burning a CD" in industry slang.

Run the Setup program

1   Double-click the Setup.exe file in the c:\vbnet03sbs\chap14\lucky\ release folder to run the setup program for your application.

The Setup.exe program starts the Windows Installer program and gives users who don't have a copy of Windows Installer on their system a chance to install it, which might require a reboot. After a moment, a dialog box entitled Welcome To The Lucky Setup Wizard appears, as shown here:

2   Click the Next button to continue the installation.

You'll see the following Select Installation Folder dialog box, which prompts you for a folder location and allows you to set additional installation options:

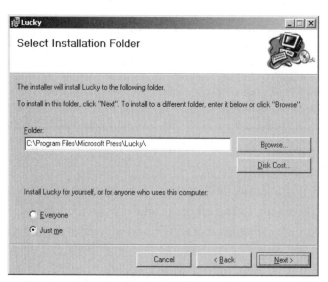

Notice that the default installation folder is c:\program files\microsoft press\lucky. The "Microsoft Press" label matches the *Author* and *Manufacturer* property settings you made earlier in this chapter by using the Properties window. The Everyone and Just Me option buttons have to do with underlying security settings in the Windows operating system.

3   Click the Everyone option button, and then click Next.

The setup program asks you to confirm your installation settings by clicking the Next button. If you're not sure, click Back to return to one or more dialog boxes to verify your selections, and then click Next until this dialog box is visible again.

4   Click Next to start the installation.

The setup program begins copying the necessary files to the folder location you specified. The program also registers the Lucky Seven application by using the system registry so that you can uninstall it later if you want to.

5   Click Close when the installation is complete.

You did it! You created a working setup program that installs your application in a professional manner.

> ▶ **Tip** If you attempt to install this application on another computer, you must make sure that the target computer meets the minimum system requirements. Applications created with Visual Studio .NET require Windows 98 or later with Internet Explorer 5.01 or later, Microsoft Windows NT 4.0 Service Pack 6a or later with Internet Explorer 5.01 or later. Windows 95 isn't supported. The target computer also requires the .NET Framework.

Run the Lucky Seven application

1 Click the Start button on the Windows taskbar, click Programs, and then click Lucky Seven.

Recall that this is the shortcut that you created by using the File System Editor.

Windows starts the program. The installation works!

> ▶ **Tip** You can also start the Lucky Seven program by browsing to the c:\program files\microsoft press\lucky folder by using Windows Explorer and then double-clicking the Lucky Seven.exe program.

2 Click the Spin button several times to play the game and verify that everything is running properly.

After 25 spins, your screen will look like this:

3 When you're finished, click the End button.

You've tested both the setup process and the final application—everything seems to be working fine!

One Step Further: Examining Setup Files and Uninstalling

As one final experiment with your installation, use Windows Explorer to examine the content of the c:\program files\microsoft press\lucky folder, and then uninstall the Lucky Seven test application. It's always a good idea to see exactly what your deployment project installed and how Add/Remove Programs in Control Panel can be used to uninstall the program files. Complete the following exercises.

Check final installation files

1 Open Windows Explorer, and browse to the c:\program files\microsoft press\lucky folder.

   This folder contains the Lucky Seven.exe program file and the Readme.txt file you included when you configured deployment project properties.

2 Click the View menu in Windows Explorer, and then click Details.

   Windows Explorer displays a more detailed file listing, which allows you to see the file sizes and attributes associated with each file. Windows Explorer will look like this:

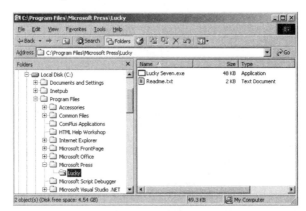

   From the detailed file listing, you can see that the Lucky Seven.exe application file itself takes up only about 48 KB of disk space. However, a significant amount of disk space will be required for the .NET Framework. The .NET Framework files will take up 30

MB of disk space or more and are primarily installed in the Windows\Microsoft.NET folder. Notice that these file sizes can vary from system to system and among different builds of the Visual Studio development suite and the .NET Framework libraries, so your exact file sizes might be different.

3   Double-click the Readme.txt file.

The simple Readme.txt file I created for the Lucky Seven program appears in the Notepad application, as shown here:

Recall that you incorporated the Readme.txt file in your deployment project earlier in this chapter. When you create your own applications, be sure to create a simple Readme.txt file that contains basic usage information, instructions for uninstalling the program, and instructions on how to contact the company for help or more information.

4   Review the file, and then close the Notepad application.

Now you'll practice uninstalling the Lucky Seven program and its support files.

Uninstall the test application

1 Click the Start button on the Windows taskbar, click Settings, and then click Control Panel.

Windows displays the Control Panel folder, containing tools for defining basic system settings and preferences.

2 Double-click Add/Remove Programs.

Add/Remove Programs allows you to install new applications or uninstall unwanted applications by using the application settings in the system registry. Because you installed the Lucky Seven application by using a setup program and the Windows Installer, Lucky is now included in the list of installed programs.

3 Locate the Lucky application in the list of installed programs.

Your screen will look like this:

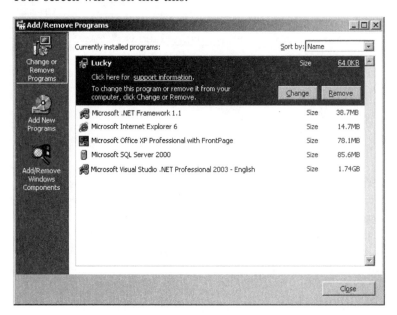

4   Click the Support Information link in the Lucky application listing.

The following dialog box appears, which contains publisher, version, and contact information. You added this information by setting properties for the deployment project earlier in the chapter.

5   Click Close to close the Support Info dialog box.

6   Click the Remove button in the Lucky application listing to uninstall the program.

7   Click Yes when you're asked to verify your decision to uninstall.

Add/Remove Programs starts the Windows Installer, which manages the uninstall process. After a few moments, the registry entries, .exe file, Readme file, shortcut, and supporting files for the Lucky Seven application are removed from the system. The Lucky listing is also removed from the list of installed programs.

8   Click Close to close Add/Remove Programs, and then close the Control Panel folder.

You're done working with deployment projects in this chapter. You now have the skills to install and uninstall Visual Basic .NET projects safely. In future chapters, you'll learn more about creating applications that are powerful, interesting, and worth deploying to friends and coworkers.

14

Deploying Applications

Lesson 14 Quick Reference

To	Do this
Create a setup program for your Visual Basic application	Open the Visual Basic solution that you want to create a setup program for, and then add a deployment project to it by clicking New Project on the File menu. Click the Setup and Deployment Projects folder, and then click a setup template or the Setup Wizard. Specify the deployment project name and location, select the Add To Solution option, and then click OK.
Automatically create an installation program for your project	Select the Setup Wizard in the Setup and Deployment Projects folder, and then specify settings in the wizard.
Adjust how the compiler will build your application	Click the Configuration Manager command on the Build menu. Specify a release build if you're preparing final installation files.
Customize deployment options	Select the deployment project in Solution Explorer, and then set its properties by using the Properties window and the Properties command on the Project menu.
Create an application shortcut	In the File System Editor, right click the Primary Output icon, and select the Shortcut To Primary Output option. Give the shortcut a name, and drag the shortcut into the User's Programs Menu folder.
Compile an application and its setup files	Click the Build Solution command on the Build menu.
Run a setup program	The mechanism for launching a setup program depends on the type of setup files you create. To run a Windows application setup that uses the Windows Installer, double-click the Setup.exe file or the .msi (Windows Installer) file.
Uninstall a Visual Basic application	Visual Basic applications installed using the Windows Installer should be uninstalled by using Add/Remove Programs in Control Panel.

Advanced User Interface Design

Chapter

15

Managing Windows Forms

In this chapter, you will learn how to:

- Add new forms to a program.
- Change the position of a form on the Microsoft Windows desktop.
- Add controls to a form at runtime.
- Change the alignment of objects within a form.
- Specify the startup object.

In Part 3, you learned how to construct sophisticated Microsoft Visual Basic .NET programs that used modules, arrays, collections, text files, and Microsoft Office applications to manage data and perform useful work. In Part 4, you'll focus again on the user interface, and you'll learn how to add multiform projects, animation effects, visual inheritance, and printing support to your Visual Basic applications.

In this chapter, you'll learn how to add additional forms to an application to handle input, output, or special messages. You'll also learn how to use the *DesktopBounds* property to size and position a form, how to add Toolbox controls to a form at runtime, how to change the alignment of objects within a form, and how to specify the form or procedure that runs when a program is started.

Upgrade Notes: What's New in Visual Basic .NET?

If you're experienced with Visual Basic 6, you'll notice some new features in Visual Basic .NET, including the following:

■ In Visual Basic .NET, you cannot set the properties of a second form in the project without having an instance variable of the form that you want to manipulate.

■ In Visual Basic 6, you could set a form's runtime position on the Windows desktop by using the graphical Form Layout window. There's no Form Layout window in Visual Basic .NET, but you can use a new form property named *DesktopBounds* to set the size and location of a form at runtime.

■ In Visual Basic 6, you could add new controls to a form at runtime by using program code, and in Visual Basic .NET you have a similar capability. The syntax changes for adding controls at runtime will be discussed in this chapter.

■ The new *Anchor* property for objects on a form specifies which sides should remain at a constant from the edges of the form when the form is resized. The new *Dock* property forces an object to remain attached to one edge of the form when the form is resized. The *Anchor* and *Dock* properties allow you to create forms in which the objects are sized accordingly as the form is resized.

■ In Visual Basic 6, you could create MDI (multiple document interface) projects by creating an MDI parent form by using the Add MDI Form command on the Project menu. In Visual Basic .NET, MDI parent forms are just regular forms that have their *IsMdiContainer* properties set to True. MDI child forms are regular forms that have their *MdiParent* properties set to the name of a parent form.

Adding New Forms to a Program

Each program you've written so far has used only one form for input and output. In many cases, one form will be sufficient for communicating with the user. But if you need to exchange more information with the user, Visual Basic lets you add additional forms to your program. Each new form is considered an object that inherits its capabilities from the *System.Windows.Forms.Form* class. The first form in a program is named Form1.vb. Subsequent forms are named Form2.vb, Form3.vb, and so on. (You can change the default name for forms in

the Add New Item dialog box, or by using Solution Explorer.) The following
table lists several practical uses for additional forms in your programs.

Each new form has a unique name and its own set of objects, properties, methods, and event procedures.

Form or forms	Description
Introductory form	A form that displays a welcome message, artwork, or copyright information when the program starts
Program instructions	A form that displays information and tips about how the program works
Dialog boxes	Custom dialog boxes that accept input and display output in the program
Document contents	A form that displays the contents of one or more files and artwork used in the program

How Forms Are Used

Visual Basic gives you significant flexibility when using forms. You can make all
the forms in a program visible at the same time, or you can load and unload
forms as the program needs them. If you display more than one form at once,
you can allow the user to switch between the forms, or you can control the
order in which the forms are used. A form that must be addressed when it's displayed on the screen is called a *dialog box*. Dialog boxes (called *modal* forms in
Visual Basic 6) retain the focus until the user clicks OK, clicks Cancel, or otherwise dispatches them. To display an existing form as a dialog box in Visual
Basic .NET, you open it by using the *ShowDialog* method.

If you want to display a form that the user can switch away from, use the *Show*
method instead of the *ShowDialog* method. In Visual Basic 6, forms that could
lose the application focus were called *non-modal*, or *modeless*, forms, and you
might still hear these terms being used. Most applications for Microsoft Windows use regular, non-modal forms when displaying information because they
give the user more flexibility, so this style is the default when you create a new
form in Microsoft Visual Studio. Because forms are simply members of the *System.Windows.Forms.Form* class, you can also create and display forms by using
program code.

For information about how the default form is defined in a Visual Basic application, examine the code in the Windows Form Designer generated code section
at the top of each new form—you've learned enough about program code at
this point to understand some of this form code.

Working with Multiple Forms

The following exercises demonstrate how you can use a second form to display Help information for the Lucky Seven program that you worked with in the previous chapter. You'll add a second form by using the Add Windows Form command on the Project menu, and you'll display the form in your program code by using the *ShowDialog* method. The second form will display the Readme.txt file that you used to display usage and Help information in Chapter 14.

Add a second form

1   Start Visual Studio, and then open the Lucky Seven project in the c:\vbnet03sbs\chap15\lucky seven folder.

The Lucky Seven project is the same slot machine game that you worked with in the previous chapter, except that it doesn't include the deployment project you created.

2   Display the primary form (Form1.vb) in the Windows Forms Designer, if it isn't already visible.

3   Click the Add Windows Form command on the Project menu to add a second form to the project.

You'll see this dialog box:

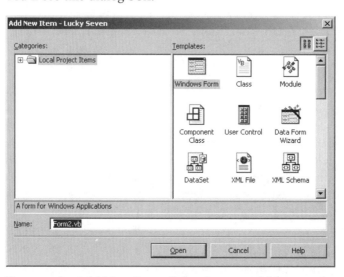

You use the Add New Item dialog box to add forms, classes, modules, and other components to your Visual Basic project. Although you selected the Add Windows Form command, forms aren't the only components listed here. (The Windows Form template is selected by default, however.) The Add New Item dialog box is flexible enough so that you can pick other project components if you change your mind.

4   Type **HelpInfo.vb** in the Name text box, and then click Open.

A second form named HelpInfo.vb is added to the Lucky Seven project, and the form appears in Solution Explorer, as shown here:

> ▶   **Tip**   You can rename or delete form files by using Solution Explorer. To rename a file, right click the file, and then click the Rename command. To remove a file from your project, right click the file, and then click the Exclude From Project command. To remove a file from your project and permanently delete it from your computer, select the file, and then press Delete.

Now you'll add some controls to the HelpInfo.vb form.

5   Use the *Label* control to draw a long label at the top of the HelpInfo.vb form. Make the label the width of the form so that it has room for a long line of text.

6   Use the *TextBox* control to create a text box object.

7   Set the *Multiline* property for the text box object to True so that you can resize the object easily.

8   Resize the text box object so that it covers most of the form.

9   Use the *Button* control to create a button at the bottom of the form.

10   Set the following properties for the objects on the HelpInfo.vb form:

Object	Property	Setting
Label1	*Text*	"Operating Instructions for Lucky Seven Slot Machine"
TextBox1	*Scrollbars*	Vertical
	Text	(empty)
Button1	*Text*	"OK"
HelpInfo.vb	*Text*	"Help"

15

Managing Windows Forms

The HelpInfo.vb form looks like this:

Now you'll enter a line of program code for the HelpInfo.vb form's *Button1_Click* event procedure.

11 Double-click the OK button to display the *Button1_Click* event procedure in the Code Editor.

12 Type the following program statement:

```
Me.DialogResult = DialogResult.OK
```

The HelpInfo.vb form acts as a dialog box in this project because it will be opened in a Form1 event procedure with the *ShowDialog* method. After the user has read the Help information displayed by the dialog box, the OK button closes the form by setting the *DialogResult* property of the current form (*Me*) to DialogResult.OK, a Visual Basic constant that indicates the dialog box has been closed and should return a value of "OK" to the calling procedure. A more sophisticated dialog box might allow for other values to be returned by parallel button event procedures, such as DialogResult.Cancel, DialogResult.No, DialogResult.Yes, and DialogResult.Abort. When the *DialogResult* property is set, however, the form is automatically closed.

13 Scroll to the top of the program code in the Code Editor. Type the following *Imports* statement:

```
Imports System.IO
```

This statement incorporates the class library containing the *StreamReader* class into the project. The *StreamReader* class isn't specifically related to defining or using additional forms—I'm just using it as a quick way to add textual information to the new form I'm using.

14 Display the HelpInfo.vb form again, and then double-click the form background.

The *HelpInfo_Load* event procedure appears in the Code Editor. This is the event procedure that runs when the form is first loaded into memory and displayed on the screen.

15 Type the following program statements:

```
Dim StreamToDisplay As StreamReader
StreamToDisplay = _
  New StreamReader("c:\vbnet03sbs\chap14\readme.txt")
TextBox1.Text = StreamToDisplay.ReadToEnd
StreamToDisplay.Close()
TextBox1.Select(0, 0)
```

Rather than type the contents of the Help file into the *Text* property of the text box object (which would take a long time), I've used the *StreamReader* class to open, read, and display the Readme.txt file from Chapter 14 in the text box object. If you worked through Chapter 14, you'll remember the Readme.txt file as a product support document with usage information about the Lucky Seven program. It contains operating instructions, uninstall information, and general contact information.

The *StreamReader* class was introduced in Chapter 12, but you haven't seen it used in an actual code sample yet. *StreamReader* is a .NET Framework alternative to opening a text file using the Visual Basic *FileOpen* function. To use *StreamReader*, you include the *System.IO* class library at the top of the code for your form. Next, declare a variable (*StreamToDisplay*) of the type *StreamReader* to hold the contents of the text file, and open the text file using a specific path. Finally, you read the contents of the text file into the *StreamToDisplay* variable by using the *ReadToEnd* method, which reads all the text in the file from the current location (the beginning of the text file) to the end of the text file and assigns it to the *Text* property of the text box object. The *StreamReader.Close* statement closes the text file, and the *Select* method removes the selection from the text in the text box object.

You're finished with the HelpInfo.vb form. Now you'll add a button object and some code to the first form.

Display the second form by using an event procedure

1   Click Form1.vb in Solution Explorer, and then click the View Designer button.

The Lucky Seven form appears in the development environment. Now you'll add a Help button to the lower right corner of the form.

2   Use the *Button* control to draw a small button object in the lower right corner of the form.

3   Use the Properties window to set the button object's *Text* property to Help.

Your form should look like this:

4   Double-click the Help button to display the *Button3_Click* event procedure in the Code Editor.

5   Type the following program statements:

```
Dim frmHelpDialog As New HelpInfo()
frmHelpDialog.ShowDialog()
```

These two program statements demonstrate how to declare and display a second form in your program code. Unlike Visual Basic 6, which allowed you to simply reference a second form in code by using its name (a technique called *implicit instantiation*), Visual Basic .NET requires that you specifically declare a variable of the form's type before you use a second form. You created the class named *HelpInfo* when you added the HelpInfo.vb form to your project; now you're using it to declare a variable named *frmHelpDialog* using the *Dim* statement.

The second program statement uses the *frmHelpDialog* variable to open the HelpInfo.vb form as a dialog box using the *ShowDialog* method. Alternatively, you could have used the *Show* method to open the form, but in that case, Visual Basic wouldn't consider HelpInfo.vb to be a dialog box; the form would be a non-modal form that the user could switch away from and return to as needed. In addition, the *DialogResult* property in the HelpInfo.vb form's *Button1_Click* event procedure wouldn't close the HelpInfo.vb form—the program statement

```
Me.Close
```

would be required instead. Keep the differences between modal and non-modal forms in mind as you build your own projects. There are differences between each type of form, and you'll find that each style provides a benefit to the user.

Now you'll run the program to see how a multiple-form application works.

Run the program

1   Click the Start button on the Standard toolbar.

> ▶   **Note**   The completed project is named Multiple Forms and is located in the c:\vbnet03sbs\chap15\multiple forms folder.

The opening Lucky Seven form appears.

2   Click the Spin button seven or eight times to play the game a little. Your screen will look like this:

3   Click the Help button on the first form.

Visual Basic opens the second form in the project, HelpInfo.vb, and displays the Readme.txt file in the text box object. The form looks like this:

4   Use the vertical scroll bar to view the entire Readme file.

5   Click the OK button to close the HelpInfo.vb form.

The form closes, and the first form becomes active again.

6   Click the Spin button a few more times, and then click the Help button again.

The HelpInfo.vb form appears again and is fully functional. Notice that you cannot activate the first form while the second form is active. This is because the second form is a dialog box or modal form, and you must address it before you can continue with the program.

7   Click the OK button, and then click the End button on the first form.

The program stops, and the development environment returns.

Using the *DialogResult* Property in the Calling Form

Although I didn't demonstrate it in the Multiple Forms sample program, you can use the *DialogResult* property that you assigned in the dialog box to great effect in a Visual Basic program. As I mentioned earlier, a more sophisticated dialog box might have offered additional buttons to the user—Cancel, Yes, No, Abort, and so on. Each dialog box button could have been associated with a different type of action in the main program. And in each of the dialog box's button event procedures, you could have assigned the *DialogResult* property for the form that corresponded to the button name, such as the following program statement:

```
Me.DialogResult = DialogResult.Cancel    'user clicked Cancel button
```

In the calling event procedure, in other words, in the *Button3_Click* event procedure of Form1, you can write additional program code to detect which button the user clicks in a dialog box. This information is passed back to the calling procedure through the *DialogResult* property, which is stored in the variable name you used to declare and instantiate the second form. For example, the following code in Form1 could be used to check whether the user clicked OK, Cancel, or another button in the dialog box. (The first two lines aren't new, but they show the variable name you need to use.)

```
Dim frmHelpDialog As New HelpInfo()
frmHelpDialog.ShowDialog()

If frmHelpDialog.DialogResult = DialogResult.OK Then
    MsgBox("The user clicked OK")
ElseIf frmHelpDialog.DialogResult = DialogResult.Cancel Then
    MsgBox("The user clicked Cancel")
Else
    MsgBox("Another button was clicked")
End If
```

By using creative event procedures that declare, open, and process dialog box choices, you can add any number of forms to your programs, and you can create a user interface that looks professional and feels flexible and user friendly.

Positioning Forms on the Windows Desktop

You've learned how to add forms to your Visual Basic project and how to open and close forms by using program code. But which tool or setting determines the placement of forms on the Windows desktop when your program runs? As you might have noticed, the placement of forms on the screen at runtime is different from the placement of forms at design time within the Visual Studio development environment. In this section, you'll learn how to position your forms just where you want them at runtime so that users see just what you want them to see.

In Visual Basic 6, a graphical tool called the Form Layout window controlled the placement of forms at runtime. You dragged a tiny form icon within the

Form Layout window to where you wanted the final form to appear at runtime, and Visual Basic recorded the screen coordinates you specified. In Visual Basic .NET, there's no Form Layout window, but you can still position your forms precisely on the Windows desktop. The tool you use isn't a graphical layout window but a property named *DesktopBounds* that's maintained for each form in your project. *DesktopBounds* can be read or set at runtime only, and it takes the dimensions of a rectangle as an argument—that is, two point pairs that specify the coordinates of the upper left corner of the window and the lower right corner of the window. The coordinate points are expressed in pixels, and the distances to the upper left and lower right corners are measured from the upper left corner of the screen. (You'll learn more about the Visual Basic coordinate system in the next chapter.) Because the *DesktopBounds* property takes a rectangle structure as an argument, it allows you to set both the size and the location of the form on the Windows desktop.

In addition to the *DesktopBounds* property, there's a simpler mechanism for setting the location of a form that you can set at design time, although it has fewer capabilities. This mechanism is the *StartPosition* property, which positions a form on the Windows desktop by using one of the following property settings: Manual, CenterScreen, WindowsDefaultLocation, WindowsDefault-Bounds, or CenterParent. The default setting for the *StartPosition* property is WindowsDefaultLocation. If you accept this setting, Visual Basic will let Windows position the form on the desktop where it chooses—usually the upper left corner of the screen.

If you set *StartPosition* to Manual, you can manually set the location of the form by using the *Location* property, in which the first number (*x*) is the distance from the left edge of the screen and the second number (*y*) is the distance from the top border of the screen. (You'll learn more about the *Location* property in the next chapter.) If you set *StartPosition* to CenterScreen, the form will appear in the middle of the Windows desktop. (This is my preferred *Start-Position* setting.) If you set *StartPosition* to WindowsDefaultBounds, the form will be resized to fit the standard window size for a Windows application, and then the form will be opened in the default location for a new Windows form. If you set *StartPosition* to CenterParent, the form will be centered within the bounds of the parent form. This final setting is especially useful in so-called MDI (multiple document interface) applications in which parent and child windows have a special relationship.

The following exercises demonstrate how you can set the *StartPosition* and *DesktopBounds* properties to position a Visual Basic form. You can use either technique to locate your forms on the Windows desktop at runtime.

Use the *StartPosition* property to position the form

1 Click the Close Solution command on the File menu, and then create a new Visual Basic Windows Application project named **My Desktop Bounds** in the c:\vbnet03sbs\chap15 folder.

2 If the project's form isn't visible, display it now.

3 Click the form to display its properties in the Properties window.

4 Set the *StartPosition* property to CenterScreen.

Changing the *StartPosition* property to CenterScreen directs Visual Basic to display the form in the center of the Windows desktop when you run the program.

5 Click the Start button to run the application.

Visual Basic loads the form and displays it in the middle of the screen, as shown here:

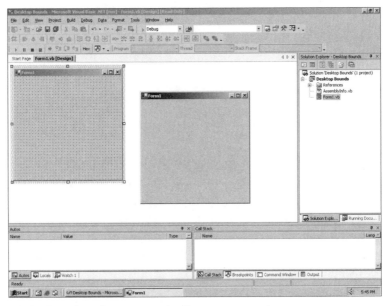

6 Click the Close button on the form to stop the program.

The development environment returns.

7 Set the *StartPosition* property to Manual.

The Manual property setting directs Visual Basic to position the form based on the values in the *Location* property.

8 Set the *Location* property to 100, 50.

The *Location* property specifies the position of the upper left corner of the form.

9 Click the Start button to run the application.

Visual Basic loads the form and then displays it on the Windows desktop 100 pixels from the left and 50 pixels from the top, as shown here:

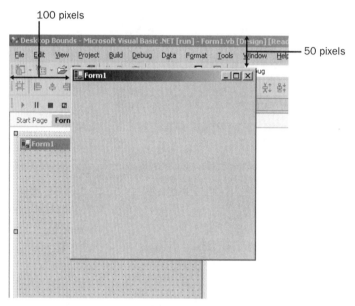

10 Click the Close button on the form to close the program.

You've experimented with a few basic *StartPosition* settings for positioning a form. Now you'll use the *DesktopBounds* property to size and position a second form window while the program is running. You'll also learn how to create a new form at runtime without using the Add Windows Form command on the Project menu.

Set the *DesktopBounds* property

1 Use the *Button* control to add a button object to the form, and then change the *Text* property of the button object to "Create Form".

2 Double-click the Create Form button to display the *Button1_Click* event procedure in the Code Editor.

3 Type the following program code:

```
'Create a second form named form2
Dim form2 As New Form

'Define the Text property and border style of the form
form2.Text = "My New Form"
form2.FormBorderStyle = FormBorderStyle.FixedDialog

'Specify that the position of the form will be set manually
form2.StartPosition = FormStartPosition.Manual

'Declare a Rectangle structure to hold the form dimensions
'Upper left corner of form (200, 100)
'Width and height of form (300, 250)
Dim Form2Rect As New Rectangle(200, 100, 300, 250)

'Set the bounds of the form using the Rectangle object
form2.DesktopBounds = Form2Rect

'Display the form as a modal dialog box
form2.ShowDialog()
```

When the user clicks the Create Form button, this event procedure creates a new form with the title "My New Form" and a fixed border style. To create a new form using program code, you use the *Dim* statement and specify a variable name for the form and the *Form* class, which is automatically included in projects as part of the *System.Windows.Forms* namespace. You can then set properties such as *Text*, *FormBorderStyle*, *StartPosition*, and *DesktopBounds*. The *StartPosition* property is set to FormStartPosition.Manual to indicate that the position will be set manually. The *DesktopBounds* property sizes and positions the form and requires an argument of type *Rectangle*. The *Rectangle* type is a structure that defines a rectangular region and is automatically included in Visual Basic projects. Using the *Dim* statement, the *Form2Rect* variable is declared of type *Rectangle* and initialized with the form position and size values. At the bottom of the event procedure, the new form is opened as a dialog box using the *ShowDialog* method.

4   Click the Start button to run the program.

> ▶ **Note**   The complete Desktop Bounds program is located in the
> c:\vbnet03sbs\chap15\desktop bounds folder.

Visual Basic displays the first form on the desktop.

5   Click the Create Form button.

Visual Basic displays the My New Form dialog box with the size and position you specified in the program code, as shown here:

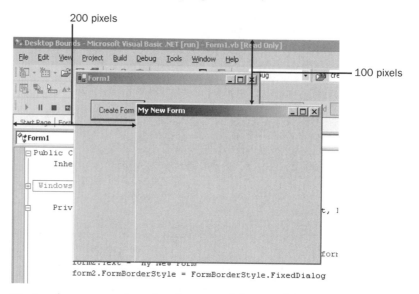

Notice that you can't resize the second form. This is because the *FormBorderStyle* was set to FixedDialog.

6   Close the second form, and then close the first form.

Your program stops running, and the development environment returns.

Minimizing, Maximizing, and Restoring Windows

In addition to establishing the size and location of a Visual Basic form, you can minimize a form on the Windows taskbar, maximize a form so that it takes up the entire screen, or restore a form to its normal shape. These settings can be changed at design time or at runtime based on current program conditions.

To allow a form to be both minimized and maximized, first verify that the form's minimize and maximize boxes are available. Using the Properties window or program code, specify the following settings:

```
MaximizeBox = True
MinimizeBox = True
```

Then, in program code or by using the Properties window, set the *Window-State* property for the form to Minimized, Maximized, or Normal. (In code, you need to add the *FormWindowState* constant, as shown below.) For example, the following program statement minimizes a form and places it on the Windows taskbar:

```
WindowState = FormWindowState.Minimized
```

If you want to control the maximum or minimum size a form can be, set the *MaximumSize* or *MinimumSize* properties at design time by using the Properties window. To set the *MaximumSize* or *MinimumSize* in code, you'll need to use a *Size* structure, shown here, similar to the *Rectangle* structure used in the previous exercise:

```
Dim FormSize As New Size(400, 300)
MaximumSize = FormSize
```

Adding Controls to a Form at Runtime

Throughout this book, you've added objects to forms by using the Toolbox and the Windows Forms Designer. However, you can also create Visual Basic objects on forms at runtime, either to save you development time or to respond to a current need in the program. For example, you might want to generate a simple dialog box containing objects to process input.

Creating objects is very simple because the fundamental classes that define controls in the Toolbox are available to all programs. Objects are declared and instantiated by using the *Dim* and *New* keywords. The following program statement shows how this process works when a new button object named *button1* is created on a form:

```
Dim button1 as New Button
```

After you create an object at runtime, you can also use code to customize it with property settings. In particular, it's useful to specify a name and location for the object because you didn't specify them manually by using the Windows Forms Designer. For example, the following program statements configure the *Text* and *Location* properties for the new *button1* object:

```
button1.Text = "Click Me"
button1.Location = New Point(20, 25)
```

Finally, your code must add the following new object to the *Controls* collection of the form where it will be created so that it becomes visible and is active in the program:

```
form2.Controls.Add(button1)
```

You can use this process to add any control in the Toolbox to a Visual Basic form. The class name you use to declare and instantiate the control is a variation of the name that appears in the *Name* property for each control.

The following exercise demonstrates how you can add a *Label* control and a *Button* control to a new form at runtime. The new form will act as a dialog box that displays the current date.

Create new Label and Button controls

1 Click the Close Solution command on the File menu, and then create a new Visual Basic Windows Application project named **My Add Controls** in the c:\vbnet03sbs\chap15 folder.

2 Display the form (Form1.vb), and then open the Properties window.

3 Use the *Button* control to add a button object to the form, and then change the *Text* property of the button object to Display Date.

4 Double-click the Display Date button to display the *Button1_Click* event procedure in the Code Editor.

5 Type the following program code:

```
'Declare new form and control objects
Dim form2 As New Form
Dim lblDate As New Label
Dim btnCancel As New Button

'Set label properties
lblDate.Text = "Current date is: " & DateString
lblDate.Size = New Size(150, 50)
lblDate.Location = New Point(80, 50)

'Set button properties
btnCancel.Text = "Cancel"
btnCancel.Location = New Point(110, 100)

'Set form properties
form2.Text = "Current Date"
form2.CancelButton = btnCancel
form2.StartPosition = FormStartPosition.CenterScreen

'Add new objects to Controls collection
form2.Controls.Add(lblDate)
form2.Controls.Add(btnCancel)

'Display form as a dialog box
form2.ShowDialog()
```

This event procedure displays a new form on the screen containing a label object and a button object. The label object contains the current date as recorded in your computer's system clock (returned through

DateString), and the *Text* property of the button object is set to "Cancel". As I mentioned earlier, you add controls to a form by declaring a variable to hold the control, setting object properties, and adding the objects to the *Controls* collection. In this exercise, I also demonstrate the *Size* and *CancelButton* properties for the first time. The *Size* property requires a *Size* structure. The *New* keyword is used to immediately create the *Size* structure. The *CancelButton* property allows the user to close the dialog box by pressing Esc or clicking the Cancel button. (The two actions are considered equivalent.)

6   Click the Start button to run the program.

▶ **Note**   The complete Add Controls program is located in the c:\vbnet03sbs\chap15\add controls folder.

Visual Basic displays the first form on the desktop.

7   Click the Display Date button.

Visual Basic displays the second form on the desktop, and this form contains the label object and the button object that you defined by using program code. The label object contains the current date, as shown here:

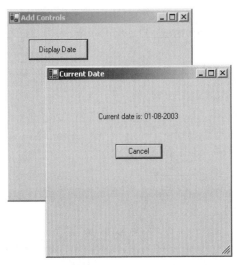

8   Click the Cancel button to close the new form.

9   Click the Display Date button again.

The new form appears as it did the first time.

10   Press Esc to close the form.

Because you set the *CancelButton* property to the *btnCancel* object, both actions (clicking Cancel and pressing Esc) produce the same result.

11 Click the Close button on the form to end the program.

The program stops, and the development environment returns.

Organizing Controls on a Form

When you add controls to a form programmatically, it takes a bit of trial and error to position the new objects so that they're aligned properly and look nice. After all, you don't have the Windows Forms Designer to help you—just the (*x*, *y*) coordinates of the *Location* and *Size* properties, which are clumsy values to work with unless you have a knack for two-dimensional thinking or have the time to run the program repeatedly to verify the placement of your objects.

Fortunately, Visual Basic .NET contains several property settings that allow you to organize objects on the form at runtime. These include the *Anchor* property, which forces an object on the form to remain at a constant distance from the specified edges of the form, and the *Dock* property, which forces an object to remain attached to one edge of the form. You can use the *Anchor* and *Dock* properties at design time, but I find that they're also very helpful when used to programmatically align objects at runtime. The following exercise shows you how these properties work.

Anchor and dock objects at runtime

1 Click the Close Solution command on the File menu, and then create a new Visual Basic Windows Application project named **My Anchor and Dock** in the c:\vbnet03sbs\chap15 folder.

2 Display the form.

3 Click the *PictureBox* control, and then add a picture box object in the top middle of the form.

4 Use the *TextBox* control to create a text box object.

5 Set the *Multiline* property for the text box object to True so that you can resize the object appropriately.

6 Resize the text box object so that it covers most of the bottom half of the form.

7 Click the *Button* control, and add a button object to the lower right corner of the form.

8   Set the following properties for the form and the objects on it:

Object	Property	Setting
PictureBox1	Image	"c:\vbnet03sbs\chap16\sun.ico"
	SizeMode	StretchImage
Button1	Text	"Align Now"
Form1	Text	"Anchor and Dock Samples"

Your form should look similar to this:

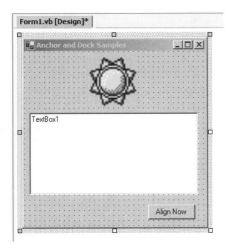

9   Double-click the Align Now button to open the *Button1_Click* event procedure in the Code Editor.

10   Type the following program code:

```
PictureBox1.Dock = DockStyle.Top
TextBox1.Anchor = AnchorStyles.Bottom Or _
  AnchorStyles.Left Or AnchorStyles.Right Or _
  AnchorStyles.Top
Button1.Anchor = AnchorStyles.Bottom Or _
  AnchorStyles.Right
```

When this event procedure is executed, the *Dock* property of the *PictureBox1* object is used to dock the picture box to the top of the form. This forces the top edge of the picture box object to touch and adhere to the top edge of the form—much as Visual Studio's own docking feature works in the development environment. The only surprising behavior here is that the picture box object is also resized so that its sides adhere to the left and right edges of the form. You'll see this behavior in the following steps.

Next, the *Anchor* property for the *TextBox1* and *Button1* objects is used. The *Anchor* property will maintain the current distance from the specified edges of the form, even if the form is resized. Note that the *Anchor* property maintains the object's current distance from the specified edges—it doesn't attach the object to the specified edges unless it's already there. In this example, I specify that the *TextBox1* object should be anchored to all four edges of the form (bottom, left, right, and top). I use the *Or* operator to combine my edge selections. I anchor the *Button1* object to the bottom and right edges of the form.

11 Click the Start button to run the program.

> ▶ **Note**   The complete Anchor and Dock program is located in the c:\vbnet03sbs\chap15\anchor and dock folder.

The form appears, just as you designed it.

12 Move the mouse pointer to the lower right corner of the form until it changes into a Resize pointer, and then enlarge the size of the form.

Notice that the size and position of the objects on the form do not change.

13 Resize the form back to its original size.

14 Click the Align Now button on the form.

The picture box object is now docked to the top edge of the form. The picture box is also resized so that its sides adhere to the left and right edges of the form, as shown here:

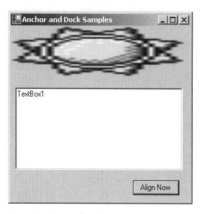

Notice that the Sun icon in the picture box is now distorted, which is a result of the docking process.

15 Enlarge the size of the form again.

As you resize the form, the picture box and text box objects are also resized. Because the text box is anchored on all four sides, the distance between the edges of the form and the text box remains constant. During the resizing activity, it also becomes apparent that the button object is being repositioned. Although the distance between the button object and the top and left edges of the form changes, the distance to the bottom and right edges remains constant, as shown here:

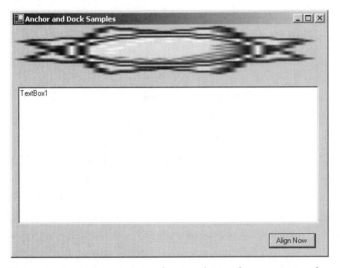

16 Experiment with the *Anchor* and *Dock* properties for a while. When you're finished, click the Close button on the form to end the program.

You now have the skills necessary to add new forms to a project, position them on the Windows desktop, populate them with new controls, and align the controls by using program code. You've gained a number of useful skills for working with forms in a Visual Basic program.

One Step Further: Specifying the Startup Object

If your project contains more than one form, which form is loaded and displayed first when you run the application? Although Visual Basic normally loads the first form that you created in a project (Form1.vb), you can actually change the form that Visual Basic loads first by adjusting a setting in the project's Property Pages dialog box. Alternatively, you can direct Visual Basic to execute a procedure named Sub Main first, which can declare public variables and load one or more forms after specific tests have been made. By modifying which form or procedure is run first, you can create a truly customized and adaptable user interface for your program.

The following exercise shows you how to change the first form, or *startup form*, that's displayed by Visual Basic when you run a program. You'll also learn how to set the startup object to a Sub Main procedure in your project.

Switch from Form1 to Form2

1 Click the Close Solution command on the File menu, and then create a new Visual Basic Windows Application project named **My Startup Form** in the c:\vbnet03sbs\chap15 folder.

2 Display Form1.vb, if it isn't already visible.

3 Click the Add Windows Form command on the Project menu.

   You'll add a new form to the project to demonstrate how switching the startup form works.

4 Click Open to add the second form (Form2.vb) to Solution Explorer.

5 Click the My Startup Form project icon in Solution Explorer, and then click Properties on the Project menu.

   The Startup Form Property Pages dialog box appears, as shown here:

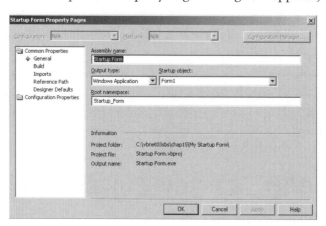

The Property Pages dialog box lets you adjust property settings that apply to the entire project. In this case, you'll use the Startup Object drop-down list box to specify a new startup form.

6 Click the Startup Object drop-down list box, and then click Form2.

Visual Basic changes the startup form in your project from Form1 to Form2. When the program runs, Form2 will be displayed, and Form1 will appear only if it's opened using the *Show* or *ShowDialog* method.

7 Click OK to close the Property Pages dialog box.

8 Click the Start button on the toolbar.

The program runs in the development environment, and Form2 appears.

9 Click the Close button on the form to end the program.

Now you'll add a Sub Main procedure to the project in a module, and you'll set the startup object to Sub Main so that execution begins in the standard module.

Start program execution with Sub Main

1 Click the Add New Item command on the Project menu, click the Module template, and then click Open to add the Module1.vb module to Solution Explorer.

2 If Module1 doesn't open in the Code Editor, select Module1.vb in Solution Explorer, and then click the View Code button.

3 Type the following code between the *Module* and *End Module* program statements:

```
Public MyForm1 As New Form1()
Public MyForm2 As New Form2()
Public Sub Main()
    MsgBox("This is Sub Main")
    'place additional program code here
    MyForm1.ShowDialog()
End Sub
```

When you add a Sub Main procedure to your project, you must add it to a standard module. The Sub Main procedure must be declared as *Public*, and it doesn't accept any arguments (except in a console application, described shortly). Note that in addition to defining the Sub Main procedure, which displays a message box and then opens Form1 as a dialog box, I also declared two public variables to represent Form1 and Form2 in the project. The *New* keyword is used to create instances of the *Form1* and *Form2* objects. In Visual Basic 6, form objects were automatically available in modules, and it wasn't necessary to create new instances.

4   Click the My Startup Form project icon in Solution Explorer, and then click Properties on the Project menu.

The Startup Form Property Pages dialog box appears.

5   Click the Startup Object drop-down list box, and then click Sub Main.

Visual Basic changes the startup object in your project from Form2 to Sub Main. When the program runs, the Sub Main procedure will be executed first, and then the Form1 window will be displayed.

6   Click OK to close the Property Pages dialog box.

7   Click the Start button on the toolbar.

The program runs in the development environment, and the Sub Main procedure is executed. You'll see this message box:

8   Click OK in the message box.

The Sub Main procedure closes the message box and displays Form1 as a new dialog box in the program.

9   Click the Close button on the form to end the program.

Although this demonstration exercise was fairly simple, you can see that Visual Basic is quite flexible in how you start your programs. You can specify a different startup form to begin your application, or you can add a Sub Main procedure to your project so that execution begins directly in program code.

▶   **Tip**   If you want to write a Visual Basic application that displays no graphical user interface at all, consider writing a console application, a project type in Visual Studio .NET that processes input and output by using a command line console (a character-based window also known as the *command prompt*). For more information about writing console applications, search for "Building Console Applications" in the Visual Basic online Help.

Lesson 15 Quick Reference

To	Do this
Add new forms to a program	Click the down arrow to the right of the Add New Item button on the Standard toolbar, and then click Add Windows Form. *or* On the Project menu, click Add Windows Form, and then click Open.

Create and modify a new form by using program code	Create the form by using the *Dim* and *New* keywords and the *Form* class, and then set any necessary properties. For example:
	<pre>Dim form2 As New Form
	form2.Text = "My New Form"</pre>

Display a form on the screen	Use the *Show* or *ShowDialog* method. For example: <pre>form2.ShowDialog()</pre>
Position a startup form on the Windows desktop	Set the *StartPosition* property to one of the available options, such as CenterScreen or CenterParent.

Size and position a startup form on the Windows desktop by using code	Set the *StartPosition* to Manual, declare a *Rectangle* structure that defines the form's size and position, and then use the *DesktopBounds* property to size and position the form on the desktop. For example:
	<pre>form2.StartPosition = FormStartPosition.Manual
	Dim Form2Rect As New Rectangle _
	  (200, 100, 300, 250)
	form2.DesktopBounds = Form2Rect</pre>

Minimize, maximize, or restore a form at runtime	Set the *MaximizeBox* and *MinimizeBox* properties for the form to True in design mode to allow for maximize and minimize operations. In the program code, set the form's *WindowState* property to FormWindowState.Minimized, FormWindowState.Maximized, or FormWindow-State.Normal when you want to change the window state of the form.

Add controls to a form at runtime	Create a control of the desired type, set its properties, and then add it to the form's *Controls* collection. For example:
	<pre>Dim button1 as New Button
	button1.Text = "Click Me"
	button1.Location = New Point(20, 25)
	form2.Controls.Add(button1)</pre>

To	Do this
Anchor an object a set distance from the specified edges of the form	Set the *Anchor* property of the object, and specify the edges you want to remain a constant distance from. Use the *Or* operator when specifying multiple edges. For example:
	``` Button1.Anchor = AnchorStyles.Bottom Or _ AnchorStyles.Right ```
Dock an object to one of the form's edges	Set the *Dock* property of the object, and specify the edge you want the object to be attached to. For example:
	``` PictureBox1.Dock = DockStyle.Top ```
Specify the startup object in a project	Click the project icon in Solution Explorer, and then click Properties on the Project menu. Specify the startup object in the Startup Object drop-down list box. (Choose either a form in the project or the Sub Main procedure.)

Chapter 16

Adding Graphics and Animation Effects

In this chapter, you will learn how to:

- Use the *System.Drawing* namespace to add graphics to your forms.

- Create animation effects on your forms.

- Expand or shrink objects on your form at runtime.

- Change the transparency of a form.

For many developers, adding artwork and special effects to an application is the most exciting—and addictive—part of programming. Fortunately, creating impressive and useful graphical effects with Microsoft Visual Basic .NET is both satisfying and easy. In this chapter, you'll learn how to add interesting "bells and whistles" to your programs. You'll learn how to create compelling artwork on a form, create simple animation effects by using *PictureBox* and *Timer* controls, and expand or contract controls at runtime by using the *Height* and *Width* properties. When you've finished, you'll have many of the skills you need to create the ultimate user interface.

Upgrade Notes: What's New in Visual Basic .NET?

If you're experienced with Visual Basic 6, you'll notice some new features in Visual Basic .NET, including the following:

- In Visual Basic 6, you used the *Line* and *Shape* controls to create simple lines, rectangles, and circles on your forms. In Visual Basic .NET, no drawing controls are provided in the Toolbox. Instead, you're encouraged to use the GDI+ graphics services directly through the *System.Drawing* namespace.

- The Visual Basic 6 keywords *Circle*, *Line*, and *PSet* have been replaced by two methods—*DrawEllipse* and *DrawLine*—and the *Point* structure in the *System.Drawing.Graphics* class.

- The default coordinate system in Visual Basic is now pixels rather than twips.

- In Visual Basic 6, many controls could be relocated, or *animated*, on the form by rapidly calling the control's *Move* method. Visual Basic .NET controls don't have a *Move* method, but they can still be relocated quickly if you update the control's *Left*, *Top*, or *Location* property or if you use the *SetBounds* method.

- Visual Basic .NET controls continue to support drag-and-drop effects, but they handle them in a different way. For example, although Visual Basic .NET continues support for the *DragDrop* event, the *DragIcon* and *DragMode* properties are no longer available.

- Microsoft Visual Studio .NET can work with more image formats than Visual Basic 6 can. In particular, the *System.Drawing.Imaging* namespace contains functions to work with the following image formats: BMP, EMF, EXIF, GIF, Icon, JPEG, MemoryBMP, PNG, TIFF, and WMF.

Adding Artwork by Using the *System.Drawing* Namespace

In Chapter 2, Chapter 3, and Chapter 7, you've experimented with adding bitmaps and icons to a form by using picture box objects. Adding ready-made artwork to your programs is easy in Visual Basic, and you've had practice doing it in several exercises. Now you'll learn how to create original artwork on your forms by using the GDI+ functions in the *System.Drawing* namespace, a new API (application programming interface) for creating graphics. The images you create can add color, shape, and texture to your forms, and they're powerful and easy to use.

Using a Form's Coordinate System

The first thing to learn about creating graphics is the layout of the form's pre-defined coordinate system. In Visual Basic, each form has its own coordinate system. The coordinate system's starting point, or *origin*, is the upper left corner of a form. The default coordinate system is made up of rows and columns of device-independent picture elements, or *pixels*, which represent the smallest points that you can locate, or *address*, on a Visual Basic form.

In the Visual Basic coordinate system, rows of pixels are aligned to the *x*-axis (horizontal axis), and columns of pixels are aligned to the *y*-axis (vertical axis). You define locations in the coordinate system by identifying the intersection of a row and a column with the notation (x, y). The (x, y) coordinates of the upper left corner of a form are always $(0, 0)$. The following illustration shows how the location for a picture box object on the form is described in the Visual Basic coordinate system:

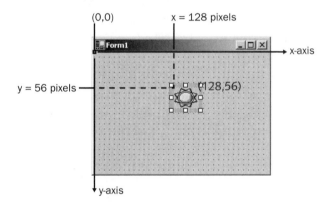

Visual Basic works along with your computer's video display driver software to determine how pixels are displayed on the form and how shapes such as lines, rectangles, curves, and circles are displayed. Occasionally, more than one pixel is turned on to display a particular shape, such as the line drawing shown in the following illustration. The logic to handle this type of rendering isn't your responsibility—it's handled by your display adapter and the drawing routines in the GDI+ graphics library. The following illustration shows a zoomed-in view of the distortion or jagged edges you sometimes see in Visual Basic and Windows applications.

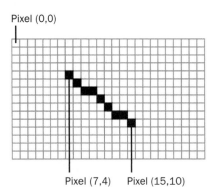

The *System.Drawing.Graphics* Class

The *System.Drawing* namespace includes numerous classes for creating artwork in your programs. In this section, you'll learn a little about the *System.Drawing.Graphics* class, which provides methods and properties for drawing shapes on your forms. You can learn about the other classes by referring to the Visual Basic .NET online Help.

Whether you're creating simple shapes or building complex drawings, it's important to be able to render many of the standard geometric shapes in your programs. The following table lists several of the fundamental drawing shapes and the methods you use in the *System.Drawing.Graphics* class to create them.

Shape	Method	Description
Line	*DrawLine*	Simple line with two points
Rectangle	*DrawRectangle*	Rectangle or square with four points
Arc	*DrawArc*	Curved line with two points (a portion of an ellipse)
Circle/Ellipse	*DrawEllipse*	Elliptical shape that's "bounded" by a rectangle
Polygon	*DrawPolygon*	Complex shape with a variable number of points and sides (stored in an array)
Curve	*DrawCurve*	A curved line that passes through a variable number of points (stored in an array); also called a cardinal spline
Bézier splines	*DrawBezier*	A curve drawn by using four points (points two and three are "control" points)

In addition to the preceding methods, which create empty or "non-filled" shapes, there are several methods that draw shapes which are automatically filled with color. These methods usually have a "Fill" prefix, such as *FillRectangle*, *FillEllipse*, and *FillPolygon*. When you use a graphics method in the *System.Drawing.Graphics* class, you need to create a *Graphics* object in your code to represent the class and either a *Pen* or *Brush* object to indicate the attributes of the shape you want to draw, such as line width and fill color. The *Pen* object is passed as one of the arguments to the methods that aren't filled with color. The *Brush* object is passed as an argument when a fill color is desired. For example, the following call to the *DrawLine* method uses a *Pen* object and four integer values to draw a line that starts at pixel (20, 30) and ends at pixel (100, 80). The *Graphics* object is declared by using the name *GraphicsFun*, and the *Pen* object is declared by using the name *PenColor*.

```
Dim GraphicsFun As System.Drawing.Graphics
Dim PenColor As New System.Drawing.Pen(System.Drawing.Color.Red)
GraphicsFun = Me.CreateGraphics
GraphicsFun.DrawLine(PenColor, 20, 30, 100, 80)
```

The syntax for the *DrawLine* method is important, but also note the three lines above it, which are required to use a method in the *System.Drawing.Graphics* class. You must create variables to represent both the *Graphics* and *Pen* objects, and the *Graphics* variable needs to be instantiated by using the *CreateGraphics* method for the Windows Form. Note that the *System.Drawing.Graphics* namespace is included in your project automatically—you don't need to include an *Imports* statement in your code to declare the necessary class.

Using the Form's *Paint* Event

If you test the previous *DrawLine* method in a program, you'll notice that the line you created lasts, or *persists*, on the form only as long as nothing else covers it up. If a dialog box appears on the form momentarily and covers the line, the line will no longer be visible when the dialog box disappears. The line will also disappear if you minimize the form window and then maximize it again. To address this shortcoming, you need to place your graphics code in the form's *Paint* event procedure so that each time the form is refreshed, the graphics will be repainted, too.

In the following exercise, you'll create three shapes on a form by using the form's *Paint* event procedure. The shapes you draw will continue to persist even if the form is covered or minimized.

Create line, rectangle, and ellipse shapes

1   Start Visual Studio, and create a new Visual Basic Windows Application project named **My Draw Shapes** in the c:\vbnet03sbs\chap16 folder.

2   Resize the form so that it's longer and wider than the default form size.

You'll need a little extra space to create the graphics shapes. You won't be using any Toolbox controls, however. You'll create the shapes by placing program code in the form's *Form1_Paint* event procedure.

3   Set the *Text* property of Form1 to Draw Shapes.

4   Click the View Code button in Solution Explorer to display the Code Editor.

5   In the Class Name drop-down list box, click Form1 Events.

Form1 Events is the list of events in your project associated with the *Form1* object.

6   In the Method Name drop-down list box, click the Paint event.

7   The *Form1_Paint* event procedure appears in the Code Editor.

This is where you type program code that should be executed when Visual Basic refreshes the form.

8   Type the following program code:

```
'Prepare GraphicsFun variable for graphics calls
Dim GraphicsFun As System.Drawing.Graphics
GraphicsFun = Me.CreateGraphics

'Use a red pen color to draw a line and an ellipse
Dim PenColor As New System.Drawing.Pen(System.Drawing.Color.Red)
GraphicsFun.DrawLine(PenColor, 20, 30, 100, 80)
GraphicsFun.DrawEllipse(PenColor, 10, 120, 200, 160)

'Use a green brush color to create a filled rectangle
Dim BrushColor As New SolidBrush(Color.Green)
GraphicsFun.FillRectangle(BrushColor, 150, 10, 250, 100)
```

This sample event procedure draws three graphic shapes on your form—a red line, a red ellipse, and a green-filled rectangle. To enable graphics programming, the routine declares a variable named *GraphicsFun* in the code and uses the *CreateGraphics* method to activate or instantiate the variable. The *PenColor* variable of type *System.Drawing.Pen* is used to set the drawing color in the line and ellipse, and the *BrushColor* variable of type *SolidBrush* is used to set the fill color in the rectangle. These examples are obviously just the tip of the graphics library iceberg—there are many more shapes, colors, and variations that you could create by using the methods in the *System.Drawing.Graphics* class.

9 Click the Start button to run the program.

> ▶ **Note** The complete Draw Shapes program is located in the c:\vbnet03sbs\chap16\draw shapes folder.

Visual Basic loads the form and executes the form's *Paint* event. Your form will look like this:

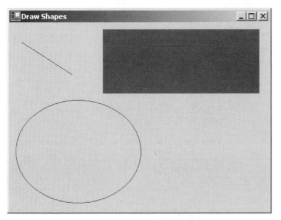

10 Minimize the form, and then restore it again.

The form's Paint event is executed again, and the graphics shapes are refreshed on the form.

11 Click the Close button to end the program.

Now you're ready to move on to some simple animation effects.

Adding Animation to Your Programs

Displaying bitmaps and drawing shapes adds visual interest to a program, but for programmers, the king of graphical effects has always been animation. *Animation* is the simulation of movement produced by rapidly displaying a series of related images on the screen. Real animation involves moving objects programmatically, and it often involves changing the size or shape of the images along the way.

In this section, you'll learn how to add simple animation to your programs. You'll learn how to update a picture box's *Top* and *Left* properties, control the rate of animation using a timer object, and sense the edge of your form's window.

Moving Objects on the Form

In Visual Basic 6, a special method named *Move* allowed you to move objects in the coordinate system. The *Move* method is no longer supported by Visual Basic .NET controls; however, you can use the following method and properties instead:

Keyword	Description
Left	This property can be used to move an object horizontally (left or right).
Top	This property can be used to move an object vertically (up or down).
Location	This property can be used to move an object to the specified location.
SetBounds	This method sets the boundaries of an object to the specified location and size.

The following sections discuss how you can use the *Left*, *Top*, and *Location* properties to move objects. For additional information about the *SetBounds* method, search for the *SetBounds* keyword in the Visual Basic online Help.

The *Left* and *Top* properties allow you to move an object. To move an object in a horizontal direction, use the *Left* property. *Left* takes the syntax

```
object.Left = horizontal
```

where *object* is the name of the object on the form that you want to move, and *horizontal* is the new horizontal, or *x*-axis, coordinate of the left edge of the object, measured in pixels. For example, the following program statement moves a picture box object to a location 300 pixels to the right of the left window edge:

```
PictureBox1.Left = 300
```

To move a relative distance to the left or right, you would add or subtract pixels from the current *Left* property setting. For example, to move an object 50 pixels to the right, you would add 50 to the *Left* property, as follows:

```
PictureBox1.Left = PictureBox1.Left + 50
```

In a similar way, you can change the vertical location of an object on a form by setting the *Top* property. The syntax for the *Top* property is

```
object.Top = vertical
```

where *object* is the name of the object on the form that you want to move, and *vertical* is the new vertical, or *y*-axis, coordinate of the top edge of the object, measured in pixels. For example, the following program statement moves a picture box object to a location 150 pixels below the window's title bar:

```
PictureBox1.Top = 150
```

Relative movements up or down are easily made by adding or subtracting pixels from the current *Top* property setting. For example, to move 30 pixels in a downward direction, you would add 30 to the current *Top* property, as follows:

```
PictureBox1.Top = PictureBox1.Top + 30
```

The *Location* Property

To move an object in both vertical and horizontal directions, it's easy enough to use a combination of the *Left* and *Top* property settings. For example, to relocate a picture box object to the (*x*, *y*) coordinates (300, 200), you'd enter the following program code:

```
PictureBox1.Left = 300
PictureBox1.Top = 200
```

However, the designers of Visual Basic .NET don't recommend using two program statements to relocate an object if you plan to make numerous object movements in a program (for example, if you plan to move an object hundreds or thousands of times during an elaborate animation effect). Instead, Microsoft recommends using the *Location* property with the syntax

```
object.Location = New Point(horizontal, vertical)
```

where *object* is the name of the object, *horizontal* is the horizontal *x*-axis coordinate, *vertical* is the vertical *y*-axis coordinate, and *Point* is a structure identifying the pixel location for the upper left corner of the object. For example, the following program statement moves a picture box object to an (*x*, *y*) coordinate of (300, 200):

```
PictureBox1.Location = New Point(300, 200)
```

To perform a relative movement using the *Location* property, the *Location.X* and *Location.Y* properties are needed. For example, the program statement

```
PictureBox1.Location = New Point(PictureBox1.Location.X - 50, _
  PictureBox1.Location.Y - 40)
```

moves the picture box object 50 pixels left and 40 pixels up on the form. Although this construction seems a bit unwieldy, it's the recommended way to relocate objects in relative movements on your form at runtime.

Creating Animation by Using a *Timer* Object

The trick to creating animation in a program is placing one or more *Location* property updates in a timer event procedure so that at set intervals the timer will cause one or more objects to drift across the screen. In Chapter 7, you learned to use a timer object to update a simple clock utility every second so that it displayed the correct time. When you create animation, you set the *Interval* property of the timer to a much faster rate—1/5 second (200 milliseconds), 1/10 second (100 milliseconds), or less. The exact rate you choose depends on how fast you want the animation to run.

Another trick is to use the *Top* and *Left* properties and the size of the form to "sense" the edges of the form. Using these values in an event procedure will let you stop the animation (disable the timer) when an object reaches the edge of the form. By using the *Top* property, the *Left* property, form size properties, and an If...Then or Select Case decision structure, you can make an object appear to bounce off one or more edges of the form.

The following exercise demonstrates how you can animate a picture box containing a Sun icon (Sun.ico) by using the *Location* property and a timer object. In this exercise, you'll use the *Top* property to detect the top of the form, and you'll use the *Size.Height* property to detect the bottom edge of the form. The Sun icon will move back and forth between these extremes each time you click a button.

Animate a Sun icon on your form

1   Click the Close Solution command on the File menu, and then create a new Visual Basic Windows Application project named **My Moving Icon** in the c:\vbnet03sbs\chap16 folder.

2   Using the *Button* control, draw two button objects in the lower left corner of the form.

3   Using the *PictureBox* control, draw a small rectangular picture box object in the lower right corner of the form. This is the object that you'll animate in the program.

4   Double-click the *Timer* control on the Windows Forms tab of the Toolbox to add it to the component tray below the form.

The timer object will be the mechanism that controls the pace of the animation. Recall that the timer object itself isn't visible on the form, so it's shown below the form in the component tray reserved for non-visible objects.

5 Set the following properties for the button, picture box, timer, and form objects:

Object	Property	Setting
Button1	*Text*	"Move Up"
Button2	*Text*	"Move Down"
PictureBox1	*Image*	"c:\vbnet03sbs\chap16\sun.ico"
	SizeMode	StretchImage
Timer1	*Enabled*	False
	Interval	75
Form1	*Text*	"Basic Animation"

After you set these properties, your form will look similar to this:

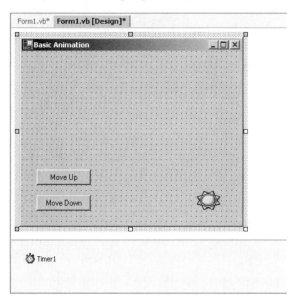

6 Double-click the Move Up button to edit its event procedure.

The *Button1_Click* event procedure appears in the Code Editor.

7 Type the following program code:

```
GoingUp = True
Timer1.Enabled = True
```

This simple event procedure sets the *GoingUp* variable to True and enables the timer object. The actual program code to move the picture box object and sense the correct direction is stored in the *Timer1_Tick* event procedure.

8   Scroll to the top of the form's program code, and below "Windows Form Designer generated code", type the following variable declaration:

```
Dim GoingUp As Boolean   'GoingUp stores current direction
```

This variable declaration makes the *GoingUp* variable available to all the event procedures in the form. I've used a Boolean variable because there are only two possible directions for movement in this program—up and down.

9   Display the form again, double-click the Move Down button, and then enter the following program code in the *Button2_Click* event procedure:

```
GoingUp = False
Timer1.Enabled = True
```

This routine is very similar to the *Button1_Click* event procedure, except that it changes the direction from up to down.

10   Display the form again, double-click the *Timer1* object, and then enter the following program code in the *Timer1_Tick* event procedure:

```
If GoingUp = True Then
    'move picture box toward the top
    If PictureBox1.Top > 10 Then
        PictureBox1.Location = New Point _
          (PictureBox1.Location.X - 10, _
          PictureBox1.Location.Y - 10)
    End If
Else
    'move picture box toward the bottom
    If PictureBox1.Top < (Me.Size.Height - 75) Then
        PictureBox1.Location = New Point _
          (PictureBox1.Location.X + 10, _
          PictureBox1.Location.Y + 10)
    End If
End If
```

As long as the timer is enabled, this If…Then decision structure is executed every 75 milliseconds. The first line in the procedure checks whether the *GoingUp* Boolean variable is set to True, indicating the icon is moving toward the top of the form. If it's set to True, the procedure moves the picture box object to a relative position 10 pixels closer to the left edge of the form and 10 pixels closer to the top edge of the form.

If the *GoingUp* variable is currently False, the decision structure moves the icon down instead. In this case, the picture box object moves until the edge of the form is detected. The height of the form can be determined by using the *Me.Size.Height* property. (I subtract 75 from the form height so that the icon is still displayed on the form.) The *Me* object in this example represents the form (*Form1*).

As you'll see when you run the program, this movement gives the icon animation a steady drifting quality. To make the icon move faster, you'd decrease the *Interval* setting for the timer object. To make the icon move slowly, change the *Interval* setting to a larger number.

Run the Moving Icon program

1   Click the Start button to run the program.

The Moving Icon program runs in the development environment.

> ▶ **Note**   The complete Moving Icon program is located in the c:\vbnet03sbs\chap16\moving icon folder.

2   Click the Move Up button.

The picture box object moves up the form on a diagonal path, as shown here:

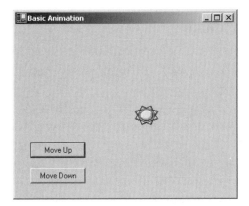

After a few moments, the button comes to rest at the upper edge of the form.

3   Click the Move Down button.

The picture box moves back down again to the lower right corner of the screen.

4   Click both buttons again several times, and ponder the animation effects.

Note that you don't need to wait for one animation effect to end before you click the next button—the *Timer1_Tick* event procedure uses the *GoingUp* variable immediately to manage your direction requests, so it doesn't matter whether the picture box has finished going in one direction. Consider this effect for a moment, and imagine how you could use a similar type of logic to build your own Visual Basic video games—you could increase or decrease the animation rates according to specific conditions or "collisions" on screen, and you could also force the animated objects to move in different directions.

5   When you're finished running the program, click the Close button on the form to stop the demonstration.

Expanding and Shrinking Objects While a Program Is Running

In addition to maintaining a *Top* property and a *Left* property, Visual Basic maintains a *Height* property and a *Width* property for most objects on a form. You can use these properties in clever ways to expand and shrink objects while a program is running. The following exercise shows you how to do it.

Expand a picture box at runtime

1   On the File menu, click the Close Solution command.

2   Create a new Visual Basic Windows Application project named **My Zoom In** in the c:\vbnet03sbs\chap16 folder.

3   Display the form, click the *PictureBox* control in the Toolbox, and then draw a small picture box object near the upper left corner of the form.

4   Set the following properties for the picture box and the form. When you set the properties for the picture box, note the current values in the *Height* and *Width* properties within the *Size* property. (You can set these at design time, too.)

Object	Property	Setting
PictureBox1	*Image*	"c:\vbnet03sbs\chap16\earth.ico"
	SizeMode	StretchImage
Form1	*Text*	"Approaching Earth"

5   Double-click the *PictureBox1* object on the form.
The *PictureBox1_Click* event procedure appears in the Code Editor.

6   Type the following program code in the *PictureBox1_Click* event procedure:

```
PictureBox1.Height = PictureBox1.Height + 15
PictureBox1.Width = PictureBox1.Width + 15
```

7   These two lines increase the height and width of the Earth icon by 15 pixels each time the user clicks the picture box. If you let your imagination run a little, watching the effect makes you feel like you're approaching Earth in a spaceship.

8   Click the Start button to run the program.

▶   **Note**   The complete Zoom In program is located in the c:\vbnet03sbs\chap16\zoom in folder.

The Earth icon appears alone on the form, as shown here:

9   Click the Earth icon several times to expand it on the screen. After 10 or 11 clicks, your screen should look similar to this:

10   When you get close enough to establish a standard orbit, click the Close button to quit the program.

The program stops, and the programming environment returns.

One Step Further: Changing Form Transparency

Interested in one last special effect? With GDI+, you can do things that were difficult or even impossible in earlier versions of Visual Basic. For example, you can make a form partially transparent so that you can see through it. Let's say you were designing a photo-display program that included a separate form that had various options to manipulate the photos. You could make the option form partially transparent so that the user could see any photos beneath it while still having access to the options.

The following exercise shows you how to change the transparency of a form. This is accomplished by changing the value of the *Opacity* property.

Set the *Opacity* property

1   On the File menu, click the Close Solution command.

2   Create a new Visual Basic Windows Application project named **My Transparent Form** in the c:\vbnet03sbs\chap16 folder.

3   Display the form, click the *Button* control in the Toolbox, and then draw two buttons on the form.

4   Set the following properties for the two buttons and the form:

Object	Property	Setting
Button1	*Text*	"Set Opacity"
Button2	*Text*	"Restore"
Form1	*Text*	"Transparent Form"

5   Double-click the Set Opacity button on the form.

6   Type the following program code in the *Button1_Click* event procedure:

```
Me.Opacity = 0.75
```

Opacity is specified as a percentage, so it has a range of 0 to 1. This line sets the *Opacity* of Form1 (*Me*) to 75 percent.

7   Display the form again, double-click the Restore button, and then enter the following program code in the *Button2_Click* event procedure:

```
Me.Opacity = 1
```

This line restores the opacity to 100 percent.

8   Click the Start button to run the program.

> ▶ **Note**   The complete Transparent Form program is located in the
> c:\vbnet03sbs\chap16\transparent form folder.

9   Click the Set Opacity button.

Notice how you can see through the form, as shown here:

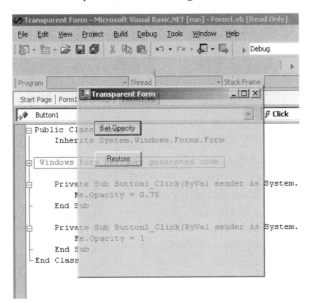

10   Click the Restore button.

The transparency effect is removed.

11   When you're done testing the transparency effect, click the Close
button to quit the program.

The program stops, and the programming environment returns.

Lesson 16 Quick Reference

To	Do this
| Create lines or shapes on a form | Use methods in the *System.Drawing.Graphics* namespace. For example, the following program statements draw an ellipse on the form:<br><br>```
Dim GraphicsFun As System.Drawing.Graphics
GraphicsFun = Me.CreateGraphics
Dim PenColor As New System.Drawing.Pen _
  (System.Drawing.Color.Red)
GraphicsFun.DrawEllipse(PenColor, 10, _
  120, 200, 160)
``` |
| Create lines or shapes that persist on the form during window redraws | Place the graphics methods in the *Paint* event procedure for the form. |
| Move an object on a form | Relocate the object by using the *Location* property, the *New* keyword, and the *Point* structure. For example:<br><br>```
PictureBox1.Location = New Point(300, 200)
``` |
Animate an object	Change the *Left*, *Top*, or *Location* properties for an object in a timer event procedure. The timer's *Interval* property controls animation speed.
Expand or shrink an object at runtime	Change the object's *Height* property or *Width* property.
Change the transparency of a form	Change the *Opacity* property.

Chapter
17

Inheriting Forms and Creating Base Classes

In this chapter, you will learn how to:

■ Use the Inheritance Picker to incorporate existing forms in your projects.

■ Create your own base classes with custom properties and methods.

■ Derive new classes from base classes by using the *Inherits* statement.

A popular buzzword among software developers today is *object-oriented programming* (OOP). Microsoft Visual Basic 4 added several object-oriented programming features to the Visual Basic language, but according to experts, Visual Basic still lagged behind the "true" OOP languages, such as Microsoft Visual C++, because it lacked *inheritance*, a mechanism that allows one class to acquire the pre-existing interface and behavior characteristics from another class. At long last, Visual Basic .NET *does* support inheritance, which means that you can build one form in the development environment and pass its characteristics and functionality on to other forms. In addition, you can build your own classes and inherit properties, methods, and events from them. In this chapter, you'll experiment with both types of inheritance. You'll learn how to integrate existing forms into your projects by using a new Microsoft Visual Studio .NET tool called the Inheritance Picker, and you'll learn how to create your own classes and derive new ones from them by using the *Inherits* statement. With these skills, you'll be able to utilize many of the forms and coding routines you've already developed, making Visual Basic programming a faster and more flexible endeavor.

Upgrade Notes: What's New in Visual Basic .NET?

If you're experienced with Visual Basic 6, you'll notice some new features in Visual Basic .NET, including the following:

■ The ability to inherit forms in the Visual Studio development environment by using the Inheritance Picker tool.

■ Classes are now defined between the *Public Class* and *End Class* keywords.

■ Several user-defined classes can now be stored in a single source file. (In Visual Basic 6, each new class had to be stored in its own file.)

■ Properties are added to classes by using a new syntax in Visual Studio .NET, and the *Property Get*, *Property Let*, and *Property Set* syntax is no longer supported.

■ The *Inherits* keyword allows a new derived class to inherit the interface and behaviors of an existing class.

Inheriting a Form by Using the Inheritance Picker

In object-oriented programming syntax, *inheritance* means having one class receive the objects, properties, methods, and other attributes of another class. As I mentioned in Chapter 15, Visual Basic goes through this process routinely when it creates a new form in the development environment. The first form in a project (*Form1*) relies on the *System.Windows.Forms.Form* class for its definition and default values. In fact, this class is identified at the top of each form with the *Inherits* keyword each time a new form is created by using the Add Windows Form command on the Project menu, as shown here:

```
Inherits
System.Windows.Forms.Form
```

Although you haven't realized it, you've been using inheritance all along to define the Windows Forms that you've been using to build Visual Basic applications. Although existing forms can be inherited by using program code as well, the designers of Visual Studio .NET considered the task to be so important that they designed a special tool in the development environment to facilitate the process. This tool is called the Inheritance Picker, and it's accessed through the

Add Inherited Form command on the Project menu. In the following exercise, you'll use the Inheritance Picker to create a second copy of a dialog box in a project.

Inherit a simple dialog box

1 Start Visual Studio, and create a new Visual Basic Windows Application project named **My Form Inheritance** in the c:\vbnet03sbs\chap17 folder.

2 Display the form in the project, and use the *Button* control to add two button objects at the bottom of the form, positioned side by side.

3 Change the *Text* properties of the *Button1* and *Button2* buttons to OK and Cancel, respectively.

4 Double-click the OK button to display the *Button1_Click* event procedure in the Code Editor.

5 Type the following program statement:

```
MsgBox("You clicked OK")
```

6 Display the form again, double-click the Cancel button, and then type the following program statement in the *Button2_Click* event procedure:

```
MsgBox("You clicked Cancel")
```

7 Display the form again, and set the *Text* property of the form to "Dialog Box".

You now have a simple form that can be used as the basis of a dialog box in a program. With some customization, you can use this basic form to process several tasks—you just need to add the controls that are specific to your individual application.

Now you'll practice inheriting the form. The first step in this process is building, or *compiling*, the project because you can inherit only from forms that are compiled into .EXE or .DLL files. Each time that the base form is recompiled, changes made to the base form are passed to the derived (inherited) form.

8 Click the Build Solution command on the Build menu.

Visual Basic compiles your project and creates an .EXE file.

9 Click the Add Inherited Form command on the Project menu.

You'll see this dialog box:

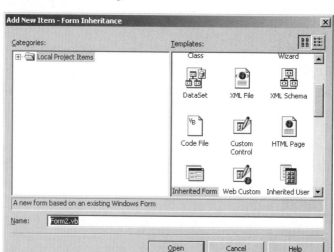

As usual, Visual Studio lists all the possible templates you could include in your projects, not just those related to inheritance. But because Inherited Form is the default selection in the Templates pane, you don't need to make any adjustments.

The Name text box at the bottom of the dialog box lets you assign a name to your inherited form; this is the name that will appear in Solution Explorer and in the filename of the form on disk.

10 Click Open to accept the default settings for the new, inherited form. Visual Studio displays the Inheritance Picker dialog box, as shown here:

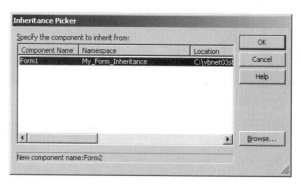

This dialog box lists all the inheritable forms in the current project. If you want to browse for other compiled forms, click the Browse button, and locate the .DLL file on your hard disk. (If you want to inherit a form that isn't a component in the current project, the form must be compiled as a .DLL file.)

11 Click Form1 in the Inheritance Picker dialog box, and then click OK.

Visual Studio creates the Form2.vb entry in Solution Explorer and displays the inherited form in the Windows Forms Designer. Notice in the following figure that the form looks identical to the Form1 window you created earlier, except that the two buttons contain tiny icons, which indicate that the objects come from an inherited source:

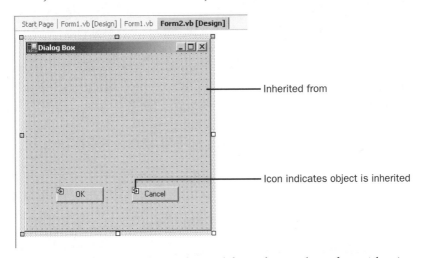

It can be difficult to tell an inherited form from a base form (the tiny inheritance icons aren't that obvious), so be sure that you use Solution Explorer and the development environment window tabs to distinguish between the forms.

Now you'll add a few new elements to the inherited form.

Customize the inherited form

1 Use the *Button* control to add a third button object to Form2 (the inherited form).

2 Set the *Text* property for the button object to "Click Me!"

3 Double-click the Click Me! button.

4 In the *Button3_Click* event procedure, type the following program statement:

```
MsgBox("This is the inherited form!")
```

5   Display Form2 again, and then try double-clicking the OK and Cancel buttons on the form.

You can't display or edit the event procedures for these inherited objects without taking additional steps that are beyond the scope of this chapter. However, you can add new objects to the form to customize it.

6   Enlarge the form.

You can also change other characteristics of the form, such as its size and location. Notice that if you use the Properties window to customize a form, the Object drop-down list box displays the form that the current form derives from.

Now set the startup object to Form2.

7   Click the My Form Inheritance project icon in Solution Explorer, and then click the Properties command on the Project menu.

The Property Pages dialog box appears.

8   Click the Startup Object drop-down list box, click Form2, and then click OK.

Now run the new project.

9   Click the Start button.

The inherited form opens, as shown here:

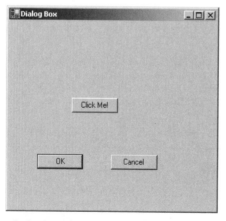

10   Click the OK button.

The inherited form runs the event procedure it inherited from Form1, and it displays the following message box:

11 Click OK, and then click the Click Me! button.

Form2 displays the inherited form message.

The inherited form has been customized to include a new object as well as the two inherited button objects. Congratulations! You've taken your first steps with inheritance by using the Inheritance Picker dialog box.

12 Click OK to close the message box, and then click Close on the form to end the program.

The program stops, and the development environment returns.

Creating Your Own Base Classes

The Inheritance Picker tool managed the inheritance process in the last exercise by creating a new class in your project named *Form2*. To build the *Form2* class, the Inheritance Picker established a link between the *Form1* class in the My Form Inheritance project and the new form. Here's what the new *Form2* class looks like in the Code Editor:

```
Public Class Form2
    Inherits My_Form_Inheritance.Form1
    ⋮
    Private Sub Button3_Click(ByVal sender As System.Object, _
      ByVal e As System.EventArgs) Handles Button3.Click
        MsgBox("This is the inherited form!")
    End Sub
End Class
```

In addition to the *Inherits* statement at the top of the form's code, the *Button3_Click* event procedure that you added is also a member of the new class. But recall for a moment that the *Form1* class itself relied on the *System.Windows.Forms.Form* class for its fundamental behavior and characteristics. So the last exercise demonstrates that one derived class (*Form2*) can inherit its functionality from a second derived class (*Form1*), which in turn inherited its core functionality from an original base class (*Form*), which is a member of the *System.Windows.Forms* namespace in the .NET Framework library.

Recognizing that classes are such a fundamental building block in Visual Basic .NET programs, one might very well ask how new classes are created and how these new classes might be inherited down the road by subsequently derived classes. To ponder these possibilities, I'll devote the remainder of this chapter to discussing the new syntax for creating classes in Visual Basic .NET and introducing how these user-defined classes might be inherited later by still more classes. Along the way, you'll learn how very useful creating your own classes can be.

17

Creating Base Classes

Nerd Alert

There's a potential danger for terminology overload when discussing class creation and inheritance. A number of very smart computer scientists have been thinking about these object-oriented programming concepts for several years, and there are numerous terms and definitions in use for the concepts that I plan to cover. However, if you stick with me, you'll find that creating classes and inheriting them is quite simple in Visual Basic .NET and that you can accomplish a lot of useful work by adding just a few lines of program code to your projects. Let's get started.

Adding a New Class to Your Project

A user-defined class allows you to define your own objects in a program—objects that have properties, methods, and events, just like the objects that Toolbox controls create on Windows Forms. To add a new class to your project, you click the Add Class command on the Project menu, and then you define the class by using program code and a few new Visual Basic keywords.

In the following exercise, you'll create a program that prompts a new employee for first name, last name, and date of birth. You'll store this information in the properties of a new class named *Person*, and you'll create a method in the class to compute the current age of the new employee. This project will teach you how to create your own classes and also how to use the classes in the event procedures of your program.

Build the Person Class project

1   Click the Close Solution command on the File menu, and then create a new Visual Basic Windows Application project named **My Person Class** in the c:\vbnet03sbs\chap17 folder.

2   Use the *Label* control to add a long label object to the top of Form1.

3   Use the *TextBox* control to draw two wide text box objects below the label object.

4   Use the *DateTimePicker* control to draw a date time picker object below the text box objects.

You last used the *DateTimePicker* control to enter dates in Chapter 3. Go to that chapter if you want a review of this control's basic methods and properties.

5 Use the *Button* control to draw a button object below the date time picker object.

6 Set the following properties for the objects on the form:

Object	Property	Setting
Label1	*Text*	"Enter employee first name, last name, and date of birth."
TextBox1	*Text*	"First name"
TextBox2	*Text*	"Last name"
Button1	*Text*	"Display Record"
Form1	*Text*	"Person Class"

7 Your form should look like this:

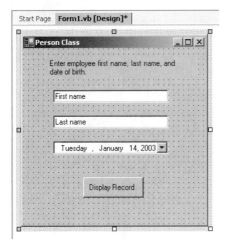

This is the basic user interface for a form that defines a new employee record in a business. (The form isn't connected to a database, so only one record can be stored at a time.) Now you'll add a class to the project to store the information in the record.

8 Click the Add Class command on the Project menu.

17

Creating Base Classes

Visual Studio displays the Add New Item dialog box, as shown here:

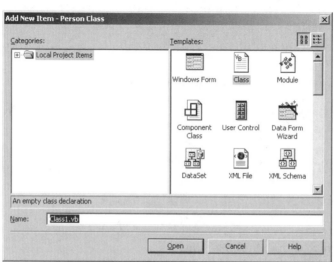

The Add New Item dialog box gives you the opportunity to name your class. As you assign a name, notice that you can store more than one class in a new class module, so you might want to specify a name that's somewhat general.

9   Type **Person.vb** in the Name text box, and then click Open.

Visual Studio opens a blank class module in the Code Editor and lists a file named Person.vb in Solution Explorer for your project, as shown here:

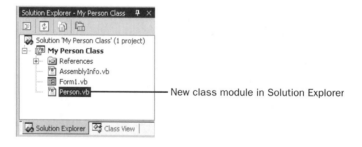

New class module in Solution Explorer

Now you'll type the definition of your class in the class module and learn a few new Visual Basic keywords. You'll follow three steps: declare class variables, create properties, and create a method.

Declare class variables

■ Below the *Public Class Person* program statement, type the following variable declarations:

```
Private Name1 As String
Private Name2 As String
```

Here you declare two variables that will be used exclusively within the class module to store the values for two string property settings. I've declared the variables by using the *Private* keyword because by convention Visual Basic programmers keep their internal class variables private—in other words, not available for inspection outside the class module itself.

Create properties

1   Below the variable declarations, type the following program statement, and press Enter:

```
Public Property FirstName() As String
```

This statement creates a property in your class named *FirstName*, which is of type *String*. When you pressed Enter, Visual Studio immediately supplied a code structure for the remaining elements in the property declaration. The required elements are a Get block, which determines what the programmers see when they check the *First-Name* property, a Set block, which determines what happens when the *FirstName* property is set or changed, and an *End Property* statement, which marks the end of the property procedure.

▶ **Note**   In Visual Basic 6, property procedures contained *Property Get*, *Property Let*, and *Property Set* code blocks. This syntax is no longer supported.

2   Fill out the property procedure structure so that it looks like the code that follows. (The elements you type are formatted in bold type.)

```
Public Property FirstName() As String
    Get
        Return Name1
    End Get
    Set(ByVal Value As String)
        Name1 = Value
    End Set
End Property
```

The *Return* keyword specifies that the *Name1* string variable will be returned when the *FirstName* property is referenced. The Set block assigns a string value to the *Name1* variable when the property is set. Notice here especially the *Value* variable, which is used in property procedures to stand for the value that's assigned to the class when a property is set. Although this syntax might look strange, trust me for now—this is how property settings are created in controls, although more sophisticated properties would add additional program logic here to test values or make computations.

3   Below the *End Property* statement, type a second property procedure for the *LastName* property in your class. It should look like the code that follows. (The bold lines are the ones you type.)

```
Public Property LastName() As String
    Get
        Return Name2
    End Get
    Set(ByVal Value As String)
        Name2 = Value
    End Set
End Property
```

This property procedure is similar to the first one, except that it uses the second string variable (*Name2*) that you declared at the top of the class.

You're finished defining the two properties in your class. Now let's move on to a method named *Age* that will determine the new employee's current age based on his or her birth date.

Create a method

● Below the *LastName* property procedure, type the following function definition:

```
Public Function Age(ByVal Birthday As Date) As Integer
    Return Int(Now.Subtract(Birthday).Days / 365.25)
End Function
```

To create a method in the class that performs a specific action, add a function or a Sub procedure to your class. Although many methods don't require arguments to accomplish their work, the *Age* method I'm defining requires a *Birthday* argument of type *Date* to complete its calculation. The method uses the *Subtract* method to subtract the new employee's birth date from the current system time, and it returns the value expressed in days divided by 365.25—the approximate length in days of a single year. The *Int* function converts this value to an integer, and this number is returned to the calling procedure via the *Return* statement—just like a typical function. (For more information about function definitions, see Chapter 10.)

Your class definition is finished! Now return to Form1, and use the new class in an event procedure.

▶ **Tip** Although it wasn't done for this example, it's wise to add some type-checking logic to the class modules in actual projects so that properties or methods that are improperly used don't trigger runtime errors that halt the program.

Create an object based on the new class

1 Click the Form1.vb icon in Solution Explorer, and then click the View Designer button.

The Form1 user interface appears.

2 Double-click the Display Record button to open the *Button1_Click* event procedure in the Code Editor.

3 Type the following program statements:

```
Dim Employee As New Person
Dim DOB As Date

Employee.FirstName = TextBox1.Text
Employee.LastName = TextBox2.Text
DOB = DateTimePicker1.Value.Date

MsgBox(Employee.FirstName & " " & Employee.LastName _
  & " is " & Employee.Age(DOB) & " years old.")
```

This routine stores the values entered by the user into an object named *Employee* that's declared as type *Person*. The *New* keyword indicates that you want to immediately create a new instance of the *Employee* object. You've declared variables often in this book—now you get to declare one based on a class you created yourself! The routine then declares a *Date* variable named *DOB* to store the date entered by the user, and the *FirstName* and *LastName* properties of the *Employee* object are set to the first and last names returned by the two text box objects on the form. The value returned by the date and time picker object is stored in the *DOB* variable, and the final program statement displays a message box containing the *FirstName* and *LastName* properties plus the age of the new employee as determined by the *Age* method, which returns an integer value when the

DOB variable is passed to it. Once you define a class in a class module, it's a simple matter to use it in an event procedure, as this routine demonstrates.

4   Click the Start button to run the program.

> ▶ **Note**   The complete Person Class program is located in the c:\vbnet03sbs\chap17\person class folder.

The user interface appears in the development environment, ready for your input.

5   Type your first name in the First Name text box and your last name in the Last Name text box.

6   Click the drop-down list arrow in the date time picker object, and scroll to your birth date (mine is March 1, 1963).

> ▶ **Tip**   You can scroll faster into the past by clicking the year field when the date time picker dialog box is open. Tiny scroll arrows appear, and you can move one year at a time backward or forward. You can also move quickly to the month you want by clicking the month field and then clicking the month in a popup menu.

Your form will look like this:

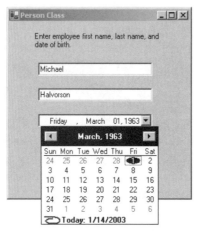

7   Click the Display Record button.

Your program stores the first name and last name values in property settings and uses the *Age* method to calculate the new employee's current age. A message box displays the result, as shown here:

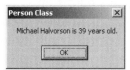

8   Click OK to close the message box, and then experiment with a few different date values, clicking Display Record each time you change the birth date field.

9   When you're finished experimenting with your new class, click the Close button on the form.

The development environment returns.

One Step Further: Inheriting a Base Class

As promised at the beginning of this chapter, I have one more trick to show you regarding user-defined classes and inheritance. Just as it's possible to inherit form classes, you can also inherit regular classes that you've defined yourself by using the Add Class command and a class module. The mechanism for inheriting a base (parent) class is to use the *Inherits* statement to include the previously defined class in a new class. You can then add additional properties or methods to the derived (child) class to distinguish it from the base class.

In the following exercise, you'll modify the My Person Class project by adding a second user-defined class to the *Person* class module. This new class, called *Teacher*, will inherit the *FirstName* property, the *LastName* property, and the *Age* method from the *Person* class and will add an additional property named *Grade* to record the grade in which the new teacher teaches.

Use the *Inherits* keyword

1   Click the Person.vb class in Solution Explorer, and then click the View Code button.

2   Scroll to the bottom of the Code Editor so that the insertion point is below the *End Class* statement.

As I mentioned earlier, you can include more than one class in a class module, as long as each class is delimited by *Public Class* and *End Class* statements. You'll create a class named *Teacher* in this class module, and you'll use the *Inherits* keyword to incorporate the method and properties you defined in the *Person* class.

3 Type the following class definition in the Code Editor. (Type the statements formatted in bold below—Visual Studio will add the remaining statements automatically.)

```
Public Class Teacher
    Inherits Person
    Private Level As Short

    Public Property Grade() As Short
        Get
            Return Level
        End Get
        Set(ByVal Value As Short)
            Level = Value
        End Set
    End Property
End Class
```

The *Inherits* statement links the *Person* class to this new class, incorporating all its variables, properties, and methods. If the *Person* class were located in a separate module or project, you could identify its location by using a namespace designation, just as you identify classes when you use the *Imports* statement at the top of a program that uses classes in the .NET Framework class libraries. Basically, I've defined the *Teacher* class as a special type of *Person* class—in addition to the *FirstName* and *LastName* properties, the *Teacher* class has a *Grade* property that records the level of student the teacher teaches.

Now you'll use the new class in the *Button1_Click* event procedure.

4 Display the *Button1_Click* event procedure in Form1.

Rather than create a new variable to hold the *Teacher* class, I'll just use the *Employee* variable as it is—the only difference will be that I can now set a *Grade* property for the new employee.

5 Modify the *Button1_Click* event procedure as follows. (The lines you need to change are formatted in bold type.)

```
Dim Employee As New Teacher
Dim DOB As Date

Employee.FirstName = TextBox1.Text
Employee.LastName = TextBox2.Text
DOB = DateTimePicker1.Value.Date
Employee.Grade = InputBox("What grade do you teach?")

MsgBox(Employee.FirstName & " " & Employee.LastName _
   & " teaches grade " & Employee.Grade)
```

In this example, I've removed the current age calculation—the *Age* method isn't used—but I did this only to keep information to a minimum in the message box. When you define properties and methods in a class, you aren't required to use them in the program code.

6 Click the Start button to run the program.

▶ **Note** The complete Class Inheritance program is located in the c:\vbnet03sbs\chap17\class inheritance folder.

The new employee form appears on the screen.

7 Type your first name in the First Name text box and your last name in the Last Name text box.

8 Click the date time picker object, and scroll to your birth date.

9 Click the Display Record button.

Your program stores the first name and last name values in property settings and then displays the following input box, which prompts the new teacher for the grade he or she teaches:

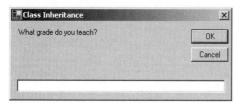

10 Type 3, and then click OK to close the input box.

The application stores the number 3 in the new *Grade* property and uses the *FirstName*, *LastName*, and *Grade* properties to display the new employee information in a confirming message box. You'll see this message:

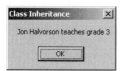

11 Experiment with a few more values if you like, and then click the Close button on the form.

The program stops, and the development environment returns. You're finished working with classes and inheritance in this chapter. Nice job!

Further Experiments with Object-Oriented Programming

If you've enjoyed this foray into object-oriented coding techniques, more fun awaits you in Visual Basic .NET Version 2003, a truly object-oriented programming language. In particular, you might want to add events to your class definitions, create default property values, and experiment with a new polymorphic feature called *method overloading*. These and other OOP features can be explored by using the Visual Basic online Help or by perusing an advanced book on Visual Basic .NET programming. (See Appendix B for a reading list.)

Lesson 17 Quick Reference

To	Do this
Inherit an existing form's interface and functionality	Click the Add Inherited Form command on the Project menu, specify a name for the inherited form, and then click Open. Use the Inheritance Picker to select the form you want to inherit, and then click OK. Note that to be eligible for inheritance, base forms must be compiled as .EXE or .DLL files. If you want to inherit a form that isn't a component in the current project, the form must be compiled as a .DLL file.
Customize an inherited form	Add Toolbox controls to the form, and set property settings. Note that you won't be able to set the properties of inherited objects on the form, however. These objects can be identified by small icons and will be inactive.
Create your own base classes	Click the Add Class command on the Project menu, specify the class name, and then click Open. Define the class in a class module by using program code.
Declare variables in a class	Use the *Private* keyword to make class variables hidden when others examine your class. For example: `Private Name1 As String`

Create a new property in the class	Define a public property procedure in the class. For example:
	`Public Property FirstName() As String`
	`    Get`
	`        Return Name1`
	`    End Get`
	`    Set(ByVal Value As String)`
	`        Name1 = Value`
	`    End Set`
	`End Property`

To	Do this
Create a new method in the class	Define a Sub or Function procedure in the class. For example:

```
Public Function Age(ByVal Birthday As Date) _
   As Integer
      Return Int(Now.Subtract(Birthday).Days _
      / 365.25)
End Function
```

To	Do this
Declare an object variable to use the class	Use the *Dim* and *New* keywords, a variable name, and the user-defined class in a program statement. For example:

```
Dim Employee As New Person
```

To	Do this
Set properties for an object variable	Use the regular syntax for setting object properties. For example:

```
Employee.FirstName = TextBox1.Text
```

To	Do this
Inherit a base class in a new class	Create a new class, and use the *Inherits* keyword to incorporate the base class's class definitions. For example:

```
Public Class Teacher
      Inherits Person
      Private Level As Short

      Public Property Grade() As Short
         Get
               Return Level
         End Get
         Set(ByVal Value As Short)
               Level = Value
         End Set
      End Property
End Class
```

Working with Printers

In this chapter, you will learn how to:

- Print graphics from a Microsoft Visual Basic program.
- Print text from a Visual Basic program.
- Print multipage documents.
- Use the Print, Page Setup, and Print Preview dialog boxes.

In the following sections, you'll complete your survey of advanced user interface components by learning how to add printer support to your Windows Forms applications. Visual Basic .NET supports printing by offering the *Print-Document* class and its many objects, methods, and properties that facilitate printing. In this chapter, you'll learn how to print graphics and text from Visual Basic programs, manage multipage printing tasks, and add printing dialog boxes to your user interface.

For my money, this chapter is one of the best in the book, with lots of practical code that you can immediately incorporate into real-world programming projects. Printing support doesn't come automatically in Visual Basic .NET, but the routines in this chapter will help you print longer text documents and display helpful dialog boxes such as Page Setup, Print, and Print Preview.

Upgrade Notes: What's New in Visual Basic .NET?

If you're experienced with Visual Basic 6, you'll notice some new features in Visual Basic .NET, including the following:

- In Visual Basic 6, printing was accomplished by using the methods and properties of the *Printer* object. For example, the *Printer.Print* method sent a string of text to the default printer. In Visual Basic .NET, printing is accomplished by using the new *PrintDocument* class, which provides more functionality than the older method but is also more complex.

- In Visual Basic 6, you had access to one predefined dialog box for printing services—the Print dialog provided by the *CommonDialog* ActiveX control. In Visual Basic .NET, you have access to several predefined dialog box controls for printing, including *PrintDialog*, *PrintPreviewDialog*, and *PageSetupDialog*.

- To implement multipage printing in Visual Basic .NET, you must create a *PrintPage* event handler that prints each page of your document one at a time. Although managing this printing process can be somewhat involved, it's simplified by services in the *System.Drawing.Printing* namespace.

Using the *PrintDocument* Class

Most Microsoft Windows applications allow users to print documents after they create them, and by now you might be wondering just how printing works in Visual Basic programs. This is one area where Visual Basic .NET has improved considerably over Visual Basic 6, although the added functionality comes at a little cost. It isn't trivial to produce printed output from Visual Basic .NET programs, and the technique you use depends on the type and amount of printed output you want to generate. In all cases, however, the fundamental mechanism that regulates printing in Visual Basic .NET is the *PrintDocument* class, which you can create in a project by adding the *PrintDocument* control to a form, or you can define it programmatically by using a few lines of Visual Basic code. The *PrintDocument* class provides several useful objects for printing text and graphics, including the *PrinterSettings* object, which contains the default print settings for a printer; the *PageSettings* object, which contains print settings for a particular page; and the *PrintPageEventArgs* object, which contains event information about the page that's about to be printed. The *PrintDocument* class is located in the *System.Drawing.Printing* namespace. If you add a *PrintDocument* control to your form, some of the objects in the *Print-Document* class are automatically incorporated into your project, but you still need to add the following *Imports* statement to the top of your form:

```
Imports System.Drawing.Printing
```

This defines *PrintPageEventArgs* and other important values.

To learn how to use the *PrintDocument* class in a program, complete the following exercise, which teaches you how to add a *PrintDocument* control to your project and use it to print a graphics file on your system.

Use the *PrintDocument* control

1   Start Microsoft Visual Studio, and create a new Visual Basic Windows Application project named **My Print Graphics** in the c:\vbnet03sbs\chap18 folder.

    A blank form appears in the Visual Studio development environment.

2   Use the *Label* control to draw a label object near the top of the form. Make the label wide enough to display one line of instructions for the user.

3   Use the *TextBox* control to draw a text box object below the label object.

    The text box object will be used to type the name of the artwork file that you want to open. A single-line text box will be sufficient.

4   Use the *Button* control to draw a button object below the text box.

    This button object will print the graphics file. Now add a *PrintDocument* control to your form.

5   Scroll down on the Windows Forms tab of the Toolbox until you see the *PrintDocument* control, and then double-click it.

    Like the *Timer* control, the *PrintDocument* control is invisible at runtime, so it's placed in the component tray beneath the form when you create it. Your project now has access to the *PrintDocument* class and its useful printing objects.

6   Set the following properties for the objects on your form:

Object	Property	Setting
Label1	*Text*	"Type the name of a graphic file to print."
TextBox1	*Text*	"c:\vbnet03sbs\chap16\sun.ico"
Button1	*Text*	"Print Graphic"
Form1	*Text*	"Print Graphics"

Your form will look like this:

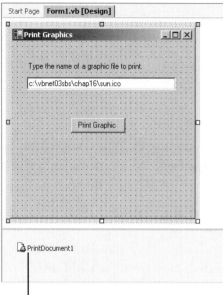

Print document object

Now add the program code necessary to print a graphic file (bitmap, icon, metafile, JPEG file, etc.).

7   Double-click the Print Graphic button.

The *Button1_Click* event procedure appears in the Code Editor.

8   Scroll to the very top of the form's code, and then type the following program statement:

```
Imports System.Drawing.Printing
```

This *Imports* statement declares the *System.Drawing.Printing* namespace, which is needed to define the *PrintPageEventArgs* object in the *PrintGraphic* procedure. The *PrintGraphic* procedure will be added in a later step. (The other *PrintDocument* objects will receive their definitions from the *PrintDocument* control.)

9   Now scroll back down to the *Button1_Click* event procedure, and then enter the following program code:

```
' Print using an error handler to catch problems
Try
    AddHandler PrintDocument1.PrintPage, AddressOf Me.PrintGraphic
    PrintDocument1.Print()    'print graphic
Catch ex As Exception   'catch printing exception
    MessageBox.Show("Sorry--there is a problem printing", _
        ex.ToString())
End Try
```

This code uses the *AddHandler* statement, which specifies that the *PrintGraphic* event handler should be called when the *PrintPage* event of the *PrintDocument1* object fires. You've seen *error handlers* in previous chapters—an *event handler* is a closely related mechanism that handles system events that aren't technically errors but that also represent crucial actions in the life cycle of an object. In this case, the event handler being specified is related to printing services, and the request comes with specific information about the page to be printed, the current printer settings, and other attributes of the *PrintDocument* class. Technically, the *AddressOf* operator is used to identify the *PrintGraphic* event handler by determining its internal address and storing it. The *AddressOf* operator implicitly creates an object known as a *delegate* that forwards calls to the appropriate event handler when an event occurs.

The third line of the previous code uses the *Print* method of the *PrintDocument1* object to send a print request to the *PrintGraphic* event procedure, a routine that you'll create in the next step. This print request is located inside a Try code block to catch any printing problems that might occur during the printing activity. Note that I'm using a slightly different syntax in the Catch block than what I introduced in Chapter 9. Here the *ex* variable is being declared of type *Exception* to get a detailed message about any errors that occur. Using the *Exception* type is another way to get at the underlying error condition that created the problem.

10 Scroll above the *Button1_Click* event procedure in the Code Editor to the general declaration space below the label "Windows Form Designer generated code". Type the following Sub procedure declaration:

```
'Sub for printing graphic
Private Sub PrintGraphic(ByVal sender As Object, _
   ByVal ev As PrintPageEventArgs)
     ' Create the graphic using DrawImage
     ev.Graphics.DrawImage(Image.FromFile(TextBox1.Text), _
       ev.Graphics.VisibleClipBounds)
     ' Specify that this is the last page to print
     ev.HasMorePages = False
End Sub
```

This is the routine that handles the printing event generated by the *PrintDocument1.Print* method. I've declared the Sub procedure within the form's code, but you can also declare the Sub as a general-purpose procedure in a standard module. Note the *ev* variable in the argument list for the *PrintGraphic* procedure—this is the crucial carrier of information about the current print page, and it's declared of type *PrintPageEventArgs*, an object in the *System.Drawing.Printing* namespace.

To actually print the graphic, the procedure uses the *Graphics.Draw-Image* method associated with the current print page, and this method loads a graphics file using the filename stored in the *Text* property of the *TextBox1* object. (By default, I set this property to c:\vbnet03sbs\chap16\sun.ico—the Sun icon you used in Chapter 16—but you can change this value at runtime and print any artwork files that you like.) Finally, I set the *ev.HasMorePages* property to False so that Visual Basic understands the print job doesn't have multiple pages.

11 Click the Save All button on the toolbar to save your changes.

Now you're ready to run the program. Before you do so, you might want to locate a few graphics files on your system that you can print. (Just jot down the paths for now and type them in.)

Run the Print Graphics program

1 Click the Start button on the toolbar.

> ▶ **Note**   The complete Print Graphics program is located in the c:\vbnet03sbs\chap18\print graphics folder.

Your program runs in the development environment. You'll see this form:

2 Turn on your printer, and verify that it's on line and has paper.

3 If you installed your sample files in the default c:\vbnet03sbs folder, click the Print Graphic button now to print the Sun.ico icon graphic.

If you didn't use the default sample file location, or if you want to print a different artwork file, modify the text box path accordingly, and then click the Print Graphic button.

The *DrawImage* method will expand the graphic to the maximum size your printer can produce on one page and then send it to the printer. (This "expansion feature" gives you a closer look at the image.) If you want to modify the location or size of your output, search the Visual Basic online Help for the Graphics.DrawImage topic, and then study the different argument variations available to you, and modify your program code.

If you look closely, you'll see the following dialog box appear when Visual Basic sends your print job to the printer:

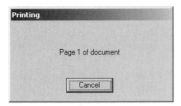

This status box is also a product of the *PrintDocument* class, and it provides users with a professional-looking print interface, including the page number for each printed page.

4 Type additional paths if you like, and then click the Print Graphic button for more printouts.

5 When you're finished experimenting with the program, click the Close button on the form.

The program stops. Not bad for your first attempt at printing from a Visual Basic program!

Printing Text from a Text Box Object

You've had a quick introduction to the *PrintDocument* control and printing graphics. Now try using a similar technique to print the contents of a text box on a Visual Basic form. In the following exercise, you'll build a project that prints text by using the *PrintDocument* class, but this time you'll define the class by using program code without adding the *PrintDocument* control to your form. In addition, you'll use the *Graphics.DrawString* method to send the entire contents of a text box object to the default printer.

▶ **Note** The following program is designed to print one page or less of text. To print multiple pages, you need to add additional program code, which will be explored later in the chapter.

Use the *Graphics.DrawString* method to print text

1   Click the Close Solution command on the File menu, and then create a new Visual Basic Windows Application project named **My Print Text** in the c:\vbnet03sbs\chap18 folder.

A blank form appears.

2   Use the *Label* control to draw a label object near the top of the form.

This label will also display a line of instructions for the user.

3   Use the *TextBox* control to draw a text box object below the label object.

The text box object will contain the text you want to print.

4   Set the *Multiline* property of the text box object to True, and then expand the text box so that it's large enough to enter several lines of text.

5   Use the *Button* control to draw a button object below the text box.

This button object will print the text file.

6   Set the following properties for the objects on your form:

Object	Property	Setting
Label1	*Text*	"Type some text in this text box object, then click Print Text."
TextBox1	*ScrollBars*	Vertical
	Text	(empty)
Button1	*Text*	"Print Text"
Form1	*Text*	"Print Text"

Your form will look like this:

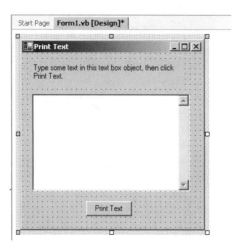

Now add the program code necessary to print the contents of the text box.

7   Double-click the Print Text button.

The *Button1_Click* event procedure appears in the Code Editor.

8   Scroll to the very top of the form's code, and then type the following *Imports* declaration:

```
Imports System.Drawing.Printing
```

This defines the *System.Drawing.Printing* namespace, which is needed to define the *PrintDocument* class and its necessary objects.

9   Now scroll back down to the *Button1_Click* event procedure, and then enter the following program code:

```
' Print using an error handler to catch problems
Try
    ' Declare PrintDoc variable of type PrintDocument
    Dim PrintDoc As New PrintDocument
    AddHandler PrintDoc.PrintPage, AddressOf Me.PrintText
    PrintDoc.Print()    'print text
Catch ex As Exception  'catch printing exception
    MessageBox.Show("Sorry--there is a problem printing", _
        ex.ToString())
End Try
```

The lines that are new or changed from the Print Graphics program are highlighted with bold formatting. Rather than add a *PrintDocument* control to your form, this time you simply created the *PrintDocument* programmatically by using the *Dim* keyword and the *PrintDocument* type, which is defined in your program when you define the *System.Drawing.Printing* namespace. From this point on, the *PrintDoc* variable represents the *PrintDocument* object, and it's used to declare the error handler and to print the text document. Note that for clarity, I renamed the Sub procedure that will handle the print event *PrintText* (rather than *PrintGraphic*).

10   Scroll above the *Button1_Click* event procedure in the Code Editor to the general declaration area. Type the following Sub procedure declaration:

```
'Sub for printing text
Private Sub PrintText(ByVal sender As Object, _
  ByVal ev As PrintPageEventArgs)
    'Use DrawString to create text in a Graphics object
    ev.Graphics.DrawString(TextBox1.Text, New Font("Arial", _
      11, FontStyle.Regular), Brushes.Black, 120, 120)
    ' Specify that this is the last page to print
    ev.HasMorePages = False
End Sub
```

18

Working with Printers

This is the routine that handles the printing event generated by the *PrintDoc.Print* method. The changes from the *PrintGraphic* procedure in the last exercise are also formatted with bold type. As you can see, when you print text you need to use a new method. Rather than use *Graphics.DrawImage*, which renders a graphics image, you must use *Graphics.DrawString*, which prints a text string. I've specified the text in the *Text* property of the text box object to print, some basic font formatting (Arial, 11 point, regular style, black color), and an (*x*, *y*) coordinate (120, 120) on the page to start drawing. This will give the printed output a default look that's similar to the text box on the screen. Like last time, I also set the *ev.HasMorePages* property to False to indicate that the print job doesn't have multiple pages.

11 Click the Save All button on the toolbar to save your changes.

Now you'll run the program to see how a text box object prints.

Run the Print Text program

1 Click the Start button on the toolbar.

> ▶ **Note**   The complete Print Text program is located in the
> c:\vbnet03sbs\chap18\print text folder.

Your program runs in the development environment.

2 Verify that your printer is on.

3 Type some sample text in the text box. If you type multiple lines, be sure to include a carriage return at the end of each line.

Wrapping isn't supported in this demonstration program—very long lines will potentially extend past the right margin. Your form should look like this:

4   Click the Print Text button.

The program displays a printing dialog box and prints the contents of your text box.

5   Modify the text box and try additional printouts, if you like.

6   When you're finished, click the Close button on the form.

The program stops. Now you know how to print both text and graphics from a program.

Printing Multipage Text Files

The printing techniques that you've just learned are useful for simple text documents, but they have a few important limitations. First, the method I used doesn't allow for long lines—in other words, text that extends beyond the right margin. Unlike the text box object, the *PrintDocument* object doesn't automatically wrap lines when they reach the edge of the paper. If you have files that don't contain carriage returns at the end of lines, you'll need to write the code that handles these long lines.

The second limitation is that the Print Text program can't print more than one page of text. Indeed, it doesn't even understand what a page of text *is*—the printing procedure simply sends the text to the default printer. If the text block is too long to fit on a single page, the additional text won't be printed. To handle multipage printouts, you need to create a virtual page of text called the *PrintPage*, and then add text to it until the page is full. When the page is full, it will be sent to the printer, and this process continues until there's no more text to print. At this point, the print job ends.

If fixing these two limitations sounds complicated, don't despair yet—there are a few handy mechanisms that help you create virtual text pages in Visual Basic and help you print text files with long lines and several pages of text. The first mechanism is the *PrintPage* event, which occurs when a page is printed. *PrintPage* receives an argument of the type *PrintPageEventArgs*, which provides you with the dimensions and characteristics of the current printer page. Another mechanism is the *Graphics.MeasureString* method. The *MeasureString* method can be used to determine how many characters and lines can fit in a rectangular area of the page. By using these mechanisms and others, it's relatively straightforward to construct procedures that process multipage print jobs.

Complete the following steps to build a program named Print File that opens text files of any length and prints them. The Print File program also demonstrates how to use the *RichTextBox*, *PrintDialog*, and *OpenFileDialog* controls. The *RichTextBox* control is a more robust version of the *TextBox* control you just used to display text. The *PrintDialog* control displays a standard Print dialog box so that you can specify various print settings. The *OpenFileDialog* control lets you select a text file for printing. (You used *OpenFileDialog* in Chapter 4.)

Manage print requests with *RichTextBox*, *OpenFileDialog*, and *PrintDialog* controls

1 Click the Close Solution command on the File menu, and then create a new Visual Basic Windows Application project named **My Print File** in the c:\vbnet03sbs\chap18 folder.

   A blank form appears.

2 Use the *Button* control in the Toolbox to draw two buttons in the upper left corner of the form.

   This program has a simple user interface, but the printing techniques you'll learn are easily adaptable to much more complex solutions.

3 Click the *RichTextBox* control in the Toolbox, and then draw a rich text box object that covers the bottom half of the form.

4 Double-click the *OpenFileDialog* control to add an open file dialog object to the component tray below your form.

   You'll use the open file dialog object to browse for text files on your system.

5 Double-click the *PrintDocument* control to add a print document object to the component tray.

   You'll use the print document object to support printing in your application.

6 Double-click the *PrintDialog* control to add a print dialog object to the component tray.

   You'll use the print dialog object to open a Print dialog box in your program.

7 Now set the following properties for the objects on your form:

Object	Property	Setting
Button1	*Name*	btnOpen
	Text	"Open"
Button2	*Name*	btnPrint
	Enabled	False
	Text	"Print"
RichTextBox1	*Text*	(empty)
Form1	*Text*	"Print File"

Your form will look like this:

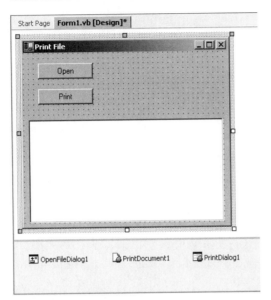

Now add the program code necessary to open the text file and print it.

8 Double-click the Open button.

The *btnOpen_Click* event procedure appears in the Code Editor.

9 Scroll to the top of the form, and enter the following code:

```
Imports System.IO  'for FileStream class
Imports System.Drawing.Printing
```

These library definitions make available the *FileStream* class and the classes for printing.

10 Move the cursor below the "Windows Form Designer generated code" tag, and then enter the following variable declarations:

```
Private PrintPageSettings As New PageSettings
Private StringToPrint As String
Private PrintFont As New Font("Arial", 10)
```

These statements define important information about the pages that will be printed.

11 Scroll to the *btnOpen_Click* event procedure, and then type the following program code:

```
Dim FilePath As String
'Display Open dialog box and select text file
OpenFileDialog1.Filter = "Text files (*.txt)|*.txt"
OpenFileDialog1.ShowDialog()
'If Cancel button not selected, load FilePath variable
If OpenFileDialog1.FileName <> "" Then
```

```
    FilePath = OpenFileDialog1.FileName
    Try
        'Read text file and load into RichTextBox1
        Dim MyFileStream As New FileStream(FilePath, FileMode.Open)
        RichTextBox1.LoadFile(MyFileStream, _
          RichTextBoxStreamType.PlainText)
        MyFileStream.Close()
        'Initialize string to print
        StringToPrint = RichTextBox1.Text
        'Enable Print button
        btnPrint.Enabled = True
    Catch ex As Exception
        'display error messages if they appear
        MessageBox.Show(ex.Message)
    End Try
End If
```

When the user clicks the Open button, this event procedure displays
an Open dialog box using a filter that displays only text files. When
the user selects a file, the filename is assigned to a public string variable named *FilePath*, which is declared at the top of the event procedure. The procedure then uses a Try...Catch error handler to load
the text file into the *RichTextBox1* object. To facilitate the loading
process, I've used the *FileStream* class and the *Open* file mode, which
places the complete contents of the text file into the *MyFileStream*
variable. Finally, the event procedure enables the Print button
(*btnPrint*) so that the user can print the file. In short, this routine
opens the file and enables the print button on the form but doesn't
do any printing itself.

Now you'll add the necessary program code to display the Print dialog box and
print the file by using logic that monitors the dimensions of the current text page.

Add code for the *btnPrint* and *PrintDocument1* objects

1   Display the form again, and then double-click the Print button
    (*btnPrint*) to display its event procedure in the Code Editor.

2   Type the following program code:

```
Try
    'Specify current page settings
    PrintDocument1.DefaultPageSettings = PrintPageSettings
    'Specify document for print dialog box and show
    StringToPrint = RichTextBox1.Text
    PrintDialog1.Document = PrintDocument1
    Dim result As DialogResult = PrintDialog1.ShowDialog()
```

```
        'If click OK, print document to printer
        If result = DialogResult.OK Then
            PrintDocument1.Print()
        End If
    Catch ex As Exception
        'Display error message
        MessageBox.Show(ex.Message)
    End Try
```

This event procedure sets the default print settings for the document and assigns the contents of the *RichTextBox1* object to the *StringTo-Print* string variable (defined at the top of the form) in case the user changes the text in the rich text box. It then opens the Print dialog box and allows the user to adjust any print settings he or she would like (printer, number of copies, the print to file option, and so on). If the user clicks the OK button, the event procedure sends this print job to the printer by issuing the following statement:

```
PrintDocument1.Print()
```

3   Display the form again, and then double-click the *PrintDocument1* object in the component tray.

Visual Studio adds the *PrintPage* event procedure for the *PrintDocument1* object.

4   Type the following program code in the *PrintDocument1_PrintPage* event procedure:

```
Dim numChars As Integer
Dim numLines As Integer
Dim stringForPage As String
Dim strFormat As New StringFormat
'Based on page setup, define drawable rectangle on page
Dim rectDraw As New RectangleF( _
    e.MarginBounds.Left, e.MarginBounds.Top, _
    e.MarginBounds.Width, e.MarginBounds.Height)
'Define area to determine how much text can fit on a page
'Make height one line shorter to ensure text doesn't clip
Dim sizeMeasure As New SizeF(e.MarginBounds.Width, _
    e.MarginBounds.Height - PrintFont.GetHeight(e.Graphics))

'When drawing long strings, break between words
strFormat.Trimming = StringTrimming.Word
'Compute how many chars and lines can fit based on sizeMeasure
e.Graphics.MeasureString(StringToPrint, PrintFont, _
    sizeMeasure, strFormat, numChars, numLines)
'Compute string that will fit on a page
stringForPage = StringToPrint.Substring(0, numChars)
'Print string on current page
e.Graphics.DrawString(stringForPage, PrintFont, _
```

```
        Brushes.Black, rectDraw, strFormat)
    'If there is more text, indicate there are more pages
    If numChars < StringToPrint.Length Then
        'Subtract text from string that has been printed
        StringToPrint = StringToPrint.Substring(numChars)
        e.HasMorePages = True
    Else
        e.HasMorePages = False
        'All text has been printed, so restore string
        StringToPrint = RichTextBox1.Text
    End If
```

This event procedure handles the actual printing of the text document, and it does so by carefully defining a printing area (or printing rectangle) based on the settings in the Page Setup dialog box. Any text that fits within this area can be printed normally; text that's outside this area needs to be wrapped to the following lines, or pages, as you'd expect from a standard Windows application.

The printing area is defined by the *rectDraw* variable, which is based on the *RectangleF* class. The *strFormat* variable and the *Trimming* method are used to trim strings that extend beyond the edge of the right margin. The actual text strings are printed by the *DrawString* method, which you've already used in this chapter. The *e.HasMore-Pages* property is used to specify whether there are additional pages to be printed. If no additional pages remain, the *HasMorePage* property is set to False, and the contents of the *StringToPrint* variable are restored to the contents of the *RichTextBox1* object.

5   Click the Save All button on the toolbar to save your changes.

That's a lot of typing! But now you're ready to run the program and see how printing text files on multiple pages works.

Run the Print File program

1   Click the Start button on the toolbar.

> ▶ **Note**   The complete Print File program is located in the
> c:\vbnet03sbs\chap18\print file folder.

Your program runs in the development environment. Notice that the Print button is currently disabled because you haven't selected a file yet.

2   Click the Open button.

The program displays an Open dialog box.

3   Browse to the c:\vbnet03sbs\chap18 folder, and then click the long-file.txt file.

Your Open dialog box will look like this:

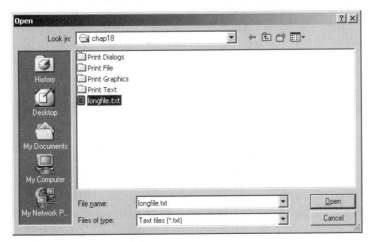

4   Click Open to select the file.

Your program loads the text file into the rich text box object on the form and then enables the Print button. This file is long and has a few lines that wrap so that you can test the wide margin and multi-page printing options. Your form will look like this:

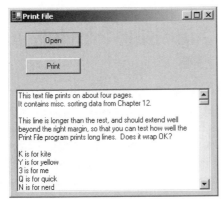

5   Verify that your printer is on, and then click the Print button.

6   Visual Basic displays the Print dialog box, as shown in the following illustration:

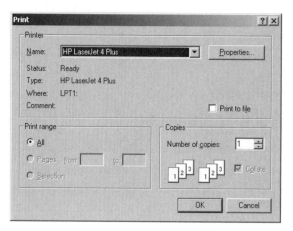

Many of the options in the Print dialog box are active, and you can experiment with them as you would a regular Windows application.

7   Click OK to print the document.

Your program submits the four-page print job to the printer. After a moment, your printer starts printing the document. As in previous exercises, a dialog box automatically appears to show you the printing status and give you an indication of how many pages your printed document will be.

8   Click the Close button on the form to stop the program.

The program stops. You've just created a set of very versatile printing routines!

One Step Further: Adding Print Preview and Page Setup Dialog Boxes

The Print File application is ready to handle several printing tasks, but its interface isn't as visual as a commercial Windows application's. You can make your program more flexible and interesting by adding a few extra dialog box options to supplement the Print dialog box you experimented with in the previous exercise. The following additional printing controls are available on the Windows Forms tab of the Toolbox, and they work much like the familiar *PrintDialog* and *OpenFileDialog* controls you've used in this book:

- *PrintPreviewDialog*, a control that displays a custom Print Preview dialog box

- *PageSetupDialog*, a control that displays a custom Page Setup dialog box

Like other dialog boxes, these printing controls can be added by using the Toolbox, or they can be created programmatically.

In the following exercise, you'll add print preview and page setup dialog boxes to the Print File program you've been working with. In the completed practice files, I've named this project Print Dialogs so that you can keep the code straight between the projects, but you can just add the dialog box features directly to the Print File project if you want.

Add *PrintPreviewDialog* and *PageSetupDialog* controls

1 Open the Print File project now from the c:\vbnet03sbs\chap18\print file folder if you didn't complete the last exercise.

   The Print File project is the starting point for this project.

2 Display the form, and then use the *Button* control to add two additional buttons to the top of the form.

3 Double-click the *PrintPreviewDialog* control on the Windows Forms tab of the Toolbox.

   A print preview dialog object is added to the component tray.

4 Double-click the *PageSetupDialog* control on the Windows Forms tab of the Toolbox.

   A page setup dialog object is added to the component tray. If the objects in the component tray obscure one another, you can drag them to a better (more visible) location, or you can right click the component tray and select Line Up Icons.

5 Set the following properties for the button objects on the form:

Object	Property	Setting
Button1	*Name*	btnSetup
	Enabled	False
	Text	"Page Setup"
Button2	*Name*	btnPreview
	Enabled	False
	Text	"Print Preview"

Working with Printers   18

Your form will look like this:

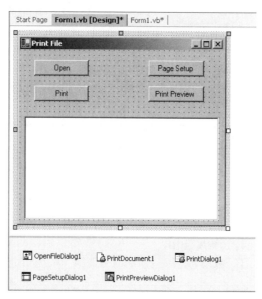

6   Double-click the Page Setup button (*btnSetup*) to display the *btnSetup_Click* event procedure in the Code Editor.

7   Type the following program code:

```
Try
    'Load page settings and display page setup dialog box
    PageSetupDialog1.PageSettings = PrintPageSettings
    PageSetupDialog1.ShowDialog()
Catch ex As Exception
    'Display error message
    MessageBox.Show(ex.Message)
End Try
```

The code for creating a Page Setup dialog box in this program is quite simple because the *PrintPageSettings* variable has already been defined at the top of the form. This variable holds the current page definition information, and when it's assigned to the *PageSettings* property of the *PageSetupDialog1* object, the *ShowDialog* method automatically loads a dialog box that allows the user to modify what the program has selected as the default page orientation, margins, and so on. The Try...Catch error handler simply handles any errors that might occur when the *ShowDialog* method is used.

8   Display the form again, and then double-click the Print Preview button (*btnPreview*) to display the *btnPreview_Click* event procedure.

9 Type the following program code:

```
Try
    'Specify current page settings
    PrintDocument1.DefaultPageSettings = PrintPageSettings
    'Specify document for print preview dialog box and show
    StringToPrint = RichTextBox1.Text
    PrintPreviewDialog1.Document = PrintDocument1
    PrintPreviewDialog1.ShowDialog()
Catch ex As Exception
    'Display error message
    MessageBox.Show(ex.Message)
End Try
```

In a similar way, the *btnPreview_Click* event procedure assigns the *PrintPageSettings* variable to the *DefaultPageSettings* property of the *PrintDocument1* object, and then it copies the text in the rich text box object to the *StringToPrint* variable and opens the Print Preview dialog box. Print Preview automatically uses the page settings data to display a visual representation of the document as it will be printed— you don't need to display this information manually.

Now you'll make a slight modification to the program code in the *btnOpen_Click* event procedure.

10 Scroll up to the *btnOpen_Click* event procedure in the Code Editor.

This is the procedure that displays the Open dialog box, opens a text file, and enables the printing buttons. Because you just added two new printing buttons, you have to add program code to enable the Page Setup and Print Preview buttons.

11 Scroll to the bottom of the event procedure, just before the final Catch code block, and locate the following program statement:

```
    btnPrint.Enabled = True
```

12 Below that statement, add the following lines of code:

```
btnSetup.Enabled = True
btnPreview.Enabled = True
```

Now your program will enable the print buttons when there's a document available to print.

13 Click the Save All button on the toolbar to save your changes.

Test the Page Setup and Print Preview features

1   Click the Start button on the toolbar.

> ▶   **Note**   The complete Print Dialogs program is located in the
>   c:\vbnet03sbs\chap18\print dialogs folder.

The program opens, and only the first button object is enabled.

2   Click the Open button, and then open the longfile.txt file in the
c:\vbnet03sbs\chap18 folder.

The remaining three button objects are now enabled, as shown here:

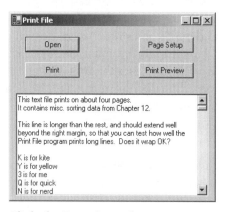

3   Click the Page Setup button.

Your program displays the Page Setup dialog box, as shown here:

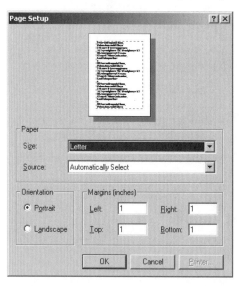

Page Setup has numerous useful options, including the ability to change the paper size and source, the orientation of the printing (Portrait or Landscape), and the page margins (Left, Right, Top, and Bottom).

4 Change the Left margin to 2, and then click OK.

The left margin will now be 2 inches.

5 Click the Print Preview button.

Your program displays the Print Preview dialog box, as shown in the following illustration:

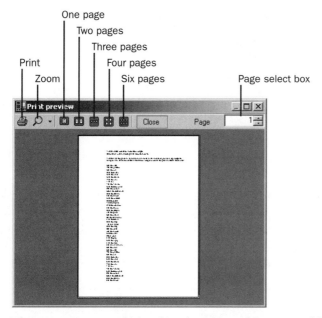

The Print Preview dialog box has several recognizable buttons and preview features, especially if you've used the Print Preview command in Microsoft Word or Microsoft Excel. The Zoom, One Page, Two Pages, Three Pages, Four Pages, Six Pages, and Page Select Box controls all work automatically in the dialog box. No program code is required to make them operate.

6 Click the Four Pages button to see your document four pages at a time.

7 Click the Maximize button on the Print Preview title bar to see the window full size.

8 Click the arrow to the right of the Zoom button, and click 150 percent.

Your screen will look like this:

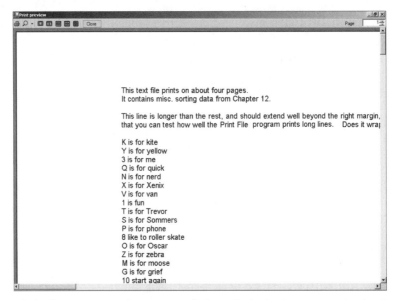

This text file prints on about four pages.
It contains misc. sorting data from Chapter 12.

This line is longer than the rest, and should extend well beyond the right margin, that you can test how well the Print File program prints long lines.   Does it wra;

K is for kite
Y is for yellow
3 is for me
Q is for quick
N is for nerd
X is for Xenix
V is for van
1 is fun
T is for Trevor
S is for Sommers
P is for phone
8 like to roller skate
O is for Oscar
Z is for zebra
M is for moose
G is for grief
10 start again

9 Click the One Page button, and then click the Up arrow in the Page Select box to view pages 2–4.

As you can see, this Print Preview window is quite impressive—and you incorporated it into your program with just a few lines of code!

10 Click the Close button to close the Print Preview dialog box, and then click the Close button to close the program. You're done working with printers for now.

Lesson 18 Quick Reference

To	Do this
Incorporate the *PrintDocument* class in your projects and prepare for printing	Add the following *Imports* statement to the top of your form: `Imports System.Drawing.Printing`

Create a printing event handler	Use the *AddHandler* statement and the *AddressOf* operator. For example:
	
	`AddHandler PrintDocument1.PrintPage, _`
	`        AddressOf Me.PrintGraphic`

To	Do this
Create a *PrintDocument* object in your project	Double-click the *PrintDocument* control on the Windows Forms tab of the Toolbox. *or* Include the following variable declaration in your program code: ```Dim PrintDoc As New PrintDocument```

Print graphics from a printing event handler	Use the *Graphics.DrawImage* method. For example:
	
	```ev.Graphics.DrawImage(Image.FromFile _```
	``` (TextBox1.Text), ev.Graphics.VisibleClipBounds)```

Print text from a printing event handler	Use the *Graphics.DrawString* method in an event handler. For example:
	
	```ev.Graphics.DrawString(TextBox1.Text, _```
	``` New Font("Arial", 11, FontStyle.Regular), _```
	``` Brushes.Black, 120, 120)```

Call a printing event handler	Use the *Print* method of an object of type *PrintDocument*. For example: ```PrintDoc.Print()```
Print multipage text documents	Write a handler for the *PrintPage* event, which receives an argument of the type *PrintPageEventArgs*. Compute the rectangular area on the page for the text, use the *MeasureString* method to determine how much text will fit on the current page, and use the *DrawString* method to print the text on the page. If additional pages are needed, set the *HasMorePages* property to True. When all text has been printed, set *HasMorePages* to False.

Open a text file by using the *FileStream* class, and load it into a *RichTextBox* object	Create a variable of type *FileStream*, specifying the path and file mode, load the stream into a *RichTextBox*, and then close the stream. For example:
	
	```Imports System.IO 'at the top of the form```
	```...```
	```Dim MyFileStream As New FileStream(_```
	``` FilePath, FileMode.Open)```
	```RichTextBox1.LoadFile(MyFileStream, _```
	``` RichTextBoxStreamType.PlainText)```
	```MyFileStream.Close()```

Display printing dialog boxes in your programs	Use the *PrintDialog*, *PrintPreviewDialog*, and *PageSetupDialog* controls on the Windows Forms tab of the Toolbox.

Database Programming

Chapter 19

Getting Started with ADO.NET

In this chapter, you will learn how to:

- Use Server Explorer to establish a connection to a database.

- Create a data adapter that extracts specific database information.

- Create a dataset to represent one or more database tables in your program.

- Use *TextBox*, *Label*, and *Button* controls to display database information and navigation controls on a Windows Form.

In Part 5, you'll learn how to work with information stored in databases. You'll learn about ADO.NET, Microsoft's newest paradigm for working with database information, and you'll learn how to display, modify, and search for database information by using a combination of program code and Windows Forms controls. Microsoft Visual Basic .NET was specifically designed to create custom interfaces, or *front ends*, for existing databases, so if you'd like to customize or dress up data that you've already created with another application, such as Microsoft Access, you can get started immediately.

In this chapter, you'll take your first steps with ADO.NET database programming. You'll use the Server Explorer window to establish a connection to an Access database on your system, you'll configure the connection by using the Data Link Properties dialog box, you'll use a data adapter to select the data table that you want to use, and you'll create a dataset based on the table that will represent a portion of the database in your program. After you've completed these preliminary steps, you'll use the *TextBox*, *Label*, and *Button* controls to display database information on a Windows Form.

Upgrade Notes: What's New in Visual Basic .NET?

If you're experienced with Visual Basic 6, you'll notice some new features in Visual Basic .NET, including the following:

- The Remote Data Objects (RDO) and ActiveX Data Objects (ADO) data access models have been replaced by the ADO.NET data access model. ADO.NET offers a wider range of data access possibilities than its predecessors and is based on a recent Microsoft data access technology.

- ADO.NET is the standard data model for all programs in Microsoft Visual Studio .NET, including Microsoft Visual Basic .NET, Microsoft Visual C++ .NET, Microsoft J# .NET, and Microsoft Visual C# .NET.

- The familiar *Data* control and ADO *Data* control are no longer available in Visual Basic .NET. To display data on a form, you typically create a data adapter and a dataset, and then add controls to your form that can display the data and allow users to navigate from one record to the next.

- In Visual Basic 6, database information was represented in a program by the recordset object. In Visual Basic .NET, database information is represented by the dataset object, a disconnected image of the database table you're accessing.

- The internal data format of ADO.NET is XML, making it easier to use existing XML data sources and to use ADO.NET in programs designed for the Web.

- In Visual Studio .NET 2003, ADO.NET gained additional connectivity in the form of the .NET Framework Data Provider for ODBC and the .NET Framework Data Provider for Oracle. These tools provide access to native ODBC providers as well as to Oracle databases using the Oracle Call Interface.

Database Programming with ADO.NET

A *database* is an organized collection of information stored in a file. You can create powerful databases by using any of a variety of database products, including Microsoft Access, Microsoft FoxPro, Btrieve, Paradox, Oracle, and Microsoft SQL Server. You can also store and transmit database information by using XML (Extensible Markup Language), a file format designed for exchanging structured data over the Internet and in other settings.

Creating and maintaining databases has become an essential task for all major corporations, government institutions, non-profit agencies, and most small businesses. Rich data resources—be they customer addresses, manufacturing inventories, account balances, employee records, donor lists, or order histories—have become the lifeblood of the business world.

Microsoft Visual Basic .NET isn't designed for creating new databases, but rather for displaying, analyzing, and manipulating the information in existing databases. Although previous versions of Visual Basic have also provided this capability, Visual Basic .NET offers a new data model called ADO.NET that provides access to an even greater number of database formats. In particular, ADO.NET has been designed for Internet use, meaning that it uses the same method for accessing local, client-server, and Internet-based data sources. As a testimony to Microsoft's goal of making ADO.NET a great technology for manipulating databases over the Internet, Microsoft has made XML—a standard defined by the World Wide Web Consortium—the internal data format of ADO.NET. Using XML in this way makes ADO.NET easier to utilize with existing Internet data sources, and it makes it easier for software vendors to write data adapters, or "providers," that convert third-party database formats to be compatible with ADO.NET.

Database Terminology

When working with databases and ADO.NET, it's important to understand some basic database terminology. *Fields* are the categories of information stored in a database. Typical fields in a customer database might include customer names, addresses, phone numbers, and comments. All the information about a particular customer or business is called a *record*. When databases are created, information is entered in tables of fields and records. Records correspond to rows in a table, and fields correspond to columns, as shown here:

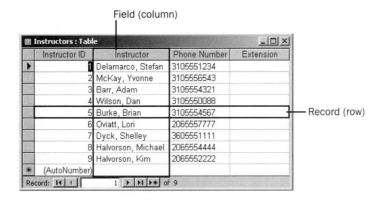

In ADO.NET, various objects are used to retrieve and modify information in a database. The following illustration shows an overview of the approach that will be covered in more detail in this chapter:

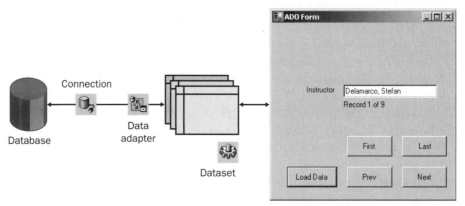

Form with bound controls

First a *connection* is made, which specifies connection information about the database. Next a *data adapter* is created, which manages retrieving data from the database and posting data changes. Then a *dataset* is created, which is a representation of one or more database tables you plan to work with in your program. (You don't manipulate the actual data, but rather a copy of it.) Information in the dataset can then be bound to controls on a form.

Working with an Access Database

In the following sections, you'll learn how to use the ADO.NET data access technology in Visual Basic .NET. You'll get started by using Server Explorer to establish a connection to a database named Students.mdb that I created in Microsoft Access. Students.mdb contains various tables of academic information that would be useful for a teacher who's tracking student coursework or a school administrator who's scheduling rooms, assigning classes, or building a time schedule. You'll learn how to create a dataset based on a table of information in the Students database, and you'll display this information on a Windows Form. When you've finished, you'll be able to put these skills to work in your own database projects.

▶ **Tip**   Although the sample in this chapter uses a Microsoft Access database, you don't have to have Microsoft Access installed. Visual Studio and ADO.NET include the necessary support to understand the Access file format as well as other formats.

Establish a connection to a database

1 Start Visual Studio .NET, and create a new Visual Basic Windows Application project named **My ADO Form** in the c:\vbnet03sbs\chap19 folder.

A new project appears in the development environment.

2 On the View menu, click the Server Explorer command.

The Server Explorer window appears in the development environment, as shown here:

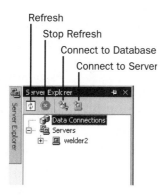

▶ **Tip** Depending on your configuration and edition of Visual Studio, the Connect To Server button and the Servers node might not be displayed. These options aren't required to complete the steps in this chapter.

Server Explorer is a graphical tool that lets you establish connections to local, client-server, or Internet-based data sources. Using Server Explorer, you can view the structure of database tables and learn more about the attributes of tables, fields, and records in a database. You can also log on to network servers and explore the databases and system services that they offer. Finally, you can drag database components, or *nodes*, from Server Explorer and drop them onto Visual Studio .NET designers, such as the Windows Forms Designer. This process creates new data components that are preconfigured to reference the database item you selected.

3   Click the Connect To Database button in Server Explorer.

Before you can manipulate the information in a database, you need to establish a connection to it. The Connect To Database button begins that process by opening the Data Link Properties dialog box, which lets you specify information about the database format, the database location and password (if necessary), and other information.

▶   **Tip**   You can also open the Data Link Properties dialog box by clicking the Connect To Database command on the Tools menu.

4   Click the Provider tab in the dialog box.

A *provider* (or *managed provider*) is an underlying database component that knows how to connect to a database and extract data from it. The two most popular types of providers offered by Visual Studio .NET are OLE DB and SQL, but there are also third-party providers available for many of the most popular database formats. In this example, you'll use the Microsoft Jet 4.0 OLE DB provider, a component designed to connect to Microsoft Access databases.

5   Click Microsoft Jet 4.0 OLE DB Provider on the Provider tab.

Your screen will look like this:

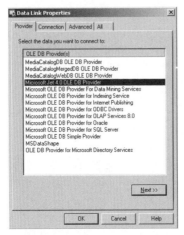

6   Click the Next button to display the Connection tab of the Data Link Properties dialog box.

Because you selected a Jet OLE DB format, which is the internal format of Microsoft Access, the Connection tab has been configured to receive information about the name, location, and logon information of an Access database.

7   Click the ellipsis button next to the Select Or Enter A Database
      Name field, select the Students.mdb database in the
      c:\vbnet03sbs\chap19 folder, and then click Open.

   Your screen will look like this:

   ▶   **Tip**   You can specify your own database if you like, but you'll need to
       modify the steps in this chapter accordingly to fit your database's struc-
       ture.

8   Click the Test Connection button on the Connection tab.

   Visual Studio attempts to establish a database connection with the
   Students.mdb database. If the message "Test Connection Succeeded"
   appears in a message box, you know the provider is working properly and that your database is structured in a recognizable format. If
   Visual Studio detects a problem at this point, verify that you're using
   an appropriate provider and that you selected a database file, and
   then try the connection again.

9   Click OK in the Test Connection Succeeded message box to continue,
      and then click OK in the Data Link Properties dialog box.

   Visual Studio completes your connection and adds a node representing your database to Server Explorer.

10 Open the Data Connections node, the ACCESS node, and finally the Tables node in Server Explorer.

To open nodes in Server Explorer, click the plus signs (+), which function as toggle switches. The structure of the Students database appears in Server Explorer, as shown here:

Server Explorer provides this great advantage: it lets you see how a database is organized graphically so that you can immediately make use of its tables, fields, and other objects.

Creating a Data Adapter

Now that you have an active database connection, you need to create a *data adapter* to extract specific information from the database for your program to use. A data adapter defines the specific information you'll use and serves as a foundation for the dataset object, which is the representation of the data you want to use in your program. Creating a data adapter is a required step when using a dataset because some databases are highly structured and have many tables to choose from—much more than you might want to make use of in a single program. You might think of a data adapter as a kind of filter for the data.

Visual Studio provides several mechanisms for creating data adapters in a program. The easiest way is to simply drag a graphical table icon from Server Explorer to the Windows Forms Designer. (This procedure creates a data adapter object in the component tray directly below the form.) However, the following exercise shows you how to create a data adapter by using a second method—a tool called the Data Adapter Configuration Wizard. This tool is easy to use, and it gives you the opportunity to fine-tune your data selection by writing a SQL SELECT statement. You launch the wizard by dragging the *Ole-DbDataAdapter* control from the Data tab of the Toolbox onto a form. Give this second method a try now.

Use the *OleDbDataAdapter* control

1 Open the Toolbox, and click the Data tab.

The Data tab contains controls that help you access data in your programs. If you're familiar with Visual Basic 6, you'll see that the *Data* and ADO *Data* controls are no longer provided. Instead, you access data by adding a data adapter object and a dataset object to your program's component tray.

> ▶ **Tip** The *OleDbConnection* and *SqlConnection* controls can also be used to establish a connection between your program and a data source on a local computer, network server, or Internet resource. However, you already created a database connection using Server Explorer in this chapter, so using the *OleDbConnection* control isn't necessary now.

2 Drag the *OleDbDataAdapter* control from the Data tab of the Toolbox to the form.

The *OleDbDataAdapter* control is designed to handle connections to Access/Jet databases and many other popular database formats. When you drag the control to your form, Visual Studio starts the Data Adapter Configuration Wizard.

3 Read the opening statement about data adapters, and then click Next.

The second wizard dialog box appears, prompting you for the name of a valid data adapter. Your screen should look like this:

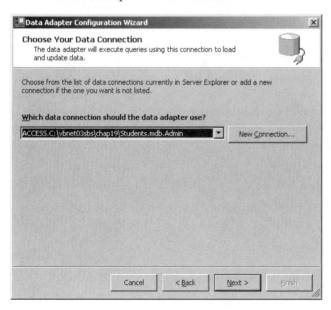

Because you already created a data connection to an Access database by using Server Explorer, the connection appears in the drop-down list box. (If you hadn't created the connection or wanted to create a new one, you could do so now by clicking the New Connection button.)

4   Click Next to continue configuring the data adapter.

You'll see the following dialog box asking you how the data adapters should access data in the database:

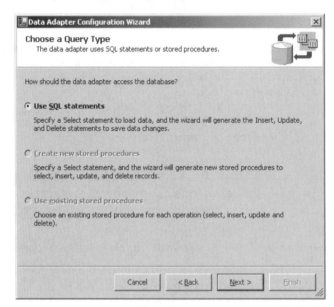

The first option, Use SQL Statements, gives you the opportunity to create a SQL SELECT statement that will fine-tune, or *filter*, the data you plan to use. For Visual Basic users who are familiar with database programming, writing Access queries, or using SQL Server, creating a SQL SELECT statement is relatively straightforward. If you're not familiar with this syntax, however, you can use the Query Builder tool to visually generate an appropriate SELECT statement. We'll use the Query Builder in the following steps.

5   Click Next to accept the Use SQL Statements option.

You'll see the following dialog box, which prompts you for a valid SQL SELECT statement:

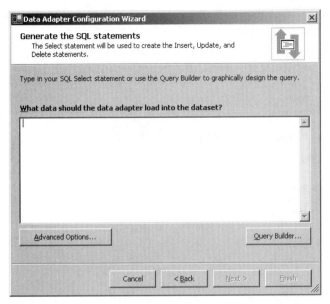

6   Click the Query Builder button to build your SELECT statement graphically.

The Add Table dialog box appears, as shown here:

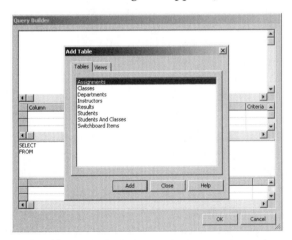

To build your SELECT statement, you need to pick one or more tables provided by the Students.mdb database.

7   Click Instructors, click Add, and then click Close.

Visual Studio displays the graphical Query Builder tool, which now contains a representation of the Instructors table.

8   In the Instructors table, click the check boxes next to the Instructor and InstructorID fields.

The Query Builder creates a SELECT statement that extracts the Instructor and InstructorID fields from the Instructors table, as shown here:

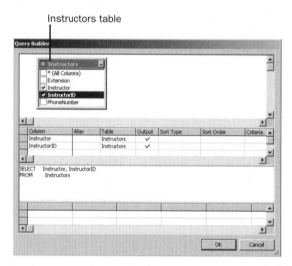

Instructors table

In this example, you're just extracting two fields from the table, but you can easily create a SQL SELECT statement that extracts several fields from one or more tables. The InstructorID field is shown in bold type because it's acting as the *primary key* for the database table.

9   Click OK to complete the SELECT statement.

The Generate The SQL Statements dialog box reappears with your new SELECT statement. (You might want to remember this simple syntax—you can use it to write your own SELECT statements without using the Query Builder in the future.)

10   Click the Finish button.

If you see a dialog box prompting you for password information, click Don't Include Password. Visual Studio adds the completed data adapter to the component tray beneath your form. Visual Studio also adds a representation of the *OleDbConnection* object to the component tray. Each object is identified by a unique number because you can have more than one data connection or data adapter in a project. Your screen looks like this:

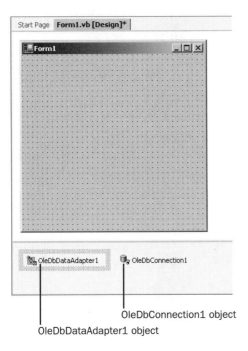

OleDbConnection1 object

OleDbDataAdapter1 object

Working with Datasets

The next step in ADO.NET database programming is creating an object that represents the data you want to use in your program. As I mentioned earlier, this object is called the dataset, and it's a representation of the data provided by the data connection object and extracted by the data adapter object. A dataset can contain information from one or more database tables, and the contents can also be the result of a SQL SELECT statement, like the one you just used to extract data from the Students.mdb database. Unlike recordsets, the mechanisms for accessing data in previous versions of Visual Basic, datasets only *represent* the data in a database—when you modify a dataset, you don't actually modify the underlying database tables until you issue a command that writes your changes back to the original database.

In the following exercise, you'll create a dataset that represents the Instructor field of the Instructors table in the Students.mdb database. As you'll see, creating a dataset is easy once you have a properly configured data adapter to build on.

Create a dataset to hold Instructor data

1   Click the form to make sure that it's active.

If the form doesn't have the focus, the command you need to create a dataset isn't available on the Data menu.

2   Click the Generate Dataset command on the Data menu.

The Generate Dataset dialog box appears.

3   In the New box, set the name of the new dataset to DsInstructors.

4   Verify that the Add This Dataset To The Designer check box is selected so that Visual Studio will add the new dataset to the component tray.

Your dialog box will look like this:

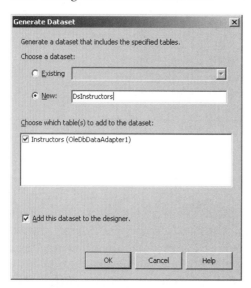

5   Click OK to create a dataset for the Instructor field and add it to your project.

The dataset appears in the component tray, as shown here:

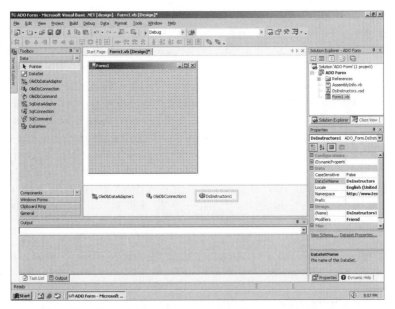

Visual Studio also adds a file named DsInstructors.xsd to Solution Explorer that represents the database *schema* you just added to your project. This schema is an XML file that describes the tables, fields, data types, and other elements in the dataset. Typed datasets have a schema (.xsd) file associated with them, but un-typed datasets don't. Typed datasets with schema files are advantageous because they enable the statement completion feature of the Visual Studio Code Editor, and they give you specific information about the fields and tables you're using.

Now that you've created a dataset, you're ready to display the records from the Instructors table on your form by using bound controls.

Using Bound Controls to Display Database Information on a Form

After several steps and procedures, you're finally ready to display some database information on your form. This is the exciting part—but how do you actually do it? Rather than re-creating an Access database table on your form, Visual Basic allows you to display only the fields and records that you want to—you can present an entire grid of database information for your users or only the specific fields that you want them to see. In addition, you can supply a navigation mechanism so that users can browse through all the records in a database, or you can display only specific records. Finally, of course, you can allow your users to modify or even delete information in the underlying database,

19

ADO.NET

or you can limit their activity to simply viewing database records. In short, Visual Basic allows you to create a database viewer, or *front end*, that presents only the information and data access features that you want your users to have. Although I haven't discussed it, most of the controls on the Windows Forms tab of the Toolbox have the built-in ability to display database information on a form. In Visual Basic terminology, these controls are typically called *bound controls*. A control is said to be bound to a data source when its *DataBindings* properties are set to valid fields (or columns) in a dataset. After the connection has been established, you can display database information by using methods and properties in the ADO.NET object model. A few of the controls on the Windows Forms tab of the Toolbox that can display database information include *TextBox*, *ComboBox*, *ListBox*, *CheckBox*, *RadioButton*, *DataGrid*, and *PictureBox*.

▶ **Tip**   For specific information about using the *DataGrid* control to display database information, see Chapter 20.

The following exercise shows how you can add a text box object to your form to display information from the Instructors table of the Students.mdb database.

Use a *TextBox* object to display data

1   Use the *TextBox* control to draw a text box object in the middle of the form.

Make the text box object wide enough to display the first and last names of a hypothetical instructor from the Students.mdb database.

2   Use the *Label* control to draw a label object to the left of the text box object.

3   Use the *Button* control to draw one button object in the lower left corner of the form.

4   Set the following property settings for the objects on the form:

Object	Property	Setting
TextBox1	*Name*	txtInstructor
	Text	(empty)
Label1	*Name*	lblInstructor
	Text	"Instructor"
	TextAlign	MiddleRight
Button1	*Name*	btnLoad
	Text	"Load Data"
Form1	*Text*	"ADO Form"

Your form should look like this:

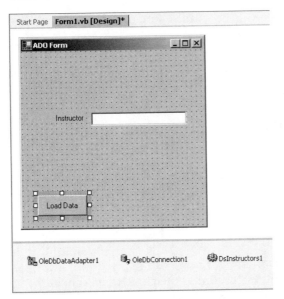

Now you'll bind the Instructor field to the text box object (*txtInstructor*).

5   Click the text box object on the form, and then open the Properties window.

I recommend that you undock and widen the Properties window so that you have plenty of room to see the structure of the Instructors table in the database.

6   Open the DataBindings category, click the *Text* property, and then click the drop-down arrow.

The Properties window displays a list of data sources that you can bind to the text box. If you've completed the previous exercises, you'll see a dataset object named *DsInstructors1* in the drop-down list box.

7   Click the plus sign (+) to expand the *DsInstructors1* dataset, and then expand the Instructors table beneath it.

You'll see the following database structure in the Properties window:

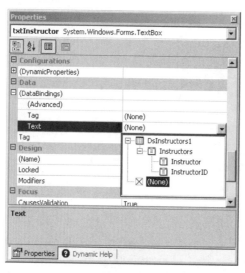

As you might recall, Instructors is the name of a table in the Students.mdb database, and Instructor is a field within the table containing the names of teachers that work at a hypothetical college.

8   Click the Instructor field to select it as the field that will be displayed in the *txtInstructor* text box. Be sure to click the "Instructor" text and not the icon; otherwise, the Instructor field won't be selected.

The dataset, table, and field names appear in the *Text* property setting of the Properties window. Now you're ready to write the program code that loads data into the dataset and displays it in the text box object.

9   Restore the Properties window, double-click the Load Data button, and then type the following program code in the *btnLoad_Click* event procedure of the Code Editor:

```
DsInstructors1.Clear()
OleDbDataAdapter1.Fill(DsInstructors1)
```

You must manually fill the data adapter with data by using the *Fill* method, which subsequently loads, or *populates*, the bound text box object on your form with information from the dataset you defined earlier. Although this might feel like an extra step, it's accomplished easily with two lines of program code. In this context, the *Clear* method is necessary so that records returned by subsequent queries to the database aren't appended to the dataset. Using ADO.NET does sometimes require additional steps that weren't needed in ADO and Visual Basic.

> ▶ **Tip**   For demonstration purposes, I've placed these two lines into a but-
> ton event procedure, but you could just as easily place them in the
> *Form1_Load* event procedure so that the text box object is populated
> when the opening form is displayed.

10 Click the Start button to run the ADO Form program.

The ADO Form program runs in the development environment.
Note that there's currently no instructor name in the text box.

11 Click the Load Data button.

After a moment, the name "Delamarco, Stefan" appears in the text
box, as shown in the following illustration. This is the first instructor
name in the Students database.

12 Click the Close button on the form to stop the program.

You've successfully displayed an instructor name from the Students
database. Now it's time to add some more sophisticated features to
your database front end.

Creating Navigation Controls

Right now, the ADO Form program displays the first instructor name in the
Students.mdb database. But how do you browse through the list of instructor
names, and how do you make jumps to the first record or the last record in the
database? ADO.NET keeps track of information about the current record and
the total number of records by using an object named the *CurrencyManager*.
There's a *CurrencyManager* object for each dataset, and each Windows Form
has a *BindingContext* object that keeps track of all the *CurrencyManager*
objects on the form.

In the following exercise, you'll create button objects named First, Last, Prev, and Next in the ADO Form program that provide basic database navigation features for the user. After you create these buttons on your form, you'll add program code to each button's *Click* event procedure that displays a different database record by using the *BindingContext* object, the *DsInstructors1* dataset, and the Instructors table. You can also customize this program code to fit your own needs by substituting my dataset and table names with parameters from your own database structure.

Add First, Last, Prev, and Next buttons

1   Display the ADO Form user interface, and then use the *Button* control to create four button objects on your form.

   Add two button objects in the middle of the form and two at the bottom of the form.

2   Set the following properties for the button objects:

Object	Property	Setting
Button1	*Name*	btnFirst
	Text	"First"
Button2	*Name*	btnLast
	Text	"Last"
Button3	*Name*	btnPrev
	Text	"Prev"
Button4	*Name*	btnNext
	Text	"Next"

Your form should look like this:

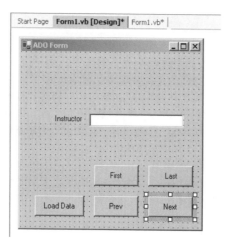

Now you'll add the program code that enables the navigation functionality of the buttons.

3   Double-click the First button.

The *btnFirst_Click* event procedure appears in the Code Editor.

4   Type the following program code:

```
Me.BindingContext(DsInstructors1, "Instructors").Position = 0
```

This is the syntax for using the *BindingContext* object to display the first record in the *DsInstructors1* dataset of the Instructors table. The program statement sets the *Position* property to 0, which changes the current record in the dataset to the first record. (Like arrays and collections, datasets start their numbering at the 0 position.) Also note the use of the *Me* object, which specifically identifies the *BindingContext* object for the current form.

5   Display the form, and then double-click the Last button.

The *btnLast_Click* event procedure appears in the Code Editor.

6   Type the following program code:

```
Me.BindingContext(DsInstructors1, "Instructors").Position = _
    Me.BindingContext(DsInstructors1, "Instructors").Count - 1
```

This long statement (broken into two lines) causes the last record in the dataset to be displayed on the form. It's a variation of the *BindingContext* statement that precedes it, but rather than setting the *Position* property to 0, this statement sets the current record to the value held in the *Count* property minus 1. *Count* is the total number of records in the dataset. One is subtracted because the dataset is zero-based.

7   Display the form, and then double-click the Prev button.

The *btnPrev_Click* event procedure appears in the Code Editor.

8   Type the following program code:

```
Me.BindingContext(DsInstructors1, "Instructors").Position -= 1
```

This statement displays the previous record in the dataset by subtracting 1 from the current record. Although this statement won't have meaning if the current record is already 0, it won't create a syntax error—ADO.NET won't let the current record be a number less than zero. Note the use of the -= syntax in this statement to decrement the *Position* property. This is the math shortcut syntax I first introduced for decrementing variables in Chapter 5.

9   Display the form, and then double-click the Next button.

The *btnNext_Click* event procedure appears in the Code Editor.

10 Type the following program code:

```
Me.BindingContext(DsInstructors1, "Instructors").Position += 1
```

This statement increments the *Position* property to display the next record in the dataset. Notice that I used the math shortcut operator += here to update the *Position* property using a minimum of program code.

Now you'll run the updated program, and test the navigation buttons you just configured.

11 Click the Start button on the Standard toolbar.

The program runs in the development environment.

12 Click the Load Data button to populate the text box on the form with the first instructor name in the dataset.

13 Click the Next button to display the next database record.

Your form will look like this:

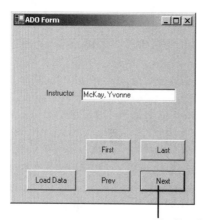

The Next button displays
the next instructor name

14 Click the Prev button to display the first record again.

15 Click the Next button several times to browse through several instructor names in the list.

16 Click the First button to display the first record in the dataset.

17 Click the Last button to display the last record in the dataset.

Notice that the program doesn't produce an error if you display the last record and then click Next. In addition, the program doesn't produce an error if you display the first record and then click Prev. This error handling is built into the *BindingContext* object.

18 Click the Close button on the form to stop the program.

One Step Further: Displaying the Current Record Position

In addition to providing basic navigation tools on your form, you might want to provide some indication of the current record number on the form, along with the total number of records in the dataset. You can accomplish this by creating a label object on the form to display the current position. The current position count is held in the *Position* property of the *BindingContext* object, as you've already learned. If you want to update the current position when each of the navigation buttons is used, you should create a procedure at the top of the form's program code to determine the current position and display it on the form.

In the following exercise, you'll create a Sub procedure named *Count* that declares two variables to track the total number of records and the current record and then displays this information by using the *Text* property of a new label named *lblCount*.

Create a *Count* procedure to display current record statistics

1. Display the form, and then use the *Label* control to draw a wide label object directly below the text box object.

2. Set the *Name* property of the label object to lblCount.

3. Set the *Text* property of the label object to "Record 0 of 0".

4. Click the View Code button in Solution Explorer to display the Code Editor.

5. Scroll to the top of the Code Editor, and place the cursor below the tag "Windows Form Designer generated code".

   By placing procedures in the *Form* class, the procedure can be accessed from anywhere within the form.

6. Type the following program code for the *Count* Sub procedure. (Note that Visual Basic adds the *End Sub* statement automatically.)

```
Private Sub Count()
    Dim Records, Current As Integer
    Records = Me.BindingContext( _
      DsInstructors1, "Instructors").Count
    Current = Me.BindingContext( _
      DsInstructors1, "Instructors").Position + 1
    lblCount.Text = "Record " & Current.ToString & " of " & _
      Records.ToString
End Sub
```

The *Count* procedure assigns the value of the *Count* property to the *Records* integer variable, and it assigns the value of the *Position* property plus 1 to the *Current* integer variable. 1 is added to the *Position* property because the list of records is zero-based (like arrays and collections)—an interesting detail for programmers, but not something that the user should see. Finally, the *Records* and *Current* variables are converted to strings and copied to the *Text* property of the *lblCount* object along with some formatting information so that the label will appear in the following format: *Record x of y*, where *x* is the value of the *Current* variable, and *y* is the value of the *Records* variable.

Now you need to add a call to the *Count* procedure to each of the five button event procedures in the ADO Form program. This is important because each button performs a navigation activity, so the label needs to be updated appropriately each time that the *Position* property changes.

7   Scroll down to the *btnFirst_Click* event procedure, add a blank line to the procedure at the bottom, and type the following procedure call:

```
Count()
```

Your event procedure should now look like this (although the first line doesn't need to be broken):

```
Private Sub btnFirst_Click(ByVal sender As System.Object, _
  ByVal e As System.EventArgs) Handles btnFirst.Click
    Me.BindingContext(DsInstructors1, "Instructors").Position = 0
    Count()
End Sub
```

8   Repeat this step by adding a call to the *Count* procedure in each of the following event procedures in your program: *btnLast_Click*, *btnPrev_Click*, *btnNext_Click*, and *btnLoad_Click*.

That's it! Now you're ready to run the program and see how the current record statistics work.

9   Click the Start button to run the program.

▶   **Note**   The complete ADO Form program is located in the c:\vbnet03sbs\chap19\ado form folder.

10 Click the Load Data button.

The form is populated with data, and the first instructor name appears. In addition, the text "Record 1 of 9" appears below the text box in the new label you created. Your form should look like this:

11 Click the Next button several times to see the current record statistics change as you scroll through the instructor records in the dataset.

12 Click the Prev, First, and Last buttons to verify that the *Count* procedure works for those navigation buttons, too.

13 Click the Close button on the program's title bar to stop the ADO Form application.

That's it! You've written your first database front end with Visual Basic and ADO.NET. Although you used a Microsoft Access database in this example, you'll find that the basic data access techniques are very similar for other types of database information, including SQL Server databases and databases stored at remote locations, such as network servers or the Internet. The reason for this similarity is the distributed architecture of ADO.NET, which uses a similar mechanism for establishing connections, configuring data adapters, and creating datasets based on diverse data resources.

Although it takes several steps to establish the basic connections and settings in an ADO.NET session, the advantage of this upfront work is that manipulating database information on a form is a very uniform process. This is the case even when the data you're using has come from a remote setting or is the result of combining different database tables or data formats. In the next chapter, you'll continue working with database information by exploring how to use the *Data-Grid* control to work with several database records at once.

Data Access in a Web Forms Environment

The data access techniques discussed in this chapter were designed for use in a Windows Forms environment—the fundamental Visual Studio designer you've used to build most of the programs in this book. However, you can also use ADO.NET programming techniques in a Web Forms environment, which allows you to share data resources over the Internet and write database front ends that are accessible through a Web browser such as Internet Explorer. The major differences between the Windows Forms environment and the Web Forms environment are covered in Chapter 22. For additional information about writing database applications in a Web Forms environment, see "Introduction to Data Access in Web Forms Pages" in the Visual Basic online Help.

Lesson 19 Quick Reference

To	Do this
Establish a connection to a database	Click the Server Explorer command on the View menu, click the Connect To Database button, and identify the database that you want to access by using the Data Link Properties dialog box.
Create a data adapter	Click the Data tab in the Toolbox, drag the *OleDbDataAdapter* control or *SqlDataAdapter* control to the form, and then specify the database information that you want to use in the Data Adapter Configuration Wizard.
Create a dataset	Click the Generate Dataset command on the Data menu, specify a name for the dataset, and then verify that the Add This Dataset To The Designer check box is selected.
Binding a Windows Forms control to an active dataset	Add a suitable control to the form, open the Properties window, and then set one of the control's *DataBinding* properties to a valid field (column) in the dataset. (One of the most useful *DataBinding* properties is *Text*.)
Fill a dataset with data and populate any bound control on a Windows Form	Place the following program statement in the event procedure that should populate the form's controls. (Substitute the adapter and dataset names with your own.) `OleDbDataAdapter1.Fill(DsInstructors1)`
Add navigation controls to a Windows Form	Create button objects on the form, and add statements that update the *Position* property of the *BindingContext* object in each button's *Click* event procedure. For example, the following program statement displays the next record in a dataset named *DsInstructors1* and in a table named *Instructors*: `Me.BindingContext(DsInstructors1, _` `  "Instructors").Position += 1`

Data Presentation Using the *DataGrid* Control

In this chapter, you will learn how to:

- Create a data grid object on a Windows Form and use it to display database records.

- Sort database records by column.

- Change the format and color of cells in a data grid.

- Permit changes in data grid cells and write updates to the underlying database.

In Chapter 19, you learned how to use Microsoft ADO.NET database programming techniques to establish a connection to a Microsoft Access database and display fields from the database on a Windows Form. You also learned how to add navigation buttons such as First, Last, Prev, and Next to the form to provide a mechanism for browsing through the records of the database. In this chapter, you'll continue working with the database programming features of Microsoft Visual Basic .NET and the useful classes and objects in ADO.NET. In particular, you'll learn how to use the *DataGrid* control, which allows you to present several fields and records of a database at once.

Upgrade Notes: What's New in Visual Basic .NET?

If you're experienced with Visual Basic 6, you'll notice some new features in Visual Basic .NET, including the following:

- In Visual Basic 6, there were several grid controls that you could use to display database information on a form, including *FlexGrid*, *Hierarchical FlexGrid*, and *DataGrid*. In Visual Basic .NET, the *DataGrid* control is the only spreadsheet-style control that's provided to display database records.

- The *DataGrid* control included with Visual Basic .NET is quite different from the *DataGrid* control included with Visual Basic 6. One important improvement is that the Visual Basic .NET *DataGrid* control doesn't require data-specific commands because the underlying data adapter and dataset objects handle all the data access functionality. However, many of the familiar properties and methods have changed in the new *DataGrid* control. For a list of these updates, see the Visual Basic .NET online Help topic entitled "DataGrid Control Changes in Visual Basic .NET."

Using *DataGrid* to Display Database Records

The *DataGrid* control presents information by establishing a grid of *rows* and *columns* on a form to display data as you might see it in a program such as Microsoft Excel or Microsoft Access. A *DataGrid* control can be used to display any type of tabular data: text, numbers, dates, or the contents of an array. In this chapter, however, you'll focus on *DataGrid*'s ability to display the fields and records of the Students.mdb database, a file of structured student information you started working with in Chapter 19. You'll start by filling a simple data grid object with text from the database, and then you'll set a few formatting options. Next you'll move on to sorting records in the data grid object and learning how to write changes in the data grid back to the underlying database.

The *DataGrid* control is connected, or *bound*, to database information through the DataGrid's *DataSource* and *DataMember* properties. These properties will contain useful information only after your program has established a connection to a valid data source by using a data adapter and a dataset object. (The tools and processes involved in this connection were described in detail in Chapter 19; if you're uncertain how to establish this connection, read the section entitled "Database Programming with ADO.NET" in that chapter.) Once a data grid object is bound to a valid data source, you can populate the object by using the *Fill* method of the data adapter object. The syntax for the *Fill* method looks like this:

```
OleDbDataAdapter1.Fill(DsInstructors1)
```

The following exercises demonstrate how you can display the Instructors table of the Students.mdb database by using a data grid object.

Establish a connection to the Instructors table

1   Start Microsoft Visual Studio .NET, and create a new Visual Basic Windows Application project named **My DataGrid Sample** in the c:\vbnet03sbs\chap20 folder.

    A new project appears in the development environment.

2   On the View menu, click the Server Explorer command.

    The Server Explorer window opens in the development environment. If you just completed the exercises in Chapter 19, there'll be a current connection to an Access database named Students.mdb in Server Explorer under the Data Connections node. If there's a red "x" on the connection, it means that the connection isn't current, but if you click the ACCESS node, it should reestablish itself.

    ▶ **Note**   If you see a valid connection to the Students.mdb database now, don't complete steps 3–7 that follow. I've included steps 3–7 only for readers who didn't complete the exercises in Chapter 19 or for those who completed the exercises some time ago and don't see a valid database connection now. If you see a valid database connection, continue working at step 8.

3   Click the Connect To Database button in Server Explorer.

    As you learned in Chapter 19, the Connect To Database button helps you establish a connection to a database in your program.

4   Click the Provider tab in the Data Link Properties dialog box, and then click the entry Microsoft Jet 4.0 OLE DB Provider.

5   Click the Next button to display the Connection tab of the Data Link Properties dialog box.

    In this tab, you'll specify the name and location of the Access database that you plan to use—Students.mdb.

6   Click the ellipsis button next to the Select Or Enter A Database Name field, select the Students.mdb database in the c:\vbnet03sbs\chap19 folder, and click Open.

7   Click OK in the Data Link Properties dialog box.

Visual Studio completes your connection and adds a node representing your database to Server Explorer.

8   Expand the Data Connections node, the ACCESS node, and then the Tables node in Server Explorer by clicking the plus signs (+).

The structure of the Students database appears in Server Explorer, as shown here:

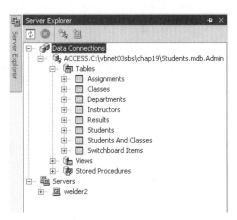

Now you'll create a data adapter for the Instructors table in the database.

9   Open the Toolbox, click the Data tab, and then drag the *OleDb-DataAdapter* control to the form.

When you drag the control to your form, Visual Studio starts the Data Adapter Configuration Wizard.

10   Click the Next button to accept the opening screen.

11   Make sure your data connection to Students.mdb is selected in the Choose Your Data Connection dialog box, and then click Next.

12   Make sure the Use SQL Statements option is selected in the Choose A Query Type dialog box, and then click Next.

You'll see a dialog box prompting you for a valid SQL SELECT statement.

13   Type the following SELECT statement in the text box:

```
SELECT
    Extension,
    Instructor,
    InstructorID,
    PhoneNumber
FROM
    Instructors
```

This statement will retrieve the Extension, Instructor, InstructorID, and PhoneNumber fields from the Instructors table of the Students.mdb database and load them into your data adapter.

Your dialog box will look like this:

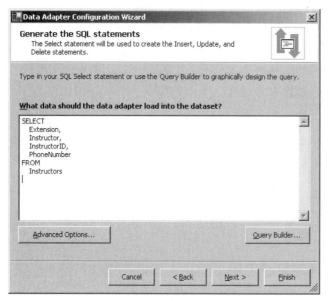

14 Click the Next button to view the wizard results.

The wizard should have successfully created the appropriate SQL statements (SELECT, INSERT, UPDATE, and DELETE) and table mappings. If there are any errors, click the Back button and verify that your SQL statement is correct.

15 Click the Finish button to add the completed data adapter and connection objects to the component tray beneath your form. If you're asked whether you want to include a password in the connection string you've created, click No.

A password isn't necessary in this sample application, but you might want to use one in future database applications as a protection mechanism. Now you'll create a dataset object to represent the Instructors table in your program.

16 Click the form to make sure that it's active, and then click the Generate Dataset command on the Data menu.

The Generate Dataset dialog box appears.

17 In the New box, set the name of the new dataset to DsInstructors.

Verify that the Add This Dataset To The Designer check box is selected so that Visual Studio will add the new dataset to the component tray.

18 Click OK to create a dataset for the Instructors table and add it to your project.

The dataset appears in the component tray with the connection and data adapter objects, as shown here:

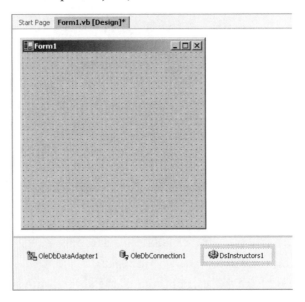

Now that you've established a connection to the Instructors table, you're ready to display the records by using a *DataGrid* control.

Create a data grid object

1 Resize the form so that it's large enough to display 4 columns and about 10 rows of data.

2 Click the Windows Forms tab in the Toolbox, and then click the *DataGrid* control.

3 Create a large data grid object on the form with the *DataGrid* control.

4 Add a *Button* control below the data grid.

Your form should look like this:

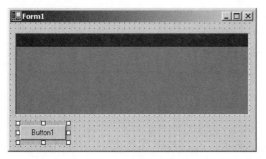

5   Click the data grid on the form, and then open the Properties window.

6   Set the *Anchor* property to all four sides, as shown here:

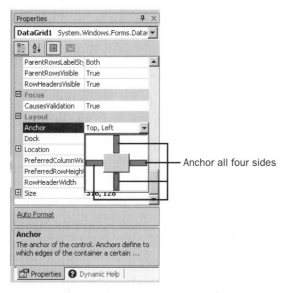

Anchor all four sides

Now you'll use the *DataSource* and *DataMember* properties to bind the data grid object to the *DsInstructors1* dataset.

7   Display the *DataSource* property options in the Properties window.

The *DataSource* property contains the name of the dataset you're displaying in the data grid. Remember that there can be more than one active dataset in a program, so you might have more than one selection here.

8   Click the *DsInstructors1* dataset (not the DsInstructors1.Instructors entry).

The Properties window looks like the following illustration as you pick the *DsInstructors1* dataset:

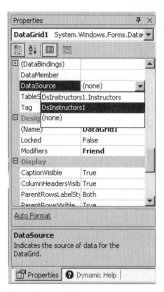

Now you'll use the *DataMember* property to specify the sublist (in this case, the table) that you want to display in the data grid.

9   Click the *DataMember* property, and then click the Instructors entry.

As soon as you specify the *DataMember* property, a grid appears in the data grid object containing the fields you specified in the Instructors table. The fields appear as columns in the grid, and a row is reserved for the first record in the dataset. When you run your program and populate the data grid with data, the specific records in the Students.mdb database will also be added to this grid.

10   Click the form and set its *Text* property to "DataGrid Sample".

11   Click *Button1* on the form, set its *Anchor* property to Bottom, Left, set its *Name* property to btnLoad, and then set its *Text* property to Load. Your form should look like this:

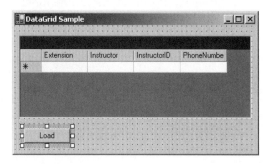

Now you'll add the program code necessary to populate the data grid. You'll add the *Fill* method to the *btnLoad_Click* event procedure.

12 Double-click the Load button to display the *btnLoad_Click* event procedure.

13 Type the following program statements:

```
DsInstructors1.Clear()
OleDbDataAdapter1.Fill(DsInstructors1)
```

The *Clear* method makes sure that no records are present in the dataset from previous queries—it clears the dataset out and prepares it for new data. The *Fill* method fills the dataset with data from the *OleDbDataAdapter1* data adapter—data from the Instructors table of the Students.mdb database.

14 Click the Save All button on the toolbar to save your changes.

You're ready to run the program.

15 Click the Start button on the Standard toolbar.

16 Click the Load button.

The data grid object is populated with data from the dataset. Your screen will look like this:

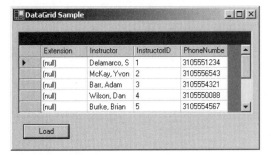

Each row in the grid represents a record of data from the Instructors table in the database. The SELECT statement that we used included all the fields (columns) in the Instructors table, but we could have easily limited the number of fields so that the entire table isn't currently visible or included in the dataset. Notice that the fields are organized in the order you placed them in your SELECT statement—you can change this order by placing the fields in the SELECT statement in a different sequence. Also note that scroll bars appear so that you can view any records that aren't immediately visible. This is a handy ease-of-use feature that comes automatically with the *Data-Grid* control.

17 Scroll down the list of records to view all the database information, which represents instructor data for a college or university.

18 Resize the form to see more of the instructor data.

Because you set the *Anchor* property for the data grid and the button, their size and position adjust accordingly.

Note that you can widen the columns of the data grid (to see their entire contents) by dragging the column cell borders to the right. The following illustration shows what the data grid looks like after the Instructor column has been widened:

Instructor column

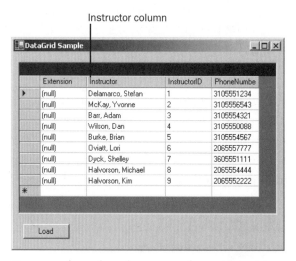

You can also take advantage of an automatic sorting feature of the *DataGrid* control when it's filled with data.

19 Click the Instructor column heading.

The data grid is sorted alphabetically by instructor name. (Barr, Adam is now first.) When database records are sorted, a sorting column, or *key*, is required—you establish this key by clicking on the column heading that you want to use for the sort.

The *DataGrid* provides visual identification for the current sort key—a tiny arrow to the right of the column header. If the arrow is pointed up, the sort order is an alphabetical A–Z list. However, you can click the column heading again and reverse the sort order, making it an alphabetical Z–A list. The arrow acts like a toggle, so you can switch back and forth between sorting directions.

▶ **Tip** Sorting is only allowed in the *DataGrid* control if the *AllowSorting* property is set to True, its default setting. If you don't want to allow sorting, set this property to False at design time.

20

Data Presentation

20   Click the Instructor column several times to see how the sort order can be switched back and forth.

21   Click other column headings such as InstructorID and PhoneNumber to sort the database by those keys.

22   When you're finished experimenting with the scrolling, resizing, and sorting features of the *DataGrid* control, click the Close button on the form to stop the program.

The program closes, and the development environment returns.

Formatting DataGrid Cells

You can control the look and orientation of several DataGrid characteristics with property settings at design time to customize the appearance of your dataset on the form. For example, you can change the default width of cells in the grid, add or remove column headers, change the grid or header background colors, and change the color of the gridlines. The following exercise steps you through some of these useful property settings.

Set data grid properties at design time

1   Display the form and click the data grid object, and then open the Properties window.

2   Set the *PreferredColumnWidth* property to 110.

A setting of 110 (measured in pixels) will provide enough room for the data in the fields in the Instructors table.

3   Set the *ColumnHeadersVisible* property to False.

This property setting will remove the field names from the table. This is useful if the field names in your database don't clearly identify their contents or if the field names contain abbreviations or words that you want to hide from your users.

4   Click the *BackColor* property, click the drop-down arrow, click the Custom tab, and then select the light yellow color for the cells of the data grid.

The *BackColor* property controls the color that appears in the background of the data grid cells. If you change this setting, it will usually produce an alternating effect (white and the color you select) from row to row in the data grid. (Note that the color that appears around the edges of the cell grid is controlled by the *BackgroundColor* property.) Remember that the default font color is black, so pick a background color that will look good with black if you change this setting. (Don't get carried away with distracting colors if you change the property from its default value.)

> ▶ **Tip**   To change the background color used for the header cells, modify the *HeaderBackColor* property.

5   Click the *GridLineColor* property, click the drop-down arrow, click the Custom tab, and then click Blue.

This property setting sets the color of the gridlines in the data grid. If you change the background color of the cells, you might also want to modify the gridline color.

Now run the program to see the effect of your formatting changes.

6   Click the Start button.

7   Click the Load button.

After a few moments, the data grid appears with information from the Instructors table.

8   Resize the form to accommodate the wider columns.

Your screen will look like this:

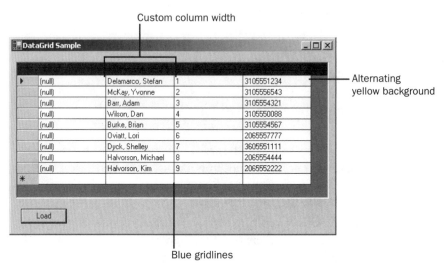

Custom column width

Alternating yellow background

Blue gridlines

Notice that the column headers are missing now but that the cells are wider and contain more room for text. Notice also the alternating yellow and white row pattern and the blue gridlines (not discernible in this book, alas, but on the screen).

9   Click the Close button on the form to stop the program.

Scan the Properties window for additional property settings and customizations—there are several possibilities if you look closely at the list of formatting options.

One Step Further: Updating the Original Database

As I mentioned earlier, the dataset object in your program is only a representation of the data in your original database. This is also true of the information stored in the data grid on your form—if the user makes a change to this data, it isn't written back to the original database unless you specifically direct the data adapter object in your program to make the change. The designers of ADO.NET and Visual Studio created this relationship to protect the original database and to allow you to manipulate data freely in your programs—whether you planned to save the changes or not.

In the following exercise, you'll examine the DataGrid *ReadOnly* property, which enables or disables changes in the data grid. You'll also learn how to use the *Update* method, which writes changes back to your original database on disk if you need this feature.

Enable updates to the database

1   Click the data grid object on the form, and then open the Properties window.

2   Scroll to the *ReadOnly* property, and examine its property setting.

If the *ReadOnly* property is set to False, the user is free to make changes to the information in data grid cells. You should keep this default setting if you want to allow your users to modify the information in the data grid so that it can be written back to the original database your program is connected to. If you want to disable editing, you would set the *ReadOnly* property to True.

Keep the default setting of False in this case—you want to test updating the underlying Students.mdb database.

3   Use the *Button* control to draw a button object near the bottom of the form.

4   Set the *Anchor* property of the button object to Bottom, Left, set the *Name* property to btnUpdate, and set the *Text* property to Update.

This is the button the user will click when he or she makes a change and wants to pass it to the underlying database.

5   Double-click the Update button, and then type the following program code in the *btnUpdate_Click* event procedure:

```
Try
    OleDbDataAdapter1.Update(DsInstructors1)
Catch ex As Exception
    MsgBox(ex.ToString)
End Try
```

This program statement uses the *Update* method of the *OleDbDataAdapter1* object to write any changes that have been made in the *DsInstructors1* dataset. When you make a change to the data grid, the data grid object automatically updates the dataset to which the data grid is bound. However, you need to take the further step of updating the data adapter in the program if you want to write the change all the way back to the underlying database.

6   Click the Start button to test your addition to the DataGrid Sample program.

> ▶ **Note**   The complete DataGrid Sample program is located in the c:\vbnet03sbs\chap20\datagrid sample folder.

7   Click the Load button.

The data grid appears with data from the Instructors table of the Students.mdb database.

8   Resize the form, and change the contents of one of the data grid cells by selecting the existing value with the mouse, pressing Delete, and then typing a new value.

As you make the change, a tiny pencil icon appears in the left row header, indicating that a change is being made. Your screen will look like this:

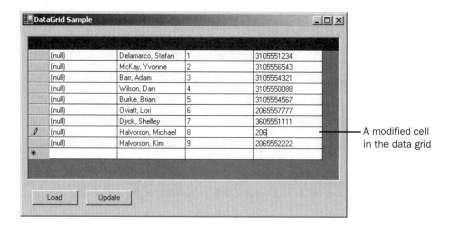

A modified cell in the data grid

When you click a different cell in the grid, the change is written to the *DsInstructors1* dataset.

9   Click the Update button.

Visual Basic uses the *Update* method of the program's data adapter object to write the changed dataset to the underlying database. The Students.mdb database is now permanently changed.

10   Click in a cell of the last row, which has a star icon in the left row header.

11   Modify the cells that have "(null)" values.

A new row appears in the grid.

12   Click the Update button.

A new row is permanently inserted in the Instructors table of the Students.mdb database.

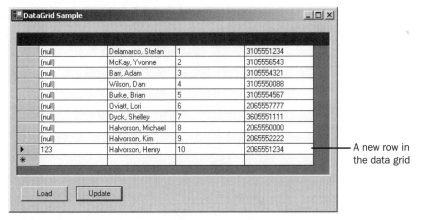
A new row in the data grid

13   Click the left row header of the row you just inserted to select the entire row, and then press the Delete key.

The row is deleted.

14   Click the Load button.

The deleted row reappears. Why is this? Didn't you just delete the row? The row was deleted from the *DsInstructors1* dataset, but the row still exists in the Students.mdb database. To permanently delete a row, you'll need to click the Update button to update the underlying database.

15   Make a few additional changes if you like, and then close the program when you're finished.

Congratulations! You've learned to display several fields and records by using the *DataGrid* control, and you've learned how to customize the data grid with property settings and how to write updates in the grid back to the original database. If you want to learn more about ADO.NET programming, consult one of the books or resources I've listed in Appendix B.

Lesson 20 Quick Reference

To	Do this
Create a data grid object on a form	Click the Windows Forms tab in the Toolbox, and then drag the *DataGrid* control from the Toolbox to your form. Resize the data grid object and set its *Anchor* property so that it's resized when the form is resized.
Bind a data grid to an active dataset in the program	Set the data grid's *DataSource* property to the dataset that you want to use, and then set the data grid's *DataMember* property to the sublist within the dataset that you want to access.

Populate a data grid with data from the dataset	Use the following program statements in an event procedure. (Change the name of the data adapter and dataset to match your particular application.)
	
	`DsInstructors1.Clear()`
	`OleDbDataAdapter1.Fill(DsInstructors1)`

Sort the records in a data grid at runtime	Click the data grid column header that you want to sort by. Visual Basic will sort the data grid alphabetically based on the column you select.
Reverse the direction of a sort	Click the data grid column header a second time to reverse the direction of the sort (from A–Z to Z–A).
Prohibit sorting in a data grid	Set the data grid's *AllowSorting* property to False.
Change the default width of data grid cells	Set the data grid's *PreferredColumnWidth* property.
Change the background color of the cells in a data grid	Set the data grid's *BackColor* property.
Prohibit changes in a data grid	Set the data grid's *ReadOnly* property to True.
Write changes made in the data grid back to the underlying database	Use the data adapter's *Update* method in an event procedure that's executed when the user wants to write the changes back to the underlying database. For example, the following program statement writes changes made to the *DsInstructors1* dataset back to the database: `OleDbDataAdapter1.Update(DsInstructors1)`

Internet Programming

Displaying HTML Documents Using Internet Explorer

In this chapter, you will learn how to:

■ Investigate the Microsoft Internet Explorer object model.

■ View HTML documents from within your application.

■ Use Internet Explorer events.

In Chapter 3, you used the *LinkLabel* control to display a Web site address on a form, and on several occasions you've used the *System.Diagnostics.Process.Start* method in code to open the default Internet browser on your system. In Part 6, you'll focus again on connecting your Microsoft Visual Basic .NET programs to the Internet. You'll learn to use the methods, properties, and events of the Internet Explorer application in a program, and you'll learn how to create Visual Basic .NET Web applications by using the controls on the Web Forms tab of the Toolbox. As you'll see, many Web programming techniques work hand in hand with the programming skills you've learned in Parts 1 through 5.

In this chapter, you'll learn how to display HTML documents in your applications by using the Internet Explorer object, a programmable component with properties, methods, and events that are available on every computer that maintains an installed copy of the Internet Explorer software. As you investigate the Internet Explorer object model, you'll learn how to add the Internet Explorer object to your Visual Basic projects and how to use Internet Explorer methods, properties, and events to display HTML documents. The advantage of using Internet Explorer directly is that you can display complex HTML documents and Web pages without writing the browser software yourself.

Upgrade Notes: What's New in Visual Basic .NET?

If you're experienced with Visual Basic 6, you'll notice some new features in Visual Basic .NET, including the following:

- The version of Internet Explorer that was shipped with the first release of Visual Basic 6 was Internet Explorer version 4. Internet Explorer version 6 is included with Visual Basic .NET 2002 and 2003. Both versions are largely compatible, so if you wrote Visual Basic 6 programs that used earlier versions of Internet Explorer, you should have little trouble compiling them under Visual Basic .NET and the new version of Internet Explorer.

- To use Internet Explorer features in a Visual Basic .NET program, you need to add a reference to the Microsoft Internet Controls object library (SHDocVw) by using the Add Reference command on the Project menu.

Getting Started with the Internet Explorer Object

Microsoft Internet Explorer is a general-purpose browser application that displays HTML documents located on the Internet or on your hard disk. Microsoft designed Internet Explorer so that you can use it as an individual application (started from the Microsoft Windows Start menu) or as a component object in a program of your own creation. Accordingly, Internet Explorer exposes its features as a collection of properties, methods, and events in a recognizable object model that you can put to work in your programs. You can investigate the Internet Explorer object model by using the Microsoft Visual Studio Object Browser.

The Internet Explorer object isn't a Toolbox control included in Microsoft Visual Basic .NET. Instead, it's a COM library that resides on all systems that have an installed copy of Internet Explorer (in other words, on all systems in which Internet Explorer is recorded and active in the system registry). Because Microsoft uses Internet Explorer to display Help files in many of its applications, you'll find the Internet Explorer object library on most systems that contain Microsoft software.

► **Important**   The version of Internet Explorer described in this chapter is version 6 (the version shipped with Visual Basic .NET 2002 and 2003). Core properties, methods, and events in the Internet Explorer object haven't changed significantly between versions. However, be sure to check which version of Internet Explorer you're using before you start this chapter. (Use the About command on the Internet Explorer Help menu.) If you have a version other than version 6, use the Object Browser to verify that it contains the properties, methods, and events that you plan to use. Like the object libraries in Microsoft Office applications, the Internet Explorer object model is updated from time to time. Undoubtedly, future versions will be a little different (and richer in terms of features).

Adding the Microsoft Internet Controls Reference to Your Application

The first step in using the Internet Explorer object is adding a COM reference to the object library in your application. You accomplish this by using the Add Reference command on the Visual Basic Project menu, as shown in the following exercise. Practice adding a reference now, if you like, or simply note the steps for later use. (The program I use in this chapter already includes this reference, but you should practice adding it now if you want to investigate the object model later in this section.)

Include the Internet Explorer object in your project

1   Start Visual Studio, and create a new Visual Basic Windows Application project named **My Explorer Objects** in the c:\vbnet03sbs\chap21 folder.

The new project is created, and a blank form appears in the Windows Forms Designer.

2   On the Project menu, click the Add Reference command.

3   Click the COM tab in the Add Reference dialog box.

4   Scroll to the Microsoft Internet Controls reference, click Microsoft Internet Controls in the dialog box, and then click Select.

Your dialog box will look similar to the following illustration:

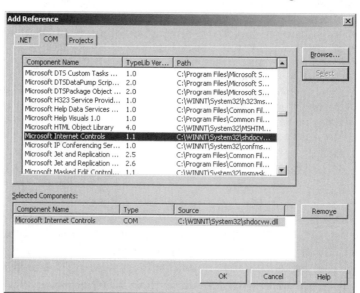

5   Click OK to add the reference to your project.

If you see the primary interoperability assembly dialog box, click Yes to allow Visual Studio to create the needed class wrapper automatically for you.

Visual Basic adds the Internet Explorer object library to your project, and the types associated with the wrapper are added to the project in Solution Explorer.

Investigating the Internet Explorer Object Model

Before you use the Internet Explorer object in a program, take a moment to examine its properties, methods, and events with the Visual Studio Object Browser. The Internet Explorer object is stored in a class named *Internet-Explorer*, which is a member of the SHDocVw library—the Microsoft Internet Controls reference you just added to your project. Within the *InternetExplorer* class are the properties, methods, and events that you can use to display HTML documents in your programs. As you learned in Chapter 13, the Object Browser is your best source of information for an object library that isn't shipped with Visual Basic. The Internet Explorer object library is a good case in point.

Use the Object Browser

1   On the View menu, click the Object Browser command. (The keyboard shortcut to display the Object Browser is F2.)

As you learned in Chapter 13, the Object Browser lists references and components in a tree hierarchy. The object hierarchy is shown in the left pane of the Object Browser, and individual members are shown in the right pane. At the bottom of the Object Browser is a pane that contains syntax information, when it's available, for the selected object.

2   Click the plus sign (+) next to the *Interop.SHDocVw* object, and then click the plus sign next to SHDocVw.

A list of the objects exposed by the Microsoft Internet Controls library fills the Objects pane, as shown here:

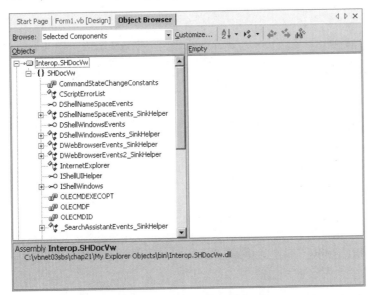

3   Scroll down the alphabetical list of objects, and then click the first object named *InternetExplorer*.

A list of the methods and properties associated with the Internet Explorer object appears in the Members pane. These are some of the commands Internet Explorer exposes for manipulating Internet Explorer.

4   Scroll down in the Members pane, and then click the *Navigate* method.

Your screen will look like this:

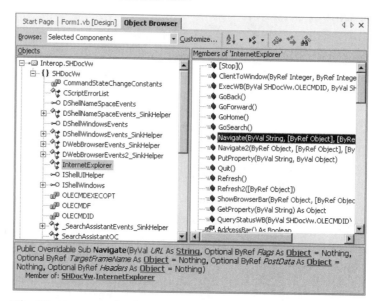

The *Navigate* method opens the URL specified in the parameter list, which can be either an Internet address or an HTML document somewhere on your system. The *Flags* argument specifies whether to add this URL to the Internet Explorer's history list or disk cache. The *TargetFrameName*, *PostData*, and *Headers* arguments describe how the HTML document should be opened and identified in the browser window. (The *Flags*, *TargetFrameName*, *PostData*, and *Headers* arguments are all optional.) Although it might appear complex, the *Navigate* method is easy to use. In many cases, it's all you'll need to view an HTML document from within your application.

5   Scroll down in the Members pane, and click the *LocationURL* property.

The *LocationURL* property contains the path of the HTML document that's currently open in the Internet Explorer browser. If you want to keep track of each Web site a user visits in a computing session, you can copy the string in the *LocationURL* property to a text box or combo box after each successful connection to a Web page.

6   Take a moment to explore other properties and methods that look interesting with the Object Browser.

7   When you're finished exploring the object model, click the Close button to quit the Object Browser.

8   Click the Save All button on the toolbar to save your changes.
    You're finished working with the My Explorer Objects project.

Displaying HTML Documents

Displaying HTML documents with the Internet Explorer object requires just a few lines of program code in a Visual Basic application. First you declare a variable in your application that represents the Internet Explorer type. You use the *New* keyword to create an instance of the Internet Explorer object. Then you display the Internet Explorer application by setting the *Visible* property of the object to True. Next you load an HTML document into Internet Explorer by issuing the *Navigate* method with a valid URL or local path as an argument. Here's what the process looks like in program code:

```
Dim Explorer As SHDocVw.InternetExplorer
Explorer = New SHDocVw.InternetExplorer()
Explorer.Visible = True
Explorer.Navigate("http://www.microsoft.com")
```

In this example, I created a variable named *Explorer* to represent the *Internet-Explorer* class in the shdocvw.dll object library. If you want to use this variable in every event procedure in your form, you could declare it as a public variable by using the *Public* keyword in a standard module or in the general declarations section of your form.

To see how the Internet Explorer object works in a program, you'll run the Show HTML demonstration that I created for this chapter. Show HTML uses a combo box to present a list of favorite Web sites to the user, and it uses Internet Explorer's *Navigate* method to display whichever HTML document the user selects.

Run the Show HTML program

1   Click the Close Solution command on the File menu.

2   Open the Show HTML project in the c:\vbnet03sbs\chap21\show html folder.

3   Click the Start button on the Standard toolbar to run the program.

Your form will look like the following illustration:

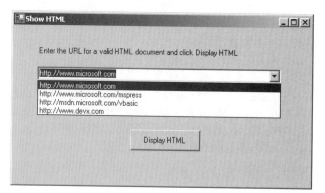

4 Click the down arrow in the combo box on the form to display a list of favorite Web sites for Visual Basic programmers.

You'll see the following list of URLs:

As you've probably noticed in your Internet browser, a combo box can be a handy control for presenting URLs to the user. In my Web applications, I usually try to display four or five URLs for users to choose from when they start their Web applications, and they can add their own favorites when they visit additional sites. The Internet addresses I've included here will connect you to a few sites that I think are of general interest to Visual Basic programmers. Feel free to use them, but note that one or two of the URLs might not be valid a year or two from now. (These things change rapidly.)

The following table lists the Web sites I present in the program:

Internet address	Description
http://www.microsoft.com	Microsoft Corporation home page
http://www.microsoft.com/mspress	Microsoft Press home page (with links for Visual Basic books)

Internet address	Description
http://msdn.microsoft.com/vbasic	Microsoft Visual Basic Programming home page
http://www.devx.com	General resources for computer programming and Visual Studio .NET

5   Click the Microsoft Visual Basic Programming home page (*http://msdn.microsoft.com/vbasic*) in the combo box.

6   Click the Display HTML button.

Visual Basic opens Internet Explorer and loads the Microsoft Visual Basic URL into the browser. If you're not on line, Internet Explorer prompts you for your Internet service provider (ISP) member ID and password with a sign-in dialog box and connects you to the Internet. (If you connect to the Internet through a corporate network, you might have a different logon process.) After a moment, you'll see the Microsoft Visual Basic home page, which will look similar to the following illustration. (Your HTML document will contain more recent information.)

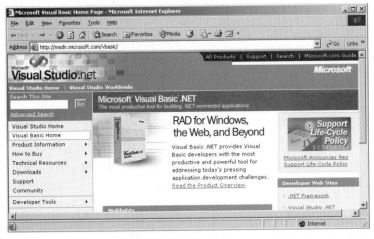

7   Maximize the Internet Explorer window if it isn't already full-size, and then click one or two links of interest to you.

The Microsoft Visual Basic Programming home page is an excellent resource for late-breaking news about programming tools, tips, conferences, books, and other information about Visual Basic.

8   After you've finished reviewing the page, close the Internet Explorer window. If you're asked whether you want to disconnect from the Internet, click No to remain connected.

9   Display the Show HTML form again.

The Show HTML program is still running, although it might have settled beneath a few other open applications by this point.

10 Place the cursor in the combo box on the Show HTML form, remove the current URL, and enter a URL of your own choosing. Then click Display HTML to open it.

In addition to entering URLs, you can also enter file paths in the combo box to display HTML documents stored on your hard disk.

11 After you've displayed three or four HTML documents, click the Close button on the Show HTML program's title bar, and then close any open Internet Explorer windows.

Now you'll take a look at the program code in the Show HTML application that utilizes the Internet Explorer object.

Examine the Internet Explorer code in Show HTML

1 View the code for Form1 in the Code Editor, and scroll to the top where general variable declarations are defined.

You'll see the following program code:

```
Public Explorer As SHDocVw.InternetExplorer
```

The Show HTML program begins by declaring a public variable named *Explorer* that will facilitate the program's connection to the Internet Explorer object. The variable type is associated with the *InternetExplorer* class in the shdocvw.dll library, which must be included in your project by using the Add Reference command on the Project menu. (I made this reference for you in this project.)

2 Display the *Button1_Click* event procedure in the Code Editor.

You'll see the following program code:

```
Private Sub Button1_Click(ByVal sender As System.Object, _
  ByVal e As System.EventArgs) Handles Button1.Click
    Explorer = New SHDocVw.InternetExplorer()
    Explorer.Visible = True
    Explorer.Navigate(ComboBox1.Text)
End Sub
```

The *Button1_Click* event procedure runs when the user clicks the Display HTML button on the form and attempts to navigate to the URL or HTML document currently specified in the combo box. The event procedure begins by assigning a new Internet Explorer object to the *Explorer* public variable. Next, the procedure makes the Internet Explorer window visible and opens a document in the browser that corresponds to the user's selection in the combo box (a value currently held in the combo box object's *Text* property) by using the *Navigate* method. At this point, the Show HTML application has completed its part of the navigation, and the user's attention is shifted to the open Internet Explorer window, which manages the connection to the Internet (if necessary) and allows the user to view the selected Web site and click any existing hyperlinks on the page.

3   Display the *Form1_Load* event procedure in the Code Editor. You'll see the following program code:

```
Private Sub Form1_Load(ByVal sender As System.Object, _
   ByVal e As System.EventArgs) Handles MyBase.Load
      'Add a few useful Web sites to the combo box at startup
      ComboBox1.Items.Add("http://www.microsoft.com")
      ComboBox1.Items.Add("http://www.microsoft.com/mspress")
      ComboBox1.Items.Add("http://msdn.microsoft.com/vbasic")
      ComboBox1.Items.Add("http://www.devx.com")
End Sub
```

When the Show HTML program loads, the user is presented with a list of several "favorite" Web sites automatically. These URLs are presented in a combo box that I configured initially in the *Form1_Load* event procedure by using the *Add* method. Feel free to add your own favorite URLs to this list by including additional *Add* statements—the combo box object includes scroll bars when necessary and can accommodate many entries.

One Step Further: Responding to Internet Explorer Events

In this chapter, you've used the *Visible* property and the *Navigate* method of the Internet Explorer object to display HTML documents. You can also take greater control of your browsing activities by responding to events that occur in the Internet Explorer object. As you might recall from previous chapters, each Visual Basic control has the ability to track status activities, or *events*, in the regular course of its operation. These events can include anything from a simple mouse movement in the *PictureBox* control (the *MouseMove* event) to notification that a key has been pressed in the *TextBox* control (the *KeyPress* event). The Internet Explorer object also produces events that you can respond to programmatically with event procedures. These include *NavigateComplete2*, *DownloadBegin*, *DownloadComplete*, *TitleChange*, *DocumentComplete*, and *OnQuit*.

If you want to use Internet Explorer events in your program, you first need to modify the statement in your program code that declares the Internet Explorer variable. Events produced by COM components aren't automatically listed in the Method Name drop-down list box of the Code Editor. However, you can include these events by using the *WithEvents* keyword when you make your variable declaration. In the Show HTML program developed in this chapter, you edit the variable declaration section of your form as follows:

```
Public WithEvents Explorer As SHDocVw.InternetExplorer
```

After you use the *WithEvents* keyword, the *Explorer* variable appears automatically in the Class Name drop-down list box in the Code Editor. When you select the *Explorer* object, its events appear in the Method Name drop-down list box. You can then select each event that you want to control and build an event procedure for it. You'll see how this works in a revision to the Show HTML program.

In the following exercise, you'll write an event procedure that adds the URL for the current Web site in Internet Explorer to the combo box object in the Show HTML program.

Use the *NavigateComplete2* event

1   If the Show HTML project isn't open, load it into the Visual Studio development environment.

   The Show HTML program is located in the c:\vbnet03sbs\chap21\show html folder.

2   Display the variable declarations section of the program in the Code Editor (the area just below the tag "Windows Form Designer generated code").

3   Add the *WithEvents* keyword to the Internet Explorer variable declaration after the *Public* keyword.

   Your object declaration should look like this:

```
Public WithEvents Explorer As SHDocVw.InternetExplorer
```

4   Move your cursor to another line so that Visual Studio can recognize the *WithEvents* change.

5   Click the Class Name drop-down list box in the Code Editor, and then click the *Explorer* object.

6   Click the Method Name drop-down list box in the Code Editor, and then click the *NavigateComplete2* event.

   The *Explorer_NavigateComplete2* event procedure and its parameters appear in the Code Editor.

7   Type the following statement in the *Explorer_NavigateComplete2* event procedure:

```
ComboBox1.Items.Add(Explorer.LocationURL)
```

Your procedure should now look like this:

```
Private Sub Explorer_NavigateComplete2(ByVal pDisp As Object, _
  ByRef URL As Object) Handles Explorer.NavigateComplete2
    ComboBox1.Items.Add(Explorer.LocationURL)
End Sub
```

The *NavigateComplete2* event occurs when the Internet Explorer object has successfully loaded the specified document into the browser—an invalid Web page or URL won't trigger the event. As a result, watching for the *NavigateComplete2* event is a useful way to keep track of the Web documents you've recently loaded. If you use the *LocationURL* property of the *Explorer* object, you can build your own history list of HTML documents. In this example, I've simply added the visited URL to the combo box on the form, so you can easily revisit the site with a mere mouse click. However, you also could store this information permanently by writing the URL to a file or a database.

8   Click the Save All button on the toolbar to save your changes.

9   Click the Start button on the Standard toolbar to run the program.

10   Click one of the Web sites listed in the combo box, and then click the Display HTML button.

11   After the connection is established, click some of the hyperlinks on the site to jump to a few new URLs.

12   Click the Show HTML program icon on the taskbar, and then click the combo box again.

The new sites you visited are added to the Show HTML combo box, as shown here:

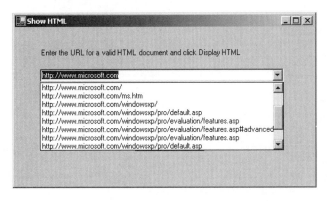

Experiment with the *NavigateComplete2* event by visiting a few more Web sites and seeing how they're added to the combo box.

13 When you're finished, close the Internet Explorer windows you have open. Then click the Close button on the Show HTML application's title bar.

You're finished working with the Internet Explorer object in this chapter. Nice job!

Chapter 21 Quick Reference

To	Do this
Add a COM reference to the Internet Explorer object library to your program	On the Project menu, click the Add Reference command, click the COM tab, click the Microsoft Internet Controls entry, click the Select button, and then click OK.
Investigate the Internet Explorer object model	Press F2 to open the Object Browser, click the plus sign (+) next to the *Interop.SHDocVw* object, and then click the plus sign next to SHDocVw. Scroll down the list of objects, and then click the object named *InternetExplorer*. Click individual members of the Internet Explorer object in the Members pane to learn more about them.

Start Internet Explorer in your program	Declare a variable of the *SHDocVw.InternetExplorer* type, create a new instance by using the *New* keyword, and set its *Visible* property to True. For example:
	
	`Dim Explorer As SHDocVw.InternetExplorer`
	`Explorer = New SHDocV\w.InternetExplorer`
	`Explorer.Visible = True`

Display a Web site with the Internet Explorer object	Use the *Navigate* method. For example: `Explorer.Navigate("http://www.microsoft.com/")`

Access the events of an external object (such as Internet Explorer)	Declare your object by using the *WithEvents* keyword. For example:
	
	`Public WithEvents Explorer As _`
	`    SHDocVw.InternetExplorer`

Using Web Forms to Build Interactive Web Applications

In this chapter, you will learn how to:

■ Create a new Web application.

■ Use the Web Forms Designer.

■ Add text and formatting effects to a Web Forms page.

■ Use Web Forms controls to make Web applications interactive.

■ Create an HTML page.

■ Use the *HyperLink* control to link one page to another within a Web application.

In Chapter 21, you learned how to display HTML pages in a Visual Basic .NET application by using Microsoft Internet Explorer. In this chapter, you'll learn how to build your own Web applications by using the Web Forms Designer that's supplied with Microsoft Visual Basic .NET. *Web Forms* is a new programming model for Internet user interfaces based on ASP.NET, the Microsoft Visual Studio .NET Framework component designed to provide state-of-the-art Internet functionality. Web Forms is a replacement for WebClasses and the DHTML Page Designer in Visual Basic 6, and it's distinct from the Windows Forms components that you've used for most of the projects in this book. Although a complete description of Web Forms and Microsoft ASP.NET isn't possible here, there's enough in common between Web Forms and Windows Forms to allow you some useful experimentation right away—even if you have little or no experience in Internet programming and HTML page design. Invest a few hours in this chapter and see if Web Forms is for you!

Upgrade Notes: What's New in Visual Basic .NET?

If you're experienced with Visual Basic 6, you'll notice some new features in Visual Basic .NET, including the following:

- A new Internet programming model called Web Forms, which is part of ASP.NET. Web Forms and the Web Forms Designer are a replacement for the Visual Basic 6 WebClasses and DHTML Page Designer, which are no longer supported in Visual Basic .NET.

- Although the Web Forms Designer is distinct from the Windows Forms Designer, both user interface tools offer similar controls and support drag-and-drop programming techniques. Because the Web Forms Designer is part of Visual Studio .NET, it's available to Visual Basic .NET, Microsoft Visual C# .NET, and Microsoft Visual J# .NET.

- Web Forms applications are designed to be displayed by Web browsers such as Internet Explorer. The controls on Web Forms are visible in the client's Web browser (in other words, on the end-user's computer), but the functionality for the controls resides on the Web server that hosts the actual Web application.

- Although many of the Web Forms controls have the same names as the Windows Forms controls, the controls aren't identical. For example, Web Forms controls have an *ID* property, rather than a *Name* property.

Inside ASP.NET

ASP.NET is Microsoft's latest Web development platform. Although ASP.NET has some similarities with the previous version, named ASP (Active Server Pages), ASP.NET has been completely redesigned based on the .NET Framework. Web Forms is the design component of ASP.NET that allows you to create and manage Internet user interfaces, commonly called Web pages or (in a more comprehensive sense) Web applications. By using Web Forms, you can create a Web application that displays a user interface, processes data, and provides many of the commands and features that a standard application for Microsoft Windows might offer. However, the Web application you create runs in a Web browser such as Internet Explorer or Netscape Navigator, and it's stored on one or more *Web servers*, which display the correct Web pages and handle most of the computing tasks required by your Web application. This distributed strategy allows your Web applications to potentially run anywhere on the Internet while residing physically in one manageable location on the Web server, on which rich data resources can also be stored.

To create a Web application in Visual Basic .NET, you create a new ASP.NET Web Application project in the Visual Studio development environment, and then use the Web Forms Designer to build one or more Web Forms that will collectively represent your program. Each Web form consists of two pieces—a Web Forms page and a code-behind file. The Web Forms page contains HTML and controls to create the user interface. The code-behind file is a code module that contains program code that "stands behind" the Web Forms page. This division is conceptually much like Windows Forms you've been creating in Visual Basic—there's a user interface component and a code module component. The code for both of these components can be stored in a single .aspx file, but typically the Web Forms page code is stored in an .aspx file and the code-behind file is stored in an .aspx.vb file. The following illustration shows a conceptual view of how an ASP.NET Web application is displayed in a Web browser:

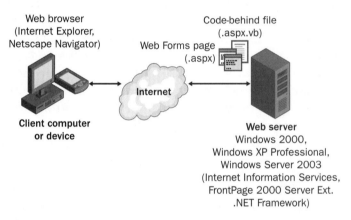

In addition to Web Forms, Web applications can contain code modules (.vb files), HTML pages (.htm files), configuration information (a Web.config file), global Web application information (a Global.asax file), and other components. You can use the Web Forms Designer and Solution Explorer to switch back and forth between these components quickly and efficiently.

Web Forms vs. Windows Forms

What are the important differences between Web Forms and Windows Forms? To begin with, Web Forms offers a slightly different programming paradigm than Windows Forms. Whereas Windows Forms uses a Windows application window as the primary user interface for a program, Web Forms presents information to the user via one or more Web pages with supporting program code.

These pages are viewed through a Web browser, and you can create them by using the Web Forms Designer.

Like a Windows Form, a Web form can include text, graphic images, buttons, list boxes, and other objects that are used to provide information, process input, or display output. However, the basic set of controls you use to create a Web Forms page isn't the same as the set Visual Studio offers on the Windows Forms tab of the Toolbox. Instead, ASP.NET Web applications must use controls on either the HTML tab or the Web Forms tab of the Toolbox. Each of the HTML and Web Forms controls has its own unique methods, properties, and events, and although there are many similarities between these controls and Windows Forms controls, there are also several important differences.

Web Forms controls are *server controls*, meaning they run and can be programmed on the Web server. Server controls can be identified on a Web form by the small green icon that appears in the upper left corner of the control at design time. HTML controls are *client controls* by default, meaning they run only within the end user's browser. HTML controls can be configured as server controls by right clicking the controls in the Web Forms Designer and selecting Run As Server Control or by setting their *Runat* attribute to Server. For now, however, you simply need to know that you can use HTML controls, Web Forms controls, or a combination of both in your Web application projects.

HTML Controls

The HTML controls are a set of older user interface controls that are supported by most Web browsers and conform closely to the early HTML standards developed for managing user interface elements on a typical Web page. They include *Button*, *Text Field*, and *Checkbox*—useful base controls for managing information on a Web page that can be represented entirely with HTML code. Indeed, you might recognize these controls if you've coded in HTML before or if you've had some experience with the Visual Basic 6 DHTML Page Designer. However, although they're easy to use and have the advantage of being a "common denominator" for most Web browsers, they're limited by the fact that they have no ability to maintain their own state unless they're configured as server controls. (In other words, the data that they contain will be lost between views of a Web page.) The following illustration shows the HTML controls offered on the HTML tab of the Toolbox in Visual Studio:

Web Forms Controls

Web Forms controls offer more features and capabilities than HTML controls. Web Forms controls are more capable than HTML controls and function in many ways like the Windows Forms controls. Indeed, many of the Web Forms controls have the same names as the Windows Forms controls and offer many of the same properties, methods, and events. In addition to simple controls such as *Button*, *TextBox*, and *Label*, more sophisticated controls such as *DataGrid*, *Calendar*, and *RequiredFieldValidator* are also provided. The following illustration shows some of the Web Forms controls on the Web Forms tab of the Toolbox:

Web Browser Support

You might be wondering, "Do these exciting new controls mean that all the users of my application will need to be using the latest, most up-to-date version of a specific Web browser? What if such an upgrade isn't possible for our Web customers?"

Visual Studio .NET Web applications don't require the latest browser—Visual Studio .NET includes a *targetSchema* property for the *DOCUMENT* object that allows you to target a specific Web browser and versions. The *targetSchema* options are Internet Explorer 3.02 / Navigator 3.0, Internet Explorer 5.0, and Navigator 4.0. The default is Internet Explorer 5.0. The value of the *targetSchema* property affects the HTML code that Visual Studio generates and the features available in Visual Studio. For example, if the *targetSchema* property is set to Internet Explorer 3.02 / Navigator 3.0 and the *pageLayout* property is set to GridLayout, HTML tables rather than cascading style sheets (CSS) are used for positioning objects.

The *targetSchema* property won't be discussed any further, but I'll use the *pageLayout* property later in this chapter. If you're interested in learning more about *targetSchema*, search the Visual Studio online Help for the topic "targetSchema."

Getting Started with a Web Application

The best way to learn about ASP.NET and Web applications is to get some hands-on practice. In the exercises in this chapter, you'll create a simple Web application. This application is a car loan calculator that determines monthly payments and displays a second Web page containing Help text. You'll begin by verifying that Visual Studio is properly configured for ASP.NET programming, and then you'll create a new Web application project. Next you'll use the Web Forms Designer to create a Web Forms page with text and links on it, and you'll add controls to the Web Forms page by using controls on the Web Forms tab of the Toolbox.

Installing the Software for ASP.NET Programming

Before you write your first ASP.NET Web application, you need to verify that you have the necessary support files on your system. ASP.NET Web applications rely on a Web server running Windows 2000, Windows XP Professional, or Windows

Server 2003 that has an installation of Microsoft Internet Information Services (IIS), the Microsoft FrontPage 2000 Server Extensions, and the .NET Framework libraries. You need to verify that you have these components installed now either locally on your own computer or through a server connection.

▶ **Important**   Windows XP Home Edition doesn't include or support IIS and the FrontPage 2000 Server Extensions, which means you cannot create ASP.NET Web applications locally by using Windows XP Home Edition. However, it's possible to create ASP.NET Web applications using Windows XP Home Edition by accessing a properly configured remote Web server. This chapter assumes that you're using Windows 2000, Windows XP Professional, or Windows Server 2003 and that your Web server is local.

Fundamentally, this is a Visual Studio .NET Setup issue—during the installation of the Visual Studio .NET software, a setup routine called Windows Component Update analyzed your system to see whether you had the capability to create local Web projects. If you didn't have the necessary support files, you were asked to install IIS and the FrontPage 2000 Server Extensions by using your original Windows 2000, Windows XP Professional, or Windows Server 2003 setup CD-ROMs. If you ignored these messages at the time and didn't install the necessary support files, you'll need to install the files now to enable your system for ASP.NET programming.

▶ **Note**   Microsoft recommends that you install IIS and the FrontPage 2000 Server Extensions before you install the .NET Framework and Visual Studio .NET because the .NET Framework must register extensions with IIS. If you install IIS and the FrontPage 2000 Server Extensions after the .NET Framework, you'll need to repair the .NET Framework as described in the following steps to ensure that it's configured properly.

If you find that you don't have IIS and the FrontPage 2000 Server Extensions installed to start programming with ASP.NET, follow these steps:

Install IIS and the FrontPage 2000 Server Extensions

1   On the Windows Start menu, click Settings, and then click Control Panel.

2   Double-click Add/Remove Programs.

3   In the Add/Remove Programs dialog box, click Add/Remove Windows Components.

4   In the Windows Components Wizard, click Internet Information Services (IIS), and then click Details.

5   If FrontPage 2000 Server Extensions and World Wide Web Server aren't already selected, click the check boxes shown in the following illustration:

▶   **Note**   If the FrontPage 2000 Server Extensions and World Wide Web Server options are already checked, your computer is probably already configured for ASP.NET programming. You can cancel the installation and continue at the section "Create a new Web application."

6   Click OK.

7   Click Next to start your installation of the files, and follow the instructions that appear.

You might be prompted to insert your Windows 2000, Windows XP Professional, or Windows Server 2003 CD-ROM during the installation process.

If it was necessary to install IIS and the FrontPage 2000 Server Extensions, follow the steps in the following procedure to repair the .NET Framework.

Repair the .NET Framework

1   If you're using Visual Studio .NET CD-ROMs, insert the Windows Component Update CD-ROM. If you're using a Visual Studio. NET DVD, insert the DVD.

If you're using CD-ROMs, a message might be displayed to insert Disk 1. Ignore this message and click OK.

2   On the Windows Start menu, click Run.

The Run dialog box appears.

3   If you're using Visual Studio .NET CD-ROMs, type the following command in one long line in the Open text box, replacing *<CDdrive>* with your CD-ROM drive letter:

```
<CDdrive>:\dotNetFramework\dotnetfx.exe /t:c:\temp
/c:"msiexec.exe /fvecms c:\temp\netfx.msi"
```

If you're using a Visual Studio .NET DVD, type the following command in one long line in the Open text box, replacing *<DVDdrive>* with your DVD drive letter:

```
<DVDdrive>:\wcu\dotNetFramework\dotnetfx.exe /t:c:\temp
/c:"msiexec.exe /fvecms c:\temp\netfx.msi"
```

4   Click OK.

A message will appear asking whether you want to install the Microsoft .NET Framework Package.

5   Click Yes.

After you complete the .NET Framework repair process, your computer should be ready for ASP.NET programming.

▶ **Note**   Because the Visual Studio .NET software installation hasn't been performed in the order that Microsoft recommends, you still might encounter problems when creating Web applications. For example, you might not be able to create a new ASP.NET Web application project, or the Web application might not display properly in a Web browser. If you still encounter problems after performing the steps in this section, check out the following resources:

Setup\WebServer.htm and Setup\WebServerInfo.htm on Visual Studio .NET CD1 or DVD

"Visual Studio .NET Software Requirements" and "Troubleshooting Web Projects" topics in the Visual Studio online Help

After you've loaded the necessary support files, you're ready to build your first ASP.NET Web application.

Create a new Web application

1   Start Visual Studio, and open the New Project dialog box.

2   In the New Project dialog box, click the ASP.NET Web Application icon in the Visual Basic Projects folder.

When you select this icon, Visual Studio will prepare the development environment and your program files for Internet programming. Creating a new ASP.NET Web application project is similar to creating a Windows Application project. However, the Name text box is disabled, and the Location text box is a different type of setting. In a Web application environment, you're directed to specify a Web server for your project or accept the default value of *http://localhost*. As I mentioned earlier, you can choose a local or remote Web server (that has the .NET Framework and supporting files installed) for your project while it's under construction, and Visual Studio will use the specified Web server to place and organize your project files. The Web server isn't identified by using a drive and folder names, but rather by using a valid Internet address (URL).

3   Enter your Web server URL and the Web application name in the Location text box. Because these steps assume your Web server is on your local machine, type **http://localhost/MyWebCalculator**.

Your screen will look this:

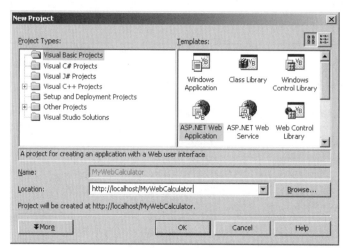

4   Click OK.

> ► **Note**   If Visual Studio displays an error while attempting to create a new ASP.NET Web application project, your setup isn't configured properly for ASP.NET programming. Review the steps in the section "Installing the Software for ASP.NET Programming" earlier in this chapter to make sure you have the proper software installed.

Visual Studio loads the Web Forms Designer and creates a Web Forms page (WebForm1.aspx) that will contain the user interface and a code-behind file (WebForm1.aspx.vb) that will contain the code for your Web application. Your screen will look like this:

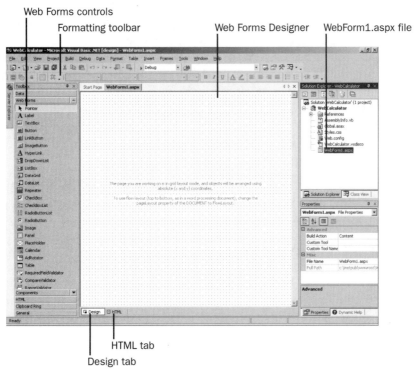

Web Forms controls

Formatting toolbar   Web Forms Designer   WebForm1.aspx file

HTML tab

Design tab

Unlike the Windows Forms Designer, the Web Forms Designer displays the Web Forms page in the center of the development environment by using a large white document window and a grid of tiny gray dots. Two tabs at the bottom of the designer (Design and HTML) allow you to change your view of this Web Forms page. The Design tab (the default view) shows you approximately how your Web Forms page will look when a Web browser displays it. When the Design tab is selected, you can choose either grid layout mode or flow layout mode to control how the objects on your Web Forms page are arranged. The message you see on the Web Forms page describes these two modes. (You'll experiment with them in the next section.)

The HTML tab at the bottom of the designer lets you view and edit the HTML code that's used to display the Web Forms page in a Web browser. If you've used Microsoft Visual InterDev or Microsoft FrontPage in the past, you'll be familiar with these two ways of displaying a Web Forms page and perhaps with some of the HTML formatting codes that control how Web Forms pages are actually displayed.

A few additional changes in Visual Studio are also worth noting at this point. Below the Standard toolbar are new Design and Formatting toolbars, which contain design and formatting options for your Web Forms page. The Web Forms tab of the Toolbox is visible on the left side of the screen and offers the Web Forms controls that you can use to customize your ASP.NET Web applications. (If you don't see the Web Forms controls, click the Web Forms tab now.) Solution Explorer on the right side of the screen contains a different list of project files for the Web application you're building. In particular, notice the WebForm1.aspx file in Solution Explorer, which contains the user interface code for this Web Forms page.

Now you're ready to add some text to the Web Forms page by using the Web Forms Designer.

Using the Web Forms Designer

Unlike a Windows Form, a Web Forms page can have text added directly to it when it's in flow layout mode in the Web Forms Designer. In flow layout mode, text appears in top-to-bottom fashion as it does in a word processor such as Microsoft Word. You can type text in flow layout mode, edit it, and then make formatting changes by using the Formatting toolbar. Manipulating text in this way is usually much faster than adding a Web Forms *Label* control to the Web page to contain the text. You'll practice entering the text for your car loan calculator in the following exercise.

Add text in flow layout mode

1   Click the Web Forms page in the Web Forms Designer, and then open the Properties window.

    You'll change the Web Forms Designer from grid layout mode to flow layout mode to facilitate text entry on the form, but before you do so you need to select the Web Forms page in the designer. When the Web Forms page is selected, the label DOCUMENT will appear in the Object drop-down list box of the Properties window.

2   Change the *pageLayout* property of the *DOCUMENT* object to FlowLayout.

Visual Studio removes the grid from the Web Forms page. You can switch between flow layout and grid layout by changing the *page-Layout* property when the *DOCUMENT* object is selected.

3   Click the Web Forms page again.

A blinking text cursor appears at the top of the Web Forms page.

4   Type **Car Loan Calculator**, and then press Enter.

Visual Studio displays the title of your Web application on the Web Forms page exactly as it will appear when you run the program in your browser.

5   Type the following sentence below the application title:

Enter the required information and click Calculate!

Now you'll format the title with bold formatting and a larger point size.

6   Select the Car Loan Calculator text.

When you select text on the form, the Formatting toolbar displays font information for the text you selected.

7   Click the Bold button on the Formatting toolbar, and set the font size to 5.

Font size isn't specified in points in Web applications, but rather in relative sizes. (Font size 5 is about 18-point type.) Your screen will look like this:

Formatting toolbar

Formatted text on Web Forms page

Now you'll examine the HTML code for the text you entered.

View the HTML for a Web Forms page

1   Click the HTML tab at the bottom of the Web Forms Designer.

The HTML tab displays the actual HTML code for your Web Forms page. To see more of the code, you might want to temporarily close the Toolbox. The HTML code for the Web Forms page looks like this:

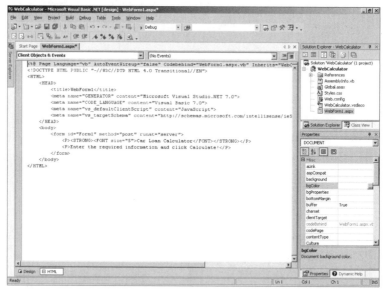

A Web Forms page is made up of file and document information, formatting codes called *HTML tags* that are enclosed in angle brackets, and the text and objects to be displayed by your Web Forms page. This Web Forms page is still rather short—it contains a header with information about the language you selected when creating the Web application, the name of any code-behind file, and any inherited forms.

The body tag identifies the beginning of the document; tags typically always appear in pairs so that you can see clearly where a section begins and ends. Notice that the "Car Loan Calculator" text appears within a line of HTML that formats the text as strong (bold) with font size 5. Below this text, the second line of text you entered is displayed.

> ▶ **Tip**   The HTML view is an actual editor, so you can change the text you entered now by using standard text editing techniques. If you know something about HTML, you can add additional formatting tags and content as well.

2   Click the Design tab to display your Web Forms page in Design view, and open the Toolbox if you closed it.

3   Select DOCUMENT in the Object drop-down list box of the Properties window.

4   Set the *pageLayout* property to GridLayout.

You're finished adding text to the Web Forms page, so you can switch from flow layout to grid layout.

Flow Layout vs. Grid Layout

Why are there two different layout modes, flow layout and grid layout? Each layout mode has advantages and disadvantages, but fundamentally, the choices are designed to give you, the Web application designer, different ways to control how a Web form looks in a Web browser. Grid layout allows you to precisely position, size, and even overlap objects on a Web Forms page. The drawback is that grid layout generates more complicated HTML to position the objects, which might not display as expected in different or older browsers. If you want your Web applications to display cleanly in the widest range of Web browsers, set the *pageLayout* property to FlowLayout and the *targetSchema* property to Internet Explorer 3.02 / Navigator 3.0.

Adding Web Forms Controls to a Web Application

Now you'll add *TextBox*, *Label*, and *Button* controls to the car loan calculator. Although these controls are located on the Web Forms tab of the Toolbox, they're very similar to the Windows Forms controls of the same name that you've used throughout this book. (I'll cover a few of the important differences coming up.) After you add the controls to the Web Forms page, you'll set property settings for the controls.

Use *TextBox, Label,* and *Button* controls

1   Display the Web Forms tab of the Toolbox if it isn't already visible, and verify that the Web Forms page is in grid layout mode. (The grid should be visible on the form.)

2   Click the Web Forms *TextBox* control, and then create a text box object on the Web Forms page below the text you entered. Align the text box object along the left margin.

Visual Studio allows you to create Web Forms controls just as you create Windows Forms controls. Because the Web Forms page is in grid layout mode, you can size and position the controls precisely, just as you can fine-tune the placement of controls on a Windows Form.

Notice the small green icon that appears in the upper left corner of the control, which indicates that this control runs on the server.

3   Create two more text box objects below the first text box.

Now you'll create labels by using the Web Forms *Label* control to identify the purpose of the text boxes.

4   Click the Web Forms *Label* control, and then draw a label object to the right of the first text box object.

5   Create two more label objects below the first label object and to the right of the second and third text box objects.

6   Use the Web Forms *Button* control to draw a button object at the bottom of the Web Forms page.

The *Button* control, like the *TextBox* and *Label* controls, is very similar to its Windows Forms counterpart. Your screen should look like this:

Green icon indicates server control

| Start Page | WebForm1.aspx* |

Car Loan Calculator

Enter the required information and click Calculate!

Label

Label

Label

Button

Now you'll set a few properties for the seven new controls you created on the Web Forms page. As you set the properties, you'll notice one important difference between Web Forms and Windows

Forms—the familiar *Name* property has been changed to *ID* in Web Forms. Despite their different names, the two properties perform the same function.

7 Set the following properties for the objects on the form:

Object	Property	Setting
TextBox1	*ID*	txtAmount
TextBox2	*ID*	txtInterest
TextBox3	*ID*	txtPayment
Label1	*ID*	lblAmount
	Text	"Loan Amount"
Label2	*ID*	lblInterest
	Text	"Interest Rate (for example, 0.09)"
Label3	*ID*	lblPayment
	Text	"Monthly Payment"
Button1	*ID*	btnCalculate
	Text	"Calculate"

Your Web Forms page will look like this:

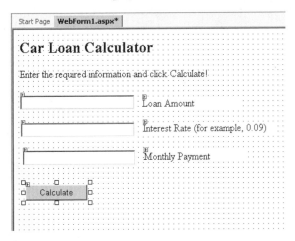

Writing Event Procedures for Web Forms Controls

You write event procedures (or event handlers) for controls on a Web Forms page by double-clicking the objects on the Web Forms page and typing the necessary program code in the Code Editor. Although the user will see the controls on the Web Forms page in his or her own Web browser, the actual code that's executed is located on the Web server and is run by the Web server. When the user clicks a button, for example, the browser typically sends the button click event back to the server, which processes the event and sends a new Web page back to the browser. Although the process seems similar to that of Windows Forms, there's actually a lot going on behind the scenes when a control is used on a Web Forms page!

In the following exercise, you'll practice creating an event procedure for the *btnCalculate* object on the Web Forms page.

Create the *btnCalculate_Click* event procedure

1   Double-click the Calculate button on the Web Forms page.

   The code-behind file (WebForm1.aspx.vb) is opened in the Code Editor, and the *btnCalculate_Click* event procedure appears.

2   Type the following program code:

```
Dim LoanPayment As Single
'Use Pmt function to determine payment for 36 month loan
LoanPayment = Pmt(txtInterest.Text / 12, 36, txtAmount.Text)
txtPayment.Text = Format(Abs(LoanPayment), "$0.00")
```

   This event procedure uses the *Pmt* function, a financial function that's part of the Visual Basic language, to determine what the monthly payment for a car loan would be by using the specified interest rate (*txtInterest.Text*), a three-year (36-month) loan period, and the specified principal amount (*txtAmount.Text*). The result is stored in the *LoanPayment* single-precision variable and then formatted with appropriate monetary formatting and displayed by using the *txtPayment* text box object on the Web page. The *Abs* (absolute value) function is used to make the loan payment a positive number—the *Pmt* function returns a negative number by default (reflecting money that's owed), but I think this formatting looks strange when it isn't part of a balance sheet.

   Notice that the program statements in the code-behind file are just regular Visual Basic code—the same stuff you've been using throughout this book. You'll even use an *Imports* statement. This process feels similar to creating a Windows application.

3   Scroll to the top of the Code Editor, and enter the following program statement as the first line of the file:

```
Imports System.Math
```

   As you learned in Chapter 5, the *Abs* function isn't included in Visual Basic by default, but it's part of the *System.Math* class in the .NET Framework, which can be included in your project via the *Imports* statement. Web applications can make use of the .NET Framework class libraries just as Windows applications can.

4   Click the Save All button on the Standard toolbar.

That's it! You've entered the program code necessary to run the car loan calculator and make your Web Forms page interactive. Now build the project and see how it works!

Build and run the Web application

1   Click the Start button on the Standard toolbar.

▶   **Note**   If an error displays here indicating that the Web server doesn't support debugging ASP.NET Web applications, it means that IIS, the FrontPage 2000 Server Extensions, and the .NET Framework aren't properly installed and configured. Review the section "Installing the Software for ASP.NET Programming" for recommendations on how to correct this.

Visual Basic builds the project and runs it by using Internet Explorer. The car loan calculator looks like this:

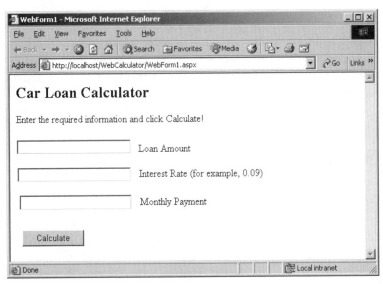

2   Type **18000** in the Loan Amount text box, and then type **0.09** in the Interest Rate text box.

You'll compute the monthly loan payment for an $18,000 loan at 9 percent interest for 36 months.

3   Click the Calculate button.

Visual Basic calculates the payment amount and displays $572.40 in the Monthly Payment text box. Your screen will look like this:

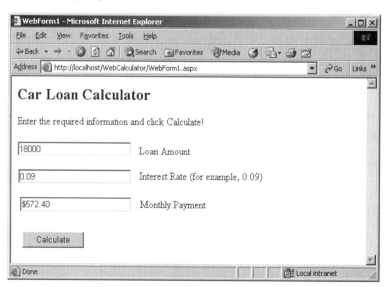

4   Close Internet Explorer.

You're finished testing your Web application for now. When Internet Explorer closes, your program is effectively ended. As you can see, building and running a Web application is basically the same as for a Windows application, except that the final application is run in the browser. You can even set break points and debug your application just as you can in a Windows application. To deploy a Web application, you'd need to copy the .aspx file and any necessary support files for the project to a properly configured virtual directory on the Web server.

Validating Input Fields on a Web Forms Page

Although this Web application is useful, it runs into problems if the user forgets to enter a principal amount or an interest rate or specifies data in the wrong format. To make this Web application more robust, consider adding one or more *validator controls* to the Web Forms page that will require user input in the proper format. The validator controls are located on the Web Forms tab of the Toolbox and include controls that require data entry in important fields (*RequiredField-Validator*), require entry in the proper range (*RangeValidator*), and so on. For information on the validator controls, search the Visual Studio online Help.

One Step Further: Creating a Link to Another Web Page

If your Web application will feature more than one Web page, you might want to use the *HyperLink* control on the Web Forms tab of the Toolbox to let your users jump from the current Web page to a new one. The *HyperLink* control places a hyperlink, which the user can click to display another Web page, on the current Web page. When you use a *HyperLink* control, you specify the text that will be hyperlinked, and you specify the desired resource to display (either a URL or a local path) by using the *NavigateUrl* property.

If you've already created the Web pages, you can add them to your Web application project and establish the proper links. If you want to create new Web pages, you can use Visual Studio .NET.

In the following exercise, you'll create a second Web page by using Visual Studio, and you'll save it in HTML format along with your other project files. The document will be a Help file that users of your Web application can access to get more information. Next you'll add a *HyperLink* control to the WebCalculator project and set the *HyperLink* control's *NavigateUrl* property to the new HTML page.

Create an HTML page

1   Click the Add HTML Page command on the Project menu.

 The Add New Item dialog box appears with the HTML Page template selected.

2   Type **WebCalculatorHelp.htm** in the Name text box, and click Open.

 The WebCalculatorHelp.htm file is added to Solution Explorer and is opened in the HTML Designer in Design view.

 Notice that the Web Forms tab is no longer displayed in the Toolbox. Because this is an HTML page, the Web Forms controls aren't supported.

3   Click the HTML page and change the *pageLayout* property in the Properties window to FlowLayout.

 Visual Studio removes the grid from the HTML page.

4   Click the HTML page to add your cursor, and type the following text:

 Car Loan Calculator

 This Car Loan Calculator program was developed for the book *Microsoft Visual Basic .NET Step by Step—Version 2003,* **by Michael Halvorson (Microsoft Press, 2003). The Web application is best viewed using Microsoft Internet Explorer version 5.0 or later.**

To learn more about how this application was created, read Chapter 22 in the book.

Operating instructions:

Type a loan amount, without dollar sign or commas, into the Loan Amount text box.

Type an interest rate in decimal format into the Interest Rate text box. Do not include the "%" sign. For example, to specify a 9% interest rate, type "0.09".

Note that this loan calculator assumes a three year, 36-month payment period.

Click the Calculate button to compute the basic monthly loan payment that does not include taxes or other bank fees.

5   Using the Formatting toolbar, add bold and italic formatting, as shown here:

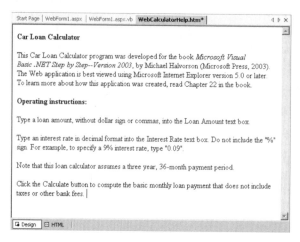

Now you'll use the *HyperLink* control to create a hyperlink on your Web Forms page that opens the WebCalculatorHelp.htm file.

Use the *HyperLink* control

1   Display the Web Forms page (WebForm1.aspx) in Design view.

2   Click the *HyperLink* control on the Web Forms tab of the Toolbox, and then draw a hyperlink object on the Web Forms page to the right of the Calculate button.

3   Set the *Text* property of the hyperlink object to "Get Help".

The *Text* property contains the text that will appear underlined on the Web Forms page as the hyperlink. You want to use words here that will make it obvious that there's a Web page available containing Help text.

4   Click the *NavigateUrl* property, and then click the ellipsis button in the second column.

Visual Studio opens the Select URL dialog box, which prompts you for the location of the Web page you want to link to.

5   Click the WebCalculatorHelp.htm file in the Contents pane.

The URL text box displays the name of the file you want to use as the hyperlink. Your dialog box will look like this:

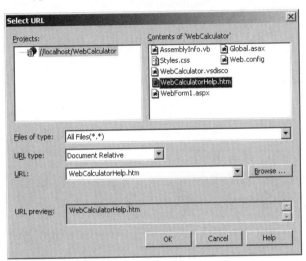

6   Click OK to set the *NavigateUrl* property.

Your Web page looks like this:

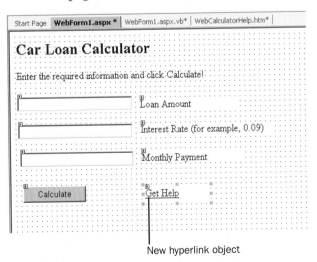

New hyperlink object

Your link is finished, and you're ready to run the WebCalculator application again.

7   Click the Save All button on the Standard toolbar.

8   Click the Start button.

> ▶   **Note**   The complete WebCalculator program is located in the c:\vbnet03sbs\chap22\webcalculator folder. See the readme file in the chap22 folder for instructions on how to configure and test the Web-Calculator program.

Visual Studio builds the Web application and runs it in Internet Explorer.

9   Compute another loan payment to verify that the original program is operating correctly. (Specify your own principal amount and interest rate this time.)

10   Now click the Get Help hyperlink to see how the *HyperLink* control works.

After a moment, Internet Explorer displays the second Web page. Your screen looks like this:

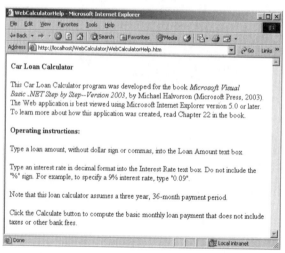

11   Read the text, and then click the Back button in Internet Explorer.

Just like any Web application, this one lets you click the Back and Forward buttons to jump from one Web page to the next.

12   When you're finished experimenting with the Web Calculator program, close Internet Explorer. You're finished working with Visual Basic .NET for now.

As you add additional HTML pages to your solution, feel free to add additional hyperlinks by using the handy *HyperLink* control. Although ASP.NET has many additional capabilities, you can see from these simple exercises how powerful Web Forms are and how similar the development process is to the Windows Forms techniques you've been learning about.

Congratulations on completing the entire *Microsoft Visual Basic .NET Step by Step—Version 2003* programming course! You're ready for more sophisticated Visual Basic .NET challenges and programming techniques. Check out the resource list in Appendix B for a few ideas about continuing your learning.

Chapter 22 Quick Reference

To	Do this
Create a new Web application	Select the ASP.NET Web Application icon in the New Project dialog box, and then specify a Web server and a project name.
Enter text on a Web Forms page or an HTML page	Use the Properties window to change the *DOCUMENT* object's *pageLayout* property to FlowLayout, and then click the page and type the text you want to add.
Format text on a Web Forms page or an HTML page	In flow layout mode, select the text on the page that you want to format, and then click a button or control on the Formatting toolbar.
View the HTML code in your Web Forms page or HTML page	Click the HTML tab at the bottom of the designer.
Display the layout grid in the Web Forms Designer or HTML Designer	Use the Properties window to change the *DOCUMENT* object's *pageLayout* property to GridLayout.
Add controls to a Web Forms page	Display the HTML or Web Forms tabs of the Toolbox, and drag controls to the Web Forms page in the Web Forms Designer.
Change the name of an object on a Web Forms page	Use the Properties window to change the object's *ID* property to a new name.
Write an event procedure for an object on a Web Forms page	Double-click the object to display the code-behind file, and write the event procedure code for the object in the Code Editor.
Verify the format of the data entered by the user into a control on a Web Forms page	Use one or more validator controls from the Web Forms tab of the Toolbox to test the data entered in an input control.

To	Do this
Run a Web application in Visual Studio	Click the Start button on the Standard toolbar. Visual Studio will build the project and load the Web application into Internet Explorer.
Create an HTML page for a project	Click the Add HTML Page command on the Project menu, and then add the new HTML page to the project. Create and format the HTML page by using the HTML Designer.
Create a link to other Web pages in your Web application	Add a Web Forms *HyperLink* control to your Web Forms page, and then set the control's *NavigateUrl* property to the address of the linked Web page.

Part

7

Appendixes

Upgrading Visual Basic 6 Programs to Visual Basic .NET 2003

In this appendix, you will learn how to:

■ Evaluate Microsoft Visual Basic 6 programs for compatibility with Visual Basic .NET.

■ Locate Internet resources for migrating applications.

■ Run the Visual Basic Upgrade Wizard to upgrade Visual Basic 6 programs to Visual Basic .NET 2003.

This book teaches Visual Basic .NET programming techniques from scratch and assumes no previous programming experience. However, many users will be coming to Visual Basic .NET with significant development time in previous versions of Visual Basic, including Visual Basic 6. So what steps do you follow if you have older Visual Basic programs that you want to convert to Visual Basic .NET 2003? Are there tools or resources that can assist in this upgrading, or *migration*, process?

This appendix identifies a few of your resources for analyzing Visual Basic 6 programs and upgrading them to Visual Basic .NET 2003. You'll learn some of the major features of Visual Basic 6 that are no longer supported in Visual Basic .NET, the strategies Microsoft recommends for migrating Visual Basic 6 applications, and the location of useful Internet resources that document the upgrading process in greater detail. You'll also learn how to use the Visual Basic Upgrade Wizard, which can automatically convert part or all of your Visual Basic 6 application to Visual Basic .NET 2003.

Assessing Visual Basic 6 Programs for Compatibility

Visual Basic .NET is a very significant revision to the Visual Basic programming language and to Microsoft Windows programming in general. This change brings numerous advantages: a revised Visual Basic language syntax, which emphasizes clear and maintainable code; the new .NET Framework class libraries, which add additional functionality and eliminate the hassle of calling Windows APIs; real object-oriented programming features, including inheritance; the new Microsoft ADO.NET database programming model, which provides access to truly distributed data sources; and new controls in the Toolbox, including the Web Forms controls for Internet programming. However, these new features come at a cost—not all Visual Basic 6 code is supported in Visual Basic .NET, and in many cases, you'll need to extensively revise existing Visual Basic 6 programs to make them compatible with Visual Basic .NET.

The decision is up to you—you can upgrade your existing Visual Basic 6 code, or you can continue to maintain some of it in Visual Basic 6, which Microsoft has announced it will continue to sell and support. For each Visual Basic 6 application, you have three choices:

- Leave your programs in Visual Basic 6 format. Microsoft continues to support Visual Basic 6 and will do so for the foreseeable future.

- Upgrade part of your Visual Basic 6 program (for example, one or more components), and interoperate with COM components created using Visual Basic 6.

- Upgrade the entire Visual Basic 6 program to Visual Basic .NET 2003.

Your decision will depend on the goals of your project. If your Visual Basic 6 application is basically complete, if you're in maintenance mode, or if your program relies on some older components that cannot easily be updated, you might want to leave the program in Visual Basic 6 format. If your application is still in development, if it will make particular use of XML or Web pages, or if it will utilize distributed data sources, upgrading the program to Visual Basic .NET 2003 will likely be cost effective.

Problematic Issues

Microsoft has provided a list of unsupported or problematic features in Visual Basic 6 that will require special consideration when you upgrade your application to Visual Basic .NET. The list includes the following features:

- **OLE Container Control.**   This ActiveX control isn't supported in Visual Basic .NET, and no replacement is available.

- **Dynamic Data Exchange.**   Dynamic Data Exchange (DDE) methods are no longer supported. Applications that depend on DDE should be revised to use another method of inter-application communication, such as the *SendMessage* API.

- **DAO or RDO Data Binding.**   Data binding to a DAO or an RDO data source isn't supported in Visual Basic .NET. The *Data* control and the *RemoteData* control are no longer available in Visual Basic .NET. Applications that rely on DAO or RDO data binding either should be updated to use ADO in Visual Basic 6 or should use ADO.NET after upgrading to Visual Basic .NET.

- **Visual Basic 5 Projects.**   Visual Basic 5 projects should be upgraded to Visual Basic 6 projects before upgrading to Visual Basic .NET. To upgrade to Visual Basic 6, open the project in Visual Basic 6, and choose to upgrade controls. Then save the project in Visual Basic 6 before upgrading to Visual Basic .NET.

- **ActiveX DHTML Page Applications.**   These are client-side Web technologies that cannot be automatically upgraded to Visual Basic .NET. These should be left in Visual Basic 6. These applications interoperate well with Visual Basic .NET technologies; you can navigate from an ActiveX DHTML page application to a Web Forms page and back.

- **ActiveX Documents.**   Like ActiveX DHTML page applications, ActiveX documents cannot be automatically upgraded to Visual Basic .NET. And as you can do between an ActiveX DHTML page application and a Web Forms page, you can navigate from an ActiveX document to a Microsoft ASP.NET Web page and back, so you can leave these applications in Visual Basic 6.

- **Property Pages.**   These aren't supported in Visual Basic .NET because the Windows Forms property browser is very flexible and can display and edit any classes, unlike the Visual Basic 6 property browser. You should reimplement the properties on property pages as standard control properties.

A

Upgrading

- **User Controls.**   User controls created with Visual Basic 6 can be used in Visual Basic .NET. Currently, modifications to user controls should be made in Visual Basic 6.

- **WebClasses.**   Visual Basic 6 WebClasses cannot be upgraded to Visual Basic .NET Web Forms. WebClasses can interoperate with Visual Basic .NET Web technologies, however—you can navigate from a Visual Basic 6 WebClass to an ASP.NET application or from an ASP.NET application to a Visual Basic 6 WebClass.

- **Visual Basic Add-Ins.**   Because Visual Basic .NET uses the Microsoft Visual Studio IDE, the object model for extensibility is significantly different from that of Visual Basic 6. Add-ins must be rewritten in Visual Basic. NET. The advantage in doing so is that the add-in will then be available to all languages.

- **Graphics.**   The Visual Basic 6 forms graphics methods, such as *Line* and *Circle*, cannot be automatically upgraded by the Visual Basic Upgrade Wizard.

- **Drag-and-Drop Functionality.**   Drag-and-drop functionality cannot be automatically upgraded by the Visual Basic Upgrade Wizard.

- **Variants.**   Visual Basic .NET no longer supports the *Variant* data type in Visual Basic 6. When an application is upgraded using the Visual Basic Upgrade Wizard, the *Variant* data type is converted to *Object*.

- **Windows APIs.**   It is still legitimate to call the Windows API directly in a Visual Basic .NET application, but many existing API calls are no longer necessary due to the increased functionality of the .NET Framework class libraries. Existing calls to the Windows API in Visual Basic 6 applications might need to be revised, although direct calls are still permissible.

Internet Resources for Migration

Microsoft is aware that upgrading existing code is an important priority, so it has assembled numerous resources on the Web to make the process easier—or at least more straightforward. The following Web site contains useful information for assessing existing Visual Basic 6 applications and converting them to Visual Basic .NET:

http://msdn.microsoft.com/vbasic/techinfo/articles/upgrade/default.asp

On this site, you'll find white papers about various aspects of upgrading Visual Basic 6 applications, technical sessions (multimedia presentations) describing important migration tools and issues, and checklists for planning the conversion process. This site changes periodically, so monitor it on a regular basis if you're upgrading one or more Visual Basic 6 applications to Visual Basic .NET.

Upgrade Steps

If you decide that upgrading your existing Visual Basic 6 applications to Visual Basic .NET is your best choice, here are the overall steps that Microsoft recommends:

1 Install Visual Basic 6 and Visual Basic .NET 2003 on the same computer.

Installing Visual Basic 6 isn't a requirement, but if the project to be upgraded uses controls or components that don't have an upgrade equivalent in Visual Basic .NET, you might encounter additional upgrade errors and warnings.

2 Compile and run your application in Visual Basic 6 first to ensure that it works correctly.

3 Run the Visual Basic Upgrade Wizard to upgrade.

4 Review the upgrade report and upgrade comments, and make any necessary modifications.

Running the Visual Basic Upgrade Wizard

Visual Studio .NET includes a special program called the Visual Basic Upgrade Wizard that can assist you in upgrading your Visual Basic 6 applications to Visual Basic .NET. The Visual Basic Upgrade Wizard isn't a complete solution for migrating Visual Basic 6 applications—the tool can handle most repetitive code changes and can even swap Visual Basic 6 controls for .NET controls on forms. But in all except the most trivial applications, you'll have some hand coding to do when the wizard is complete.

The Visual Basic Upgrade Wizard starts automatically when you try to load a Visual Basic 6 application in Visual Studio .NET. It creates a new Visual Basic .NET project for the original application and then migrates as much code as possible. When the wizard cannot upgrade a feature, it adds comments to the program code identifying issues that you'll need to address later. The wizard also creates an upgrade report listing general issues related to the migration and any problems it wasn't able to fix. The following exercise demonstrates how the Visual Basic Upgrade Wizard works. In the example, I'll open and upgrade a Visual Basic 6 project named Alarm.vbp, which uses a *Timer* control, *TextBox* controls, and *Button* controls to create a personal appointment reminder that notifies users when it's time for an important meeting. Because the program doesn't use features that aren't supported in Visual Basic .NET, the upgrade is relatively straightforward. Within Visual Basic 6, the Alarm project looks like this:

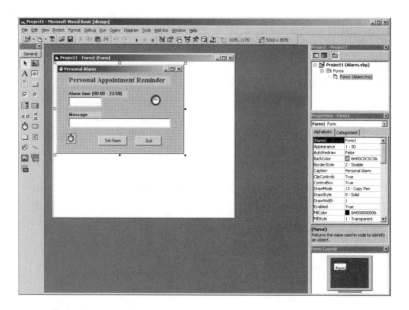

▶   **Note**   Because the Alarm Visual Basic 6 project doesn't use any unsupported features, it isn't necessary to have Visual Basic 6 installed to follow these upgrade steps.

Upgrade the Alarm program

1   Start Visual Studio .NET 2003, and open the Alarm.vbp project in the c:\vbnet03sbs\appa\alarmvb6 folder.

Visual Studio recognizes that Alarm.vbp is a Visual Basic 6 project, and it starts the Visual Basic Upgrade Wizard to upgrade the project to Visual Basic .NET. You'll see this dialog box:

▶ **Note**   If your edition of Visual Studio .NET doesn't include the Visual Basic Upgrade Wizard, a message box will be displayed indicating that Visual Basic 6 migration isn't supported.

As the dialog box indicates, the Visual Basic Upgrade Wizard assists in the migration process by creating a new Visual Basic .NET project for the Visual Basic 6 application, copying form and class files to the project and converting them to the new format and issuing an upgrade report that identifies additional work items. The upgrade report is added to the Visual Basic .NET project so that it's easy to locate and read.

2   Click Next to start the conversion.

The wizard asks you some questions about the format of your project and its component contents. Your screen will look like the following illustration:

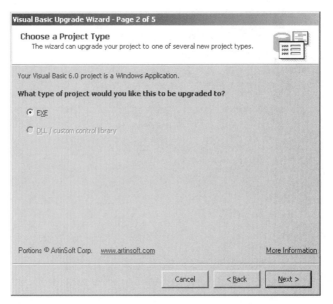

In this example, EXE format was selected by default for the Alarm application because the tool is an application program and not a DLL (dynamic link library).

3   Click Next to continue the upgrade process.

The wizard prompts you for a location for the new Visual Basic .NET project. The default folder is a subfolder within your original project folder, as shown in this dialog box:

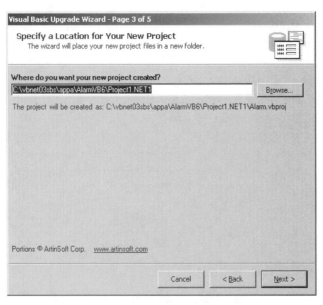

4   Click the Next button, and then click Yes if you're prompted to create a new folder.

5   Change the new project path to **c:\vbnet03sbs\appa\my alarmvb.net**

This will place the upgraded Visual Basic .NET project in a new folder named My AlarmVB.NET in the appa folder.

6   Click Next again to begin the upgrade process.

The Visual Basic Upgrade Wizard invokes the upgrade engine and steps through the Alarm project's form and code to convert the controls to .NET controls, to update the program code to conform to Visual Basic .NET specifications, and to create an upgrade report. The upgrade report is saved in HTML format and is named _UpgradeReport.htm.

After a few minutes, the wizard closes, and the new Visual Basic .NET project appears in the Visual Studio development environment. The new project's contents are listed in Solution Explorer.

7   If the form isn't visible, select Alarm.vb now in Solution Explorer and click the View Designer button.

Your screen will look like this:

Upgrade Report

Alarm.vb

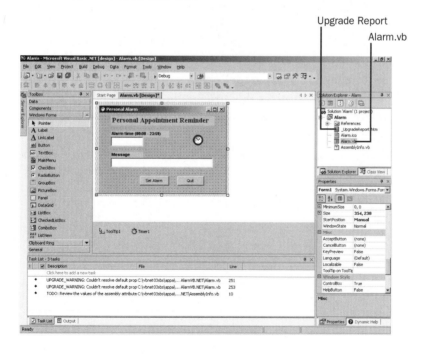

If you compare this figure with the first one in this appendix (the Alarm project loaded in Visual Basic 6), a few characteristics of the Visual Basic Upgrade Wizard become apparent. First, although the wizard accurately sized the form and its objects, the fonts used on the form aren't an exact match and will need to be adjusted in Visual Studio .NET to display the proper user interface. Second, the Visual Basic 6 controls were upgraded to .NET controls. The *Label* and *TextBox* controls were upgraded to their equivalent .NET versions. The *CommandButton* controls are now *Button* controls, even though they still have the "Command" name. The *Image* control showing the clock was upgraded to a .NET *PictureBox* control. Visual Studio .NET doesn't have an *Image* control, and graphic files are now displayed using just the *PictureBox* control. The *Timer* control was upgraded to the .NET version, and it now appears in the component tray.

Finally, the wizard has added a *ToolTip* control to the component tray below the form. In Visual Basic 6, many controls had a *ToolTip-Text* property to display a tool tip for an individual control. Visual Studio .NET has a different mechanism to display tool tips and uses a single *ToolTip* control to manage tool tips for all the controls on a form. Because many Visual Basic 6 controls had the *ToolTipText* property, even if it was empty, the Visual Basic Upgrade Wizard adds it as a matter of course to upgraded Visual Basic 6 projects.

8   Double-click the _UpgradeReport.htm file in Solution Explorer.

Visual Studio displays the formatted upgrade report, giving you an opportunity to review the issues that remain in the migration of this application.

9   If necessary, close the Toolbox to get more space, and then open the Global Issues and Alarm.vb sections by clicking the plus signs (+) to read the detailed report.

Your screen will look like this:

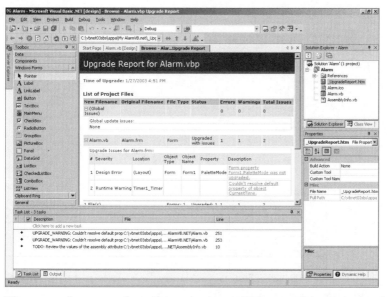

The upgrade report describes any upgrade issues. For example, the *PaletteMode* property for the form wasn't upgraded, and the default property for the *Timer1* object couldn't be resolved. If you click on the Description hyperlinks, additional documentation about the issue is displayed.

10 Click Alarm.vb in Solution Explorer, and click the View Code button to display the Alarm code in the Code Editor.

Near the top of the Code Editor, you'll see a collapsed Upgrade Support section. This section includes code to assist in the Visual Basic 6 compatibility. As you scan through the program code, you'll see comments that flag potential issues, as shown on the following page.

Upgrading

Upgrade Support section

Upgrade comments

These upgrade comments describe the issue and typically contain a hyperlink for additional documentation, which you can see if you scroll the Code Editor to the right. For example:

```
'UPGRADE_WARNING: Couldn't resolve default property of object
  CurrentTime. Click for more:
  'ms-help://MS.VSCC.2003/commoner/redir/redirect.htm?key
    word="vbup1037"'
```

Realizing that some upgrade problems might be confusing, Microsoft has engineered the Visual Basic Upgrade Wizard to insert hyperlinks to where there is more information.

Run the upgraded Alarm program

1 Click the Start button on the Standard toolbar.

A Save File As dialog box appears asking for a location and a name for the Alarm solution file.

2 Click Save to accept the default name of Alarm.sln in the AlarmVB.NET folder.

The Personal Alarm form appears! Even though the upgrade included warnings, it didn't include errors that required modifications to the code.

3   Type a time in the Alarm Time text box that's a couple of minutes in the future. Specify the time by using a military format, where 8:00 a.m. is specified as 08:00 and 1:00 p.m. is specified as 13:00.

4   Type a short message in the Message text box, such as **Upgraded to Visual Basic .NET!**, and then click the Set Alarm button.

Patiently wait for the time to pass, and you should see your message appear; it will look similar to this one:

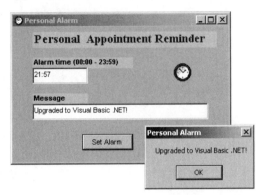

5   Click OK, and then click Quit to close the program.

In this simple case, the Visual Basic 6 project was upgraded, and it didn't require modifications to run. However, most upgrades will require some modifications to compile and run without error. You'll also typically need to make some user interface adjustments and perform careful testing to ensure the program works the same as it does in Visual Basic 6. In my opinion, the benefits of upgrading most projects using the Visual Basic Upgrade Wizard outweigh the potential disadvantages, but you'll need to assess this for your own projects on a case-by-case basis. Best of luck!

A

Upgrading

Where to Go for More Information

In this appendix, you will learn how to:

■ Search Web sites for information about Microsoft Visual Basic .NET.

■ Locate additional books about Visual Basic .NET programming.

This book has presented beginning, intermediate, and advanced Visual Basic .NET programming techniques with the aim of making you a confident software developer and Microsoft Windows programmer. Now that you've experimented with many of the tools and features in Visual Basic .NET 2003, you're ready for more advanced topics and the full breadth of the Microsoft Visual Studio .NET 2003 development suite. If you have your sights set on a career in Visual Basic programming, you might also want to test your proficiency by preparing for a certified exam in Visual Basic .NET development. In this appendix, you'll learn about additional resources for Visual Basic .NET programming, including helpful Web sites on the Internet, a source for certification information, and books that you can use to expand your Visual Basic .NET programming skills.

Visual Basic .NET Web Sites

The Web is a boon to programmers and is definitely the fastest mechanism for gathering information about Visual Basic .NET and related technologies. In the following section, I list several of the Web sites that I use to learn about new products and services related to Visual Basic .NET. As you use this list, note that the Internet address and contents of each site change from time to time, so the sites might not appear exactly as I've described them. Considering the constant ebb and flow of the Internet, it's also a good idea to search for "Visual Basic" or "Visual Studio .NET" occasionally to see what new information is available.

http://msdn.microsoft.com/vbasic/

The Microsoft Corporation Visual Basic home page is the best overall site for documentation, breaking news, conference information, and product support for Visual Basic .NET. This site will give you up-to-date information about the entire Visual Basic product line and will let you know how new operating systems, applications, and programming tools affect Visual Basic development. From the Visual Basic home page, you can also click on support links for the remaining Visual Studio .NET tools.

http://www.devx.com/

DevX is a commercial Web site devoted to numerous Windows development topics and issues, including Visual Studio .NET and Visual Basic .NET programming. Discussion groups of professional Visual Basic .NET programmers provide peer-to-peer interaction and feedback for many development issues. In addition, the DevX Marketplace offers books, controls, and third-party tools for sale.

http://www.microsoft.com/mspress/

The Microsoft Press home page offers the newest books on Visual Basic .NET 2003 programming from Microsoft Press authors. Check here for new books about Microsoft Visual C# .NET, Microsoft Visual C++ .NET, and Microsoft Visual J# .NET as well. You can also download freebies and send mail to Microsoft Press.

http://www.microsoft.com/traincert/

This is the Microsoft corporate Web site for software training and services, including testing and certification. Over the last few years, many Visual Basic programmers have found that they can better demonstrate their development skills to potential employers if they pass one or more certification examinations and earn a Microsoft certified credential, such as the MCP (Microsoft Certified Professional), MCSE (Microsoft Certified Systems Engineer), or MCSA (Microsoft Certified Systems Administrator). Visit this Web site to learn more about your certification options.

http://communities2.microsoft.com/home/

This is a site of newsgroup communities for many Microsoft software products, including the tools in the Visual Studio .NET 2003 family. Currently, Visual Studio .NET newsgroup topics are listed in the Enterprise Development Newsgroups category under the keywords "vb," "vc," "dotnet," "vsnet," and "vstudio."

Books for Visual Basic .NET Programming

Printed books about Visual Basic .NET programming provide in-depth sources of information and self-paced training that Web sites can supplement but not replace. As you seek to expand your Visual Basic .NET programming skills, I recommend that you consult the following sources of printed information (listed here by category). Note that this isn't a complete bibliography of Visual Basic .NET titles, but it is a list that's representative of the books available in English at the time of the initial release of Visual Basic .NET 2003.

Visual Basic .NET Programming

- *Inside Microsoft Visual Studio .NET 2003*, by Brian Johnson, Craig Skibo, and Marc Young (Microsoft Press, ISBN 0-7356-1874-7).
- *Programming Microsoft Visual Basic .NET*, by Francesco Balena (Microsoft Press, ISBN 0-7356-1375-3).
- *Coding Techniques for Microsoft Visual Basic .NET*, by John Connell (Microsoft Press, ISBN 0-7356-1254-4).
- *Visual Basic .NET Codemaster's Library*, by Matt Tagliaferri (Sybex, ISBN 0-7821-4103-X).
- *Professional VB .NET*, by Fred Barwell, Richard Blair, Richard Case, Jonathan Crossland, Bill Forgey, Whitney Hankison, Billy Hollis, Rockford Lhotka, Tim McCarthy, Jan D. Narkiewicz, Jonathan Pinnock, Rama Ramachandran, Matthew Reynolds, John Roth, Bill Sempf, Bill Sheldon, and Scott Short (Wrox Press, ISBN 1-8610-0497-4).
- *Microsoft Visual Basic .NET Programmer's Cookbook*, by Matthew MacDonald (Microsoft Press, ISBN 0-7356-1931-X).
- *Upgrading Microsoft Visual Basic 6.0 to Microsoft Visual Basic .NET*, by Ed Robinson, Michael Bond, and Robert Ian Oliver (Microsoft Press, ISBN 0-7356-1587-X).
- *Practical Standards for Microsoft Visual Basic .NET*, by James Foxall (Microsoft Press, ISBN 0-7356-1356-7).

B

Where to Go

- *OOP: Building Reusable Components with Microsoft Visual Basic .NET*, by Ken Spencer, Tom Eberhard, and John Alexander (Microsoft Press, ISBN 0-7356-1379-6).
- *OOP with Microsoft Visual Basic .NET and Microsoft Visual C# .NET Step by Step*, by Robin A. Reynolds-Haertle (Microsoft Press, ISBN 0-7356-1568-3).

Web Programming with ASP.NET

- *Microsoft ASP.NET Programming with Microsoft Visual Basic .NET Version 2003 Step by Step*, by G. Andrew Duthie (Microsoft Press, ISBN 0-7356-1934-4).
- *Programming Microsoft ASP.NET*, by Dino Esposito (Microsoft Press, ISBN 0-7356-1903-4).
- *Microsoft ASP.NET Coding Strategies with the Microsoft ASP.NET Team*, by Matthew Gibbs and Rob Howard (Microsoft Press, ISBN 0-7356-1900-X).
- *Beginning ASP.NET Using VB .NET*, by Rob Birdwell, Ollie Cornes, Chris Goode, John Kauffman, Ajoy Krishnamoorthy, Juan T. Llibre, Christopher L. Miller, Neil Raybould, David Sussman, and Chris Ullman (Wrox Press, ISBN 1-8610-0504-0).
- *Teach Yourself ASP.NET in 21 Days*, by Chris Payne and Scott Mitchell (Sams, ISBN 0-6723-2168-8).

Database Programming with ADO.NET

- *Microsoft ADO.NET Step by Step*, by Rebecca M. Riordan (Microsoft Press, ISBN 0-7356-1236-6).
- *Programming Microsoft SQL Server 2000 with Microsoft Visual Basic .NET*, by Rick Dobson (Microsoft Press, ISBN 0-7356-1535-7).
- *Microsoft ADO.NET (Core Reference)*, by David Sceppa (Microsoft Press, ISBN 0-7356-1423-7).

Visual Basic for Applications Programming

- *Microsoft Excel 2002 Visual Basic for Applications Step by Step*, by Reed Jacobson (Microsoft Press, ISBN 0-7356-1359-1).
- *Excel 2002 Power Programming with VBA*, by John Walkenbach (Hungry Minds, ISBN 0-7645-4799-2).
- *Microsoft Access 2002 Visual Basic for Applications Step by Step*, by Evan Callahan (Microsoft Press, ISBN 0-7356-1358-3).

B

Where to Go

Upgrading Index

This index provides an alphabetical guide to many of the upgrading topics in this book. It is designed to help readers who are familiar with Visual Basic 6 identify the new features in Visual Basic .NET Version 2003 and use them to upgrade their applications. Scan both the Upgrade Topic and Description columns to find topics that you are curious about, and then turn to the page number indicated for a discussion of the upgrading material. Note that a comprehensive index following this table offers additional information about Visual Basic .NET Version 2003 features and programming skills.

Index

Symbols

A

C

About the Author

Michael Halvorson is the author or co-author of 30 books, including *Microsoft Office XP Inside Out*, *Microsoft Visual Basic 6.0, Professional Step By Step, Second Edition*, *Learn Microsoft Visual Basic 6.0 Now*, and *Microsoft Word 97/Visual Basic Step by Step*. Michael has a bachelor's degree in Computer Science from Pacific Lutheran University in Tacoma, Washington, and master's and doctoral degrees in History from the University of Washington in Seattle. He was employed at Microsoft Corporation

Photo by Kim Halvorson

from 1985 to 1993. Now he divides his time between developing innovative software solutions with Visual Basic .NET and teaching college courses in European history. Michael is also the editor of *Loharano (The Water Spring): Missionary Tales from Madagascar* (Warren & Howe Publishers, 2003), a collection of essays about Lutheran missionary activity in 19th century Madagascar. He lives in Seattle with his wife and two boys.

Protractor Triangle

The word navigation traditionally meant the art or science of conducting ships and other watercraft from one place to another. A device commonly used in navigation is the protractor triangle. It plots courses accurately in tight spaces when used with a parallel rule or course plotter. It's essential for easily measuring right angles, celestial azimuth angles, and lines of position. With its protractor scales, the triangle is easily aligned in any direction with a chart meridian.

At Microsoft Press, we use tools to illustrate our books for software developers and IT professionals. Tools very simply and powerfully symbolize human inventiveness. They're a metaphor for people extending their capabilities, precision, and reach. From simple calipers and pliers to digital micrometers and lasers, these stylized illustrations give each book a visual identity, and a personality to the series. With tools and knowledge, there's no limit to creativity and innovation. Our tagline says it all: *the tools you need to put technology to work*.

The manuscript for this book was prepared and submitted to Microsoft Press in electronic form. Pages were composed by Microsoft Press using Adobe FrameMaker+SGML for Windows, with text in Sabon and display type in ITC Franklin Gothic. Composed pages were delivered to the printer as electronic pre-press files.

Cover designer:	Methodologie, Inc.
Interior Graphic Designer:	James D. Kramer
Principal Compositor:	Elizabeth Hansford
Interior Graphic Artist:	Michael Kloepfer
Principal Copy Editor:	Sandi Resnick
Proofreader:	nSight, Inc.
Indexer:	Richard Shrout

Get the expert guidance you need to succeed in .NET Framework development with *Visual Basic .NET!*

Applied Microsoft® .NET Framework Programming in Microsoft Visual Basic® .NET
U.S.A. $49.99
Canada $72.99
ISBN: 0-7356-1787-2

The Microsoft .NET Framework provides powerful technologies such as ASP.NET Web Forms, XML Web services, and Windows® Forms to simplify developing applications and components that work seamlessly on the Internet. This book shows how to make the most of the .NET Framework's common language runtime (CLR). Written by two highly respected developer/writers, it's intended for anyone who understands OOP concepts such as data abstraction, inheritance, and polymorphism. The book clearly explains the extensible type system of the CLR, examines how the CLR manages the behavior of types, and explores how an application manipulates types. While focusing on Visual Basic .NET, its in-depth explanations and concepts apply equally to all programming languages that target the .NET Framework.

microsoft.com/mspress

MICROSOFT LICENSE AGREEMENT
Book Companion CD

IMPORTANT—READ CAREFULLY: This Microsoft End-User License Agreement ("EULA") is a legal agreement between you (either an individual or an entity) and Microsoft Corporation for the Microsoft product identified above, which includes computer software and may include associated media, printed materials, and "online" or electronic documentation ("SOFTWARE PRODUCT"). Any component included within the SOFTWARE PRODUCT that is accompanied by a separate End-User License Agreement shall be governed by such agreement and not the terms set forth below. By installing, copying, or otherwise using the SOFTWARE PRODUCT, you agree to be bound by the terms of this EULA. If you do not agree to the terms of this EULA, you are not authorized to install, copy, or otherwise use the SOFTWARE PRODUCT; you may, however, return the SOFTWARE PRODUCT, along with all printed materials and other items that form a part of the Microsoft product that includes the SOFTWARE PRODUCT, to the place you obtained them for a full refund.

SOFTWARE PRODUCT LICENSE

The SOFTWARE PRODUCT is protected by United States copyright laws and international copyright treaties, as well as other intellectual property laws and treaties. The SOFTWARE PRODUCT is licensed, not sold.

1. **GRANT OF LICENSE.** This EULA grants you the following rights:

   a. **Software Product.** You may install and use one copy of the SOFTWARE PRODUCT on a single computer. The primary user of the computer on which the SOFTWARE PRODUCT is installed may make a second copy for his or her exclusive use on a portable computer.

   b. **Storage/Network Use.** You may also store or install a copy of the SOFTWARE PRODUCT on a storage device, such as a network server, used only to install or run the SOFTWARE PRODUCT on your other computers over an internal network; however, you must acquire and dedicate a license for each separate computer on which the SOFTWARE PRODUCT is installed or run from the storage device. A license for the SOFTWARE PRODUCT may not be shared or used concurrently on different computers.

   c. **License Pak.** If you have acquired this EULA in a Microsoft License Pak, you may make the number of additional copies of the computer software portion of the SOFTWARE PRODUCT authorized on the printed copy of this EULA, and you may use each copy in the manner specified above. You are also entitled to make a corresponding number of secondary copies for portable computer use as specified above.

   d. **Sample Code.** Solely with respect to portions, if any, of the SOFTWARE PRODUCT that are identified within the SOFTWARE PRODUCT as sample code (the "SAMPLE CODE"):

      i. **Use and Modification.** Microsoft grants you the right to use and modify the source code version of the SAMPLE CODE, *provided* you comply with subsection (d)(iii) below. You may not distribute the SAMPLE CODE, or any modified version of the SAMPLE CODE, in source code form.

      ii. **Redistributable Files.** Provided you comply with subsection (d)(iii) below, Microsoft grants you a nonexclusive, royalty-free right to reproduce and distribute the object code version of the SAMPLE CODE and of any modified SAMPLE CODE, other than SAMPLE CODE, or any modified version thereof, designated as not redistributable in the Readme file that forms a part of the SOFTWARE PRODUCT (the "Non-Redistributable Sample Code"). All SAMPLE CODE other than the Non-Redistributable Sample Code is collectively referred to as the "REDISTRIBUTABLES."

      iii. **Redistribution Requirements.** If you redistribute the REDISTRIBUTABLES, you agree to: (i) distribute the REDISTRIBUTABLES in object code form only in conjunction with and as a part of your software application product; (ii) not use Microsoft's name, logo, or trademarks to market your software application product; (iii) include a valid copyright notice on your software application product; (iv) indemnify, hold harmless, and defend Microsoft from and against any claims or lawsuits, including attorney's fees, that arise or result from the use or distribution of your software application product; and (v) not permit further distribution of the REDISTRIBUTABLES by your end user. Contact Microsoft for the applicable royalties due and other licensing terms for all other uses and/or distribution of the REDISTRIBUTABLES.

2. **DESCRIPTION OF OTHER RIGHTS AND LIMITATIONS.**

   • **Limitations on Reverse Engineering, Decompilation, and Disassembly.** You may not reverse engineer, decompile, or disassemble the SOFTWARE PRODUCT, except and only to the extent that such activity is expressly permitted by applicable law notwithstanding this limitation.

   • **Separation of Components.** The SOFTWARE PRODUCT is licensed as a single product. Its component parts may not be separated for use on more than one computer.

   • **Rental.** You may not rent, lease, or lend the SOFTWARE PRODUCT.

- **Support Services.** Microsoft may, but is not obligated to, provide you with support services related to the SOFTWARE PRODUCT ("Support Services"). Use of Support Services is governed by the Microsoft policies and programs described in the user manual, in "online" documentation, and/or in other Microsoft-provided materials. Any supplemental software code provided to you as part of the Support Services shall be considered part of the SOFTWARE PRODUCT and subject to the terms and conditions of this EULA. With respect to technical information you provide to Microsoft as part of the Support Services, Microsoft may use such information for its business purposes, including for product support and development. Microsoft will not utilize such technical information in a form that personally identifies you.

- **Software Transfer.** You may permanently transfer all of your rights under this EULA, provided you retain no copies, you transfer all of the SOFTWARE PRODUCT (including all component parts, the media and printed materials, any upgrades, this EULA, and, if applicable, the Certificate of Authenticity), **and** the recipient agrees to the terms of this EULA.

- **Termination.** Without prejudice to any other rights, Microsoft may terminate this EULA if you fail to comply with the terms and conditions of this EULA. In such event, you must destroy all copies of the SOFTWARE PRODUCT and all of its component parts.

3. **COPYRIGHT.** All title and copyrights in and to the SOFTWARE PRODUCT (including but not limited to any images, photographs, animations, video, audio, music, text, SAMPLE CODE, REDISTRIBUTABLES, and "applets" incorporated into the SOFTWARE PRODUCT) and any copies of the SOFTWARE PRODUCT are owned by Microsoft or its suppliers. The SOFTWARE PRODUCT is protected by copyright laws and international treaty provisions. Therefore, you must treat the SOFTWARE PRODUCT like any other copyrighted material **except** that you may install the SOFTWARE PRODUCT on a single computer provided you keep the original solely for backup or archival purposes. You may not copy the printed materials accompanying the SOFTWARE PRODUCT.

4. **U.S. GOVERNMENT RESTRICTED RIGHTS.** The SOFTWARE PRODUCT and documentation are provided with RESTRICTED RIGHTS. Use, duplication, or disclosure by the Government is subject to restrictions as set forth in subparagraph (c)(1)(ii) of the Rights in Technical Data and Computer Software clause at DFARS 252.227-7013 or subparagraphs (c)(1) and (2) of the Commercial Computer Software—Restricted Rights at 48 CFR 52.227-19, as applicable. Manufacturer is Microsoft Corporation/One Microsoft Way/Redmond, WA 98052-6399.

5. **EXPORT RESTRICTIONS.** You agree that you will not export or re-export the SOFTWARE PRODUCT, any part thereof, or any process or service that is the direct product of the SOFTWARE PRODUCT (the foregoing collectively referred to as the "Restricted Components"), to any country, person, entity, or end user subject to U.S. export restrictions. You specifically agree not to export or re-export any of the Restricted Components (i) to any country to which the U.S. has embargoed or restricted the export of goods or services, which currently include, but are not necessarily limited to, Cuba, Iran, Iraq, Libya, North Korea, Sudan, and Syria, or to any national of any such country, wherever located, who intends to transmit or transport the Restricted Components back to such country; (ii) to any end user who you know or have reason to know will utilize the Restricted Components in the design, development, or production of nuclear, chemical, or biological weapons; or (iii) to any end user who has been prohibited from participating in U.S. export transactions by any federal agency of the U.S. government. You warrant and represent that neither the BXA nor any other U.S. federal agency has suspended, revoked, or denied your export privileges.

PN 097-0002296